The Papers of
Thomas Jefferson

VOLUME 11, which covers the period from 1 January to 6 August 1787, continues the account of Jefferson's mission as minister to France.

From February through June 1787 Jefferson made his first major tour on the continent of Europe, and the record of this journey to southern France and northern Italy is contained in the delightful "Notes of a Tour . . ." in this volume. Perhaps Jefferson is here revealed most clearly, for he traveled incognito, alone, separated from family and countrymen, and was completely free to do as he wished and seek out the people he wanted to see—scholars, merchants, abbés, peasants, farmers. The trip was essentially a tour to study the social, economic, and agricultural aspects of the region, and Jefferson was interested in all he saw, from Roman antiquities and the beauties of the countryside to the production of rice and wine and cheese; from the numerous mechanical devices and gadgets which intrigued him (for many of which he made drawings which are reproduced here) to the workings of a canal.

Shortly after his return from the southern tour, Jefferson's daughter Polly journeyed from Virginia to join her parent, and the account of this experience, much of it charmingly conveyed in letters from Abigail Adams, with whom she stayed in London while further transport was being arranged, is another pic-

THE PAPERS OF
Thomas Jefferson

Volume 11
1 January to 6 August 1787

JULIAN P. BOYD, EDITOR

MINA R. BRYAN AND FREDRICK AANDAHL
ASSOCIATE EDITORS

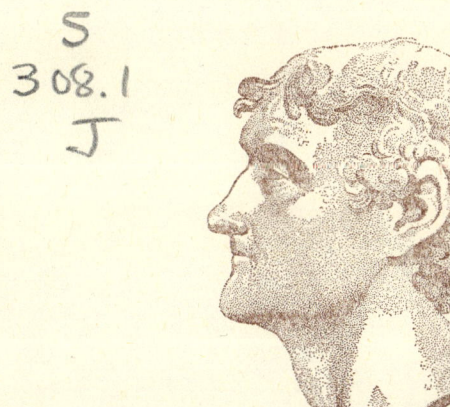

PRINCETON, NEW JERSEY
PRINCETON UNIVERSITY PRESS
1955

Copyright, 1955, by Princeton University Press
London: Geoffrey Cumberlege, Oxford University Press
L.C. CARD 50-7486

Printed in the United States of America by
Princeton University Press, Princeton, New Jersey

DEDICATED TO THE MEMORY OF

ADOLPH S. OCHS

PUBLISHER OF THE NEW YORK TIMES

1896-1935

WHO BY THE EXAMPLE OF A RESPONSIBLE

PRESS ENLARGED AND FORTIFIED

THE JEFFERSONIAN CONCEPT

OF A FREE PRESS

ADVISORY COMMITTEE

FISKE KIMBALL, *CHAIRMAN*
FRANCIS L. BERKELEY, JR.
SOLON J. BUCK
L. H. BUTTERFIELD
GILBERT CHINARD
HENRY STEELE COMMAGER
HAROLD W. DODDS
LUTHER H. EVANS
A. WHITNEY GRISWOLD
BRECKINRIDGE LONG
ARCHIBALD MACLEISH
DUMAS MALONE
BERNARD MAYO
RICARDO A. MESTRES
SAMUEL E. MORISON
HOWARD W. SMITH
DATUS C. SMITH, JR.
IPHIGENE OCHS SULZBERGER
WILLIAM J. VAN SCHREEVEN
LAWRENCE C. WROTH
JOHN C. WYLLIE

CONSULTANTS AND STAFF

PROFESSOR ARCHIBALD T. MACALLISTER, *Consultant in Italian*
PROFESSOR RAYMOND S. WILLIS, *Consultant in Spanish*
FRANCE C. RICE, *Consultant in French*
HOWARD C. RICE, JR., *Consultant*, Princeton University Library
DOROTHY S. EATON, *Consultant*, The Library of Congress
LAURA B. STEVENS, *Assistant Editor*

GUIDE TO EDITORIAL APPARATUS

1. TEXTUAL DEVICES

The following devices are employed throughout the work to clarify the presentation of the text.

[...], [....]	One or two words missing and not conjecturable.
[...]¹, [....]¹	More than two words missing and not conjecturable; subjoined footnote estimates number of words missing.
[ ]	Number or part of a number missing or illegible.
[roman]	Conjectural reading for missing or illegible matter. A question mark follows when the reading is doubtful.
[*italic*]	Editorial comment inserted in the text.
⟨*italic*⟩	Matter deleted in the MS but restored in our text.
[ ]	Record entry for letters not found.

2. DESCRIPTIVE SYMBOLS

The following symbols are employed throughout the work to describe the various kinds of manuscript originals. When a series of versions is recorded, *the first to be recorded is the version used for the printed text.*

Dft	draft (usually a composition or rough draft; later drafts, when identifiable as such, are designated "2d Dft," &c.)
Dupl	duplicate
MS	manuscript (arbitrarily applied to most documents other than letters)
N	note, notes (memoranda, fragments, &c.)
PoC	polygraph copy
PrC	press copy
RC	recipient's copy
SC	stylograph copy
Tripl	triplicate

All manuscripts of the above types are assumed to be in the hand of the author of the document to which the descriptive symbol pertains. If not, that fact is stated. On the other hand, the follow-

GUIDE TO EDITORIAL APPARATUS

ing types of manuscripts are assumed *not* to be in the hand of the author, and exceptions will be noted:

FC   file copy (applied to all forms of retained copies, such as letter-book copies, clerks' copies, &c.)

Tr   transcript (applied to both contemporary and later copies; period of transcription, unless clear by implication, will be given when known)

3. LOCATION SYMBOLS

The locations of documents printed in this edition from originals in private hands, from originals held by institutions outside the United States, and from printed sources are recorded in self-explanatory form in the descriptive note following each document. The locations of documents printed from originals held by public institutions in the United States are recorded by means of the symbols used in the National Union Catalog in the Library of Congress; an explanation of how these symbols are formed is given above, Vol. 1: xl. The list of symbols appearing in each volume is limited to the institutions represented by documents printed or referred to in that and previous volumes.

CLU	William Andrews Clark Memorial Library, University of California at Los Angeles
CSmH	Henry E. Huntington Library, San Marino, California
Ct	Connecticut State Library, Hartford, Connecticut
CtY	Yale University Library
DLC	Library of Congress
DNA	The National Archives
G-Ar	Georgia Department of Archives and History, Atlanta
ICHi	Chicago Historical Society, Chicago
IHi	Illinois State Historical Library, Springfield
MB	Boston Public Library, Boston
MH	Harvard University Library
MHi	Massachusetts Historical Society, Boston
MHi:AMT	Adams Family Papers, deposited by the Adams Manuscript Trust in Massachusetts Historical Society
MdAA	Maryland Hall of Records, Annapolis

GUIDE TO EDITORIAL APPARATUS

MdAN	U.S. Naval Academy Library
MeHi	Maine Historical Society, Portland
MiU-C	William L. Clements Library, University of Michigan
MoSHi	Missouri Historical Society, St. Louis
MWA	American Antiquarian Society, Worcester
NBu	Buffalo Public Library, Buffalo, New York
NcU	University of North Carolina Library
NHi	New-York Historical Society, New York City
NK-Iselin	Letters to and from John Jay bearing this symbol are used by permission of the Estate of Eleanor Jay Iselin.
NN	New York Public Library, New York City
NNC	Columbia University Libraries
NNP	Pierpont Morgan Library, New York City
NNS	New York Society Library, New York City
NcD	Duke University Library
NjP	Princeton University Library
PBL	Lehigh University Library
PHC	Haverford College Library
PHi	Historical Society of Pennsylvania, Philadelphia
PPAP	American Philosophical Society, Philadelphia
PPL-R	Library Company of Philadelphia, Ridgway Branch
PU	University of Pennsylvania Library
RPA	Rhode Island Department of State, Providence
RPB	Brown University Library
Vi	Virginia State Library, Richmond
ViHi	Virginia Historical Society, Richmond
ViU	University of Virginia Library
ViW	College of William and Mary Library
ViWC	Colonial Williamsburg, Inc.
WHi	State Historical Society of Wisconsin, Madison

4. OTHER ABBREVIATIONS

The following abbreviations are commonly employed in the annotation throughout the work.

Second Series   The topical series to be published at the end of this edition, comprising those materials which are best suited to a classified rather than a chronological arrangement (see Vol. 1: xv-xvi).

GUIDE TO EDITORIAL APPARATUS

TJ Thomas Jefferson
TJ Editorial Files Photoduplicates and other editorial materials in the office of *The Papers of Thomas Jefferson*, Princeton University Library
TJ Papers Jefferson Papers (Applied to a collection of manuscripts when the precise location of a given document must be furnished, and always preceded by the symbol for the institutional repository; thus "DLC: TJ Papers, 4:628-9" represents a document in the Library of Congress, Jefferson Papers, volume 4, pages 628 and 629.)
PCC Papers of the Continental Congress, in the National Archives
RG Record Group (Used in designating the location of documents in the National Archives.)
SJL Jefferson's "Summary Journal of letters" written and received (in DLC: TJ Papers)
SJPL "Summary Journal of Public Letters," an incomplete list of letters written by TJ from 16 Apr. 1784 to 31 Dec. 1793, with brief summaries, in an amanuensis' hand (in DLC: TJ Papers, at end of SJL).
V Ecu
ƒ Florin
£ Pound sterling or livre, depending upon context (in doubtful cases, a clarifying note will be given)
s Shilling or sou
d Penny or denier
₶ Livre Tournois
℞ Per (occasionally used for pro, pre)

5. SHORT TITLES

The following list includes only those short titles of works cited with great frequency, and therefore in very abbreviated form, throughout this edition. Their expanded forms are given here only in the degree of fullness needed for unmistakable identification. Since it is impossible to anticipate all the works to be cited in such very abbreviated form, the list is appropriately revised from volume to volume.

Atlas of Amer. Hist., Scribner, 1943 James Truslow Adams and R. V. Coleman, *Atlas of American History*, N.Y., 1943
Barbary Wars Dudley W. Knox, ed., *Naval Documents Related to the United States Wars with the Barbary Powers*
Betts, *Farm Book* Edwin M. Betts, ed., *Thomas Jefferson's Farm Book*

GUIDE TO EDITORIAL APPARATUS

Betts, *Garden Book*   Edwin M. Betts, ed., *Thomas Jefferson's Garden Book*

Biog. Dir. Cong.   *Biographical Directory of Congress, 1774-1927*

B.M. Cat.   British Museum, *General Catalogue of Printed Books*, London, 1931—. Also, *The British Museum Catalogue of Printed Books 1881-1900*, Ann Arbor, 1946

B.N. Cat.   *Catalogue général des livres imprimés de la Bibliothèque Nationale. Auteurs.*

Burnett, *Letters of Members*   Edmund C. Burnett, ed., *Letters of Members of the Continental Congress*

Cal. Franklin Papers   *Calendar of the Papers of Benjamin Franklin in the Library of the American Philosophical Society*, ed. I. Minis Hays

CVSP   *Calendar of Virginia State Papers . . . Preserved in the Capitol at Richmond*

DAB   *Dictionary of American Biography*

DAE   *Dictionary of American English*

DAH   *Dictionary of American History*

DNB   *Dictionary of National Biography*

Dipl. Corr., 1783-89   *The Diplomatic Correspondence of the United States of America, from the Signing of the Definitive Treaty of Peace . . . to the Adoption of the Constitution*, Washington, Blair & Rives, 1837, 3 vol.

Evans   Charles Evans, *American Bibliography*

Ford   Paul Leicester Ford, ed., *The Writings of Thomas Jefferson*, "Letterpress Edition," N.Y., 1892-1899.

Freeman, *Washington*   Douglas Southall Freeman, *George Washington*

Fry-Jefferson Map   *The Fry & Jefferson Map of Virginia and Maryland: A Facsimile of the First Edition*, Princeton, 1950

Gottschalk, *Lafayette, 1783-89*   Louis Gottschalk, *Lafayette between the American Revolution and the French Revolution (1783-1789)*, Chicago, 1950

Gournay   *Tableau général du commerce, des marchands, négocians, armateurs, &c., . . . années 1789 & 1790*, Paris, n.d.

HAW   Henry A. Washington, ed., *The Writings of Thomas Jefferson*, Washington, 1853-1854

Hening   William W. Hening, *The Statutes at Large; Being a Collection of All the Laws of Virginia*

Henry, *Henry*   William Wirt Henry, *Patrick Henry, Life, Correspondence and Speeches*

[xi]

JCC *Journals of the Continental Congress, 1774-1789*, ed. W. C. Ford and others, Washington, 1904-1937

JHD *Journal of the House of Delegates of the Commonwealth of Virginia* (cited by session and date of publication)

Jefferson Correspondence, Bixby *Thomas Jefferson Correspondence Printed from the Originals in the Collections of William K. Bixby*, ed. W. C. Ford, Boston, 1916

Johnston, "Jefferson Bibliography" Richard H. Johnston, "A Contribution to a Bibliography of Thomas Jefferson," *Writings of Thomas Jefferson*, ed. Lipscomb and Bergh, xx, separately paged following the Index.

L & B Andrew A. Lipscomb and Albert E. Bergh, eds., *The Writings of Thomas Jefferson*, "Memorial Edition," Washington, 1903-1904

L.C. Cat. *A Catalogue of Books Represented by Library of Congress Printed Cards*, Ann Arbor, 1942-1946; also *Supplement*, 1948.

Library Catalogue, 1783 Jefferson's MS list of books owned and wanted in 1783 (original in Massachusetts Historical Society)

Library Catalogue, 1815 *Catalogue of the Library of the United States*, Washington, 1815

Library Catalogue, 1829 *Catalogue. President Jefferson's Library*, Washington, 1829

MVHR *Mississippi Valley Historical Review*

OED *A New English Dictionary on Historical Principles*, Oxford, 1888-1933

PMHB *The Pennsylvania Magazine of History and Biography*

Randall, *Life* Henry S. Randall, *The Life of Thomas Jefferson*

Randolph, *Domestic Life* Sarah N. Randolph, *The Domestic Life of Thomas Jefferson*

Sabin Joseph Sabin and others, *Bibliotheca Americana. A Dictionary of Books Relating to America*

Sowerby *Catalogue of the Library of Thomas Jefferson*, compiled with annotations by E. Millicent Sowerby, Washington, 1952-53

Swem, *Index* E. G. Swem, *Virginia Historical Index*

Swem, "Va. Bibliog." Earl G. Swem, "A Bibliography of Virginia," Virginia State Library, *Bulletin*, VIII, X, XII (1915-1919)

TJR Thomas Jefferson Randolph, ed., *Memoir, Correspondence, and Miscellanies, from the Papers of Thomas Jefferson*, Charlottesville, 1829

GUIDE TO EDITORIAL APPARATUS

Tucker, *Life*   George Tucker, *The Life of Thomas Jefferson*, Philadelphia, 1837

Tyler, *Va. Biog.*   Lyon G. Tyler, *Encyclopedia of Virginia Biography*

Tyler's Quart.   *Tyler's Quarterly Historical and Genealogical Magazine*

VMHB   *Virginia Magazine of History and Biography*

Wharton, *Dipl. Corr. Am. Rev.*   *The Revolutionary Diplomatic Correspondence of the United States*, ed. Francis Wharton

WMQ   *William and Mary Quarterly*

CONTENTS

Guide to Editorial Apparatus	vii
Jefferson Chronology	2

1787

From Maria Cosway, *1 January*	3
From H. Fizeaux & Cie., *1 January*	5
From Thomas Boylston, *2 January*	5
From Goltz, *2 January*	6
From Brissot de Warville, with Enclosure, *3 January*	6
From Etienne Clavière, *3 January*	9
From Le Couteulx & Cie., *3 January*	10
To Alexander McCaul, *4 January*	10
From C. W. F. Dumas, *5 January*	12
To William Jones, *5 January*	14
From Chartier de Lotbinière, *5 January*	18
To Samuel Osgood, *5 January*	18
From José da Maia, *5 January*	20
From Thomas Barclay, *6 January*	20
Thomas Barclay to the American Commissioners, *6 January*	21
From S. & J. H. Delap, *6 January*	22
From Jean Nicolas Démeunier, *6 January*	23
From Ferdinand Grand, *6 January*	24
〚To Abigail Adams, *7 January*〛	24
To Calonne, *7 January*	25
To Colonia, *7 January*	25
To Matthew Boulton, *8 January*	26
From Duler, *8 January*	26
From R. & A. Garvey, *8 January*	26
From C. W. F. Dumas, *9 January*	27
From George Gilmer, *9 January*	27
To John Jay, *9 January*	29
〚To Pierre Louis Lacretelle, *9 January*〛	34
From Elizabeth Blair Thompson, *10 January*	34
To John Adams, *11 January*	35
To John Bondfield, *11 January*	36
To David S. Franks, *11 January*	36
From the Abbé Morellet *[11? January]*	37
From R. & A. Garvey, *12 January*	38

CONTENTS

To Philippe-Denis Pierres, *12 January*	38
From Mrs. Rider, *13 January*	39
To Ferdinand Grand, *14 January*	39
To an Agent of Antoine-Félix Wuibert, *14 January*	40
To Harcourt, *14 January*	40
To Louis Guillaume Otto, *14 January*	42
To St. John de Crèvecoeur, *15 January*	43
From Philippe-Denis Pierres, *15 January*	45
To Abigail Adams Smith, *15 January*	45
To William Stephens Smith, *15 January*	46
〚From John Bondfield, *16 January*〛	47
From Carburi, *16 January*	47
To Edward Carrington, *16 January*	48
From Champagni *[17? January]*	50
To S. & J. H. Delap, *17 January*	51
To Duler, *17 January*	51
To Jean Durival, *17 January*	52
From Miguel de Lardizábel y Uribe, *17 January*	52
From Segond, *17 January*	53
To John Adams, *19 January*	54
To Champagni *[19 January]*	54
From Chevallié Fils, *19 January*	55
To R. & A. Garvey, *19 January*	55
To François Soulés, *19 January*	56
〚To the Abbé Morellet, *19 January*〛	56
To Elizabeth Blair Thompson, *19 January*	56
From Charles Burney, *20 January*	58
From Jean Durival, *20 January*	60
From Uriah Forrest, *20 January*	60
From Madame de Tessé, *21 January*	60
From William Jones, *22 January*	61
〚From Tarbé, *22 January*〛	62
From St. Victour & Bettinger, *23 January*	62
From C. W. F. Dumas, *23 January*	62
From Madame de Tessé, *23 January*	65
From John Adams, *25 January*	65
From R. & A. Garvey, *25 January*	67
From Le Veillard *[before 26 January]*	67
From John Sullivan, *26 January*	68
From John Sullivan, *26 January*	68
From Benjamin Vaughan, with Enclosure, *26 January*	69
The American Commissioners to John Jay, *27 January*	77

[xvi]

CONTENTS

The American Commissioners to Taher Fennish, *27 January*	79
To Hilliard d'Aubertueil, *27 January*	80
To Gelhais, *27 January*	81
From De Langeac, *27 January*	81
〚From Schweighauser & Dobrée, *27 January*〛	82
To Segond, *27 January*	82
From Edmund Randolph, *28 January*	83
From Edmund Randolph, *28 January*	84
To John Stockdale, *28 January*	85
To Anthony Vieyra [*28 January*]	85
From Abigail Adams, *29 January*	86
From William Cunningham, *29 January*	88
To R. & A. Garvey, *29 January*	88
From Thomas Haddaway, *29 January*	89
From Rochambeau, *29 January*	89
From Rosaubo, *29 January*	90
From William Stephens Smith, *29 January*	90
To Zachariah Loreilhe, *30 January*	92
To James Madison, *30 January*	92
From Thomas Silbey, *30 January*	98
From André Limozin, *31 January*	98
From Partout [*January?*]	98
From George Wythe, *January*	99
To Cunningham and Haddaway, *1 February*	99
To John Jay, *1 February*	99
From Louis Le Pelletier, *1 February*	104
From Puisaye, *1 February*	105
To John Stockdale, *1 February*	107
To the Commissioners of the Treasury, *1 February*	108
To Mary Barclay, *2 February*	108
From C. W. F. Dumas, *2 February*	109
From Mademoiselle de Lausanne, *2 February*	109
〚From Alexander McCaul, *2 February*〛	109
To François Soulés, *2 February*	110
From André Limozin, *3 February*	110
To Christian Frederick Michaelis and Others, *4 February*	111
From Henry Champion, *5 February*	112
From Degaseq, with Enclosure, *5 February*	112
From Anthony Garvey, *5 February*	116
From Madame de Tott [*early February*]	117
To John Adams, *6 February*	118
From Mary Barclay, *6 February*	119

CONTENTS

To William Drayton, 6 February	119
To John Banister, 7 February	120
To John Banister, Jr., with Enclosure, 7 February	121
To Anne Willing Bingham, 7 February	122
To the Governor of Virginia, 7 February	124
To James Madison, 7 February	125
To David S. Franks, 8 February	125
To John Jay, 8 February	126
To André Limozin, 8 February	127
To C. W. F. Dumas, 9 February	127
From John Jay, 9 February	129
〚From John Banister, Jr., 10 February〛	132
Thomas Barclay to the American Commissioners, 10 February	132
From Thomas Barclay, 10 February	133
From David S. Franks, 10 February	135
〚To Madame de Doradour, 11 February〛	136
From Duler, 11 February	136
From David S. Franks, 11 February	136
To André Limozin, 11 February	138
To De Puisaye, 11 February	139
To Tarbé, 11 February	139
To Vergennes, 11 February	140
To Charles Burney, 12 February	140
To Borgnis DesBordes, Frères, 12 February	141
To Schweighauser & Dobrée, 12 February	141
From C. W. F. Dumas, 13 February	142
From André Limozin, 13 February	142
From John Stockdale, 13 February	143
To John Adams, 14 February	143
To John Jay, 14 February	144
To John Jay, 14 February	144
From John Jay, 14 February	145
To André Limozin, 14 February	145
From Louis Guillaume Otto, 14 February	146
From Maria Cosway, 15 February	148
From L. J. M. Daubenton, 15 February	151
From Louis Le Pelletier, 15 February	151
From James Madison, 15 February	152
From John Trumbull, 15 February	155
To Simon Bérard, 16 February	156
From Simon Bérard, 16 February	157
To Henry Champion, 16 February	157

[xviii]

CONTENTS

From C. W. F. Dumas, *16 February*	158
To Philip Mazzei, *16 February*	159
From the Commissioners of the Treasury, *16 February*	159
From Vandenyver Frères, *16 February*	161
From Benjamin Vaughan, *16 February*	162
From Froullé, *17 February*	163
To Thomas Barclay, *18 February*	163
To William Carmichael, *18 February*	164
To De Corny, *18 February*	165
To the Prévôt des Marchands et Echevins de Paris, *18 February*	165
From André Limozin, *18 February*	166
From Anne Blair Banister, *19 February*	166
To Alexander McCaul, *19 February*	167
To William Stephens Smith, *19 February*	168
To John Adams, *20 February*	169
From John Adams, *20 February*	170
From De Corny, *20 February*	170
From William Gordon, *20 February*	172
To Barradelle, *21 February*	173
From Henry Champion, *21 February*	173
To Abigail Adams, *22 February*	174
To De Langeac, *22 February*	175
To John Adams, *23 February*	176
To Mrs. Champernoune, *23 February*	178
To John Jay, *23 February*	179
To Eliza House Trist, *23 February*	180
To John Trumbull, *23 February*	181
To Michel Capitaine, *25 February*	182
From D'Hancarville, *25 February*	182
〚From William Jones, *25 February*〛	182
To Richard Peters, *26 February*	182
To John Stockdale, *27 February*	183
To John Adams, *28 February*	184
Jefferson's Letter of Credit from Ferdinand Grand [*ca. 28 February*]	184
To Ferdinand Grand, *28 February*	185
From Richard Paul Jodrell, *28 February*	186
To Lafayette, *28 February*	186
To Madame de Tessé, *28 February*	187
To Madame de Tott, *28 February*	187
To St. John de Crèvecoeur [*ca. February*]	188
From John Adams, *1 March*	188

CONTENTS

From Elias Hasket Derby, *1 March*	191
From Alexander Donald, *1 March*	193
From Benjamin Vaughan *[ca. 1 March]*	195
C. W. F. Dumas to William Short, *2 March*	195
C. W. F. Dumas to William Short, *2 March*	197
From Lavoisier, *3 March*	197
From De Saint-Paterne, *3 March*	198
From Madame de Tott, *4 March*	198
From Gaudenzio Clerici, *5 March*	199
〚To Visly, *6 March*〛	200
From De Guichén, *7 March*	200
From Benjamin Hawkins, *8 March*	201
From Martha Jefferson, *8 February [i.e., March]*	203
From Brissot de Warville, with Enclosure, *8 March*	204
〚From Alexander McCaul, *9 March*〛	206
From Sir John Sinclair, *9 March*	206
From Madame de Tessé, *11 February [i.e., March]*	206
From William Short, *12 March*	207
To Parent, *13 March*	211
From William Short, *14 March*	213
〚To Adrien Petit, *15 March*〛	214
To William Short, *15 March*	214
〚From Adrien Petit, *17 March*〛	216
From John Ledyard, *19 March*	216
From James Madison, *19 March*	219
To José da Maia, *19 March*	225
To Madame de Tessé, *20 March*	226
From Richard Cary, *21 March*	228
William Short to the Governor of Virginia, *21 March*	230
William Short to John Jay, *21 March*	231
From William Short, *22 March*	232
From the Governor of Georgia, *23 March*	235
From William Carmichael, *25 March*	236
From Martha Jefferson, *25 March*	238
From William Short, *26 March*	239
From Edward Bancroft, *27 March*	242
〚From Buffon, *27 March*〛	243
To Adrien Petit, *27 March*	243
C. W. F. Dumas to William Short, *27 March*	243
To William Short, *27 March*	246
From John Blair, *28 March*	248
To Martha Jefferson, *28 March*	250

CONTENTS

From the Rev. James Madison [ca. 28 March]	252
To William Short, 29 March	253
From John Bondfield, 30 March	255
From Francis Eppes, 30 March	255
From Ferdinand Grand [ca. 30 March]	257
From Madame de Tessé, 30 March	257
From Elizabeth Wayles Eppes [31 March]	260
From Mary Jefferson [ca. 31 March]	260
From André Limozin, 31 March	261
[From Adrien Petit, 31 March]	261
To Chastellux, 4 April	261
From Ralph Izard, 4 April	262
From the Papal Nuncio, 4 April	266
To Philip Mazzei, 4 April	266
From William Short, 4 April	267
[To John Banister, 5 April]	270
From Pierre Poinsot des Essarts, 5 April	270
To Madame de Tott, 5 April	270
From William Macarty, 6 April	273
From Rigoley d'Ogny, 6 April	274
From William Short, 6 April	274
To Martha Jefferson, 7 April	277
[From Adrien Petit, 7 April]	278
From David Ramsay, 7 April	279
To William Short, 7 April	280
From Martha Jefferson, 9 April	281
From Jacques Nicolas Mayeux, 9 April	282
From A. E. van Braam Houckgeest, 10 April	283
To Lafayette, 11 April	283
From Louis Guillaume Otto, 11 April	285
To William Short, 12 April	287
To the Abbés Arnoux and Chalut, 12 April	287
From Francis Hopkinson, 14 April	288
From Francis Hopkinson, 14 April	290
[From Adrien Petit, 14 April]	291
From Thomas Mann Randolph, Jr., 14 April	291
From David Rittenhouse, 14 April	293
From Francis Hopkinson, 15 April	294
From St. John de Crèvecoeur, 16 April	294
From David Ramsay, 16 April	295
From John Sullivan, 16 April	295
From Thomas Brand Hollis, 17 April	297

CONTENTS

From Philip Mazzei, *17 April*	297
[From John Sullivan, *17 April*]	298
From John Adams, *18 April*	298
From Peter Carr, *18 April*	299
From Castries, *19 April*	300
From Benjamin Franklin, *19 April*	301
[From St. Victour, *19 April*]	302
From Bellon, *21 April*	302
From the Abbés Arnoux and Chalut, *23 April*	303
From John Banister, Jr., *23 April*	303
From David S. Franks, *23 April*	305
From David Hartley, *23 April*	306
From James Madison, *23 April*	307
From Edward Carrington, *24 April*	310
From John Jay, *24 April*	312
From William Short, *24 April*	315
From William Hay, *26 April*	318
From John Sullivan, with Account of Expenses for Obtaining Moose Skeleton, *26 April*	320
From John Sullivan, *27 April*	321
From Richard O'Bryen, *28 April*	321
From Charles Thomson, *28 April*	323
From Chastellux, *29 April*	324
From John Sullivan, *30 April*	326
To William Short, *1 May*	326
From James Currie, *2 May*	327
From William Fleming, *2 May*	330
From Peter J. Bergius, *3 May*	331
To Castries, *3 May*	332
From William Hay, *3 May*	332
From Martha Jefferson, *3 May*	333
To Rigoley d'Ogny, *3 May*	334
From Edmund Randolph, *3 May*	335
From American Traders in Guadeloupe, *3 May*	336
To Ferdinand Grand, *4 May*	337
From Delahais, *4 May*	337
To John Jay, *4 May*	338
From Edmund Randolph, *4 May*	344
To William Short, *4 May*	344
William Short to John Jay, *4 May*	345
To Thomas Barclay, *5 May*	347
To Martha Jefferson, *5 May*	348

CONTENTS

From André Limozin, 5 May	349
To William Short, 5 May	349
To Edward Bancroft, 6 May	351
From John Banister, Sr., and Anne Blair Banister, 6 May	351
To Jean Baptiste Guide, 6 May	352
To Philip Mazzei, 6 May	354
To St. Victour & Bettinger, 6 May	355
To George Wythe, 6 May	355
From Elizabeth Wayles Eppes [7 May]	356
From William Short, 8 May	356
From Stephen Cathalan, Jr., 9 May	358
From John Sullivan, 9 May	359
From John Ammonet, 10 May	360
From G. A. Auckler, 11 May	360
[From the Abbé Guibert, 14 May]	361
From William Short, 14 May	361
From James Madison, 15 May	363
John Stockdale to William Short, 15 May	364
From Ferdinand Grand, 19 May	364
From William Stephens Smith, 19 May	365
From Madame de Tott, 19 May	367
From John Lamb, 20 May	368
To Martha Jefferson, 21 May	369
From James Maury, 21 May	370
To William Short, 21 May	371
From William Short, 21 May	373
From William Drayton, 22 May	374
From André Limozin, 22 May	375
From Robert Montgomery, 22 May	376
From Ferdinand Grand, 23 May	377
[From the Abbé Gaubert, 25 May]	377
[From Wilt, Delmestre & Cie., 25 May]	377
To John Banister, Jr., 26 May	377
To William Carmichael, 26 May	378
To Francis Eppes, 26 May	378
From Robert Montgomery, 26 May	379
From G. Pin, 26 May	379
To William Stephens Smith, 26 May	380
From Martha Jefferson, 27 May	380
From William Short, 29 May	381
From John Sullivan, 29 May	384
From Miguel de Lardizábel y Uribe, 30 May	384

[xxiii]

CONTENTS

From George Washington, *30 May*	385
From Jeudy de l'Hommande, *31 May*	391
From Anne Willing Bingham, *1 June*	392
From J. P. P. Derieux, *1 June*	394
To Martha Jefferson, *1 June*	394
To William Short, *1 June*	395
From Feger, Gramont & Cie., *2 June*	396
From C. W. F. Dumas, *5 June*	397
From John Churchman, with a Memorial on Magnetic Declinations, *6 June*	397
From Lafayette, *6 June*	399
From James Madison, *6 June*	400
From Charles Thomson, *6 June*	403
From Eliza House Trist, *6 June*	403
From C. W. F. Dumas, *7 June*	405
From John Rutledge, *7 June*	405
From C. W. F. Dumas, *8 June*	406
From Edward Carrington, *9 June*	407
From Richard Claiborne, with Enclosure, *9 June*	411
From Benjamin Hawkins, *9 June*	413
Notes of a Tour into the Southern Parts of France, &c., *3 March to 11 June*	415
From Dr. Lambert, *11 June*	464
From Thomas Barclay, *12 June*	466
From Thomas Barclay, *12 June*	467
From Motture, *12 June*	468
〚To Cassini, *13 June*〛	468
〚To Champion, *13 June*〛	468
From Richard Claiborne, *13 June*	468
〚To the Abbé Gaubert, *13 June*〛	469
To William Carmichael, *14 June*	469
To C. W. F. Dumas, *14 June*	471
To Martha Jefferson, *14 June*	472
To Parent, *14 June*	472
From Joel Barlow, *15 June*	473
From Wilt, Delmestre & Cie., *15 June*	474
To the Commissioners of the Treasury, *17 June*	474
To Du Pin d'Assarts, *18 June*	476
To John Banister, Jr., *19 June*	476
To Thomas Barclay, *19 June*	477
To Feger, Gramont & Cie., *19 June*	479
From the Abbés Arnoux and Chalut, *20 June*	479

CONTENTS

To William Macarty, *20 June*	479
To James Madison, *20 June*	480
From Parent, *20 June*	484
From Richard Claiborne, *21 June*	485
To George Rogers Clark, *21 June*	487
To John Jay, *21 June*	487
To Barrois, *22 June*	500
From John and Lucy Ludwell Paradise, *22 June*	501
To R. & A. Garvey, *24 June*	501
From Abigail Adams, *26 June*	501
From Abigail Adams, *27 June*	502
To Martha Jefferson, *28 June*	503
From Thomas Barclay, *29 June*	504
From R. & A. Garvey, *29 June*	506
From Pierre Bon, *30 June*	506
From Stephen Cathalan, Sr., *30 June*	507
To Madame de Corny, *30 June*	509
From C. W. F. Dumas, *30 June*	510
From Feger, Gramont & Cie., *30 June*	510
From William Stephens Smith, *30 June*	511
From Vernes, *30 June*	513
To Abigail Adams, *1 July*	514
To John Adams, *1 July*	515
To Matthew Boulton, *1 July*	518
To Richard Claiborne, *1 July*	518
To Maria Cosway, *1 July*	519
To Anne Cleland Kinloch, *1 July*	520
To John Stockdale, with Orders for Books, *1 July*	521
To John Bondfield, *2 July*	524
To Francis Eppes, *2 July*	524
To William Gordon, *2 July*	525
To David Hartley, *2 July*	525
To Thomas Brand Hollis, *2 July*	527
To Richard Paul Jodrell, *2 July*	527
From Lormerie, *2 July*	528
To James Maury, *2 July*	528
To the Abbé Morellet, *2 July*	529
Jefferson's Instructions to Adrien Petit *[ca. 2 July]*	531
To Sir John Sinclair, *2 July*	532
To Benjamin Vaughan, *2 July*	532
From Villedeuil, *2 July*	533
To Wilt, Delmestre & Cie., *2 July*	534

CONTENTS

From Thomas Barclay [ca. 3 July]	534
From John Bondfield, 3 July	538
Jefferson's Observations on Calonne's Letter Concerning American Trade [ca. 3 July]	539
From the Abbé Morellet [3 July]	542
From André Pepin, 3 July	543
To André Pepin, 3 July	543
To Thomas Barclay, 4 July	544
[From Clesle, 4 July]	545
To Feger, Gramont & Cie., 4 July	545
From Lanchon Frères & Cie., 4 July	546
To André Limozin, 4 July	546
[From Parent, 4 July]	546
To Hérault, 5 July	547
John Jay to William Short, 5 July	549
To Villedeuil, 5 July	550
From Abigail Adams, 6 July	550
From Thomas Barclay, 6 July	552
To Dr. Lambert, 3 July	552
To Miguel de Lardizábel y Uribe, with Enclosure, 6 July	553
To Lormerie, 6 July	554
To Robert Montgomery, 6 July	555
To G. Pin, 6 July	555
From Andrew Ramsay, 6 July	556
To Thomas Mann Randolph, Jr., 6 July	556
To G. A. Auckler, 7 July	559
[To Guillaume Delahaye, 7 July]	559
To Pierre Poinsot des Essarts, 7 July	559
From Thomas Barclay, 8 July	560
From Francis Hopkinson, 8 July	561
From William Macarty, 8 July	563
To Abbé d'Arnal, 9 July	563
From William Carmichael, 9 July	565
From Maria Cosway, 9 July	567
From Madame de Corny, 9 July	569
To Jan Ingenhousz, 9 July	570
To Lanchon Frères & Cie., 9 July	571
From Wilt, Delmestre & Cie., 9 July	571
To Abigail Adams, 10 July	572
From Abigail Adams, with List of Purchases for Mary Jefferson, 10 July	572
From John Adams, 10 July	575

[xxvi]

CONTENTS

From Blumendorf, *10 July*	575
From C. W. F. Dumas, *10 July*	576
From John Stockdale, *10 July*	576
From John Trumbull, *10 July*	578
From Nathaniel Barrett, *11 July*	578
From Richard Claiborne, *11 July*	579
From Abigail Adams Smith, *11 July*	580
From C. W. F. Dumas, *12 July*	581
From Ladevese, *12 July*	582
Thomas Barclay to the American Commissioners, *13 July*	582
[From John Stockdale, *13 July*]	584
From Thomas Barclay [*14 July*]	584
From Gaudenzio Clerici, *14 July*	585
From Feger, Gramont & Cie., *14 July*	587
To Edward Rutledge, *14 July*	587
From Frederick Soffer, *14 July*	589
To Wilt, Delmestre & Cie., *14 July*	589
Notes on the Rice Trade Supplied by Jean Jacques Bérard & Cie.	590
To Abigail Adams, *16 July*	592
From Thomas Barclay, *16 July*	593
From Joseph Fenwick, *16 July*	594
To John Trumbull, *16 July*	594
To John Adams, *17 July*	595
From John Bondfield, *17 July*	596
To La Boullaye, *17 July*	596
From Dr. Lambert, *17 July*	596
To André Limozin, *17 July*	597
To John Stockdale, *17 July*	597
To John Trumbull, *17 July*	598
To Adam Walker, *17 July*	599
To La Boullaye, *18 July*	599
From James Madison, *18 July*	600
From Burrill Carnes, *19 July*	601
From Guillaume Delahaye, *20 July*	603
From Langlade, *20 July*	604
From André Limozin, *20 July*	604
To Stephen Cathalan, Jr., *21 July*	605
To Joseph Fenwick, *21 July*	606
From R. & A. Garvey, *21 July*	607
From Ferdinand Grand, *21 July*	607
To William Macarty, *21 July*	608

[xxvii]

CONTENTS

To Parent, *21 July*	608
To Ferdinand Grand, *22 July*	609
To the Rhode Island Delegates in Congress, *22 July*	609
To John Adams, *23 July*	610
To Mary Jefferson Bolling, *23 July*	612
To H. Fizeaux & Cie., *23 July*	613
To Ladevese, *23 July*	613
To Montmorin, *23 July*	614
To Abigail Adams Smith, *23 July*	618
From John Jay, *24 July*	618
From Robert Montgomery, *24 July*	620
To Moustier, *24 July*	621
From Moustier, *24 July*	622
From the Abbé de Reymond de St. Maurice, *24 July*	622
To Martha Jefferson Carr, *25 July*	623
From Mantel Duchoqueltz, *25 July*	624
To John Stockdale, *25 July*	624
To Nathaniel Barrett, *26 July*	625
[From John Sandford Dart, *26 July*]	625
From Thomas Barclay, *27 July*	625
From John Jay, with Enclosure, *27 July*	627
From John Jay, *27 July*	629
From André Limozin, *27 July*	629
From James Monroe, *27 July*	630
To John Adams, *28 July*	632
To Alexander Donald, *28 July*	632
To Elizabeth Wayles Eppes, *28 July*	634
To John Wayles Eppes, *28 July*	635
To Henry Skipwith, *28 July*	635
To La Boullaye, *29 July*	637
From John Ledyard, *29 July*	637
To Nicholas Lewis, *29 July*	639
To André Limozin, *29 July*	642
[From St. Victour, *29 July*]	643
From Thomas Barclay, *30 July*	643
To William Drayton, *30 July*	644
To Francis Eppes, *30 July*	650
From Parent, *30 July*	654
From Mainville, *[ca. July]*	655
From Madame Oster *[July]*	655
To Francis Hopkinson, with Enclosure, *1 August*	655
To Ralph Izard, *1 August*	659

CONTENTS

From André Limozin, *1 August*	660
From Abbé Morellet, *1 August*	661
[From Thomas Barclay, *2 August*]	662
To James Madison, with Enclosure, *2 August*	662
To Thomas Barclay, with Enclosure, *3 August*	669
To Thomas Barclay, *3 August*	671
From Zachariah Loreilhe [3] *August*	671
To Edmund Randolph, *3 August*	672
To the Governor of Virginia, *3 August*	673
From William Stephens Smith, *3 August*	674
From Stael de Holstein, *3 August*	675
From John Stockdale, *3 August*	676
From Wilt, Delmestre & Cie., *3 August*	677
To Edward Carrington, *4 August*	678
From Madame de Corny, *4 August*	680
To James Currie, *4 August*	681
To Benjamin Hawkins, *4 August*	683
To William Hay, *4 August*	685
To David Ramsay, *4 August*	686
To James Monroe, *5 August*	687
To the Commissioners of the Treasury, *5 August*	689
To Anne Blair Banister, *6 August*	691
To John Banister, Sr., *6 August*	691
To St. John de Crèvecoeur, *6 August*	692
To Benjamin Franklin, *6 August*	693
To John Hannum Gibbons, *6 August*	693
To John Jay, *6 August*	693
To André Limozin, *6 August*	700
To John Rutledge, *6 August*	700

ILLUSTRATIONS

FOLLOWING PAGE 414

"ECU DE CALONNE," 1786

A specimen of the experimental French crown, in silver, executed by Jean Pierre Droz in 1786. On 7 Jan. 1787, Jefferson made the following entry in his Account Book: "pd for one Drost's coins 9f"; this was probably one of the two coins which Jefferson sent to Congress by David S. Franks, in the hope that Congress would negotiate with Droz for removing to America and undertaking coinage there. The economy of the process by which the two faces and the edge of the coin were struck at one time, together with the perfection of the result, excited the interest of Jefferson, Boulton, and others in the new machine invented by Droz. Jay did not acknowledge receipt of the coins that Jefferson sent; they have not been found among the objects connected with the Papers of the Continental Congress; and evidently they have not survived. See TJ to John Jay, 9 Jan. and 1 Feb. 1787. (Courtesy of the Bibliothèque Nationale, Cabinet des Médailles, through Howard C. Rice, Jr.)

MARIUS AT MINTURNES

Jefferson was deeply moved by this painting of Jean Germain Drouais (1763-1788), son and student of François Hubert Drouais, who joined the school of Louis David and accompanied David to Rome in 1785. While in Rome Drouais sent several paintings to Paris, among them the picture of Marius. He died of a fever in Rome in 1788. Though Jefferson was perceptive enough to choose Houdon to do the statue of Washington and to have it executed in modern dress; though he associated with the Cosways, Trumbull, Peale, and other artists; and though he was a diligent student of the fine arts, he was led by popular enthusiasm into an extravagant estimate of Drouais' painting and then forced to retreat from an unfamiliar and not wholly congenial ground when Madame de Tott advanced a contrary opinion. For this revealing incident, compare the reproduction of Drouais' "Marius at Minturnes" with TJ to Mme. de Tott, 28 Feb.; Mme. de Tott to TJ, 4 Mch.; TJ to Mme. de Tott, 5 Apr. 1787. (Courtesy of The Louvre, and Archives Photographiques, through U.S. Information Service, Paris.)

PARIS IN 1787

A detail of a map of Paris, entitled, "Nouveau Plan Routier de la Ville et Faubourgs de Paris, avec ses Principaux Edifices par M. Pichon," engraved by Glot and published by

[xxxi]

ILLUSTRATIONS

FOLLOWING PAGE 414

Esnauts and Rapilly, Paris, 1787. The Hôtel de Langeac (not shown in this section) is located west of the Champs Elysées (center, left). North of the Rue Saint-Honoré is the Place de Louis le Grand or Place Vendôme, a residential section much favored by the bankers and farmers-general; toward the right is the Palais Royal, the fashionable center of Paris; still farther right, the circular "Halle au Bled." The Pont Royal (center, right) was the main link between the Faubourg Saint Honoré on the Right Bank and the Faubourg Saint Germain on the Left Bank. Along the Left Bank of the Seine, to the west of the Pont Royal, the site of the Hôtel de Salm is indicated by the word "chantiers," i.e. construction (see TJ to Mme. de Tessé, 20 Mch. 1787). Also to the west of the Pont Royal, on the Rue de Grenelle, is the Abbaye Royale de Pentemont, the school attended by Martha and Mary Jefferson. Below this, in the Rue de Varenne, near the corner of the Rue de Bourgogne, and next door to the Hôtel de Castries, is the Hôtel de Tessé, the town residence of Lafayette's aunt and Jefferson's friend, the Comtesse de Tessé. On the Left Bank, at the extreme right-hand edge of the map, near the tip of the Ile de la Cité, is the Hôtel de la Monnaie, where Condorcet, as director of the Mint, resided. Slightly to the west of this, between the Rue de Seine and the Rue des Petits Augustins, is the Hôtel de La Rochefoucauld, where Jefferson was a frequent visitor. It was in the Rue des Petits Augustins, at the Hôtel d' Orléans, that Jefferson spent several weeks in the autumn of 1784, shortly after his arrival in Paris. (Photo by Rigal, courtesy of the Bibliothèque Historique de la Ville de Paris, through Howard C. Rice, Jr.)

"ROUGH NOTES OF JOURNEY THROUGH CHAMPAGNE, BURGUNDY, BEAUJOLOIS"

Jefferson's daily memoranda for the first part of his journey through southern France. These notes, together with similar notes for the latter part of his journey and copies of his letters during his absence from Paris, were later incorporated in his fair copy of "Memorandums taken on a journey from Paris into the Southern parts of France and Northern of Italy, in the year 1787," q.v. under 10 June 1787. (Courtesy of the Massachusetts Historical Society.)

The following six illustrations of places visited by Jefferson on his tour into the southern parts of France have all been reproduced from plates in the *Voyage Pittoresque de la France*, compiled by Laborde, Guettard, and Béguillet, Paris, 1784-1802. The plans for this voluminous work were laid in 1780

ILLUSTRATIONS

FOLLOWING PAGE 414

by Jean-Benjamin de Laborde and the first portfolios were published in 1784. The work was interrupted by the French Revolution and the final volumes were not published until 1802. The engravings reproduced here were all made by François Denis Née or under his supervision. The drawings from which the engravings were taken were executed in the 1780's and therefore represent the scenes essentially as Jefferson saw them. For a full bibliographical description of this work, see André Mongland, *La France Révolutionnaire et Impériale*, Grenoble, v (1938), 921-69. (Courtesy of The Boston Athenaeum.)

CHATEAU DE VERMANTON, NEAR AUXERRE

From a drawing by Lallemand, Plate No. 53, Bourgogne. See Notes of a Tour, 3 Mch. (p. 415)

CHATEAU DE CHAGNY, BETWEEN BEAUNE AND CHALONS

From a drawing by Lallemand, Plate No. 64, Bourgogne. See Notes of a Tour, 7-8 Mch. (p. 416-18).

MACON

From a drawing by Lallemand, Plate No. 35, Bourgogne. See Notes of a Tour, 9 Mch. (p. 418).

PONT DU GARD

From a drawing by Genillion, Plate No. 69, Provence. See Notes of a Tour, 19-23 Mch. (p. 424).

AIX-EN-PROVENCE

From a drawing by Meunier, Plate No. 2, Départ. des Bouches du Rhône. See Notes of a Tour, 25-28 Mch. (p. 426-7).

FOUNTAIN OF VAUCLUSE AND ENVIRONS

From a drawing by Genillion, Plate No. 76, Provence. See Notes of a Tour, 8 May (p. 443).

MAP OF THE CANAL OF LANGUEDOC

This map, printed at Paris by Dezauche in 1787, was enclosed in Jefferson's letter to George Washington, 2 May 1788, together with the relevant extracts of the memoranda of his tour. The Canal of Languedoc was one of the primary objectives of his journey and the detailed memoranda he accumulated on the construction and navigation of the canal comprise a large portion of the Notes of a Tour (p. 446-54). (Courtesy of the Library of Congress.)

[xxxiii]

Volume 11

1 January to 6 August 1787

JEFFERSON CHRONOLOGY
1743 · 1826

1743.	Born at Shadwell.
1772.	Married Martha Wayles Skelton.
1775-76.	In Continental Congress.
1776-79.	In Virginia House of Delegates.
1779-81.	Governor of Virginia.
1782.	His wife died.
1783-84.	In Continental Congress.
1784-89.	In France as commissioner and minister.
1790-93.	U.S. Secretary of State.
1797-1801.	Vice President of the United States.
1801-09.	President of the United States.
1826.	Died at Monticello.

VOLUME 11
1 January to 6 August 1787

9 January. Recommended Droz's new method of coinage to Jay.
27 January. With Adams, reported to Congress on the success of Barclay's negotiations with Morocco.
28 February. Departed on journey to southern France and northern Italy.
15 March. At Lyons.
20 March. At Nîmes.
29 March. Went from Aix to Marseilles.
11 April. At Nice.
20 April. At Milan.
23 April. At Rozzano.
25 April. At Genoa.
4 May. At Marseilles. Reported to Jay on Italian rice and possibility of Brazilian revolt against Portugal.
15-21 May. On the Canal of Languedoc.
24 May. At Bordeaux.
1 June. At Nantes.
10 June. Returned to Paris.
June. Mary Jefferson arrived in London and stayed with Mrs. John Adams.
July. Mary Jefferson brought to Paris by Petit.

THE PAPERS OF
THOMAS JEFFERSON

From Maria Cosway

[Stim]at.mo: Amico   Londra 1 Gennaio 1787

Ho aspettato con infinita ansietà la lunga lettera che m'annunziò, ma non so per qual delitto devo provar la penitenza di Tantalo, la credo ogni giorno vicina, ma quel giorno non arriva mai; nella sua ultima lettera d'un secolo passato mi dice aver ricevuta *una* mia lettera, ne o scritte fino tre, che mi ricordi, tutte dirette all' Banchiere secondo l'indirizzo che mi dette Mr. Trumbull. La perdita e mia, perche mi priva di quei momenti che sacrifica in leggere le mie lettere, mi richiamo per qualche instante alla sua memoria, e mi giustifica nel desiderio che o di farli i miei complimenti e di presentarli quelle attenzioni che lei tanto si merita per la sua compiacenza, ed amicizia per me; e quel che mi preme ancor di piu non mi dice come sta, se il suo braccio e guarito, se a ricevuto un libro di musica che gli mandai, tempo fà, * * * Eccoli soggetti bastanti da impiegare due linee, che la conseguenza non è interessante che a me e che puo scrivere per farmi piacere.

Sono la peggio persona del mondo per mandar *Novità* sicchè non entrerò mai in quel soggetto; sono sensibile alla severità della stagione; a quest'ingrato clima, e alla malinconia del Paese; forse mi par piu severo adesso, doppo i mesi allegri che passai in Parigi ove tutto è allegro, sono suscettibile e tutto quel che mi sta attorno a gran potere a magnetisarmi. Se tengo piu dalla Natura d'un senso, e quello di malinconia, secondo gli oggetti che mi stanno attorno, si puo dissipare o accrescere. Tale e l'influenza sopra la suscettibilità. Sono circondata da amabili Persone, Amici, e tutto quel che è lusinghevole, ma passo piu tempo in casa e posso dir che i piaceri vengono in traccia a me, perche non gli vado cercando altrove. Tutto il giorno dipingo, ed esercito la mia fantasia a tutto quel che indica, e tale e il piacere nella Pittura quando si a la libertà di seguire solo quando il desiderio c'inspira; la sera la passo generalmente in esercitarmi alla musica, e una amabile società rende l'armonia perfetta, ed ambi si uniscono a produrre il vero

1 JANUARY 1787

passatempo. Non son stata all' Opera, ma sento che e cattiva, non vado mai all Teatro, ed o piu piacere in ricusare ogni altro divertimento e impegni, che di accettarli. Ma cosa serve tutto questo preambolo, quando cominciai avevo intenzione di dir solo due parole, per confessar la verità voglio tenermi all' suo esempio; non voglio scancellare quel che o scritto perche sono riconoscente all' piacere che mi a procurato in conversar con lei, ma voglio esser crudele a me stessa e mortificarmi privandomi di continuar di più e finir con assicurarla che sono sempre con l'istessa stima ed affezione, Sua Um.ma: serva e vera amica, M.C.

RC (MHi). Recorded in SJL as received 8 Jan. 1787.

Translation: [Esteemed] friend, I have awaited with infinite anxiety the long letter which you announced to me, but I do not know for what crime I must experience the punishment of Tantalus, every day I believe it near, but that day never comes; in your last letter of a century ago you tell me you have received *one* letter of mine, I have written as many as three of them, as I recall, all directed to the banker according to the address which Mr. Trumbull gave me. The loss is mine, because it deprives me of those moments which you sacrifice in reading my letters, I recall myself for a few instants to your memory, and it justifies me in the desire which I have to pay you my compliments and to offer you those attentions which you so well deserve through your kindness and friendship for me; and what concerns me still more you do not tell me how you are, whether your arm is cured, whether you have received a book of music which I sent you some time ago * * * Here are subjects enough for you to fill two lines, whose import is of interest only to me and which you may write to please me.—I am the worst person in the world for sending *news* since I never enter upon that subject; I am sensitive to the severity of the season; to this unpleasant climate, and to the melancholy of this country; perhaps it seems more severe now, after the gay months I spent in Paris where everything is gay, I am susceptible and everything that surrounds me has great power to magnetize me. If I am more endowed by nature with any one sense, it is that of melancholy, according to the objects which surround me, it may be dissipated or increased. Such is the influence upon susceptibility. I am surrounded by amiable persons, friends, and everything that is flattering, I spend more time at home and I may say that pleasures come in search of me, because I do not go hunting for them elsewhere. All day I paint, and exercise my fancy on anything which it points out, and such is the pleasure in painting when one is free to follow only when desire inspires us; the evening I generally spend in practicing music, and a charming society makes the harmony perfect, and both unite to produce the true pastime. I have not been to the opera, but I hear that it is bad, I never go to the theater, and I take more pleasure in declining every other pastime and engagements, than in accepting them. But for what does all this preamble serve, when I began I intended to say only two words, to confess the truth I wish to hold myself to your example; I do not wish to erase what I have written because I am grateful for the pleasure which it has brought me in conversing with you, but I wish to be cruel to myself and mortify myself by depriving myself of continuing further and finish by assuring you that I am always with the same esteem and affection your most humble servant and true friend.

From H. Fizeaux & Cie.

Monsr.   Amsterdam le 1. Janr. 1787

Nous avons l'honneur de vous prévenir, qu'en remboursement des interets échus d'un emprunt de ƒ51000. à 5 p% pour les Etats unis de l'Amerique Septentrionale, nous fournissons ce jour sur

M. Grand à Paris, notre traite de   V. 1893.1.6 à 3 usances,
faisant au change de $52\frac{5}{16}$ Bo.ƒ2475.14.8

ce qui balance cet objet suivant la Notte que nous joignons ici; Nous vous prions Monsieur de vouloir bien autoriser ce Banquier à l'acceuil de nôtre traite, et pour qu'il en soit passé écriture de nôtre conformité.

Nous saisissons au même tems cette occasion pour vous prévenir que le remboursement de cet emprunt echeoit le 1e. Janvr. 1788; afin que vous presices, dans l'intervale, les mésures qui vous paraitront necessaires pour nous   [1] des fonds qu'exige ce payement.

Nous avons l'honneur d'etre avec la plus parfaite consideration Monsieur &c.,   H. Fizeaux & Co.

Tr (DNA: PCC, No. 107, i). Recorded in sjl as received 11 Jan. 1787. Enclosure (DLC): "la Notte" included an item as follows: "Agio a 3 p% . . . "74.5.8" which balanced the total of ƒ2550, being the whole of the interest at 5% on ƒ51,000. This item is explained by the fact that accounts were usually kept in either current money (sometimes called *Cassa*) or bank money, commonly referred to as *Banco* (or abbreviated as *Bo.* as in the above instance). *Banco* was preferred and therefore bore a premium called *Agio* (Kelly, *Universal Cambist*, London, 1811, i, 13).

[1] Blank in MS; "fournir" probably intended.

From Thomas Boylston

Sr.   London Jany. 2. 1787

I am favor'd with a Letter, adviseing me of your success in the reduction of the duties on Whale Spermacoeti Oil, which was the Object of my pursuit last Winter at Paris, and left undetermined, under your care and vigilance to perfect and carry to the happy issue, its now arrived at. Mr. Garvey who favors me with this inteligence, does not say, whether the Oil I had in the Diana, and paid this duty, receives the benefit of this reduction or not. I presume and don't doubt it does; it was on that Oils Account the application was first made, and rested with the Minister to deside upon.

I must beg the favor of your attention to any necessary steps, to secure the repayment of it to me, and leave no room for Objections arising to any lapse of time on Account of my absence, or want of a Seasonable application made in my behalf. An Order from Court or the Minister to the Collector of the Customs who received it, to refund the Money, seems to me a ready, and direct method to be taken in this case. However you are undoubtedly the best judge of the necessary steps to be taken, and beg the favor of your kind aid and assistance in it.

I propose being in Paris as soon as possible and presume it will be some time in Feby. In the mean while the honor of a line from you on this business will be most gratefully acknowledge by Sr. Your most Obliged hume. Serv., THO BOYLSTON

RC (DLC); endorsed. Recorded in SJL as received 8 Jan. 1787.

From Goltz

Le 2. janvier

Le Cte. de Goltz reçoit tout à l'heure les exemplaires de l'Acte de La Virginie, que Monsieur Jefferson a La bonté de lui envoÿer et s'empresse de Lui en faire tous ses remerciemens et de renouveler les assurances de Sa consideration distinguée pour Lui.

RC (MHi); without indication of the year, but presumably 1787, since TJ was at this time still distributing copies of the Virginia Act for Establishing Religious Freedom. Not recorded in SJL. Baron de Goltz was envoy extraordinary from Prussia in 1786-1788 (*Almanach Royal*).

From Brissot de Warville, with Enclosure

MONSIEUR   Chancellerie d'orléans ce 3 Janvier lan 1787.

J'ai L'honneur de Vous adresser ci Joint Les questions sur les fonds publics des Etats unis dont je Vous ai parlé. Vous m'avés fait esperer, ainsi que M. decrevecoeur, que Vous pourriés en Vous adressant au treasury Board du Congrès nous procurer une reponse complete et exacte sur tous Les points.

Cette reponse est singulierement importante pour fonder le credit des Etats unis, et Je ne doute point que mon digne ami Claviere avec son ami d'Amsterdam ne parviennent à Leur etablir un grand credit, quand une fois, ils auront des Lumieres sufisantes sur leur situation.

Vous Voudrés donc bien, Monsieur, Mettre ces questions au Nombre de Vos depeches prochaines et me faire parvenir ou à M. Claviere La reponse aussitot qu'elle sera dans vos mains.[1]

[6]

3 JANUARY 1787

J'ai Communiqué à M. Le Marquis du Crest Le resultat de La derniere conversation que J'ai eu l'honneur d'avoir avec Vous. La reponse de M. de V——— ne L'effraie point, et Il est Convenu qu'après avoir eu L'honneur de Vous faire une Visite ainsi qu'à Monsr. Le Marquis De la fayette, il concerteroit un rendès vous, avec vous et avec lui, pour determiner La Marche à prendre. En atendant ce moment je m'ocupe du memoire à presenter aux Ministres.

Puisque Je viens de Nommer M. Le Mis. de la fayette, Voulés Vous bien me permettre de me feliciter avec vous et avec tous Les amis du bien public de sa Nomination pour L'assemblée prochaine. Je ne sais pas à qui elle fait plus d'honneur, ou aux ministres ou à Lui; mais Je sais à qui ce choix fera du bien. C'est au peuple.

Aussitôt que J'aurai un Moment de Libre, Je m'empresserai de vous porter Les plans que Je vous ai promis.

Je suis avec respect Monsieur Votre très humble et très obeissant serviteur,   Brissot de Warville

ENCLOSURE
Questions Sur Les fonds Publics des Etats unis

On Suppose que le Congrès des Etats unis d'Amérique met quelqu'importance à leur établir un bon Credit en Europe. Ils ne peuvent y trouver que de grands avantages. La grande affaire des Américains est sans contredit les déffrichemens, et ces déffrichemens demandent toujours plus de Numeraire parce qu'ils le répandent sur une plus grande étendue de Païs. Il sera donc avantageux aux Americains de donner à leurs papiers un tel credit qu'il puisse se placer dans les Etats de l'Europe, où l'argent est très abondant, et dans ceux où le Commerce peut les admettre; car ces papiers pourroient venir chercher l'argent Européen de plusieurs manieres, soit directement et par voye d'emprunt, soit indirectement, et en retour de fournitures Europeennes lorsque les productions Americaines ne suffiroient pas au moment même pour les payer.

La constitution Republicaine est, de toutes, celle qui favorise le mieux un Crédit public; et sous ce point de vue les Etats unis ont droit au Crédit le plus étendu puisqu'il s'apuie sur un sol immense fertilisé par la liberté.

Mais dans ce moment, soit par la malice de leurs ennemis, soit par les difficultés qui s'élèvent entr'eux sur leurs dettes et leurs régulations intérieures, on ne peut pas encore faire naître en Europe en faveur des Americains une confiance générale. Une infinité de faits, vrais ou faux, ou mal representés, donnent des ombrages perpétuels, et font croire à beaucoup de gens que les Américains eux mêmes ne sont pas encore persuadés de l'importance de leur credit au dehors, ou ne connoissent pas toute l'étendue des égards dus aux maximes que fondent et maintiennent le Credit public.

3 JANUARY 1787

Il seroit donc très nécéssaire d'avoir, tant de la part du congrès que de la chambre de la Trésorerie, toutes les instructions nécessaires pour se former des Idées justes sur l'état présent des dettes Americaines intérieures et extérieures; sur la maniere dont elles sont considérées en général et en particulier, par la réunion des Etats, et par chacun d'eux individuellement, et pour juger s'il y a des dettes dont le remboursement soit considéré sous des degrés differens de certitude.

Les fonds (Stocks) Americains se divisent en effets continentaux, et effets particuliers à chaque Etat.

On desire Sur les premiers d'avoir

Leur Liste.
Leur Origine.
Le Capital.
La forme.
Le terme de remboursement s'il y en a.
Par qui il est payé.
Quand, Comment, ou?
Quels sont ceux qui ont cours dans le Commerce?
S'il y en a qui soyent reçus aux payemens des taxes, ou qui servent à ce payement?
Est-il dû des arrerages et en quelle quantité?
Sur quel Objet chaque emprunt ou fond continental est-il hypothequé?

Les mêmes questions sont à repondre sur les fonds particuliers à chaque état; et s'il y en a de ceux ci qui soient reçus dans tous les Etats, on desire d'en avoir la liste; comme aussi de connoitre ceux qui n'y sont pas reçus et qu'elle en est la raison?

On desireroit aussi d'avoir la liste des prix auxquels tous les differens effets Américains se négocient actuellement, et la distinction de ceux dont le rembours prochain est le plus probable.

Enfin, cette question regarde plus particulierement le Congrès.

On demande quel intérêt le Congrès accorderoit à des particuliers qui lui preteroient de l'argent, à la condition de n'en pouvoir être remboursé qu'en fonds de terres appartenantes au Congrès, et dans le cours d'un certain nombre d'années, que le Congrès designeroit, et qui ne devroit pas être trop court.

Si de pareils emprunts pouvoient avoir lieu, ils exigeroient la determination d'une certaine étendue de terres avantageusement situées pour le commerce et la culture, lesquelles seroient reservées pour acquitter ces emprunts, en déterminant d'avance la maniere dont les porteurs de ces effets pourroient en prendre possession.

Si une telle idée peut s'apliquer à un Plan quelconque, d'une exécution sure et facile, et qu'il soit possible de lui donner une forme séduisante pour ceux qui cherchent à varier l'employ de leur argent, il ne seroit pas impossible que cette maniere d'emprunter ne reussit en Europe, surtout si le produit de tels emprunts servoit à aquitter des parties de dettes etrangères, parce qu'alors ils donneroient lieu à des traités entre des particuliers et les Etats même à qui le Congrès a des avances à rembourser.

Mais il faudroit que les Plans de tels Emprunts arrivassent en Europe avec des pleins pouvoirs aux Ambassadeurs du Congrès de traiter, et meme de pouvoir admettre certaines modifications, et y engager le Congrès, s'il s'en presentoit de convenables aux préteurs, sans être nuisibles aux interest des Etats unis.

RC (DLC); endorsed. Tr (DLC); extract in the hand of William Short. Recorded in SJL as received 4 Jan. 1787. Enclosure (MoSHi); undated and at head of text in Brissot's hand: "Questions Sur les fonds Publics des Etats unis." Tr (DLC); in Short's hand, also without date.

[1] Text of Tr ends at this point.

From Étienne Clavière

Monsieur L'Ambassadeur   Paris Le 3. J. 1787.

J'ay l'honneur de vous envoyer un petit mémoire, que Monsieur de Warville m'a dit que vous voudriez bien faire passer en Amérique. Je crois une reponse à ce mémoire utile à vos Etats si elle est bien Circonstanciée.

Je ne puis voir sans douleur, comme sans étonnement, qu'en Amérique, où il y a tant de lumières, on s'écarte encore des vrais principes sur le papier monoye. Toute contrainte est diamétralement oposée à son credit et sans crédit c'est une peste qui fait des ravages affreux sur les propriétés et sur les mœurs. Il introduit un esprit d'agiotage qui devient bientot une cruelle usure. Comment ne voit-on pas que Les monoye d'or et d'argent ne tirent leur credit que de l'usage qu'on peut en faire partout? Et le papier monoye a-t-il cet avantage? Quand la liberté de le refuse[r] ne peut pas L'accréditer, il n'en faut point faire, car toute situation, *dans la paix*, est préfférable à celle où l'on ordonne la circulation forceé du papier.

Pardonnes ces reflexions à un pauvre républicain dépaysé qui ne cessera d'aimer et d'adorer la liberté dont il ne peut plus jouïr, et qui éprouve une cruelle douleur lorsqu'il voit qu'elle se calomnie par ignorance.

Agrées mes voeux pour votre bonheur et votre Contentement dans cette nouvelle année et les suivantes.

Je suis avec respect Monsieur l'Ambassadeur Votre très humble & très obeïssant serviteur,   E Claviere

RC (MoSHi); endorsed. Recorded in SJL as received 4 Jan. 1787.
The petit mémoire enclosed by Claviere has not been identified. It may have been his *Lettre à l'auteur du Mercure politique par les auteurs du traité intitulé: De la France et des Etats-Unis*, 1787.

From Le Couteulx & Cie.

SIR   Paris 3 Jany. 1787

By the inclosed from Mr. Barrett, your Excellency will observe that no order has been as yet officially given to the farmers people at Ruan, relative to the Relaxation of the Duties, which they have perceived upon an American Oil Spermaceti Cargoe, much less have they had the necessary Orders relative to the entire taking off of them in those, that come for Account of Mr. Barrett's Contract. It would be then Sir, of a very urging Moment to have your Excellency interfere in this Affair and write to Mr. de Calonne that he should order the farmers to give at Ruan the necessary Orders in favor of Mr. Barrett's Contract, as he has promised it already in the printed Letter written by him to your Excellency and that he should give your Excellency at the same time an Answer by writing that could in the mean Time serve Mr. Barrett as a Title to refuse himself to the Payment of the Duties, without running the Risks of being prosecuted by the Agents of the farm.

I profit of this Occasion to repeat myself at the Obedience of your Excellency & subscribe myself Your most obedt. hble. Servt.,

LE COUTEULX & CIE.

RC (DLC). Recorded in SJL as received 5 Jan. 1787. Enclosure: Barrett to TJ, 25 Dec. 1786.

To Alexander McCaul

DEAR SIR   Paris Jan. 4. 1787.

In the letter which I had the honor of addressing you from London on the 19th. of April 1786 I informed you that I had left my estate in the hands of a Mr. Eppes and a Mr. Lewis, who were first to clear off some debts which had been necessarily contracted during the war, and afterwards to apply the whole profits to the paiment of my debt to you (by which I mean that to the several firms with which you were connected) and of my part of a debt due from Mr. Wayles's estate to Farrell & Jones of Bristol. Being anxious to begin the paiment of these two debts, and finding that it would be too long postponed if the residuary ones were to be paid merely from the annual profits of the estate, a number of slaves have been sold, and I have lately received information from Messrs. Eppes and Lewis that the proceeds of that sale with the profits of the estate to the end of 1786 would pay off the whole of the residuary

4 JANUARY 1787

debts. As we are now therefore clear of embarrassments to pursue our principal object, I am desirous of arranging with you such just and practicable conditions as will ascertain to you the receipt of your debt, and give me the satisfaction of knowing that you are contented. What the laws of Virginia are, or may be, will in no wise influence my conduct. Substantial justice is my object, as decided by reason, and not by authority or compulsion.

The article of interest may make a difficulty. I had the honour of observing to you, in my former letter, that I thought it just I should pay it for all the time preceding the war, and all the time subsequent to it. But that for the time during the war I did not consider myself as bound in justice to pay. This includes the period from the commencement of hostilities Apr. 19. 1775. to their cessation Apr. 19. 1783, being exactly eight years. To the reasons against this paiment which apply in favor of the whole mass of American debtors, I added the peculiar circumstance of having already lost the debt, principal and interest, by endeavoring to pay it by the sale of lands and by the depreciation of their price: and also a second loss of an equal sum by Ld. Cornwallis's barbarous and useless depredations. I will therefore refer you to that letter, to save the repetition here of those reasons which absolve me in justice from the paiment of this portion of interest. In law, our courts have uniformly decided that the treaty of peace stipulates the paiment of the principal only and not of any interest whatever.

This article being once settled, I would propose to divide the clear proceeds of my estate (in which there are from 80. to 100. labouring slaves) between yourself and Farrell & Jones, one third to you and two thirds to them: and that the crop of this present year 1787. shall constitute the first paiment. That crop you know cannot be got to the warehouse completely till May of the next year, and I presume that three months more will be little enough to send it to Europe, or to sell it in Virginia and remit the money. So that I could not safely answer for placing the proceeds in your hands till the month of August, and so annually every August afterwards till the debt shall be paid. It will always be both my interest and my wish to get it to you as much sooner as possible, and probably a part of it may always be paid some months sooner. If the assigning the profits in general terms may seem to you too vague, I am willing to fix the annual paiment at a sum certain. But that I may not fall short of my engagement, I shall name it somewhat less than I suppose may be counted on. I shall fix your part at two hundred pounds sterling annually: and as you know our

5 JANUARY 1787

crops of tobacco to be incertain, I should reserve a right, if they should fall short one year, to make it up the ensuing one, without being supposed to have failed in my engagement. But I would be obliged every second year to pay any arrearages of the preceding one together with the full sum for the current year: so that once in every two years the annual paiment should be fully paid up.

I do not know what the balance is; having for a long time before the war had no settlement, yet there can be no difficulty in making that settlement, and in the mean while the paiments may proceed without affecting the right of either party to have a just settlement.

If you think proper to accede to these propositions, be so good as to say so at the foot of a copy of this letter. On my receipt of that, I will send you an acknolegement of it, which shall render this present letter obligatory on me for the paiment of the debt before mentioned, and interest, at the epochs and in the proportions beforementioned, excepting always the interest during the war. This done, you may count on my faithful execution of it.

I avail myself of this, as of every other occasion of recalling myself to your friendly recollection, and of assuring you of the sentiments of perfect esteem and attachment with which I am Dear Sir your most obedt. & most humble servant,

Th: Jefferson

PrC (DLC); endorsed. BE SO GOOD AS TO SAY SO AT THE FOOT OF A COPY OF THIS LETTER: This means that TJ enclosed a second PrC, but it has not been found.

From C. W. F. Dumas

Monsieur Lahaie 5e. Janv. 1786 [i.e., 1787]

Je suis affecté de l'accident qui, faisant souffrir votre Excellence, m'avoit privé de l'honneur de sa correspondance. J'espere qu'une main si précieuse à l'Amerique, à vos Amis, à l'Humanité, se remettra tout-à-fait, et apprendrai avec joie que Votre Excellence est hors de souffrance.

J'ai vérifié et trouvé conformes les dates de mes Lettres jusqu'au 1er. Dec. inclus, où étoit No. 13 pour Mr. Jay.—V. E. doit avoir reçu depuis, No. 14, du 2 au 6. Dec. au même. No. 15 du 22 Dec. au même. et puis une du 29 Dec. à V. E.

J'attends réponse de Mr. De la Fayette à celles qu'il doit avoir reçues de moi en date du 8, du 9 et du 22 Dec: étant surtout en peine de celle du 9.

5 JANUARY 1787

J'ai écrit à Mr. Luzac ce qu'il falloit pour donner au public une idée juste dans son papier des petits mouvemens qui ont eu lieu en Amérique. Je l'ai prié aussi confidemment, de supprimer la Piece falsifiée, si elle lui parvient.

Quant à la question que V. E. me propose, son importance m'impose la nécessité de demander au moins une quinzaine de jours pour en donner mon opinion. Je ferai dans cet intervalle un voyage exprès pour cela à Amsterdam, afin de m'y aboucher là-dessus avec une personne de confiance, de la discrétion de laquelle, ainsi que de ses dispositions pour les Etats-Unis, je suis sûr, et je sonderai ce terrain avec toute la prudence et la délicatesse requise. J'ignore si maintenant tous les Etats se sont mis entierement en regle quant au Revenu qu'il faut au Congrès pour payer les Intérêts de la Dette commune tant interne qu'externe. Si cela est, cela donnera certainement le plus grand poids et relief à la proposition. En attendant que je puisses la meurir et en parler avec plus de connoissance de cause, il est bon que cela reste secret entre V. E. et moi; tout comme, lorsque le projet auroit pris quelque consistence, il n'en seroit que mieux que son exécution ne passât par d'autres mains que celles de V. E. et les miennes. J'ai de fortes raisons pour dire cela et suis avec grand respect De V. E. le très humble & très obeisst. serviteur,
C W F Dumas

RC (DLC); endorsed. FC (Rijksarchief, The Hague, Dumas Papers; photostats in DLC); date corrected to "1787" by overwriting. Entry in SJL of its receipt on 11 Jan. 1787 reads: "Dumas. Haie. Jan. 5. (1786 for 1787)." There is no mention of an enclosure, but Dumas must have sent with this letter his "No. 16" for Congress which he had told TJ (Dumas to TJ, 29 Dec. 1786) he did not wish to send by post. This was Dumas' letter to Jay of 1 Jan. 1787, containing his "*Divinatio quarto*" in which he inserted a "Pro-Memoria" that had been drawn up the 23rd of December, translated the 24th, and transmitted to the same person who received the first memoir, a copy of which was in Dumas' despatch No. 14 of Dec. 2nd; and stating that the negotiations started by Rayneval and Goertz had fallen through; that the States General, suspended during the holidays, would reassemble on the 16th; that a crisis is at hand, and Rayneval probably only awaits the last courier sent to Versailles in order to return, thoroughly put out at the stubbornness of the prince; that there are to be no more diplomatic conversations, but categorical measures will be taken; that Dumas was obliged at the end of December to draw on Willink, Nicolas and Jacob Van Staphorst for part of the arrears due him according to the act of Congress of Oct. 14th, 1785; that his situation is miserable: "Me laissera-t-on succomber et périr lentement?"; and that Goertz has returned from Nijmegen "Veritablement et au pied de la lettre *rebus infectis*." This letter is among those listed as missing in *Dipl. Corr.*, 1783-89, III, 541; although dated 1 Jan. it includes a continuation of events in Holland up through 6 Jan. 1787.

LA PIECE FALSIFIÉE: That is, the letter from TJ to Jay, 27 May 1786, which TJ claimed was "mutilated" in its publication in American newspapers. Dumas may have spoken to Luzac about suppressing the piece if it should come to him, as TJ had requested, for there is no letter recorded in Dumas' letter book covering this subject, and none has been found in the Luzac Papers at the University of Leiden. The present letter was enclosed in one to

[13]

Brantzen, ambassador of the States General at Versailles, to whom Dumas wrote on 4 Jan. 1787 asking permission to continue the practice for the time being: "J'ai besoin d'écrire quelques Lettres à Mr. Jefferson et de les soustraire pendant quelques temps [. . . ⟨indiscrets⟩] à etre ouvertes en chemin. Je prends la Liberté de commencer par l'incluse sous le couvert de V.E., espérant que V.E. me la pardonnera et me permettra de la continuer" (FC, Rijksarchief, The Hague, Dumas Papers; photostats in DLC).

To William Jones

Sir   Paris Jan. 5. 1787.

When I had the pleasure of seeing you in London, I mentioned to you that the affairs of Mr. Wayles's estate were left to be ultimately settled by Mr. Eppes, the only acting executor; that I had left in his hands also and in those of a Mr. Lewis the part of Mr. Wayles's estate which came to me, together with my own: that they were first to clear off some debts which had been necessarily contracted during the war, and would after that apply the whole profits to the paiment of my part of Mr. Wayles's debt to you, and to a debt of mine to Kippen & co. of Glasgow. Being anxious to begin the paiment of these two debts, and finding that it would be too long postponed if the residuary ones were to be paid merely from the annual profits of the estate, a number of slaves have been sold, and I have lately received information from Messrs. Eppes and Lewis that the proceeds of that sale, with the profits of the estate to the end of 1781.[1] would pay off the whole of the residuary debts. As we are now therefore clear of embarassment to pursue our principal object, I am desirous of arranging with you, such just and practicable conditions as will ascertain to you the terms at which you will receive my part of your debt, and give me the satisfaction of knowing that you are contented. What the laws of Virginia are, or may be, will in no wise influence my conduct. Substantial justice is my object, as decided by reason, and not by authority or compulsion.

The first question which arises is as to the article of interest. For all the time preceding the war, and all subsequent to it, I think it reasonable that interest should be paid; but equally unreasonable during the war. Interest is a compensation for the use of money. Your money in my hands is in the form of lands and negroes. From these, during the war, no use, no profits could be derived. Tobacco is the article they produce. That can only be turned into money at a foreign market. But the moment it went out of our ports for that purpose, it was captured either by the king's ships or by those of individuals. The consequence was that tobacco, worth from twenty to thirty shillings the hundred, sold generally in Virginia during the war for five shillings. This price it is known will not maintain the labourer and pay his taxes. There was no surplus of profit then to pay an interest. In the mean while we stood insurers of the lives of the labourers and of the ultimate issue of the war. He who attempted during the war to remit either his principal or interest, must have expected to remit three times to make one paiment; because it is supposed that two out of three parts of the shipments were taken. It was not possible then for the debtor to derive any profit from the money which might enable him to pay an interest, nor yet to get rid of the principal by remitting it to his creditor. With respect to the Creditors in Great Britain they mostly turned their attention to privateering, and, arming the vessels they had before emploied in trading with us, they captured on the seas, not only the produce of the farms of their debtors, but of those of the whole state. They thus paid themselves by capture more than their annual interest and we lost more. Some merchants indeed did not engage in privateering. These lost their interest but we did not gain it. It fell into the hands of their countrymen. It cannot therefore be demanded of us. As between these merchants and their debtors it is the case where, a loss being incurred, each party may justifiably endeavor to shift it from himself. Each has an equal right to avoid it. One party can never expect the other to yeild a thing to which he has as good a right as the demander. We even think he has a better right than the demander in the present instance. This loss has been occasioned by the fault of the nation which was creditor. Our right to avoid it then stands on less exceptionable ground than theirs. But it will be said that each party thought the other the aggressor. In these disputes there is but one umpire, and that has decided the question where the world in general thought the right laid.

Besides these reasons in favor of the general mass of debtors, I have some peculiar to my own case. In the year 1776. before a shilling of paper money was issued, I sold lands to the amount of £4200 in order to pay these two debts. I offered the bonds of the purchasers to your agent Mr. Evans, if he would acquit me, and accept of the purchasers as debtors, in my place. They were as sure as myself. Had he done it, these debts, being turned over to you, would have been saved to you by the treaty of peace. But he declined it. Great sums of paper money were afterwards issued. This depreciated, and paiment was made me in this money when

5 JANUARY 1787

it was but a shadow. Our laws do not entitle their own citizens to require repaiment in these cases, tho the treaty authorizes the British creditor to do it. Here then I lost the principal and interest once. Again, Ld. Cornwallis encamped 10. days on an estate of mine at Elk-island, having his headquarters in my house. He burned all the tobacco houses and barns on the farm, with the produce of the former year in them. He burnt all the inclosures, and wasted the feilds in which the crop of that year was growing (it was the month of June). He killed or carried off every living animal, cutting the throats of those which were too young for service. Of the slaves he carried away thirty. The useless and barbarous injury he did me in that instance was more than would have paid your debt, principal and interest. Thus I lost it a second time. Still I will lay my shoulder assiduously to the paiment of it a third time. In doing this however I think yourself will be of opinion I am authorized in justice to clear it of every article not demandeable in strict right. Of this nature I consider interest during the war.

Another question is as to the paper money I deposited in the treasury of Virginia towards the discharge of this debt. I before observed that I had sold lands to the amount of 4200£ before a shilling of paper money was emitted, with a view to pay this debt. I received this money in depreciated paper. The state was then calling on those who owed money to British subjects to bring it into the treasury, engaging to pay a like sum to the creditor at the end of the war. I carried the identical money therefore to the treasury, where it was applied, as all the money of the same description was to the support of the war. Subsequent events have been such that the state cannot, and ought not to pay the same nominal sum in gold or silver which they received in paper, nor is it certain what they will do. My intention being, and having always been, that, whatever the state decides, you shall receive my part of your debt fully, I am ready to remove all difficulty arising from this deposit, to take back to myself the demand against the state, and to consider the deposit as originally made for myself and not for you.

These two articles of interest and paper money being thus settled, I would propose to divide the clear proceeds of the estate (in which there are from 80. to 100 labouring slaves) between yourself and Kippen & co., two thirds to you and one third to them: and that the crop of this present year 1787 shall constitute the first paiment. That crop you know cannot be got to the warehouse completely till May of the next year and I suppose that three

5 JANUARY 1787

months more will be little enough to send it to Europe, or to sell it in Virginia and remit the money. So that I could not safely answer for placing the proceeds in your hands till the month of August, and so annually every August afterwards till the debt shall be paid. It will always be both my interest and my wish to get it to you as much sooner as possible, and probably a part of it may always be paid some months sooner. If the assigning the profits in general terms may seem to you too vague, I am willing to fix the annual paiment at a sum certain. But that I may not fall short of my engagement, I shall name it somewhat less than I suppose may be counted on. I shall fix your part at four hundred pounds sterling annually. And as you know our crops of tobacco to be incertain, I should reserve a right if they fall short one year, to make it up the ensuing one, without being supposed to have failed in my engagement. But every other year at least all arrearages shall be fully paid up.

My part of this debt of Mr. Wayles's estate being one third, I should require that in proportion as I pay my third, I shall stand discharged as to the other two thirds, so that the paiment of every hundred pounds shall discharge me as to three hundred pounds of the undivided debt. The other gentlemen have equal means of paying, equal desires, and more skill in affairs. Their parts of the debt therefore are at least as sure as mine: and my great object is, in case of any accident to myself, to leave my family uninvolved with any matters whatever.

I do not know what the balance of this debt is. The last account current I saw was before the war, making the whole balance, principal and interest somewhere about nine thousand pounds: and after this there were upwards of four hundred hogsheads of tobacco and some paiments in money to be credited. However this settlement can admit of no difficulty: and in the mean time the paiments may proceed without affecting the right of either party to have a just settlement.

Upon the whole then I propose that on your part you relinquish the claim to interest during the war, say from the commencement of hostilities April 19. 1775. to their cessation April 19. 1783. being exactly eight years: and that in proportion as I pay my third I shall be acquitted as to the other two thirds. On my part I take on myself the loss of the paper money deposited in the treasury, I agree to pay interest previous and subsequent to the war, and oblige myself to remit to you for that and the principal four hundred pounds sterling annually, till my third of the whole debt

5 JANUARY 1787

shall be fully paid; and I will begin these paiments in August of the next year.

If you think proper to accede to these propositions, be so good as to say so at the foot of a copy of this letter. On my receipt of that, I will send you an acknowlegement of it, which shall render this present letter obligatory on me. In which case you may count on my faithful execution of this undertaking.

I have the honour to be with great respect Sir Your most obedient & most humble servant,

TH: JEFFERSON

RC (NN); endorsed. PrC (DLC). Entry in SJL reads: "[Jan.] 5. Jones Wm. (Bristol)," to distinguish him from William Jones of London. TJ enclosed a second PrC OF THIS LETTER as he did in his to McCaul of 4 Jan. 1787, but it has not been found.

When the question of TJ's debts to British merchants (and those that devolved upon him in the Wayles estate) became political matters at a later date, this letter was "produced in court by Jones's agent, and afterwards published in the Aurora," whence it was also published by John Wood, *History of the Administration of John Adams*, New York, 1802, p. 442-9.

[1] Thus in MS; 1786 was intended; see TJ to McCaul, 4 Jan. 1787.

From Chartier de Lotbinière

Paris, rue de Bourgogne No. 78, au Coin de la rue de Varenne, 5 Jan. 1787. Asks TJ for an appointment during the next week to confer about a letter he had received from John Jay, dated 15 Aug. preceding.

RC (DLC); 2 p.; in French; endorsed. Not recorded in SJL.

Jay's letter was in response to one from Lotbinière of 11 Mch. 1786 concerning his claim to the seigniories of Alainville and Hocquart on Lake Champlain, a subject, he reminded Jay, that Vergennes took a great interest in and had more than once recommended to the attention of the United States. Lotbinière had also urged Jay to give the benefit of his protection to his son who was coming to America to claim lands in Massachusetts. Jay replied that all titles and claims to lands lying within any of the states had to be determined by its laws and that Congress could not with propriety interfere in such matters; he promised to give his "friendly attentions" to Lotbinière's son, but added: "In this Country protection and personal Influence, whether more or less, are no avail in our judicial proceedings and decisions, which are entirely directed and governed by the Laws of the Land" (copies of this exchange were sent by Lotbinière to Vergennes, and are to be found in Arch. Aff. Etr., Corr. Pol., E.-U., XXXI; Tr in DLC).

To Samuel Osgood

DEAR SIR
Paris Jan. 5. 1787.

I am desired to forward to you the inclosed queries, and to ask the favor of you to give such an answer to them as may not give you too much trouble. Those which stand foremost on the paper can be addressed only to your complaisance; but the last may possibly be interesting to your department, and to the United states: I mean those which suggest the possibility of borrowing money in Europe, the principal of which shall be ultimately paiable in land, and in the mean time a good interest. You know best whether the suggestion can be turned to any profit, and whether it will be worth while to introduce any proposition to Congress thereon. Among the possible shapes into which a matter of this kind may be formed, the following is one. Let us suppose the public lands to be worth a dollar, hard money, the acre. If we should ask of a monied man the loan of 100 dollars, paiable with 100 acres of land at the end of 10. years, and in the mean time an interest of 5. per cent, this would be more disadvantageous to the lender than a common loan paiable ultimately in cash. But if we should say we will deliver you the 100 acres of land immediately, which is in fact an immediate paiment of the principal, and will nevertheless pay your interest of 5. per cent for 10. years, this offers a superior advantage, and might tempt money holders. But what should we in fact receive in this way for our lands? $37\frac{1}{4}$ dollars being left in Europe on an interest of 5. per cent would pay annually the interest of the 100 for 10. years. There would remain then only $62\frac{3}{4}$ dollars for the 100 acres of land, that is to say about two thirds of it's price. Congress can best determine whether any circumstances in our situation should induce us to get rid of any of our debts in that way. I beg you to understand that I have named rates of interest, term of paiment and price of land merely to state the case, and without the least knowlege that a loan could be obtained on these terms. It remains to inform you from whom this suggestion comes. The person from whom I receive them is a Monsr. Claviere, connected with the monied men of Amsterdam. He is, on behalf of a company there, actually treating with the Comptroller general here for the purchase of our debt to this country at a considerable discount. Whether he has in idea any thing like a loan to us on terms such as I have above spoken of I know not; nor do I know that he is authorised to make the suggestion he has made. If the thing should be deemed worthy the attention of Congress, they can only consider it as a possibility and take measures to avail themselves of it if the possibility turns out in their favor, and not to be disappointed if it does not. Claviere's proposition not being formal enough for me to make an official communication of it, you will make what use of it you see best. I am with very sincere esteem & attachment, Dear Sir, your most obedient & most humble servant, TH: JEFFERSON

5 JANUARY 1787

PrC (DLC). Enclosure: Queries concerning the public funds of the United States, printed above as enclosure to Brissot de Warville to TJ, 4 Jan. 1787.

From José da Maia

MONSEGNEUR   à Montpellier 5 de Janvier 1787

La nouvelle, que je viens d'avoir l'honeur de recevoir de Votre voyage dans cette partie de France, m'a fait un tres grand plaisir, et je m'en felicite; puisque je voyois, qu'il m'etoit tres essentiel d'avoir l'honeur de Vous parler, et l'etat de ma santé ne me permettoit pas de faire le voyage de Paris. Si je pouvois savoir le jour de Votre arrivée à Nismes, et votre logement, je ne manquerois pas d'avoir l'honeur d'y aller Vous rencontrer, ce que je suis pret à faire dans quelque autre, où il Vous faira plaisir: et pour cela je n'attends que Vos commandemens. En attendant je me flate d'être avec le plus grand respect Monsegneur Votre tres humble et obeissant serviteur,   VENDEK

RC (DLC); endorsed. Entry in SJL, noting its receipt on 15 Jan. 1787, reads: "Vendek (Maya Barbalho Dr) Monpelier Jan. 5." See TJ to José da Maia, 26 Dec. 1786.

From Thomas Barclay

DEAR SIR   Alicante 6th. Janry. 1787.

The inclos'd letter to you and Mr. Adams of this date contains every thing that occurs relative to my business here, and the Day after tomorrow I shall leave it and remain at Madrid untill I can decide on the necessity of going to Coruña. The objects there are the Effects belonging to the United States left by Mr. Guillon and the proceeds of some prizes carried in by Capt. Cunyingham. It is three years since attempts have been made to settle these matters by correspondence and from appearances at present Nothing but an application to this Government will extort it. After consulting Mr. Carmichael I will abide by his opinion. I have been for some time a little uneasy respecting your state of health, but as Col: Franks has written me a few lines I think it probable if you had been indispos'd he wou'd have mention'd it. I sincerely wish you many returns of the year attended with Health and Happiness. When Col: Franks left Spain for Paris I paid him 1266 livres for which he promis'd to account with you. After deducting his Expences the balance will not be great but you will have the

[20]

Goodness to receive it, or to save you trouble he may pay it to Mrs. Barclay. He also promis'd to place in your hands as soon as he wou'd get to Paris an account of his last voyage from America. But as he does not mention either of these Settlements I take it for granted they are neither of them Made. Inclos'd is a letter for him which please to send and if agreeable, you will have the Goodness to tell him there is a necessity for his furnishing the account of his voyage to Europe.

It will give me great pleasure to receive a line from you under cover to Mr. Carmichael. Mean time I am Dr. Sir Your most obedt. hble. Servant,
THOS BARCLAY

RC (DLC); in an unidentified hand, signed by Barclay; endorsed. Recorded in SJL as received 27 Jan. 1787. Enclosures: (1) Barclay to the Commissioners, 6 Jan. 1787. (2) A letter to Franks, presumably from Barclay, not found.

Thomas Barclay to the American Commissioners

GENTLEMEN Alicante 6 Jany. 1787

I Have Not had the pleasure of addressing You since My arrival at this place, being hitherto without any thing to say worth Your Attention. Mr. Lamb was Embarked for Minorca before I got here, but as he is in Correspondance with Mr. Montgomery, I was in hopes of learning through that Channel, the possibility of our Meeting before I shou'd return to France, a Matter that I am of opinion might have been attended with some Advantages. But the Letters which he has lately written Hold out Nothing, and therefore I Contented My self with writing to him the Motives which Induced me to Come here, and am without any Expectation of seeing him. As the Spanish Portugueze and Neapolitan Ministers were preparing to Embark from Carthagena, I went and passed one Day at that place in hopes of learning something that Might be useful, and I took that opportunity of Impressing on the Mind of the Count D'Espilly, some Matters that had before been talked over at Madrid and the Escurial, and I left him seemingly in the Best Disposition towards our People at Algiers, and very Ready to obey the Instructions Concerning us which the Count de Florida Blanca had given him. Since my Return from Carthagena I have Received letters from thence informing me that the Count D'Espilly has Orders from Court not to proceed to Algiers without Further Instructions, as the Plague is at Constantina within Fifty leagues of that place. But as it was lately reported that the Dey, who is very far advanced in Years was much Indisposed, it is no ways Improbable that this Circumstance may have had its weight, for the Knowledge of the Plague being at Constantina is Not New. It was Even beleived before I left Africa that the City of Bona was Depopulated with that Distemper. However this May Be, I most Sincerely wish the Negociations respecting our Country Cou'd go Hand in Hand with those of the European Powers, For there is no Doubt that when the Barbary States have made peace with them, they will Turn all their Views towards Us, and If another Capture or Two be made, the Terms of Peace will be Risen most Extravagantly. I shall make no appology to you Gentlemen for Communicating whatever has occur'd to me on this Subject, and as it is probable I shall not have occasion again to Resume it, I will now add that I know No American subject in Spain or France—Mr. Jefferson is out of the Question—So adequate to the Task of negociating at Algiers, as is Mr. Carmichael. I am Perfectly Convinced that when it is Renew'd He ought if Possible to undertake it and I Beg leave to Recommend this Hint to Your serious Consideration. I am sure Mr. Carmichael has No objects under his Care half so Interesting, and if His situation will permit, he ought Not to Hestitate.

I wish much to Know your sentiments of the Treaty with Morocco. Though it is Not Quite as Good as I Desire, It is as much so as I Cou'd make it. I Beg you will Favor me with Your Opinion when you are at Leisure. The answer from Coruna is what I Feared it wou'd be—No ways Decisive. It is Two or Three Years since Mr. Carmichael Endeavord to Procure a Settlement, and I much Fear I shall be obliged to Go and Force one.

I am with Great Respect and Esteem Gentlemen Your Most obed. and Very Huml. Servant, THOS BARCLAY

RC (DLC); addressed: "Their Excellencies John Adams and Thomas Jefferson Esqrs. Paris"; endorsed by TJ. Tr (DNA: PCC, No. 107, I). Recorded in SJL as received 27 Jan. 1787.

From S. & J. H. Delap

SIR   Bordeaux 6 January 1787

In the month of March 1785, Thomas Barclay Esquire appointed by the Honorable Congress of the United States of America to Audit the accounts of the different particulars who transacted business for that honorable body, called upon us for our accounts, which we furnished him to transmit them, and on which there is a balance due us of £79945. 4. Tournois; we have since been Deprived of any answer, 'tho he gave us every reason to expect we should be immediately paid. We have therefore to request your letting us know, if you have received any orders relative to the payment of our account, or to whom we are to apply for same. Our present situation is such, that it absolutely requires our taking some active measures to extricate ourselves from the Embarras, into which we were plunged by the great advances we enter'd into, for Numbers of Gentlemen on your Continent, who since our misfortunes have never deigned to remit us a Sous or even answer our letters. There is due us by private persons in America upwards of Four hundred Thousand livers Tournois, exclusive of what the Congress owes us, payable in France, and about Three hundred Thousand Dollars that we are possessed of in Loan Office certificates &c. We should esteem it a particular favor when you do us the honor of answering us, to let us know if there is any prospect of this paper ever being paid, and on what footing. For your Government we hand you inclosed Copy of the account settled with Thomas Barclay Esqr. to whom we exhibited the different orders of Congress in vertue of which we made these advances.

We have the honor to be with great respect Sir, Your most obedient Humble Servants, S & J. H. DELAP

RC (DLC); endorsed. Recorded in SJL as received 17 Jan. 1787. Enclosure: Account of S. & J. H. Delap with the U.S. to 7 Mch. 1785 (DLC), showing balance due of 79,945 livres tournois.

From Jean Nicolas Démeunier

Rue Ste Anne no. 87 Le 6 Janvier

Les abonnés au Sallon des Echecs ont reçu une Lettre pareille à Celle qu'a reçu Monsieur Jefferson. On est Le Maitre de ne pas renouveller Son abonnement, et M. Démeunier dira que Les affaires et L'eloignement de Monsieur Jefferson ne Lui permettent pas de renouveller Le Sien.

On Sera Faché de perdre L'esperance de voir Monsieur Jefferson, Mais c'est une chose toute simple, dont il ne doit pas s'occuper davantage. M. Démeunier Le prie d'agréer mille Tendres et respectueux Complimens. Il desire toujours L'histoire du nouvel hampshire et M. Massei qui L'a emprunté devroit bien L'envoyér

Rue Ste anne no. 87 ou Faire dire, quel Jour, et en quel endroit, on pourroit L'envoyer chercher.

P.S. M. Démeunier en rendant Justice à La Constitution du nouvel hampshire qui Lui paroit très belle, et d'une precision et d'une netteté remarquables, S'est permis de demander, Si elle a Formé Le Conseil executif de La Maniere La plus avantageuse? Pour Separer davantage Les individus qui exercent La puissance Legislative, Judiciaire, ou executrice, il est Tenté de croire, qu'on Auroît du choisir pour Les Membres du Conseil executif des hommes qui ne Fussent ni dans Le Senat, ni dans La chambre des représentans; il voit bien Les raisons qui ont determiné Le nouvel hampshire, et Les Autres provinces, mais il voit aussi beaucoup de raisons en Faveur de L'opinion Contraire, et il voit surtout une petite Contradiction, avec Les articles de declarations des droits, qui ordonnent expressement de separer Les trois pouvoirs, et de Les separer Le plus qu'il est possible.

M. Démeunier Soumet cette idée aux Lumieres de Monsieur Jefferson; il seroit bien Aise de Savoir, Si on n'y a pas Songé; ou Si on y a Songé, pourquoi on ne L'a pas adopté.

RC (DLC); endorsed; undated. Not recorded in SJL. The date is established by internal evidence; e.g., TJ was not admitted to the SALLON DES ECHECS until Feb. 1786 (see Account Book under date of 6 Feb. 1786) and it was on 6 Jan. 1786 that Démeunier first wrote him; the letter that TJ received in common with other ABONNÉS has not been found.

From Ferdinand Grand

MONSIEUR   Paris le 6. Janvier 1787.

J'ai l'honneur de vous informer que Mrs. Hy. Fizeaux & Cie. se sont prévalus sur moi le 1er. de ce mois pour le 11 avril de £5679.1.6. qu'ils m'avisent être pour compte des Etats unis. Veuillez me faire savoir, Monsieur, si je dois acceuillir cette traitte et en débiter les états.

J'ai l'honneur d'etre avec une parfaite considération Monsieur Votre très humble & très obéissant Serviteur,   GRAND

RC (DLC); endorsed. Not recorded in SJL.

To Abigail Adams

[*Paris, 7 Jan. 1787.* Recorded in SJL under this date. Not found; but see Mrs. Adams' reply, 29 Jan. 1787.]

To Calonne

[SIR] Paris Jan. 7. 1787.

I had the honour on the 2d. of November last to acknowlege the receipt of your Excellency's letter of October the 22d. wherein you were so good as to communicate to me the arrangements which the king had been pleased to make for the encouragement of the commerce of the United states of America with his subjects. I immediately made known the same to the Agents of the United States in the several seaports of this kingdom, that they might give information thereof to the persons concerned in that commerce. Unacquainted with the forms in which his Majesty usually declares his will in cases of this kind, and the manner in which it is communicated to the Officers of the customs at the seaports, I am unable to answer those agents who inform me that the officers of the customs and farms do not as yet consider themselves bound to conform to the new regulations. I take the liberty therefore of solliciting your Excellency's interposition for the issuing such orders as may be necessary for carrying into effect the gracious intentions of the king, and of repeating the assurance of those sentiments of perfect respect and esteem with which I have the honour to be your Excellency's most obedient & most humble servant,

TH: JEFFERSON

PrC (DLC).

THOSE AGENTS WHO INFORM ME: See, among others, Boylston to TJ, 2 Jan. 1787 and Le Couteulx to TJ, 3 Jan. 1787. On the whole problem of implementing Calonne's regulations of 22 Oct. 1786, see Short to TJ, 4 Apr. 1787; Short to Jay, 4 May 1787; TJ to Jay, 21 June 1787; Villedeuil to TJ, 2 July 1787; Barrett to TJ, 11 July 1787.

To Colonia

7me. Janvier 1787.

Monsieur Jefferson avoit l'honneur, il y a quelques jours de faire passer à Monsieur de Colonia un passeport pour l'expedition des armes à l'etat de Virginie, signé par sa majesté le roi, mais manquant la signature de son excellence Monsieur le Comtrolleur general: et il prenoit la liberté de supplier Monsieur de Colonia de lui procurer la signature de ce Ministre. Peut il oser de le prier, quand cette formalité sera supplée, de vouloir bien lui faire repasser le passeport par le moyen de la petite poste? Il a l'honneur de lui renouveller les assurances de sa consideration distinguée pour lui.

PrC (DLC); endorsed.

To Matthew Boulton

Paris Jan. 8. 1787.

Mr. Jefferson's compliments to Mr. Boulton and will beg the favor of him, when he shall be arrived in England, to have an estimate made of the cost of the underwritten articles, plated in the best manner, with a plain bead, and to send him the estimate to Paris. If Mr. Jefferson should on the estimate decide to buy them, he will take the liberty of addressing a letter to Mr. Boulton for them.

2. Soup-terreens middlesized, say 11. Inches long.
2. dishes for the terreens to stand in.
10. dishes, round, of $10\frac{1}{2}$ Inches diameter.
2. dishes, oval, 16 I. long, $10\frac{1}{2}$ I. wide.
4. dishes, oval, 12 I. long, 9 I. wide.

PrC (MHi); endorsed.

From Duler

Rouen, 8 Jan. 1787. TJ's letter has emboldened him to state that he did not expect aid in securing a position in "any Bureau at Paris"; hopes he can secure a position in England or France "in some of the American affairs" or possibly "a place of Consul for the french nation in some of the American Ports"; sends testimonial as to character from D'Anmours of Baltimore, which, though in French, he thinks TJ may "perfectly understand" and which he asks to have returned; can supply other testimonials respecting "my morals and Capacity in the line of trade and sea affairs."

RC (DLC); 2 p.; endorsed. Recorded in SJL as received 10 Jan. 1787. Enclosure not found.

From R. & A. Garvey

Sir Roüen 8 January 1787

We are desired by Mr. Thoms. Boylston to apply to your Excellency, and to beg the favour of you, to take such Measures as may be necessary, to secure him the repayment of the duties which he paid last year on his oil, which is an object of £9252: its in Consequence of the letter M. de Callonne wrote your Excellency the 22d. of last october, which you forwarded me the 29th. same Month, that Mr. Boylston thinks himself entitled to call for said restitution; we cant say in what light his demand May be seen, but we think that its possible he May recover the Money under the Patronage and protection of your Excellency. We have the Honour to be Sir Your Excellencys most humble & most obedient Servants, ROBT. & ANT. GARVEY

RC (MHi); endorsed. Recorded in SJL as received 11 Jan. 1787.

From C. W. F. Dumas

MONSIEUR Lahaie 9e. Janv. 1787

En conséquence de ma derniere, qui doit être parvenue à V.E. par Mr. Brantsen, sous le couvert de qui je L'ai mise, je me propose d'aller là où j'ai dit, sonder le terrain discretement, dans 5 ou 6 jours d'ici.

Dès que Votre Excellence saura quelque chose de positif sur l'accession finale et complete de l'Etat de N. York, aux mesures des autres, il sera bon et il importe qu'Elle Veuille bien m'en donner connoissance d'abord.

Je suis toujours avec grand respect, De Votre Excellence Le très-humble & très-obéissant Serviteur, C W F DUMAS

RC (DLC). FC (Rijksarchief, The Hague, Dumas Papers; photostats in DLC). Recorded in SJL as received 14 Jan. 1787. Evidently this also was enclosed in one to MR. BRANTSEN (see note to Dumas to TJ, 5 Jan. 1787).

From George Gilmer

DEAR SIR Pen Park 9th. January 1787

Your kind attention to me in sending the Vegitable system gave me great pleasure; and could only have been increased by a line from you. This may be a reproof for my inattention that you may have thought me guilty of, in not writing to you. Believe I have often wrote, and should more frequent could my sheding ink furnish you one moments satisfaction, but too late have I discovered the misfortune of not laying up a large stock of contemplative treasure, the true foundation of all sublunary satisfaction. A large purchase of this fund, might have given me powers that would have merited your friendship, but as I can have no claim from the head, let a warm and affectionate heart, beg the continuance of your esteem, which reluctates your distance, and augures from your sweet little olive branch intending for Paris must lament a long absence. This Idea is the more distressing at this period

9 JANUARY 1787

because I wish your able opinion on a subject of moment, and were it possible for you to rob weighty matters to procure a moments leizure flatter myself you'l cheerfully render me service and excuse the trouble which you would not have received was it not for the variety and contradictory opinions of the learned on this side the water.

My old friend Mr. George Harmer Il est non plus. In his last will he gives and bequeaths unto Doctr. George Gilmer of Albemarle County All the Estate called Marrowbone in the county of Henry, containing by estimation two Thousand five hundred and eighty five acres of land. Likewise one other tract of land in said county called horse pasture containing by estimation two Thousand five hundred acres. 12. Sepr. 1786.

Also another tract in the county aforesaid containing by estimation six hundred and sixty seven and one half acres of land called poisoned feild. Other property to be sold to pay his debts, balance to be remitted his nephew John Lambert out of which he is to pay his sister five hundred pounds.

Since recording this will there was found one wrote in his own hand amongst his papers in which all his estate given him by his brother is returned to him. This will I conjecture to have been executed in Bristol dated 26 Decr. 1779.

In his pockett book wrote in his own hand was found another will with a copy drawn by Henry Tazwell Esqr. To this effect.

In the name of God amen. I George Harmer of the commonwealth of Virginia being perfectly well and of sound mind and memory do make and ordain my last will and testament in manner and form following that is to say.

All the estate both real and personal that I possess or am entitled to in the commonwealth of Virginia I hereby give and devise unto my friend Thomas Mann Randolph of Tuckaho and Henry Tazwell of the City of Williamsburg in Trust upon these conditions, that when John Harmer my brother now a subject of the king of Great Britain shall be capable of acquiring property in this country, that they or the survivor of them do convey or cause to be conveyed to him in fee simple a good and indefeasable title in the said Estate and in case the said John Harmer should not be capable of acquiring such right before his death then that my said trustees or the survivor of them do convey the said Estate in manner aforesaid to John Lambert son of my sister Hannah Lambert when he shall be capable of acquiring property in this country, and in case John Lambert should not before his death be capable of acquiring

[28]

9 JANUARY 1787

a title to the said estate then I direct the same to be conveyed to my sister Hannah Lambert if she in her lifetime can acquire property in this country.

But if the said John Harmer, John Lambert and Hannah Lambert should all die before they can acquire any property legally in this country then I desire that my trustees aforesaid may cause the said Estate of every kind to be sold and the money arising from each sale together with intermediate profits of the said estate shall be by them remitted to the Mayor and Corporation of the City of Bristol in England to be by them distributed according to the laws of England to the right Heirs of my said Sister Hannah Lambert to whom I hereby give all such excepting the sum of one hundred pounds lawful money to each of the aforementioned trustees, which shall be paid out of the first money arising from the sales aforementioned or from the profits arising to my heirs, in witness whereof I have hereunto set my hand and affixed my seal this twenty fifth day of June one thousand seven hundred and eighty two.

RC (DLC); unsigned; endorsed: "Gilmer George." Recorded in SJL as received 11 June 1787.

Despite the abrupt ending of this letter and the absence of a signature or a complementary close, it is clear that this is the whole of the text as TJ received it. For, in his reply of 12 Aug. 1787, TJ described it as unsigned and said that for this and other reasons he had ascribed the letter to John Harmer and had so endorsed it. He added: "I sat down to answer it to John Harmer, and now for the first time discover marks of it's being yours." There is no endorsement or deleted endorsement on the letter save that indicated above, but TJ's first and erroneous endorsement was probably made on the address leaf which—as was the case with so many of the address leaves of letters written to TJ—was later detached and used for scrap paper. The SWEET LITTLE OLIVE BRANCH was Mary Jefferson, who was, however reluctantly, INTENDING FOR PARIS.

To John Jay

SIR Paris Jan. 9. 1787.

My last of Dec. 31. acknowleged the receipt of yours of Oct. 12. as the present does those of Oct. 3d. 9th. and 27th. together with the resolution of Congress of Octob. 16. on the claim of Shweighauser. I will proceed in this business on the return of Mr. Barclay, who being fully acquainted with all the circumstances, will be enabled to give me that information the want of which might lead me to do wrong on the one side or the other.

Information of the signature of the treaty with Marocco has been long on it's passage to you. I will beg leave to recur to dates, that you may see that no part of it has been derived from me. The

[29]

9 JANUARY 1787

first notice I had of it was in a letter from Mr. Barclay dated Daralbeyda August 11th. I received this on the 13th. of September. No secure conveyance offered till the 26th. of the same month, being 13. days after my receipt of it. In my letter of that date, which went by the way of London, I had the honour to inclose you a copy of Mr. Barclay's letter. The conveyance of the treaty itself is suffering a delay here at present, which all my anxiety cannot prevent. Colo. Franks's baggage, which came by water from Cadiz to Rouen, has been long and hourly expected. The moment it arrives he will set out to London to have duplicates of the treaty signed by Mr. Adams, and from thence he will proceed to New-York. The Chevalier del Pinto, who treated with us on behalf of Portugal, being resident at London, I have presumed that the causes of the delay of that treaty had been made known to Mr. Adams, and by him communicated to you. I will write to him by Colo. Franks in order that you may be answered on that subject.

The publication of the inclosed extract from my letter of May 27. 1786. will, I fear, have very mischeivous effects. It will tend to draw on the Count de Vergennes the formidable phalanx of the Farms: to prevent his committing himself to me in any conversation which he does not mean for the publick papers: to inspire the same diffidence into all other ministers with whom I might have to transact business: to defeat the little hope, if any hope existed, of getting rid of the farm on the article of tobacco; and to damp that freedom of communication which the resolution of Congress of May 3. 1784. was intended to reestablish.

Observing by the proceedings of Congress that they are about to establish a coinage, I think it my duty to inform them, that a Swiss, of the name of Drost, established here, has invented a method of striking the two faces and the edge of a coin at one stroke. By this and other simplifications of the process of coinage he is enabled to coin from 25000 to 30000 peices a day, with the assistance of only two persons, the peices of metal being first prepared. I send you by Colo. Franks three coins of gold, silver and copper, which you will percieve to be perfect medals: and I can assure you from having seen him coin many, that every peice is as perfect as these. There has certainly never yet been seen any coin, in any country, comparable to this. The best workmen in this way acknolege that his is like a new art. Coin should always be made in the highest perfection possible because it is a great guard against the danger of false coinage. This man would be willing to furnish his implements to Congress, and if they please, he will

9 JANUARY 1787

go over and instruct a person to carry on the work: nor do I beleive he would ask any thing unreasonable. It would be very desireable that in the institution of a new coinage, we could set out on so perfect a plan as this, and the more so, as while the work is so exquisitely done, it is done cheaper.

I will certainly do the best I can for the reformation of the Consular Convention, being persuaded that our states would be very unwilling to conform their laws either to the Convention, or to the Scheme. But it is too difficult, and too delicate to form sanguine hopes. However that there may be room to reduce the convention as much as circumstances will admit, will it not be expedient for Congress to give me powers, in which there shall be no reference to the scheme? The powers sent me, oblige me to produce that scheme, and certainly the moment it is produced, they will not abate a tittle from it. If they recollect the scheme and insist on it, we can but conclude it: but if they have forgotten it (which may be) and are willing to reconsider the whole subject, perhaps we may get rid of something the more of it. As the delay is not injurious to us, because the Convention whenever and however made is to put us in a worse state than we are in now, I shall venture to defer saying a word on the subject till I can hear from you in answer to this. The full powers may be sufficiently guarded by private instructions to me not to go beyond the former scheme. This delay may be well enough ascribed (whenever I shall have received new powers) to a journey I had before apprised the minister that I should be obliged to take to some mineral waters in the South of France, to see if by their aid I may recover the use of my right hand, of which a dislocation about 4. months ago threatens to deprive me in a great measure. The Surgeons have long insisted on this measure. I shall return by Bourdeaux, Nantes and Lorient to get the necessary information for finishing our commercial regulations here. Permit me however to ask as immediately as possible an answer either affirmative or negative as Congress shall think best, and to ascribe the delay on which I venture to my desire to do what is for the best.

I send you a copy of the late Marine regulations of this country. There are things in it which may become interesting to us. Particularly what relates to the establishment of a marine militia, and their classification.

You will have seen in the publick papers that the king has called an Assembly of the Notables of his country. This has not been done for 160 years past. Of course it calls up all the attention of the people. The objects of this assembly are not named. Several are conjectured. The tolerating the Protestant religion; removing all the internal custom houses to the frontier; equalising the gabels on salt thro' the kingdom; the sale of the king's domains to raise money; or finally the effecting this necessary end by some other means, are talked of. But in truth nothing is known about it. This government practises secrecy so systematically that it never publishes it's purposes or it's proceedings sooner or more extensively than necessary. I send you a pamphlet which giving an account of the last Assemblée des notables, may give an idea of what the present will be.

A great desire prevails here of encouraging manufactures. The famous Boulton & Watts, who are at the head of the plated manufactures of Birmingham, the steam mills of London, Copying presses and other mechanical works, have been here. It is said also that Wedgwood has been here, who is famous for his steel manufactories and an earthen ware in the antique stile: but as to this last person I am not certain. It cannot, I believe, be doubted, but that they came at the request of government, and that they will be induced to establish similar manufactures here. The transferring hither those manufactures which contribute so much to draw our commerce to England, will have a great tendency to strengthen our connections with this country, and loosen them with that.

The enfranchising the port of Honfleur at the mouth of the Seine, for multiplying the connections with us, is at present an object. It meets with opposition in the ministry; but I am in hopes it will prevail. If natural causes operate, uninfluenced by accidental circumstances, Bourdeaux and Honfleur or Havre must ultimately take the greatest part of our commerce. The former by the Garonne and canal of Languedoc opens the Southern provinces to us, the latter the Northern ones and Paris. Honfleur will be peculiarly advantageous for our rice, and whale oil, of which the principal consumption is at Paris. Being free, they can be re-exported when the market here shall happen to be overstocked.

The labours of the ensuing summer will close the Eastern half of the harbour of Cherbourg, which will contain and protect forty sail of the line. It has from 50 to 35 feet water next to the cones, shallowing gradually to the shore. Between this and Dunkirk the navigation of the channel will be rendered much safer in the event of a war with England, and invasions on that country become more practicable.

9 JANUARY 1787

The gazettes of France and Leyden to the present date accompany this. I have the honour to be with sentiments of the most perfect esteem & respect, Sir, your most obedient & most humble servant,

TH: JEFFERSON

PrC (DLC). Tr (DNA: PCC, No. 107, I). Enclosures: (1) Extract from an unidentified American newspaper containing TJ's letter to Jay, 27 May 1786 (see notes there). (2) The "late Marine regulations" that TJ enclosed may have been a copy of *Ordonnances et Règlemens concernant la Marine,* Paris, 1786 (Sowerby, No. 2222) and that relating "to the establishment of a marine militia" may have been the arrêt of 5 Sep. 1782 for the "création d'une milice maritime" (*Recueil Général des Anciennes Lois Françaises,* Paris, 1827, XXVII, p. 224, No. 1692). (3) The "pamphlet . . . giving an account of the last Assemblée des notables" has not been identified. (4) Various unidentified "gazettes of France and Leyden."

The recipient's copies of TJ's despatches to Jay from France are missing for the year 1787; only those from Short to Jay of 21 Mch., 4 May, and 19 Sep. 1787 are present in DNA: PCC, No. 87. In the Daily Journals or Despatch Books of the Office of Foreign Affairs, 1784-1790 (DNA: PCC, No. 127), there are entries showing that Jay received eighteen despatches from TJ during the year. These were dated 9 Jan.; 1, 8, 14 (bis), and 23 Feb.; 4 May; 21 June; 6 and 15 Aug.; 19, 22 (bis), and 24 Sep.; 3 and 7 Nov.; and 21 and 31 Dec. 1787. The following communication to the editors from Dr. Carl L. Lokke, Chief of the Foreign Affairs Division, the National Archives, of 29 Oct. 1954, is of interest: "When did the original despatches of 1787 disappear? It is possible to pinpoint the time within a year or two. William A. Weaver obviously had the despatches at hand (either originals or copies) when he compiled the *Diplomatic Correspondence of the United States of America, 1783-89* (7 vols., Washington, 1833-34; new edition, 3 vols., printed 1837, published 1855), as all of them are included in this publication except those dated November 7 and December 21, 1787. (He may have had all of them in 1833 and merely decided not to include these two in the publication.) But he did not have the original despatches when, in the summer and fall of 1834, he arranged, bound (mounted), and prepared 'a summary descriptive list' of the Papers of the Continental Congress. The Jefferson despatches for 1787 are not mounted with others received from Jefferson (PCC, No. 87). Weaver's summary descriptive list of the papers, printed by Blair in 1835 under the title, *Catalogue of Manuscript Books,* states moreover, under PCC, No. 87, that 'most of the correspondence of 1787 is missing.' (Information from Dorothy Eaton, Library of Congress.) It would have been more accurate to say that all of the despatches of 1787 from the United States Legation in Paris are missing except three from William Short. Did Weaver make a point of calling attention to the missing Jefferson despatches because they had disappeared so recently? We do not know the answer. John Laurens' original despatches, January 3—September 6, 1781 also are missing, yet Weaver fails to note the fact."

TJ did not send THREE COINS OF GOLD, SILVER AND COPPER by Franks, but only those of gold and silver (for notes on the experimental "écu de Calonne" struck by J.-P. Droz, see TJ to Jay, 1 Feb. 1787). To the various VERY MISCHEIVOUS EFFECTS that TJ feared as a result of the indiscreet and unauthorized publication of his letter to Jay might possibly be added the very dilatory and reluctant implementation of the trade regulations as set forth in Calonne's letter to TJ of 22 Oct. 1786. TJ himself was the author of the RESOLUTION OF CONGRESS OF MAY 3. 1784. which placed all letters of ministers at all times under an injunction of secrecy "except as to such parts of them as Congress shall by special permission allow to be published or communicated" and Congress had on 7 Aug. 1786 taken off "The injunction of Secresy . . . from this letter of May 27 from Mr. Jefferson and the papers accompanying it as far as relates to the tobacco Contract" (Vol. 7: 207; JCC, XXXI, 488). YOURS OF OCT. . . . 9TH was Jay's to the president of Congress, not to TJ.

[33]

To Pierre Louis Lacretelle

[*Paris, 9 Jan. 1787.* Recorded in SJL. Not found; it may possibly have related to Lacretelle's *Discours sur le préjugé des peines infamantes, couronnés à l'Académie de Metz*, Paris, 1784, of which TJ possessed a copy (Sowerby, No. 2362).]

From Elizabeth Blair Thompson

Titchfield the 10 of Janry. 87

Two years last summer I experienced a sever mortification; that of not seeing my old friend, and acquaintence Mr: Jefferson, when he did me the favor of calling: my stuped servant ought to have told you that I was confined up stairs with a little one, (I had just lost,) instead of saying I was not at home: that Captn. and Miss Thompson was not is true; but had I known *you* was in the *house*, I should not have denyed my self the pleasure of seeing you, and should certainly have interduced you into my Bed Chamber. Captn. T. set out the next day in hopes of meeting of you, but had the mortification of hearing you were gone: I dont know that I was ever more vexed, for believe me I should have rejoyced much to see you; and I flatter my self if ever you come to this country again, you will do us the favor of spending some time with us; where you will always find a sincere welcome. I have not very lately heard from our friends in America, but my last letters was from my sister Cary: her Son, and his Amiable Lady were then her visitors; and in pretty good health, tho the little Boy had bad Eyes: but its most probable you have heard since that account. I wish they lived in a more healthy situation then Richneck, where I fear they will seldom enjoy health for any time together. You will excuse I hope the trouble I am about to give you; which is to beg of you (if you can,) to give us some information of Mr. John Banister; who we have not heard of for some time: in his last, which I think was dated at Nantes, but I am not quite sure, for we were involved at the time in great distress, on account of Miss Thompson's last illness; one of the most amiable creatures that ever Parent was blesst with: she had long been in a decline, and she was released the day after Xmas from a World, where she had known *little else then pain.* In our distress, we have laid his letter, where we cannot find it; but I think he does not say where we shall find him, and we are very uneasy about him, as he tells us he had then another severe attack; and as it is some time since, we fear he may still be too ill to write. If you can inform us where he is, and what state of health he is in; you will greatly oblige us.

I have never heard what family you have, or if any part of them are with you; but I sincerely hope if you have any, they may be all comforts to you. Mine is greatly increased, I have two Sons and four Daughters living; beside two I lost in their in[fancy.] My eldest Son, almost begins to write man; and is ente[ring] our Navy; which I hope he will be a credit to. Captn. Thompson, tho he has not the pleasure of being known to you, begs to unite with me in respectfull good wishes, and believe me: I shall always be happy to hear of your welfare, and I am with great sincerity your obliged, Friend & Humble St:, ELIZA: THOMPSON

RC (DLC); slightly mutilated. Recorded in SJL as received 17 Jan. 1787.
MY SISTER CARY: Sarah Blair (1738-1804), sister of Elizabeth Blair Thompson, was the wife of Wilson Miles Cary.
MY ELDEST SON, ALMOST BEGINS TO WRITE MAN: The allusion is to an expression in Samuel Richardson, *The History of Sir Charles Grandison*, London, 1762, 4th ed., II, Letter iv, p. 48: "I never feared man, since I could write man."

To John Adams

DEAR SIR Paris Jan. 11. 1787

Mr. Jay, in his last letter to me, observes that they hear nothing further of the treaty with Portugal. I have taken the liberty of telling him that I will write to you on the subject, and that he may expect to hear from you on it by the present conveyance. The Chevalier del Pinto being at London, I presume he has, or can inform you why it is delayed on their part. I will thank you also for the information he shall give you.

There is here an order of priests called the Mathurins, the object of whose institution is the begging of alms for the redemption of captives. About 18. months ago they redeemed 300, which cost them about 1500 livres a peice. They have agents residing in the Barbary states, who are constantly employed in searching and contracting for the captives of their nation, and they redeem at a lower price than any other people can. It occurred to me that their agency might be engaged for our prisoners at Algiers. I have had interviews with them, and the last night a long one with the General of the order. They offer their services with all the benignity and cordiality possible. The General told me he could not expect to redeem our prisoners as cheap as their own, but that he would use all the means in his power to do it on the best terms possible, which will be the better as there shall be the less suspicion that he acts for our public. I told him I would write to you on the subject, and speak to him again. What do you think of employing them, limiting them to a certain price, as 300 dollars for instance, or any other sum you think proper? He will write immediately to his instruments there, and in two or three months we can know the event. He will deliver them at Marseilles, Cadiz, or where we please, at our expence. The money remaining of the fund destined to the Barbary business may I suppose be drawn on for this object. Write me your opinion if you please, on this subject, finally, fully, and immediately, that, if you approve the proposition, I may enter into arrangements with the General before my departure for the waters of Aix, which will be about the beginning of February.

I have the honour to be with very sincere esteem and respect Dear Sir your most obedient & most humble servt.,

TH: JEFFERSON

RC (MHi: AMT); endorsed in part: "ansd. Jan. 25." PrC (DLC).

To John Bondfield

SIR   Paris Jan. 11. 1787.

In the moment of receiving your letter inclosing the passport, which wanted the Comptroller's signature, I inclosed it to his bureau to obtain that ceremony. It is but this instant returned to me, and in the same I take the liberty of inclosing it to you and of assuring you of the esteem & respect with which I have the honour to be Sir Your most obedient & most humble servt.,

TH: JEFFERSON

PrC (DLC).   See TJ to Calonne, 20 Dec. 1786 and 7 Jan. 1787. If Calonne sent the passport under a covering letter, it has not been found.

To David S. Franks

Thursday Jan. 11. 1787

My anxiety, my dear Sir, on the detention of the Marocco treaty, is inexpressible. However cogent and necessary the motives which detain you, I should be deemed inexcusable were I to let so safe an opportunity as that by Colo. Blackden pass without sending the papers on to London. Mr. Jay complained that a treaty signed in June was not ratified in October. What will they say when they shall observe that the same treaty does not reach them till March, nine months? In the mean time our whole commerce is paying a heavy tax for insurance till it's publication. Can you fix a day as early as Monday or Tuesday for your departure whether your baggage arrives or not? Or would you rather decline the going with the papers? In the former case, if your baggage does not arrive before your departure, any orders you may think proper to leave respecting it shall be punctually executed. I can send it to Mr. Limosin at Havre so that it may go to America in the February packet. I shall see you at the Marquis's to-day and we will speak about this matter.

PrC (DLC); unsigned.

MR. JAY COMPLAINED in his to TJ of 27 Oct. 1786. In none of his letters to Jay subsequent to Franks' arrival in Paris early in December had TJ explained that Franks was in Paris or why he was detained. The question of personal baggage, as TJ clearly implies in the present letter, was of no importance in so urgent a matter of state, but the threatened use of COLO. BLACKDEN would not have been so safe an expedient as TJ had reason to think (see Short to TJ, 21 and 29 May 1787; Claiborne to TJ, 21 June 1787).

From the Abbé Morellet

MONSIEUR jeudy [11? Jan. 1787?]

Mr. de Crevecoeur m'a dit hier que dans la lecture plus suivie que vous avez faite de notre traduction vous aves eté mécontent de quelques articles où je vous ai mal entendu et de l'insertion que j'ai faite dans votre texte des notes de Mr. Thomson et peut etre de quelques autres points. Je vous prie de m'envoyer les corrections que vous croires necessaires. Je ferai faire des cartons. Quant aux notes si j'ai mal fait de les placer dans le texte c'est un mal aujourd'hui irremediable mais je vous en avois demandé la permission et vous me l'avies accordée. S'il y a quelque autre faute de ma part à laquelle on puisse apporter remede vous n'aves qu'à ordonner. J'oubliois de vous dire que les notes de Mr. Thomson etant toujours distinguées de votre texte par des crochets qui les enferment il me semble que le lieu qu'elles occuppent dans l'ouvrage est bien indifferent. Faites moi savoir vos intentions je m'y conformerai avec le zele que j'aurai toujours à vous montrer mon respectueux devouement. J'ai l'honneur d'etre avec respect Monsieur Votre très humble et très obéissant Serviteur,

L'ABBÉ MORELLET

RC (DLC); endorsed: "Morellet Abbé"; undated and not recorded in SJL, but evidently sent to TJ before he dispatched to Morellet the 7-page list of "Errors in the Abbé Morellet's translation of the Notes on Virginia the correction of which is indispensable" (PrC in DLC: TJ Papers, 27: 4717-

[37]

23); this list, with an excellent commentary, has been published by Joseph M. Carrière in "The Manuscript of Jefferson's Unpublished Errata List for Abbé Morellet's Translation of the *Notes on Virginia*," *Papers of the Bibliographical Society University of Virginia*, I (1948-9), 1-24. It bears at the head of the text the date "January 19. 1787." which Carrière accepts without question and which may indeed be correct, but the following facts may be noted: (1) this date is in a different ink from that of the press copy; (2) it is in a different form from that usually employed by TJ (on this date he wrote several letters, all of which were dated "Jan. 19. 1787," which was his customary form); (3) it was presumably added later, perhaps on the basis of an entry in SJL; and (4) it does not appear to be in TJ's hand. Nevertheless, the Editors incline to the opinion that the date inscribed on this errata list is the correct one. If this is so, Morellet's letter must have been written several days earlier, for if it had been written on the "jeudy" immediately preceding 19 Jan. 1787, TJ would have had only twenty-four hours, more or less, in which to compile the seventy errors that he listed so carefully in parallel columns. For this reason, the "jeudy" of the week preceding has been conjectured as the probable date of Morellet's letter.

The list of errata and LES CARTONS made in Morellet's edition will be discussed in the Second Series, where a critical edition of *Notes on Virginia* will appear.

From R. & A. Garvey

SIR   Rouen 12th. January 1787

We have the honor to remitt you Inclosed the notes of our disbursments for your Excellency importing £59.5 which have taken the liberty to value on you at sight order of Messr. Perregaux & Co. which please to own.

With the small Case of Books there was an Acquit à Caution de Librairie which beg you'll send for to the Customhouse or the Chambre Sindicalle and return it us.

We are on all your and Friends Commands very respectfully Sir Your Excellency's most humble & very obedient Servants,

             ROBT. & ANT. GARVEY

RC (MHi). Recorded in SJL as received 14 Jan. 1787. Enclosure (MHi): Account of expenses of handling two cases received from London "par le sloop Anglais l'Aventure Capne John Damon," and also a case of books received from Barclay "par la Rosalie Capne Fauqueux," totalling 59 livres 5 sols. There is also in MHi a draft on TJ to the order of Perregaux & Cie. dated 12 Jan. 1787 for this amount.

To Philippe-Denis Pierres

            Paris 12me. Janvier 1787.

M. Jefferson prie Monsieur Pierre de vouloir bien lui envoyer les feuilles qu'il a eu la bonté de faire imprimer pour lui. Il a l'honneur de lui demander s'il seroit possible de procurer pour la presse d'imprimerie que Monsieur Pierre a eu la complaisance de se charger de faire faire pour M. Jefferson, les characteres charmantes de Didot, de deux grandeurs, c'est à dire, de la plus petite, et de la Moyenne? Si M. Jefferson demanderoit des Messrs. Foulis de Glasgow, des characteres Grecques, est il bien sur qu'on pourroit les accommoder à une presse quelconque? Dans ce cas M. Jefferson prieroit Monsr. Pierre de vouloir bien lui indiquer la nombre de chaque caractere qu'il doit faire venir de ces Messieurs.

PrC (MHi); endorsed.

From Mrs. Rider

Hotel de la Chine 13 Janvier 1787

Mrs. Rider is infinitely obliged to Mr. Jefferson for his very kind attention. She has not as yet met with apartmens that would suit Her. From the description Mr. J—n gives of those He has seen they appear to be just what She wants. She proposes going tomorrow morning to see them.

RC (MHi). Not recorded in SJL.

To Ferdinand Grand

Sir   Paris Jan. 14.

A person called here to-day, while I was out, and left the inclosed note for me, on the subject of Colo. Wuibert's money. He left word at the same time that he would call at your office tomorrow for an answer. I have written him the inclosed answer, but as he did not leave his name or address, I am unable to write an address on it. I will beg the favor of you to let it lye in your office till he comes, and have it delivered to him, with such explanations as to the mode in which Wuibert's money was remitted as you are able to give him.

I have the honour to be with much respect & esteem Sir, your most obedt. humble servt.,   TH: JEFFERSON

PrC (DLC); without indication of the year. Not recorded in SJL. Enclosures: The note from Col. Wuibert's agent is missing, but see TJ's reply of this date, which also was enclosed.

To an Agent of Antoine-Félix Wuibert

Sir   Paris Jan. 14. 1787.

I received Colo. Wuibert's letter and power of attorney on the 16th. of February 1786. I wrote immediately to Mr. Thevenard at l'Orient to obtain an order for his money. I was called to England in the month of March and returned here the last day of April. I found Mr. Thevenard's answer here on my return. From that time till the 22d. of May was taken up in discussions with which you are acquainted. On the 22d. of May I wrote to Colo. Wuibert, inclosing Mr. Grand's letter authorizing him to receive his money at the Cape. Of this letter I inclose you a copy. It was directed to him, as he expressly instructed, chez M. le Marquis de Galiffet à 6. miles du Cap. Français; I wrote a second letter to him June 3. inclosing papers from Monsr. Troyes. The whole were sent to L'Orient to be forwarded from thence to the Cape. The date of his letter Sep. 4. at Philadelphia gives room to presume he had left the Cape before the receipt of mine. You will percieve by these dates, Sir, that his business has not been forgotten by me, and, by the copy of my letter, that I have avoided touching his money. If, with your answer to him, you will be so good as to send him this letter, he will perceive that I served him diligently. I have the honour to be Sir your very humble servt.,   Th: Jefferson

PrC (DLC); without indication of addressee. Recorded in SJL as being a letter to "anonymous, viz. to one, unknown, on Wuibert's affair." Enclosure: TJ to Wuibert, 22 May 1786. Enclosed in TJ to Grand, this date. TJ's letter to Wuibert of 3 June and Wuibert's to TJ of 4 Sep. 1786 have not been found.

To Harcourt

Sir   Paris Jan. 14. 1787.

In the conversation with which you were pleased to honor me a few days ago,[1] on the enfranchisement of the port of Honfleur, I took the liberty of observing that I was not instructed by my constituents to make any proposition on that subject. That it would be agreeable to them however I must suppose, because it will offer the following advantages.

1. It is a convenient entrepot for furnishing us with the manufactures of the Northern parts of France and particularly of Paris, and for recieving and distributing the productions of our country in exchange.

2. Cowes, on the opposite side of the channel, has heretofore

been the deposit for a considerable part of our productions, landed in Great Britain in the first instance, but intended for re-exportation. From thence our rice particularly has been distributed to France and other parts of Europe. I am not certain whether our tobaccos were deposited there or carried to London to be sorted for the different markets.[2] To draw this business from Cowes, no place is so favorably situated as Honfleur.

3. It would be a convenient deposit for our Whale oil, of which after the supply of Paris, there will be a surplus for re-exportation.

4. Should our Fur trade be recovered out of the hands of the English, it will naturally come to Honfleur, as the Out-port of Paris.

5. Salt is an important article in all our return-cargoes; because, being carried as ballast, it's freight costs nothing. But on account of some regulations, with which I am not well acquainted, it cannot at present be shipped to advantage from any port in the Seyne.

6. Our vessels being built sharp, for swift sailing, suffer extremely in most of the Western ports of France, in which they are left on dry ground at every ebb of the tide. But at Honfleur, I am told, they can ride in bold water, on a good bottom, and near the shore, at all times.

These facts may perhaps throw some light on the question in which, for the good of both countries, you are pleased to interest yourself. I take the liberty therefore of barely mentioning them, and with the more pleasure as it furnishes me an occasion of assuring you of those sentiments of respect and[3]

PrC (DLC); at foot of text: "à Monsieur le Duc d'Harcourt, gouverneur du Dauphin"; complimentary close and signature lacking. Tr (DLC: TJ Papers, 235: 42125); a French translation in hand of St. John de Crèvecoeur; without date or indication of addressee, and lacking part of complimentary close and signature. Tr (DLC); copy of the foregoing French translation; in Short's hand, with one correction by TJ; endorsed by TJ: "Freeport   Duc de Harcourt"; also without date or indication of addressee.

Mitchell, *Crèvecoeur*, p. 152, suggests that TJ drafted the above text and gave it to Crèvecoeur, who was collaborating with him in the matter of the enfranchisement of the port of Honfleur, to be translated into French; that Short then copied it off, TJ signed and dated it (possibly after 14 Jan.), and the prototype of the above-described copy by Short was then dispatched to Harcourt. However, there seems to be no satisfactory explanation for the presence in TJ Papers of the three texts above, even if it is assumed—as the editors believe to be the case—that on 14 Jan. TJ sent to Harcourt the prototype of the above PrC in English. For if this were done, why should Crèvecoeur have translated it in view of the fact that TJ himself occasionally wrote in French and Short often translated for him? Assuming that Crèvecoeur did translate it, why should Short have copied that translation? Having done so, why did he not copy it precisely at the close (see note 3)? Why, too, did TJ make the alteration in Short's text? If TJ did in fact send a French text to Harcourt, why did he not retain the customary press copy instead of Short's transcript? The Editors believe that Crèvecoeur's translation and Short's copy of it may have been intended for distribution among the merchants who were interested in the enfranchisement of Honfleur, or for some other purpose. But this still does not explain the absence of a date and the incomplete complimentary close in both copies or the correction in Short's.

[1] The phrase "a few days ago" does not appear in translation in either of the French texts. This may suggest that Crèvecoeur made the translation some time after 14 Jan.

[2] Short's copy and its prototype read: "Je ne suis pas sûr que nos tabacs y aient eté deposés. Je crois qu'ils etoient conduits à Londres afin d'y être ⟨frêtés⟩ assortis pour les differents marchés." The word "frêtés" (copied from "freittés" in Crèvecoeur's translation) was struck out by TJ, who interlined the word "assortis."

[3] Complimentary close in Crèvecoeur's translation reads: ". . . des Sentiments de respect & destime avec lesquels Jay l'honeur detre." Short's copy ends: ". . . des sentimens de . . ." Short's spelling and punctuation were more correct in general than Crèvecoeur's.

To Louis Guillaume Otto

SIR   Paris Jan. 14. 1787.

I have been honoured with your letter of Oct. 15. and thank you for the intelligence it contained. I am able to make you but an unequal return for it, your friends here being so much more in condition to communicate to you interesting intelligence. With respect to the affairs of Holland they do not promise arrangement. The interest which the King of Prussia takes in the affairs of the Stadholder seem to threaten an interruption of his cordiality with this country. The misunderstanding between the kings of Spain and Naples, and a projected visit of the latter to Vienna, with the known influence of his queen over him are matter for some jealousy.

As to domestic news, the assembly des Notables occupies all conversation. What will be the subjects of their deliberation is not yet declared. The establishment of provincial assemblies, tolerating the protestant religion, removing the internal barriers to the frontiers, equalizing the Gabels, sale of the kings domains, and in short every other possible reformation, are conjectured by different persons. I send you a pamphlet on the last assembly of Notables, from which ideas are formed as to what this will be. Possibly you may receive the same from some of your friends. I send you also what it is less likely you should get from them, because it is next to impossible to get it at all. That is a late memoire by Linguet which has produced his perpetual exile from this country. To these I add a report written by M. Bailly on the subject of the Hotel-dieu of Paris which has met a very general approbation. These are things for the day only. I recollect no work of any dignity which has been lately published. We shall very soon receive another volume of mineralogy from M. de Buffon; and a 3d. vol. of the Cultivateur Americain is in the Press. So is a history of the American war by a Monsr. Soulés, the two first volumes of which, coming down to the capture of Burgoyne I have seen, and think better than any other I have seen. Mazzei will print soon 2. or 3. vols. 8vo. of Recherches historiques et politiques sur les etats unis d'Amerique, which are sensible.

We are flattered with the hope that the packet boats will hereafter sail monthly from Havre, the first being to sail on the 10th. of the next month. This is very desireable indeed: as it will furnish more frequent opportunities of correspondence between the two countries. If I can be made useful to you in any line whatever here, it will make me very happy; being with sincere esteem & respect, Sir, your most obedient & most humble servt.,

TH: JEFFERSON

PrC (DLC). Enclosures: (1) Copy of Simon Nicolas Henri Linguet's *Mémoire au Roi par M. Linguet, concernant ses réclamations actuellement pendants au Parlement de Paris*, London, 1786. (2) Jean-Sylvain Bailly, *Extrait des registres de l'Académie royale des sciences, du 22 Novembre 1786. Rapport des commissaires chargés par l'Académie de l'examen du projet d'un nouvel Hôtel-Dieu*, Paris, 1786. (3) The "pamphlet on the last assembly of Notables" has not been identified.

To St. John de Crèvecoeur

DEAR SIR   Paris Jan. 15. 1787.

I see by the Journal of this morning that they are robbing us of another of our inventions to give it to the English. The writer indeed only admits them to have revived what he thinks was known to the Greeks, that is the making the circumference of a wheel of one single peice. The farmers in New Jersey were the first who practised it, and they practised it commonly. Dr. Franklin, in one of his trips to London, mentioned this practice to the man, now in London, who has the patent for making those wheels (I forget his name.) The idea struck him. The Doctor promised to go to his shop and assist him in trying to make the wheel of one peice. The Jersey farmers did it by cutting a young sapling, and bending it, while green and juicy, into a circle; and leaving it so till it became perfectly seasoned. But in London there are no saplings. The difficulty was then to give to old wood the pliancy of young. The Doctor and the workman laboured together some weeks, and succeeded, and the man obtained a patent for it which has made his fortune. I was in his shop in London, he told me the whole story

15 JANUARY 1787

himself, and acknowleged, not only the origin of the idea, but how much the assistance of Dr. Franklin had contributed to perform the operation on dry wood. He spoke of him with love and gratitude. I think I have had a similar account from Dr. Franklin, but cannot be certain quite. I know that being in Philadelphia when the first set of patent wheels arrived from London, and were spoken of by the gentleman (an Englishman) who brought them as a wonderful discovery. The idea of it's being a new discovery was laughed at by the Philadelphians, who in their Sunday parties across the Delaware had seen every farmer's cart mounted on such wheels. The writer in the paper supposes the English workman got his idea from Homer. But it is more likely that the Jersey farmer got the idea from thence, because ours are the only farmers who can read Homer: because too the Jersey practice is precisely that stated by Homer; the English practice very different. Homer's words are (comparing a young hero killed by Ajax to a poplar felled by a workman)———

$$\mathring{o}\ \delta'\ \epsilon\nu\ \kappa o\nu\iota\eta\varsigma\iota,\ \chi\alpha\mu\alpha\iota\ \pi\epsilon\sigma\epsilon\nu,\ \alpha\iota\gamma\epsilon\iota\rho o\varsigma\ \mathring{\omega}\varsigma,$$
$$\text{'H}\ \rho\alpha\ \tau'\epsilon\nu\ \epsilon\iota\alpha\mu\epsilon\nu\eta\ \epsilon\lambda\epsilon o\varsigma\ \mu\epsilon\gamma\alpha\lambda o\iota o\ \pi\epsilon\phi\upsilon\kappa\epsilon$$
$$\Lambda\epsilon\iota\eta\ \alpha\tau\alpha\rho\ \tau\epsilon\ \mathring{o}\iota\ o\zeta o\iota\ \epsilon\pi'\ \alpha\kappa\rho o\tau\alpha\tau\eta\ \pi\epsilon\phi\upsilon\alpha\sigma\iota$$
$$T\eta\nu\ \mu\epsilon\nu\ \theta\mathring{\alpha}\rho\mu\alpha\tau o\pi\eta\gamma o\varsigma\ \alpha\nu\eta\rho\ \alpha\iota\theta\omega\nu\iota\ \varsigma\iota\delta\eta\rho\tilde{\omega}$$
$$E\xi\epsilon\tau\alpha\mu'\ o\phi\rho\alpha\ \iota\tau\upsilon\nu\ \kappa\alpha\mu\psi\eta\ \pi\epsilon\rho\iota\kappa\alpha\lambda\lambda\ddot{\epsilon}\iota\ \delta\iota\phi\rho\wp,$$
$$\text{'H}\ \mu\epsilon\nu\ \tau'\alpha\zeta o\mu\epsilon\nu\eta\ \kappa\epsilon\iota\tau\alpha\iota\ \pi o\tau\alpha\mu o\iota o\ \pi\alpha\rho\ o\chi\theta\alpha\varsigma \quad 4.\ \text{Il}.\ 482.$$

literally thus 'he fell on the ground, like a poplar, which has grown, smooth, in the wet part of a great meadow; with it's branches shooting from it's summit. But the Chariot-maker with his sharp axe, has felled it, that he may bend a wheel for a beautiful chariot. It lies drying on the banks of the river.' Observe the circumstances which coincide with the Jersey practice. 1. It is a tree growing in a moist place, full of juices, and easily bent. 2. It is cut while green. 3. It is bent into the circumference of a wheel. 4. It is left to dry in that form. You, who write French well and readily, should write a line for the Journal to reclaim the honour of our farmers. Adieu. Your's affectionately,   TH: JEFFERSON

RC (Saint-John de Crèvecoeur, Montesquieu-sur-Losse, La Plagne, France, 1947). PrC (DLC).

TJ might not have objected to the article in THE JOURNAL OF THIS MORNING (*Journal de Paris*, 15 Jan. 1787) if its author had confined himself to the interpretation of a passage in *The Iliad* as meaning that the process of making a wheel of a single piece of wood was known to the Greeks; but the writer had gone on to say: "L'on en a pourtant fait honneur, n'aguères, à un Anglois, comme d'une invention nouvelle." This was sufficient to arouse TJ's patriotic feelings, and the present MS resulted.—As TJ had requested, Crèvecoeur made a translation of this letter, with some interesting variations and interpolations; the most famous passage, as rewritten by Crèvecoeur, reads: "L'Auteur de ce paragraphe suppose même que le Charron Anglois avoit tiré cette idée d'Homère. Il est bien plus vraisemblable que ces Cultivateurs l'ont puisée dans cette source; cette classe d'hommes étant dans ce moment la seule au sein de laquelle on puisse trouver des hommes qui entendent et lisent cet ancien Auteur. La méthode Angloise est d'ailleurs bien différente, puisqu'on ne se sert à Londres que de bois sec, au lieu qu'Homère ne parle que d'arbres jeunes et verds, tels que sont ceux qui couvrent une grande partie de notre continent." This joint production by TJ and Crèvecoeur was published in the *Journal de Paris*, 31 Jan. 1787, and was signed "Un Américain."—I WAS IN HIS SHOP IN LONDON: TJ visited the shop with John Adams during Apr. 1786 after their return from a tour of the English gardens. "Since my return," wrote Adams, "I have been over Blackfriar's Bridge to see Viny's manufacture of patent wheels made of bent timber" (Adams, *Works*, ed. C. F. Adams, III, 394-6; see also TJ to Thomson, 22 Apr. 1786, note).

From Philippe-Denis Pierres

MONSIEUR   Paris, le 15 Janvier 1787.

J'ai l'honneur de vous adresser les cartons dont vous avez desiré l'impression. Je souhaitte que vous en soyez satisfait.

Quant aux Caracteres que vous demandez pour accompagner la petite Presse, je ne crois pas qu'il soit nécessaire de choisir ceux des *Didot* et des *Foulis*: J'en ai qui ont été gravés par *Garamond*, et dont la beauté ne cede en rien à ceux-là. Si cependant, Monsieur, vous tenez à cette idée, ayez la bonté de me la faire savoir, et alors vous voudriez bien vous adresser à eux mêmes; mais je n'en vois point la nécessité. Il seroit d'ailleurs difficile de déterminer le nombre qu'il faudroit de chaque caractere, attendu qu'il faut que les cases soient faites avant cela.

Agréez, Monsieur, Les assurances du respect infini avec lequel je suis, Monsieur, Votre Très-humble et très-obéissant serviteur,

PIERRES

RC (MHi); endorsed. Not recorded in SJL.

To Abigail Adams Smith

Paris Jan. 15. 1787.

Mr. Jefferson has the honour to present his compliments to Mrs. Smith and to send her the two pair of Corsets she desired. He wishes they may be suitable, as Mrs. Smith omitted to send her measure. Times are altered since Mademoiselle de Sanson had the honour of knowing her. Should they be too small however, she will be so good as to lay them by a while. There are ebbs as well as flows in this world. When the mountain refused to come to Mahomet, he went to the mountain. Mr. Jefferson wishes Mrs. Smith a happy new year, and abundance of happier ones still to follow it. He begs leave to assure her of his esteem and respect, and that he shall always be happy to be rendered useful to her by being charged with her commands.

PrC (MHi). See Mrs. Smith to TJ, 2 Dec. 1786.

To William Stephens Smith

Dear Sir Paris Jan. 15. 1787.

Colo. Franks's delay here, occasioned by that of his baggage, gives me an opportunity of acknowleging the receipt of the map. I am now occupied in correcting it. I have got thro about two thirds of the map and have a list of 172 errors, so that we may expect in the whole about 250, and I reckon only those which are material. Small and immaterial changes of orthography I do not correct. Except as to the errors, the work is fairly and neatly done. I shall try to have the corrections made by a French workman. If he cannot do it. I must send it again to Mr. Neele to be done. I think it is long since you were so kind as to give me notice that the second copying press was sent off. But I have never heard a tittle of it. I will be obliged to you if you will be so good as to let me know how, by whom, and to what place it was directed, that I may give orders to search for it, before my departure to the waters of Aix, which will be within a fortnight or three weeks. I will thank you at the same time for what an Architect here describes to me in the following words 'un ruban, contenû dans du cuivre, sur lequel est marqué le pied Anglois.' It is a portable measure, made for travellers to carry in their pockets in order to measure bridges, arches, buildings &c. He sais I should have two, one of about 20. feet, the other 50 feet. I suppose they are to be found in the Mathematical shops. I must trouble you to send me two by the Diligence, and in time for my journey. I must beg the favor of you to get me also from Lee's at Hammersmith the following plants: 12. of the Acer rubrum. 12. of the Quercus Phellos, and 5. Liriodendron tulipiferum. I do not mean that this should cost you any other trouble than to send the inclosed note to Lee, let him know you will pay his bill, and press his instantaneous execution of it.

You will have heard that the king has called an assembly of

Notables, which has not been done for 160. years. The objects are not known: the following are conjectured. To establish provincial assemblies: tolerate the Protestant religion; remove all the internal douanes to the frontiers; equalise the Gabels; and sell the crown lands. I send you an account of the last assembleé des Notables, which will give you an idea of the present one. The king names the members ad libitum, our friend de la Fayette is one, and is the youngest man but one in it, and that one is named on account of a charge he has. The Dutch affairs promise no arrangement: and it has been feared that the K. of Prussia might be shifted into the Austrian scale.

I take the liberty of putting under your cover some letters which I will only trouble you to send to the post office. I am with very sincere esteem, dear Sir, Your friend & servant,

TH: JEFFERSON

P.S. The letter which is sealed and without a superscription, is for a Mr. Vaughan whose Christian name I have forgot. It is he who went with us to the king's museum. He is married. We dined at his house, at least Mr. Adams and myself did, and I dined in company with him at the M. of Lansdowne's. From these descriptions perhaps you will be able to put the superscription on the letter.

RC (PHC); endorsed in part: "ansr. Jany. 29." PrC (DLC). TJ's "inclosed note to Lee" is missing; of the other enclosures, only his letter "to Mr. Vaughan" (q.v. under 29 Dec. 1786, TJ to Benjamin Vaughan) has been identified.

From John Bondfield

[*Bordeaux, 16 Jan. 1787.* Recorded in SJL as received 21 Jan. 1787. Not found; but see St. Victour & Bettinger to TJ, 23 Jan. 1787.]

From Carburi

à Paris ce 16 Janv. 1787.

Ms. de Carburi presente ses respects à Mr. Jefferson, il lui envoye les 4 demibouteilles qu'il demande, et 4 autres demibouteilles d'autres vins de la Grece à fin qu'il choisisse ceux qui lui plairont d'avantage.

Tous ces vins reviennent à 6 francs la Boutteille de Pinte.

RC (MHi); endorsed: "Carburi Comte de." Not recorded in SJL.

To Edward Carrington

DEAR SIR Paris Jan. 16. 1787.

Incertain whether you might be at New York at the moment of Colo. Franks's arrival, I have inclosed my private letters for Virginia under cover to our delegation in general, which otherwise I would have taken the liberty to inclose particularly to you, as best acquainted with the situation of the persons to whom they are addressed. Should this find you at New York, I will still ask your attention to them. The two large packages addressed to Colo. N. Lewis contain seeds, not valuable enough to pay postage, but which I would wish to be sent by the stage, or any similar quick conveyance. The letters to Colo. Lewis and Mr. Eppes (who take care of my affairs) are particularly interesting to me. The package for Colo. Richd. Cary our judge of Admiralty near Hampton, contains seeds and roots, not to be sent by post. Whether they had better go by the stage, or by water, you will be the best judge. I beg your pardon for giving you this trouble. But my situation and your goodness will I hope excuse it.

In my letter to Mr. Jay I have mentioned the meeting of the Notables appointed for the 29th. inst. It is now put off to the 7th. or 8th. of next month. This event, which will hardly excite any attention in America, is deemed here the most important one which has taken place in their civil line during the present century. Some promise their country great things from it, some nothing. Our friend de la fayette was placed on the list originally. Afterwards his name disappeared: but finally was reinstated. This shews that his character here is not considered as an indifferent one; and that it excites agitation. His education in our school has drawn on him a very jealous eye from a court whose principles are the most absolute despotism. But I hope he has nearly passed his crisis. The king, who is a good man, is favorably disposed towards him: and he is supported by powerful family connections, and by the public good will. He is the youngest man of the Notables, except one whose office placed him on the list.

The Count de Vergennes has within these ten days had a very severe attack of what is deemed an unfixed gout. He has been well enough however to do business to-day. But anxieties for him are not yet quieted. He is a great and good minister, and an accident to him might endanger the peace of Europe.

The tumults in America, I expected would have produced in Europe an unfavorable opinion of our political state. But it has not. On the contrary, the small effect of those tumults seems to have given more confidence in the firmness of our governments. The interposition of the people themselves on the side of government has had a great effect on the opinion here. I am persuaded myself that the good sense of the people will always be found to be the best army. They may be led astray for a moment, but will soon correct themselves. The people are the only censors of their governors: and even their errors will tend to keep these to the true principles of their institution. To punish these errors too severely would be to suppress the only safeguard of the public liberty. The way to prevent these irregular interpositions of the people is to give them full information of their affairs thro' the channel of the public papers, and to contrive that those papers should penetrate the whole mass of the people. The basis of our governments being the opinion of the people, the very first object should be to keep that right; and were it left to me to decide whether we should have a government without newspapers, or newspapers without a government, I should not hesitate a moment to prefer the latter. But I should mean that every man should receive those papers and be capable of reading them. I am convinced that those societies (as the Indians) which live without government enjoy in their general mass an infinitely greater degree of happiness than those who live under European governments. Among the former, public opinion is in the place of law, and restrains morals as powerfully as laws ever did any where. Among the latter, under pretence of governing they have divided their nations into two classes, wolves and sheep. I do not exaggerate. This is a true picture of Europe. Cherish therefore the spirit of our people, and keep alive their attention. Do not be too severe upon their errors, but reclaim them by enlightening them. If once they become inattentive to the public affairs, you and I, and Congress, and Assemblies, judges and governors shall all become wolves. It seems to be the law of our general nature, in spite of individual exceptions; and experience declares that man is the only animal which devours his own kind, for I can apply no milder term to the governments of Europe, and to the general prey of the rich on the poor.—The want of news has led me into disquisition instead of narration, forgetting you have every day enough of that. I shall be happy to hear from you some times, only observing that whatever passes thro' the post is read, and that when you write what should be read by myself only, you must be so good as to confide your letter to some passenger or officer of the packet. I will ask your permission to write to you sometimes, and to assure you of

17 JANUARY 1787

the esteem & respect with which I have the honour to be Dear Sir your most obedient & most humble servt.,

TH: JEFFERSON

PrC (DLC).

It may not have been altogether a want of news that led TJ into DISQUISITION INSTEAD OF NARRATION. The oft-quoted opinions that he inserted in a letter to one whose character he understood very well from the days of his governorship may have been as calculated as was TJ's selection of a correspondent in Congress to supply, in part at least, the place formerly occupied by Madison and Monroe. William Short seems to have been the intermediary on this occasion. "Some time ago Sir," he wrote Carrington on 3 Nov. 1786, "I took the liberty of advising Mr. Jefferson to write to you in order to the commencement of a correspondence, as he wished to have an intimate one with some of his friends in Congress" (DLC: Short Papers). This may have been TJ's manner of inquiring indirectly whether such a correspondence would be agreeable. Even before the correspondence was opened, Short gave Carrington an opinion on American foreign relations that might have been only TJ's echo: "What will be the principal deliberations of Congress during this winter? What have the states done respecting the investiture of Congress with powers for regulating the commerce? What are the probabilities of the fœderal finances being well arranged? These my dear Sir are subjects which inquiet much some of our friends on this side of the Atlantic. They frequently talk to me on them, and I confess I some times find it very difficult to satisfy all their doubts and difficulties. I wish you would put it in my power to do this for their sakes as well as my own.—We want in America Sir, but open arrangements taken for the establishment of federal credit, to become the most envied nation on earth. This is what is agreed on all hands here, but what would surprize you is, to see how few there are who suppose the continental union can subsist. The British news-papers which have an universal circulation in Europe, have found means to make it generally believed that there is nothing but distress, disorder and discontent in America. Their lies have been so often told, that they are believed now by themselves, and there is no question that some of the most able men in England, are fully persuaded that America would be glad at this moment to throw herself back into the arms of Britain.— Were the foreign debts once paid public credit would be re-established immediately on a footing to give the lye to all these suppositions, for where there is public credit, it is difficult to be persuaded that there is public discontent, disorder and distress" (same).

From Champagni

Paris, Wednesday [17? *Jan.* 1787]. He is a French citizen who wishes to buy some land in the United States; asks for information about procedure and for advice concerning the location of lands; realizes that the value of land varies according to its location and that land in the Philadelphia vicinity is the most expensive; however, that is the neighborhood he prefers but does not know whether an investment of 100,000 francs in land and an additional amount for Negroes would yield a reasonable profit. If the cost of land in Pennsylvania is too high, would like advice about another situation in a good climate. The latitude of Virginia would be acceptable but he does not know whether land there is expensive or whether the residents are "trouble par les sauvages qui, selon ce que disent nos gazètes, inquiètent terriblement les colons de vos frontières." Would also like to know in what form he should carry his money; whether French, Spanish or English money is most

[50]

advantageous; whether commercial intercourse is well enough established with some French firm to enable him to carry a letter of credit; whether trade is easy in the United States; what products are the most lucrative; whether it would be cheaper to transport a dozen Negroes from French Guiana, where he has property, than to purchase them in America. Asks pardon for asking so many questions; has "une envie éxtrême d'habiter le païs de la liberté, païs ou l'home conserve sa naturèl dignité." If it is too much trouble to reply by letter, asks for an appointment.

RC (DLC); p. 4.; in French; endorsed. Undated except for the day of the week and not recorded in SJL; assigned to this date from internal evidence and TJ's reply of 19 Jan. 1787.

To S. & J. H. Delap

GENTLEMEN   Paris Jan. 17. 1787.

I am honoured this day by the receipt of your letter of the 6th. instant. Having nothing to do with the matters of account of the United states in Europe, it is out of my power to say any thing to you as to the paiment of the balance due to you. Yet I think it would be proper for you to write to the 'Commissioners of the treasury' at New York on the subject. They are the persons who are to pay it, and as their board has been created since the debt was contracted, they may possibly need information on the subject.

As to your loan office certificates, you would do well to commit them to some correspondent in America. They will be settled by the table of depreciation at their true worth in gold or silver at the time the paper dollars were lent. On that true value the interest has been paid, and continues to be paid to the creditors annually in America. That the principal will also be paid, is as sure as any future fact can be. The epoch is not fixed. It is expected that the state of New York will shortly accede to the impost which has been proposed. When that shall be done, that impost will suffice to pay the interest and sink the principal in a very few years. I have the honour to be with much respect, Gentlemen, your most obedt. humble servt.,   TH: JEFFERSON

PrC (DLC); at foot of text: "Messrs. S. & J. H. Delap merchts. Bordeaux."

To Duler

SIR   Paris Jan. 17. 1787.

I have the honour of now returning to you the certificate of the Chevalier Danmours, in your favour. The testimony of that gentle-

[51]

man, with whose worth I am well acquainted, would have satisfied me of yours, had any testimony been wanting. It adds another to the list of many worthy persons whom I am unable to assist; for I declare to you that I know no way on earth in which I can be useful to you. To give you false hopes, would be to injure and not to serve you. I beg you to be assured of my wishes for your success, and of the respect with which I have the honor to be Sir your most obedt. & most humble servt., TH: JEFFERSON

PrC (DLC); at foot of text: "M. Duler. chez M. Rochet Negt. à Rouen." On the enclosed "certificate," see Duler to TJ, 8 Jan. 1787.

To Jean Durival

SIR Paris Jan. 17. 1787.

You were pleased, in behalf of a friend, to ask information of me on the subject of the money of the United states of America, and I had the honour of informing you, by letter of Nov. 7. that no regulations of their coin had then been made by Congress, as far as I knew. They had however entered into resolutions on that subject which have since come to hand. A translation of these will be found in the Leyden gazette of some few weeks ago. But it will be necessary to make the following corrections on the gazette.

The gazette dates the resolutions Oct. 10. but they were of Aug. 8.

It gives only 365.64 grains of pure silver to the dollar. It should be 375.64. It states the pound of silver with it's alloy to be worth 9.99 dollars only: whereas it is fixed at 13.777 dollars. And the pound of gold with it's alloy being worth 209.77 dollars gives the proportion of silver to gold as 1. to 15.225. These corrections being made, the resolutions as stated in the Leyden gazette may be confided in.

I have the honour to be with much respect Sir your most obedt. & most humble servt., TH: JEFFERSON

PrC (DLC).

From Miguel de Lardizábel y Uribe

MONSR. 17 Janvr. 87

J'ai etè hier chez vous sans me rapeller que vous seriez à Versailles. Je partirai lundi, c'est pour quoi je vous prie d'avoir pret la

17 JANUARY 1787

boite des machines à pouvoir me l'envoyer samedi porchain. Demain au soir j'irai prendre vos ordres, et à même tems m'essayer dans votre grande machine à imprimer une page. Je suis avec tout le respect et avec tout l'attachemt. possible Mr. Votre très humb. et très obeisst. servr.,
MICHEL DE LARDIZABEL

RC (MHi); endorsed: "Lardizabal, Don Miguel de"; addressed to TJ "à la Grille de Chaillot." Not recorded in SJL.

The BOITE DES MACHINES that Lardizábel wished TJ to have ready against his departure on Monday contained one of the portable copying presses that TJ had asked him to convey as a gift to Carmichael (TJ to Carmichael, 26 Dec. 1786; possibly another press was included in the box). Lardizábel's remark that he would attempt DANS VOTRE GRANDE MACHINE À IMPRIMER UNE PAGE simply meant that TJ would give him a lesson in the technique of operating the large copying press.— Lardizábel was the brother of Manuel de Lardizábel y Uribe, Spanish author whose work on penology was in TJ's library: *Discurso sobre las penas contrahido á las leyes criminales de España, para facilitar su reforma* (Madrid, 1782); Sowerby, No. 2422.

From Segond

Beausset-en-Provence, 17 Jan. 1787. A friend, charged with collecting for him the interest due on his account with the United States, informs him that Mr. Grand has received no funds for that purpose; the payment is now two years in arrears; asks how long this will continue. "Aprés avoir exposé nos jours à la [service] de vos etats, avoir coopéré à la grande œuvre de votre independance, n'est il pour naturel de compter sur un revenu Si justement acquis? Quand pendant une geurre tres longue nous nous some privé de toute jouissance, que nous n'avons même procuré l'absolu necessaire qu'a nos depens, n'est il pas horrible que les etats mettent tant de lenteur à liquidés une creance qu'ils ont si authentiquement reconue bien acquise; qu'ils n'en payent pas même l'interets? S'ils [avaient] quelque idée de justice, trois années de paix ne les [. . . .]" Not expecting such a lack of good faith, he borrowed 1,800 francs for his trip to Paris; is being pressed for the payment of the loan and, as always, eager to satisfy his obligations, asks TJ to draw an order on Mr. Grand for payment or, if TJ prefers, he will accept a personal note. Justice demands that he be saved from the embarrassing position in which the default of the United States has thrown him.

Tr (DNA: PCC, No. 107, I); 2 p. Recorded in SJL as received 25 Jan. 1787; enclosed in TJ to John Jay, 1 Feb. 1787. An English translation is printed in *Dipl. Corr., 1783-89*, II, 30-1, but with omissions.

The Chevalier de Segond (1758-1832) was a native of Beausset in Provence who volunteered in the American army in 1777. He was made a captain in the Pulaski Legion in 1778 and fought at Brandywine, Germantown, Whitemarsh, and in the Southern campaign, being captured at Charleston in 1780. He served in Holland from 1785 to 1788; in Russia from 1788 to the end of 1790; and after a short period with the French armies, 1791 to 1793, he deserted to Austria (Lasseray, *Les Français sous les treize étoiles*, p. 410-2).

[53]

To John Adams

Sir Paris Jan. 19. 1787.

Colo. Franks having occasion for fifty pounds sterling to enable him to pursue his journey to London and New York, Mr. Grand has furnished him with that sum, for the reimbursement whereof I have drawn on you in his favor, and have to pray you to honour that draught and to charge it against the fund appropriated to the negociations with Marocco, as expended in that business. I have the honour to be with the most perfect esteem & respect, Sir, Your most obedient & most humble servt., Th: Jefferson

RC (MHi: AMT); endorsed by Adams: "Letter of advice of a Bill of 50£ in favor of Mr. Grand indorsed to Lane Son & Fraser. Bill accepted by me 30. Jan. for Franks's Expences." PrC (DLC).

To Champagni

[Paris, 19 Jan. 1787]

Vous me faites l'honneur, Monsieur, de demander mes conseils sur le projet que vous avez conçu, de vendre vos biens ici, et d'aller vous etablir en Amerique. Je vous repeterai ce que j'ai eu l'honneur de conseiller à d'autres, qui en ont eté dans la suite tres contents. C'est de ne vendre ici, qu'après que vous vous auriez rendu en Amerique, que vous auriez bien parcouru les etats dont le climat est temperé, que vous auriez examiné par vous meme le sol, le prix, la societé, et toutes les circonstances qui entreroient pour quelque chose dans votre decision. C'est selon votre gout que doit se faire cette decision, et il n'y a personne qui peut la faire aussi bien que vous meme. Si vous trouverez que vous pouvez y etre plus heureux qu'ici, vos amis vendront vos biens d'ici, deposeront l'argent chez un banquier connu, et en tirant sur ce banquier des billets d'exchange là bas, on vous donnera de l'argent contant, et vous y gagnerez meme quelque chose. Si pourtant vous preferez de vendre avant d'avoir vu ce païs-la, vous ferez bien de deposer l'argent semblablement chez un banquier connu. Messrs. le Couteulx, Monsieur Grand, Monsieur Perigaux sont bien connus en Amerique. J'ai l'honneur d'etre, avec bien de respect, Monsieur votre tres humble et tres obeissant serviteur,

Th: Jefferson

PrC (MoSHi); endorsed; at foot of text: "M. le Chevr. de Champagni. hotel d'Auvergne. Quai des Augustins." The date has been supplied from an entry in SJL for a letter to Champagni of this date.

From Chevallié Fils

Monsieur   L'Orient le 19 Janvier 1787.

Arrivé hier au Soir de Newyork, Je m'enpresse à remettre à Votre Excellence, deux lettres de Mr. James Madisson, et Saisir cette occasion de vous presenter mes très humbles remerciments des renseignements dont vous honnorates mon Pere Négociant á Rochefort en Janvier 1785 et qui ont descidé mon passage en amerique pour recouvrer les fonds qui luy etoient dûs par l'Etat de Virginie. L'assemblée de cet Etat, Sans repondre entiérement à mes prétensions, a cependant traité ma demande plus favorablement que celle d'aucun créancier; aussi Si mon pere, peu satisfait de ce traitement, Veut mon retour aux Etats unis, je ne manquerai pas de prendre vos ordres et reclamer l'appuy de Votre protection. Je suis avec respect De Votre Excellence Le très humble & très obéissant Serviteur,   Chevallié fils
à Rochefort

RC (DLC); endorsed. Recorded in SJL as received 24 Jan. 1787. Enclosures: James Madison to TJ, 25 Nov. and 4 Dec. 1786.

Chevallié's acknowledgement of the renseignements dont vous honnorates mon pere refers, no doubt, to TJ's letters to Franklin of 25 Nov. and 1 Dec. 1784, which Chevallié père replied to in his to TJ of 17 Mch. 1785.

To R. & A. Garvey

Gentlemen   Paris Jan. 19. 1787.

I am honoured with your letter of Jan. 8. on the subject of the duties paid by Mr. Boylston on his cargo of whale oil, but being about to take a journey which will absent me from Paris three months, it will be necessary for Mr. Boylston to desire his correspondent at this place to undertake the sollicitation of that reimbursement.

Your bill for 59^{tt} 5s has been presented to-day and paid. I sent to the Douane to ask your Acquit à caution. They said they thought they had sent it to you lately; but desired, if you had not received it, that you would be so good as to send me a description of it, by it's number &c. as usual, and they will immediately deliver me for you a proper discharge. I will thank you to send me this immediately as I would wish to see it settled myself before my departure.

I expect a box or two containing another copying press from London very shortly. Indeed I suspect it is already lodged either at

[55]

19 JANUARY 1787

Rouen or Havre. I shall thank you for your care of it, as I do for the past, and have the honour to be with much esteem Gentlemen your most obedt. humble servt., TH: JEFFERSON

PrC (DLC).

To François Soulés

SIR   Paris Jan. 19. 1787.

I have the honour of inclosing to you the sheets on the subject of Wyoming. I have had a long conversation with M. Crevecoeur on them. He knows well that canton. He was in the neighborhood of the place when it was destroyed, saw great numbers of the fugitives, aided them with his waggons, and had the story from all their mouths. He committed notes to writing in the moment, which are now in Normandy at his father's. He has written for them, and they will be here in 5. or 6. days, when he promises to put them into my hands. He says there will be a great deal to alter in your narration, and that it must assume a different face, more favorable both to the British and Indians. His veracity may be relied on, and I told him I was sure your object was truth, and to render your work estimable by that character, that I thought you would wait, and readily make any changes upon evidence which should be satisfactory to you. The moment I receive his notes I will communicate them to you; I have the honour to be with much respect Sir Your most obedt. humble servt., TH: JEFFERSON

PrC (DLC). Enclosure: Either MS or proof sheets of Soulés' *Histoire des Troubles de l'Amérique Anglaise*; Soulés may have sent proof sheets of the account of the Battle of Wyoming of 3 July 1778, for, as finally published, the story occupied only p. 9-17 of Volume III—that is, the last half of the first sheet (sig. A) and the first page of the second (sig. B)—and this included a good bit of matter about the Connecticut-Pennsylvania disputes in the Wyoming Valley and a description of the region that could only have been added after TJ sent Crèvecoeur's notes (see TJ to Soulés, 2 Feb. 1787).

To the Abbé Morellet

[*Paris, 19 Jan. 1787.* Entry in SJL reads: "Morellet l'Abbé." Not found; but see Morellet to TJ, 11? Jan. 1787.]

To Elizabeth Blair Thompson

DEAR MADAM   Paris Jan. 19. 1787.

I am this day honoured with your favour of the 10th. instant and have the happiness to inform you that Mr. Bannister has been

19 JANUARY 1787

here near two months, and appears to enjoy as perfect health as any person can. I am in hopes he will have no more relapses.—I am much obliged by your kind expressions of concern at the accident which prevented me the honour of seeing you at Titchfeild. Certainly if I had suspected your being in the house I should have pressed for a permission to see you. The accident of my daughter's being taken ill a little before we made land, occasioned my going ashore on your side of the channel to procure medical aid, and the gentleman who attended her, gave me the first information of your living in the neighborhood. A fair wind offering to cross the channel the day after I had been to Titchfeild, left me no longer at liberty to indulge my wish of making another effort to see you. I am sincerely pleased to hear you have been able to raise so many blessings for the autumn of life, for by this term I am sure your children will deserve to be named. Some years ago (I am afraid to say how many) we should have thought this but an awkward congratulation: but we have both lived to learn that there is no subject which affords more just ground for it. My history, since I had the pleasure of seeing you last, would have been as happy a one as I could have asked, could the objects of my affection have been immortal. But all the favors of fortune have been embittered by domestic losses. Of six children I have lost four, and finally their mother. This happened too in the moment when I had retired from all public business, determined to enjoy the remainder of life in the bosom of my family. I have been induced to enter again on a stage I had quitted, merely to absent myself from scenes where I had been happier than I ever can be again. I have one daughter 14. years of age, now with me, and expect the other over in the spring. She is 10. years old. The time of my stay in Europe is unfixed; but I love my own country too much to stay from it long. I went to London the last summer under a commission, the object of which was to endeavor to heal the wounds of affection between the two countries. It proved unsuccesful. I wished an occasion of taking Titchfeild in my way back: but circumstances did not permit it: and I think it rather improbable I should ever cross the channel again. Perhaps the wish to see your friends may one day tempt you to revisit the country which possesses them. In that event I may hope to meet you there. Be assured that there is none who would meet you with more sincere affection. The friendships contracted earliest in life, are those which stand by us the longest. The happy hours and days I have passed in your company are recollected with infinite sensibility. To talk them over again, would

20 JANUARY 1787

be to renew them. But to complete this enjoyment it should be in the same circle: some chasms indeed are made in that; but the greater part are still living. I have no late news from our friends in Virginia. You know that indolence is one of the characteristics of that country. They write seldom and little. I shall be happy at all times to hear of your welfare, and of that of all who are dear to you. Be so good as to make my respects acceptable to Captain Thompson and to be assured of the sincerity of those sentiments of friendship & esteem with which I have the honour to be Dear Madam your affectionate humble servant,

TH: JEFFERSON

PrC (DLC).

From Charles Burney

SIR   London, Jany. 20th. 1787.

Few things have given me more concern than the not being able sooner to give you a satisfactory account of the Harpsichord and its Machinery, which I had the honour to bespeak for you, last Summer. I visited Kirkman from time to time whenever I came to town, and saw the Instrument in every stage of its construction. The wood was chosen with great care; the Lid is solid, as you desired, and no part has been veneered or inlaid that could possibly be avoided, or which could receive the least injury from vicissi[tu]de of climate. I got the Instrument out of Kirkman's hands, very completely finished, as far as concerned his part of the business, in Autumn; and by a little management prevailed on him to send it to Walker, with tolerable good humour. Walker undertook to place his Machine for the Celestine Stop upon it, with great readiness, finding for whom the Instrument was made: as I discovered that he had had the honour of conversing with you about the difficulties and objections on the Subject of his Stop. I was glad of this, as it made him more alert and solicitous to execute his part well. He told me that he had little doubt but that he could put his machinery in motion by clock-work, with very little use of a Pedal. I let him alone to meditate and work at his leisure till the Month of November, when I began to be uneasy lest you should imagine the commission had been neglected on my Part. Walker was still in high spirits about the success of his new Machine, and only waited for the Clock-maker's part of the work. Last month the new Machine was applied; and though infinitely superior to the

[58]

old, the motion given to it by a single stroke or pressure of the foot, was not so durable as I wished, or as Walker expected. He had difficulties in placing, and covering his machine, after it was made; as well as in regulating its operations. At length, after long delays, some occasioned by real difficulties, and others by having, like all his brethren, projectors, too many pursuits at a time, the machine has received all the perfection he can give it. He has promised to describe its powers, and the means of exhibiting them, in a paper which will accompany the Instrument. The Resin will, he says, be easily brushed off the strings, if adhesion from damp is not suffered to take place, by neglecting to clean the strings too long. As a Harpsichord I never heard a better instrument or felt a more even and pleasant touch. The Tone is full, sweet, and equally good through the whole scale. And as to Walkers stop, it is much more easily used than any I ever tried. It will not suit things[1] of execution, but is not confined to mere Psalmody, as was the Case at the first invention. The machine or species of Bow is sooner and more easily brought into contact, than formerly, and is not so subject to produce a *Scream* by over pressure of the keys. It is perfectly sweet, and at a little distance *Organic*: that is it reminds one of the best and most expressive part of an organ, the Swell. On the degree of pressure depends not only the durability of tone, but its force. It will require much exercise to find out, and display, all the beauties of this stop. You, Sir, are speculative Musician sufficient to know the truth of this assertion, and to avail yourself of it.   As to the Question you ask concerning the superiority of organs made in England or France? I can only answer that as far as I have seen, heard, or examined, this mechanism of the English is infinitely superior, as well as the tone of the Solo-stops. Green, the organ builder here, is a very ingenious and experimental man; and not only makes dayly discoveries and improvements himself, but readily adopts those that may be made or recommended to him by others. *Pour la forme* and ornaments the Fr. will doubtless beat us; mais, *pour le fond*, I think we always *had*, and still *have* it all to Nothing against the rest of Europe. We are Notorious for want of invention—yet give us but a principle to work on, and we are sure of leaving an invention better than we find it. I write now in too great a hurry to describe the contents of such a Chamber organ as you have in meditation. About £100 would I think supply all that is wanting in such an Instrument. Fine stops, well-voiced, and chosen, will produce better Effects in a small space, than crowds of such course or unmeaning pipes as

20 JANUARY 1787

are usually crammed into Chamber organs of any Size. If I can be of the least further use in this or any other commiss[ion] in my Power, I beg you not to spare me, being with great respect & regard, Sir your obedient & most humble Servant,

CHAS. BURNEY

RC (DLC); addressed; endorsed: "Burney Dr." Recorded in SJL as received 2 Feb. 1787.

[1] Thus in MS; Burney probably intended to write: "things difficult of execution."

From Jean Durival

Versailles, 20 Jan. 1787. Acknowledges receipt of information on the coinage of the U.S., which he will forward to "M. Des Rotours Premier Commis des Monnoyes à Paris" for use in his book now in preparation. Des Rotours will be grateful for any further information TJ may procure on that subject; his address is: "rue Neuve de Luxembourg No. 29."

RC (DLC); 2 p.; in French; endorsed. Recorded in SJL as received 21 Jan. 1787.

From Uriah Forrest

Georgetown, Md., 20 Jan. 1787. Introducing the bearer, Joseph Fenwick, his "particular Friend, a Man of the best Character and Connexions." Forrest will spend remainder of winter and spring in New York and will communicate with TJ from there.

RC (MHi); 2 p.; endorsed. Recorded in SJL as received 25 May 1787 at Bordeaux.

From Madame de Tessé

a Paris ce 21 janvier

Monsieur jefferson est supplié d'accepter à la fois les excuses et les Regrets d'un hopital entier. Mr. de Tessé est condamné par l'ordre du medecin a garder sa chambre pour un gros Rhume. Me. de Tott, excessivement souffrante depuis plusieurs jours, a tellement fatigué par l'inquietude la fragile constitution de Me. de Tessé quelle se trouve ce matin hors d'etat de sortir. Le chagrin quils eprouvent de manquer une occasion qui leur etoit si chere merite quelque pitié et les engage a se flatter que Monsieur jefferson voudra bien leur en accorder le dedommagement a son Retour des

[60]

eaux. L'espoir de trouver Mademoiselle jefferson chés Monsieur son pere ajoute au malheur de toute la famille.

Mr. Short verra ici pourquoi Me. de Tessé a eté privée deux fois du plaisir de le voir. Elle etoit retenue près de Me. de Tott trop souffrante pour recevoir quelqu'un.

RC (DLC); without indication of the year. The date has been established from Madame de Tessé's reference to TJ's imminent journey to the EAUX of southern France. Not recorded in SJL.

From William Jones

SR.   London Jany. 22nd. 1787

On account of the hurry of previous business, I have been prevented from finishing your Perspective Machine as soon as I wished, but herewith you receive it, and in a State which I presume will not be unacceptable. I have improved it, by adding the few requisites for a Drawing Board, which make it a complete Instrument. The use of the several parts of the Machine I presume will be obvious to you, viz. the T. and Bevil Square for drawing Parallel lines in all Directions. The box scale frame, for confining down the paper (which should be rather damp when first put down) on the board. The scale serving as a guide to the distance of the parallel lines. The Steel Pin at the corner of the Box is to be put in a hole in one of the joints to keep the brass frame upright when necessary. There is a groove in the brass frame, to contain a Pane of Glass mentioned by Ferguson. I made the frame square for an obvious reason viz. to admit the whole of the board, as the drawing of a Machine &c. when placed near the Instrument may require a larger space, than the Arches admit of. A Friend has informed me Sir that Monsr. Guyot, has lately published a very pleasant Work, entitled Récréations Physiques et Mathematiques, in 3 Vos. Octavo, containing a selection of many very curious and entertaining experiments [in] Electricity, Magnetism &c. I expect very shortly some copies of his book from him having ordered them 3 Months ago. If you think it worth while to call on him, as he is [a] curious man I have written underneath the Direction of his Address.

I am Sr. Your Obliged Humble Servt.,   WM. JONES

Monsr. Guyot, directeur des Postes, rue francois Pres la rue mauconseil No. 12.

RC (DLC); addressed; endorsed: "Jones Wm. (Mathematic)." Recorded in

22 JANUARY 1787

sjl as received 26 Mch. 1787 at Aix. For the misfortunes which happened to this letter and the accompanying apparatus, see Smith to TJ, 29 Jan. 1787 and TJ to Smith, 19 Feb. 1787.

From Tarbé

[Rouen, 22 Jan. 1787. Recorded in sjl as received 24 Jan. 1787. Not found; but it must have enclosed an undated statement (MoSHi; endorsed "Tarbé") to the amount of £34.19.6 for the cost of handling a barrel of wine sent from Bordeaux by Le Veillard to TJ; see TJ to Tarbé, 11 Feb. 1787.]

From St. Victour & Bettinger

Paris, 23 Jan. 1787. Enclosing copy of certificate dated 2 Nov. 1786 of the artillery officer, Dubois d'Escordal, at the manufactory of arms at Tulle for 27 boxes containing 820 rifles at 27^{tt} 10s. or a total of 22,550^{tt}; also a copy of a letter from Bondfield at Bordeaux to Bettinger, 16 Jan. 1787, acknowledging receipt of the shipment. They request payment by TJ and will provide the person in charge of the cases with their receipt, the original of the certificate, and Bondfield's letter.

RC (Vi); 2 p.; in French. Recorded in sjl as received 24 Jan. 1787. Enclosures: (1) Certificate as described (missing). (2) Bondfield to Bettinger, 16 Jan. 1787 (Vi).

From C. W. F. Dumas

Monsieur   LaHaie 23e. Janv. *1787*

De retour d'Amsterdam, je me hâte de répondre à la question confidentielle que m'a fait votre Excellence dans sa Lettre du 25 Decembre dernier.

S'il y auroit moyen de négocier en Hollande de l'Argent pour les Etats-Unis, afin de rembourser les 24 millions tournois qu'on doit à la France?

J'ai consulté là des amis intimes, dont je suis sûr, non seulement quant à la Discrétion, qui sera scrupuleusement observée, mais aussi quant à la capacité, honnêteté et suffisance parfaite pour l'exécution même d'une telle entreprise: Et voici le Résultat de nos entretiens, couché par écrit à Amsterdam le 20 et le 21, quoique je le transcrive et date comme ci-dessus.

Pour ce qui est du Crédit du Congrès, il est certain que peu à peu il s'établit sur un pied solide: Ce qui y contribue grandement, c'est l'acquit régulier des Intérêts dans le temps précis de leur échéance, et spécialement aussi celui des Primes de la Négociation de deux Millions de florins en argent, que le Congrès avoit le choix de faire en obligations nouvelles. On pense même que ce Crédit seroit parvenu dès-à-présent au point, que l'on eût pu en toute assurance donner des encouragemens à des Négociations ultérieures, et des promesses touchant leur réussite, si les Papiers Anglois ne continuoient de débiter sur l'état des affaires en Amérique des Avis très-propres à donner la fievre aux Rentiers, et certains Gazettiers de ce pays de les adopter avidement dans leurs papiers. Ces derniers appartiennent à la Faction de ceux qui, traversant tant qu'ils peuvent les efforts qu'on fait pour rétablir la Liberté civile en ce pays, s'imaginent que la reproduction continuelle d'images qui représentent les émeutes et commotions populaires (lesquelles selon eux ont lieu en Amérique), doit dégoûter les esprits ici de la pensée de s'en tenir à une Constitution ou le Peuple ait quelque influence dans le Gouvernement. Quoique l'on ne craigne guere que ces méchants atteignent leur but en ceci, il n'en est pas moins facheux que leur artifice fasse assez d'impression sur nombre de personnes peu instruites, pour leur faire soupçonner que, vu de pareils troubles, une pareille confusion, une telle foiblesse du Gouvernement en Amérique, il ne soit pas prudent de lui accorder un grand Crédit. Il est possible de ramener les plus sensés à des idées plus saines; mais le grand nombre des Rentiers l'est peu, et se laisse aller au préjugé plutôt qu'à la raison.

Il est donc impossible d'assurer positivement que l'on feroit avec succès une nouvelle Négociation, ni d'en déterminer la somme et les conditions. Ce qui ajoute à l'incertitude, et fait craindre qu'en tout cas ces conditions ne fussent très-onéreuses, c'est que l'on n'ignore pas ici que la Dette interne du Congrès en Amérique peut être achetée *à un prix*[1] tel que les Acheteurs y trouvent incomparablement plus de profit qu'on ne leur en accorderoit ici; tandis que la solidité de cette Dette interne est tout aussi bonne que celle de la Dette externe.

Ce qu'il y auroit donc, selon mes amis, de mieux à faire, seroit de se charger ici de la prétention de la France aux conditions qu'on pourroit stipuler, accompagnées d'un petit sacrifice de la part de ce Royaume, avec la Liberté de négocier ici l'argent pour un nombre limité d'années sur le *Crédit du Congrès* et sous la *Garantie de la France*. Cette derniere condition, où l'on ne voit rien que d'honorable pour le Congrès, influeroit beaucoup *sur l'Intérêt*, que l'on obtiendroit *moindre* en ce cas qu'autrement on ne pourroit le faire dans les circonstances présentes par les raisons apportées ci-dessus: et de cette maniere on pourroit en même temps *reculer de quelques années les termes du remboursement* qui vont bientôt écheoir; ce qui, ce semble, conviendroit fort au Congrès. On croit aussi que le sacrifice que la France feroit pour cela ne sauroit y mettre obstacle: car cette opération ne laisseroit pas que de verser une somme considérable dans son Trésor, qu'elle ne seroit point obligée de restituer, et qui par conséquent ne tourneroit point à la charge du Royaume. Aussi ne s'attend-on pas de la part de la France à la moindre difficulté pour accorder cette Garantie; attendu que cette Cour-là est très exactement au fait de l'état des affaires Américaines, et qu'elle a intérêt de les maintenir.

Si l'on avoit quelque inclination pour ce Plan, mes Amis entreront volontiers en pourparler là-dessus, et examineront alors le degré de possibilité à trouver toute la Somme dans un temps limité: ce qui est un point dont on ne peut s'occuper, pour le déterminer, qu'en s'ouvrant et traitant là-dessus avec d'autres gens.—Ils pensent que pour peu que les conditions soient établies d'une maniere acceptable, on trouveroit d'abord promptement 3 à 4 Millions de Florins d'Hollande (6 à 8 Millions de Livres tournois, ou 12 à 16 cent mille Dollars).

P.S. Nous nous sommes ultérieurement et sous le sceau du secret, entretenus sur la question ci-dessus avec un des hommes les plus experts dans la matiere. Il a confirmé absolument notre avis; en ajoutant seulement que si l'on se déterminoit *promptement* à quelque chose, le *sacrifice* en question seroit très-petit, et même, qu'il pourroit être *bonifié* par une diminution sur l'Intérêt. La raison de cela est l'abondance[2] actuelle d'argent. Mais comme cela peut changer en peu de temps, il faudroit se déterminer le plutôt possible.

En réfléchissant à tout cela pendant mon retour, il m'a semblé que Votre Excellence et Mr. le Ms. De la Fayette pourroient, puisqu'il ne s'agiroit que d'acheter la Dette due à la France, rendre un grand service et à la France et aux Etats-Unis, en secondant et favorisant cette vente, de maniere à réserver au Congrès l'*Option* de reculer de quelques années le Remboursement, sans qu'il soit nécessaire de perdre un temps précieux, peut-être irrévocable, à consulter d'avance le Congrès: Car de cette maniere, la France étant libre de vendre ou endosser la Dette pour remplir son trésor, et le Congrès de profiter de l'Option, il ne seroit fait tort quelconque à personne, on profiteroit de la bonne occasion, et chacun seroit aidé, puisque l'*Option* équivaudroit à l'*Emprunt* en question, et seroit même plus avantageuse. Si Votre Excellence goûte mon opinion, et veut me donner ses ordres après avoir conféré et agréé, si ce n'est Ministériellement, au moins personnellement, avec les Ministres en France, j'irai les exécuter sur le champ à Amsterdam, et ferai connoître à Votre Excellence la Maison consultée, contre laquelle je sais d'avance que ni les dits Ministres, ni Votre Excellence ne feront aucune objection.

Je suis avec le plus respectueux dévouement, De Votre Excellence Le très-humble et très-obéissant serviteur,

C W F Dumas

RC (DLC); endorsed. FC (Rijksarchief, The Hague, Dumas Papers; photostats in DLC). Tr (DNA: PCC, No. 107, 1); with several copyist's errors. Translation printed in *Dipl. Corr., 1783-89*, II, 31-3.

1 In both RC and FC the following is written in the margin: "On m'a assuré et promis de me faire voir, qu'on peut l'avoir à Amsterdam a 9 p% de profit net par an."

2 In both RC and FC the following is written in the margin: "Provenant de la rentrée *ordinaire* des Intérêts ici, et pour le coup encore *extraordinairement* des Remboursemens que fait la Russie et de ce que ni les Anglois ni les François n'ont pas encore ouvert quelque nouvel Emprunt."

From Madame de Tessé

a Paris ce 23 janvier.

Mr. de Tesse est presqu'entierement gueri de son Rhume. Me. de Tott souffre beaucoup moins, mais elle souffre encore trop pour que Me. de Tessé puisse se Retablir. Elles seront fort heureuses la premiere fois que Monsieur jefferson voudra bien leur donner l'occasion de lui Renouveller l'assurance de l'attachement bien sincère et bien profond qu'elles lui ont consacré.

RC (DLC); without indication of the year (see Madame de Tessé to TJ, 21 Jan. [1787]). Not recorded in SJL.

From John Adams

Dear Sir Grosvenor Square Jan. 25. 1787

I have received your Letters of December 20. and Jan. 11. by Coll. Franks. The whole of the Business shall be dispatched, and Coll. Franks sent to Congress as you propose, as soon as possible. I have prepared a Draught of a joint Letter to Mr. Barclay and signed it, concerning Mr. Lamb, and shall inclose it to you with this. As to the Treaty with Portugal, the Chevalier De Pinto's

25 JANUARY 1787

Courier whom he sent off when you were here, is still in Lisbon. He is a confidential Domestick of De Pinto and calls every day, at the Ministers office in Lisbon but can get no answer. De Pinto is very uneasy, makes apologies when he sees me, but can do no more. He says Mr. De Melo has been sick and the Queen in the Country, and that Falkner could obtain no audience for these Causes till December.—I suppose the Treaty of Commerce between France and England has astonished Portugal, and divided the Court into Parties, so that neither administration can be settled, nor a system adopted relative to Spain France, England or America. Congress are always informed of Facts as soon as they happen, and it is not to be expected that we should write Letters every Day to tell them, that Events have not happened. As to the Reasons why the Treaty is not signed, they know at New York as well as you and I know, or even as De Pinto knows them.

The charitable, the humane, the Christian Mathurins deserve our kindest Thanks, and we should be highly obliged to them if they could discover at what Price, our Countrymen may be redeemed: but I dont think we have Authority to advance the Money without the further orders of Congress. There is no Court, or Government, that redeems its Citizens unless by a Treaty of Peace. This is left to private Connections and benevolent Societies. If Congress redeem these, it will be a Precedent for all others, and although I might[1] in Congress vote for Setting the Precedent, and making it a Rule, Yet I dont think that as Subordinate Ministers We have a Right to do it. The Money remaining, must in February be applied to the Payment of Interest, and We must absolutely come to a full Stop in all Expences relating to Barbary Matters untill further orders of Congress. Lamb has drawn on me for Three thousand two hundred and twelve Pounds, twelve shillings.[2] Mr. Barclay has drawn a great sum, £4020..0..0 according to the Minutes inclosed.

If Congress thought the original appointment of Lamb censurable they had reason. But you and I were not censurable. We found him ready appointed to our hands. I never saw him nor heard of him.—He ever was and still is as indifferent to me, as a Mohawk Indian. But as he came from Congress with their Dispatches of such importance, I supposed it was expected We should appoint him.—There is no harm done.—If Congress had sent the ablest Member of their own Body, at such a Time and under such pecuniary Limitations he would have done no better. With great and sincere Esteem I have the honour to be, dear Sir, your most obedient and most humble Servant, JOHN ADAMS

RC (DLC); endorsed. FC (MHi: AMT); in W. S. Smith's hand. Recorded in SJL as received 2 Feb. 1787. Enclosures: (1) Adams' "Draught of a joint Letter to Mr. Barclay" has not been found, and in fact may never have been sent to Barclay by TJ, who mistakenly thought David Franks had included it with the other papers on the Morocco negotiations that the latter carried to Le Havre; TJ's letters to Barclay and Carmichael give no indication that he had found it, as Franks suggested, in his own study (see TJ's two letters to Franks, 11 Feb. 1787; TJ to Barclay and TJ to Carmichael, both dated 18 Feb. 1787; Carmichael to TJ, 25 Mch. 1787). (2) The account current of Barclay, listing twenty-one drafts accepted by Adams between 7 Oct. 1785 and 21 Dec. 1786, to the amount of £4020, to which was added the total of all drafts drawn by Lamb, making in all £7232-12-0 (DLC).

[1] Adams first wrote "would," then deleted it and interlined "might."
[2] Adams first wrote "Two thousand Nine hundred Pounds" and then altered this to read as above, possibly to accommodate a new draft by Lamb.

From R. & A. Garvey

SIR Rouen 25 January 1787

The acquit for your Excellencys things has not been returned; they would not Give a duplicate of it; the original one is No. 1477 and is dated the 21 october 1786: we shall be much obliged to you to Give the necessary orders about it before your departure, for if it is not returned discharged, or some other document to serve in its stead, it will be attended with very disagreable Consequences, which its proper to avoid.

Great Care shall be taken of the Boxes you Expect, and your orders for their ultimate expedition duly attended to. We remain with respect Sir Your Excellencys most humble & most obedient Servants, ROBT. & ANT. GARVEY

RC (MHi); endorsed. Not recorded in SJL.

From Le Veillard

[Before 26 Jan. 1787]

Monsieur de Jefferson a du recevoir ces jours cy de Mr. Tarbé negotiant à Rouen que Le vin de Cahuzac est en route et doit arriver ces jours cy. Mr. Tarbé aura vraisemblablement joint à son avis le mémoire des droits et frais depuis Bordeaux jusquà Rouen pour les quels il aura tiré un mandat payable à vue et qu'on presentera à monsieur Jefferson. Outre cela il y aura à payer la Voiture depuis Rouen et les droits dentrée à paris dont le Voiturier

26 JANUARY 1787

lui presentera le memoire pour en estre remboursé. Il ne restera plus que le prix du vin et de sa route jusqu'à Bordeaux qui est de 98ᵗᵗ et que m. leVeillard se chargera de faire tenir au vendeur. La barrique est de 250 bouteilles, par consequent ce vin qui est excellent n'ira peut estre qu'à 15 ou 16s. la pinte.

M. LeVeillard assure de son respect monsieur Jefferson. Il auroit eu l'honeur de le voir, si sa sante qui a ete miserable depuis 3 mois le luy eut permis. Il le prie de luy faire savoir s'il na pas eu des nouvelles d'amérique et s'il auroit une occasion pour y envoyer un paquet de quelques livres. M. L. V. a eu hier des lettres du 13 Xbre. Mr. Frank., bien portan[t].

RC (MoSHi); without signature or date; in Le Veillard's hand; memorandum of costs on verso in TJ's hand. The date has been assigned from TJ's entries in his Account Book under 26 Jan. 1787, which read: "pd. Tarbé's draught for portage of wine de Cahusac 35ƒ." and "pd. Le Veillard for the same wine 98ƒ. Note the barrel contains 250 bottles, and this was for the wine delivered at Bourdeaux" (see also the entry for Tarbé to TJ, 22 Jan., and TJ to Tarbé, 11 Feb. 1787).

From John Sullivan

Sir   Portsmouth Jany. 26th. 1787

Perhaps you may think it strange that I have not forwarded the Articles I promised, but want of opportunity prevented till I found it in my power to forward to your Excellency the whole Skeleton of a Moose which is now on Connecticut River and I expect it in a sleigh as soon as the Roads are broken through the snow which is now very Deep and no time shall be Lost in forwarding the same to your Excellency.

I have the honor to be with great respect your Excellencys most obedt. & very humble Servt.,   JNO. SULLIVAN

RC (DLC); endorsed: "Sullivan Genl." Recorded in SJL as received 16 June 1787.

From John Sullivan

                                       Portsmouth New Hampshire
Sir   Jany. 26th. 1787

I have the honor to inclose your Excellency a petition from Mr. Darby to his most Christian majesty respecting a vessell condemned at port au prince with Copies of Depositions to Support the facts therein alledged. Your Excellencey will at once Discover

[68]

26 JANUARY 1787

how Injuriously Mr. Darbey has been treated and how by the Art and Design of the Two French Merchants mentioned he has suffered a Loss which must almost ruin him: may I entreat your Excellency to Interest your self in his favour at the Court of France, where the original Petition and Depositions are forwarded.

I have the honor to be with the most Lively Sentiments of Esteem Your Excellenceys most obedt. and very Humble Servt.,

JNO. SULLIVAN

RC (DLC). Recorded in SJL as received 16 June 1787. Enclosures (DLC): (1) Petition of Elias Hasket Derby to the king of France, dated at Salem, Mass., 24 Jan. 1787, stating that in April of 1786 he had dispatched the brig *Nancy*, Ichabod Nichols, master, to the French West Indies with a "very valuable Cargo" in order to carry on "a Trade there Agreably to the established Laws"; that at Port au Prince Nichols met with one of Derby's snows laden with lumber; that "Messrs. Barrere & La Maire, Merchants of that place agreed for the purchase of both Cargoes at a price certain," agreeing to pay in sugars at a stipulated price; that Nichols fulfilled his part of the contract only to find "to his extreme mortification and Disappointment . . . they had no intention to perform their engagement, which they now alledged to be impossible"; that in his dilemma Nichols had been persuaded to accept the merchants' proposal "that his Snow should be conveyed to one of them, and made a French Bottom, and that they would lade on board a Cargo to the amount of the Debt and clear out the Vessell for Nantes"; that the transfer was made, the vessel loaded with 410,000 pounds of sugar, 4,000 pounds of coffee, 7,400 pounds of cotton, &c. so that the value of vessel and cargo amounted to a total of 230,473 livres, and clearance papers obtained for a voyage to Nantes; that, soon after, the vessel was seized "under a pretext of her being bound to the Continent of America," and, after "Mr. La Maire appeared as Owner" and made what seemed to be a feeble opposition as claimant, the snow was condemned by the admiralty court; that an appeal was made but the verdict confirmed, "although some of the Judges, and the most learned Lawyers were clearly of opinion that the Vessell being still in port, there was not any transgression of the Law"; that it appears the merchants were interested in the condemnation, since their captain was the informer, caused the seizure, "and immediately Fled apparently to avoid the Public Odium and Indignation"; and that the petitioner now has "no resource but in that Royall power and Goodness . . . to relieve the distressed and Injured." (2) Notarized deposition of Ichabod Nichols, dated at Portsmouth, N.H., 4 Dec. 1786, testifying to the same facts. (3) Notarized deposition of Richard Tibbets, mariner, of Portsmouth, N.H., dated 16 Nov. 1786, testifying that he was at Port au Prince in the summer of 1786 and "present at a conversation between Captain Ichabod Nichols and Messrs. Barrière and Lemaire" when the latter offered to purchase the cargoes of the *Nancy* and the snow, of which he, Tibbetts, was master; and that he also heard the merchants tell Nichols "it would be more for their Interest and his to make a French Bottom of his Vessell," to which, "after a good deal of persuasion on their part he consented."—Sullivan's covering letter and its enclosures were sent to TJ by Derby with his letter of 1 Mch. 1787, q.v.

From Benjamin Vaughan, with Enclosure

DEAR SIR Jeffries Square London Jany. 26. 1787.

I was honoured with your letter of the 29th. of December only last night, and take the first moment of answering it, presuming

[69]

26 JANUARY 1787

to offer a few remarks on the objects you have in view, by way of preface.

It appears that many mistakes respecting the animal and vegetable productions of America have arisen from the precipitancy of European philosophers in deciding upon slight evidence; as well as from the propensity of mankind to extend partial into general conclusions. Your notes respecting Virginia furnish ample proofs of this.

Those Europeans however who have disparaged the New World have not only been imperfectly acquainted with their subject; but seem to have overlooked the original destitute state of Europe which is said to have borrowed many of its valuable animals and vegetables from other countries. We hear of a Ceres, a Bacchus, and a Minerva deified for the introduction of corn, of wine, and of oil into our quarter of the globe; and we can very easily credit these traditions from the accounts given of the gradual spread of the two latter productions in the Southern parts of Europe. We are not able (it is said) in this island of Great Britain to boast of a single fruit as indigenous among the number that now appear at our tables, and it is clear from authentic accounts, that we have as little claim to the original of most of our esculent vegetables, which are now so common. I must add that the species both of our fruits and common esculent vegetables are still very few in number, though we have taken some pains to traverse the globe to collect or add to them, and have likewise called in experienced art to our assistance. It is observable also that several of our present English fruits have had their reputed origin from the neighbourhood of the *Black Sea*, whose climate bears a very particular resemblance to those parts of Eastern North America which lie in correspondent latitudes. I may add that from various authentic relations, Eastern North America appears to exhibit (notwithstanding the opinions that have been entertained respecting it) a fair Model in general of the climate of all the *inland* and *Eastern* quarters of our Northern Hemisphere.

I have sometimes thought that if Eastern North America had been peopled by old and civilized nations, some ages before the birth of Christ, and had at that time accumulated in it (wherever the climates were analagous) not only the productions (vegetable and animal) of the Western and Southern parts of its double continent, but those from China and Japan, in addition to all those productions which accident, as well as diligence and art might have enabled it to discover and propagate within itself: I have thought that if a people, so circumstanced in those parts, had at that period discovered Western Europe, similar remarks would probably have occurred (after a time) among *their* speculative philosophers, on the rude and ill provided condition of the New World (as our part of it would then have been called). A civilized Chinese, given to speculation and theory, might in similar terms now speak of Western North America; though Western North America, there is good reason to think, is the exact counterpart, as to climate, of Europe and part of Africa. Indeed it is to be hoped that in future ages it *will* become alike civilized and alike abounding in the good things of this life with Western Europe, and when that period arrives, the voyages of Cook will be read with the same degree of curiosity by Western Americans with which Western Europeans now peruse the accounts of Germany, Gaul and England given by Tacitus and Cæsar. Certain it is, that Europeans in general do not at present think worse of America than some of the Greeks and Romans formerly thought of those parts of Europe, which now make the most brilliant figure of any countries upon the globe.

I do not mean to suggest by any of these remarks, that there are not certain considerable and characteristic distinctions between the climate of this quarter of the world and that of your own. But every circumstance of this sort, were it to be entered into, would come under a separate head of discussion. All that I mean to affirm is, that there is nothing peculiar and ill-fated in your own climate and soil, compared with that of the globe *at large*; and that nature, after she has had proper time to make a full display of herself, will be found as provident to you, as to the Northern Hemisphere in general. Indeed it has never appeared her intention to accumulate all her favours upon any one situation: her gifts are dispersed; and men are to be made acquainted and united among each other, by their attempts to assemble and exchange them.

I am truly happy to see that in your work, you have with so much success combated the opinions of certain European philosophers on some of these subjects respecting Eastern America. I think the *Recherches sur Les Americains* contain nearly three volumes of errors, believed in Europe because boldly asserted, and till lately never controverted. Monsr. De Buffon and the abbé Raynal in particular among the French, and Dr. Robertson and others with us, have largely imbibed these errors; but the time

26 JANUARY 1787

has arrived when science, industry and art on your side of the water, will soon furnish materials to overthrow the whole of them, and even to efface their memory.

As to the supposed humidity of the atmosphere of Eastern North America, compared with that of Europe, (your desire of enquiring into which gave occasion to the letter you have done me the honour to write) European philosophers seem to have formed their conclusion respecting this subject principally from three sources. First, from the excessive vehemence of the rains which fall at times in the colonized parts of Eastern America, especially to the Southward. Next from the cultivated parts of the West Indies (a supposed appendage of the part of America in question) being divided into small islands exposed to the sea air. And lastly from the inhabitants of all our colonies having generally chosen for the seat of their plantations and settlements the banks of the sea or of rivers; or else low lands, swamps and mill ponds; either for the sake of cheap carriage and easy cultivation, or of the advantages for machinery afforded by such situations; preferring the speedy acquisition of wealth, to health and happiness, and the other slower, though more permanent and substantial modes of attaining riches. I do not defend the necessity of the last of these causes; I think it an opprobrium to my American friends, and that it much more deserves legislative attention in each particular state, than matters of trade, or other matters of a more delicate nature which legislators seldom treat with any success. But after allowing for all these causes in their fullest extent, I cannot but incline to the opinion which yourself and Dr. Franklin have assumed on the subject alluded to, as far as respects the Eastern and probably the internal parts of North America.

Trusting to your kind forgiveness of a few observations made in favour of a country from which I am in part descended, I shall now have the pleasure of attending more immediately to the particulars respecting which you did me the honour to apply to me.

I have been some time acquainted with Dr. Franklins observations on Hygrometers, since published in the second volume of the Philadelphian Philosophical Transactions. He showed me the manuscript when in an unfinished state, in which it had long lain by neglected, and which occasioned me to express considerable regret, and I had the pleasure to find that the paper was soon after completed and forwarded to Mr. Nairne. I think it in his usual manner, novel, sagacious, and simple; and it appears the more useful, as extreme diversity of opinion, if not difficulty has long prevailed respecting hygrometers constructed upon other principles.

Mr. Nairne made an instrument pursuant to Dr. Franklins hint, of which he some time ago favoured me with a drawing and description, a copy of which I have annexed. My objection to the plan of this instrument, though otherwise ingenious, is, that the motion of the pin produces greater changes in the position of the smaller arm and consequently of the index, when the smaller arm is at *right angles* to the line of motion of the pin, than when oblique.* The remedy of this difficulty must either lie in certain complex machinery annexed to the arm, or in a complex division of the scale to which the index points: but as the result sought after, is made to depend upon the comparison of two instruments, the less complex the plan is, the better.

I have therefore been led to employ Dr. Franklin's principles in a manner more simple. As the case of the shutter of the magnet-box seemed to prove that a small plate of wood, cut thin, might exhibit considerable variations of dimension across the grain, I at first directed a number of such plates to be cut square, two of the sides of which should run parallel to the grain or fibre of the wood; and the other two to be at right angles; designing to make the invariable serve as measures to the variable sides. But as a small scale might leave room for doubts, and if the squares were much enlarged, other inconveniences might arise, I directed a thin and narrow stripe, or fillet of wood, to be cut across the grain of the widest plank of Mahogony that could be found; and that from the same wood a staff should be cut, in which the fibres should run longitudinally; the staff being both solid and long enough to allow of a groove in it for the purpose of receiving the fillet. (The fillet having the cross grain, would thus lie freely in the groove of the

---

* That is, if from *f*. be drawn lines intersecting equal portions of the line *a*

those center lines which decline most from a right angle with *a*, will form the smallest *angles* respectively at *f* with the contiguous radii. But it is upon the equality of the *angles* at *f*, and not of the *portions* of motion along the line *a*, that the equal motions of the index will depend.

staff which is oppositely grained, nearly as a pocket comb lies in its tortoise shell case.) The staff being made a little longer than the fillet, when the two were brought to coincide at one of their extremities, it would be easy to mark upon the staff the standard point, to which the other end of the fillet reached in the standard country; and afterwards, to mark the point to which the fillet should stretch or shrink in other countries, accordingly as they were moister or drier.

An instrument of this kind, which, by being composed of two parts, carries along with it its own standard and allows its changes to be reduced into well known and ordinary measures, I had the pleasure about a fortnight ago to send to Mr. White, who is appointed principal surgeon to attend the proposed expedition with our convicts to Botany Bay in the South Seas. It is one of its advantages, that any carpenter can easily construct the like out of any kind of wood.

I was sorry not to have been able to inspect the instrument sent to Mr. White. But Messrs. Nairne & Blunt, who made it, having undertaken to make a second for me, I have the honour to request your acceptance of it, Coll. Smith offering the means of conveying it to you.

I have had no trial of this little contrivance, but I foresee several *precautions* necessary to be observed. The first is, that of placing the instrument in corresponding situations in the countries of trial; since considerable differences may arise from the neighbourhood of the sea and other waters, or from swampy or mountainous situations; and other differences again from the apartments in which the instruments are preserved, either as to their being with or without fires, their aspect, elevation from the ground, and other circumstances. A second precaution is, that of noting the state of the weather, or the season at the period of observation; for it is well known, for instance, that the doors and windows of houses will shut more or less closely, according to the state of the air as to humidity, at different periods in the same country. A third precaution is, that of using for the construction of the instrument none but seasoned wood. It is partly owing to a neglect of this that the floor of the room where I now write, has large openings between each of its boards; though neither the boards, nor the rafters that run across the boards, appear to have altered in their dimensions longitudinally; and in like manner that the door of a deal box (in which, when lined with baize, fire arms may long be kept dry and free from rust) and which is fastened to the wainscot of my bedroom, has shrunk considerably cross ways, though two wooden bars, that stretch across this door at right angles, appear to retain their original dimensions: (These effects being also partly owing to the removal of the wood from an open timber yard, or carpenters shed, into a warm inhabited house). The warping of the parts of the instrument may call for a fourth precaution; and to remedy this defect, when it takes place in the filleting, the filleting may be measured when laid under the pressure of a moderate weight; while the shape of the staff may be best preserved by giving it such a degree of solidity as shall produce compensations to the action of any one part of its substance against any other part of it. The filleting may be two inches wide and $\frac{1}{10}$ inch thick, as recommended by Dr. Franklin, and a section across the staff may form a square of 2. or 3 inches.

Should the supposition, that certain woods do not vary in their longitudinal dimensions prove untrue, it will not affect the credit to be given to the instrument in question, provided the variation is different in its degree from that occurring crosswise.

I am pleased with the ingenuity of Mr. Rittenhouse's idea, which was perfectly new to me; but I fear the variations of no two hygrometers, on his plan of construction can be depended upon as at all corresponding, which is certainly one objection to it; and I think a second objection to it is, that the degrees of variation in the same instrument, must be far from being equable in their measurement, compared with the degrees of change taking place in the atmosphere.

I have ordered a box of magnets from Messrs. Nairne & Blunt, similar to that which was in the possession of Dr. Franklin, which will accompany the hygrometer, its case being formed out of the same piece of wood above described.

During the last summer I made use of a thermometer with a fine tube, in which I found it difficult in some situations readily to mark the station of the quicksilver. I placed white paper behind the tube with some advantage, till it occurred to me to put a stripe of thick black paint upon the back of the tube, the breadth of which was about ⅙ only of the tube's circumference. The optical effect of this was curious enough; for though the place of the black paint could scarcely be seen when the thermometer was viewed sideways; yet in front the whole of the glass appeared as dark as ink. The result was that the quicksilver losing no rays of light, and the tube within having much less luminous reflection than before, I could in many situations of the light and of the thermometer, discover the thread of quicksilver to much greater advantage than usual. I take the liberty to add to my packet through Coll. Smith, a thermometer on which this operation has been performed. I find that another device practiced upon thermometers with the same view, has been to flatten the bore in which the thread of the quicksilver lies, in order to increase the breadth of the thread to the eye; the advantage of which operation I have never had an opportunity of ascertaining; but I know that some who have used it, have since laid it aside. The most advantageous view that can be had of the thread of the thermometer, is certainly by bringing in light upon the tube from the back of its scale, or using a scale that is transparent, or by marking the degrees upon the tube itself; but as it is not always practicable thus to bring in the light from behind, I think that to some persons and in some cases the contrivance of the paint abovementioned may be of use. Indeed I am not sure whether it may not in some measure be combined with the use of the slit in the scale, so as to allow of both advantages in the instrument at different moments. I have sometimes thought also, that if the polish were removed from some parts of the glass tube, it might produce some good effect. But my time does not allow me to try many experiments.

If I suspend the execution of what respects the hygrometer you have desired to be sent to you, till you repeat your directions on the subject, I hope you will not be put to any disappointment by the liberty I take in this particular.

With very great respect & esteem, I have the honour to be your Excellency's most obedient and most humble servant,

BENJN. VAUGHAN

ENCLOSURE

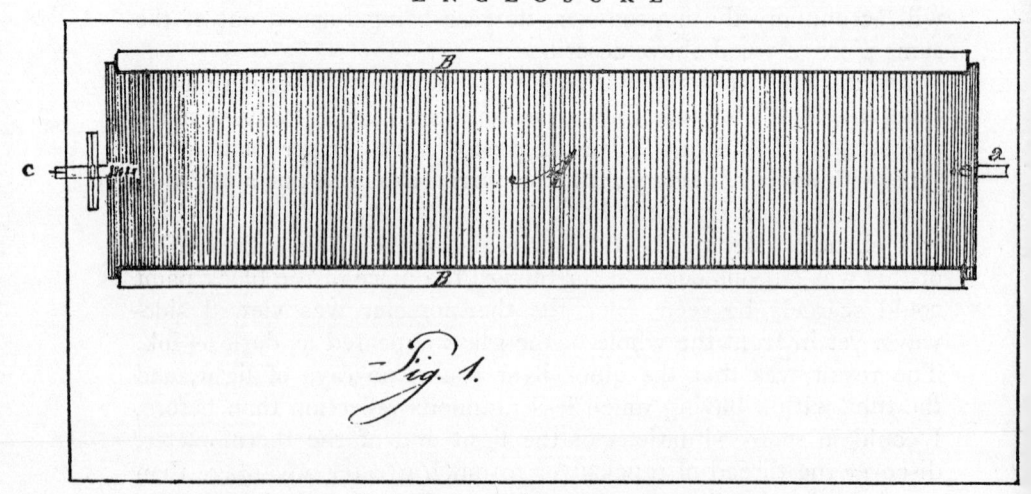

Fig. I. (being one side of the instrument)
A A piece of about 12 inches long and 2 broad cut crosswise to the

27 JANUARY 1787

grain of the wood, which slides freely between the pieces of wood *BB* forming grooves for it.

C Is a screw for adjusting the piece of wood *A* to the frame of the instrument, so that the index may point to the proper division when first made.

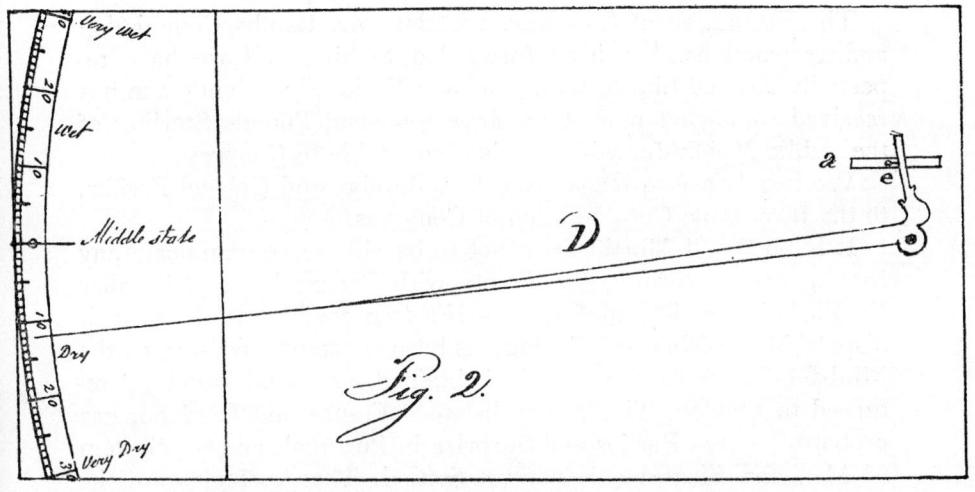

Fig. II. (being the other side of the instrument.)

a Is a slit to admit the pin *e* to move freely, which pin by being fast in the piece of wood *A* moves with it, as it shortens or lengthens, and by pressing against the short end of the index *D*, causes it to move up or down according as the weather is moist or dry. The result is shewn on the divided arch at the other end of the index.

RC (DLC). Enclosure (DLC). This letter was enclosed in Vaughan's to TJ of 5 Apr. 1788; see also Vaughan to TJ, 16 Feb. 1787 and TJ to Vaughan, 2 July 1787.

The American Commissioners to John Jay

SIR   London Jany. 27th. 1787.[1]

We had the honour of transmitting to Congress, Copies of the Commission and Instructions, which in pursuance of the Authority delegated to us, were given to Mr. Barclay, to conduct a negotiation with Morocco.[2]

Mr. Barclay has conducted that Business to a happy Conclusion, and has brought with him Testimonials of his prudent Conduct, from the Emperor of Morocco and his Minister, so clear and full, that we flatter ourselves Mr. Barclay will receive, the Approbation of Congress. Mr. Barclay has received somewhat more than four Thousand Pounds sterling, for the Expences of Presents and all other Things. Colonel Franks, who accompanied Mr. Barclay in

[77]

his tedious Journeys, and difficult Negotiations, in the Character of Secretary, will be dispatched to Congress, and will have the honour of delivering this Letter, together with the Treaty, the Emperors Letter to Congress, and a variety of other Papers, relative to this Mission, a Schedule of which is annexed.

The Resolution of Congress, vacating Mr. Lambs Commission and Instructions, has been forwarded to him, and we have repeatedly advised him to return to New York. That Gentleman has received somewhat more than three thousand Pounds Sterling of the public Money for which he is accountable to Congress.

We beg Leave to recommend Mr. Barclay and Colonel Franks, to the favourable Consideration of Congress.

It is no Small Mortification not to be able to communicate any Intelligence concerning the Treaty with Portugal. The Chevalier De Pinto is equally uninformed.—His own confidential Domestick dispatch'd to Lisbon last Spring has been constantly waiting on the Minister for an Answer, but has obtained none, and is not yet returned to London. The Treaty between France and England, has probably excited Parties and Surprize in Portugal, and the System of Men and Measures is not yet Settled. The Apologies are the Queens Absence in the Country and the Prime Ministers Indisposition.

The Article of Money is become so scarce and prescious that we shall be obliged to suspend all further Proceedings in the Barbary Business, even for the Redemption of Prisoners untill we shall be honoured with fresh Instructions from Congress.

With great Respect we have the Honour to be, Sir, your most obedient and most humble Servants,

London Jan. 27. 1787. JOHN ADAMS

RC (DNA: PCC, No. 84); in John Adams' hand, with one alteration by TJ; signed and dated by Adams only; endorsed by Charles Thomson: "Letter 24 Jany. 1787 Mr. J. Adams." Tr (DNA: PCC, No. 104). Enclosures: Barclay to American Commissioners, 2 Oct. 1786 (and its enclosures), 7 Nov., and 15 Nov. 1786.

This letter is printed in *Dipl. Corr., 1783-89*, II, 693-4, as addressed by Adams only, while C. F. Adams in *Works of John Adams*, VIII, 525, designates it as from the Commissioners. From TJ's single correction in the text it is evident that the letter was reviewed by him; his failure to sign it—an omission that happened also in the instance of the Commissioners' letter to Taher Fennish, following—can only be attributed to his haste in assembling the dispatches which David Franks was to carry to America (see TJ's two letters to Franks, 8 Feb. 1787). Though the date is uncertain, TJ very likely reviewed the letter on or immediately after 2 Feb. 1787, the date on which Franks returned from London with Adams' letter of 25 Jan. 1787, in which the present letter was enclosed.

[1] This date was added by the clerk in the office of foreign affairs who transcribed the Tr in PCC, No. 104.

[2] TJ substituted this word for Adams' incorrect "Algiers."

The American Commissioners to Taher Fennish

To His Excellency, Sidi Hadq Taher Ben Abdelhack Fennish, in the Service of His Majesty the Emperor of Morocco

We have recieved with high satisfaction the letter, which your Excellency by the command of His Majesty the Emperor of Morocco, did us the honor to write us, on the first day of the blessed month Ramadan twelve hundred and transmitted to us, by the Honorable Thomas Barclay Esqr., who was sent to your court, in order to negociate an amicable treaty of peace and commerce, between His Majesty the Emperor of Morocco and all his dominions, and those of the United States of America. We are happy to learn that this matter has been fortunately concluded to the satisfaction of all parties. The contents of the treaty we have learned from the said envoy, the honorable Thomas Barclay Esqr. to whom His Imperial Majesty delivered it together with a letter to the United States.

It is with the most respectful satisfaction that we learn from your Excellency, that the conduct of our said Envoy, the Honorable Thomas Barclay Esqr. has the entire approbation of His Imperial Majesty, and that he has behaved with integrity and honor since his arrival in His Imperial Majesty's Dominions and above all that His Imperial Majesty has been graciously pleased to give him two honorable favourable and unparalleled audiences, signifying His Majesty's perfect satisfaction at his conduct.

We pray your Excellency, if you think proper, to express to His Imperial Majesty the high sense we entertain of His Majesty's friendship to the United States of America and of his goodness to the said Honorable Thomas Barclay.

And we request of your Excellency to accept of our sincere thanks for the kind assistance you have given to the said envoy in the course of these negociations. With much pleasure we learn that your Excellency is charged with the affairs of our country, by His Imperial Majesty, at his Court and doubt not that your Excellency will do all that lies in your power to promote the friendly intercourse that is so happily begun.

We shall transmit, without delay, to the Honourable the Congress of the United States an account of all these proceedings and entertain the fullest assurance that they will recieve in due time the approbation of that August Assembly.

May the Providence of the one Almighty God, whose Kingdom

27 JANUARY 1787

is the only existing one protect your Excellency. With great Respect we have the Honour to be Your Excellency's most obedient & most humble servants,
London. Jan. 27. 1787.

JOHN ADAMS

Tr (DLC); in William Short's hand, with only Adams' dating and signature recorded. FC (MHi: AMT); undated; in Adams' hand, with several variations in phraseology not noted here. The differences between the text prepared by Adams and that copied by Short resulted from TJ's effort to make the latter conform to expressions used by Taher Fennish in his communication of 28 June 1786; for example, where Adams had written "May the Providence of God Almighty, protect your Excellency," TJ altered the expression to read as it does above in the final paragraph. These corrections were so numerous that TJ caused Short to make a fair copy—which, however, he neglected to sign (see note to Commissioners to Jay, preceding, and Carmichael to TJ, 25 Mch. 1787).

This letter was included by mistake among the American despatches carried by Franks to Le Havre on 8 Feb., but TJ discovered the error in time (see TJ to Banister, 7 Feb. 1787; TJ's two letters to Franks, 8 Feb. 1787; and Franks to TJ, 10 and 11 Feb. 1787).

To Hilliard d'Auberteuil

SIR
Paris Jan. 27. 1787.

I duly received the letter you did me the honour to write, and the verses therein inclosed on the subject of the M. de la Fayette. I have taken measures to present the public with this acceptable present; but the newspapers here are slow in complying with the applications addressed to them. It is not for a stranger to decide on the merit of poetry in a language foreign to him. Were I to presume to do it in this instance, I should certainly assign to this composition a high degree of approbation.

I wish it were in my power to furnish you with any materials for the history on which you are engaged. But I brought no papers of that kind with me from America. In a letter you did me the honour of writing me some time ago, you seemed to suppose it possible you might go to America in quest of materials. Should you execute this idea, I should with great pleasure give any assistance in my power to obtain access for you to the several deposits of materials which are in that country. I have the honour to be with great respect Sir your most obedient & most humble servant,

TH: JEFFERSON

PrC (DLC). If TJ took MEASURES TO PRESENT THE PUBLIC WITH THIS ACCEPTABLE PRESENT, the evidence and result of his doing so have not been found.

To Gelhais

Monsieur   Paris 27me. Janvier 1787.

Un quartier du loyer de la maison de M. le comte de Langeac etant echu ce mois ci, je lui ai prevenu des titres de la demande que vous avez eu la complaisance de m'adresser. Mais il m'a montré un arret de surseance par lequel les reclamations de ses creanciers contre lui sont suspendues. A cet arret, emandant de l'autorité supreme du païs, c'est de mon devoir de me conformer aussi. Je lui ai payé donc le loyer comme á l'ordinaire. J'ai l'honneur de vous renvoyer le titre que vous m'avez confié, et j'aurois eté tres charmé si les circonstances m'auroient permis de me preter plus efficacement á vos justes demandes. J'ai l'honneur d'etre avec une consideration trés distinguée, Monsieur, votre trés humble et trés obeissant serviteur,   Th: Jefferson

PrC (DLC); endorsed. Enclosure not found. See TJ to De Langeac, 12 Oct. 1786; TJ to Gelhais, 7 Dec. 1786.

From De Langeac

ce 27 janvier 1787

Le nommé savisse est venu me trouver, monsieur pour me prier d'interceder vos bontés pour lui, qu'il est bien faché davoir perdû; vous aves surement de bonnes Raisons pour vous en plaindre et le renvoÿer, mais je serois bien flatté et bien reconnoissant si à ma consideration et sur la priere que je vous en fais vous voulies bien lui pardonner. Si vous ne voules vous rendre absolument à mes sollicitations je vous demande en grace pour mon compte particulier de trouver bon quil continüe à faire votre jardin. J'ai confiance en sa maniere de soigner Les arbres. C'etoit une de mes conditions en louant ma maison et votre homme d'affaires m'en donna dans le tems parole de votre part et je m'en rapportai à tout ce quil me dit en votre nom sans croire quil fut nécessaire de le faire inserer dans le bail par devant notaire n'y dans le Sous seing privé particulier. C'est ainsi que j'en ai agis pour le cautionement et les autres precautions d'usage que mes gens d'affaires vouloient me faire prendre et dont jai crû, Monsieur, n'avoir pas besoin avec vous. Si vous n'aves pas des Raisons trop fortes pour ne pas pardonner au nommé savisse je vous demande avec instances de m'en faire le Sacrifice le connoissant depuis longtems pour un garçon honnête fidel, laborieux et attaché.

27 JANUARY 1787

J'ai lhonneur d'etre avec la plus parfaite consideration Monsieur Votre trés humble et tres obeissant serviteur,

LE CTE. DE LESPINASSE LANGEAC

RC (MHi); endorsed. Not recorded in SJL.

SAVISSE: The name of the gardener is doubtful; it may be as given, or it may be "foresse," "favesse," "soresse," "savesse," or a variation of these with the first "e" replaced by an "i." TJ's Account Books from the time of leasing the Hôtel de Langeac do not give the name of the gardener, and evidently TJ did not yield to De Langeac's appeal. On TJ's return in July the gardener's place appears to have been taken by one Nomenie.

From Schweighauser & Dobrée

[[Nantes, 27 Jan. 1787. Recorded in SJL as received 31 Jan. 1787. Not found, but see TJ's reply, 12 Feb. 1787. Enclosure: Copy of the resolution of Congress of 16 Oct. 1786 directing TJ to adjust the claim of Daniel Schweighauser against the United States "in such manner as he shall judge most for the interest and honor of the said states; and that the property of the United States in the custody of the . . . claimant, be applied towards the discharge of the balance, if any, which shall be found due" (JCC, XXXI, 878-9).]

To Segond

Paris Jan. 27. 1787.

I have duly received the letter with which you have been pleased to honour me, complaining of the nonpaiment of interest on the sum due to you from the United States. I feel with great sensibility the weight of these complaints; but it is neither in my province, nor in my power, to remedy them. I am no ways authorised to interfere with the money matters of the U.S. in Europe. These rest altogether between the Commissioners of the treasury of the U.S. at New York, and their bankers in Europe. Being informed however from Mr. Grand that the funds appropriated to the paiment of the foreign officers were exhausted, I took the liberty of representing strongly to the Commissioners the motives which should urge them to furnish new supplies. They assured me, in answer, that they would do it the first moment it should be in their power. I am perfectly persuaded they will: however I shall immediately forward to them the letter you have been pleased to address to me: and will observe to you that it is to them alone, or to Congress, to whom you can make any future applications with effect.

I have the honour to be with much respect, Sir, your most obedient & most humble servant, TH: JEFFERSON

PrC (DLC); at foot of text: "Le Chevalr. de Segond."

From Edmund Randolph

SIR   Richmond January 28. 1787.

When I came lately into office, I found two letters from your excellency to my predecessor unanswered. I cannot ascertain the dates, being at present unable to have recourse to them; but the subject of this address will point to the letters themselves.

The executive are much indebted to you for your humane attention to Mercier: and I am authorized to assure you, that your disbursements shall be repaid by this commonwealth. His family is unknown to us; but I have circulated in the place of his former residence such information of his distress, as will reach the ears of his relations, if he has any there.

Altho' a special vote was not taken in council concerning the cancelling of the Marquis's signature to Mr. Littlepage's note, the propriety of the step seemed to be universally assented to. For myself, I should have been really mortified, had it remained attached to the obligation. It was presented to the treasurer and Mr. Benjamin Lewis; the former of whom said, that he had never received a shilling towards discharging it, and the latter, that he should not pay a shilling for that purpose. A formal protest is not sent; because it is presumed, that Mr. Littlepage will acquiesce in my statement of the facts. Every effort in our power shall be made for the remittance of the funds, to be applied to the purchase of arms. We sincerely thank you for your exertions; and if it would not add too much to the trouble already given, we beg your excellency to direct an inquiry to be made for the bayonets, which by mistake, we suppose, were omitted, when the late importation of arms was sent off. I mention this omission from the report of Colo. Meriwether, our military assistant, who possibly may not have minutely examined the Cases: and they are not now within my own reach.

I beg you to put yourself to no inconvenience, if you should wish to take a credit for the money advanced for the directors of the public buildings. I have pressed the treasurer, however, to replace it in your hands by the first oppurtunity. I trust this will be shortly done.

I have the honor sir to be with the highest respect and esteem yr. excellency's mo. ob. & very hbl. serv.,

EDM: RANDOLPH

RC (DLC). Recorded in SJL as received 3 May 1787 at Aix-en-Provence.

TJ'S TWO LETTERS . . . TO MY PREDECESSOR were those to the governor of Virginia of 9 Aug. and 12 Aug. 1786, to the first of which TJ added a postscript dated 13 Aug. pertaining to MERCIER.

From Edmund Randolph

DEAR SIR Richmond January 28. 1787

The new arrangement, to which my aversion to the law has lately given birth, throws me into a new scene, which leaves me at leisure to testify my respect for you, by transmitting any intelligence, occurring here, worthy of your notice.

At present, however, political action has ceased, and this state is in perfect tranquillity; the assembly having risen about a fortnight ago, and the public mind being at rest on the subject of paper-money. It has been defeated, indeed, on the first erection of its crest. But the year may possibly not pass away, before the number of its enemies will be found to be diminished. What if a certain popular leader should espouse it? And the same men, who refused to expedite the administration of justice, clogged as it now is, should return in the delegation? I suggest this as a suspicion only. It is to be developed by time alone.

Our capitol rears its head, to the approbation of most people: but I tremble, lest we should have committed some blunder in proportion. The danger of this I mentioned in my letter to you of July last: but from the indolence of our superintendant he has never finished the draught, which I desired for your inspection. The outward walls are raised above the windows of the first story, and we have obtained a vote of 6000£ on the contingent fund, towards this work. This sum may truly be called depreciated paper, warrants on this fund being exchanged for cash at one half. From this circumstance we shall have our eyes fixed on the accommodation of the legislature in this building at their next cession having experienced their hardiness in supplying us, and foreseeing the probable effect of rousing their pride to finish a house, in which they themselves sit.

Being engaged in preparing for an official visit to the naval offices below, I shall for the present only beg you, to inform Mr.

Mazzei that I have remitted him money—wrote to him in the summer—am settling with Mr. Webb—and shall give him a full detail very soon.

You will oblige me too by offering my best respects to Mr. Short, and to be assured that I am dear sir with the greatest sincerity yr. friend and serv: EDM: RANDOLPH

RC (MHi); endorsed. Recorded in SJL as received 3 May 1787 at Aix-en-Provence. The CERTAIN POPULAR LEADER was Patrick Henry.

To John Stockdale

SIR   Paris Jan. 28.—87.

I will thank you to send me by the Diligence Sterne's works complete, 5. vols. 12mo. published by Cadell 1780. I name this edition because it brings all his works into the smallest compass of any one I have seen. If you know of any edition still smaller I would prefer it, elegantly bound.

A friend here has desired me to procure there two peices of Pope, viz, 'Happy the man whose wish and care &c.' and 'Vital spark of heavenly flame &c.' set to musick for the harpsichord, if they have been ever set to music, as I think they have. Will you be so good as to have enquiry made at some of the music shops, and forward them to me by the Diligence, or, if not too bulky, by the post. I shall set out on my journey the 15th. of February, within which time I shall hope to receive these articles. I have never heard whether you sent the books to Virginia which I desired long ago. I remember you had to get some of them from Scotland.

I am Sir your very humble servt., TH: JEFFERSON

PrC (DLC); endorsed.

To Anthony Vieyra

[28 Jan. 1787]

Mr. Jefferson has the honour of presenting his compliments to Mr. Vieyra and is sorry to have been out of the way when he did him the honour to call on him yesterday. He returns him the copy of his book which he had been so kind as to leave with him, and which Mr. Jefferson has gone over with much satisfaction, and with a conviction of the great erudition of it's author.

29 JANUARY 1787

PrC (MoSHi); not dated; at foot of text: "M. Antonius Vieyra L.L.B. &c." The date has been supplied from SJL and from internal evidence (see Vieyra to TJ, 15 Aug. 1787).

From Abigail Adams

MY DEAR SIR　　　　　　　　　　London Janry. 29th. 1787

I received by Col. Franks your obliging favour and am very sorry to find your wrist[1] still continues lame; I have known very salutary effects produced by the use of British oil upon a spraind joint.[2] I have sent a servant to see if I can procure some. You may rest assured that if it does no good: it will not do any injury.

With regard to the Tumults in my Native state which you inquire about, I wish I could say that report had exaggerated them. It is too true Sir that they have been carried to so allarming a Height as to stop the Courts of justice in several Counties. Ignorant, wrestless desperadoes, without conscience or principals, have led a deluded multitude to follow their standard, under pretence of grievences which have no existance but in their immaginations. Some of them were crying out for a paper currency, some for an equal distribution of property, some were for annihilating all debts, others complaning that the Senate was a useless Branch of Government, that the Court of common pleas was unnecessary, and that the sitting of the General Court in Boston was a grievance. By this list you will see the materials which compose this rebellion, and the necessity there is of the wisest and most vigorus measures to quell and suppress it. Instead of that laudible spirit which you approve, which makes a people watchfull over their Liberties and alert in the defence of them, these mobish insurgents are for sapping the foundation, and distroying the whole fabrick at once.— But as these people make only a small part of the state, when compared to the more sensible and judicious, and altho they create a just allarm and give much trouble and uneasiness, I cannot help flattering myself that they will prove sallutary to the state at large, by leading to an investigation of the causes which have produced these commotions. Luxery and extravagance[3] both in furniture and dress had pervaded all orders of our Countrymen and women, and was hastning fast to sap their independance by involving every class of citizens in distress, and accumulating debts upon them which they were unable to discharge.[4] Vanity was becoming a more powerfull principal than patriotism. The lower order of the

[86]

29 JANUARY 1787

community were prest for taxes,[5] and tho possest of landed property they were unable to answer the demand, whilst those who possest money were fearfull of lending, least the mad cry of the mob[6] should force the Legislature upon a measure very different from the touch of Midas.[7]

By the papers I send you, you will see the beneficial effects already produced. An act of the Legislature laying duties of 15 per cent upon many articles of British manufacture and totally prohibiting others—a number of Vollunteers Lawyers physicians and Merchants from Boston made up a party of Light horse commanded by Col. Hitchbourn, Leit. Col. Jackson and Higgenson, and went out in persuit of the insurgents and were fortunate enough to take 3 of their principal Leaders, Shattucks Parker and Page. Shattucks defended himself and was wounded in his knee with a broadsword. He is in Jail in Boston and will no doubt be made an example of.[8]

Your request my dear sir with respect to your Daughter shall be punctually attended to, and you may be assured of every attention in my power towards her.

You will be so kind as to present my Love to Miss Jefferson, compliments to the Marquiss and his Lady. I am really conscience smitten that I have never written to that amiable Lady, whose politeness and attention to me deserved my acknowledgment.[9]

The little balance which you stated in a former Letter in my favour, when an opportunity offers I should like to have in Black Lace at about 8 or 9 Livres pr. Ell. Tho late in the Month, I hope it will not be thought out of season to offer my best wishes for the Health, Long Life and prosperity of yourself and family, or to assure you of the Sincere Esteem & Friendship with which I am Your's &c. &c.,
A. ADAMS

RC (DLC); addressed in David S. Franks' hand; endorsed. Recorded in SJL as received 2 Feb. 1787. Dft (MHi: AMT); with many variations in phraseology and some modifications in substance. For comment on this letter, see note to TJ's reply, 22 Feb. 1787.

[1] Dft reads "arms."
[2] At this point, instead of the two following sentences, Dft reads: "which I would recommend to your use. One thing you may be assured of which is that it will not do harm."
[3] Instead of the passage beginning "I cannot help flattering myself" and ending at this point, Dft reads: "I do not doubt but in the end the Commotions will prove Salutary to the state at large by ⟨controuling⟩ Luxery and extravagance," &c.
[4] Preceding eleven words not in Dft.
[5] Dft adds "and Debts."
[6] Dft reads: "the cry of the people."
[7] Dft has the following paragraph at this point, omitted in RC: "The disturbances which have taken place have roused from their Lethargy the Supine and the Indolent animated the Brave and taught wisdom to our Rulers."
[8] This paragraph in Dft reads as follows: "You will see by the papers I send that [a party] of Vollunteers from Boston commanded by Col. Hitchburn

with Mr. Jackson whom you remember to have seen in France and Mr. Higgenson formerly a Member of Congress Let Cols. went out in persuit of Shattucks and his party whom with two other leaders they took after some resistance in which Shattucks was wounded in his knee with a broad Sword. The other two submitted without resistance.... It is not unlikely that some examples must be made before the riots will be totally quelled and peace and good order restored." (The omitted sentence in this passage repeats, with slight variation in phraseology, the statement about the Act of the General Court laying a duty of 15 per cent. on British goods.)

9 Dft ends at this point with the following deletion and complimentary close: "⟨but I have such a Number of Correspondents in America, all of whom think⟩ Believe me dear Sir with the highest esteem Your &c &c A Adams."

From William Cunningham

Le Havre, 29 Jan. 1787. Is a native of New York, where his wife and parents reside; requests assistance in procuring passage on "the ship Les Deriux Freres which is to sail for New York on the 10th. of Next Month." Has applied to Ruellan to obtain passage, but "he says it is impossible even to go as a foremast hand without paying 160 Livres which is not in my power to Comply with." Was mate of the ship *Marianne*, James Martin, master, from Virginia laden with tobacco consigned to Ruellan. Ship has been seized for debts contracted by her former captain and all "Hands ... discharged from the Ship on the 20th. instant." Has been absent for fifteen months, and "having been Cast away and Lost the Vessell I then Commanded ... has reduced my Circumstances." Charles Thomson, secretary of Congress, is an intimate friend of his father. "When the Ship may arrive off the Port of N York and no pilot offers I am Capable of taking Charge of her to the City."

RC (DLC); 1 p. Recorded in SJL as received 1 Feb. 1787.

To R. & A. Garvey

GENTLEMEN   Paris Jan. 29. 1787.

I have now the honour to inclose you a paper from the Douane equivalent to the Acquit a caution which they have mislaid. They insist that the variation between the Acquit described in this paper, and that described in your letter proceeds from an error in the latter, and that no such Acquit á caution as you describe has been transmitted to them. I wish however the error may not be with them: tho' they took a good degree of pains in searching. If this paper does not suffice to discharge you, I must give you the trouble of writing to me again, as I shall still have time enough before my departure to have it rectified if it can be done.

Will you be so good as to inform me whether any Diligence plies regularly between Rouen and Havre, at what days and hours it departs from and arrives at each post, and the price of a place. This information becomes necessary to me since the establishment of the packets at Havre, as I may have occasion to send couriers to Havre, and to receive them from there. I have the honour to be with much esteem & respect, Gentlemen, your most obedt. humble servt.,

TH: JEFFERSON

PrC (DLC). The enclosed "paper from the Douane" has not been identified. TJ also enclosed with this letter a memorandum (MHi), outlining the information he desired concerning the schedule of the diligence, with blanks to be filled in; this copy, with the blanks completed, was returned to TJ as an enclosure in Garvey's letter of 5 Feb. 1787.

From Thomas Haddaway

Le Havre, 29 Jan. 1787. With "these few illiterate Lines" he is compelled by necessity to ask TJ's assistance in getting to America. Was mate on the brig *Sally,* Shuball Coffin, master, from Nantucket. Is willing to work his passage across, but has been told "to procure an order from you." Is a native of Boston. Assures TJ that he will "ever while Life Be ready and Willing to Compensate . . . for your Goodness." He has little cash, and "Lodgings are High and Diet likewise." Wishes reply to be directed to Captain James Martin, care of Ruellan.

RC (DLC); 1 p.; in the hand of William Cunningham. Recorded in SJL as received 1 Feb. 1787.

From Rochambeau

Paris ce 29. Janvier

Le Cte. de Rochambeau est au desespoir de ne pouvoir se rendre à l'invitation de Monsieur Jefferson pour le vendredi 2. de ce mois.[1] Il doit être ce jour là à Versailles pour la ceremonie de l'ordre du Saint Esprit. Il a l'honneur de lui faire mille tendres complimens, et de lui faire part que sa belle fille vient d'accoucher heureusement d'un garçon.

RC (PU); addressed in part: "à la Bassein de Chaillot, à Paris"; without date, but obviously written in 1787 since that was the only year in which Feb. 2 fell on a Friday during the period of TJ's stay in France. Also, it was in 1787 that Rochambeau's only grandson was born (Jean-Edmond Weelen, *Rochambeau Father and Son,* New York, 1936, p. 182, 183). TJ's invitation to which this is a reply has not been found.

[1] Thus in MS, an error for "du mois prochain."

From Rosaubo

29 Jan. [1787]. Declines TJ's dinner invitation for the following Friday, because of his prior engagement with the Marquis de la Guiche.

RC (MHi); 1 p.; in French; dated only: "ce lundy 29 janvier" (see note to Rochambeau to TJ, this date); addressed. TJ's invitation to which this is a reply has not been found.

From William Stephens Smith

London January 29th. 1787.

No my dear Sir it is not me. It is impossible that my heart would ever permit me to pen a line to you, charged with the reflection which that line single and alone seems formed to admit of. When in haste I said I had no more letters in my file unanswered and therefore should not trouble you farther, I intended to hold up this Idea, that I could only spare the time for the necessary business contained in your favours. When that was done, I hoped you would attribute my stoping short to want of time. I seriously feel for your misfortune, and have sent up prayers for your recovery.—The harpsicord is finished and inclosed is Dr. Burney's Letter on the subject. It shall be dispatched by the first Vessel. Mr. Franks takes charge of the Instrument which Jones has made for you. You will find his Letter explanatory packed with it. Your other slipers and a pair of shoes for Mr. Short accompany it. I do not like the appearances in the eastern States, nor the construction you put on the raising of troops in them to fight the *Shawanese.* I hope there will not be any necessity for spilling of Blood, for there is no knowing where it will end. If there is an appearance of it, may we not shelter ourselves from the horror and inconvenience of internal Commotion by turning the tide on these Britons by a formal declaration of War. They are at the botom of it, and merit our highest indignation. But the subject distresses me beyond measure, and I still think the good sense of the people will render harshness and severity unnecessary.—On the receipt of yours of the 20th. ulto. which I began to answer, I set out as a pilgrim doing pennance, and walked to Hammersmith, and sent the Acer rubrum and the Liriodendron tulipefer but the Quercus Phellos is not to be had in Europe. After this walk I felt a little as if I had got rid of the crime which so strangely beset me, that nothing but an exertion to serve you could have shaken off. Forget and forgive

29 JANUARY 1787

my errors and accept of my thanks for the map. I will guard it with great attention, and give particular directions on the subject of its publication. It is very valuable and shall be done in the best manner possible.

I am very sorry that there are so many errors in Neles map. If you think best to send it back, it shall be immediately attended to. The second copying press shall be strictly enquired after. Its direction must have been to Mr. Garvey at Rouen, but I will be more particular when I can get a sight of Mr. Woodmason. I have not yet been able to get the measure you ask for and Franks is in a terrible fret to be off, and Mr. A. has not been behind hand in furnishing me with employment, but I will not loose sight of it.— The Letters which you sent are all put in the proper channels to reach their respective address. And now my dear sir having replyed fully (1.2.3.4.5.6.7.8.9.10) to your two favours of the 20th. of Decr. and of the 15th. inst. I will only mention that I was happy in cultivating the acquaintance of Monsieur Tronchin who presented your Introductory Letter of May 17. 1786. I was much pleased with him and shall pursue your advise respecting him—and now shall in confidence say a little of myself and if you can with good conscience grant it take the liberty of asking your protection and Countenance to my pursuits. Mr. Franks convey's to Congress Mr. Adam's request to be recalled from this Court, or their permission to return after the expiration of his present Commission, and at the same time recommends and solicits for your humble servant the appointment of Charge des affairs and as much higher as they think proper. Letters from you to your friends in and out of Congress would be very flattering to me, and have great weight in procuring the advance sought for. I need say no more, confident that you will do every thing to serve me, consistant with the interest of our Country. Mr. Adams's intention had better not be spoke of in Europe, tho' it will be no secreet when the Letters arrive in america as he has wrote private and positive Letters to his friends of his determination of retiring. I am Dr. Sir with great respect & esteem Your obliged Humble Servt.,

W. S. SMITH

RC (DLC); endorsed. Recorded in SJL as received 2 Feb. 1787. Enclosure: Charles Burney to TJ, 20 Jan. 1787.

For the significance of THAT LINE, see TJ to Smith, 20 Dec. 1787, and note. Jones' LETTER EXPLANATORY is that of 22 Jan. 1787. For the significance of the expression "(1. 2. 3. 4. 5. 6. 7. 8. 9. 10)," see Smith to TJ, 21 May 1786; Adams to TJ, 6 June 1786, note 2; and TJ to Madison, 30 Jan. 1787.

To Zachariah Loreilhe

SIR   Paris Jan. 30. 1787.

A letter from a friend of mine in S. Carolina informs me that, with that letter, he sends some plants, addressed to the care of Monsr. Otto, Chargé des affaires of France at New York. The letter is come to hand, but no plants. Fearing they may remain on board the Packet boat last arrived at L'Orient, or neglected in some warehouse, I take the liberty of asking your friendly enquiries after them, as I value them much. If by any means you can find them out, and forward them to me immediately it will confer a great obligation on Sir your most obedient & most humble servt.,

                                           TH: JEFFERSON

PrC (MHi); endorsed. See Ramsay to TJ, 8 Nov. 1786.

To James Madison

DEAR SIR   Paris Jan. 30. 1787.

My last to you was of the 16th of Dec. since which I have received yours of Nov. 25. and Dec. 4. which afforded me, as your letters always do, a treat on matters public, individual and oeconomical. I am impatient to learn your sentiments on the late troubles in the Eastern states. So far as I have yet seen, they do not appear to threaten serious consequences. Those states have suffered by the stoppage of the channels of their commerce, which have not yet found other issues. This must render money scarce, and make the people uneasy. This uneasiness has produced acts absolutely unjustifiable: but I hope they will provoke no severities from their governments. A consciousness of those in power that their administration of the public affairs has been honest, may perhaps produce too great a degree of indignation: and those characters wherein fear predominates over hope may apprehend too much from these instances of irregularity. They may conclude too hastily that nature has formed man insusceptible of any other government but that of force, a conclusion not founded in truth, nor experience. Societies exist under three forms sufficiently distinguishable. 1. Without government, as among our Indians. 2. Under governments wherein the will of every one has a just influence, as is the case in England in a slight degree, and in our states in a great one. 3. Under governments of force: as is the case in all other monarchies and in

30 JANUARY 1787

most of the other republics. To have an idea of the curse of existence under these last, they must be seen. It is a government of wolves over sheep. It is a problem, not clear in my mind, that the 1st. condition is not the best. But I believe it to be inconsistent with any great degree of population. The second state has a great deal of good in it. The mass of mankind under that enjoys a precious degree of liberty and happiness. It has it's evils too: the principal of which is the turbulence to which it is subject. But weigh this against the oppressions of monarchy, and it becomes nothing. Malo periculosam, libertatem quam quietam servitutem. Even this evil is productive of good. It prevents the degeneracy of government, and nourishes a general attention to the public affairs. I hold it that a little rebellion now and then is a good thing, and as necessary in the political world as storms in the physical. Unsuccesful rebellions indeed generally establish the incroachments on the rights of the people which have produced them. An observation of this truth should render honest republican governors so mild in their punishment of rebellions, as not to discourage them too much. It is a medecine necessary for the sound health of government. If these transactions give me no uneasiness, I feel very differently at another peice of intelligence, to wit, the possibility that the navigation of the Missisipi may be abandoned to Spain. I never had any interest Westward of the Alleghaney; and I never will have any. But I have had great opportunities of knowing the character of the people who inhabit that country. And I will venture to say that the act which abandons the navigation of the Missisipi is an act of separation between the Eastern and Western country. It is a relinquishment of five parts out of eight of the territory of the United States, an abandonment of the fairest subject for the paiment of our public debts, and the chaining those debts on our own necks in perpetuum. I have the utmost confidence in the honest intentions of those who concur in this measure; but I lament their want of acquaintance with the character and physical advantages of the people who, right or wrong, will suppose their interests sacrificed on this occasion to the contrary interests of that part of the confederacy in possession of present power. If they declare themselves a separate people, we are incapable of a single effort to retain them. Our citizens can never be induced, either as militia or as souldiers, to go there to cut the throats of their own brothers and sons, or rather[1] to be themselves the subjects instead of the perpetrators of the parricide. Nor would that country quit the cost of being retained against the will of it's inhabitants, could it be done. But it cannot be done.

30 JANUARY 1787

They are able already to rescue the navigation of the Missisipi out of the hands of Spain, and to add New Orleans to their own territory. They will be joined by the inhabitants of Louisiana. This will bring on a war between them and Spain; and that will produce the question with us whether it will not be worth our while to become parties with them in the war, in order to reunite them with us, and thus correct our error? And were I to permit my forebodings to go one step futher, I should predict that the inhabitants of the U.S. would force their rulers to take the affirmative of that question. I wish I may be mistaken in all these opinions.

We have for some time expected that the Chevalier de la Luzerne would obtain a promotion in the diplomatic line, by being appointed to some of the courts where this country keeps an Ambassador. But none of the vacancies taking place which had been counted on, I think the present disposition is to require his return to his station in America. He told me himself lately, that he should return in the spring. I have never pressed this matter on the court, tho' I knew it to be desireable and desired on our part: because if the compulsion on him to return had been the work of Congress, he would have returned in such ill temper with them as to disappoint them in the good they expected from it. He would for ever have laid at their door his failure of promotion. I did not press it for another reason, which is that I have great reason to beleive that the character of the Count de Moutier, who would go were the Chevalier to be otherwise provided for, would give the most perfect satisfaction in America.—As you are now returned into Congress it will become of importance that you should form a just estimate of certain public characters; on which therefore I will give you such notes as my knowlege of them has furnished me with. You will compare them with the materials you are otherwise possessed of, and decide on a view of the whole. You know the opinion I *formerly*[2] entertained of *my friend Mr. Adams.* Yourself and the governor were the first who *shook* that opinion. I afterwards saw proofs which *convicted* him of a degree of *vanity*, and of a *blindness* to it, of which no germ *had appeared* in Congress. A *7-months'* intimacy with him *here* and *as* many *weeks* in *London* have given me opportunities of studying him closely. *He is vain, irritable and a bad calculator of* the force and probable effect of the motives which govern men. This is *all* the *ill* which can possibly be *said of him.* He is as disinterested as the being which made him: he is profound in his views: and accurate in his judgment *except where knowledge of the world* is necessary to form a judgment. He is so amiable, that I pronounce you will love him if ever you become acquainted with him. He would be, as he was, a great man in *Congress*.[3] *Mr. Carmichael* is I think very little *known* in *America*. I never *saw him* and while I was *in Congress I* formed rather a *disadvantageous idea* of him. His letters, received then, shewed him *vain* and more attentive to *ceremony* and *etiquette* than we suppose men *of sense* should be. I have now a constant correspondence with him, and find *him* a little *hypocondriac* and *discontented*. He possesses very *good understanding* tho' not of the *first order. I have* had great opportunities of *searching into* his *character* and have availed myself *of it*. Many persons of different nations *coming* from *Madrid* to *Paris* all speak of *him as* in *high esteem* and *I think* it certain that he has more of the *Count de Florid. B's friendship* than any *diplomatic* character at *that court*. As long as this *minister* is in *office Carmichael* can do *more than* any other *person who* could be *sent there*. You will see *Franks and* doubtless he will be *asking some appointment*. I wish there may be any one for *which* he is *fit*. He is *light, indiscreet, [act]ive*,[4] *honest, affectionate*. Tho' *Bingham* is not in *diplomatic office* yet as he wishes to be so I will mention such circumstances of *him as you might* otherwise be *deceived in. He* will make *you believe he* was on the most intimate footing with the first *characters in Europe* and versed in the *secrets* of every *cabinet*. Not a word of this *is true. He* had a rage for being *presented* to *great men* and had no *modesty* in the methods by which he could effect it. If *he obtained access* afterwards, it was with such as who were susceptible of impression from the *beauty of his wife*. I must *except* the *Marquis de Bouilli*[5] who had been an *old acquaintance*. The *Marquis de Lafayette* is a most valuable *auxiliary to me*. His *zeal* is unbounded, and his *we[ight]*[4] with those in *power great*. His *education* having been merely *military, commerce* was an unknown feild to him. But his good sense enabling him to *comprehend* perfectly whatever is *explained to him, his agency* has been very *efficacious. He* has a great deal of *sound genius*, is well *remarked* by the *king* and rising in *popularity. He* has nothing against *him but* the *suspicion of republican principles*. I think he will one day *be of* the *ministry*. His *foible* is a *canine appetite for popularity and fame*. But he will get *above* this. *The Count de Vergennes* is *ill*. The possibility of his *recovery* renders it dangerous for *us to express a doubt but* he is *in danger*. He is *a great Minister* in *European affairs* but has very *imperfect ideas* of ours [and] *no confidence in* them. His *devotion to* the principles of *pure despotism* render him *unaffectionate to*

30 JANUARY 1787

our governments but *his fear* of *England makes him value us* as a *make weight*. He is *cool, reserved in political conversation, free* and *familiar* on other *subjects*, and a very *attentive, aggreeable person* to *do business with*. It is impossible to have a clearer, better *organised head* but *age* has *chilled his heart.* Nothing should be spared on our part to attach this country to us. It is the only one on which we can rely for support under every event. It's inhabitants love us more I think than they do any other nation on earth. This is very much the effect of the good dispositions with which the French officers returned. In a former letter I mentioned to you the dislocation of my wrist. I can make not the least use of it, except for the single article of writing, tho' it is going on five months since the accident happened. I have great anxieties lest I should never recover any considerable use of it. I shall, by the advice of my Surgeons, set out in a fortnight for the waters of Aix in Provence. I chose these out of several they proposed to me, because if they fail to be effectual, my journey will not be useless altogether. It will give me an opportunity of examining the canal of Languedoc and of acquiring knowlege of that species of navigation which may be useful hereafter: but more immediately it will enable me to take the tour of the ports concerned in commerce with us, to examine on the spot the defects of the late regulations respecting our commerce, to learn the further improvements which may be made on it, and, on my return, to get this business finished. I shall be absent between two and three months, unless any thing happens to recall me here sooner, which may always be effected in ten days, in whatever part of my route I may be. In speaking of *characters* I omitted *those of Reyneval and Henin*, the *two eyes* of *M. de Vergennes*. The *former* is the most important *character because possessing* the most of the *confidence* of the *Count, he* is rather *cunning* than *wise*. *His* views of things being neither *great* nor *liberal he governs* himself by *principles* which he has *learnt* by *rote* and is *fit only* for the *details* of *execution. His heart* is susceptible of *little passions* but not of *good ones. He* is *brother* in *law* to *M. Gerard* from whom he received *disadvantageous impressions* of *us which* cannot be *effaced. He* has much *duplicity. Henin* is a *philosopher sincere, friendly, liberal, learned, beloved* by every *body*, the *other* by *nobody. I think* it a great *misfortune* that the *United States* are in the *department* of the *former*. As particulars of this kind may be useful to you in your present situation, I may hereafter continue the chapter. I know it safely lodged in your discretion.

Feb. 5.

Since writing thus far *Franks* is *returned* from *England*. *I learn that Mr. Adams desires to be recalled and that Smith should be appointed charge des affairs* there. It is not for me to decide whether any *diplomatic character* should be *kept* at a *court* which *keeps* none with *us*. You can judge of *Smith's abilities* by *his letters*. They are not of the *first order* but they are *good*. For his *honesty* he is like our friend *Monroe*. Turn his *soul* wrong side outwards and there is not a speck on it. *He* has one *foible*, an *excessive inflammability* of *temper*, but he feels it when it comes on, and has *resolution enough* to *suppress* it, and to *remain silent* till it *passes* over.

I send you by Colo. Franks your pocket telescope, walking stick, and chemical box. The two former could not be combined together. The latter could not be had in the form you referred to. Having a great desire to have a portable copying machine, and being satisfied from some experiments that the principle of the large machine might be applied in a small one, I planned one when in England and had it made. It answers perfectly. I have since set a workman to making them here, and they are in such demand that he has his hands full. Being assured that you will be pleased to have one, when you shall have tried it's convenience, I send you one by Colo. Franks. The machine costs 96 livres, the appendages 24. livres, and I send you paper and ink for 12 livres, in all 132 livres. There is a printed paper of directions: but you must expect to make many essays before you succeed perfectly. A soft brush, like a shaving brush, is more convenient than the sponge. You can get as much ink and paper as you please from London. The paper costs a guinea a ream.

RC (DLC: Madison Papers); unsigned; endorsed; partly in code. PrC (DLC: TJ Papers); accompanied in TJ Papers, 28:4767 by a list giving the coded passages *en clair*, from which one or two minor errors of encoding have been silently corrected.

[1] At this point TJ deleted the clause "have their own throats cut by them" and rephrased it as above.

[2] This and subsequent words in italics are written in code and have been decoded by the editors, employing Code No. 9.

[3] TJ deleted the word "Congress" at the bottom of a page and then wrote the code symbol for the word at the top of the next.

[4] TJ omitted the code symbol for the letters in square brackets (supplied), but these have been added from the list *en clair*.

[5] The name was first writtten out, then heavily deleted; Ford, IV, 366, does not indicate that the name was in code and gives it as "the Marquis de Bonclearren"; the above reading is verified by the list *en clair*.

From Thomas Silbey

Le Havre, 30 Jan. 1787. Was a carpenter on board the ship *Marianne*, James Martin, master; "the Ship has been paid off by Reason of her being laid up"; has a wife and family in Virginia and desires TJ to procure for him a passage "in the Ship La Deriux Frear" sailing 10 Feb. for New York.

RC (DLC); 2 p.; addressed; endorsed; postmarked "HAVRE." Recorded in SJL as received 3 Feb. 1787. Enclosure (DLC): Certificate by James Martin, dated 30 Jan. 1787, of Silbey's service on the *Marianne* and of his having a family in Virginia.

From André Limozin

Le Havre, 31 Jan. 1787. Has no doubt but that TJ has been informed packets are established in that port and that the first will sail 10 Feb. for New York. Offers to perform any commissions for him. Is "really astonished that there is no Carolina rice sent from America to our Market. There is at present a very great demand here and in all our Neighbourhood for that article and not a Single Barrell remains unsold."

RC (MHi); 2 p.; endorsed. Recorded in SJL as received 3 Feb. 1787.

From Partout

[Jan. 1787?]

The Cook returned and told he would accept of my terms whatever they would be: I answerd he should consult nothing but his own convenience: I told him I thought M. Jefs. would be disposed to give him fifty guineas a year for teaching another the cookery. Aggreed.

He observed a sufficient quantity of linnen and kitchen utensils should be furnished only for his use, and in greater quantity than in the English cookerey which does not require as many as ours. I aggreed.

He desired a suply of bier or toddy or brandy for the days when he should have an extraordinary business. I left it to Mr. Jeffson.

The man comes for an answer in half an hour. As a number of small affairs press on me I hope M. Jepherson will excuse the paper, Style and Writer.

RC (MHi); undated, unaddressed, and unsigned; in an unidentified hand; endorsed by TJ: "Partout, cook." The identity of Partout has not been established, but he may have been the "old cook" of the Prince of Conde (see Mazzei to TJ, 17 Apr. 1787; TJ to Mazzei, 6 May 1787) or he may have been the person who engaged the patissier to instruct James in the art of pastry-cooking early in Jan. 1787 (an entry in Account Book for 10 Jan. 1787 reads: "[pd Petit] for James's apprenticeship with patissier" 72f.). The letter could not have been written by Petit, who evidently wrote only a labored French.

From George Wythe

G. W. TO MR. J. Williamsburgh, januar. 1787.

Would not the figures to which one must advert in studying geometry, formed of wood, metal, or ivory, be more instructive than those, which are delineated on paper? If you think so, and if such figures can be procured where you are, i wish to know the cost of them, that i may remit money to pay for them, when i will beg the favour of you to send them to me.

RC (DLC); endorsed: "Wyth George." Recorded in SJL as received 31 May 1787 at Nantes.

To Cunningham and Haddaway

GENTLEMEN Paris Feb. 1. 1787.

I am sorry to be obliged to inform you that I am not able to procure an order for your being permitted to work your passage back to America, nor able otherwise to comply with your desires, being neither invested with the power, nor furnished with the means of doing it. I imagine you have come under particular contracts with your captains, which doubtless they will either perform, or make satisfaction for. Capt. Coffin is here, and returns in the packet. I will speak to him, and recommend you to his attention. Perhaps also if you apply to Mr. Limozin, who acts as our Consul at Havre, he may be able to advise you how to get back. I am Gentlemen your most obedient humble servt.,

TH: JEFFERSON

PrC (DLC); at foot of text: "Messieurs Thomas Haddaway & William Cuningham."

To John Jay

SIR Paris Feb. 1. 1787.

My last letters were of the 31st. of Decemb. and 9th. of January, since which last date I have been honoured with yours of

[99]

December the 13th. and 14th. I shall pay immediate attention to your instructions relative to the S. Carolina frigate. I had the honour of informing you of an improvement in the art of coining made here by one Drost, and of sending you by Colo. Franks a specimen of his execution in gold and silver. I expected to have sent also a coin of copper. The inclosed note from Drost will explain the reason why this was not sent. It will let you see also that he may be employed; as I suppose he is not so certain as he was of being engaged here. Mr. Grand, who knows him, gives me reason to believe he may be engaged reasonably. Congress will decide whether it be worth their attention.

In some of my former letters I suggested an opportunity of obliging this court by borrowing as much money in Holland as would pay the debt due here, if such a loan could be obtained; as to which I was altogether ignorant. To save time, I wrote to Mr. Dumas, to know whether he thought it probable a loan could be obtained, enjoining him the strictest secrecy, and informing him I was making the enquiry merely of my own motion and without instruction. I inclose you his answer. He thinks purchasers of the debt could be found, with a sacrifice of a small part of the capital, and a postponement be obtained of some of the first reimbursements. The proposition for an immediate adoption of this measure by me, was probably urged on his mind by a desire to serve our country more than a strict attention to my duty and the magnitude of the object. I hope on the contrary that, if it should be thought worth a trial, it may be put into the hands of Mr. Adams who knows the ground, and is known there, and whose former succesful negociations in this line would give better[1] founded hopes of success on this occasion.

I formerly mentioned to you the hopes of preferment entertained by the Chevalr. de la Luzerne. They have been baffled by events, none of the vacancies taking place which had been expected. Had I pressed his being ordered back, I have reason to believe the order would have been given. But he would have gone back in ill humour with Congress, he would have laid for ever at their door the failure of a promotion then viewed as certain, and this might have excited dispositions that would have disappointed us of the good we hoped from his return. The line I have observed with him has been to make him sensible that nothing was more desired by Congress than his return, but that they would not willingly press it so as to defeat him of a personal advantage. He sees his prospects fail, and will return in the approaching spring, unless something unexpected should turn up in his favor. In this case the Count de Moutier has the promise of succeeding to him, and, if I do not mistake his character, he would give great satisfaction. So that I think you may count on seeing the one or the other by midsummer.

It had been suspected that France and England might adopt those concerted regulations of commerce for their West Indies, of which your letter expresses some apprehensions. But the expressions in the 4. 5. 7. 11. 18. and other articles of their treaty, which communicate to the English the privileges of the most favored *European* nation only, has lessened if not removed those fears. They have clearly reserved a right of favoring specially any nation not European, and there is no nation out of Europe who could so probably have been in their eye at that time as ours. They are wise. They must see it probable at least that any concert with England will be but of short duration: and they could hardly propose to sacrifice for that a connection with us which may be perpetual.

We have been for some days in much inquietude for the Count de Vergennes. He is very seriously ill. Nature seems struggling to decide his disease into a gout. A swelled foot at present gives us a hope of this issue. His loss would at all times have been great: but it would be immense during the critical poise of European affairs, existing at this moment.   I inclose you a letter from one of the foreign officers complaining of the nonpaiment of their interest. It is only one out of many I have received. This is accompanied by a second copy of the Moorish declaration sent me by Mr. Barclay. He went to Alicant to settle with Mr. Lamb: but, on his arrival there, found he was gone to Minorca. A copy of his letter will inform you of this circumstance, and of some others relative to Algiers, with his opinion on them. Whatever the states may enable Congress to do for obtaining the peace of that country, it is a separate question whether they will redeem our captives, how, and at what price? If they decide to redeem them, I will beg leave to observe that it is of great importance that the first redemption be made at as low a price as possible, because it will form the future tariff. If these pyrates find that they can have a very great price for Americans, they will abandon proportionably their pursuits against other nations to direct them towards ours. That the choice of Congress may be enlarged as to the instruments they may use for effecting the redemption, I think it my duty to inform them that there is here an order of priests called the Mathurins, the object of whose institution is to beg alms for the redemption of captives. They keep members always in Barbary searching out the captives of their own country, and redeem I beleive on better terms than any other body, public or private. It occurred to me that their agency might be obtained for the redemption of our prisoners at Algiers. I obtained conferences with the General and with some members of the order. The General, with all the benevolence and cordiality possible, undertook to act for us if we should desire it. He told me that their last considerable redemption was of about 300 prisoners, who cost them somewhat upwards of 1500 livres apeice. But that they should not be able to redeem ours as cheap as they do their own; and that it must be absolutely unknown that the public concern themselves in the operation, or the price would be greatly enhanced. The difference of religion was not once mentioned, nor did it appear to me to be thought of. It was a silent reclamation and acknowlegement of fraternity between two religions of the same family, which historical events of antient date had rendered more hostile to one another than to their common adversaries. I informed the general that I should communicate the good dispositions of his order to those who alone had the authority to decide whatever related to our captives. Mr. Carmichael informs me that monies have been advanced for the support of our prisoners at Algiers which ought to be replaced. I infer from the context of his letter, that these advances have been made by the court of Madrid. I submit the information to Congress.

A treaty of commerce is certainly concluded between France and Russia. The particulars of it are yet secret.

I inclose the gazettes of France and Leyden to this date, and have the honor of assuring you of those sentiments of perfect esteem & respect with which I am Sir your most obedient & most humble servant,
TH: JEFFERSON

PrC (DLC). Tr (DNA: PCC, No. 107, I). Enclosures: (1) J. P. Droz to [Ferdinand Grand], 16 Jan. 1787, advising that he is no longer permitted to make "la pieces d'or que vous me demandez" without running the risk of displeasing government and requesting him to inform TJ; that he has not had time to work on the report promised on his request concerning "la fabrication des monnoyes"; that he is resolved more than ever to accept suitable offers of employment, even if this meant emigrating to a foreign land; that, therefore, if Congress wished to make a reasonable proposal, he would set up for them "toutes les machines necessaire pour fabriequier les plus belles monnoyes qu'il ayt encore peutêtre éxisté, et aussi avec beaucoup moins de fraix"; that he thought it would suffice in the report to make an estimate of the cost of making the machine in France for shipment to America; that it was extremely difficult to determine a proper price for the coinage of specie and all he could do would be to give assurance that it could be done at a price below that prevailing in France; that he would be willing to take charge of the machines, the coins, and the engraving, but wished not to be connected with the melting and alloy of gold and silver since he would have enough to do with setting up the machines, laminating, cutting, adjusting the blanks, and striking; and that he would soon have all of the information necessary to complete "le petit memoire" and he would bring it and confer with him immediately (Tr in DNA: PCC, No. 107, I, with the obviously erroneous caption: "Monsr. Droz to Mr. Jefferson"; the addressee was very probably Grand, since it was through him that TJ communicated with Droz in 1787 and later; see TJ to Grand, 23 Apr. 1790). (2) Dumas to TJ, 23 Jan. 1787. (3) Fizeaux & Cie. to TJ, 1 Jan. 1787. (4) Segond to TJ, 17 Jan. 1787. (5) The "second copy of the Moorish declaration" was enclosed in Barclay to TJ, 4 Dec. 1786 (see note there). (6) Barclay to Commissioners, 6 Jan. 1787.

The gold and silver specimens of the experimental "ecu de Calonne" executed by Jean Pierre Droz in 1786 and conveyed to America BY COLO. FRANKS are not preserved among the Papers of the Continental Congress and evidently have not survived; see illustration of a specimen in silver in this volume. Droz, whose name TJ probably attempted to render phonetically by spelling DROST or Drozt, was born at La Chaux-de-Fond, Canton of Neuchâtel, Switzerland, and died in Paris in 1823. He was an engraver of medals, coiner, and inventor of the machine for striking the two faces and edge of a coin at a single stroke (see TJ to Jay, 9 Jan. 1787, and, for TJ's subsequent efforts to bring Droz to America, TJ to Grand, 23 Apr. 1790; Grand to TJ, 25 Aug. 1790; TJ to Short, 25 Apr., 29 Aug., 24 Nov. 1791; TJ to Pinckney, 14 June 1792, 20 Apr. 1793; TJ to Washington, 30 Dec. 1793). Grand, Matthew Boulton, and TJ were present at the Hôtel des Monnaies when Droz gave a demonstration of his machine. Sir John Sinclair later claimed the credit for having brought Boulton and Droz together: "the improved machines for coining money, invented by Monsieur Droz, a native of Switzerland . . . were at that time unknown in England. I prevailed on M. Droz to explain his plans to Mr. Boulton of Birmingham, and was thus the means of introducing this superior mode of coinage into the British Mint" (*Correspondence of . . . Sir John Sinclair*, London, 1831, I, xxxii). Thus it is possible that Sinclair was with TJ, Grand, and Boulton at the time of the demonstration. James Watt, Boulton's partner who was with him in Paris late in 1786, was also among those present (H. W. Dickinson, *Matthew Boulton*, Cambridge, 1937, p. 124, 136, 206). An account of the Hôtel des Monnaies in Sebastien Mercier's *Tableau de Paris* (Amsterdam, 1788), p. 145, contains the follow reference to Droz: "J'ai regret que l'on n'ait point fait usage de l'invention du sieur Droz de Neufchâtel, graveur intelligent. Ill avoit perfectionné une machine qui, d'un seul coup de balancier, marquoit la pièce et la tranche en même-temps. Elle avoit la double utilité d'offrir une monnoie d'une beauté parfaite, et de déjouer les faux-monnoyeurs, qui se seroient trouvés dans l'impossibilité de l'imiter. Ce dernier avantage est bien supérieur à l'autre; car il n'y a rien de plus rare et de plus heureux en politique, que de pouvoir prévenir et épargner le crime à des malheureux." When the French government failed to employ Droz's method, Boulton, who was as enthusiastic about the invention as TJ, "engaged Mr. Droz at a very great expence to engrave the original puncheons and matrices for the proposed" copper coinage of halfpenny pieces in England "and to superintend the execution of it" (Dickinson, *Boulton*, p. 137). Despite the fact that Boulton paid Droz a "high salary," he was nevertheless able to report to a committee of the privy council that he could execute the halfpenny coinage at a cost not above half that incurred by the royal Mint in producing the coin then current and to endeavor to produce "more excellent coin than had ever been seen, and establishing an effectual check upon those who counterfeit it" (same, p. 137). Boulton applied steam power to the machines and introduced a number of improvements; Droz's split collar in six parts for forming the edge of a coin was found to be difficult to manage and faulty in execution; Droz himself was, according to Watt, "of a troublesome disposition" though a "good die sinker," and he was dismissed (same, p. 206). Possibly Droz's chief influence on the development of better coinage was exerted through the stimulus that he gave to Boulton. "Much ingenuity, time and great expence were required to perfect the application of the steam engine to coining," wrote James Watt of his partner, "in all of which Mr. B[oulton] acted the principal part and gave life to the whole." (Same, p. 206.)

[1] This word interlined in substitution for "well," deleted.

[103]

From Louis Le Pelletier

Monsieur   Paris le 1er. fevrier 1787

J'ai l'honneur de vous adresser une expédition des procès verbaux des deux séances des 15 et 28 7bre: dernier de la réception et de l'inauguration du buste de M. le Marquis de la fayette, à l'hôtel de ville de Paris, de l'enrégistrement fait de la lettre par laquelle Mr. le Baron de Breteüil a annoncé au Corps de Ville les intentions du Roi sur cet objet, de la lettre que vous avez écrite, Monsieur, et enfin de la deliberation prise par les Etats de Virginie.

J'ai été bien touché de l'indisposition qui vous a empêché de nous transmettre vous même ce gage intéressant de l'opinion et des sentimens de vos compatriotes. Soyez près d'eux l'interprète de tous ceux qui nous animaient en ce moment, des vœux que nous formerons toujours pour que l'amérique Septentrionale et les Etats de Virginie voient accroître leurs forces en éloignant de leurs mœurs et de leurs foyers ce qui a porté le germe de la destruction parmi les plus grands Etats. C'est en conservant cette simplicité, cette pureté primitive qui sont les bases et les garants de la prospérité publique que vous atteindrez au dégré de splendeur que vous promettent vos sages constitutions et dont votre alliance avec notre auguste Monarque est le gage. Assurez de l'attachement immuable de cette Capitale tous ces hommes vertueux qui ont travaillé si efficacement à la gloire et au bonheur de leur patrie, et recevez, Monsieur, les mêmes témoignages qui vous sont dûs personnellement à tant de titres. Soyez persuadé que J'éprouve une satisfaction bien véritable en joignant l'expression de tous mes sentimens à ceux dont Je suis dans cette circonstance l'organe auprès de vous.

J'ai l'honneur d'être avec un respectueux attachement Monsieur, de votre Excellence, Le très humble et très obéissant serviteur,

Le Pelletier

RC (Vi); in a clerk's hand, signed by Le Pelletier. Enclosure (Vi): MS copy consisting of thirty pages in a clerk's hand, signed by Veytard, *greffier en chef*, bearing at its head the word "Duplicata" and the caption "Procès verbal de la Réception et de l'Inauguration du buste de Mr. le Marquis de la fayette a l'hôtel de Ville de Paris"; endorsed in part "Feby 7th. 1787. No. 6." The date in the endorsement refers to TJ's letter of transmittal to Edmund Randolph and "No. 6" refers to the number given it as an enclosure in Randolph's letter of transmittal to the Speaker of the House of Delegates, 15 Oct. 1786. Le Pelletier's letter and its enclosure were evidently handed to TJ by De Corny and were enclosed by TJ in his to Madison of 7 Feb. 1787, along with the unsealed letter to Randolph (see TJ to De Corny, 18 Feb. 1787). Another copy of the proceedings, in parchment, was enclosed in De Corny's letter to TJ of 20 Feb. 1787, and TJ was requested to bring the matter to a close by sending this official copy to America by the first opportunity. Having already dispatched the "Duplicata" that Le Pelletier transmitted, and being in the midst of preparations for his tour of Southern France, TJ instructed Short to send this parchment copy to Gov. Randolph. Short did so by the March packet, and Randolph received it in Philadelphia where he was attending the Federal Convention. He in turn forwarded it to Lt. Gov. Beverly Randolph, describing it as "only ... a repetition of the stile in which the Marquis' bust was inaugurated" (see Le Pelletier to TJ, 15 Feb. 1787; TJ to De Corny, 18 Feb. 1787; TJ to the Prévôt des Marchands, &c., 18 Feb. 1787; De Corny to TJ, 20 Feb. 1787; Short to Gov. of Virginia, 21 Mch. 1787; Madison to TJ, 23 Apr. 1787; JHD, Oct. 1787, 1828 edn., p. 3; CVSP, IV, 290; see also Vol. 10: 414-16).

From Puisaye

MONSIEUR 1er. De Fevrier 1787.

Il est des situations bien douloureuses dans la vie, il est aussi quelques consolations. Au milieu des maux qui m'accablent, j'en ai trouvé dans la lecture des Lettres d'un Cultivateur americain. Ecrasé sous le poids du malheur, j'ai cru que Vos heureuses Contrées pouroient devenir Pour moi un azile ou je finirois en paix le Reste d'une Carriere dont tous les instants Furent marqués par L'infortunne.

Je suis né d'une des plus anciennes familles nobles de ma province, j'ai embrassé comme mes ayeux le parti des armes. J'en ai parcouru Les devoirs avec honneur et je puis dire que je m'y suis distingué. J'ai eu le desir de faire usage de mes talends et de contribuer de mon Sang à La liberté de L'amerique; sans doutte, Par une suitte de ma mauvaise fortune, je n'ai pu éffectuer Ce desir. Peut être Serois-je heureux maintenant, jaurois du moins mérité à quelque titre d'être admis au rang de Vos Concytoyens. J'ai mené jusqu'ici une Conduitte éxempte de tout Reproche. Mes peres m'avoient Laissé une fortunne Suffisante pour mettre ma viellesse à l'abri du Besoin. Avec tout cela, Monsieur, je suis sur le point d'Eprouver La misere et toutes les humiliations auxquelles La naissance, Dont je suis, éxpose celui que la fortunne persécute, dans un paÿs ou ce préjugé est dans toute sa force.

Le détail des circonstances qui me privent des Ressources que jetois en droit d'attendre pour prix de mes services seroit trop long pour trouver place ici. Il résulte en partie de Raisons qui font honneur à mon caractere, d'un autre Côté j'appartiens à la maison de Rohan et cela fait Beaucoup.

La privation de ma fortune Résulte d'un procès intanté sur la qualité de ma possession, elle m'avoit été transmise Comme Noble, je la Possedois à Ce titre. Dans la Discussion elle à été

[105]

jugée Roturiere. Vous ignorés ces distinctions; j'ai été condamné à la Restitutions des deux tiers envers mes cohéritiers, en 14. années de jouissances de ces deux tiers, ce qui, joint aux frais d'un procès qui dure depuis dix ans, réduit Ce qui me restera à peu pres à rien. Voila, Monsieur, L'état de mes affaires. Voÿons maintenant si je suis Propre au nouveau genre d'éxistance que je me propose d'embrasser.

J'ai 41 an accomplis, je jouis d'une santé robuste, je suis fort, vigoureux et actif. J'entends L'œconomie Ruralle de mon païs, je suis sobre en toutes manieres, je vis à La campagne, Depuis cinq ans je me livre au travail le plus pénible. Comme je ne l'ai jamais fait par besoin, je n'y ai jamais mis de suitte, mais il est nécessaire à mon Bonheur, et je lui dois sans doutte la bonne santé dont je jouis. Je scai manier la Beche, la hache, La Verloppe, je forge et travaille le fer et L'acier. Grossierement, je peux construire un chariot de tout point, le conduire, le charger, décharger, etc. Je scai ferrer un cheval, le saigner, le médicamenter au Besoin, j'en connois tous les Défauts et presque toutes les maladies. Je scai faire la plus grande partie des outils, du charpentier et du maréchal, tous les ustencilles de la campagne, soit de Bois, de fer, ou d'acier. J'ai une teinture de Geometrie pratique et de mécaniques. Voila tous mes talens. Je ne scai ny Labourer, ny faucher, et je n'entends rien au commerce. En fondant le Superflu des mes éffets, en vendant le peu de fonds qui me restera, ce sera Beaucoup si je parviens à Rassembler une somme de quatre à cinq mille livres tournois. Voila toute L'étenduë de mes facultés.

Actuellement, Monsieur, je Reclame votre asistance et vos conseils. Dois-je adopter votre patrie? Suis-je Propre a devenir américain? Quel sort puis-je me faire dans ce nouvel émisphere? Quels sont Les obstacles que J'ai à surmonter. Il s'en présente naturellement deux, la langue, et Le nom français qui, dit-on, n'est pas accueilli chés vous aussi favorablement que Les autres nations, mais je suis né allemand.

Je pourois mendier des secours dans ma patrie, j'aime à croire que j'en obtiendrois, mais je ne veux être à charge à personne. Je Rougirois de charger un autre que moi du soin de mon éxistance. Comme homme j'ai droit à la pitié de mes semblables, à Leurs bons offices et à leurs conseils. Je ne veux rien de plus. J'entrevois un terme à mes malheurs, j'ai Besoin d'un guide pour me conduire dans la Route que je dois suivre pour y atteindre. C'est à vous, Monsieur, que je m'adresse, me refuserès Vous, non. J'ai des titres, je suis malheureux. Vous pouvès me parler franchement, je prèvois une grande partie des difficultés, elles ne m'effraÿent point, j'ai du courage, de la patience, de l'énergie. Je me soumettrai à tout. Je laisserai derriere moi toute espece de préjugé, depuis Longtemps j'en suis éxempt. Je présume, avec raison, que J'ai Besoin d'un noviciat, que je dois travailler pour autrui avant de travailler pour moi, cela me paroit indispensable, ne fut-ce que pour apprendre la langue.

Au reste, Monsieur, il Vous importe de savoir que je ne présenterai nulle part que ce soit sans des titres qui répondront de ma conduitte et qui apprendront que j'ai toujours cheri et pratiqué L'honneur et la vertu.

Puissiès vous, Monsieur, mettre quelque interêt à me conduire dans votre patrie. Peut être un jour auriès Vous la satisfaction de jouir de ma Reconnoissance et de mon Bonheur.

J'attends de vos nouvelles avec la plus grande impatïence.

J'ai L'honneur d'etre avec Respect Monsieur Votre tres humble et tres obeissant serviteur, DE PUISAYE

RC (MoSHi); at foot of text: "Mon adresse est. À Mr. de Puisaye encien Cpne. de Cavallerie à Beaufossé proche le Mêle sur Sarte en normandie au Mêle sur sarte"; endorsed. Recorded in SJL as received 7 Feb. 1787.

To John Stockdale

SIR   Paris Feb. 1. 1787.

You have two or three times proposed to me the printing my Notes on Virginia. I never did intend to have them made public, because they are little interesting to the rest of the world. But as a translation of them is coming out, I have concluded to let the original appear also. I have therefore corrected a copy, and made some additions. I have moreover had a map engraved, which is worth more than the book. If you chuse to print the work I will send you the corrected copy, and when it shall be nearly printed I will send the plate of the map. I would not chuse that it should be put under a patent, nor that there should be a tittle altered, added, nor omitted. It would be necessary to have a small half sheet map engraved of the country of Virginia as when first discovered. This map is only to be found in Smith's history of Virginia, a thin folio, now very rare.   I was not able to find that work here, but surely it can be found in London. An exact copy of the map is all that would be wanting. I leave this place about the 11th. or 12th. Be so good as to let me know whether you chuse to print

this work under the conditions before named. If I receive your answer in the affirmative before I set out, I will send you immediately the copy. It is an octavo of 391. pages. The American Atlas is come safe to hand. I am Sir your very humble servt.,
TH: JEFFERSON

P.S. It is not necessary to observe that as I have been at the expence of engraving the large map, I should expect to be paid for those you should have occasion for, a shilling a peice.

PrC (DLC); endorsed.

To the Commissioners of the Treasury

GENTLEMEN   Paris Feb. 1, 1787.

Colo. Franks, who acted as Secretary to Mr. Barclay on his mission to Marocco, having occasion for money for his journey, I furnished him with fifty pounds sterling by draught on the fund appropriated to those purposes, for which I now inclose you his receipt. Mr. Barclay settled his account to the time of his being at Madrid on his return, of which, I presume, one or both those gentlemen will render you account.

I have the honour to be with sentiments of the most perfect esteem & respect Gentlemen your most obedient & most humble servant,
TH: JEFFERSON

PrC (DLC). Enclosure not found.

To Mary Barclay

Paris Feb. 2. 1787.

You could not have obliged me more, my dear Madam, than by the friendly application you have made. The thousand livres shall be delivered into the hands of any person you will be so good as to direct to call for them; or to any person you please in Paris at a moment's warning. My last letter from Mr. Barclay was dated Alicant Jan. 6. He was well, and was to set out in two days for Madrid, from whence he had some expectations of going to Corunna. I have the honour to be with very sincere esteem & respect Dr. Madam your most obedt. humble servt.,
TH: JEFFERSON

PrC (MHi). Mrs. Barclay's letter to which this was a reply has not been found; see Mrs. Barclay to TJ, 6 Feb. 1787.
The FRIENDLY APPLICATION, if in writing, has not been found.

From C. W. F. Dumas

The Hague, 2 Feb. 1787. Is "toujours en peine de 3 choses": the healing of TJ's hand; the fate of a letter he sent some time ago through Du Muy for Lafayette; and the fate of two letters, especially the second, that he wrote to TJ and entrusted to Ambassador Brantzen. He writes at the Hôtel de France, "un moment avant que Mr. l'Ambr. ferme son paquet et expédie Son Courier."

RC (DLC); 2 p.; in French; endorsed. Recorded in SJL as received 9 Feb. 1787. The postscript to TJ's letter of 9 Feb. in reply to this suggests that, though not indicated in the text of the present letter, Dumas had accompanied this with certain papers for America; since TJ was Dumas' usual medium for dispatching his communications to Jay and Congress, it is probable that at least one enclosure was Dumas' letter to Jay of 26 Jan. 1787 (brief extract in Dumas Letter Book, Rijksarchief, The Hague; photostat in DLC).

The letter for LAFAYETTE was one of 8 Dec. 1786; the letter of 5 Jan. 1787 to TJ was entrusted to BRANTZEN; possibly the second letter referred to was that of 23 Jan. 1787.

From Mademoiselle de Lausanne

Paris, 2 Feb. 1787. As a token of appreciation of services "your lordship has rendered us," she sends TJ a letter from Eliza Livingston which she received in reply to the letter TJ forwarded for her; asks to have it returned. In executing a work she has undertaken at the suggestion of her friends, she needs a "collection of journals and strange gazettes"; has no way to procure those from America; asks TJ to lend them to her as they come out, as well as other "works which it produces whatever they may be, but the mathematics and marine"; would send for them at the beginning of every month; anything entrusted to her would be returned and the "news should be retaken, the all with the greatest exactness." Hopes TJ will grant her request because this would give her renewed opportunities of expressing her esteem for him.

RC (MHi); 4 p.; at foot of text: "Mlle de Lauzanne rue Ste avoye No 12"; endorsed; TJ used the final blank page for making arithmetical calculations. Not recorded in SJL. The enclosed letter from Eliza Livingston to Mlle. de Lausanne has not been identified.

From Alexander McCaul

[*Glasgow, 2 Feb. 1787.* Recorded in SJL as received 14 Feb. 1787. Not found, but see TJ to McCaul, 4 Jan. and 19 Feb. 1787.]

To François Soulés

SIR   Feb. 2.

I send you the papers M. de Crevecoeur sent to Normandy for. The account of the destruction of Wyoming begins page 40. You may rely certainly on the author's facts, and you will be easily able to separate from them his reflections. You can best judge whether an account of that interesting settlement, condensed into a few lines might not form an agreeable episode in your history, and prepare the mind more awfully for it's final catastrophe. I will thank you to return these papers as soon as you are done with them that I may restore them to the hands of M. de Crevecoeur before my departure which will now be in a few days. I have the honor to be Sir your most obedt. humble servt.,

TH: JEFFERSON

PrC (DLC); without indication of the year, but date is established from an entry in SJL for 2 Feb. 1787. Enclosure: St. John de Crèvecoeur's manuscript *Susquehanna*, a document of 48 pages, of which THE ACCOUNT . . . OF WYOMING BEGINS PAGE 40 (see TJ to Soulès, 19 Jan. 1787; Howard C. Rice, *Le Cultivateur Amèricain* [Paris, 1933], p. 154, 230).

From André Limozin

Le Havre, 3 Feb. 1787. Has had no letter from TJ since his own of 31 Jan.; encloses a letter from "Mr. Oster of Richmond by my ship Le Bailly de Suffren Captn. Cleret," which left Portmouth, Va., 4 Jan. 1787 with cargo of 315 hogsheads of tobacco "for Mr. Robert Morris's account. She had a fine Passage. . . . an exceeding good fine fast sailing Ship." Has received a letter from Barclay at Alicant asking his ideas "relating to what would be the most profitable to the American trade in France Knowing perfectly well that I have a great experience in business." Will forward his ideas to Barclay under cover to TJ as soon as his health improves.

RC (MHi); 4 p.; endorsed. Recorded in SJL as received 6 Feb. 1787. The enclosed letter from Martin Oster, French consul at Richmond, has not been found, but it was probably in reply to that from TJ to him of 19 Nov. 1786. No such letter is recorded in SJL as having been received with Limozin's, the only other on that date being Wythe's letter of 22 Dec. 1786. Despite this omission in SJL, the present letter probably covered letters from both Oster and Wythe, for TJ's acknowledgement on 8 Feb. 1787 refers to "your favor of the 3d. inst. and . . . the letters it covered."

To Christian Frederick Michaelis and Others

SIR   Feb. 4. 1787

The American Philosophical Society having heretofore done themselves the honour of naming you one of their members, the President has been pleased to transmit to me the Diploma made out in the forms used by the society, and authenticated by their seal. I do myself the honour of forwarding it to you and at the same time of assuring you of the sentiments of esteem & respect with which I have the honour to be Sir Your most obedient & most humble servant,   TH: JEFFERSON

RC (MWA); without indication of addressee; in William Short's hand, signed by TJ. PrC (DLC); dated "Paris Feb.4.1787"; at foot of text Short copied off the following list of names of persons to whom the letter was addressed, each with its appropriate certificate of membership in the American Philosophical Society:
"MM.
1. Christian Frederick Michaelis. M.D. of Gottenberg [1785]
2. Forbern Bergman. Prof. Math. Stockholm [1773]
3. Lavoisier. of the Acad. of Sciences. Paris [1775]
4. Abbé [Felice] Fontana—Director of the Great Duke's Cabinet of natural history [1783]
5. Tim. Baron de Kleingstedt. Councillor of State to the Empress of Russia [1773]
6. Abbé [Jean F.] de Rosier of the Acad. of Sciences at Lyons [1775]
7. Le Roux [1775]
8. Christian Magee. L.L.D. of Heidelberg
9. Gerbier. [Thibert Garbier] chez Messrs. les Abbés Chalut et Arnaud [1786]
10. Chevalier Grenchon [Granchain] of Paris [1786]
11. Gastellier. [René G. Gastelier] M.D. at Montgaris [Montargis] [1786]
12. Grival. [Guillaume Grivell] Paris [1786]
13. Doctor Noel [Nicolas Noël] Paris [1786]
14. Abbé [Jean L.] Soulavie. France [1786]
15. Peter Bergius M.D. Prof. Nat. hist. Stockholm [before 1769]
16. Christian Meyer. Astronomer to his Serene Highness the Elector Palatine [1777]
17. Signor Famitz of Naples [before 1769]
18. Major Frederick F.S. de Brahm, Triers [1784]
19. Charles Magnus Wrangel D.D. of Sweden [before 1769]
20. Duke de la Rochefoucault [1786]
21. Count de Buffon [before 1769]
22. M. de Condorcet [1775]
23. [Isaac] Jamineau, English Consul at Naples [before 1769]
24. Daubenton [1775]
25. Count Guichen. [1785]."

Entry in SJL reads: "American Phil. Society, new members of, here, circular."

TJ evidently received Vol. II of *Transactions of the American Philosophical Society* between 23 Dec. 1786 and the date of the present circular (see TJ to Franklin, 23 Oct. 1786). Franklin's letter of transmittal of 8 Oct. 1786 only mentions "several Diplomas for foreign gentlemen" without specifying the number. Vol. II of the *Transactions* lists only the names of those given above under numbers 1, 2, 3, 4, 5, 6, 7, 18, 24, and 25 (p. xxvii-xxviii); those whose names appear under numbers 8, 15, 17, 19, 21, and 23 are listed among foreign members in Vol. I (1770) of *Transactions* (p. xxii). The name of CHRISTIAN MAGEE appears as given in same, but this must have been a confusion with CHRISTIAN MEYER; the

[111]

name of the former does not appear in *Year Book 1948* of the American Philosophical Society wherein all former resident and foreign members are listed, but the name of the latter does (p. 404). The year in which each of the above was elected a member of the American Philosophical Society is supplied from the list in same, together with full names when given. For the confusion in respect to TJ's own certificate of membership, see Vol. 4: 544-6. See Lavoisier to TJ, 3 Mch. 1787, and Daubenton to TJ, 15 Feb. 1787.

From Henry Champion

SIR   L'Orient 5th. feby, 1787

Mr. Loreilhe being now at Bordeaux, your Letter of the 30th. past came to my hand, respecting the Plants sent you from S. Carolina care of Mr. Otto. They must certainly be Ship'd on board the Courier de L'Europe Captain Seonville which was the last Packet arriv'd from New York, but as that Vessel arriv'd at the Island of Groix twelve miles from hence, the Captain had his orders to proceed with all possible dispatch to Havre de Grace from whence the Packet is now to depart. He only sent on shore the Passengers, and Letters, consequently the roots have been left on board. I have enquir'd of the Commissary who has charge of that department, but he has seen nothing directed to your Excellency. I am convinced your Excellency will find them at Havre de Grace. I am Your Excellencys Most obt. & Most Huml. Serv.,

HY. CHAMPION

RC (MHi); endorsed: "Loreilhé." Recorded in SJL as received 11 Feb. from "Champion Henry."

From Degaseq, with Enclosure

MONSIEUR   rue des Prouvaires à Paris ce 5. fevrier 1787.

Vous aves vu sans doute Dans le Mercure de france No. 34, du 26 aout 1786 un extrait d'un ouvrage de Mr. Payne contre l'établissment du papier monoie dans vos états unis. Comme le redacteur du Mercure a prétendu que chaque ligne de cette ouvrage portoit avec elle un caractere dévideuse qu'il n'était pas permis de contester, j'ay cru devoir lui prouver le contraire. A raison de la publicité de cet extrait, et de la sensation qu'il a faite dans le public, j'ay demandé vainement que ma reponse fut inseree dans ce même journal. Comme cette matière interesse directement les Etats unis, j'ay l'honneur de vous l'adresser, parceque si vous n'y trouvés pas d'inconvenient, personne n'a plus de qualité que vous, pour exiger que cette pièce soit rendue publique.

[112]

5 FEBRUARY 1787

J'ay l'honneur d'etre avec le plus profond respect, Monsieur, Votre très humble et très Obéissant serviteur,

DEGASEQ

ancien Cer. au pnt. De guienne

RC (DLC). Not recorded in SJL.

ENCLOSURE

Dans ce moment interessant où toutes les nations de l'europe s'occupent de l'administration de leurs finances, nous avons cru necessaire de repondre à l'extrait d'un ouvrage de *Mr. Payne* contre l'etablissement du *papier monoie* dans les états unis, inseré dans le Mercure de france No. 34. du 26. aout 1786.

L'argent, dit M. Payne, d'après un bon allemand, *est de l'argent, et le papier du papier*. Mais qu'elle idée attache-t-il à cette expression? Si on considere l'argent et le papier comme une matière de convention il y a certainement une très grande différence de l'une à l'autre. Si on les considere comme un signe représentatif, et empreints du même sceau de l'autorité, ils auront une égale valeur, et produiront le même effet dans la circulation et dans les moyens.

Il ne s'agit que de determiner le vrai point de vue sous lequel on doit envisager le papier monoie. Si son émission devenoit un abus, attendu la facilité de le fabriquer, l'etat ressembleroit alors parfaitement à l'alchimiste dont parle M. Payne, qui auroit trouvé la pierre philosophale, puisque cette grande decouverte auroit les mêmes inconvenients que l'abus du papier monoie, en raison de la profusion illimitée de l'or qui en seroit le resultat.

On ne présupposera pas qu'un état, quelqu'il soit, établisse sans cause une nouvelle propriété factice telle que le papier monoie, où tel autre engagement. Il faut de necessité absolue que ce soit, où pour se liberer d'une dette deja contractée, et dont la circulation des effets représentatifs le generoit, où pour suppléer à la rareté des especes courantes, et faciliter par cette création d'un numeraire fictif les moyens d'échanges pour toutes especes de productions.

Or, dans ces deux cas, on est bien éloigné de voir les suites funestes qu'a prétendu demontrer M. Payne dans la création du papier.

Le papier monoie est un engagement d'etat représentant une somme plus où moins considerable d'especes courantes, pour avoir cours *comme elles*, sans *avoir besoin d'echanges en especes sonantes dans l'achat des productions, si ce n'est pour le plus où le moins de leur valeur au-dessus de celle dudit papier*.

L'etat qui fait la mise dehors d'un tel papier repond de sa valeur comme de tout autre engagement. Il n'y a de difference du prémier au dernier qu'en ce que l'un ne produit point d'interet dans l'echange où dans l'agiotage, et que l'autre au contraire éprouve tous ces inconvenients.

Ce papier monoie est donc comme tout autre papier, *où est écrite une obligation d'une valeur quelconque de la part du gouvernement qui l'a contracté, et signé*.

[113]

5 FEBRUARY 1787

C'est de plus *une promesse de payement en especes*, et il équivaut dans tous les cas à une semblable promesse, puisqu'on acquiert avec ledit papier tout ce qu'on peut acquérir avec le numeraire qu'il représente. Certainement M. Payne lui-même ne contesteroit pas que le gouvernement qui le donne n'est pas en état de le paier, où ne veut pas le paier; et alors il vaut donc invinciblement la somme pour laquelle il est donné.

M. Payne auroit raison dans son sisteme de proscription du papier chés un gouvernement insolvable, mais peut-il et oseroit-il dire que le sien seroit dans cette hipothèse? Il n'y a de gouvernement insolvable que celui qui veut et qui peut l'être impunement par sa constitution, tel qu'un état despote. C'est là seulement qu'on peut dire avec vérité qu'il est une grande difference *entre des papiers pris et donnés comme engagements de particuliers à particuliers, et des papiers mis en circulation par cet état comme argent.*

Mais, ches un peuple où toutes les volontés sont libres, et concourent au même but, celui du bonheur public, il est impossible que l'engagement d'un particulier, quel qu'il soit, vaille celui de l'état, en quelque forme qu'il puisse être conçu. Il est incroyable qu'on ait pu avancer une telle proposition.

Il est évident que quand un état est oberé, sa liberation doit necessairement sortir du travail et de l'industrie de son peuple. Le meilleur moyen pour y parvenir sera donc celui qui augmentera ce travail et cette industrie.

Or, une masse considerable de propriétés factices telles que sont les engagements publics portant interet, devient necessairement une surcharge sur le sol et sur l'industrie. C'est par consequent une surcharge sur le produit annuel de l'un et de l'autre. Cette masse est donc infiniment nuisible et la plus contraire au travail du peuple.

Diminuer cette propriété, changer les engagements d'état qui la constitue, en créer d'autres qui sans faire aucun tort, ni aucunes injustices, retranchent où détruisent en entier cette masse de propriété factice, c'est evidement augmenter le travail du peuple et dans la culture et dans l'industrie. C'est par consequent travailler doublement à liberer l'état.

Tels sont dans le prémier cas les effets que produit le papier monoie, car supposons que cet état doive trente milions pour lesquels ses engagements circulent dans le public, et necessitent une surcharge annuelle de taxe de quinze cent mille livres pour les interets. Supposons encore qu'on crée 30. milions de papier monoie pour solder lesdits effets, et que l'employ en soit exactement appliqué à la solde susdite.

Nous disons qu'alors l'état se met évidement au pair de sa depense, et qu'il gagne de plus le 1,500,000^{lt} d'interets annuels qu'il avoit à paier. Nous disons, que si cet état est assés sage pour continuer la même taxe pendant quinze ans, il est évident qu'il peut racheter chaque année pour 1,500,000^{lt} desdits papiers et les bruler. Il est de plus en plus évident qu'à la fin d'un tel delai *fixe*, il se trouvera et liberé de l'ancienne dette de 30. milions et, ce qui est plus avantageux encore, liberé même du moyen avec lequel il l'avoit acquité

Ce dernier point est inestimable. En ce qu'il fait de l'emission du *papier monoie* un veritable *emprunt viager* de l'état à l'état lui-même, sans aucun interet, sans aucune surcharge ni pour le peuple ni pour le gouvernement, et sans aucune crainte pour *sa perpetuité*, puisque dans un état sage et libre, on en verra évidemment l'extinction *annuelle et successive* et que la volonté d'un despote ne la perpetuera pas à son gré. Cette circonstance est impossible dans un tel établissement, parceque *l'extinction* dudit papier une fois legalement établie, comme *son admission*, il suffiroit du prémier manquement à la loi pour lui ravir irrevocablement la confiance publique.

On ne peut se dissimuler que quand une nation est parvenue à un certain periode d'accablement par la multiplicité de ses alienations en propriétés factices il faut où qu'on ait recours à de moyens violents et douloureux, tels que la reduction des dites propriétés, où si ces moyens qui n'affectent qu'une partie des individus de l'état, sont injustes, il faut bien prendre celui de l'augmentation des taxes qui les affectent tous; où enfin, si personne ne veut être victime dans ces circonstances, il faut user forcement de resourses extraordinaires pour retablir le parfait équilibre et rendre à la nation toute sa force, et tôute sa vigueur.

Dans le second cas où le papier monoie seroit établi seulement pour suppléer à la rareté des especes, il rempliroit egalement le but proposé, parce qu'il tiendroit lieu du numeraire réel pendant le temps de son admission. Qu'est-ce qui pouroit empecher en effet l'engagement d'un état comme celui d'un particulier d'avoir cours dans l'échange? Ce ne pouroit être que l'insolvabilité réelle du debiteur, où la possibilité préjugée certaine de son insolvabilité. Or on demande si dans un état sage et libre, et qui n'a point de dette, comme nous le supposons, il peut y avoir un doute quelconque sur sa solvabilité? Et si la certitude existe, qu'est-ce qui peut empecher le cours public de ce numeraire fictif?

Ce n'est point de l'or et de l'argent, dira-t-on, ce n'est que du *papier*. Et la valeur d'un papier quelconque *n'est pas en lui-même, mais seulement dans l'obligation où est la personne qui l'a contracté de le paier*. Mais l'état qui l'a contracté et signé, ne vaut-il pas un particulier? Oseroit-on repondre negativement? Est-ce parce que le dit papier ne se paie pas journellement en argent? Mais, s'il est paié en équivalent, en objets réels dont l'argent n'est que la representation, qu'importe, puisque l'effet est absolument le même. Peut-on dire alors que le papier circulant de cette manière *n'arrive pas sans cesse et à la place et à la personne où et de laquelle l'argent doit être tiré*, puisqu'étant ainsi sagement constitué, il arrive constament à sa représentation.

Nous scavons qu'un peuple dans l'état des choses ne peut pas se passer d'or. C'est aujourdhuy chés les nations diverses un bien où un mal necessaire pour la facilité des échanges. Mais nous soutenons affirmativement qu'il ne peut jamais être qu'un objet de convention entre les hommes, que l'argent comme le papier monoie, où tel autre signe représentatif des objets réels, ne sera jamais qu'une propriété factice et non une propriété réelle, qui n'existe que dans le sol, et dans les bras de ces mêmes hommes.

Nous avons évidement demontré que le papier monoie peut supléer dans un état ainsi constitué à la rareté des especes pendant un temps limité, et qu'il doit avoir cours comme elles, et avec une egale confiance. Nous ajoutons encore que l'émission d'un tel papier où de tel autre numeraire fictif ne peut concourir en rien à repousser les metaux d'un état quelconque.

Que l'or soit où ne soit pas une des productions du sol, il n'en est pas moins vrai qu'une nation ne le conserve où ne le fait venir chés elle que par l'abondance où la disette des autres productions du sol et de l'industrie necessaires à l'existence, qu'elle se procure dans son sol même, et par les bras de ses individus. Quand une nation vend plus aux autres nations qu'elle n'achete d'elles, alors, comme les metaux servent à acquiter la Balance des échanges respectifs, il faut necessairement, si cette balance lui est favorable qu'on lui apporte chés elle les metaux destinés à la représenter.

De la il résulte évidement que si les états unis où l'un d'eux vendent aux autres plus qu'ils n'achètent, les métaux viendront forcement chés eux, et que, quoiqu'on fasse il est impossible qu'ils en sortent.

On conclut enfin que quoique le papier monoie ainsi établi ait et doive avoir pendant sa durée une valeur egale au numeraire réel qu'il représente, il n'en est pas moins vrai qu'il a besoin de loix coactives pour lui donner cours, et en empecher les abus. N'en a-t-il pas fallu pour l'or et l'argent dans leur introduction primitive, et n'en faut-il pas encore?

Ainsi donc il ne s'ensuit pas de ce que le *papier monoie* établi comme nous l'avons dit, ait et doive avoir réellement la même valeur que les metaux, qu'il n'ait aussi besoin de loix coactives pour avoir cours chés tous les individus quelconques. Mais il s'ensuit très demonstrativement qu'il n'a nullement besoin de ces loix pour les hommes sages et bons patriotes. Et c'est là ce qui nous fait conclure en dernier analise que l'émission du papier monoie pour supléer à la rareté des especes, renferme tous les avantages possibles sans inconvenients.

D'après tout ce que nous venons de dire, nous ne concevons pas comment le rédacteur du Mercure a pu trouver le caractere d'evidence dans chacune des lignes de l'ouvrage de M. Payne contre l'introduction du papier monoie dans les états unis de l'amerique.

MS (DLC: TJ Papers, 24: 4095-8); in Degaseq's hand.

From Anthony Garvey

Sir   Roüen 5 February 1787

I have Received the Honour of your Excellency's letter with the acquit which is in rule.

There is a regular Dilly that Gos from hence to Havre (Saturday Excepted). It returns likewise every day (Saturday Excepted). The fare is 16^{lt} 4 for a Place.

M. Boylstons Claim for return of the duty Paid on his oil, is the more favourable, that with the neat proceeds of his said cargo, he bought Sugars at Havre which he sent to Boston, the first opperation of the Kind that ever was practised.

5 FEBRUARY 1787

May I beg the favour of your Excellency to order the Inclosed to be forwarded to M. Barclay by first occasion. I have the honour to be Your Excellencys most humble & most obedient Servant,

ANTHY. GARVEY

RC (MHi); endorsed: Garvey, the Diligence to Havre." Enclosures: (1) A completed form that had been set by TJ and probably enclosed in his to Garvey of 29 Jan. 1787, the hours of arrival and departure being in Garvey's hand and the remainder of the text in TJ's, reading as follows: "Le moment du depart de Paris a 11 heures preciser du Matin. Le moment de l'arrivée à Rouen a 8 heures du Matin. Le moment du depart de Rouen 10 heures du Soir. Le moment de l'arrivée à Havre a Midy" (MHi). (2) The enclosure for Barclay has not been identified.

From Madame de Tott

[Early Feb. 1787?]

Il est très vrai, Monsieur, que depuis que j'ai eu l'honneur de vous voir, J'ai été plusieurs Jours Sans Souffrir. Il y en a eu quelqu'uns ou J'ai eu des ressentiments assez Vifs de mes premieres souffrances, particulièrement hier. Je n'en pouvois pas deviner la cause mais Je crois que L'expédition pour L'amérique m'est une suffisante. Vous êtes très occupé, Vos prieres sont nécéssairement moins ferventes pendant quelques Jours. Voilà l'explication de mes souffrances d'hier, qu'en dites Vous Monsieur? Cette Solution ne Vous parroit-elle pas probante? Quand a La question géographique J'espere y Répondre d'une manière assez *Satisfaisante* quand J'aurai Le bonheur de Vous Voir. Permettez moi en attendant de Vous Remercier de Votre charmante petite Lettre, de Vous dire combien Je suis touchée de L'interêt que Vous Voulez bien prendre a ma santé et de Vous Supplier de Venir Recevoir Le plutôt possible L'assurance de tous Les Sentiments de Reconnoissance, d'attachement et d'admiration avec Lesquels Je serai toute ma Vie Votre très humble et très Obeïssante Servante,

LA CTESSE. DE TOTT

RC (MHi); endorsed by TJ: "de Tott. Mde. la Comtesse"; undated, but since Madame de Tott was ill in January 1787 and since TJ was obliged to write a great many letters for America early in February (which may account for the allusion to "L'expédition pour L'amérique" that kept TJ very occupied), it is possible that this was written about that time (see Madame de Tessé to TJ, 21 and 23 Jan. 1787).

To John Adams

Dear Sir   Paris Feb. 6. 1787.

Your favors by Colo. Franks have come safely to hand. He will set out from hence the 8th. inst. the packet being to sail from Havre the 10th. I inclose you the copy of a letter lately received from Mr. Barclay, and of the paper it inclosed. In a letter from Mr. Carmichael is a postscript dated Dec. 25. in the following words 'since writing the preceding, the Portuguese Ambassador has pressed me to hint that the present moment is favorable to push our treaty with his court.' In the body of the letter he sais 'the Ct. d'Expilly has promised me to continue his attention to our prisoners during his stay at Algiers, and I have also engaged the Consul of Spain who remains there on his return to take care of them. Advances have been made for their support which ought to be refunded.' I suppose that these advances have been made by order of Mr. Lamb, and that, his powers being at an end, it will be incumbent on us to take measures on that subject. The Count de Vergennes is extremely ill. His disease is gouty. We have for some days had hopes it would fix itself decidedly in the foot. It shews itself there at times, as also in the shoulder, the stomach &c. Monsr. de Calonnes is likewise ill; but his complaints are of a rheumatic kind which he has often had before. The illness of these two ministers has occasioned the postponement of the Assembly of the Notables to the 14th. and probably will yet postpone it. Nothing is yet known of the objects of that meeting. I send you a pamphlet giving a summary account of all the meetings of a general nature which have taken place heretofore. The treaty between Russia and this country is certainly concluded; but it's contents are not yet known. I shall set out for the waters of Aix on the 15th. instant, so that I am unable to say when and whence I shall have the honour of addressing you again. But I take measures for the conveying to me on my road all letters, so that should any thing extraordinary require it, I can at all times be recalled to Paris in a fortnight. I shall hope to hear from you at times as if I were in Paris. I thank you much for the valuable present of your book. The subject of it is interesting and I am sure it is well treated. I shall take it on my journey that I may have time to study it. You told me once you had had thoughts of writing on the subject of hereditary aristocracy. I wish you would carry it into execution. It would make a proper sequel to the present work. I wish

6 FEBRUARY 1787

you all possible happiness and have the honour to be with sentiments of sincere esteem & affection, Dear Sir, your most obedient & most humble servant, TH: JEFFERSON

RC (MHi: AMT); endorsed. PrC (DLC). Enclosure: Barclay to Commissioners, 6 Jan. 1786.

Adams' FAVORS BY COLO. FRANKS evidently included Adams to TJ, 25 Jan. 1787; draft of Commissioners to Barclay, 25 Jan. 1787 (missing); draft of Commissioners to Taher Fennish, 27 Jan. 1787; and draft of Commissioners to Jay, 27 Jan. 1787. The first of these was received on 2 Feb. 1787, and presumably the others arrived at the same time. Franks also evidently brought a copy of Adams' VALUABLE . . . BOOK, *Defence of the Constitutions of the United States* (London, 1787).

From Mary Barclay

SIR   St. Germain-en-Laye 6 febry. 1787

I am infinitely obliged and thankfull for your friendly and ready compliance with the request in my last, and as I have not a proper person to send for the money have taken the liberty to draw on you at sight, should there be any thing improper in this mode, I beg you will attribute it to my ignorance in matters of this kind, and believe me to be with sincere respect and esteem Sir your most obedt. humble Servant,   M BARCLAY

RC (MHi); endorsed: "Barclay Mrs." Not recorded in SJL. Mrs. Barclay's letter containing the request has not been found, but see TJ to her, 2 Feb. 1787.

To William Drayton

SIR   Paris Feb. 6. 1787.

I had the honour of addressing you on the 6th. of May last by Mr. McQuin, and of sending you by the same gentleman some seed of the Sulla, or Spanish St. foin. I hope it has succeeded, as some seeds of the same parcel which I sowed in my garden have vegetated well and gave me an opportunity of seeing that it is a most luxuriant grass. It's success in the climate of Malta seems to ensure it with you. The present serves to inform you that I send with it, to the care of your delegates in Congress, some acorns of the Cork oak. I am told they must not be covered above two inches deep. Their being pierced by the worm will not affect their power of vegetating. I am just setting out on a journey to the South of France. Should any objects present themselves in the course of my journey which may promise to forward the views of the society, I shall with great pleasure avail you of them, and take every possible

[119]

occasion of assuring you of the sentiments of esteem & respect with which I have the honour to be Sir Your most obedt. & most humble servt.,
                Th: Jefferson

PrC (DLC); at foot of text: "Wm. Henry Drayton esq."; entry in SJL under this date also shows that the letter was addressed to "Drayton W.H." TJ erred in this: his letter of THE 6TH. OF MAY LAST had been correctly sent to William Drayton (1732-1790), chief justice of South Carolina and double first cousin of William Henry Drayton, who had died in 1779.

To John Banister

Dear Sir   Paris Feb. 7. 1787.

A former letter which I wrote to announce the arrival of your son in Paris in good health has failed to go by the occasion which was expected. He will have the happiness therefore of announcing that good news in person. I congratulate you on his character which is substantially good. He has never I think done an imprudent thing since he left you, unless we call by that name, as I believe we must, his having for the first time yeilded to the allurements of Paris and spent during his stay here a great deal more than you had proposed. He has been sincerely afflicted by it, and it is that which has made him adopt the sudden resolution of leaving the place and going home. Yet were he my son, I should be glad of it. He has bought lessons of which he will profit thro' life, and be able to profit his children and friends. They have done him no injury but to his purse. I think it will contribute more to his future good than the same money in the form of property. His mind will be oppressed till you relieve him by an explanation, which I beseech you to do in the first moment. The post which a parent may take most advantageous for his child is that of his bosom friend. I know your way of thinking too well to doubt your concurrence in this. I too have transgressed your instructions; but it was to relieve him from embarrasment, not to lead him into it. He has no suspicion that I write to you on this subject; but my duty to both required it. Present my friendship to Mrs. Bannister and accept assurances of it yourself from Dr. Sir your mo. obed. humble servt.,   Th: Jefferson

PrC (DLC); at foot of text: "Colo. Bannister."
For the loan that TJ advanced to young Banister to RELIEVE HIM FROM EMBARRASMENT, see the letter following and, for a final statement of the account, TJ to Eppes, 11 Mch. 1792, and its enclosure.

To John Banister, Jr., with Enclosure

Dear Sir   Paris Feb. 7. 1787.

I inclose you fifteen hundred livres being all the money I have in this moment. I must beg the favor of you to leave me your accounts to pay to the amount of your balance. My reason is this. Being to set out on my journey within a week, I shall then have occasion to draw money from my banker for the paiment of my own accounts, and would wish to make one draught of the whole. Nevertheless if it should make any odds with you, I will send to him for the balance of what you want, being desirous to accomodate you and to assure you of the esteem with which I am Dr. Sir Your sincere friend & servt.,   Th: Jefferson

P.S. I shall be at home till 8. o'clock to-night, and shall hope to see you either before that, or tomorrow morning. I do not think you can safely postpone your setting out longer than noon tomorrow. I do not say this with respect to yourself but to Colo. Franks whose failure in his passage would be too important to be risked.

ENCLOSURE

February 7. 1787.

Annona. Papaw
Andromeda arborea. Redbud
Azalea nudiflora. Wild honeysuckle.
Acer negundo. Ash leaved Maple
Cornus florida. Dogwood
Chionanthus virginica. Fringe tree.
Cupressus disticha. Cypress.
Crataegus tomentosa. Haw.
Diospyros virginiana. Persimmon.
Fraxinus Americana. Ash
Gleditsia triacanthos. Honey pod locust.
Juglans nigra. Black walnut
White walnut
Juniperus virginica. Red Cedar.
Kalmia. Green ivy.
*Liriodendron tulipifera. Poplar.
Liquidambar styraciflua. Sweet gum
Laurus Sassafras. Sassafras

Magnolia glauca. Swamp laurel.
Magnolia tripetala. Umbrella tree.
Prunus virginiana. Wild cherry.
Phytolacca decandra. Poke.
*Quercus phellos. Willow leaved oak.
Quercus virginiana. Live oak
Rhus. Sumach
Robinia pseudo-acacia. Locust.
*Bignonia sempervirens. Yellow jasmine
*Pyrus coronaria. Wild crab apple.
A dozen plants (not seeds) of each kind, and of each of those marked* two dozen.
Red birds
Opossums male & female } living
A pair of the largest bucks horns which can possibly be found. Two skins also, the one taken when the deer is red, the other

when he is blue, with the jaws & teeth & the feet left in the skin.

A pair of the largest elk horns. The skin would also be acceptable if it could be got.

Method of packing the plants.

Take the plants up by the roots, leaving good roots. Trim off all the boughs, and cut the stems to the length of your box. Near the tip end of every plant cut a number of notches which will serve as a label, giving the same number to all the plants of the same species. Where the plant is too small to be notched, notch a separate stick and tye it to the plant. Make a list on paper of the plants by their names and number of notches.

Take fresh moss just gathered, lay a layer of it at the bottom of the box 2. inches thick. Then put in a layer of plants, putting those of the same kind together and laying them side by side. Then put on them a layer of moss 1. inch thick, then a layer of plants and again of moss alternately, finishing with a layer of moss 2. inches thick, or more if more be necessary to fill the box. Large roots must be separately wrapped in moss.

These plants must come in some vessel bound to Havre or Honfleur and must be addressed to the care of Monsieur Limozin at Havre. It will be absolutely useless to send them to any other port. They should leave Virginia during the months of November and December. If they come sooner the heat of the season will destroy them: if later they will not arrive in time to be planted.

PrC (DLC); at foot of text: "Mr. Bannister." Recorded in SJL as addressed to "Bannister J. junr." Enclosure (PrC in DLC; at foot of first page: "Mr. Bannister"); although catalogued in DLC as if an enclosure in the preceding letter to Col. John Banister, the reference to "Mr. Bannister" at the foot of the first page of this list of plants indicates that TJ intended it for the son; also, it probably was not an actual enclosure but may have been handed to young Banister on the eve of his departure from Paris. In the PrC in DLC the list and the directions occupy two separate pages, but the original may have been on a single leaf.

To Anne Willing Bingham

Paris Feb. 7. 1787.

I know, Madam, that the twelvemonth is not yet expired; but it will be, nearly, before this will have the honour of being put into your hands. You are then engaged to tell me truly and honestly whether you do not find the tranquil pleasures of America preferable to the empty bustle of Paris. For to what does that bustle tend? At eleven o'clock it is day chez Madame. The curtains are drawn. Propped on bolsters and pillows, and her head scratched into a little order, the bulletins of the sick are read, and the billets of the well. She writes to some of her acquaintance and receives the

7 FEBRUARY 1787

visits of others. If the morning is not very thronged, she is able to get out and hobble round the cage of the Palais royal: but she must hobble quickly, for the Coeffeur's turn is come; and a tremendous turn it is! Happy, if he does not make her arrive when dinner is half over! The torpitude of digestion a little passed, she flutters half an hour thro' the streets by way of paying visits, and then to the Spectacles. These finished, another half hour is devoted to dodging in and out of the doors of her very sincere friends, and away to supper. After supper cards; and after cards bed, to rise at noon the next day, and to tread, like a mill-horse, the same trodden circle over again. Thus the days of life are consumed, one by one, without an object beyond the present moment: ever flying from the ennui of that, yet carrying it with us; eternally in pursuit of happiness which keeps eternally before us. If death or a bankruptcy happen to trip us out of the circle, it is matter for the buz of the evening, and is completely forgotten by the next morning.

In America, on the other hand, the society of your husband, the fond cares for the children, the arrangements of the house, the improvements of the grounds fill every moment with a healthy and an useful activity. Every exertion is encouraging, because to present amusement it joins the promise of some future good. The intervals of leisure are filled by the society of real friends, whose affections are not thinned to cob-web by being spread over a thousand objects.—This is the picture in the light it is presented to my mind; now let me have it in yours. If we do not concur this year, we shall the next: or if not then, in a year or two more. You see I am determined not to suppose myself mistaken. To let you see that Paris is not changed in it's pursuits since it was honoured with your presence, I send you it's monthly history. But this relating only to the embellishments of their persons I must add that those of the city go on well also. A new bridge, for example, is begun at the Place Louis Quinze; the old ones are clearing of the rubbish which encumbered them in the form of houses; new hospitals erecting; magnificent walls of inclosure and Custom houses at their entrance &c. &c. &c.—I know of no interesting change among those whom you honoured with your acquaintance, unless Monsr. de Saint James was of that number. His bankruptcy and taking asylum in the Bastile have furnished matter of astonishment. His garden at the Pont de Neuilly, where, on seventeen acres of ground he had laid out fifty thousand Louis, will probably sell for somewhat less money.—The workmen of Paris are making rapid strides towards English perfection. Would you believe that in the course

7 FEBRUARY 1787

of the last two years they have learnt even to surpass their London rivals in some articles? Commission me to have you a Phaeton made, and if it is not as much handsomer than a London one, as that is than a Fiacre, send it back to me. Shall I fill the box with caps, bonnets &c? not of my own chusing, but—I was going to say of Mademoiselle Bertin's, forgetting for the moment that she too is bankrupt. They shall be chosen then by whom you please; or, if you are altogether non plus-ed by her eclipse, we will call an assembleé des Notables to help you out of the difficulty, as is now the fashion. In short, honour me with your commands of any kind, and they shall be faithfully executed. The packets, now established from Havre to New York, furnish good opportunities of sending whatever you wish.

I shall end where I began, like a Paris day, reminding you of your engagement to write me a letter of respectable length, an engagement the more precious to me as it has furnished me the occasion, after presenting my respects to Mr. Bingham, of assuring you of the sincerity of those sentiments of esteem & respect with which I have the honour to be, dear Madam, your most obedient & most humble servt.,　　　　　　　　　　　　Th: Jefferson

PrC (DLC). The enclosed "monthly history" has not been identified, but it was evidently a journal devoted to fashions (see Mrs. Bingham to TJ, 1 June 1787).
For another and contrasting opinion by TJ of MR. BINGHAM and his beautiful wife, see TJ to Madison, 30 Jan. 1787.

To the Governor of Virginia

Paris Feb. 7. 1787.

I have the honour of inclosing to your Excellency a report of the proceedings on the inauguration of the bust of the Marquis de la Fayette in this city. This has been attended with a considerable, but a necessary delay. The principle that the King is the sole fountain of honour in this country, opposed a barrier to our desires which threatened to be insurmountable. No instance of a similar proposition from a foreign power had occurred in their history. The admitting it in this case is a singular proof of the king's friendly dispositions towards the States of America, and of his personal esteem for the character of the Marquis de la Fayette.

I take this the earliest occasion of congratulating my country on your Excellency's appointment to the chair of government, and of assuring you with great sincerity of those sentiments of perfect

[124]

8 FEBRUARY 1787

esteem & respect with which I have the honour to be your Excellency's most obedient and most humble servant,

TH: JEFFERSON

RC (Vi); at foot of text: "H.E. Governor Randolph." PrC (DLC). Enclosure: Louis Le Pelletier to TJ, 1 Feb. 1787, and its enclosure, both of which were enclosed unsealed in TJ to Madison, this date. See also Short to Randolph, 21 Mch. 1787.

To James Madison

DEAR SIR   Paris Feb. 7. 1787.

I leave the inclosed open for your perusal and that of your Collegues and others to whom you may chuse to shew it; only taking care that neither copies nor extracts be taken. Be so good, when you are done with it, as to stick a wafer in it and forward it to the Governor.

I am with sincere esteem Dr. Sir your friend & servt.,

TH: JEFFERSON

P.S. I do not know whether you are acquainted with young Bannister who goes by the packet. He is of good understanding and of infinite worth. I have letters and papers to the 15th. of Decemb. yet neither these nor those of any person I can meet with inform us who is President of Congress.

RC (DLC: Madison Papers); without indication of addressee; endorsed. Not recorded in SJL. Enclosure: TJ to governor of Virginia, 7 Feb. 1787, and its enclosures (see note there).

To David S. Franks

DEAR SIR   Paris Feb. 8. 1787. 8 o'clock P.M.

I discover that by mistake you have among the papers some that are not destined for America. I recollect
1. a letter intended for a jo[int] one from Mr. Adams and myself to Mr. Barclay
2. another intended to be joint to Fennish the Marocco minister
3. one of the ratified treaties signed by Mr. Adams and myself. [One copy of the last?] should go to Congress, the [other copy is?] to be sent to Mr. Barclay. Perhaps there may be other papers but I do not recollect [them?]. I had put them between the red marocco cover [and the lid of the box, in]tending when I gave you the box to [take away these papers?]. Be so good as to search for

[125]

them and return them to me by post with any others which on view you may be sensible should have been retained. I have written by the Diligence which goes off [at eight to]night and promised the driver 6. livres if he delivers the letter to you before the packet sails. Be so good as to ask the favor of Mr. Limozin to pay it, and I will replace it with him. This goes by post. Health, happiness, and a good passage to you both, and am Dr. Sir your friend & servt.,   TH: JEFFERSON

PrC (MHi); MS faded, some words being supplied by the editors with reference to the first of the two letters written to Franks on this date.

Franks's acknowledgment of a letter of the 8th indicates that only one was received (Franks to TJ, 11 Feb. 1787), and only one is recorded in SJL. But two variant texts exist, the other (PrC in DLC) reading as follows: "I suspect that among the papers you took from hence were two letters, the one intended for a joint one from Mr. Adams and myself to Mr. Barclay, and the other intended to be joint likewise to the Marocco minister. I think you will find these stuffed in between the red marocco [cover] of the treaty box and the lid of the box. Pray search for them and return them to me by the first post. Perhaps there may be in the same place some other papers not intended for America: tho I recollect no others. Health, happiness, & a fair passage to you & am with esteem Dr. Sir your friend & servt, Th:Jefferson—P.S. Be so good as to write me a line of your safe arrival the moment you land in America." The text given above is probably that which Franks received, and the absence of a postscript to it may be attributed to the fact that TJ was writing in haste at the very moment the *diligence* was scheduled to depart.

To John Jay

SIR   Paris Feb. 8. 1787.

The packet being to sail the day after tomorrow, I have awaited the last possible moment of writing by her, in hopes I might be able to announce some favorable change in the situation of the Count de Vergennes. But none has occurred, and in the mean time he has become weaker by the continuance of his illness. Tho' not desperately ill, he is dangerously so. The Comptroller General M. de Calonnes has been very ill also, but he is getting well. These circumstances have occasioned the postponement of the assemblée des notables to the 14th. inst. and will probably occasion a further postponement. As I shall set out this day sennight for the waters of Aix, you will probably hear the issue of the Ct. de Vergenne's illness thro' some other channel before I shall have the honour of addressing you again. I may observe the same as to the final decision for the effranchisement of Honfleur[1] which is in a fair way of being speedily concluded. The exertions of Monsr. de Crevecoeur, and particularly his influence with the Duke d'Harcourt, the principal instrument in effecting it, have been of chief consequence in this matter.

I have the honour to be with the most perfect esteem and respect, Sir, your most obedient & most humble servant,

TH. JEFFERSON

PrC (DLC). Tr (DNA: PCC, No. 107, II).

[1] This word interlined in substitution for "Havre," deleted.

To André Limozin

SIR   Paris Feb. 8. 1787

I am honoured with your favor of the 3d. inst. and thank you for the letters it covered. This will be handed you by two American gentlemen Colo. Franks and Mr. Bannister, who propose to go passengers in the packet, and whom I beg leave to recommend to your notice. I shall set out this day sennight for the South of France and probably shall be absent from Paris two or three months. Mr. Short, my secretary will remain here, will always know where I shall be, and will forward to me all dispatches, so that the functions of my office will[1] be attended to as if I were here; with only a little more delay.

I have the honour to be with the highest esteem & respect Sir your most obedient & most humble servt.,   TH. JEFFERSON

PrC (DLC).

[1] This word interlined in substitution for "may," deleted.

To C. W. F. Dumas

SIR   Paris Feb. 9. 1787.

My last to you was dated Dec. 25. since which I have been honoured with your several favors of Dec. 29. Jan. 5. 9. and 23. I thought that your affairs could not be more interesting than they have been for a considerable time. Yet in the present moment they are become more so by the apparent withdrawing of so considerable a personage in the drama as the K. of P. To increase this interest another person, whose importance scarcely admits calculation, is in a situation which fills us with alarm. Nature is struggling to relieve him by a decided gout; she has my sincere prayers to aid her, as I am persuaded she has yours. I have letters and papers from America as late as the 15th. of December. The govern-

9 FEBRUARY 1787

ment of Massachusets had imprisoned three of the leaders of their insurgents. The insurgents being collected to the number of three or four hundred, had sent in their petition to their government praying another act of pardon for their leaders and themselves and on this condition offering to go every man home and conduct himself dutifully afterward. This is the latest intelligence.

I thank you for your attention to the question I had taken the liberty of proposing to you. I think with you that it would be adviseable to have our debt transferred to individuals of your country, provided it can be done without any loss to this country. There could and would be no objection to the guarantee remaining as you propose, and a postponement of the first paiments of capital would surely be a convenience to us. For tho' the resources of the U.S. are great and growing, and their dispositions good, yet their machine is new, and they have not got it to go well. It is the object of their general wish at present, and they are all in movement to set it in a good train, but their movements are necessarily slow. They will surely effect it in the end because all have the same end in view, the difficulty being only to get all the 13. states to agree on the same means. Divesting myself of every partiality, and speaking from that thorough knolege which I have of the country, their resources, and their principles, I had rather trust money in their hands than in that of any government on earth: because tho' for a while the paiments of the interest might be less regular, yet the final reimbursement of the capital would be more sure.

I set out next week for the South of France, to try whether some mineral waters in that quarter, much recommended, will restore the use of my hand. I shall be absent from Paris two or three months; but I take arrangements for the regular receipt of your favors as if I were here. It will be better however for you to put your letters to Mr. Jay under cover to Mr. Short who remains here and will forward them. I have thought it my duty to submit to Congress the proposition about the French debt, and may expect their answer in four months. I have the honour to be with sincere esteem & respect Sir your most obedient & most humble servt.,

TH. JEFFERSON

P.S. After writing the preceding your favor of the 2d. of February is put into my hand. It was 24. hours too late to go by the packet which sails from Havre tomorrow. The periods of the departure of the packets from Havre are every six weeks, to wit

Feb. 10. Mar. 25. May 10. June 25. Aug. 10. Sep. 25. Nov. 10. Dec. 25. I shall always send a courier to Havre a few days before. You may perhaps find it convenient to accomodate your future dispatches to these periods. As to the 1st. inquiry you kindly make in your letter relative to my hand, it is a little better and very little. The 2d. relative to the letter sent to the M. de la fayette his absence disables me from answering. The 3d. relative to your letters sent thro the channel of your Ambassador is answered by that part of the preceding letter which specifies the dates of those I have received. I beg leave to renew my assurances of esteem & respect.

TH: J.

PrC (DLC).

From John Jay

DR. SIR   New York 9th. February 1787.

Since my last to you of the 14th. December I have been honored with yours of the 26th. September last, which with the Papers that it enclosed have been laid before Congress, but neither on that nor any of your late Letters have any Orders as yet been made.

The annual Election produces much Delay in Affairs. From that Time to this scarcely any Thing has been done. It was not until last Week that, seven States being represented, a President was elected—the Choice fell on Major General St. Clair. They have much back Business to dispatch—several Reports on important Subjects from the different Departments, are to be considered and decided upon. A Form of Government so constructed has Inconveniences, which I think[1] will continue to operate against the public or national Interest until some Cause not easy to be predicted shall produce such a Modification of it, as that the legislative, judicial and executive Business of Government, may be consigned to three proper and distinct Departments.

The Struggles for and against the Impost remain but promise little. The States in general pay little Attention to Requisitions, and I fear that our Debts foreign and domestic will not soon be provided for in a Manner satisfactory to our Creditors. The Evils to be expected from such Delays are less difficult to be foreseen than obviated. Our Governments want Energy, and there is Reason to fear that too much has been expected from the Virtue and good Sense of the People.

You will receive herewith enclosed a Letter from Congress to

9 FEBRUARY 1787

his most Christian Majesty, with a Copy of it for your Information. It is in Answer to one received from him, and should have been of Earlier Date had Congress sooner convened. Be pleased to explain this Circumstance to the Minister.

The public Papers herewith sent contain all we at present know respecting the Troubles in Massachusetts. Whether they will soon be terminated, or what Events they may yet produce, is perfectly uncertain; and the more so as we are yet to ascertain, whether and how far they may be encouraged by our Neighbours.

I enclose a Copy of a Letter from Mr. Otto, formally contradicting the Report of an Exchange between France and Spain for the Floridas. That Report had excited Attention, and given Pleasure to Ante-Gallicans.

Our Apprehensions of an Indian War still continue, for we are at a Loss to determine, whether the present Continuance of Peace is to be ascribed to the Season, or their pacific Intentions.

We have not yet received the Morocco Treaty. As soon as it arrives I am persuaded that Congress will take the earliest Opportunity of making their Acknowledgments to the friendly Powers that promoted it. Mr. Lamb is still absent. He doubtless has received the Order of Congress directing his Return, either from you and Mr. Adams, or directly from me.

Congress has not yet given any Orders respecting further Negociations with the Barbary States, nor can I venture to say what their Sentiments will be on that Head. I am equally at a Loss to judge what they will direct respecting Treaties of Commerce with the Emperor and other European Powers. For my part I think and have recommended, that Commissions and Instructions should be sent you and Mr. Adams for those Purposes. In my Opinion such Treaties for short Terms might be advantageous. The Time is not yet come for us to expect the best. The Distance of that Period will however depend much on ourselves.

With very sincere Esteem and Regard, I am Dr. Sir your most obt. & hble servt, JOHN JAY

FC (DNA: PCC, No. 121). Dft (NK-Iselin). Recorded in SJL as received 6 Apr. 1787 at Marseilles. Enclosures: (1) Congress' congratulatory letter to Louis XVI in response to his of 9 July 1786 announcing the birth of a princess (text printed in JCC, XXXII, 15). (2) Louis Guillaume Otto to Jay, 21 Dec. 1786 (printed in Burnett, *Letters of Members*, VIII, No. 576, note 7).

The LETTER FROM MR. OTTO that Jay forwarded to TJ was read in Congress only on 2 Feb. 1787 after seven states had assembled and made it possible for that body to function, but two weeks earlier Jay had released it to the press, thereby causing Otto acute embarrassment in much the same way that Jay had distressed TJ by publishing the latter's dispatch of 27 May 1786. This action also provoked resentment in a Congress already embittered over his conduct of negotiations with Gardoqui. Otto had sent to Vergennes on 23 Apr. 1786 news of the report that Louisiana was to be exchanged for a French possession in the West Indies, and on 25 Aug. 1786 Vergennes replied that such an exchange had never been in question and that, if the report should arise again, Otto would "be pleased to deny it formally" (*Dipl. Corr., 1783-89*, I, 241; Dft of Vergennes' instructions is in Arch. Aff. Etr., Corr. Pol., E.-U., XXXII; transcripts in DLC, where the passage quoted reads: "et si l'on vous en parle encore, vous démentirez formellement"). Otto's letter to Jay appeared in the *New York Journal*, 18 Jan. and the *New York Packet*, 19 Jan. 1787. Otto, greatly disturbed, wrote at once to Vergennes explaining the background of the episode. He said that the false news of the exchange of Louisiana for a French possession in the Antilles (published in *Pa. Journ.*, 6 Jan. 1787 on "the most indisputable authorities from France and Spain"; Burnett, *Letters of Members*, VIII, No. 576, note 7) had scarcely appeared when two gazettes printed the same day a pretended treaty by which France was put in possession of the two Floridas on condition of closing the Mississippi to the Americans and of keeping there a considerable body of troops to prevent any invasion of Spanish territory (the *New York Packet* of 16 Jan. 1787 described the article concerning the Mississippi as being secret). Otto thought that it was easy to guess the authors and object of this fabrication, but reported that even the best informed Americans and those most attached to France were deceived by the apparently authentic form of the treaty; that he had vainly tried to assure members of Congress and principal citizens of New York that this "treaty" was entirely forged in England, but they replied that the news had been repeated so often and accompanied with so many plausible circumstances they could not doubt its authenticity. He had followed Vergennes' instructions of the previous August, but even this had not quieted the fears. At that point, he stated, Jay had requested a written extract of these instructions relative to an exchange of Louisiana; he had complied and Jay "n'a eu rien de plus presse que de le faire imprimer," whereupon the clamors "ont cesse sur le champ," the "treaty" was regarded as false on every hand, and praise for the wisdom and good policy of France took the place of the intemperate criticism and suspicion that had prevailed such a short time before. (Otto gave no indication to Vergennes that his letter had been written almost a month before Jay "rushed" it into print; that the first publication of the false treaty had taken place only two days before Otto's letter appeared; and that, at the time of his reporting to Vergennes, scarcely twenty-four hours had elapsed between Jay's hasty action and the effective quieting of clamors!) Otto further stated that, while Jay's publication of the extract had produced the most prompt and salutary effect, he himself was so troubled with the liberty Jay had taken that he had frankly expressed his displeasure and had told Jay that, because of this episode, he would be obliged in future to maintain "une reserve extrême a son égard." Jay justified himself by arguing that the popular ferment was so great as to require the weight of Vergennes' name to discredit the "fausses nouvelles que des Emissaires Anglois ne cessoient de repandre en Amerique"; that there would always be found in America a very considerable party favorably disposed toward England and engaged in trying to detach the United States from France; and that in order to make France's cession of Louisiana still more odious, this party had spread the rumor that Louis XVI, disappointed in his hope of full reimbursement for American loans, had decided to retake Louisiana, gain a foothold on the continent, and at his leisure take possession of Georgia and Carolina as compensation for his losses. Otto reported further that Congress very strongly disapproved of the precipitation of Jay, thinking that he had no right to publish any information addressed to him. "Mais," concluded Otto, "je n'en aurai pas moins desormais le plus grand soin de ne faire à ce Ministre que des communications verbales toutes les fois que Vous ne m'aures pas ordonné expressement de traiter avec lui par ecrit." Even so, Otto thought that Jay's grave apprehensions about the menace of English emissaries appeared well founded. He reported that he had noticed insinuations against France or prejudicial to the Franco-American alliance appearing with frequency in the gazettes after the arrival of the English consul, Sir John Temple; that at first he disregarded these publications, but as they became more and more insidious he decided to answer them moderately and without trusting anyone to translate his paragraphs; that Temple had seized the moment of publication of the Anglo-French treaty of commerce in order to play upon American fears of any rapprochement between those two nations, deploring the fate of the United States as the ultimate victim of this coalition; that these adroit lamentations came from Boston, Rhode Island, and Philadelphia, but that he could always recognize "la plume ou du moins la politique de M. Temple"; that Temple affected in public and in the presence of members of Congress to be most amicable toward Otto, while speaking of the important consequences of the treaty and inferring from it that the "systeme de l'Europe etoit tout-à-fait changé et que les forces reunies des deux nations les plus puissantes feroient desormais la loi à l'Univers entier" (Otto to Vergennes, 19 Jan. 1787; Arch. Aff. Etr., Corr. Pol., E.-U., Vol. XXXII; transcripts in DLC). When this troubled account with its unconvincing chronology arrived in Paris on 23 Mch. 1787, the astute minister to whom it was addressed was already dead.

By a strange coincidence Jay had allowed about a month to elapse before publishing either TJ's letter of 27 May 1786 or Otto's of 21 Dec. 1786 (see Vol. 9:588, note), and in both instances the delay and the fact of publication are alike unexplained. It may not be without significance that one instance brought acute embarrassment to the American minister in France and the other an equally acute embarrassment to the French chargé in America, a fact that perhaps places in proper perspective Jay's solicitous concern about the dangers to be expected from the "Emissaires Anglois."

[1] In Dft Jay first wrote, then deleted, "despair."

From John Banister, Jr.

[[*Le Havre, 10 Feb. 1787.* Recorded in SJL as received 14 Feb. 1787. Not found, but for its contents, see TJ to John Dunbar, 15 Dec. 1789.]]

Thomas Barclay to the American Commissioners

GENTLEMEN   Alicante 10th. February 1787.

Since I wrote to you from hence the 6th. of last month I have been much aflicted with the Rheumatism in my loins which confin'd me to my bed with pains great beyond Discription. I am now free of them, and shall leave this place in a few Days. Upon further reflection, I thought it best not to abandon the Idea of meeting Mr. Lamb, and therefore I wrote to him at Port Mahon that I wou'd go to Valencia and from thence to Barcelona, if he wou'd embark for this last place and meet me there. I informd him that my orders from Congress were to make a settlement with all the people in Europe who are employ'd or who have been employ'd in their Service, and that the Ministers at London and Paris wish that I may be able to comply with the Desire, which He com-

[132]

municated to them of having his account settled here, and I desir'd him to answer me by one letter address'd for me at Valencia and another at Barcelona. If his business or health will not permit him to see me, I will probably go to Madrid from Valencia or perhaps to France from Barcelona, but my movements will in some measure be govern'd by the necessity I shall find myself under of going to Coruña. The Gentlemen with whom my business lyes there have not by any means comply'd with my request. They acknowledge that there is some property belonging to the Prizes carried in by Captain Cunnyngham in their hands but they have applyed it towards the discharge of Expences incurred by the South Carolina Frigate commanded by Commodore Gillon, and with respect to the public Effects left by him, little can be known from what they write.

I fear nothing will ever be recover'd of any consequence from these effects or from this ballance. Yet having them pointed out as objects to be attended to, I am unwilling to leave anything undone on my part. In the mean time I shall communicate to the Secretary of foreign Affairs what I have collected on these subjects, and determine hereafter whether I shall pass to Coruña or not. I receiv'd a letter from Mr. Jefferson Dated the 26th.[1] of December, in which he says he will write to Mr. Adams to join him in desiring Mr. Lamb to settle his accounts, a Circumstance that proves very agreeable to me, However willing Mr. Lamb may be to do it without such a letter. I am Gentlemen with the greatest respect and Esteem, Your most obedt. Servant, THOS. BARCLAY

The Count D'Espilly &c. sail'd from this Bay about ten Days ago for Algier.

RC (DLC); in an unidentified hand, signed by Barclay; endorsed. Tr (DLC); in William Short's hand. Recorded in SJL as received 25 Feb. 1787. Enclosed in Barclay to TJ of this date, following; Barclay also wrote a separate letter to Adams on this date (MHi: AMT).

[1] Thus in RC and Tr; the correct date is 27 Dec.

From Thomas Barclay

DEAR SIR Alicante, 10th. Febry. 1787.

I had the pleasure of receiving your obliging Letter of the 27th. of December, and if my endeavours to serve our Country well have the flattering effects you suppose, I shall think my Journey to Morocco one of the happiest Incidents of my life. I am very glad to learn that you are recovering from the Injury which your wrist receiv'd, and hope it is possible we may meet on the road, but at present I am so little my own Master, and so much govern'd by circumstances that I have not even an Idea how I shall reach Paris; and on the Subject of my movements I can add nothing to the annex'd copy of what I have written to you and Mr. Adams by this Day's post, but that I shall endeavour to embark for America in April or May.—I will not now trouble you with any thing on the Subject of Messrs. Schweighauser's accounts but that the Sums which they charge were all certainly paid on the Alliance frigate at L'Orient, but at a time when the Court of France had taken the care of those advances on itself, and Mr. Schweighauser's Agent at L'Orient paid them not only in direct opposition to the orders of Dr. Franklin, but to those of Mr. Schweighauser himself and those orders were given before the Disbursements were paid. An Attachment was laid on the Effects of the United States at Nantes by which I believe a very heavy loss will fall on them, as I think a number of new Arms imported from Holland are perish'd through want of care. I consulted a Merchant at Nantes concerning the propriety of leaving the whole transactions to the determination of three or four disinterested men, and his answer was, "that if the dispute was between two Individuals there would be no doubt of its being determin'd against Mr. Schweighauser. But at present there is on one Side the Public of America, and on the other a private Individual whose fortune might be affected by the Determination. And this Consideration will have great weight with any Arbitrator we cou'd find." The papers relative to this affair are put up together in my office at St. Germains, and if any accident shou'd prevent me from having the pleasure of seeing you, it will be very necessary for you to take and examine them previous to your making a Settlement. They contain the Correspondence between Doctor Franklin and Mr. Schweighauser which was continued by Mr. Dobré after the Death of his Father in law. A List of the articles under attachment I left with you previous to my Departure.—Why has not Mr. Dobré as the Representative of Mr. Schweighauser push'd the affair to a legal Tryal if he can do it. Are Goods under attachment to lye for ever on hand, or untill they perish. I suppose I have applied at the least five or six times personally to the Marechal de Castries for an order that these arms (which were attachd before the Peace was compleated) shoud be deliver'd up to me that they might be transported to America, and I once demanded them at Nantes by a Lawyer in order to lay the foundation of a Suit for Damages. The lawyer went beyond his orders, and summon'd Mr. Dobré to a tryal before the Consular Court. With the summons the matter ended, neither Mr. Dobrè nor myself appear'd at that Court, and Monsieur De Castries said that as I had taken the affair out of the hands of the Council at Versailles by calling Mr. Dobrè to an account at Nantes, it woud not be proper in him to intermedle.

The Whole affair was Stated by me to Doctor Franklin and by him I believe to M. De Castries, but nothing was since done in it. I am of opinion that Mr. Dobrè shou'd long since have applied to the Court of France for the payment of these advances, and perhaps the letter which M. De Sartine wrote when the Alliance was lent by Dr. Franklin, might entitle him to recover his Demand. For M. De Sartine expressly promis'd, as Doctor Franklin inform'd me, that the Alliance Disbursments shou'd be paid by the Court of France, and I suppose the only objection that wou'd be made, must be, that as the Court had an Agent of their own at L'Orient, Mr. Schweighauser had no business to Intermeddle in the Supplies, especially after he was forbid. I meant only to have touch'd slightly on this matter but I have been drawn on. And if I do not see you, it may be all necessary. I shall trespass no longer on your time than to assure you of the truth wherewith I am Dr. Sir Your obedt. & oblig'd h'ble Servant,

THOS. BARCLAY

My Right Thumb is Very painful to me.

RC (DLC); in an unidentified hand, with the signature and postscript in Barclay's hand. Recorded in SJL as received 25 Feb. 1787. Enclosure: Barclay to Commissioners, this date.

From David S. Franks

DEAR SIR   Havre le 10th. Feb. 1787

We came here late last night, the roads and a broken Cariage having retarded us on the way longer than we had any reason to expect. On looking over my Papers this morning I found that the ratification of the Treaty together with the Letter to Taher Fennish to be sent to Morocco were in the Box. I therefore take the offer of Mr. Limosin to send them to you by the first safe hand. Permit me my dear Sir at parting to assure you that my Heart feels every Sentiment of gratitude and attachment to you for the many marks of Friendship which you have shewn me since my stay in France

11 FEBRUARY 1787

and that it will always be my endeavor to merit the good opinion I flatter myself you have of me. I pray you would be so kind as to present my best Respects to Mr. Short and believe me Dear Sir Your Excellys. most obt. obliged Sert., D: S. FRANKS

I believe we shall sail in a few hours—beg you woud forward the inclosed Letter.

I do myself the pleasure of inclosing you a Note which may by an accident serve to acquit my pecuniary obligations to you.

RC (DLC); endorsed. Recorded in SJL as received 14 Feb. Enclosures not found.

To Madame de Doradour

[*Paris, 11 Feb. 1787.* Recorded in SJL under this date. Not found.]

From Duler

Rouen, 11 Feb. 1787. He is grateful to TJ, for "few of my Country men equal in rank and fortune to you, would have thought it worth their while even of answering my letter." Since mid-January he has been employed by a mercantile establishment, with a salary of 4,000 livres a year. Asks if arrangement has been made for payment of interest on U.S. loan certificates; receipt of his share would benefit his family.

RC (DLC); 2 p.; at foot of text is Duler's address: "at Messrs. Elie Lefebvre freres Roüan"; endorsed. Recorded in SJL as received 3 May 1787 at Aix-en-Provence.

From David S. Franks

DEAR SIR   Havre de Grace 11th. Feby. 1787

Before I had received your Excellency's Letter of the 8th. I had made up the inclosed Packet and had given it to Mr. Limousin who had promised to send it by the first safe hand but as you desire the papers may be sent by Post I now forward them to you; I mean the Copy ratified of the Treaty with the letter to Taher Fennish. That intended for Mr. Barclay is not among my Papers. I have made the most exact search for it in Vain. I think it must be where the Box containing the Treaty used to stand, nigh the fire place in your Study.

[136]

11 FEBRUARY 1787

I do myself the Honor of sending you a rough draft of a Letter I had written to Mr. Jay; fortunately I have not now any occasion to send it, as by contrary winds the Packet is detained and we have got (with much difficulty) Permission to imbark. It appears that after the Ships Books are closed at 5 o'clock in the Evening of the 9th. of every Month, that no person can be admitted on board even tho' the Vessel should be detained a day or two by any accident; dispatches from any foreign Minister coming under the same Circumstances unless accompanied by an order from the Mar. de Castries would be rejected. The Letter I intended for Mr. Jay I should have been obliged to have smuggled into the Ship.

This Regulation must be productive of many disappointments and must serve to disgust our Countrymen from embarking on French Packet Boats. Capt. Daborelle informs me that at L'Orient no such rule was followed, that before the ship left the Coast any Passenger or Packet might be put on board. I thought it my Duty to inform Your Excellency of this Circumstance as it might have occasioned you some disappointment. If the French Ministry means to encourage this Communication between the two Countries they should remove every *natural* impediment in their power, and avoid throwing any Bars in the way. Bad Ships and but indifferent Seamen I reckon among the former and the regulation before mentioned and some others among the Latter.—The Ship we are now going to imbark in is by no means a bad one in point of strength but as to sailing I suppose that no Ship in France can be much more dull. —We have seen the Vessel built in America and which is to sail next month for the West Indies. It is hardly possible to form at a distance a proper Idea of the difference on Comparison. She is the most beautiful Vessel I ever saw.

Another Circumstance I beg leave to mention to Your Excellency and which will not a little contribute to throw her Countrymen further at a distance from sailing in French Packets. I mean the impertinence of the Director Mr. Ruellan, whose conduct to us under any other Circumstances would have procured him a proper Chastisement.—I am informed that he has also on several Occasions treated the American Crews in a very arbitrary and unbecoming manner and that many of them thereby have deserted from their Ship. He seems to enjoy an universal bad character.

We have repacked your Acorns as you directed and with great Care. I pray my best Compliments to Mr. Short and am Dear Sir with much Respect & Esteem Your Excellency's most obt. obliged Servant, DAVD. S. FRANKS

11 FEBRUARY 1787

In all probability we shall be detained some days more as the wind is contrary and very violent. Should be glad of a Line from Your Excellency.

RC (DLC); endorsed. Recorded in SJL as received 14 Feb. 1787. Enclosure (DLC): Draft of Franks to Jay, dated at Le Havre "10th Feby. 1787 12 oClock," stating that he had arrived at that port "last night at 11 oClock in Consequence of the advice and Permission of their Excellencies Mr. Adams and Mr. Jefferson charged with the Treaty made by Mr. Barclay with the Emperor of Morocco"; that he had applied to the master of the packet boat for passage and had been referred to the director of the packet boats, who in turn referred him to the intendant of the marine, who sent him back to the director where he was "peremptorily refused"; that he then communicated his credentials to both gentlemen and represented to them "the ill consequences which might arrise from the Treaty not going in this Paquet and with all the arguments that I could possibly make use of urged them to allow me to embark"; that Limozin had used his considerable influence "to as little purpose"; that as the packet would not leave until three in the afternoon, Franks thought it his duty to inform Jay of the reason for his "not embarking with the Treaty by this opportunity"; that he hoped Jay would be assured he had done everything he could to board the vessel "and that no detention of the Pacquet Boat was requested or desired by me, being in every point at 6 oClock this morning ready to embark"; and that he would write immediately to TJ and follow his orders.

The beautiful VESSEL BUILT IN AMERICA may have been Limozin's *Bailli de Suffren*, a remarkably fast ship that had just arrived from Virginia (see Limozin to TJ, 3 Feb. 1787).

To André Limozin

SIR   Paris Feb. 11. 1787

A friend in S. Carolina sent a letter and a box of plants for me to Mr. Otto, chargé des affaires of France at New York. The letter came by the packet the Courier de l'Europe, and was sent to me from l'Orient. I presume Mr. Otto sent the box of plants by the same conveiance but as the packet received orders on her arrival at l'Orient to repair immediately to Havre, she landed only her passengers and letters, and proceeded to Havre, where I suppose she is now and that she has there the box of plants for me. I leave Paris the 16th. instant, and it is very interesting for me to receive that box before I go. You will oblige me extremely if you can have it sought out in the instant of receiving this, and forwarded by the first Diligence to me here. I beg your pardon for troubling you so much: but these plants are precious, and have already come from S. Carolina to N. York, from N. York to Lorient, and from Lorient to Havre. There is danger therefore of their losing their vegetative power by delay, and my departure renders that delay still more interesting. I am with very much esteem & respect Sir your most obedient & most humble servt.   TH: JEFFERSON

PrC (MHi); endorsed.

To De Puisaye

Paris Feb. 11. 1787.

Les talents que vous possedez, Monsieur, doivent bien vous faire reussir en Amerique, comme partout ailleurs. Vous ne pouvez pas manquer d'y trouver à quoi les occuper. Vous avez bien prevu que la manque de la langue du païs vous fera eprouver des difficultés. Je vous assure qu'ils ne seront pas mediocres, et je vous parle de ma propre experience. Il faudra aussi vous preparer d'y rencontrer des usages bien differentes de celles de la France. Mais le nom François, qu'on estime infiniment en Amerique, sera votre passeport, et vous assurera un bon accueil partout. Il y a en tout tems des batimens particuliers qui partent de Bourdeaux, Nantes, Lorient et Havre pour les differents ports des etats unis et il y a aussi un paquetbote du roy qui partira toutes les six semaines de Havre pour la Nouvelle York. Les climats les plus resemblants à ceux auxquels vous etes accoutumé sont ceux de la Nouvelle York, la Nouvelle Jersey, La Pensylvanie et Delaware. Je vous souhaite Monsieur le succès le plus complet, et je vous assure des sentiments de respect et d'estime avec lesquels j'ai l'honneur d'etre Monsieur votre tres humble et tres obeissant serviteur,

TH: JEFFERSON

PrC (MoSHi); endorsed; at foot of text: "Monsr. de Puisaye, ancien Capitaine de Cavalerie à Beaufossé proche le Mêle sur Sarte [en Normandie, au] Mêle sur Sarte."

To Tarbé

Paris 11me. Fevr. 1787.

J'ai l'honneur, Monsieur, d'accuser la reception de la lettre que vous m'avez fait celui de m'ecrire, et de vous informer que votre billet d'echange a eté presenté et payé, et que le vin est arrivé á sa destination. Je vous prie de vouloir bien agreer mes sinceres remerciments pour toutes vos bontés et les assurances des sentiments d'estime et de respect avec lesquels j'ai l'honneur d'etre Monsieur votre tres humble et tres obeissant serviteur,

TH: JEFFERSON

PrC (MoSHi); endorsed. Tarbé's letter of 22 Jan. 1787, to which the present is a reply, is recorded in SJL as having been received on 27 Jan.; it has not been found.

To Vergennes

Sir   Paris Feb. 11. 1787.

My hand recovering very slowly from the effects of it's dislocation, I am advised by the Surgeons to try the waters of Aix in Provence. From thence I think it possible I may go as far as Nice. As circumstances might arise under which a passport might be useful, I take the liberty of troubling your Excellency for one. I propose to set out on Thursday next.

I would at the same time ask an enfranchisement for three barriques of common wine, and one of wine de liqueur, one of which is arrived at Paris, and the other three are soon expected there. They are for my own use.

With my sincere prayers for the speedy reestablishment of your health, I have the honor to assure you of those sentiments of perfect esteem & respect with which I am your Excellency's most obedient and most humble servant,   Th: Jefferson

PrC (MoSHi). This is accompanied by a faded PrC of a declaration, undated but possibly written a day or so after the present letter, in French and in TJ's hand, wherein TJ certified that he had requested of "M. le Comte de Vergennes un passeport pour la franchise d'une barrique de vin ordinaire contenant 250 bouteilles, arrivée à la douane de cette ville à notre adresse," and promised to transmit the passport to "Monsieur Richard" as soon as it was received.

To Charles Burney

Sir   Paris Feb. 12. 1787

I have been honoured with your favor of the 20th. of January, and am now to return you my sincere thanks for your very kind attention to the instrument I had desired. Your goodness has induced you to give yourself a great deal more trouble about it than I would have presumed to propose to you. I only meant to intrude on your time so far as to give a general instruction to the workmen. Besides the value of the thing therefore, it will have an additional one with me, of the nature of that which a good catholic affixes to the relick of a saint. As I shall set out within three or four days on a journey of two or three months, I shall propose to Colo. Smith, if the instrument is not already embarked, not to send it till about the 1st. of April when it will be less liable to be injured by bad weather.   A friend of mine in America (the same who improved the quilling of the harpsichord) writes me word he is succeeding in some improvements he had proposed for the Harmonica. However imperfect this instrument is for the general mass of musical compositions, yet for those of a certain character it is delicious.—We are all standing a tip-toe here to see what is to be done by the assembly of Notables. Nothing certain has yet transpired as to the objects to be proposed to them. The sickness of the ministers continues to retard the meeting. I have the honor to be

PrC (DLC); endorsed; at foot of text: "Dr. Burney"; lacks part of complimentary close and signature (on which, see Vol. 9: 217, note 1).

TJ's FRIEND . . . IN AMERICA was Francis Hopkinson; see Hopkinson to TJ, 28 June 1786.

To Borgnis Desbordes, Frères

GENTLEMEN   Paris Feb. 12. 1787.

Mr. Barclay the American Consul general for France being at present out of the kingdom, I have given orders to Mr. Grand, banker at Paris, to pay your draught for one hundred and eighty six livres advanced by you for the relief of the shipwrecked Americans. I thank you for your attention to these unfortunate people. It will rest with Mr. Barclay to give such future directions as he shall think proper for cases of this kind, which properly fall within the Consular department. A certainty that your kindness will meet his thanks, and that my interference in his absence will be approved, has engaged me to do it without any hesitation. I am just setting out on a journey of two or three months, but Mr. Grand, as I have before mentioned will pay your draught for the 186. livres whenever you shall be pleased to make it. I have the honour to be with sentiments of the most perfect esteem & respect Gentlemen your most obedient & most humble servant,

TH: JEFFERSON

RC (Carl G. Anthon, Iowa City, Ia., 1955); addressed; the following notation, in a French clerk's hand, appears in the margin of the page: "Du 24 fevrier 1787 Tiré une Lettre de Change a vüe de la somme de 186.^{lt} sur M. Grand pour solde des avances faittes aux nauffragés de La Lucie." PrC (DLC).

To Schweighauser & Dobrée

GENTLEMEN   Paris Feb. 12. 1787

I have received the order of Congress for the settlement of your accounts, of which order you were pleased to send me a copy

13 FEBRUARY 1787

in your favor of Jan. 27. I have reason to expect still an additional order on the same subject. This will probably arrive by the time I shall have compleated a journey into the South of France which my health obliges me to take. I purpose to return by the way of Bourdeaux and Nantes, at which last mentioned place I shall have the honour of seeing you, and of taking arrangements for the settlement with as little delay and trouble to you as possible. I have the honour to be Gentlemen your most obedient and most humble servant, TH: JEFFERSON

PrC (DLC). The letter from Schweighauser & Dobrée of 27 Jan. and its enclosure, of which the present is an acknowledgement, have not been found, but the letter was recorded in SJL as having been received on 31 Jan. 1787.

From C. W. F. Dumas

The Hague, 13 Feb. 1787. He will write on other subjects by the next regular mail; the present only serves to cover the enclosed.

RC (DLC); 1 p.; in French. Recorded in SJL as received 18 Feb. 1787. Enclosure (Dumas Letter Book, Rijksarchief, The Hague; photostats in DLC): Dumas to Jay, 13 Feb. 1787, reporting on political affairs in The Netherlands and advising that he had drawn on Willink & Van Staphorst for 2,500 florins to be charged against arrearages due him by Congress (text, together with several enclosures sent by Dumas to Jay, printed in *Dipl. Corr., 1783-89*, III, 549-64).

From André Limozin

Le Havre, 13 Feb. 1787. TJ's two letters of 8 and 11 Feb. have duly come to hand, the first by "Colo. Franks and Mr. Bannister, who are still waiting for a Fair wind to Sett of on board the Packet bound for New York." On receipt of the second he waited on "Mr. De Sionville Captn. of the Packet Le Courier de l'Europe," who remembered only a small box "containing Plants, which he delivered to Mr. Berard in Lorient, but unhappily he could not recollect by whom that Box was Shippd in New York, neither to whom it was directed for in France"; he could only recall that it contained plants. Since Short will be in Paris during TJ's absence, Limozin will continue to address his letters there.

RC (MHi); endorsed; bears a notation in TJ's hand which reads: "Berard administrateur de la compagnie des Indes rue Michautiere" (this notation was no doubt made in connection with TJ's letter to Bérard of 16 Feb. 1787; see also Bérard to TJ, 6 May 1786, and note there). Recorded in SJL as received 15 Feb. 1787.

[142]

From John Stockdale

Sir Piccadilly London 13th. Febry. 1787.

I duly received your favor's of Janry. 28th. and Febry. the 1st. and have sent the Articles agreable to your Order by this Nights Coach which I hope you'll receive in time. I sent part of the Books to America a long time since by the Gentleman you desir'd, but have not been able to get the remainder. I shall be happy to receive your corrected Copy, which shall be neatly and correctly Printed and Published, according to your desire, without one tittle of Alteration, tho' I know there is some bitter Pills relative to our Country. As I shall not be above three Weeks in Printing the Work, it may not be amiss to send the Plate at the same time, as they will take some time to Work; I think a shilling for the Use of the Plate, for working each Copy, a very great Price, and I am afraid much higher than the Work will bear, but this I leave entirely to your consideration. I intend to Print 500 Copies, which from the Merit of the Work and the advantage of your Name, I hope will be sold, but all things are uncertain. In short, all that I wish, is to be the Publisher of your work and to be indemnified, without paying any regard to the Profit. I am with great Respect Sir Your much obliged & very hble. Servt., JOHN STOCKDALE

RC (MHi); endorsed. Recorded in SJL as received 18 Feb. 1787.

To John Adams

DEAR SIR Paris Feb. 14. 1787

As I propose to write you on business by Mr. Cairnes who will set out in a few days for London, the object of the present letter is only to inform you that the Count de Vergennes died yesterday morning and that the Count de Montmorin is appointed his successor: and further to beg the favor of you to forward the inclosed by the first vessel from London. I set out on my journey on Sunday the 18th. I have the honour to be with sentiments of very sincere affection & respect Dear Sir Your most obedient & most humble servt., TH: JEFFERSON

RC (MHi: AMT); endorsed. PrC (DLC). Enclosure: TJ's first letter to Jay, this date.

To John Jay

Sir   Paris Feb. 14. 1787

In the letter of the 8th. instant which I had the honour of writing you, I informed you that the Count de Vergennes was dangerously ill. He died yesterday morning, and the Count de Montmorin is appointed his successor. Your personal knowlege of this gentleman renders it unnecessary for me to say any thing of him.

Mr. Morris, during his office, being authorized to have the medals and swords executed which had been ordered by Congress, he authorised Colo. Humphreys to take measures here for the execution. Colo. Humphreys did so; and the swords were finished in time for him to carry them. The medals not being finished, he desired me to attend to them. The workman who was to make that of Genl. Green, brought me yesterday, the medal in gold, twenty three in copper, and the dye. Mr. Short, during my absence, will avail himself of the first occasion which shall offer of forwarding the medals to you. I must beg leave through you to ask the pleasure of Congress as to the number they would chuse to have struck. Perhaps they might be willing to deposit one of each person in every college of the U.S. Perhaps they might chuse to give a series of them to each of the crowned heads of Europe, which would be an acceptable present to them. They will be pleased to decide. In the mean time I have sealed up the dye, and shall retain it till I am honoured with their orders as to this medal and the others also when they shall be finished. I have the honour to be with sentiments of the most perfect esteem & respect, Sir, your most obedt. & most humble servt.,   Th: Jefferson

PrC (DLC). Tr (DNA: PCC, No. 107, ii). Enclosed in TJ to John Adams, this date.

To John Jay

Sir   Paris Feb. 14. 1787

In the letter of the 8th. instant which I had the honour of writing you, I informed you of the illness of the Count de Vergennes. In one of the present date which I send by the way of London, I have notified to you his death which happened yesterday morning, and that the Count de Montmorin is appointed his successor, with whose character you are personally acquainted. As the winds have been contrary for the sailing of the Packet and this may possibly

14 FEBRUARY 1787

reach Havre by post in time to be put on board, I avail myself of that chance of conveying you the above information.

I have the honour to be with sentiments of the most perfect esteem & respect Sir Your most obedient & most humble servt.,

TH: JEFFERSON

PrC (DLC). Tr (DNA: PCC, No. 107, II). Enclosed in TJ to Limozin, this date.

From John Jay

DR. SIR New York 14th. February 1787

I understand that a Visit will be paid you by a Gentleman who is to be married to a Lady in this Town, and her Friends request the Favor of me to mention him in my Letters to you.

The Gentleman's Name is John Josh. Bauer a Lieutenant in his Imperial Majesty's Navy, and late Captain of the imperial East India Company's Ships Count de Cobensel and Count Belgioioso.

I have not the pleasure of being personally acquainted with this Gentleman, but from the Commissions he has had, and from some other Testimonials I have seen, I infer that he is a Gentleman of Merit. With great and sincere Esteem and Regard, I am &c.,

JOHN JAY

FC (DNA: PCC, No. 121). Recorded in SJL as received 6 Apr. 1787 at Marseilles.

To André Limozin

SIR Paris Feb. 14. 1787

The inclosed letter is to announce to Congress the death of the Count de Vergennes and appointment of the Count de Montmorin to succeed him. As the winds seem to have been contrary to the sailing of the packet boat, I send it by post and beg the favor of you to deliver it to Colo. Franks if he is not gone; and if he is, to send it by the first vessel. I have received duly the papers which Colo. Franks sent me by post. I have the honor to be with sentiments of perfect esteem & respect Sir your most obedt. & most humble servt.,

TH: JEFFERSON

PrC (DLC). Enclosure: TJ's second letter to Jay, this date.

[145]

From Louis Guillaume Otto

Monsieur A Newyork le 14. Fevr. 1787.

Vous apprendrés probablement par un autre canal que la Virginie vient de mettre des droits extraordinaires sur les liqueurs Spiritueuses à l'exception des eaux de vie de France. M. Madison qui ne fait qu'arriver ici m'assure que la même faveur a été accordée à nos vins, mais je n'ai pas encore vû l'acte qui concerne cet article. Je ne puis ignorer que les raports de Votre Excellence contribuent beaucoup aux dispositions que la Virginie manifeste à notre egard et je ne neglige aucune occasion d'en rendre compte à ma Cour. Il est heureux que les interêts des Etats unis en France ayent été confiés à un Ministre aussi attentif à cultiver la bonne intelligence qui subsiste entre les deux nations.

Vous trouverés, Monsieur, dans les gazettes tous les details relatifs à la revolte de Shayse et de ses partisans. Ses troupes ont été entierement dispersées par le Gal. Lincoln; mais je n'ose encore me flatter que la fermentation est tout à fait calmée. On croit assés generalement que la Legislature du Massachussets sera enfin obligée de faire du papier monnoye et d'avoir egard aux autres griefs, vrais ou imaginaires, des Insurgens.

Un Capitaine Americain, Monsieur, vient de trouver sur une isle dont il cache le nom, des pelleteries très precieuses, qu'il se propose d'envoyer en Chine. Son Batiment est encore mouillé dans la rivière du Nord et doit partir incessament. On dit que ces fourrures ressemblent à celles que l'equipage du Cape.Cook a vendues à Canton à un prix exorbitant. Si cette découverte est aussi importante qu'on le presume elle deviendra pour les Etats unis une nouvelle source de richesses. Comme les armateurs gardent le plus profond silence, on n'en a encore qu'une connoissance très vague. Je suis tenté de croire que l'Isle en question est une des Falklands puisque differens navigateurs et entre autres Wallis et Carteret font mention de fourrures qu'ils y ont trouvées. Vous n'ignorés pas, Monsieur, que la pêche de la Baleine attire beaucoup d'Americains vers ces isles et qu'ils y ont même fait quelques etablissemens passagers.

Plusieurs Caroliniens, Monsieur, desirent de faire passer leurs ris en France; mais pour les rendre convenables à nos marchés, ils ont besoin de Vos bons offices. Vous rendriés un très grand service aux liaisons commerciales des deux nations en faisant passer en Amerique tous les renseignemens que Vous pourrés Vous procurer

14 FEBRUARY 1787

sur cette matiere. M. Ed. Rutledge et d'autres Caroliniens doivent Vous en avoir ecrit.

L'Etat de Frankland vient de se reunir à la Caroline du Nord et la tranquillité paroit tout-à-fait retablie de ce coté la.

J'ai l'honneur d'être avec le plus respectueux attachement Monsieur de Votre Excellence le très humble et très obeisst. serviteur,

OTTO

RC (DLC); endorsed. Recorded in SJL as received 6 Apr. 1787 at Marseilles.

JE NE NEGLIGE AUCUNE OCCASION D'EN RENDRE COMPTE À MA COUR: A few days earlier Otto had sent to Vergennes a remarkable tribute to TJ's influence in promoting Franco-American relations, particularly as exercised through his private letters to America: "M. Jefferson, Monseigneur, est pour nous en Virginie ce que M. Franklin a toujours été en Pensylvanie c'est à dire le Panegyriste le plus infatigable de la france. Les Deleguès de cet Etat me traitent avec la plus grande confiance et ils ont soin de m'informer de toutes les mesures qui peuvent interesser directement ou indirectement les sujets de S.M. ou d'importance nationale. Leur Etat vient denous donner une nouvelle preuve de son attachement en mettant des droits extraordinaires sur toutes les liqueurs etrangers *à l'exception des eaux de vie de France* importées dans des batimens françois ou Americains. Un autre acte qui n'est pas encore publié etend la même faveur *aux vins de france*. On avoit proposé dans l'Assemblée de mettre des droits trés considerable sur les soiries etrangeres et d'en excepter les etoffes françoises; la chambre basse avoit deja donné son consentement à cette motion, mais la difficulté d'empêcher la contrebande des Etats Voisins l'a fait rejeter par le Senat. Ces bonnes dispositions sont evidemment dues à la lettre de M. de Calonne à M. Jefferson que j'ai eu soin de faire publier dans toutes les gazettes; un Delegué m'a assuré qu'on n'a eu connoissance de cette lettre que la veille de la redaction des nouvelles loix et que dés ce moment les membres de l'Assemblée etoient unanimement resolus d'accorder à notre commerce toutes les faveurs qui peuvent se concilier avec les interêts particuliers de la Virginie. C'est principalement par sa correspondance particuliere que M. Jefferson s'efforce de conserver en Amerique les sentiments de reconnoissance que plusieurs de ses collegues en Europe ont pris tant de peine à etouffer. Je suis persuadé, Monseigneur, que la satisfaction que vous en temoignerés à ce Ministre produira le meilleur effet et qu'il ne manquera pas d'en rendre compte à ses Constituans. Toutes les mesures prises en france en faveur du commerce Americain operent sur le champ sur l'espri des assemblées legislatives et chaque sacrifice de notre part est immediatement suivi par une compensation" (Otto to Vergennes, 10 Feb. 1787; Arch. Aff. Etr., Corr. Pol., E.-U., Vol. XXXII; Tr in DLC; received [by Montmorin] 23 Mch. 1787). This conclusion was doubtless optimistic, but Otto's appraisal of TJ's influence and good dispositions was undoubtedly accurate. However the enthusiasm with which Otto reported here and in previous months was probably due in part to the fact that Virginia delegates took pains to convey the nature of TJ's communications to Otto in the certain knowledge that this would in turn be transmitted back to the French court—which was precisely what Otto was advising in this dispatch to Vergennes, thus closing the circle of an endless promotion of good will. In this sort of private and unofficial diplomacy, James Madison was very adept; the information in Otto's dispatch of 10 Feb. parallels that in Madison's to TJ of 15 Feb. 1787 so closely as to indicate that he was the "Delegué" who had assured Otto of Virginia's good dispositions. See note to Madison to TJ, 19 Mch. 1787.

From Maria Cosway

London 15 Feb. 1787

I have the pleasure of receiving two [letters from you, and though th]ey are very short, I must content Myself, and lament Much fo[r the] reason that deprivd Me of their usual length. I must confess that the begining of your corrispondence has made Me an enfant gatée. I shall never recover to be reasonable in My expectations, and shall feel disapointed whenever your letters are not as long as the first was. Thus you are the occasion of a continual reproching disposition in Me. It is a disagreable One. It will teaze you to a hatread towards Me, notwithstanding your partiality you have had for Me till now. Nothing disobliges More than a disatisfied Mind, and thou' my fault is occasion'd by yourself you will be the most distant to allow it. I trust that your friendship would wish to see Me perfect, and Mine to be so, but diffects are, or are not, Most conspicuous according to the feel we have about the Objects which Mislead them. We may be apt to feel our own, as to discover them in others, and in both, one of the humane weakness we are subject to. [This trait of ch]aracter, we both possess it, you to [. . .][1] thought, I for suffering patiently those not bestow'd [or be]gruje them, and silence My pretensions with due consciousness; I feel at present an inclination to Make you an endless letter but have not yet determin'd what subject to begin with. Shall I continue this reproching stile; quote all the what's, and why's, out of Jeremias's lamentations, then present you with some outlines of Job for Consolation? Of all the torments, temptations, and weariness, the female has always been the principal and most powerfull object, and this is to be the most fear'd by you at present, from my pen. Are you to be painted in future ages sitting solitary and sad, on the beautifull Monticello tormented by the shadow of a woman who will present you a deform'd rod, twisted and broken, instead of the emblematical instrument belonging to the Muses, held by Genius, inspired by wit, from which all that is pleasing, beautifull and happy can be describ'd to entertain, and satisfy a Mind capable of investigating every Minutia of a lively immagination and interesting descriptions.—[I have wro]t this in Memoria of the Many pages [you wrote in reply to the scr]awls adress'd to you by One who has only a good intention to [apolo]gies for such long insipid Chit chat, that follows more the dictates of her own pleasure, than the feeling of understanding: Allegories are allways very far fecht. I don't like to follow the subject, though

[148]

15 FEBRUARY 1787

I Might find something to explain My Ideas. Supose I turn to relate to you the debats of Parlement? Was I a good politition I could entertain you Much. What do you think of a famous speach Sheridan has made which lasted five hours? which has astonished every body which has Made the subject of conversation and admiration of the whole Town. Nothing has been taulk'd of for Many days but his Speach. The Whole House applauded him at the Moment. Each Member Complimented him when they rouse. Pitt Made him the highest encomioms, and only poor Mr. Hastings sufferd for the power of his eloquence; all went against him, though nothing can be decided yet. Mr. H. was with Mr. Cosway at the very Moment [the speech was] going on. He seemd perfectly easy, talk[ing of a variet]y of subjects with great tranquility and cheerfulness. The second day he was the same, but on the third seem'd very Much affected and agitated. All his friends give him the greatest Character of humanity, generosity and feelings, amiable in his Maner. He seems in short totaly different from the disposition of cruelty they accuse him of. From Parlementary discussions it is time to tell you I have ben reading with great pleasure your description of America. It is wrot by *you*, but Nature represents all the scenes to Me in reality. Therefore dont take any thing on yourself. I must refer to your Name to Make it the More valuable to Me but she is your rival, you her usurper. Oh how I wish My self in those delightful places! Those enchanted Grotto's! Those Magnificent Mountains rivers, &c. &c.! Why am I not a Man that I could sett out immediatly and satisfy My Curiosity, indulge My sight with wonders!—[Since I have been] in Lond[on there have been a great man]y little parties. I have [attended only a very few of][2] them. I am grown so excessively indolent, that I [do not go] out for Months together. All the Morning I paint whatev[er] presents it self most pleasing to Me. Some times I have beautifull Objects to paint from and add historical Characters to Make them More interesting. Female and infantine beauty is the Most perfect Object to see. Sometimes I indulge More Malincholy subjects. History rappresents her self sometimes in the horrid, in the grand, the sublime, the sentimental, the pathetik. I attempt, I exercise and end by being witness of My own dissapointment and incapacity of executing, the Poet, the Historian, or my own conceptions of immagination. Thus the Mornings are spent regretting they are not longer, to have More time to attempt again in Search of better success, or thinking they have been too long and have afforded me Many Moments of uneasiness, anxiety and a testimony of my not

15 FEBRUARY 1787

being able to do any thing.—[I devote my eveni]ng[s to] Music and then I am Much [visited by] the first Professors who come very often to play, every evening Something new, and all perfect in their different kind. And to add to Compleat the pleasure a small society of agreable friends frequently Come to see me. In this Manner you see that I am More attached to My home, than going in search of amusement out, where nothing but crowded assemblies, uncomfortable heat, and not the least pleasure in Meeting every body, not being able to enjoy any conversation. The Operas are very bad tho' Rubinelli and Madme. Mosa are the first singers, the danceres are very bad. All this I say from report as I have not been yet.—Pray tell me Something about Madme. de Polignac. They make a great deal about it here. We hardly hear any thing else, and the stories are so different from one another that it [is] impossible to guess the real one. She is expected in England. I send this letter by a gentleman whom I think you will like. He is a spaniard. I am partial to that Nation as I know several that are very agreable. He is going to Paris Secretary of Ambassy [of his] Court. He has travell'd Mu[ch . . . .] If I should be happy enough to come again in the Sum[mer to] Paris I hope we shall pass many agreable days. I am in a Millio[n] fears about it. Mr. Cosway still keeps his intention, but how man[y] chances from our inclinations to the execution of our will! Poor D'Ancarville has been very ill. I received a very long letter from him appointing himself My *Corrispondant* at Paris. I know a Gentleman who has banished My faith in this occasion for he flatter'd me with hopes which I have seen fail. However I have accepted his offer. I shall see if I find a second disapointment.

Is it not time to finish My letter? Perhaps I should go on but I must send this to the gentleman who is to take it.

I hope you are quite well by this time, that your hand will tell me so by a line. I must be reasonable, but give me leave to remind you how Much pleasure you will give, to remember Sometimes with friendship One who will be sensible and gratfull of it as is yours Sincerly,
MARIA COSWAY

RC (MHi); mutilated; the MS consists of two sheets of four pages each, of which the text occupies the first seven pages, the last being blank; date-line appears at foot of text. Recorded in SJL as received 25 Feb. 1787, though TJ received it through D'Hancarville rather than at the hands of the Spaniard (D'Hancarville to TJ, 25 Feb. 1787).

The first and second sheets of this letter are now separated in MHi, but both internal evidence and the character of the mutilations at the top of each prove that they form part of the same letter. These mutilations (evidently produced by rodents) are present in other early letters from Mrs. Cosway, and their configurations are such as to prove that he—or perhaps his heirs—kept her letters together, since no others in his correspondence seem to bear this particular kind of mutilation. Evidently, then, her letters were also kept separate from his principal files, but in a place less secure from what Arthur Agard, Queen Elizabeth's archivist, described as one of the chief enemies of manuscripts. These mutilations in the present letter account for the loss of from a word or two to almost a whole line; the conjectural readings in some instances (see notes below) may not be the only or even the correct readings, but they are offered as the Editors' best guess as to the words that would fit Mrs. Cosway's somewhat discursive style. Most of the text of this letter is printed in Randolph, *Domestic Life*, p. 89-92, under date of 15 Feb. 1788, but the conjectural readings (not indicated) differ from those given here and are at variance at times with the space involved and remnants of descenders of missing words.

The TWO . . . VERY SHORT letters from TJ are those of 29 Nov. and 24 Dec. 1786. Sheridan's FAMOUS SPEACH was delivered on 7 Feb. 1787. The allusion to TJ's DESCRIPTION OF AMERICA is the only evidence that TJ had presented to Mrs. Cosway a copy of *Notes on Virginia*; her copy has not been found.

[1] About three words missing; no remnants of descenders are present. A possible reading is: "you to compliment me in thought," but there are other equally plausible alternatives that might fit the involved language of this passage. Randolph, *Domestic Life*, p. 90, omits this entire sentence.

[2] Randolph, *Domestic Life*, p. 91, reads: "I go to very few parties. I have a dislike for them, &c." This is clearly in error, for almost all of the first line of the fifth page and about half of the second line are missing. This and the two preceding conjectural readings for this passage may allow alternative phrasing, but they seem approximately correct in substance.

From L. J. M. Daubenton

MONSIEUR   A Paris le 15. fevrier 1787

Je suis très flaté de lhonneur que m'a fait la Société philosophique d'Amérique en me recevant au nombre de ses membres, et je vous dois bien des remercimens de la bonté que vous avez eu de m'envoyer le diplome de ma nomination. Je vous prie, Monsieur, de vouloir bien faire tenir à M. franklin la lettre ci jointe par laquelle je témoigne a la Societé toute la satisfaction que j'ai d'y être admis.

Je suis fort aise d'avoir cette occasion de vous témoigner le respect avec lequel j'ai l'honneur d'être, Monsieur, Votre très humble et très obéïssant Serviteur,   DAUBENTON

RC (DLC); endorsed. Enclosure not found.

From Louis Le Pelletier

Paris, 15 Feb. 1787. As requested by TJ, he has forwarded a copy of the minutes of the ceremony at the Hotel de Ville for the unveiling of the bust of Lafayette. Having received no acknowledgement, he

[151]

fears that the packet may have been lost. If so, he will have another copy made.

RC (MHi); 2 p.; in French; endorsed: "Prevot des marchands." Not recorded in SJL. See note to Le Pelletier to TJ, 1 Feb. 1787.

From James Madison

DEAR SIR   New York Feby. 15th. 1787

My last was from Richmond of the 4th. of December, and contained a sketch of our legislative proceedings prior to that date. The principal proceedings of subsequent date relate as nearly as I can recollect 1st. to a rejection of the Bill on crimes and punishments, which after being altered so as to remove most of the objections as was thought, was lost by a single vote. The rage against Horse stealers had a great influence on the fate of the Bill. Our old bloody code is by this event fully restored, the prerogative of conditional pardon having been taken from the Executive by a Judgment of the Court of Appeals, and the temporary law granting it to them having expired and been left unrevived. I am not without hope that the rejected bill will find a more favorable disposition in the next Assembly. 2dly. to the bill for diffusing knowledge. It went through two readings by a small majority and was not pushed to a third one. The necessity of a systematic provision on the subject was admitted on all hands. The objections against that particular provision were 1. the expence, which was alledged to exceed the ability of the people. 2. the difficulty of executing it in the present sparse settlement of the Country. 3. the inequality of the districts as contended by the Western members. The latter objection is of little weight and might have been easily removed if it had been urged in an early stage of the discussion. The bill now rests on the same footing with the other unpassed bills in the Revisal. 3dly. to the Revisal at large. It was found impossible to get thro' the system at the late session for several reasons. 1. the changes which have taken place since its compilement, in our affairs and our laws, particularly those relating to our Courts, called for changes in some of the bills which could not be made with safety by the Legislature. 2. the pressure of other business which tho' of less importance in itself, yet was more interesting for the moment. 3. the alarm excited by an approach toward the Execution Bill which subjects land to the payment of debts. This bill could not have been carried, was too important to be lost, and even

[152]

15 FEBRUARY 1787

too difficult to be amended without destroying its texture. 4. the danger of passing the Repealing Bill at the end of the Code before the operation of the various amendments &c. made by the Assembly could be leisurely examined by competent Judges. Under these circumstances it was thought best to hand over the residue of the work to our successors, and in order to have it made compleat, Mr. Pendleton, Mr. Wythe and Blair were appointed a Committee to amend the unpassed bills and also[1] to prepare a supplemental revision of the laws which have been passed since the original work was executed. It became a critical question with the friends of the Revisal whether the parts of the Revisal actually passed should be suspended in the mean time, or left to take their operation. The first plan was strongly recommended by the advantage of giving effect to the system at once, and by the inconveniency arising from the latter of leaving the old laws to a constructive repeal only. The latter notwithstanding was preferred as putting the adopted bills out of the reach of a succeeding Assembly, which might possibly be unfriendly to the system altogether. There was good reason to suspect Mr. *Henry*[2] who will certainly be *then a member*. By suffering the bills which have passed to take effect in the meantime it will be extremely difficult to get rid of them. 4thly. Religion. The Act incorporating the protestant Episcopal Church excited the most pointed opposition from the other sects. They even pushed their attacks against the reservation of the Glebes &c. to the Church exclusively. The latter circumstance involved the Legislature in some embarrassment. The result was a repeal of the Act, with a saving of the property. 5th. the district Courts. After a great struggle they were lost in the House of Delegates by a single voice. 6thly. taxes; the attempts to reduce former taxes were baffled, and sundry new taxes added; on lawyers 1/10 of their fees, on Clerks of Courts 1/4 of do., on doctors a small tax, a tax on houses in towns so as to level their burden with that of real estate in the Country, very heavy taxes on riding carriages, &c. Besides those an additional duty of 2. per Ct. ad valorem on all merchandizes imported in vessels of nations not in treaty with the U.S., an additional duty of 4d. on every gallon of wine except French wines, and of 2d. on every gallon of distilled spirits except French brandies which are made duty free. The exceptions in favor of France were the effect of the sentiments and regulations communicated to you by Mr. Calonne. A printed copy of the communication was received the last day of the Session in a newspaper from N. York and made a warm impression on the Assembly. Some of the

15 FEBRUARY 1787

taxes are liable to objections, and were much complained of. With the additional duties on trade they will considerably enhance our revenue. I should have mentioned a duty of 6s. per Hhd. on Tobacco for complying with a special requisition of Congress for supporting the corps of men raised for the public security. 7th. The Mississippi. At the date of my last the House of Delegates only had entered into Resolutions against a surrender of the right of navigating it. The Senate shortly after concurred. The States South of Virga. still adhere as far as I can learn to the same ideas as have governed Virginia. N. Jersey one of the States in Congress which was on the opposite side has now instructed her Delegates against surrendering to Spain the navigation of the River even for a limited time. And Pena. it is expected will do the same. I am told that Mr. *Jay* has *not ventured to proceed in his project* and I suppose will *not now do it*. 8th. The Convention for amending the federal Constitution. At the date of my last Virga. had passed an act for appointing deputies. The deputation consists of Genl. Washington, Mr. Henry late Governor, Mr. Randolph present Governor, Mr. Blair, Mr. Wythe, Col. Mason and Js. M. North Carola. has also made an appointment including her present and late Governor. S.C. it is expected by her delegates in Congress will not fail to follow these examples. Maryland has determined I just hear to appoint but has not yet agreed on her deputies. Delaware, Penna. and N. Jy. have made respectable appointments. N. York has not yet decided on the point. Her Assembly has just rejected the impost which has an unpropitious aspect. It is not clear however that she may not yet accede to the other measures. Connecticut has a great aversion to Conventions, and is otherwise habitually disinclined to abridge her State prerogatives. Her concurrence nevertheless is not despaired of. Massts. it is said will concur, though hitherto not well inclined. N. Hampshire will probably do as she does. Rhode Island can be relied on for nothing that is good. On all great points she must sooner or later bend to Massts. and Connecticut.

Having but just come to this place I do not undertake to give you any general view of American affairs, or of the particular state of things in Massts. The omission is probably of little consequence as information of this sort must fall within your correspondence with the office of foreign affairs. I shall not however plead this consideration for a future letter when I hope to be more able to write fully.

Mr. Fitzhugh has paid into my hands for your use £58-6-8.

Virga. currency in discharge of 1000 livres advanced to him in France. He was anxious to have settled it according to the actual exchange instead of the legal one of 33⅓ on the British standard, and even proposed the addition of interest. I did not hesitate to conclude that I should fulfill your intentions by rejecting both. I have sent to Mrs. Carr £25 for the use of your nephews as you directed. The balance is in my hands subject to your orders tho' I shall venture to apply it in the same way if I should be apprized of its being necessary to prevent interruption to the studies of the young gentlemen. My last informed you of the progress &c. of Master Peter. I have since received from the president of Hampden Sydney a letter containing the following paragraph. "Dabney Carr is a boy of very promising genius and very diligent application. He conducts himself with a good deal of prudence, and I hope will answer the expectations of his friends. I was afraid at first that he was dull or indolent from his appearance, but I find myself agreeably disappointed. His principal study at present is the Latin language, but he is also obliged to pay some attention to his native tongue."

I remain Dr. Sir Yr. Affecte. friend, Js. MADISON Jr.

RC (DLC: Madison Papers); endorsed. Recorded in SJL as received 3 May 1787 at Aix-en-Provence.

[1] The passage "made compleat, Mr. Pendleton . . . the unpassed bills and also" is interlined in substitution for the following words, which were deleted (probably contemporaneously): "compleated to this time Mr. Pendleton, Mr. Wythe and Mr. Blair were appointed."

[2] This and subsequent words in italics are written in code and were decoded interlineally by TJ; decoding verified by the editors, employing Code No. 9.

From John Trumbull

DR. SIR London Febry. 15th. 1787.

I recev'd your Letter of Inquiries about the Relations of Mrs. Trist some weeks ago. I found that Mr. Rt. Trist of Arundel St. Strand was living, but not being in Town, I thought it better to wait his return than to make my application to any others of the Family. I have at last seen him this morning. He informs me that the legacy is left as you mention and not only so, but that the son of Mrs. N. Trist is next heir to the Uncles who have no male Children, and possess £3000, a year. Mr. Trist expresses a doubt whether the Child be living, because the Family, particularly Mrs. Champernone and himself have repeatedly written to Mrs. Trist this information and as often requested her either to send the Child over to them, or to come herself with him, that He might be educated among the Family: to which letters she has not, as He says return'd any explicit Answer, tho She sometimes has written to them.

Further, He has inquir'd of several people from America about the child, some of whom have inform'd him that he *is* dead, in which case the Legacy and Estates remain in the Branches of the Family here: in short He seem'd dissatisfied, that any enquiry such as I made, should come from Mrs. Trist, when she was already inform'd the same from him, that she had returnd no answer to the request of the Family to send or bring her Son to them, and in short had for some time been silent as to him.

As this Idea of the Childs death seems to prevail in the Family, and as Mrs. Champernone has appeared so friendly, would it not be adviseable for you to write to her, especially as She has a considerable Fortune £1000 a year in her own Gift. I should indeed think it wise in Mrs. T. if she has such invitations to come over with her Son. The Gentleman whom I have seen assures me she will be receivd with great affection by all the Family.

I shall send you the clause of the will and Names of the Executors as soon as I can procure them: and shall be happy if I can be of any use on this or any other occasion to you or your friends.

Mrs. Cosway who will write you in a few days, and on whose Table I write this, charges me to assure you of her Esteem and to present in her name every good wish.—To her's permit me to [add] mine and to assure you that I am most sincerely & gratefully Your servant & friend,   Jno. Trumbull

 RC (DLC); addressed to "Mr. Jefferson a la Grille de chaillot Paris," and noted as sent by "Grand." Not recorded in SJL.

To Simon Bérard

Sir   Paris Feb. 16. 1787.

A friend of mine in Charlestown sent me a box of plants and a letter to New York to the care of Mr. Otto, Chargé des affaires of France there who delivered them to Capt. Sionville of the packet Courier de l'Europe. The letter came to hand without the box of plants. I wrote to Mr. Champion of L'Orient to ask the favor of him to enquire for the box. He wrote me word the vessel was gone on to Havre. I then wrote to Mr. Limosin of Havre who enquired of the Captain for the box. He answered that he well remembered having such a box delivered him, but had forgotten by whom and for whom, and that being without a direction, he had delivered it to Mr. Berard at Lorient. I enter into these details, Sir, in hopes you will have the goodness to write to Mr. Berard by tomorrow's post if possible, and to procure the plants to be sent on to me by the first Diligence to Paris. I shall gladly repay any expence they may occasion. I fear the delay may destroy their vegetative power. I am just setting out on a long journey but Mr. Short my secretary, will receive them in my absence. I beg your pardon for the trouble I am giving you, but the honor of the little acquaintance I have had with you encouraged me to take this liberty. I am with much respect Sir Your most obedt. humble servt.,

TH: JEFFERSON

PrC (DLC); endorsed: "Berard."

From Simon Bérard

East India house Rue de Grammont
16th: feby: 1787.

I am very happy in the opportunity you Give me of being of some utility to you. I shall write by to morrow's Post to my brother at l'orient and recommend the Plants may be sent to you by the first diligence.

I am with much Respect Sir Your most obedient and Humble Servant,

S. BERARD

RC (DLC); endorsed. Not recorded in SJL.

To Henry Champion

SIR Paris Feb. 16. 1787.

On receipt of the letter you were so kind as to write me, I wrote to M. Limozin to make enquiry for the box of plants which was the subject of the letter with which I troubled you. He called on Capt. Sionville of the packet the Courier de l'Europe, who informed him he did bring such a box of plants, that having forgot from whom he received them and for whom they were intended, and there being, as he thinks, no address on the box, he had delivered them to Monsr. Berard of L'Orient. I must therefore pray you, Sir, to apply to Mr. Berard for them and to forward them to me by the Diligence, taking measures to prevent their being stopped at any of the Douanes by the way. Any expence which has attended or which shall attend them I will thankfully repay. I shall set out in three days for the South of France, but Mr. Short, my secretary, will receive all dispatches in my absence and forward them to me. He will receive also this box of plants and dispose of them according to my directions. I have the honour to be Sir your most obedt. humble servt., TH: JEFFERSON

PrC (MHi); endorsed.

From C. W. F. Dumas

MONSIEUR Lahaie 16 fevr. 1787

Depuis Ma Lettre du 1er. Dec. dernier qui est la dernière de celles dont Votre Excellence ma accusé la réception dans la sienne du 25, Elle doit avoir reçu No. 14 à 18, du 2 au 6, 22 Dec., 1er. et 26 Janv. et 13 fevr. pour le Congrès, comme aussi les miennes pour Votre Excellence des 1er.,[1] 5e. et 23 Janvr. dernier.

Voici No. 19 de ce jour, dont l'important contenu m'a paru valoir la peine d'une Dépêche exprès.

Je joins ici une Gazette Angloise, que V.E. gardera pour Elle-même. On me l'a envoyée d'Amstm. avec permission d'en disposer. V.E. verra par l'article marqué d'une †, ce dont il s'agit.

Je languis d'apprendre que la main de votre Exce. est parfaitement guérie: comme aussi, ce que V.E. pense du contenu de ma Lettre du 23 Janvr. dernier.—Comme il s'y agit d'un projet qui, sauf meilleur avis, me paroît avantageux et aux Et. Unis, et à la France, tant par lui-même que parce qu'il rempliroit outre cela indirectement par l'Option proposée, l'objet de l'Emprunt que m'a proposé V.E., si l'affaire se trouvoit agréér entre V.E. et le Ministere de Fce., et qu'il ne fallût, pour l'accélérer, qu'une course à Paris, V.E. n'auroit qu'à ordonner. Je serois prêt à la faire avec celui qui m'a fourni le projet, et qui l'exécuteroit.

Je suis toujours avec le plus respectueux dévouement, De Votre Excellence, Le très humble & très obéissant serviteur,

CWF DUMAS

RC (DLC). FC (Dumas Letter Book, Rijksarchief, The Hague; photostat in DLC); differs in phraseology, one instance of which is noted below. Not recorded in SJL. Enclosures: (1) Dumas to Jay, 16 Feb. 1787 (same), giving a list of commissioners appointed to instruct the Prince of Orange, classified by Dumas as "good men" (eight); "those of a contrary character" (two); and those "merely passable" (five); text printed in *Dipl. Corr.*, *1783-89*, III, 564-5. (2) The marked copy of the "Gazette Angloise" has not been identified.

[1] There is no record of a letter from Dumas to TJ of this date; undoubtedly an error for the letter of 29 Dec. 1786, which is the date given in FC.

To Philip Mazzei

Feb. 16. 1787.

Anacreon.
Sophocles.
Aeschylus.
Euripides.
Aristophanes.
Seneca's tragedies.
Terence.
Plautus.
Lucian.
Horace.
Epictetus.
Xenophon's memorabilia.
Plato.
Aeschines' Socratic dialogues.
Cicero's Philosophical works.
Seneca's philosophical works.

Antoninus.
Xenophon's Cyropaedia.
————'s Hellenics.
————'s Anabasis.
Herodotus.
Thucydides.
Quintus Curtius.
Justin.
Diodorus Siculus.
Dyonisius Halicarnassus.
Polybius.
Sallust.
Caesar.
Suetonius.
Plutarch's lives.
Cornelius Nepos.

Will Mr. Mazzei be so good as to write to some friend in Italy to inform him whose translations into Italian of the above authors, are the best: and also to denote by the addition of the figures 1. 2. 3. &c. which are of the 1st. degree of merit, which are only 2d. rates, 3d. ra[tes] and which are the best of the small editions of them, for his very humble servt.,   TH: JEFFERSON

PrC (DLC).

From the Commissioners of the Treasury

SIR   Board of Treasury   February 16. 1787.

We are favored with your Letter of the 12th. of August last acknowledging the Receipt of ours of the 9th. of May and[1] 25th. of June last, and advising us of your having received of Captain Paul Jones the sum of One hundred and twelve thousand, one hundred and seventy two Livres, two Sols and four deniers, being the balance which that Officer states to be due on the Prize money by him received of the Court of France. With respect to the Claims of Captain Jones they can only be decided on by the United States in Congress, who no doubt will be disposed to give all the weight to the pretentions of that officer to which they may be justly entitled.

16 FEBRUARY 1787

Enclosed you will receive a certified Copy of an Act of the United States in Congress, directing and authoriseing you to cause the claim of the representatives of the late Mr. Daniel Schweighauser of Nantes against the United States of America to be adjusted in such manner as you should judge most for the Honor and Interest of the United States, together with the Documents which we conceive necessary for throwing proper Light on this Claim. You will observe that you are directed to apply to the discharge of the balance (if any) which may be found due to the Estate of Mr. Schweighauser the property which has been attached on account of this Claim; to what amount that property is, we cannot from any documents in this Office ascertain, or whether it consists of any other objects than the Arms belonging to the United States, which were in the Arsenal of Nantes. You will oblige us in obtaining a particular Abstract of the property referred to in the Act of Congress and in forwarding it to us as soon as possible together with the issue of the claim submitted to your adjustment.

We are sorry to observe that the Monies received by Captain Jones (after the deductions made from it) falls far short of the Sum which we supposed you would have received; and that part of these funds had been employed in reimbursing to Mr. Grand the sums which at your instance he had advanced for the objects mentioned in your letter amounting to 66,719 Livres.

No Account of Mr. Grands disbursements has been received at this Office since the 18th. July 1785. We presume that we shall receive them shortly, when we shall direct the proper entries to be made on these disbursements.

With respect to the payment made on the drafts of Mr. Dumas, Agent for the United States at the Hague, unless it was by your direction we know of no reason that Mr. Grand had for honoring these Drafts. As soon as we can ascertain the monies received by that Gentleman we will endeavor to make arrangements for the payment of his Salary in Holland, in future so that there may be no necessity of his drawing on Mr. Grand.

Our immediate attention shall be turned to making a proper remittance for your Salary for the present year, but it is necessary to observe that the public em[barr]assments for want of revenue encrease so rapidly, that it will be with the greatest difficulty that we shall be able to pay the expences of the Civil Establishment during the present year: all hopes of our being able to make any Remittances to the Foreign Officers or for the payment of Interest &c. due on the French Loans are entirely vanished. The State of New York has rejected the reccom[men]dation of the United States in Congress to grant the Impost agreeably to the general System proposed by the Act of the 18th. April 1783, whilst some late proceedings of the Legislature of Pennsylvania, with respect to Requisitions, baffle all expectations of any effectual supply from that source: As we presume however that you will receive the Political detail of the situation of this Country from the Department of Foreign Affairs, we shall forbear dwelling on a subject the reflection on which from the nature of the trust reposed [in us] fills us with continual anxiety.

We have the Honor to be Sir, with great Respect Your Obedt. Hble. Servts.,

SAMUEL OSGOOD
WALTER LIVINGSTON
ARTHUR LEE

RC (DLC); in a clerk's hand, signed by Osgood, Livingston, and Lee; endorsed: "Treasury board." Recorded in SJL as received 3 May 1787 at Aix-en-Provence. Enclosures: Only the resolution of Congress, 16 Oct. 1786 (Tr in DNA: PCC, No. 59, IV; text printed in JCC, XXXI, 878-9) has been identified. TJ had already received a copy of this resolution through Jay before the present letter was written (see TJ to Schweighauser & Dobrée, 12 Feb. 1787).

[1] Thus in MS; it should read "on the." There is no record of a letter from the Commissioners to TJ of 25 June 1786; TJ on 12 Aug. 1786 wrote: "Your favor of May 9. came to hand on the 25th. of June."

From Vandenyver Frères

[Paris] Ce 16 fev.

Mm. Vandenyver freres auront besoin de nouveaux ordres de Mm. Willink & Staphorst pour remettre a M. Jefferson Largent quil desireroit recevoir sur ce qui lui reste de bon sur le credit que les dits Sieurs avoient ouvert en Sa faveur chez Vandenyver en 1785. Ils ecrivent en consequence a Mm. Willink et feront part a Monsieur Grand de leur reponse.

RC (MHi: AMT); without indication of the year, but see TJ to Adams, 20 Feb. 1787, in which he refers to the present letter as an "answer," presumably to one he had written. Neither his to Vandenyver Frères (missing) nor theirs to him is recorded in SJL.

From Benjamin Vaughan

SIR *Jeffries Square* London, Feby. 16, 1787.

I have been honored with your letter of the 29th: of Decr., though it arrived four weeks after its date. The very day after I received it, I began a long answer, which only waits for Messrs. Nairne & Blunt's execution of what is mentioned in it, to be forwarded to you through Col. Smith; for it is too bulky for the post. I hope it will leave my hands tomorrow, and convince you of the anxiety I have to attend to any communication or directions you may think proper to favor me with.

It is very true that Dr. Herschell has discovered two satellites to the Georgium Sidus; one revolving in about a week, the other in about a fortnight; but by his account to us their orbit does not seem favorable for affording us eclipses. He discovered them last month by means of some new advantages he had given to one of his instruments, for he had never been able to discover them before. His *great* instrument will still take some little time to perfect; and it is hard to say what is not to be expected from it, if it succeeds. He will have all the world before him, and a certainty that nobody can for some time have the same advantages. This is a more honest monopoly than some others that could be named. I am happy that these satellites are not to be discovered without the best instruments, for it will be a criterion to the instruments of every country and a disgrace to those that are deficient, which will tend to the improvement of astronomy generally, and little be lost with respect to the present object, which seems most interesting at present as a spectacle of curiosity.

Dr. Herschell has promised me an account of these satellites for the Philadelphian Philosophical Society, of which he has lately been elected member.

I know of nothing very mate[rial] here at this moment, (which you are [not] likely to learn from other quarters,) on other subjects. I have the honor to be, with great respect & esteem, Your Excellency's Most obedient & most humble servt.,

BENJN. VAUGHAN

RC (DLC); addressed and endorsed. Recorded in SJL as received 21 Feb. 1787.

From Froullé

Paris, 17 Feb. 1787. TJ had informed him that a person of his acquaintance had also received a copy of the work of "Monsieur aDams sur les Constitutions de l'Amerique"; wishes to know if he may be permitted to inquire the name of that person and to borrow his copy while awaiting that ordered for him by TJ from a London bookseller. If his request "n'est point indiscrete" he would like to have a reply by the bearer.

RC (DLC); 1 p.; in French. Not recorded in SJL; see TJ to Stockdale, 27 Feb. 1787; Stockdale to Short, 15 May 1787.

To Thomas Barclay

Dear Sir   Paris Feb. 18. 1787

I am now to acknowlege your separate favors of Dec. 4. and Jan. 6. and the joint one to Mr. Adams and myself of Jan. 6. This last has been communicated to Congress and to Mr. Adams. You have my full and hearty approbation of the treaty you obtained from Marocco, which is better and on better terms than I expected. Mr. Adams and myself have annexed our confirmation to two of the copies, one of which is gone to Congress, the other with a joint letter to Fennish I now inclose to Mr. Carmichael, apprehending you are not in Madrid. I concur clearly with you in opinion that for many reasons Mr. Carmichael would be a proper person to negotiate our business with Algiers, if it be negotiable with such means as we possess. I have expressed this opinion in my letters to America: but I am sure we cannot raise the money necessary. Colo. Franks was gone to London before I received your letter. He returned and embarked in the packet from Havre, but nothing was done on the subject of accounts or money. I was unlucky enough to dislocate my right wrist five months ago, and tho' it was well set, I can yet make no use of it but to write. I am advised to try mineral waters, and those of Aix in Provence being as much recommended as any others, I am induced to go to them by the desire of making the tour of the ports with which we trade, Marseilles, Bourdeaux, Nantes &c. I set out in two days and shall be absent three months. The packets are finally fixed at Havre. They sail every six weeks. Honfleur will I think certainly be made a free port: and I flatter myself will become the center for much of our trade and particularly of that of our rice. The death of Ct. de Vergennes and appointment of Monsr. de Montmorin will reach

[163]

18 FEBRUARY 1787

you before this letter does. I have letters &c. from America as late as the 15th. of Dec. The insurgents of Massachusets had prayed pardon for themselves and their leaders in jail, and on these terms had offered to retire and live peaceably at home. Mrs. Barclay and your family are well, except that they are somewhat apprehensive of a film growing over the eye of your youngest daughter. But should it do so, it will be easily removed. I have the honour to be with much esteem & respect Dr. Sir your most obedt. & most humble servt., TH: JEFFERSON

PrC (DLC).

To William Carmichael

DEAR SIR Paris Feb. 18. 1787

My last to you was dated Dec. 26. since which I have been honoured with yours of Dec. 17. I now inclose you a duplicate of the vote for the recall of Mr. Lamb. I take the liberty also of putting under cover to you our confirmation of the Marocco treaty together with a joint letter to Fennish. The fear that Mr. Barclay might not be at Madrid has occasioned my giving you this trouble as well as that of addressing the letter properly, and of having it transmitted.

I have received from Mr. Jay sundry despatches relative to the frigate the S. Carolina, and to a claim against the court of Madrid founded on the aid of that vessel in taking the Bahama and Providence islands: with an instruction from Congress to confer with the Prince of Luxemburg and get him to interest the Duke de la Vauguyon to join you in your sollicitations of this matter. This is accordingly done, and you will have the aid of the Duke. The dispatches relative to this subject I have sealed up and addressed to you, but they will be delivered to the Duke de la Vauguyon to find a safe occasion of forwarding them.   My last news from America was of the 15th. of Decemb. The insurgents of Massachusets had sent in a petition to their government, praying the release of their leaders in jail, and an act of pardon for themselves, and offering thereon to retire every man to his home and to live submissively. You will have heard of the death of the Ct. de Vergennes, and appointment of Monsr. de Montmorin. I was unlucky enough five months ago to dislocate my right wrist, and tho' well set, I have as yet no use of it except that I can write, but in pain. I am advised to try the use of mineral waters, and those of Aix in Provence being as much recommended as any others, I combine with this object a design of making the tour of those seaports with which we trade, Marseilles, Bourdeaux, Nantes &c. and shall set out the day after tomorrow, and expect to be absent three months. This may probably prevent my having the honor of writing to you during that interval, unless any thing extraordinary should arise. I take measures for the receipt of all letters addressed to me as regularly as were I here. I have the honour to be with sentiments of the most perfect esteem & respect Sir your most obedient & most humble servt., TH: JEFFERSON

PrC (DLC). Enclosures: (1) Copy of resolution of Congress of 26 Sep. 1786, revoking Lamb's commission (JCC, XXXI, 692). (2) Attested copy of Treaty with Morocco (see Vol. 10: 426, note). (3) Commissioners to Taher Fennish, 27 Jan. 1787.

To De Corny

DEAR SIR   Paris Feb. 18. 1787.

The inclosed letter to the Prevot des Marchands et echevins de Paris is to acknolege the receipt of the report which you were so kind as to put into my hands, and which I immediately forwarded to the Governor of Virginia. As the letter is written in English, and will therefore need your explanation, I take the liberty of passing it thro' your hands, and even of praying you to put the address on it, lest I should err in that. I do this with the more pleasure as it gives me occasion to renew my thanks to you for the zeal and energy with which your aid has been afforded, as well as my assurances of the esteem & respect with which I have the honour to be Sir Your most obedient & most humble servant,

TH: JEFFERSON

PrC (DLC). Enclosure follows.

To the Prévôt des Marchands et Echevins de Paris

SIR   Paris Feb. 18. 1787.

I am now to acknolege the receipt of the letter with which you have been pleased to honour me, together with the report on the inauguration of the bust of the Major General the Marquis de la

Fayette. I availed myself of an opportunity which offered, in the moment, of transmitting them to the state of Virginia, with a faithful representation of the favor with which the Prevot des marchands et echevins de Paris received their proposition, the zeal with which it was pursued, and the dignity of it's ultimate execution. Knowing the attachment of my country to the character which was the subject of that transaction, and the price they will set on the attentions of the Magistracy of Paris, I am safe in assuring you that they will feel themselves infinitely obliged on this occasion.

The interest you are pleased to take in the happiness of our infant states, your judicious admonitions as to the means of preserving it, and the terms in which you particularly honor some of their members, require my personal thanks, which I humbly offer with all those sentiments of homage and respect with which I have the honor to be, Sir, your most obedient & most humble servant, TH: JEFFERSON

PrC (DLC); enclosed in preceding. See note to Le Pelletier to TJ, 1 Feb. 1787.

From André Limozin

Le Havre, 18 Feb. 1787. Wrote to TJ on 13 Feb.; received TJ's of 14th with enclosed letter for Jay too late for the packet, which sailed "yesterday very early in the morning at least three hours before the Letters were delivered out of the Post Office." Will forward them by the next. Wishes TJ a good journey and "a safe return in a good health."

RC (MHi); 2 p.; endorsed. Not recorded in SJL.

From Anne Blair Banister

DEAR SIR   Battersea, Feby. 19th: 1787.

On the score of old acquaintance, and a knowledge of your humane disposition, I am emboldned to entreat your favor in behalf of Mrs. Oster (the French Consuls Lady) who has been misrepresented by her cruell Husband to the Minister. The inclosed therefore is her Vindication—and which necessity *alone* wou'd have extorted from her. It is left open for your perusal; when having so done, flatter myself you can have no scruple in presenting it as directed. It is not (be assured) from an ill judged opinion of my own, that I have *dared* to be thus troublesome; I *know* her estimation in *every* Family (of any distinction) throughout Williamsburg; while *He*, by arts to injure her, is as *universally* despised. From a delicacy that no one ought to interfere between Man and Wife, this worthy distrest Lady is suffering in a strange Country—all her Letters suppress'd, and no prospect of redress *unless* the liberty I have taken with you, shou'd have the desired effect. That it may, I cannot forbear being very sanguine. Yet, forgive me if I urge this matter too far; since I never felt more Interested for another in my Life, having seen her distress, her diffidence to make known her ill treatment (which became *too* obvious to hide) and withall, her *good* Sense and *sweetness* of disposition, that must *naturally* excite pity, and render her an object worthy attention. I wou'd not however (anxious as I am) have you swerve from the dictates of your own superior Judgement, being conscious upon this, as well as on every other occasion, of its propriety; in submission therefore that I trust wholly, relying on the Friendship with which you formerly Honor'd me (and in a late Letter to my better half kindly renew'd) to pardon this freedom. We have just received a Letter from Mr. J. Banister, with the pleasing Information of his returning Health. Shou'd he be in your Neighborhood, do me the favor to present me Affectionately to him, as well as your amiable Daughter. I make no doubt but some of your Correspondents, have already acquainted you with the irreparable loss of your Friend at Rosewell. His *much* Loved Fanny has taken her final leave! That Health and Happiness may be your attendants thro' Life, are among those wishes that will ever be uppermost in the Mind of Yours with perfect Sincerity, A. BANISTER

RC (DLC); endorsed: "Bannister Ann. recd. at Paris June 11." Recorded in SJL under date of receipt. Enclosure not found. Dupl (DLC); dated 20 Feb. 1787; differs somewhat from RC in phraseology. Recorded in SJL as received on 30 June 1787. See Banister to TJ, 6 May 1787.

The LATE LETTER TO MY BETTER HALF (Dupl reads "late letter to Mr. Banister") was that from TJ to Banister of 14 Aug. 1786 with its postscript to Mrs. Banister in which he said that he would be "very happy . . . to renew an acquaintance which he has always held among the most precious of those he has ever made."

To Alexander McCaul

DEAR SIR Paris Feb. 19. 1787.

Your favor of the 2d. inst. is duly received. I agree chearfully to the alteration you propose, in our terms, for converting the current into sterling money. It will guard against injustice, should

[167]

the madness of paper money invade our assembly. I send you the inclosed paper finally settling this business. I am not well acquainted with the situation of your matter in Virginia. I had hoped that Mr. Lyle's bill in Chancery had suspended the effect of the escheat law till the treaty of peace had put it out of danger. I wrote, while in London, to a friend very powerful in our assembly, and as just as powerful, in case any thing could be done there. Not even the sufferers by escheats can condemn them more than I do, and have always done. Principle therefore as well as friendship will render it very pleasing to me if I can be instrumental in preventing your being affected by them: being with very sincere sentiments of esteem and respect Dear Sir Your most obedient & most humble servt., Th: Jefferson

P.S. I shall be glad to know by a line that this gets safe to hand.

PrC (DLC); endorsed. Enclosure not found, but see TJ to McCaul, 4 Jan. 1787. McCaul's favor of the 2d. inst. has not been found, but it is recorded in SJL as received 14 Feb. The letter that TJ wrote to a friend very powerful was that to Madison of 25 Apr. 1786.

To William Stephens Smith

Dear Sir   Paris Feb. 19. 1787.

I have duly received your favor of Jan. 29. and Dr. Burney's which was inclosed in it. If the harpsichord be not sent off, perhaps it may as well await the last of March or beginning of April when it may be less exposed to rains. But it is not material. I shall be absent till the 1st. of May. Franks was unlucky with the instrument made by Jones. It was stolen out of his carriage in the neighborhood of Dover. Payne at Dover assured him he should be able to recover it. Perhaps he might be spurred to it by a letter from you if you would be so good as to write him one. The plants came in perfect order. No news yet of the second press. So much for business.

I did really expect that that ungracious, rascally court would wear out the patience of Mr. Adams. Long habits of doing business together and of doing it easily and smoothly, will render me sincerely sensible of his loss. And I fear we shall lose him on the other side the water also; for I shall consider it as a loss, if, instead of going to Congress, he should be buried in some office. With respect to yourself I have had the pleasure of writing what both duty and inclination concurred in dictating. I wish you with all my

20 FEBRUARY 1787

heart every success you can desire. The Notables meet on Thursday next. I wait to see the causes declared for which they are convened. Not a word has yet transpired. I am in hopes our new Minister has very friendly dispositions towards our country. He has the reputation of being a very honest man. His son married the neice of the Chevalier Luzerne. Perhaps this may make some promotion for the Chevalier and prevent his return to America.—Remember Mr. Adams's picture, I pray you; and Sir Walter Raleigh's too. When they shall be ready, I would wish to receive them with my own which Mr. Brown has. Let me know if you please how stand our accounts. There must now be a balance due to you, which I will remit you the moment you inform me of it, or I will pay it to your draught. That for Jones's instrument has been duly honored. Present me in friendly terms to Mrs. Smith & the little Hans & be assured of the esteem & affection with which I am Dr. Sir Your friend & servt., TH: JEFFERSON

PrC (DLC); endorsed.

To John Adams

DEAR SIR Paris Feb. 20. 1787.

I am now to acknoledge the receipt of your favor of Jan. 25. Colo. Franks sailed in the packet of this month from Havre for New York. This arrangement of the packets opens a direct communication between Paris and America, and if we succeed as I expect we shall in getting Honfleur made a freeport, I hope to see that place become the deposit for our Whale oil, rice, tobacco and furs, and that from thence what is not wanted in this country may be distributed to others.   You remember giving me a letter of credit on Messrs. Willink and Staphorst for 1000 guineas to pay for the swords and medals. When the swords were finished I drew on the Vandemjvers, with whom the money was deposited for 6500 livres to pay for the swords. They paid it. A medal is now finished, and others will very soon be: but these gentlemen say they must have fresh orders. In the mean time the workmen complain. Will you be so good as to draw in favor of Mr. Grand on Willink &c. for the balance of the thousand guineas (which is about the sum that will be necessary) and send the bill to Mr. Grand, who in my absence will negotiate it and pay the workmen. I inclose you Vandemjers answer.   The meeting of the Notables

[169]

on Thursday and the necessity of paying my court to our new minister will detain me till Friday and perhaps till Tuesday next. Nothing is known yet of the objects of this assembly. I inclose you two new pamphlets relative to it: and will inform you of whatever I can discover relative to it during my stay.

I learn with real pain the resolution you have taken of quitting Europe. Your presence on this side the Atlantic gave me a confidence that if any difficulties should arise within my department, I should always have one to advise with on whose counsels I could rely. I shall now feel bewidowed. I do not wonder at your being tired out by the conduct of the court you are at. But is there not room to do a great deal of good for us in Holland in the department of money? No one can do it so well as yourself. But you have taken your resolution I am sure on mature consideration, and I have nothing to offer therefore but my regrets. It any thing transpires from the Notables before my departure worth communication, you shall yet hear from me. In the mean time believe me to be with sincere esteem & respect Dr. Sir your most obedt. & most humble servt., TH: JEFFERSON

RC (MHi: AMT); endorsed in part: "ansd. March 1. 1787." PrC (DLC). Enclosure: Vandenyver Frères to TJ, 16 Feb. 1787. The enclosed pamphlets have not been identified.

From John Adams

DEAR SIR Grosvenor Square Feb. 20. 1787

Dr. Gordon who is about publishing his Proposals for printing his History desires a Letter to you.—I told him that he might depend upon your good offices without any Letter, but as no harm will be done by complying with his Desire I beg Leave to introduce him, and to recommend his History to your Patronage in France.

With equal affection, Esteem and respect, I have the Honour to be, Sir your most obedient humble Servant, JOHN ADAMS

RC (DLC); endorsed. Recorded in SJL as received 26 Mch. 1787 at Aix-en-Provence.

From De Corny

DEAR SIR Paris Le 20. fevrier 1787

The inclosed Report in parchement is to be sent to you, trusted to your Excellency's cares, and immediately forwarded to the State of Virginia. I take the Liberty of passing it thro' your hands and even of praying you to put it at End By the first opportunity. I do that with the more pleasure as it affords me occasion to renew thousand assurances of the Esteem, respect and friendship with which I have the honor to be for ever Dear Sir Your Excellency's the most obedient and most humble servant, DE CORNY

P.S. I sent for you, to the Mis. de la Fayette, 70 printed copies of the report, in order of being forwarded to the North america. But M. le Mis. de la Fayette desires for himself, the notoriousness and distribution of it could be prevented. I owe comply to his Will. You may, for your own account settle this matter with him.

RC (DLC). Not recorded in SJL. Enclosure: Le Pelletier to TJ, 1 Feb. 1787 and its enclosure (see note there).

For a bibliographical and historical account of the publication of the *Procés-Verbaux*, which bears the imprint "Philadelphia: Printed by M. Carey and Co. Front-Street, West-Side, near Market-Street. 1786," see Gilbert Chinard's "Notes and Appendix" to a reprint of the unique copy owned by Stuart W. Jackson as set forth in *Bulletin de L'Institut Français de Washington*, new ser., No. 4, Dec. 1954, p. 67-110.

There is no evidence that TJ actually sent any of the printed texts to America or that he took any part in procuring publication there. This is surprising in view of his frequent and full testimonials in letters to Jay, Washington, and Madison about the valuable assistance rendered by Lafayette in promoting American interests in France and in view of his interest in procuring European publication (see TJ to Rayneval, 30 Sep. 1786). The factual summary that TJ caused to be printed in the *Gazette de Leide* stands in marked contrast to the extraordinary record set forth in the proceedings themselves. According to the latter, the *prévôt des marchands et echevins* at a meeting on 15 Sep. 1786, at which a letter was read from Baron de Breteuil conveying the king's permission for the bust to be presented, directed Veytard to notify the deans of the counsellors of the city that the date had been fixed for the ceremony and to inform them that, "comme la modestie des personnes principalement interessées à cette cérémonie a sollicité qu'elle fut faite sans éclat, le Bureau a cru devoir se dispenser à l'égard des Compagnies d'une Convocation en regle." This would seem to mean that both TJ and Lafayette, perhaps through De Corny, had made the request for a ceremony "sans eclat," for they were certainly the principals. Both, ironically, were absent from the occasion: three days after the meeting on 15 Sep., TJ suffered the accident to his wrist that confined him to his room and, though Lafayette had spent about two weeks in Paris in September, he departed for Auvergne before the ceremonies on the 28th. Short took TJ's place in the great hall of the Hôtel de Ville amid circumstances that may have made TJ grateful for the injury that pleaded his excuse—though that injury did not prevent him, scarcely a week later and at the cost of a night of excruciating pain, from making an excursion with Maria Cosway on the eve of her departure from Paris. Short had long since given TJ and friends in Virginia an account of the ceremony, but Le Pelletier's enclosure included not only all of the relevant documents but also an exact description of the arrangements and the ceremony "sans eclat." In the great hall of the Hôtel de Ville there was arranged a long phalanx of benches for the audience, at the upper end of which were two armchairs for Le Pelletier and Short and six others for the *échevins*, all of them in crimson velvet adorned with gold lace. Toward the upper end of the phalanx, before a table covered with crimson velvet and facing the *prévôt*, was the seat for the *procureur du roi* (De Corny); on the other side of the table, its back to the *prévôt's* chair, was the seat of the *greffier en chef*, also covered with crimson velvet and gold lace. In a recess the bust of Lafayette rested on a table under a velvet veil. The officials were in their ceremonial

[171]

robes and the *huissiers* in livery. They, the counsellors, minor officials, and the audience entered the hall under an arch of crossed arms held by two ranks of guards and took their places, Houdon beside the bust. Then Short, "membre au Conseil des Etats de Virginie chargé de réprésenter S. E. M. de Jefferson, Ministre plénipotentiaire des Etats-Unis, retenu chez luy pour cause de maladie," arrived at the Hôtel de Ville where he had been received within the entrance by two *huissiers*. These, preceded by a sergeant and four guards, conducted him up the grand stairway, where, at the landing, he was met by the *greffier en chef*. The procession then continued into the great hall, through the phalanx of benches and up to the *prévôt*, where Short saluted the officials and sat down, covering himself, as did the officials. He then presented TJ's letter of 27 Sep. 1786, which Le Pelletier accepted in a speech in which he declared that the act of Virginia was "un hommage aussi honorable que les services qui l'obtiennent ont été distingué." Le Pelletier handed TJ's letter and the Virginia resolution to Veytard, who read them in French. When this was done, De Corny pronounced his remarkable address (see Vol. 10: 414-5) which he concluded by formally requesting, in the name of the king and of the city, that the letter of Baron de Breteuil and of TJ, as well as the Virginia resolution, be recorded in the "Registre des actes Importantes de l'hôtel de Ville" and that the bust of Lafayette "soit placé dans la grande salle destinée aux Elections et aux séances publiques dans un lieu apparent." Le Pelletier then called for the advice of the *échevins*, who gave their approval by acclamation, whereupon he requested Houdon to place the bust on the mantel at the back of the great hall. At the same instant the bust was unveiled and borne between two files of guards to the place designated, "au bruit des Trumpettes et des Timbales et d'une Musique militaire" and to the applause of the audience. "Many tears were shed at the moment of the music commencing and the placing of the bust," Short declared (Short to William Nelson, 25 Oct. 1786; DLC: Short Papers). Following this climactic moment of the ceremony, Short was conducted by some of the *échevins*, guards, and *huissiers* to the entrance of the Hôtel de Ville. A month later he reported that the "sensation [the proceedings] made in Paris is inconceivable" (same).

From William Gordon

Sir   London Feby. 20. 1787

I promised myself the honour of being introduced to your Excellency by a letter which my friend general Gates gave me, before I had the pleasure of hearing You was appointed ambassador to the court of Versailles. Ere I could reach home in the neighbourhood of Boston You had sailed for France. I have therefore applied to his Excellency John Adams for a few introductory lines, recommending at the same time to your patronage a work which has long engaged my attention, and which I mean should go to the press the beginning of October, and continue printing till finished, if Heaven indulges me with health. Suffer me to request the favour of your support; and that You will forward to the Marquis Le Fayette the parcel directed for him, as I am a stranger to his place of residence. I remain with the sincerest respect Your Excellency's most humble servant,   WILLIAM GORDON

RC (DLC); endorsed. Recorded in SJL as received 26 Mch. 1787 at Aix-en-Provence.

The letter to TJ from GENERAL GATES has not been found; it was presumably written in 1783 or early in 1784 when Gordon was still in America (he returned to England in 1786, having been in America since 1770). The WORK recommended was Gordon's *The History of the Rise, Progress, and Establishment, of the Independence of the Thirteen Colonies*, 4 vols., London, 1788. For a summary of TJ's assistance to Gordon, see Sowerby, No. 487, which includes excerpts from TJ to Gordon, 2 July 1787; 16 July, 2 Sep. 1788; and 18 Mch. 1789; Gordon to TJ, 6 Sep. 1787; 24 Apr., 8 July, and 15 Aug. 1788, qq.v.

To Barradelle

Paris. 21me. Fevrier. 87.

Devant faire incessamment, Monsieur, une longue voiage, mes occupations ne m'ont pas permis de repondre plutot à la lettre que vous m'avez fait l'honneur de m'ecrire. C'est vrai que j'avois trouvé votre Microscope superieure à toutes celles que j'avois vue. Mais avant de la voir, j'en avois acheté une à Londres, moins parfaite vraiment, mais qui suffit aux petites experiences d'une personne qui ne s'y est jamais beaucoup occupé, et qui actuellement, et pour des années à venir, ne pourra s'y occuper du tout. Ainsi, vous voyez Monsieur, que quoique votre instrument soit parfait dans son genre, ce ne pourroit m'etre actuellement d'aucune utilité: et l'acquisition entraineroit une sacrifice qui me seroit incommode dans ce moment. Dans tout autre cas je m'aurai preté bien volontiers à votre commodité, au desir de vous etre utile, et aux sentiments d'estime avec lesquels j'ai l'honneur d'etre Monsieur votre tres humble et tres obeissant serviteur, TH: JEFFERSON

PrC (MHi); endorsed by TJ: "Monsr. Delle Barre." Recorded in SJL as addressed to: "Barre del." Gournay, p. 586, under "Ingenieurs fabricans brevetés du roi, approuvés par l'académie des sciences," lists "Barradelle, l'aîné, quai de l'Horloge, Instr. de mathem.", who was undoubtedly the person to whom the present letter was addressed in response to one from Barradelle (missing).

From Henry Champion

L'Orient, 21 Feb. 1787. Received TJ's of 16th and immediately called on Bérard, who said TJ had already written him [i.e., his brother Simon Bérard on 16 Feb.] "respecting the Box of Plants left in his hands by Captn. Sionville"; that he had the box; and that he would forward it by the first *diligence*. He expects TJ will hear from Bérard this post.

RC (MHi); 2 p.; endorsed: "Champion for Loreilhe." TJ recorded this letter in SJL as being dated "Feb. 1" and received 26 Feb. 1787.

[173]

To Abigail Adams

DEAR MADAM　　　　　　　　　　　Paris Feb. 22. 1787.

I am to acknolege the honor of your letter of Jan. 29. and of the papers you were so good as to send me. They were the latest I had seen or have yet seen. They left off too in a critical moment; just at the point where the Malcontents make their submission on condition of pardon, and before the answer of government was known. I hope they pardoned them. The spirit of resistance to government is so valuable on certain occasions, that I wish it to be always kept alive. It will often be exercised when wrong, but better so than not to be exercised at all. I like a little rebellion now and then. It is like a storm in the Atmosphere. It is wonderful that no letter or paper tells us who is president of Congress, tho' there are letters in Paris to the beginning of January. I suppose I shall hear when I come back from my journey, which will be eight months after he will have been chosen. And yet they complain of us for not giving them intelligence. Our Notables assembled to-day, and I hope before the departure of Mr. Cairnes I shall have heard something of their proceedings worth communicating to Mr. Adams. The most remarkeable effect of this convention as yet is the number of puns and bon mots it has generated. I think were they all collected it would make a more voluminous work than the Encyclopedie. This occasion, more than any thing I have seen, convinces me that this nation is incapable of any serious effort but under the word of command. The people at large view every object only as it may furnish puns and bon mots; and I pronounce that a good punster would disarm the whole nation were they ever so seriously disposed to revolt. Indeed, Madam, they are gone. When a measure so capable of doing good as the calling the Notables is treated with so much ridicule, we may conclude the nation desperate, and in charity pray that heaven may send them good kings.— The bridge at the place Louis XV. is begun. The hotel dieu is to be abandoned and new ones to be built. The old houses on the old bridges are in a course of demolition. This is all I know of Paris. We are about to lose the Count d'Aranda, who has desired and obtained his recall. Fernand Nunnez, before destined for London is to come here. The Abbés Arnoux and Chalut are well. The Dutchess Danville somewhat recovered from the loss of her daughter. Mrs. Barrett very homesick, and fancying herself otherwise sick. They will probably remove to Honfleur. This is all our news. I have only to add then that Mr. Cairnes has taken charge of 15. aunes of black lace for you at 9 livres the aune, purchased by Petit and therefore I hope better purchased than some things have been for you; and that I am with sincere esteem Dear Madam your affectionate humble servt.,　　　　　　　　　　　TH: JEFFERSON

RC (MHi: AMT). PrC (DLC); endorsed.

TJ's famous and oft-quoted statement—I LIKE A LITTLE REBELLION NOW AND THEN—cannot properly be understood unless taken in the context of his correspondence with John and Abigail Adams in the weeks preceding the time it was written. On 30 Nov. 1786 John Adams, assuming that TJ had heard of Shays's Rebellion through the public press, casually urged him not to be alarmed "at the late Turbulence in New England." TJ received this on 20 Dec., the very day that he also received Jay's disturbing letter of 27 Oct. about the Massachusetts insurgents. He replied to Adams at once saying that he had not been initially alarmed by public reports, but that Jay had "really affected" him with his pessimistic account and Adams had set him "to rights." He repeated this to Mrs. Adams in his letter of 21 Dec. 1786, but added sentences which showed his characteristic desire "to see the people awake and alert" and his confidence in their good sense. Mrs. Adams bristled in disagreement and undertook to explain the rebellion more fully to TJ, who clearly, in her view, misunderstood its nature; her letter of 29 Jan. 1787 (preceded by a carefully phrased draft with one revealing passage that she decided to eliminate from the text sent to TJ) must have surprised him by the vigor of her exposition. But this did not deter him from making a calm, though more extreme, reaffirmation of his belief. His expressed hope that the MALCONTENTS would be pardoned may have been mere coincidence—or it may possibly have reflected his understanding of the lady whom he admired and liked so much—but the fact is that it was in direct opposition to the suppressed passage in Mrs. Adams' letter, for she had thought it not unlikely that "some examples must be made before the riots will be totally quelled and peace and good order restored." Mrs. Adams did not reply or write again until she received little Mary Jefferson late in June, when she revealed the warm and kindly facet of her character that TJ found much more congenial than her political views. Possibly, too, TJ's extreme statement may be in part a reaction to the views on aristocracy set forth in John Adams' *Defence of the American Constitutions*, a book that he had just received (TJ to Adams, 6 Feb. 1787).

To De Langeac

à Paris ce 22me. Fevrier 1787.

Monsieur le Comte, par les affaires dont une voiage projettée m'a accablé il y a quelque tems, je n'ai pas pu repondre plutot à la lettre que vous m'avez fait l'honneur de m'ecrire. C'est vrai que pendant que nous etions en traité pour votre maison, vous m'avez proposé qu'au lieu de 7500.tt que j'offrois pour le loyer, je donnerois 8000.tt et que vous payeriez les gages d'un jardinier. Je me suis trouvé obligé de m'y refuser, parcequ'un domestique qui ne dependroit de son maître ni pour ses gages, ni pour sa place, ne devroit etre bien utile, ni bien complaisant. La proposition etoit abandonné donc, et le bail signé. Quelques jours après mon etablissement içi, j'ai fait un arrangement avec le jardinier qui venoit de sortir de votre service. Je

23 FEBRUARY 1787

trouvois bientôt que le jardin, qui est tout en arbres, ne lui donnoit presque rien à faire. La repugnance toutefois de congedier un domestique, quoique il m'etoit absolument inutile, m'en a fait reculer le moment un an et demi. Enfin je l'ai averti de tacher de se placer. Je ne l'ai pas pressé de sortir dans le moment. Au contraire je pensois de lui donner un tems convenable pour chercher son etablissement, en lui payant ses gages en attendant, et lui permettant de rester ici.

Ce n'est pas donc, comme on vous a fait croire Monsieur, pour une offence quelconque que je me propose de le congedier. Votre lettre, dans ce cas, lui auroit bien valu sa grace, et ce m'auroit fait un veritable plaisir de pouvoir vous temoigner mes egards par cette complaisance. Mais c'est un arrangement oeconomique et necessaire. A un autre fois, Monsieur, je serai infiniment charmé de trouver une occasion où je pourrai vous prouver combien je souhaite de me preter à vos desirs, et combien sinceres sont les sentiments de respect avec lesquels j'ai l'honneur d'etre Monsieur votre tres humble et tres obeissant serviteur,

TH: JEFFERSON

PrC (DLC); endorsed.

For De Langeac's appeal in behalf of his former gardener, see his letter to TJ of 27 Jan. 1787. QUELQUES JOURS APRÈS MON ETABLISSEMENT IÇI: An entry in Account Book shows that on 4 Nov. 1785 TJ paid the "Jardinier 17 days @ 45f-25-10," which would have put the date of employment around 14 Oct., since the 17 days all fell in that month. However, TJ did not move into the Hôtel de Langeac until 17 Oct. 1785. The discrepancy is probably explained by the fact that TJ made the engagement with the gardener a few days after moving into the new quarters, but paid him for the whole time that had elapsed since the former tenant moved out.

To John Adams

DEAR SIR Paris Feb. 23. 1787

The Notables met yesterday. The king opened the assembly with a short speech, wherein he expressed his inclination to consult with them on the affairs of his kingdom, to receive their opinions on the plans he had digested, and to endeavor to imitate the head of his family Henry IV. whose name is so dear to the nation. The speech was affectionate. The Guarde des sceaux spoke about 20 minutes, complimented the Clergy, the Noblesse, the Magistrates and tiers etats. The Comptroller general spoke about an hour. He enumerated the expences necessary to arrange his department when he came to it, he said his returns had been minutely laid before the king, he took a review of the preceding administrations, and more par-

23 FEBRUARY 1787

ticularly of Mr. Neckar's, he detailed the improvements which had been made, he portrayed the present state of the finances, and sketched the several schemes proposed for their improvement; he spoke on a change in the form of the taxes, the removal of the interior custom houses to the frontiers, provincial administrations and some other objects. The assembly was then divided into Committees. To-day there was to be another grand assembly, the plans more fully explained and referred to the discussion of the Committees. The grand assembly will meet once a week and vote individually. The propriety of my attending the first audience day of Count Montmorin, which will not be till the 27th. retards my departure till then.

I have read your book with infinite satisfaction and improvement. It will do great good in America. It's learning and it's good sense will I hope make it an institute for our politicians, old as well as young. There is one opinion in it however, which I will ask you to reconsider, because it appears to me not entirely accurate, and not likely to do good. Pa. 362. 'Congress is not a legislative, but a diplomatic assembly.' Separating into parts the whole[1] sovereignty of our states, some of these parts are yeilded to Congress. Upon these I should think them[2] both legislative and executive; and that they would have been judiciary also, had not the Confederation required them for certain purposes to appoint a judiciary. It has accordingly been the decision of our courts that the Confederation is a part of the law of the land, and superior in authority to the ordinary laws, because it cannot be altered by the legislature of any one state. I doubt whether they are at all a diplomatic assembly. On the first news of this work, there were proposals to translate it. Fearing it might be murdered in that operation, I endeavored to secure a good translator. This is done, and I lend him my copy to translate from. It will be immediately announced to prevent others attempting it. I am with sincere esteem & respect Dear Sir Your most obedt. & most humble servt.,

TH: JEFFERSON

RC (MHi: AMT); endorsed, in part: "ansd. March. 1. 1787." PrC (DLC).

TJ approached the bookseller Frouillé with the idea of getting Adams' *Defence of the Constitutions of the United States* published. No evidence has been found that it was IMMEDIATELY ANNOUNCED, and the first French edition is apparently that with notes and commentary by De la Croix, *Défense des Constitutions Americaines*, Paris, 1792. (See also Adams to TJ, 1 Mch. 1787; TJ to Adams, 23 July 1787.)

[1] TJ first wrote "all the sovereignty," &c. and then altered the passage by overwriting to read as above.

[2] Preceding four words interlined in substitution for "they are," deleted.

To Mrs. Champernoune

MADAM   Paris Feb. 23. 1787.

Tho' I have not the honor of being known to you by name even, yet the interest you have been so good as to take in behalf of the persons who will be the subject of this letter, encourage me to take the liberty of addressing it to you. The late Mr. Trist of America was your brother, and I learn from his widow that you had been pleased to take notice of her and of her son by way of letter. Well acquainted with both, knowing the uncommon worth and good sense of the mother, and the promising genius of the son, and proposing to pay a visit to England the last spring, I wrote to Mrs. Trist for information as to the relations of her son Hore Browse Trist, and the places of their residence. I meant to have taken the liberty of waiting on such of them as I could, and of informing them how hopeful a member of their family was rising up in America. Unluckily I did not receive her answer till I had returned from England. I therefore desired a gentleman, a friend of mine, in London to make some enquiries of the family, and particularly of Mr. Richard Trist of Arundel street London. The result of these enquiries is that letters and invitations have been sent to Mrs. Trist to bring her son to England, that these have not been answered, and that it has even been said the son was dead. My last letter from Mrs. Trist was of the 24th. of July last, when he was alive and well, and I am certain had any accident happened to him since, I should have heard of it. The letters written to her, and the invitations which any of the family may have been so good as to have given her, may have miscarried, or that may have been the fate of her answers to them. I know the respect she entertains for the family too well, to suppose she could have neglected to answer any letter received from them. She is a most excellent mother, judicious and prudent, and devoting her whole existence to the care of her son. She has hitherto been able to supply the expences of his education which has been well conducted: but as he makes further progress these expences will increase, and she is not rich. I fear the possibility therefore that his education may suffer. He is a beautiful boy, of mild dispositions, and fine genius, and as far as can be judged at his age, we may rely that he will do honour to his family, be the station, to which he may be called in that, ever so honorable. The friendly notice you have been already pleased to take, Madam, of the widow and son of your brother, assure me that you will excuse the disinterested testimony of a stranger, whose sufficient reward it will be if he can be any ways instrumental in restoring an interesting boy to the bosom of his family. Should you think proper to write to Mrs. Trist, I offer my service towards having the letter carried, so that no miscarriage shall take place. For this purpose I take the liberty of giving you my address below, and of adding assurances of the respect with which I have the honor to be Madam your most obedient & most humble servant, TH: JEFFERSON

A Monsieur Jefferson Ministre plenipotentiaire des etats unis d'Amerique á Paris

PrC (MoSHi); endorsed. Enclosed in TJ to Trumbull, this date.

To John Jay

SIR   Paris Feb. 23. 1787.

The assemblée des Notables being an event in the history of this country which excites notice, I have supposed it would not be disagreeable to you to learn it's immediate objects, tho no ways connected with our interests. The assembly met yesterday; the king in a short but affectionate speech informed them of his wish to consult with them on the plans he had digested, and on the general good of his people, and his desire to imitate the head of his family, Henry IV, whose memory is so dear to the nation. The Garde des Sceaux then spoke about twenty minutes, chiefly in compliment to the orders present. The Comptroller general in a speech of about an hour opened the budget, and enlarged on the several subjects which will be under their deliberation. He explained the situation of the finances at his accession to office, the expences which their arrangement had rendered necessary, their present state with the improvements made in them, the several plans which had been proposed for their further improvement, a change in the form of some of their taxes, the removal of the interior customhouses to the frontiers, and the institution of Provincial assemblies. The assembly was then divided into committees with a prince of the blood at the head of each. In this form they are to discuss separately the subjects which will be submitted to them. Their decision will be reported by two members to the Minister, who on view of the separate decisions of all the committees, will make such changes in his plans as will best accomodate them to their views without too much departing from his own, and will then submit them to the vote (but I believe not to the debate) of the General assembly, which will be convened for this purpose one day in every week, and will vote individually.

The event of the count de Vergennes' death, of which I had the honour to inform you in two letters of the 14th. inst., the appointment of the Count de Montmorin, and the propriety of my attending at his first audience which will be on the 27th. have retarded the journey I had proposed, a few days. I shall hope on my return to meet here new powers for the Consular convention, as under those I have it will be impossible to make the change in the convention which may be wished for. I have the honor to be with sentiments of the most perfect esteem & respect, Sir, your most obedient & most humble servant, TH: JEFFERSON

PrC (DLC). Tr (DNA: PCC, No. 107, II).

To Eliza House Trist

DEAR MADAM   Paris Feb. 23. 1787.

I must refer you to my letter of Dec. 15. for the reason why I had not asked of you sooner some information of Browse's relations in England and of their residence. Having received that information from you after my return from England, I wrote to my friend Mr. Trumbul to make such enquiries as he could. I inclose you a copy of his letter containing the result of these enquiries. You will perceive that either the letters of the family to you or your answers to them have miscarried, that they have made enquiries and given you invitations to which they have not received answers, and that they even doubt Browse's being alive. I shall write as Mr. Trumbul advises, to Mrs. Champernon by this conveiance, and I imagine you will write not only to her but to Mr. Trist of London. How far it may be eligible to commit yourself, by a voiage to England, to the invitation of the family you alone can judge. If you have not received such invitations, and they are sincere in desiring your presence, my letter to Mrs. Champernon shall produce a repetition of them. The prospects of your son there seem to be very fair, and doubtless would be much improved were he put into the hands of the family. The opportunities of education there too are as good, perhaps, as in America: only more attention would be requisite to prevent his being diverted from his studies, and a judicious plan of study pursued. No doubt your presence would be of infinite value to him, and probably the voiage would cost you less pain than the separation from him. I am just setting out on a journey of three months to the South of France. If Mrs. Champernon therefore should honor me with an answer, my absence may occasion it's coming late to you. If I can be useful to you in this or any other business, command me freely. I will act for you as I would for myself, but with more diligence. Should you come to England I think you would come and pay a visit to our good allies. I need not tell you how much pleasure it would give to Patsy and myself. Perhaps before that time I shall have received my other daughter, who I hope will sail in May. Pressed with many letters which must go off with this, I have only time to add [ass]urances of my sincere friendship for you, and of the sentiments of respect & esteem with which I am Dear Madam your affectionate friend & servt.,

TH: JEFFERSON

PrC (MHi); endorsed. Enclosure: Copy of Trumbull to TJ, 15 Feb. 1787.

To John Trumbull

DEAR SIR Paris Feb. 23. 1787.

I thank you for the trouble you have been so good as to take in the case of Mrs. Trist. I have sent her a copy of your letter and I now trouble you with a letter to Mrs. Champernoune. If we do some good by these enquiries we shall share the happiness of it. The illness and death of the Count de Vergennes have retarded my departure on my journey till the 27th. I foresee nothing to hinder it then: and expect to be absent three months. This will almost bring about the time of your return to Paris, for I take for granted you will come to the exhibitions of the Salon. Your apartment here will expect you, and that you become a part of our family again. Tell Mrs. Cosway she is an inconstant. She was to have been in Paris long ago, but she has deceived us. The first evening that I find myself seated in a comfortable inn, warm, solitary, and pensive, I [will] invite her to sup, and will commit our conversation to writing. It will be a very scolding one on my part. In the mean time lay all my affections at her feet, desire her to write to me to comfort me on my journey, as I take measures for the forwarding my letters safely. Accept yourself assurances of the esteem of Dear Sir, your friend & servt., TH: JEFFERSON

PrC (DLC); endorsed. Enclosure: TJ to Mrs. Champernoune, 23 Feb. 1787.

To Michel Capitaine

Paris Feb. 25. 1787.

Je viens de recevoir, Monsieur, de Monsieur Peters une lettre de change sur votre compte pour 4755ᵗᵗ-14s, qu'il me prie de vous remet[tre]. Je partirai pour la Provence dans deux jours, et je laisserai la lettre de change dans les mains de Monsieur Short, mon Secretaire, qui aura l'honneur de la livrer à vos mains si vous aurez la bonté de la lui demander. J'ai l'honneur d'etre avec bien de respect Monsieur votre tres humble et trés obeissant serviteur,

TH: JEFFERSON

PrC (MHi). See Peters to TJ, 1 Oct. 1786. J.-B. Le Roux, agent for Capitaine, gave a receipt to SHORT on 7 Mch. 1787 for ᵗᵗ4755ᵗᵗ-14s. (MHi).

From D'Hancarville

Paris, 25 Feb. 1787. Encloses a letter from "l'aimable Mde. Coswai" which he would have brought but he has been confined to his chamber for four months: "son mal est l'effet d'une entorse a la jambe, pareille à celle que Mr. Jefferson s'est donnée à la main. Il apprend avec déplaisir que l'effet de cette derniere se fait encore ressentir." Count de Moustier will make his apologies, and he promises himself to call on TJ when he returns from the southern provinces.

RC (DLC); 1 p.; in French. Recorded in SJL as received 25 Feb. 1787. Enclosure: Maria Cosway to TJ, 15 Feb. 1787.

From William Jones

[*Bristol, 25 Feb. 1787.* Recorded in SJL as received 26 Mch. 1787, at Aix-en-Provence. Not found, but see TJ to Jones of 5 Jan. 1787.]

To Richard Peters

DEAR SIR   Paris Feb. 26. 1787.

Your favor of Octob. 1. covering the letter and bill to Captn. Capitaine did not come to my hands till yesterday. I wrote to him immediately to inform him it should be delivered him at any moment.   We talk and think of nothing here but the Assemblée des Notables. Were all the puns collected to which this assembly has given rise, I think they would make a larger volume than the Encyclopedie. The government is said to want eighty millions of

[182]

27 FEBRUARY 1787

livres revenue more than they have and they propose to give to the people provincial administrations and to make other improvements. It is a pity they had not more of the virtue called oeconomy, of which we have something to spare. I hope the company of Mrs. Peters and your little ones have cured all your aches and pains both of body and mind. That you and they may continue for ever clear of them is the sincere prayer of Dr. Sir your friend & servt.,

TH: JEFFERSON

PrC (DLC); MS faded, and a number of words have been overwritten in a later hand, probably that of H. A. Washington (see Vol. 10: 288, note 1).

TJ was aware that Peters would be interested in THE PUNS . . . TO WHICH THIS ASSEMBLY HAS GIVEN RISE, since Peters was a famous punster.

To John Stockdale

SIR Paris Feb. 27. 1787.

By the Diligence of tomorrow I will send you a corrected copy of my Notes, which I will pray you to print precisely as they are, without additions, alterations, preface, or any thing else but what is there. They will require a very accurate corrector of the press, because they are filled with tables, which will become absolutely useless if they are not printed with a perfect accuracy. I beg you therefore to have the most particular attention paid to the correcting of the press. With respect to the plate of the map, it is impossible to send it at the same time. It was engraved in London, and on examination I found a prodigious number of orthographical errors. Being determined that it shall not go out with a single error, an engraver is now closely employed in correcting them. He promises to have it finished the next week, say by the 10th. of March: but I suppose you must expect he will not be punctual to a day. The map will be worth more than the book, because it is very particular, made on the best materials which exist, and is of a very convenient size, bringing the states of Virginia, Maryland, Delaware and Pennsylvania into a single sheet. It will make the book sell. I think it would be worth your while to print 400 copies of the book for America, sending 200. to Richmond in Virginia, and 200 to Philadelphia. If you have no correspondents there, you might send those for Richmond to Mr. James Buchanan merchant there, and those for Philadelphia to Aitken bookseller there. These are men on whose punctuality you may depend. But they should[1] be restrained from selling but for ready money: so that you may always find in their hands either the money or the books. I set out on

28 FEBRUARY 1787

my journey tomorrow: but Mr. Short, my secretary, remains here, and will hasten, and forward the plate to you by the Diligence.

Be so good as to send by the next Diligence a copy of Mr. Adams's book on the American constitutions printed by Dilly, in boards, it being for a bookseller here. I am Sir your very humble servt., TH: JEFFERSON

PrC (DLC).
The ENGRAVER of the corrected map for *Notes on Virginia* was far from being PUNCTUAL TO A DAY: he returned the plate only upon TJ's insistent demands after TJ had returned from the South of France (see TJ to Barrois, 22 June 1787).

[1] This word is interlined in substitution for "must," deleted.

To John Adams

DEAR SIR Paris Feb. 28. 1787.

The inclosed letter is come to hand since I had the honour of addressing you last. Will you be so good as to forward a copy to Mr. Jay? The assembly of Notables is held to secrecy, so that little transpires and this floats among so much incertain matter that we know not what can be depended on. 80. millions more of annual revenue and provincial assemblies are the certain objects. The giving to the protestants a civil state will be effected without recurrence to the Notables. I am now in the moment of my departure and have therefore only time to add assurances of the esteem & respect with which I have the honor to be Dear Sir your most obedient humble servt., TH: JEFFERSON

PrC (DLC). Enclosure: Barclay to the American Commissioners, 10 Feb. 1787, received by TJ on 25 Feb. 1787.

Jefferson's Letter of Credit from Ferdinand Grand

MESSIEURS [ca. 28 Feb. 1787]

Cette lettre vous sera rendue par Monsieur Jefferson, un des Cytoiens les plus respectables de l'Etat de Virginie, à la personne duquel je suis extrêmement attaché par tous les motifs qui sont faits pour inspirer l'estime et la considération. Je viens dans ces sentiments reclamer votre empressement et vos égards pour cet Ami dans le voyage qu'il entreprend dans vos provinces, et vous prier, Messieurs, de fournir à ses besoins contre ses doubles quittances, du moment des quelles je ne manquerai pas de vous tenir Compte avec reconnoissance. J'en aurai Surtout pour l'attention que vous voudrez bien avoir à ma Recommandation et je serai toujours charmé de pouvoir vous prouver à mon tour le dévouement reciproque avec lequel J'ai L'honneur d'être Messieurs Votre très humble et très obéissant Serviteur, GRAND

MS (DLC); undated; in a clerk's hand, signed by Grand; with list of addresses: "A Messieurs Finguerlin & Scherer à Lyon   J. L. Brethoul à Marseilles   Le Clerc & Cie. à Nice   Feger Gramont & Cie. à Bordeaux   Burnet Durand & De la Marche à Montpellier." An entry in TJ's Account Book under 15 Mch. reads: "recd. of Messrs. Fingerlin & co. on Mr. Grand's letter of credit 750.ᵗᵗ" &c., while in TJ's rough memoranda of the journey (CSmH), under the entry for 6 Mch. 1787, there is a list of names with addresses of persons he apparently intended to visit, including all of the addressees of the present letter. The original letters of credit of which the present is a retained file copy have not been found.

It will be noted that TJ was travelling as a private citizen, not as minister from the United States.

To Ferdinand Grand

SIR   Paris Feb. 28. 1787.

This serves to advise you that I have taken the liberty of drawing on you for the following sums paiable at the dates and to the persons here mentioned.

       in favor of Petit - - - - 1450.ᵗᵗ paiable immediately
       in favor of do. - - - - 600. paiable April 1st.
       in favor of do. - - - - 600. paiable May 1st.
       in favor of the Ct. de Langeac 1875. paiable April 15.
All those orders bear date this day.

I expect that Mr. Carmichael will draw soon for a quarter's salary which ought to be paid. I have written to Mr. Adams to send you an order to receive of Van Staphorst & Willink a sum somewhere about six hundred guineas, which be pleased to receive of them so soon as you shall have the order, and place it to the credit of the United States. It is intended to make good draughts which will be made on you in favor of the workmen employed in making medals.

I am just in the moment of my departure, and have therefore only time to thank you for the letters you have been so kind as to favor me with, and to assure you of the esteem & respect with which I have the honor to be Sir your very humble servant,

TH: JEFFERSON

PrC (DLC).

From Richard Paul Jodrell

Berners Street, London. 28th. Febry. 1787.

The Author of The Persian Heroine, having received from Mr. Jefferson Mr. Wythe's book of Virginia, intreats his acceptance of the inclosed Tragedy.

RC (MHi); endorsed: "Joddrell." Recorded in SJL as received 25 May 1787 at Bordeaux. The enclosed quarto edition of Jodrell's *The Persian Heroine*, London, 1786, was probably not received with the covering letter but left at the Hôtel de Langeac with other books and letters brought by Smith in TJ's absence on his southern tour (Smith to TJ, 19 May 1787).

TJ's inscription to Jodrell in a presentation copy of *Notes on Virginia* had led the latter to suppose George Wythe its author (see note to Wythe to TJ, 10 Feb. 1786).

To Lafayette

Paris Feb. 28. 1787.

I am just now, my dear Sir, in the moment of my departure. Monsr. de Montmorin having given us audience at Paris yesterday, I missed the opportunity of seeing you once more. I am extremely pleased with his modesty, the simplicity of his manners, and his dispositions towards us. I promise myself a great deal of satisfaction in doing business with him. I hope he will not give ear to any unfriendly suggestions. I flatter myself I shall hear from you sometimes. Send your letters to my hotel as usual and they will be forwarded to me. I wish you success in your meeting. I should form better hopes of it if it were divided into two houses instead of seven. Keeping the good model of your neighboring country before your eyes you may get on step by step towards a good constitution. Tho' that model is not perfect, yet as it would unite more suffrages than any new one which could be proposed, it is better to make that the object. If every advance is to be purchased by filling the royal coffers with gold, it will be gold well employed. The king, who means so well, should be encouraged to repeat these assemblies. You see how we republicans are apt to preach when we get on politics. Adieu my dear friend.

Yours affectionately,
TH: JEFFERSON

PrC (DLC).

To Madame de Tessé

Paris Feb. 28. 1787.

If you will be so good, Madam, as to send to my hotel any letters with which you will be pleased to honour and relieve me on my journey, Mr. Short if he is here will take care to forward them, and with the more care as coming from you. If he should not be here, they will be forwarded by a servant who has charge of the house. My letters will be sent to me by post twice a week.

I have had the pleasure to learn from Mr. Berard of Lorient that he has our box of Magnolia and Dionæas safe; that he will send it by the first Diligence; and take measures to prevent their being stopped or opened on the road, at the Douanes. This information was dated the 21st. of February, and as the Diligence is fifteen days on the road, we may expect them from the 7th. to the 14th. of March. My servant will carry them to you the moment they arrive, as well as any other parcels of seeds or plants, should any others escape thru all the dangers and difficulties which beset them.   I set out on my journey in the moment of writing this. It is a moment of powerful sensibility for your goodness and friendship, wherein I feel how precious they are to my heart, and with how affectionate an esteem & respect I have the honor to be Madam, your most obedient & most humble servant,

TH: JEFFERSON

PrC (MoSHi).

If TJ received a letter from MR. BERARD OF LORIENT dated the 21st, it has not been found; it is probable that TJ only had in mind information received from Bérard through Champion's letter of 21 Feb. 1787, q.v.

To Madame de Tott

Paris Feb. 28. 1787.

Have you been, Madam, to see the superb picture now exhibiting in the rue Ste. Nicaise, No. 9. chez Mde. Drouay? It is that of Marius in the moment when the souldier [ente]rs to assassinate him. It is made by her son, a student at Rome under the care of David, and is much in David's manner. All Paris is running to see it, and really it appears to me to have extraordinary merit. It fixed me like a statue a quarter of an hour, or half an hour, I do [not] know which, for I lost all ideas of time, "even the consciousness of my existence." If you have not been, let me engage you to go, for I think it will give you pleasure. Write me your judgment on it: it will serve to rectify my own, which as I have told you is a bad one, and needs a guide. It will multiply too the occasions of my hearing from you; occasions which I claim by promise, and which will strew some roses in the lengthy road I am to travel. That your road, through life, may be covered with roses, is the sincere prayer of him who has the honour to mingle his Adieus with sentiments of the most affectionate esteem and respect, TH: JEFFERSON

PrC (MoSHi); MS faded, illegible words supplied in brackets.

A reproduction of the painting by Drouais that all Paris was running to see is to be found in this volume. On 17 Mch. 1787 the *Journal de Paris* made the following comment: "Le Tableau de *Marius* de M. *Drouais* a attiré chez Mme sa Mère un concours extraordinaire et a paru justifier l'opinion avantageuse qu'on avoit conçue du talent de ce jeune Artiste sur son premier ouvrage."

To St. John de Crèvecoeur

DEAR SIR [ca. Feb. 1787]

I return you your papers with many thinks. Monsr. de Chalut who has shewn me many civilities, being desirous of sending some packages of pictures to Charles town I advised him to send them by the packet from Havre to New York, and to have them reimbarked thence to Charles town. He asks me for a correspondent at New York to whom he may address them. Knowing that men of the same language and nation can always give the best satisfaction to each other, I will beg your permission to let them be addressed to your deputy at N. York. Will you be so good as to give me a line to him, desiring him to take the trouble of receiving and reshipping them? If you could send me such a line by the return of the bearer it would much oblige Dr Sir Your friend & servt TH: JEFFERSON

RC (Louis St. John de Crèvecoeur, Montesquieu-sur-Losse, France, 1947); not dated and not recorded in SJL, but evidently written soon after TJ received back from Soulès the "papers" respecting the Wyoming massacre that had been lent to the latter through TJ's good offices (see TJ to Soulès, 2 Feb. 1787) and were also enclosed in the present letter.

From John Adams

DEAR SIR London March 1. 1787

I am much obliged to you for your favours of Feb. 20. and 23 by Mr. Carnes, and the curious Pamphlets.

Opening a direct Communication between Paris and America will facilitate the Trade of the two Countries, very much, and the new Treaty between France and England, will promote it still more. John Bull dont see it, and if he dont see a Thing at first, you know it is a rule with him ever after wards to swear that it dont exist, even when he does both see it and feel it.

I have this moment written to Messrs. Willinks and Vanstaphorsts to remit to you or Mr. Grand in your absence, what remains to be received to make up the Thousand Guineas for the Swords and Medals, you having before drawn for 6500 Livres tournois, as part of them.

My Resolution of Quitting Europe, has been taken upon mature deliberation: but really upon motives of Necessity, as much at least as Choice.—Congress cannot consistent with their own honour and Dignity, renew my Commission to this Court—and I assure you, I should hold it so inconsistent with my own honour and Dignity little as that may be, that if it were possible for Congress to forget theirs I would not forget mine, but send their Commission back to them, unless a Minister were sent from his Britannic Majesty to Congress.

As to a Residence in Holland, that Climate is so destructive to my health, that I could never bear it: and I am sure it would be fatal to her, on whom depends all the satisfaction that I have in Life. No Consideration would tempt me to think of removing to that Country with my Family.

For a Man who has been thirty Years rolling like a stone never three years in the same Place, it is no very pleasant Speculation, to cross the seas with a Family, in a State of Uncertainty what is to be his fate; what reception he shall meet at home; whether he shall set down in private Life to his Plough; or push into turbulent Scenes of Sedition and Tumult; whether be sent to Congress, or a Convention or God knows what.—If it lay in my Power, I would take a Vow, to retire to my little Turnip yard, and never again quit it.—I feel very often a violent disposition to take some Resolution and swear to it. But upon the whole, it is best to preserve my Liberty to do as I please according to Circumstances.

The approbation you express in general of my poor Volume, is a vast consolation to me. It is an hazardous Enterprize, and will be an unpopular Work in America for a long time.—When I am dead, it may be regretted that such Advice was not taken in the season of it.—But as I have made it early in life and all along a

Rule to conceal nothing from the People which appeared to me material for their Happiness and Prosperity, however unpopular it might be at the time, or with particular Parties, I am determined not now to begin to flatter popular Prejudices and Party Passions however they may be countenanced by great authorities.

The Opinion you Object to p. 362, "that Congress is not a legislative but a diplomatic assembly" I should wish to have considered as a Problem, rather for Consideration, than as an opinion: and as a Problem too, relative to the Confederation as it now stands, rather than to any other Plan that may be in Contemplation of the States. It is a most difficult Topick, and no Man at a distance can judge of it, so well as those in America. If the Book Should be translated into french, I wish you would insert this, in a Note. You have laid me under great obligation, by taking the trouble to Secure a Good Translator.—If the Thing is worth translating at all, it will not surely bare to loose any Thing by the Translation.— But will not the Government proscribe[1] it?—If I should get well home, and Spend a few Years in Retirement, I shall pursue this subject, somewhat further: but I hope never to be left, again, to publish so hasty a Production as this. A Work upon the Subject you mention, *Nobility in general*, which I once hinted to you a wish to see handled at large would be too extensive and Splendid for my means and Forces. It would require many Books which I have not, and a more critical Knowledge both of ancient and modern Languages than at my Age a Man can aspire to.—There are but two Circumstances, which will be regretted by me, when I leave Europe. One is the oppertunity of Searching any questions of this kind, in any books that may be wanted, and the other will be the Interruption of that intimate[2] Correspondence with you, which is one of the most agreable Events in my Life. There are four or five Persons here, with whom I hold a friendly Intercourse and shall leave with some degree of Pain but I am not at home in this Country.

With every affectionate and friendly Sentiment I am and shall be in this world and the future yours, JOHN ADAMS

RC (DLC); endorsed. FC (MHi: AMT); in W. S. Smith's hand, with differences in phraseology, two of which are noted below.

[1] FC reads "prohibit."
[2] FC reads "immediate."

From Elias Hasket Derby

SIR Salem, 1st. March, 1787

I have the Honor of inclosing You a letter from Our mutual Friend the Honble. John Sullivan Esqr. President of the State of New Hampshire, Incloseing Copy of a Petition from me to His most Christian Majesty, with depositions of Captain Nichols who had the transacting the bussiness at Port au Prince, and Capt. Tibbetts who was Comander of Capt. Nichols's Vessell before she was conveyed to Mr. LeMaire the French Merchant there, to support said Petition. And many more depositions may be obtained purporting the same from several American Masters of Vessels that were present at the time. By these papers you will see the method taken by these People to defraud Capt. Nichols of His and my Interest. I will not trespass on your time and patience by comenting on the papers. I have received two papers from the West Indies, Copys of which I now inclose you. One a letter from Mr. LeMaire to Mr. Francis De la Ville Merchant Nantz dated Port au Prince 16th. Augt. 1786, acknowledging the Debt, and directing Him to deliver Vessell, and Cargo, to Capt. Nichols, or to follow his directions relating the Interest. The other an Obligation given by Mr. J. Marc Barrere dated the 31st. Aug. 1786, wherein He obliges Himself to prosecute the Appeal, and supposes there is reason to think that the Judgement will be reversed, and promises to hold Himself accountable to Capt. Nichols or His order for the same, deducting the charges that may attend the prosecution; compareing these two papers their Art may be seen. Le Maire is the first of the House and Consigns the Vessell, and Cargo to Messrs. De la Ville as by His letter of the 16th. Augt. 86. After she is Condemned, J. Marc Barrere on the 31st. day of August, 86, gives an Obligation to Capt. Nichols to prosecute an Appeal, and account with Him, or Order, for what may be recoverd. I would observe that Monsr. Le Maire was the man to whom Capt. Nichols made over his Vessel, and the only One that He put any confidence in, that taking alltogather there is the greatest Appearance of Fraud, and design, that if the Interest was recover'd the Originall Owners should not be benifited by it. Mr. Le Maire, or Barrere, or both, have had the address to keep every other paper relating the concern from Capt. Nichols's hand.

J. M. Barrere's obligation shows that they promised Capt. Nichols to persue his claim to France, and Capt: Nichols has informed me that they promised Him to write Me from Time, to Time of Their Doings, but I have not as yet received a line from them, and by what I hear from that way, I do not expect they will write me on the Subject.

They have all the papers, and vouchers in their possession, and not prosicuting the Appeal to France, I have no remedy left but by Petitioning His Most Christian Majesty, and for that purpose I now inclose to my Son Elias Hasket Derby who is now in France the petition to the King with the several papers accompanying it. Should there be any inaccuracy, in any of the Forms, or Expressions made use of, my Ignorance I hope will be my Apoligy.

Presuming on your Excellencys readiness to Assist the Injured and Oppress'd, especially a Citizen of America, I have directed my Son to wait on Your Excellency, and I flatter myself you will direct a youth unacqainted with the Etiquette of Courts, and seeking redress for an injured Father the steps properest to be taken to lay His complaint at His Majestys feet.

Any Assistance you may Afford my Son in this Transaction, will greatly Oblige, & be highly esteem'd by Your Excellency's most Obedient, & very Humble Servant,

ELIAS HASKET DERBY

RC (DLC). Recorded in SJL as received 16 June 1787. Enclosures: (1) Sullivan to TJ, 26 Jan. 1787 (second letter), and its enclosures. (2) Notarized copy of Le Maire to Francis de la Ville, Port au Prince, 16 Aug. 1786 (DLC), stating that he owes 160,000 livres to Captain Nichols payable in island produce, but that on account of the scarcity of specie and the prohibition against exporting thence to a foreign port anything but molasses or taffia, he has decided to purchase the *Neptune* from Nichols; and that the vessel had been "loaded and Consigned to you for, and on Account of Mr. Nichols whose orders I desire you may follow with strictest sense, being persuaded that in Case markets should be low with you he will again reload the same Cargo," in which case De la Ville was to deliver to Nichols "the Vessel & Cargo in her present situation"; Le Maire reiterated: "I would moreover observe to you that these Goods were shipped for his Account and Risque, my Debt with him being discharged by this Remittance. I again repeat that you are to hold all at his disposal." (3) Notarized copy of the declaration signed J. Marc Barrere, Port au Prince, 31 Aug. 1786 (DLC), in which he states that as "the Snow Neptune Capt Vavasuer formerly the Lydia Capt Richard Tibbets the property of Capt Ichabod Nichols" had been seized with her cargo and condemned by the admiralty court "on Suspicion of Illicit and Contraband Trade," and as there was reason to believe an appeal would be made to have the judgment nullified in France, he would do everything possible to have the judgment set aside and, if this were done, he would hold himself accountable to Nichols for the vessel and cargo. (4) A declaration dated at Boston, 22 Feb. 1787, signed by John Lowell, Samuel Phillips, Jr., Nathaniel Gorham, and Elbridge Gerry, stating: "We the undersigners do hereby certify that We are well acquainted with Elias Hasket Derby Esqr. of Salem and do consider him as one of the first Merchants in this Commonwealth for respectability and honor in his dealings, and as a Gentleman to whose representations or declarations full Credit is justly do" (clerk's copy, signed by those named, in DLC, attested by Gov. James Bowdoin under the seal of the Commonwealth, who certified that Phillips was president of the Massachusetts Senate,

Gorham late president and at that time a member of Congress, and Gerry and Lowell late members of Congress; signed by Bowdoin, and also dated 22 Feb. 1787).

From Alexander Donald

DEAR SIR Richmond 1st. March 1787

In the multiplicity of important business, which must take up your time and attention, I am almost affraid to trouble you with this letter. But recollecting with much satisfaction, your former Friendship, I trust that your good nature will pardon me for intrudeing upon your time, and haveing the honour of being a Citizen of this State, and being deeply interested in its Welfare, I hope you will not think me impertinent in communicateing to you the following information.

In consequence of the Agreement with the Farmers General of France on the 24th. May last, for to recieve from 12. to 15,000 hhds. of Tobacco over and above the quantity contracted for with Mr. Morris at the same prices which are paid to him, provided the Tobacco was sent direct from the place of its growth, in French or American vessels, several speculations have already been made, and I have lately chartered a large Ship to send to Havre de Grace, but I am much allarmed at being lately informed that every possible obstacle is thrown in the way of carrying the resolutions of the Committee of Berni into effect. Some cargoes have been refused, and those that have been accepted, has been at an inferiour price to what Mr. Morris recieves for Tobacco shipt from the very same Rivers. I hope this information is not founded. But if it is, many individuals will suffer severely by their confidence, and it will be a great loss to the Publick, For the prices allowed Mr. Morris appeared so tempting, that many Gentlemen were induced to speculate to France. The consequence has been a very considerable rise in the price of Tobacco at all the lower warehouses on this River, as well as at Petersburg, and upon Rappk. and Potowmack, from which places Mr. Alexander chiefly draws his quantity. He ships very little from this place, or Pages (where you and myself have passed some happy days). I will take the liberty of writing my Partner Mr. Robt. Burton in London, that if there is any obstacles in the way of receiveing the Cargo of Tobacco which my Friends are now shipping for Havre, to apply to you for your Friendly and effectual interposition. For tho Mr. Morris's contract is at an end this year, yet if the Farmers General or their

[193]

1 MARCH 1787

Agents, have it in their power to evade the receiveing all Tobacco that does not come from Mr. Morris or his Agents, your spirited exertions in behalf of this State and Maryland will be rendered nugatory, and of no effect, and the Tobacco Trade to France, must remain to all intents and purposes, a monopoly in the hands of Mr. M. and his Friends, as it has done since the conclusion of the War. And they may buy the inferiour qualities in this Country at any price they please.

I will not presume to trouble you with my opinion of the Political situation of the United States. That you will no doubt be informed of by those who are more adequate to the Task. But I cannot help expressing great uneasyness at the disturbances in the Eastern States. And it gives me pain to add, that the People in this State will in the course of a year or two, be unable even to pay the taxes, unless there is a possibility of falling upon some happy plan of moderateing their extravagance, and encourageing their industry. I am sure you will blush for your Countrymen, when I assure you that in this, and all the other Towns in this State, we are supplied by our Sister States to the Eastward, with the most of our Hay, Cabbages, Potatoes, onions &c. and that they even send us Lime, Bricks, and frameing for Houses ready for setting up. Many a time I laugh at my Friends for their want of industry.

Last Fall I was up in Albermarle and passed a very happy week with our Friend Jack Walker, and his *Cara Sposa*. I had the Honour of forwarding a letter to you lately from him.

It would be presumptuous in me to make you an offer of my services here, but I beg you will do me the Justice to believe, that it would make me happy, if I could serve you either here or in London, and I can add, that my Partner's sentiments perfectly accord with mine.

I am with great respect & esteem Dear Sir Your mo: obt. humb St.,
A DONALD

RC (DLC); endorsed. Recorded in SJL as received 11 June 1787.

ALEXANDER was Morris's agent in Virginia in the purchase of tobacco. The LETTER TO YOU from John Walker must not have been that of 4 Feb. 1786, which Donald would scarcely have referred to as having been forwarded lately. TJ had received Walker's of 4 Feb. on 23 June 1786, and, since it spoke of the death of his daughter, it is possible that TJ replied during the latter part of 1786 and that Walker wrote again. However, no such letters are recorded in SJL or have been found. In the light of the politically inspired charges of a later day concerning TJ's relations with Mrs. Walker (see Malone, *Jefferson the Virginian*, "The Walker Affair, 1768-1809," p. 447-51), it is important to note that the letter of 4 Feb. 1786 addressed TJ as "My Dear Friend" and that Walker assured TJ "Mrs. Walker . . . begs to be affectionately remember'd to you and Miss Patsy."

From Benjamin Vaughan

SIR [ca. 1 Mch. 1787]

I take the liberty to introduce to your acquaintance, Mr. Garnett of Bristol, a gentleman who is particularly recommended to me by my particular connection Mr. Richard Bright of Bristol, as his friend and a person of very good character. His object with you, will be to make you acquainted with an invention of his (for which himself and the Revd. Mr. Milton have obtained a patent here) for relieving friction upon the axes of wheels &c. Its simplicity will soon enable you to determine how far it may be useful in the United States; and your protection of the invention and its author, in case you should approve it, will give you a pleasure, which I am happy in being the means of bringing to your Excellency's notice. I have the honor to be with great respect, Your Excellency's Most obedient & most humble servt., BENJN. VAUGHAN

RC (DLC); undated; endorsed. The date has been assigned from Short's letter to TJ of 6 Apr. 1787 which reads in part: "A Mr. Garnett . . . brought some letters and left a card for you two or three weeks past"; and from an entry in SJL recording the receipt of an undated letter from Vaughan on 26 Mch. 1787 at Aix-en-Provence (see also TJ to Vaughan, 2 July 1787).

C. W. F. Dumas to William Short

MONSIEUR LaHaie 2e Mars 1787

J'ai l'honneur de vous adresser l'incluse pour le Congrès, toujours ouverte, ainsi que celles qui suivront, afin que S. E. M. Jefferson ait la satisfaction à son retour de voir ce que vous jugerez à propos d'en noter ou extraire pour le tenir au courant des affaires de ce pays.

Je suppose, Monsieur, que vous savez ce que c'est que l'*Ouverture* dont je parle dans l'incluse. Mais il est de mon devoir, tant envers, Mr. Jefferson qu'envers d'autres à qui je dois le secret de vous prier de me marquer très clairement et promptement que vous le savez, afin que je puisse non seulement vous écrire plus explicitement là-dessus moi-même, mais aussi vous adresser une Lettre qu'on écrira peut-être à ce sujet à Mr. Jefferson, pour qu'il puisse, ou vous, Monsieur, pendant son absence, donner connoissance au Congrès du contenu par le paquebot qui partira du Havre le 25 de ce mois.

Veuillez me faire part des bonnes nouvelles que vous aurez

2 MARCH 1787

de la santé de Mr. Jefferson, et de lui faire parvenir mes voeux à cet égard et mes respects. Mr. Massey est-il toujours à Paris? Il a, avec vous, les meilleurs complimens de ma famille et de celui qui a l'honneur d'être, avec la plus parfaite estime et considération, Monsieur, Votre très-humble & très obéissant serviteur

C W F Dumas

RC (DLC: Short Papers); endorsed: "Dumas — Mar.2.87. [received] — 10." FC (Rijksarchief, The Hague, Dumas Papers; photostats in DLC). Enclosure (FC in same): Dumas to Jay, 27 Feb. 1787, with a postscript added on 2 Mch. 1787 (printed in *Dipl. Corr., 1783-89*, III, 565-7); forwarded by Short to Jay, 21 Mch. 1787.

L'OUVERTURE DONT JE PARLE DANS L'INCLUSE: This was the proposal concerning the purchase of the American debt to France by Holland bankers (see TJ to Jay, 1 Feb. 1787); as translated and printed in *Dipl. Corr., 1783-89*, III, 565-6, Dumas's comment on the OUVERTURE in his letter to Jay reads: "Mr. Jefferson has, I know, sent to Congress by the last packet from Havre a most important proposition, which came through me to him; but I am ignorant whether it was addressed to your department. In any case, I think it necessary to inform you, sir, that the affair, which will be most favorable to the United States, as well as agreeable to France, must be carried on with the utmost secrecy, not only in America but also in Europe, especially at Amsterdam, at which place it is most essential to its success, that no one should be made acquainted with it, nor authorized by Congress to act upon it, except Mr. Jefferson and myself, under his orders. In this case, Congress would only have to acquiesce in a most admirable arrangement." Short was well informed about this matter, and when the present letter was received by him on 10 Mch., he made extracts bearing the following caption: "Extracts from M. Dumas's letters to Mr. Jay, taken by his request for the perusal of M. Jefferson"; the MS in which Short recorded these extracts of Dumas' letter of "March 2" also included brief extracts of Dumas' letters to Jay of 23 and 30 Mch. 1787 (DLC: Short Papers). Dumas' understandable injunction to secrecy was useless; for, ten days earlier, Otto in New York had reported the facts of this OUVERTURE to Vergennes: "Une compagnie de negocians hollandois ayant fait transmettre au Congrès un projet de rembourser sur le champ la dette des Etats unis envers la france et de se nantir de la creance de S.M., cette assemblée en a renvoyé l'examen au Bureau de la tresorier. Ce Bureau, Monseigneur, est bien eloigné d'approuver la proposition des hollandois. Dans le raport qu'il a remis au Congrès il commence par analyser les vues que ces negocians peuvent avoir en se chargeant d'une dette qui dans ce moment ci est presque desesperée. Il lui paroit probable que les hollandois n'ont fait cette offre que parce qu'ils esperent se faire payer en denrées et s'emparer pendant plusieurs années d'une espece de monopole en Amerique. Les Commissaires pensent que le Congrès n'a aucun interêt de changer la nature d'une dette qui a toujours été regardee par les Americains comme sacrée puisqu'elle a été contractée non seulement envers leur bienfaieur mais pour suppleer aux besoins les plus pressans de la confederation, qu'en transferant cette creance aux hollandois elle cesseroit d'être aussi respectable et les peuples sentiroient beaucoup moins la nécessité de se liberer; qu'il est très heureux pour le Congrès d'avoir une grand dette à payer, parceque sans ce lien commun la confederation perdroit bientot toute son importance par le refus des peuples de suvenir aux besoins du gouvernement general, mais que la consideration des grands services rendus par la france foruniroit toujours de puissans motifs pour disposer les peuples à remplir les engagemens pris par le Congrès, qu'il ne paroit pas d'ailleurs que S.M.F. Chret. soit instruite de cette proposition et qu'elle pourroit être offensée d'une demarche aussi importante, qui devoit dans tous les cas avoir son approbation avant de produire aucun effet; que S.M. paroit avoir egard à la confusion actuelle des affaires en Amerique et qu'Elle attendra vraisemblablement une epoque plus favorable pour demander les arrerages qui lui sont dus. Les Commissaires proposent donc de rejeter entierement le projet des hollandois. Cette affaire, Monseigneur, est encore tres secrete et ce n'est qu'avec beaucoup de peine que j'ai pu me procurer les details que j'ai l'honneur de Vous transmettre. Le Congres n'a pas encore pris de resolution" (Otto to Vergennes, 17 Feb. 1787; Arch. Aff. Etr., Paris, Corr. Pol., E.-U., XXXII; Tr in DLC; endorsed as received 23 Mch. 1787). Two days after Otto wrote, the Commissioners of the Treasury—Samuel Osgood, Walter Livingston, and Arthur Lee—submitted their report on the proposal that TJ had transmitted to them in his letter of 26 Sep. 1786 (JCC, XXXII, 65). It may have been one of these who gave Otto the information of the "tres secrete" nature of the report.

C. W. F. Dumas to William Short

MONSIEUR Lahaie 2e. Mars 1787

Cette nuit part pour Paris Mr. le Rh. Gr. de Salm, chargé d'affaires les plus importantes pour cette Republique et pour la France. Il aura la bonté de vous remettre une Lettre de ma part. Il auroit bien des choses à dire à S.E. Mr. Jefferson. Je l'ai averti qu'on étoit absent, mais qu'il pouvoit s'ouvrir à vous en toute confiance, comme s'il le faisoit à Mr. Jefferson lui-même. Celle-ci est pour vous prévenir que vous pouvez avoir la même confiance envers lui sur ce qu'il vous dira des affaires de la republique, de la France et de moi. J'ai l'honneur d'être avec la plus sincere estime & considération Monsieur Votre trés humble et trés-obeissant serviteur C. W. F. DUMAS

RC (DLC: Short Papers); endorsed in part: "2 March. [received] 9 [Mch.]." FC (Rijksarchief, The Hague, Dumas Papers; photostats in DLC); several variations in phraseology; the name of the Rhinegrave de Salm is heavily scored out.

From Lavoisier

MONSIEUR Paris 3. mars 1787

J'ai été pénétré de reconnoissance en recevant avec la lettre dont vous m'avés honoré Le Diplôme qui me donne le titre de Membre de la Société Philosophique de Philadelphie. Un Zèle ardent pour tout ce qui peut contribuer à la destruction des Erreurs et aux progrès des connoissances humaines; Une grande vénération pour Les grands hommes qui ont rendu La Liberté aux habitans d'une des plus belles parties de l'Univers, Voila les Seuls titres que J'avois à offrir à la Société. Animé depuis Longtems des mêmes vües qu'elle, Je m'honorerai de l'association à la quelle Elle veut bien m'appeller. Je ferai tous mes Efforts pour m'Elever Jusqu'a Elle pour partager Ses nobles travaux et pour concourir avec Elle à tout ce qui peut rendre Les hommes meilleurs et plus heureux.

3 MARCH 1787

J'ai L'honneur d'etre très respectueusement Monsieur Votre très humble et très Obéissant Serviteur, LAVOISIER

RC (ViWC). Recorded in SJL as received 26 Mch. 1787 at Aix-en-Provence.

From De Saint-Paterne

MONSIEUR A Versailles le 3. mars 1787.

Les vertus de Mr. Washington m'ont inspiré le désir de faire des vers pour son Portrait; j'ai l'honneur de vous les envoyer avec la lettre que je vous supplie de faire parvenir à Messieurs les membres du *Congrès*, si vous la jugez favorablement. Je remets ma cause entre vos mains, et quelque soit vôtre jugement il ne diminuera rien des sentiments reconnoissants et respectueux avec lesquels j'ai l'honneur d'être, Monsieur Vôtre trés humble et trés obéissant serviteur,

DE SAINT-PATERNE
officier de la grande Fauconnerie,
cour des princes.

RC (DLC); endorsed. Recorded in SJL as received 26 Mch. 1787 at Aix-en-Provence. Enclosures not identified.

From Madame de Tott

A Paris ce 4. mars *1787*.

J'ai suivi Le conseil que Vous avez eu la bonté de me donner, Monsieur; J'ai été voir Le tableau de Mr. Drouai et J'en ai été Vraiment étonnée; mais puisque Vous Voulez absolument que je Vous dise Les Remarques que J'ai faites, quoique Vous Soyez parfaitement en état de Le Juger Vous même, et par Le gout exquis que Vous avez sur tout, et par l'étendue de Vos connoissances, Je Vais Vous Obeïr.—Je trouve Le soldat admirable, Le ton de sa couleur est harmonieux et fort, son Attitude est parfaitement belle, parfaitement naturelle; en Un mot L'ensemble de sa personne est Vraiment le grand genre de L'histoire. Quant à marius, ce n'est pas La figure ni Le corps de marius de L'histoire Romaine. Infiniment plus instruit que moi Vous aurez sans-doute été plus frappé de La figure délicate et presque chétive qu'on donne à cet homme célèbre. Il me semble qu'on dît qu'il avoit une figure commune, mais très caracterisée et qu'elle approchoit plus de La ferocité, que de La délicatesse qu'il y a dans Le marius de Mr. Drouai, quoiqu'il lui ait donné une expression très forte. Son bras, ses Jambes et son Corps sont trop blancs, sa Draperie qui a des beautés est d'un ton de couleur trop entier, Le bras sur Lequel il est appuyé est trop nonchalant, trop tranquille pour L'action de L'autre et pour L'expression de La figure.—Voila Monsieur Les défauts que j'ai trouvé dans Un tableau qui est cependant fait pour produire La plus grande sensation et qui annonce Le plus grand talent dans son auteur. Permettez moi, actuellement que je Vous ai Obeï, de Vous parler Un peu du plaisir que j'ai eu en Recevant une Marque de Votre souvenir Le Jour de Votre départ, permettez moi de Vous exprimer ma Reconnoissance, et de Vous Remercier de tout ce que Votre Lettre a d'Obligeant. L'assemblée des notables nous prive du plaisir de Voir Mr. de La Fayette, Mr. Short se trouve mieux à St. Germain qu'à Paris, et comme nous ne pouvons avoir de Vos nouvelles que par l'un de ses Messieurs, nous en serons privées Jusqu'à ce que Vous ayez La bonté de nous en donner Vous même. Veuillez bien Vous Rappeller Monsieur La promesse que Vous nous avez faite et agréer L'assurance de tous Les sentiments que je Vous ai Voués pour La Vie.

RC (MoSHi); unsigned; endorsed: "Tott Mde. de." Recorded in SJL as received 26 Mch. 1787 at Aix-en-Provence.

From Gaudenzio Clerici

SIR Novara the 5th. March 1787

I hope the temperature of the air of Provence has made you less sensible of the inconstancy and gloominess of the winter. Tho', I must not tell You, Sir, that it is but a weak participation that Provence makes of the serenity and mildness of an Italian Climate. Pardon my impertinence, Sir. Will you resist the temptation? You have but a step, Sir, from Aix to the Garden of Europe, and to the Country of Brutus and Cicero. Will you have nothing to say from your own observations of modern Italy and of modern Italians? You will see they are neither so bad as Sharp and Smollet would have made their Countrimen believe, nor so good as I wished once at annapolis to represent them to you. Come, Sir, give an impartial look, and let a philosophical tear drop wherever you see Miseries and Wretchedness multiplied by the hand of Oppression. Oh! How often you will turn your thoughts upon the Land of Cabot and mutter to your Countrymen O fortunati nimium ec:!

In truth, a little we had of that. Too much I have seen on the

6 MARCH 1787

other side of the great water: we should both countries in my opinion be better.—I do not know whether too much Liberty is not worse than too little to live in society.

I saw my mother and my friends, who received me with a mixt of joy and wonder to see me back from that "Undiscovered Country" from whose bourn, according to their notion no traveller returns. They are never satisfied to hear me talk of americans and american Liberty. When I tell them that america is the Country that produces and makes Philosophers, and that the generality of the inhabitants know better men and books than we do, they say it savours of a Paradox but they believe [it] at last to be a fact. I shall not trouble you as often I would wish with my letters for I know your affairs will not permit you to extend your correspondence to mere matters of Curiosity and compliments. Although I flatter myself to receive the honor of a line from you, Sir, to know your State of Health since your change of Climate, give me leave in the mean time with all possible candor to express my ambition to continue the honor of being what I always prided to be since the happy moment of my being acquainted with You, Sir, Your very respectful Sert., GAUDENZIO CLERICI

P.S. I request to direct Turin pour Novare.

RC (DLC); endorsed. Recorded in SJL as received 26 Mch. 1787 at Aix-en-Provence.

To Visly

[Dijon, 6 Mch. 1787. Under this date in TJ's rough journal of his journey through Southern France and Italy (CSmH) there is an entry reading: "wrote Presdt. de Visly letter recommendation Hayward." Not found.]

From De Guichén

MONSIEUR a morllaix ce 7 mars *1787*

Je récois avec la plus vive sensibilitté, la lettre dont votre excellance a bien voullu m'honnorer; et m'annoncer la grace que MM. de la Sociétté philosophique de philadelphie ont eu la bonté de m'admettre membre de leur tres respectable sociétté. Je sens Monsieur tout le prix d'une favoeur aussi particulliere; que mes faibles tallants ne me permettoit pas d'esperer; et aux quels je ne puis supléer, que par les sentiments de la plus parffaicte reconnaiscance,

[200]

et par la scinceritté de la part que je prendray toujours à ce qui poura l'intteresser. Perméttés moy de suplier votre excellance, d'avoir la complaisance d'estre l'interprètte de la puréttés de ses sentiments; et de prendre la libértté en leur presantant mes plus profonds respectueux hommages, de les suplier d'agreer mes tres humbles et parffaicts remerciments, d'un choix aussi honnorable que flatteur pour moy, qui ne me laisse rien à desirer que les ocasions de le meritter.

Jay l'honneur d'estre avec un tres profond respec de votre excellance Monsieur Votre tres humble et tres obeissant serviteur,

LE CTE. DE GUICHÉN

RC (DLC). Recorded in SJL as received 26 Mch. 1787 at Aix-en-Provence.

From Benjamin Hawkins

DEAR SIR   New-York 8th. March 1787

I have had within a few days the pleasure to receive your favor of the 13th august. It was received at the office of Foreign affairs in Novr. and has been traveling since southwardly and Northwardly to meet with me. I have been attentive to your other request, and expect I shall be able to send you a few plants of the Dionaea muscipula some time this Spring. Mr. de la Forest who returns to France promises to take charge of them: and a very attentive worthy man is to send me a dozen or more from Wilmington in small earthen pots. I will also send you some of the seed as soon as it is practicable. I shall send you by Mr. de la Forest the little Vocabulary of the Cherokee and Choctaw tongues: and such other information as I may receive. I have a letter from Mr. McGillivray which gives room to hope by that period he will have answered fully the part I allotted to him.

We are not here in so profound a calm as in Europe. The uneasinesses which have existed in Massachusets for some time past grew into a serious opposition to that Government, and they are now by the vigorous though not timely opposition of the government put in train of adjustment. The Southern States are more tranquil, and are emerging fast into order; and if the Foederal Government can be made efficient the revolution will be a blessing to them. Virginia taking the lead for this most desirable object proposed a convention to be in may next at Philadelphia. North Carolina and some other States have followed her example and Congress on the

8 MARCH 1787

21st. of February recommended it to all as the most probable mean of establishing a firm national Government.

Spain availing herself of probable conjectures bids far to be the first power who will strengthen our bonds of Union. Unmindful of her true interest, she seems determined to oppose her partial contracted policy, to that generous reciprocity of mutual good offices, which being the basis of our friendship would be a never failing guarantee to both Nations. She has seized some of our boats on the Mississipi and refuses us absolutely the navigation thereof. Our citizens view this as an infraction of their rights. The States of Virginia, North Carolina, New Jersey and some others have expressed it in strong terms; the words of North Carolina are "That their delegates be instructed to oppose in the most unequivocal terms any attempt that may be made to barter or surrender to any Nation the right of this State to the free and common Navigation of the Mississipi, and in case any such surrender should take place, that they should be instructed to protest against the same, as an unjust depravation of the right of this State, and one which Congress are not authorized to make by the articles of confederation."

This arose from this additional circumstance. *Seven*[1] *states* only *counting from the east have repealed the article in favor of the Missisipi in the instructions to* Mr. *Jay and he* is now at full liberty to *shut up or not the Missisipi* and he appears to me to approve of it for the *period of twenty years*. Should this take place, I know not what consequences may ensue. Our Western citizens will feel much alarmed for their situation. They will have less *confidence in the justice of Congress* and be disposed to *carve* for *themselves*. They are already numerous and daily increasing. For a *violation of a treaty Congress would be immediately responsible* and probably our western citizens might *skirmish for some years without bringing about an open rupture and within eight or ten we would be able to support our right. What can be done? You may eventually be able to do something*. If the French court had the Floridas and would establish an entrepôt at New-Orleans or some other place equally convenient on a liberal scale, it would certainly be of the first consequence to them, in a commercial point of view, as we should consume their manufactures principally, in return for the raw materials which we could supply them with in abundance. With Spain somthing could be done if we had a man of great abilities and prudence at Madrid there to treat; here I am sure we

8 MARCH 1787

have nothing to hope as I conjecture Mr. Gardoqui has duped himself and consequently given such an impression of things here as to lead his court to be very sanguine in their expectations. And *he does not appear to me to be a man of a noble mind enough to acknowledge his error* and to give that true complexion which he has certainly learnt to discover.

I have used the cypher of our friend Mr. Madison. He, expecting shortly an opportunity more certain than the present postpones writing untill then, and he presents you his most respectful compliments. Your acquaintance Mr. Nash is dead and I am in Congress in his stead.

I am with sincere esteem & regard & Friendship Dear Sir your most obedient hle. Servt.,   BENJAMIN HAWKINS

RC (DLC); endorsed; partly in code. Recorded in SJL as received 3 May 1787 at Aix-en-Provence.

THE LITTLE VOCABULARY OF THE CHEROKEE AND CHOCTAW TONGUES may be that which bears the caption in an unidentified hand: "A Vocabulary of the Cherokee (over hill) and Choctaw languages communicated to Mr. Jefferson by Col. Benjamin Hawkins"

(PPAP), though it bears an endorsement in TJ's hand as follows: "This vocabulary was from Benjamin Hawkins, probably before 1784."

[1] This and the following words in italics are written in code and have been decoded by the editors, employing Code No. 9.

From Martha Jefferson

Panthemont february [i.e., March] 8 1787

Being disapointed in my expectation of receiving a letter from my dear papa, I have resolved to break so painful a silence by giving you an example that I hope you will follow, particularly as you know how much pleasure your letters give me. I hope your wrist is better and[1] I am inclined to think that your voyage is rather for your pleasure than for your health. However I hope it will answer both purposes. I will now tell you how I go on with my masters. I have began a beautiful tune with balbastre, done a very pretty landskip with Pariseau, a little man playing on the violin, and began another beautiful landskape. I go on very slowly with my *tite live*, its being in such ancient italian that I can not read with out my master and very little with him even. As for the dansing master I intend to leave him off as soon as my month is finished. Tell me if you are still determined that I shall dine at the abesse's table. If you are I shall at the end of my quarter. The kings speach and that of the eveque de Narbone has been copied all over the convent. As for Monseur he rose up to speak but sat down again

8 MARCH 1787

with out daring to open his lips. I know no news but supose Mr. Short will write you enough for him and me too. Mde. Thaubenen desires her compliments to you. Adieu my dear papa. I am afraid you will not be able to read my scrawl, but I have not the time of coppying it over again. Therefore I must beg your indulgence and assure [you] of the tender affection of yours, M Jefferson

Pray write often and long letters.

RC (MHi); endorsed. Entry in SJL at Aix-en-Provence under 26 Mch. 1787 reads "Jefferson Martha. Panthemont. Feb. (for Mar.) 8."

MY TITE LIVE: This was Titus Livius' history of the Roman people (see Martha to TJ, 25 Mch. 1787), of which TJ possessed the 15th-century translation in Italian by Jacopo Nardi, *Le Deche di T. Livio Padovano delle Historie Romane* (Venice, 1562). TJ's copy of this work was bound in three volumes for him and has some passages underscored in red crayon and some in pencil (Sowerby, No. 53). Such marking was uncharacteristic of him; this may possibly have been the identical copy that Martha struggled over. Some of its leaves are unopened.

[1] This word interlined in substitution for "but," deleted.

From Brissot de Warville, with Enclosure

Monsieur   Paris ce 8e. Mars 1787

C'est autant à l'ami de l'humanité, qu'au digne representant d'une grande confédération Républicaine, que je prens la liberté d'adresser par ordre de la Société Gallo-Américaine, le prospectus qui annonce son existence et ses principes. Le but de cet établissement nous est un sur garant de la faveur que vous voudrés bien lui accorder. Nous la reclamerons quelquefois, afin de nous mettre à portée d'étendre les liaisons entre votre Païs et le notre, liaisons qui ne peuvent prendre de consistance qu'autant qu'elles seront précédées de lumieres générales, et repandre ces lumieres est nôtre principal objet; lorsque nos réglemens seront imprimés, je m'empresserai de vous en envoyer un exemplaire.

Je suis avec respect Monsieur Votre très humble et très obeissant serviteur, Brissot de Warville
Secret. de la Soc. Gall. am.
à La Chancellerie d'orléans

P.S. Messrs. Crevecoeur et Claviere en sont avec moi Les fondateurs.

ENCLOSURE

Prospectus de la société Gallo-Américaine.

La France a par ses armes contribué à affermir l'indépendance de l'Amérique libre.

[204]

Un traité de commerce fondé sur l'intérêt des deux contrées doit les unir de plus en plus intimement.

Le bien moral & politique des deux nations doit être l'objet & le résultat principal de ces liaisons de commerce.

Elles ne peuvent s'étendre qu'en mettant ces deux contrées à portée de mieux se connoître l'une & l'autre, qu'en rapprochant l'individu françois de l'individu américain.

Rien n'est donc plus nécessaire que de fixer un point, un centre, où l'on dépose tout ce qui se fait de bien dans chaque nation. Notre Société formera ce centre.

Il faut, par exemple, qu'en France on sache tout ce qui se passe dans les États-Unis, qu'on y enregistre tout ce qui s'y fait d'utile, qu'on le répande & qu'ensuite la Société emploie tout son influence pour faire adopter les institutions utiles.

Tel est un des objets de la Société Gallo-Américaine qu'on établit à Paris; telles sont les considérations qui lui ont donné naissance.

S'il s'en forme une semblable dans l'Amérique libre, comme il y a lieu de le croire, elle s'occupera du soin de répandre dans l'Amérique, tout ce que le génie françois peut découvrir d'utile, tout ce que l'administration françoise peut réaliser de bien.

Il seroit inutile de détailler les avantages qui résulteront pour les deux pays de l'établissement de pareilles Sociétés.

Il est plus nécessaire d'indiquer les objets principaux dont la Société Gallo-Américaine doit s'occuper à Paris.

Le commerce réciproque des deux pays, fixera sur-tout l'attention de la Société. Elle s'occupera des recherches qui peuvent l'éclairer, des moyens qui peuvent en applanir les obstacles.

L'état de l'agriculture, les canaux nouveaux, les inventions utiles, les progrès de l'industrie, de l'esprit humain, de la législation soit fédérale, soit politique, soit civile des États-Unis. Voilà les points les plus importans, sur lesquels se portera son attention.

Pour les connoître, elle fera venir de l'Amérique libre, les gazettes, les journaux, les livres, les actes de législation, les journaux du congrès, &c. & tout ce qui pourra l'éclairer. Elle en formera un répertoire toujours ouvert aux hommes qui voudront ou s'instruire ou instruire le public.

Elle se procurera des correspondances avec les Sociétés d'Amérique qui s'occupent d'objets utiles: elle accueillera dans ses assemblées, les Américains que leurs affaires ameneront en France, & que leurs connoissances mettront à portée de donner des instructions.

D'un autre côté, pour faire connoître sans cesse en Europe l'état de l'Amérique libre, la Société prendra tous les moyens possibles pour faire publier d'après l'avis de l'assemblée, soit dans les gazettes & journaux du continent, soit dans des ouvrages particuliers, soit autrement, le résultat de ses recherches.

L'utilité des deux mondes: voilà le but de cette Société, tout ce qui se rapporte à ce but, pourra fixer son attention. Elle sera composée d'hommes de tout pays, de toute profession, de toute religion, pourvu qu'ils soient capables de s'occuper constamment & sérieusement du bien de l'humanité.

9 MARCH 1787

RC (DLC); endorsed. Recorded in SJL as received 26 Mch. 1787 at Aix-en-Provence. Enclosure (DLC); printed text, three numbered pages; endorsed by TJ on blank fourth page: "Warville."

From Alexander McCaul

[*Glasgow, 9 Mch. 1787*. Recorded in SJL as received 28 Mch. 1787 at Aix-en-Provence. Not found.]

From Sir John Sinclair

DEAR SIR   Whitehall 9th March. 1787

Accept the inclosed sketch of the journey I made last summer. I hope the strain is better, and that you have had no reason, on that account to quit Paris, and believe me Yours, with very sincere regard,   JOHN SINCLAIR

RC (DLC); endorsed. Recorded in SJL as received 26 Mch. 1787 at Aix-en-Provence. Enclosure not identified.

From Madame de Tessé

a Paris ce 11 fevrier [i.e., March]

Comme vous semblés m'avoir choisie, Monsieur, pour exercer plus particulièrement votre bienfaisance, j'ai attendu la Reception de vos dernières libéralités pour avoir l'honneur de vous écrire. J'ai cru ne pouvoir me présenter d'une manière plus avantageuse qu'en vous annonçant que la fortune avoit secondé vos vues et que les plants de caroline étoient arrivés en bon état. C'est ce que je puis vous attester aujourd'huy en vous offrant l'hommage de ma Reconnoissance. La meilleure partie des magnolia a parfaitement soutenu le voyage et les dionea m'ont paru en végétation dans leurs petites mottes. J'en garde deux dans ma chambre à Paris, pour les soigner journellement moi même, jusqu'à ce que j'aille m'établir à Châville où je vais aujourd'huy planter les autres. J'avois menacé Mr. Short de vous avertir s'il demeuroit toute votre absence éloigné de Paris, il a bien voulu diner hier chés moi et m'assurer que ce n'étoit pas le produit de sa crainte. L'avantage de passer sa jeunesse près de vous, secondant en Lui les dons de la nature, j'aime à présager ce qu'il sera un jour, pour sa famille et son païs. Il m'a trouvé dans un de ces mouvemens d'effervescence qu'excite

[206]

l'assemblée des notables. Je me suis livrée devant lui à une conversation un peu vive contre un homme qui n'est pas favorable à Mr. de la Fayette; il seroit embarassé de vous faire savoir quelque chose de positif sur le Résultat des délibérations. On ne s'est encore expliqué que sur les objets d'une moindre importance. L'impôt, qui est sans doute le principal, peut être Levé, mais ne peut être approuvé qu'avec la preuve qu'il est absolument nécessaire. Le controlleur général s'apuie sur ce qu'elle a été fournie au Roy, et les notables sur ce que le Roy peut être trompé dans ce moment cy, comme Mr. de Calonne assure qu'il l'a été par le compte Rendu de Mr. Necker, qui démontroit que la Recette étoit au pair de la dépense, quoiqu'au dire de Mr. de Calonne le déficit fut alors de trente à quarante millions. On n'entrevoit pas le moment où le controlleur général se décidera à donner ses comptes, ni les notables leur avis sans les avoir obtenus, ce qui fait juger que l'assemblée se prolongera beaucoup. Si vous daignés vous Rapeller que vous avés bien voulu me souhaiter une petite terre en Virginie, je serai aussitôt dispensée de vous imposer mon opinion particulière et vous approuverés que je me livre uniquement à la culture de mon jardin. Me. de Tott, qui a déjà eu l'honneur de vous écrire, me charge de joindre l'honneur de tous ses sentimens à celui de la vive Reconnoissance et de l'attachement profond avec lequel j'ai l'honneur d'être, Monsieur, votre tres humble et tres obeissante servante, NOAILLES DE TESSÉ

RC (DLC). Recorded in SJL as received 26 Mch. 1787 at Aix-en-Provence; entry reads: "Tessé Mde. de. Paris. Feb. (for Mar.) 11."

From William Short

MY DEAR SIR   Paris March 12. 1787

This letter with the others inclosed would have been sent two days sooner but for a mistake in the post-days of Aix. I waited until saturday without writing because I wished to be able to give you some information of your map; and from saturday until to-morrow the post does not set out for Aix.—The engraver kept his word and went through all your corrections in the course of the last week. Saturday I went over the three first parallels of latitude with him at his house and found only nineteen errors. This gave me great hopes for the rest, but my expectations have been in some measure disappointed. I employed yesterday in going over the remainder of the map at home. The errors amount to sixty three

12 MARCH 1787

in the whole. I returned the map to the engraver with the corrections marked, yesterday, and he promised that they should be finished to-day: most of them will be easily rectified. It is only in the quarter of Malverne hills that there can be any difficulty. I am to go to his house in the course of the day to explain that part to him; so that to-morrow without fail the engraver's part will be finished. —The next thing is the striking off the two hundred and fifty copies for yourself. I take it for granted it is to be on the same paper with the proof sheet, as you said nothing to the contrary. You said nothing to me Sir on the arrangements you made with the engraver and of course I know not what he is to be paid. I have consulted Mr. Petit, on this subject; he says that you said nothing to him about it. I think it probable from some hints the engraver dropped the other day that he will speak to me more clearly on the affair to-day. I imagine from the nature of the work that no price could have been fixed with him before your departure, and in that case that it is a case of conscience with him.—Mr. Demarra, the person who employed the engraver I believe, and who thinks he has some merit in the matter asked me the other evening at the Abbe Morelets to give him one of the maps as the only recompense that he desired for his trouble. I had no right to give what did not belong to me, and yet as he talked of recompense I did not know how to answer in the negative, and some answer being necessary, I was obliged to say yes.

Twelve letters Sir are herewith inclosed to you. One of them is of a size and shape which made me doubt whether it was made up of letters only or other papers, and of course I doubted whether you would chuse it should be sent in this manner. If I have done wrong in sending it I hope you will excuse it as I have no data by which to determine the nature of its contents. With respect to a parcel of magnets sent from London I have had no hesitation in retaining them. But I am at a loss with respect to Lackington's catalogue: it came by the diligence and might be sent to you in the same manner if I had your address. I beg you to say what you would wish to be done in such cases. There is inclosed also a letter from Miss Jefferson, one from Mde. de Tott, and another from Mde. de Tessé. The latter undoubtedly contains a repeating dose of what I had the day before yesterday at her house. You will easily suppose the nature of it when I tell you that she had recieved the seeds expected from L'Orient a few hours before I got there. They must have been at least twenty days on the road, for Mde. de Tessé recieved them the same day of their arrival at Paris.

12 MARCH 1787

Mr. Petit desires I will let you know that your horse, which you had never put to the cabriolet goes in it *comme un bijou*. From the beginning he has made no resistance and shews that he has been accustomed to it. Mr. Petit drives him into Paris every day and purposes doing the same with the other also as he has recovered from his sickness which was for one while alarming. He has been well taken care of and indeed they are all properly attended to.

I recieved yesterday letters from Virginia via London. Among them is one from Mr. F. Skipwith as late as the 26. Jany. He gave to me a list of the acts passed at the late session of Assembly. You will see how numerous they are; but it is probable the number is not thought sufficient since the Adjournment is to the last of this month only. Mr. Skipwith gives me some account also of a late dreadful fire in Richmond. It has consumed all the houses on both sides the main street from Currie's dwelling house to Truehearts long store, whether these incluse I cannot say, but rather suppose not from a recollection of their situation. Mr. Skipwith adds that the principal sufferers among my acquaintance are Dr. Currie— Dr. Foushee, £400 a year rent in his houses. Nothing now remains to this poor and perfectly honest man, who seems pursued by fate, but the ground on which his houses stood and his profession, with this a wife and family to support. I feel for his distresses really in the most afflicting manner. Mr. Skipwith seems also more affected by them, than by his own.—The loss of his company is estimated at £5000 in goods and £2000 in houses. Another misfortune which he had not heard of when he wrote me, and which I learned yesterday, from Mr. Ogilvy who inclosed me the letters from Virginia, is the failure of Mr. Eyre an old and well established merchant of London with whom Mr. Skipwith had entered into partnership. Mr. Ogilvy thinks this will irrecoverably ruin the credit of the company. I have never felt myself so sincerely distressed by the pecuniary losses of a friend. There is a something in the fortunes of those who have been always struggling against unfavorable circumstances and situations in life that attaches us much more to them, than to those who, sailing under prosperous gales, have never met with a storm.—Mr. Ogilvy adds that he has written to Mr. Skipwith to desire his immediate return to London in order to put his deranged affairs into a train of settlement. This circumstance joined to a paragraph in Mr. Skipwith's letter will shew you that there is a certainty your daughter Polly will come to Europe under his care.—Mr. Skipwith after desiring me to inform you that your daughter and the family of Eppington were in perfect health, says

12 MARCH 1787

he has lately recieved a letter from Mr. Eppes desiring he would take charge of Miss Polly in case it was his intention to return to Europe in the Spring. He adds the pleasure it would have given him had that been the case: but as it was not he had advised Mr. Eppes to send her under the care of Capt. Roberts of the Judith Randolph, an exceedingly prudent and gentlemanly man. I know not if this is the same of whom Mr. Eppes has already spoken to you.

I recieved two days ago by the Rhinegrave of Salm, a letter from Mr. Dumas inclosing one for Mr. Jay. He tells me that this is sent open that I may read it and extract from it such parts as you would chuse to see on your return here. He desires me also to let him know If I know what is meant by the *ouverture* of which he speaks, in order that he may write to me confidentially on the subject, and send me such information as may be proper to forward to Congress in your absence. I have answered him in the affirmative, and have taken the extracts from his letter as he requested.

I wrote to M. de Reyneval after your departure and have recieved the two passeports; one has been given to Petit, the other is inclosed to you.

I have been forced by M. de Crevecoeur and Mr. Barrett to engage to press again M. de Colonia; and in consequence wrote him a letter this morning desiring he would give me a rendezvous. He was not at home, so that I have as yet no answer. I have been induced into this measure not so much from an expectation of success as to avoid the appearance of neglect and inattention in the eyes of those gentlemen, whom I cannot bring to believe that I have not the honor of being Chargé des affaires under the commission of Congress and of course cannot be known of right to any of these bureaux, except as sent in the character of a common messenger. M. de Crevecoeur insists with obstinacy that if I do not succeed with M. de Colonia I must go to Versailles to pay a visit to the Duke of Harcourt. You will readily concieve how disagreeable the alternative of risquing to do an impropriety or of meeting the censures of M. de Crevecoeur, M. Barrett, and all the American merchants who are suffering or may suffer by this affair. I am very anxious my dear Sir to hear from you, as well to know whether you feel any good effects from your journey as to satisfy the incessant enquiries of all your friends here whom I see. None of whom however can be half so much attached to you either by the ties of affection or gratitude as Your friend & servant,

W Short

13 MARCH 1787

I saw M. de la fayette yesterday morning at his house. He hopes you will not follow the example of M. de Simiane (the husband of the beauty of that name) who lately put an end to himself by a *coup de pistolet* at Aix.

RC (DLC); endorsed. PrC (DLC: Short Papers). Recorded in SJL as received 26 Mch. 1787 at Aix-en-Provence. Enclosures: In addition to the three from Martha (8 Mch.), Madame de Tott (4 Mch.), and Madame de Tessé (11 Mch.), Short enclosed the following TWELVE LETTERS from Adams (20 Feb. and 1 Mch.), Clerici (5 Mch.), Gordon (20 Feb.), Guichen (7 Mch.), Jones (25 Feb.), Jones (22 Jan.), Lavoisier (3 Mch.), St. Paterne (3 Mch.), Sir John Sinclair (9 Mch.), Vaughan (ca. 1 Mch.), Warville (8 Mch.). In addition to these fifteen and the present covering letter, TJ also received on 26 Mch. at Aix one from Petit (17 Mch.) and another from Short (14 Mch.).

For the TWO PASSEPORTS (one of which Short enclosed in the present letter), see TJ to Vergennes, 11 Feb. 1787. The MAGNETS were sent by Vaughan (see Vaughan to TJ, 26 Jan. 1787). The PARAGRAPH IN MR. SKIPWITH'S LETTER reads: "I must urge my most affectionate Compliments to Mr. Jefferson, with information that his Daughter and the family of Eppington were in good health. I have lately received a letter from Mr. Eppes requesting that I would take charge of his Daughter on a passage to London, should my Intention be to return in the Spring. This not being the case I have recommended a mode of Conveyance which I imagine Mr. Eppes will approve of, and that is to entrust her with Capt. Roberts of the Judy Randolph.—This Vessel is commodious and safe and Roberts is an exceeding prudent, gentlemanly Man. Polly will of course be sent to the particular Care of Colo. Smith or Mr. Adams, who will no doubt have an Opportunity of conveying her in some eligible way to Paris." Skipwith enclosed the LIST OF THE ACTS PASSED, and Short evidently forwarded the same list in the present letter, though he neglected to add another bit of information in Skipwith's letter that would have interested TJ: "They have also voted £6,000 towards compleating the Capitol, to be raised out of what they call the 2 ⅌Cent Fund."

To Parent

MONSIEUR   à Lyons ce 13 me. Mars. 1787.

Quoique Monsieur de la Tour nous a demandé pour son vin de Monrachet plus que nous n'avions attendu, encore je me propose de prendre une feuillette de celui de l'année 1782. dont nous avons gouté chez lui le 8me. de ce mois, au prix qu'il nous a nommé, c'est à dire à 275^{tt} pour la feuillette. Vous avez bien voulu vous charger de ces petites commissions pour moi. Je vous prie donc Monsieur d'en acheter une de ces memes feuillettes tout de suite. Vous aurez la bonté de tirer sur Messieurs Finguerlin et Scherer banquiers à Lyons pour le montant du vin, des bouteilles, du transport à Paris, des autres petits frais, et de vos propres peines. Quand vous saurez que ces Messieurs auront duement payé la somme pour laquelle vous tirerez sur eux, vous aurez la bonté de faire mettre le vin en bouteilles, et de le faire transporter à Paris

[211]

13 MARCH 1787

à l'adresse de *Monsieur Jefferson, ministre plenipotentiaire des etats unis d'Amerique, à la grille des champs elysées, à Paris*. Mes vins n'etant pas sujets à payer les droits d'entrée à Paris, il faudra que le voiturier les depose aux bureaux de la douane de Paris, et que vous le chargiez en arrivant, d'en avertir Monsieur Petit, mon maitre d'hotel, à fin qu'il aille les retirer de la douane. Il faudra encore, pour que nous soyons plus surs, que vous ayez la bonté d'ecrire un mot par poste à Monsieur Petit, pour lui avertir du jour que le vin doit arriver à Paris, et de la voiture qui en sera chargé, et de lui remettre l'incluse avec votre lettre. Quoique je ne serai pas à Paris qu'au mois de Mai prochain, meme je souhaite que nous nous profitons de la saison favorable, en y faisant transporter le vin tout de suite.

Vous avez [eu aussi] la bonté, [Monsieur, de me dire] que vous vous chargeriez de me faire passer des ceps de vigne à Paris. Je vous en prie donc de vouloir bien me procurer une douzaine de ceps des vignes dont on fait le vin de Monrachet, et autant de celles du vin de Vougeau, ou de Chambertin. Vous aurez bien le soin de les faire tirer de ces vignobles vous meme à fin d'eviter toute possibilité de manquer des veritables especes. Vous les enverrez par la meme voiture, et les annoncerez aussi dans votre lettre à Monsieur Petit. Il ne faudra pas qu'ils soient laissés à la douane, mais que le voiturier les porte chez moi à Monsieur Petit, quand il ira l'avertir de l'arrivée du vin.   Comme je me propose de me profiter de vos bonnes offices quand j'aurai besoin des vins de la Bourgogne, je vous prierai de vous donner la peine de me detailler par ecrit les qualités et les prix de ceux de Chambertin, Vougeau, Romanie, Veaune, Nuys, Beaune, Pommard, Voulenay, Meursault et Monrachet. Je vous charge de cette peine, crainte d'avoir mal entendu ce que vous m'avez deja dit ladessus, et qu'en demandant de ces vins ci-après je pourrai manquer des qualités que j'attendrois, sans les renseignemens ulterieures que vous etes bien dans le cas de me donner. Je crois particulierement que vous m'avez dit que les vins des vignobles qui touchent à celles de Monrachet sont precisement de la meme qualité des vins de Monrachet, et que l'on pourroit les acheter à beaucoup meilleure marché. Dites moi, je vous prie, si je vous aurai bien entendu, et si l'on pourroit conter ladessus.

Voila, Monsieur, bien de la peine. Mais je souhaite que vous vous en dedommagerez dans l'effet que vous tirerez sur Messrs. Finguerlin et Scherer. Je désire que vous vous contentiez, et je ne crains pas de me remettre á vous-meme. J'aurai un veritable

plaisir á trouver des occasions de vous etre utile et je suis avec bien de l'estime, Monsieur, votre trés humble et trés obeissant serviteur,
TH: JEFFERSON

PrC (MHi); at foot of first page: "Monsieur Parent, maitre tonnelier à Beaune, fauxbourgs Bretonniere." Enclosure: Probably TJ to Petit, 15 Mch. 1787 (missing); but see TJ to Petit, 27 Mch. 1787 and Short to TJ, 22 Mch. 1787.

On 9 Apr. 1787 Parent wrote to Petit as TJ here requests, advising him that the wine should reach Paris on 17 or 18 Apr.; that the carrier's name was Teuriet, from Saincaize; that he should be paid 34 livres 10 sols and not more; that he would have sent vines if the season had not been so far advanced, but would send some in October (MHi). Parent made no mention of an enclosure such as TJ had directed him to send AVEC VOTRE LETTRE, a fact which may explain why TJ's letter to Petit of 15 Mch. has not been found.

From William Short

MY DEAR SIR   Paris March 14. 1787

In my letter the day before yesterday I mentioned to you the progress I had made with the engraver. Yesterday his part of the work was entirely completed. I have employed him to have 250 copies taken for you, not knowing any better mode of having it done as you left no directions with me respecting it. He enquired of me yesterday if I was charged with the payment of these matters &c. I have told him that his disbursements for the paper and striking the maps should be refunded him immediately. With respect to the corrections he had made I should write to know your intentions. I could not learn from him what would be his demand—the nearest I could get to it was "nous arrangerons cela quand vous aurez des nouvelles de M. Jefferson."

Young Walton has come to Paris and purposes sailing on this packet. I only heard of it this morning and saw him to-day for the first time.

Pio was here this morning. He is quite unhappy about you and cannot concieve that you are in existence as you have not written since your departure. He is the more uneasy as you set off alone. He has figured it to himself as a most daring enterprize and thinks much danger is to [be] apprehended in it. A thousand accidents may happen—"Ou peut tomber malade sur la route enfin" and in such a case what could a man do. In short I suppose nothing could bring him to believe himself equal to such an undertaking. Although I have not the same alarms with Monsr. de Pio yet I hope you do not doubt of my anxiety to hear from you, and my desire to know that you recieve the wished for benefit from the change

15 MARCH 1787

of air. For be assured my dear Sir no body can be more attached to your health and happiness than Your sincere friend,

W SHORT

RC (DLC); endorsed. PrC (DLC: Short Papers). Recorded in SJL as received 26 Mch. 1787 at Aix-en-Provence.

To Adrien Petit

[*Lyons, 15 Mch. 1787.* Recorded in SJL under this date. Not found; but see TJ to Petit, 27 Mch.; TJ to Parent, 13 Mch.; and Short to TJ, 22 Mch. 1787.]

To William Short

DEAR SIR   Lyons Mar. 15. 1787.

So far all is well. No complaints; except against the weather-maker, who has pelted me with rain, hail, and snow, almost from the moment of my departure to my arrival here. Now and then a few gleamings of sunshine to chear me by the way. Such is this life: and such too will be the next, if there be another, and we may judge of the future by the past. My road led me about 60 miles through Champagne, mostly a corn country, lying in large hills of the colour and size of those in the neighborhood of Elkhill. The plains of the Yonne are of the same colour, that is to say, a brownish red; a singular circumstance to me, as our plains on the water side are always black or grey. The people here were ill clothed, and looked ill, and I observed the women performing the heavy labours of husbandry; an unequivocal proof of extreme poverty. In Burgundy and Beaujolois they do only light work in the feilds, being principally occupied within doors. In these counties they were well clothed and appeared to be well fed. Here the hills become mountains, larger than those of Champagne, more abrupt, more red and stony. I passed thro about 180 miles of Burgundy; it resembles extremely our red mountainous country, but is rather more stony, all in corn and vine. I mounted a bidet, put a peasant on another and rambled thro' their most celebrated vineyards, going into the houses of the labourers, cellars of the Vignerons, and mixing and conversing with them as much as I could. The same in Beaujolois, where nature has spread it's richest gifts in profusion. On the right we had fine mountain sides lying in easy slopes, in

15 MARCH 1787

corn and vine, and on the left the rich extensive plains of the Saone in corn and pasture. This is the richest country I ever beheld. I passed some time at the Chateau de Laye Epinaye, a seignory of about 15,000 acres, in vine, corn, pasture and wood, a rich and beautiful scene. I was entertained by Madame de Laye with a hospitality, a goodness and an ease which was charming, and left her with regret. I beg of you to present to the good Abbés Chalut and Arnoud my thanks for their introduction to this family: indeed I should be obliged to you if you could see Monsr. de Laye and express to him how sensible I am of my obligation to him for the letter to Madame de Laye, and of her attention and civilities. I have been much indebted here too for the letters from the Abbés, tho' the shortness of my stay does not give me time to avail myself of all their effect. A constant tempest confined me to the house the first day: the second, I determined to see every thing within my plan before delivering my letters, that I might do as much, in as little time, as possible. The third and fourth have been filled up with all the attentions they would admit, and I am now on the wing, as soon as this letter is closed. I enter into these details because they are necessary to justify me to the Abbés for the little time I had left to profit of the good dispositions of their friends. Six or seven hundred leagues still before me, and circumscribed in time, I am obliged to hasten my movements. I have not visited at all the manufactures of this place: because a knowlege of them would be useless, and would extrude from the memory other things more worth retaining. Architecture, painting, sculpture, antiquities, agriculture, the condition of the labouring poor fill all my moments. Hitherto I have derived as much satisfaction and even delight from my journey as I could propose to myself. The plan of having servants who know nothing of me, places me perfectly at my ease. I intended to have taken a new one at every principal city, to have carried him on to serve me on the road to the next and there changed him. But the one I brought forward from Dijon is so good a one that I expect to keep him through the greater part of the journey, taking additionally a valet de place wherever I stay a day or two. You shall hear from me from Aix where I hope to meet letters from you giving me news both great and small. Present me affectionately to my friends and more particularly to Madame de Tessé and Madame de Tott: and accept assurances of my perfect esteem & friendship to yourself. Adieu.

RC (ViW); unsigned; endorsed in part: "Jefferson March 15 [received] 18." PrC (DLC). On the LETTERS FROM THE ABBES (not found), see TJ to Arnoux and Chalut, 12 Apr. 1787.—Shortly after receiving the present letter, Short wrote to James Madison: "Mr. Jefferson's absence preventing his writing to you by this Packet, I suppose it may not be disagreeable to you to hear of him from other hands. He left this place the last of February, in order to see whether the waters of Aix would be of service to his wrist put out of place some months ago, and I fear badly set. I received a letter from him on the 15th. [sic] when he had got as far as Lyons. He was much pleased with his journey that far. He had attended very particularly to the soil, agriculture, and condition of the labouring poor, in Champagne, Burgundy, and Beaujolois. The latter he considers as the 'richest country' he ever beheld.—He observed in Champagne that the low grounds were of a brownish red—a singular circumstance to an American, as in that country they are always black or grey." Short also informed Madison of Lafayette's preoccupation with the business of the Assembly of Notables and said that in a letter just received, Lafayette had asked him "to let his friends in America know that he is well—which by the bye is not true"; and that his preoccupation with business prevented his writing by the favorable opportunity afforded by Walton. Perhaps remembering Madison's opinion of Lafayette (see notes to Madison to TJ, 17 Oct. 1784), Short added: "I mention this circumstance to you Sir because I know there are none of his friends south of the Potowmac, to whom he is more attached than yourself, or any whose correspondence he values more" (Short to Madison, 23 Mch. 1787; PrC in DLC: Short Papers).

From Adrien Petit

〚*Paris, 17 Mch. 1787*. Recorded in SJL 26 Mch. 1787 as received at Aix-en-Provence. Not found.〛

From John Ledyard

Sir St. Petersbourg March 19th. 1787

It will be one of the remaining pleasures of my life to thank you for the many instances of your friendship to me and wherever I am to pursue you incessantly with the tale of my gratitude.

If Mr. Barclay should be at Paris let him rank with you as my next friend: I hardly know how to estimate the goodness of the Marquis la Fayette to me, but I think a french nobleman of the first character in his country never did more to serve an obscure citizen of another than the Marquis has done for me: and I am as sure that it is impossible (without some kind of soul made express for the purpose) that an obscure citizen in such a situation can be more gratefull than I am: may he be told so and with my Compliments to his Lady. My Compliments wait on Mr. Short, Commodore Jones and Colo. Franks if at Paris—with thanks for their favours also. If I was sure Mr. Barclay was at Paris I would write him, for no man less acquainted with him esteems him more than I do, believing verily that of such as him consisteth the kingdom

19 MARCH 1787

of heaven. I cannot tell you by what means I came to Petersbourg, and hardly know by what means I shall quit it in the further prossecution of my tour round the world by Land: if I have any merit in the affair it is perseverence, for most severely have I been buffeted, and yet still am I even more obstinate than before—and fate as obstinate continues her assaults. How the matter will terminate I know not: the most probable Conjecture is that I shall Succeed, and be kicked round the world as I have hitherto been from England thro Denmark, thro Sweeden, thro Sweedish lapland, Sweedish finland and the most unfrequented parts of Russian finland to this Aurora Borealis of a City. I cannot give you a history of myself since I saw you, or since I wrote you last: however abridged, it would be too long: upon the whole, mankind have used me well, and tho I have as yet reached only the first stage of my journey, I feel myself much indebted to that urbanity which I always thought more general than many think it to be, and was it not for the villianous laws and bad examples of some Governments I have passed thro, I am persuaded that I should have been able to have given you still better accounts of our fellow creatures.

But I am hastning to those countries where goodness if natural to the human heart will appear independant of example and furnish an Annecdote of the character of man not unworthy the attention of him who wrote the declaration of American Independence.

I did not hear of the death of Monsieur de Vergenes untill I arived here. Permit me to express my regret at the loss of so great a man and of so good a Man. Permit me also to congratulate you as the minister of my Country on account of the additional commercial privileges granted by france to america and to send you my ardent wishes that the friendly spirit which dictated them may last forever: I was extremely pleased at reading this account, and to heighten the satisfaction I felt I found the name of la Fayette there. There was a report a few days ago of which I have heard nothing since,[1] that the french ships under the Command Capt. Lapereux had arived at Kamchatka. There is an equipment now on foot here for that ocean and it is first to *visit* the N. W. Coast of America: it is to consist of four ships. This and the equipment that went from here 12 months since by land to Kamchatka are to cooperate in a design of some sort in the northern pacific Ocean—the lord knows what—nor does it matter what with me—nor need it with you, or any other Minister or any Potentate southward of 50° of Latitude. I can only say that you are in no danger of having the luxurious repose of your charming climates disturbed by a

19 MARCH 1787

second incursion of either Goth Vandal Hun or Scythian. I dined to day with Doctr. Pallas Professor of Natural history &c. &c.—an Accomplished Sweed: my friend: has been all thro European and asiatic Russia. I find the little french I have of infinite service to me: I could not do with out it. It is a most extraordinary language: I believe that wolves, rocks, woods and snow understand it, for I have addressed them in it and they have all been very complaisant to me.[2] But I dined in a shirt that I had worn *four* days. I have but *two*: and I suppose when I write you next I shall have none.

We had a Scythian at table that belongs to the royal society of Physicians here: the moment the savage knew me, and my designs he became my friend and it will be by his generous assistance joined with that of Doctr. Pallas that I shall be able to procure a *royal passport* without which I can not stir: but this must be done thro the application of the french Minister (there being no American one here) and to whose secretary I shall apply with Dr. Pallas to morrow: and beg liberty to Make use of your name and the Marquis la fayettes as to my character. As all my Letters of recommendation have been English and as I have been hitherto used by them with the greatest kindness and respect I first applied to the English Embassy: but without success: the ostensible apology was that the present political moment between England and Russia would make it disagreeable for the English minister to ask any favour: but I saw the reason—the true reason in the specula of the secretarys eye—and so damn his eyes—which in this case particularly I concieve to be polite language: I hate ill nature and pity a fool.

Sir, I have waited on the Secretary of the french embassy who will dispatch my Letter with one of his accompanying it to the Count Segur to morrow morning. I will endeavour to write you again before I leave Petersbourg and give you some further accounts of myself.—In the meantime I wish you health. I have wrote a very short Letter to the Marquis. Adieu!

I have the honor to be with respect & friendship Sr. Your much obliged & most obt. & most hbl. Servt., LEDYARD

RC (NHi); addressed and endorsed. Tr (Mrs. Jane Ledyard Remington, Cazenovia, N.Y., 1951). Recorded in SJL as received 25 May 1787 at Bordeaux.

[1] Preceding seven words are not in Tr.
[2] This and preceding sentence are not in Tr.

[218]

From James Madison

DEAR SIR N. York. March 19th. 1787.

My last was of the 15th. of Feby, and went by the packet. This will go to England in the care of a French gentleman who will consign it to the care of Mr. Adams.

The appointments for the Convention go on auspiciously. Since my last Georgia, S. Carolina, N. York, Massts. and N. Hampshire have come into the measure. The first and the last of these States have commissioned their delegates to Congress, as their representatives in Convention. The deputation of Massts. consists of Messrs. Gohram, Dana, King, Gerry, and Strong. That of N. York, Messrs. Hamilton, Yates and Lansing. That of S. Carolina, Messrs. J. Rutlidge, Laurens, Pinkney (General) Butler, and Chas. Pinkney lately member of Congress. The States which have not yet appointed are R. Island, Connecticut, and Maryland. The last has taken measures which prove her intention to appoint, and the two former it is not doubted will follow the example of their neighbours. I just learn from the Governor of Virginia that Mr. Henry has resigned his place in the deputation from that State, and that Genl. Nelson is put into it by the Executive who were authorised to fill vacancies. The Governor, Mr. Wythe and Mr. Blair will attend, and some hopes are entertained of Col. Mason's attendance. Genl. Washington has prudently authorised no expectations of his attendance, but has not either precluded himself absolutely from stepping into the field if the crisis should demand it. What may be the result of this political experiment cannot be foreseen. The difficulties which present themselves are on one side almost sufficient to dismay the most sanguine, whilst on the other side the most timid are compelled to encounter them by the mortal diseases of the existing constitution. These diseases need not be pointed out to you who so well understand them. Suffice it to say that they[1] are at present marked by symptoms which are truly alarming, which have tainted the faith of the most orthodox republicans, and which challenge from the votaries of liberty every concession in favor of stable Government not infringing fundamental principles, as the only security against an opposite extreme of our present situation.[2] I think myself that it will be expedient in the first place to lay the foundation of the new system in such a ratification by the people themselves of the several States as will render it clearly paramount to their Legislative authorities. 2dly. Over and above the positive power of regulating trade and sundry other matters in which uniformity is proper, to arm the federal head with a negative *in all cases whatsoever* on the local legislatures. Without this defensive power experience and reflection have satisfied me that however ample the federal powers may be made, or however Clearly their boundaries may be delineated, on paper, they will be easily and continually baffled by the Legislative sovereignties of the States. The effects of this provision would be not only to guard the national rights and interests against invasion, but also to restrain the States from thwarting and molesting each other, and even from oppressing the minority within themselves by paper money and other unrighteous measures which favor the interest of the majority. In order to render the exercise of such a negative prerogative convenient, an emanation of it must be vested[3] in some set of men within the several States so far as to enable them to give a temporary sanction to laws of immediate necessity.[4] 3dly. to change the principle of Representation in the federal system. Whilst the execution of the Acts of Congress depends on the several legislatures, the equality of votes does not destroy the inequality of importance and influence in the States. But in case of such an augmentation of the federal power as will render it efficient without the intervention of the Legislatures, a vote in the general Councils from Delaware would be of equal value with one from Massts. or Virginia. This change therefore is just. I think also it will be practicable.[5] A majority of the States concieve that they will be gainers by it. It is recommended to the Eastern States by the actual superiority of their populousness, and to the Southern by their expected superiority. And if a majority of the larger States concur, the fewer and smaller States must finally bend to them. This point being gained, many of the objections now urged in the leading States against renunciations of power will vanish. 4thly. to organise the federal powers in such a manner as not to blend together those which ought to be exercised by separate departments. The limited powers now vested in Congress are frequently mismanaged from the want of such a distribution of them. What would be the case, under an enlargement not only of the powers, but the number, of the federal Representatives?—These are some of the leading ideas which have occurred to me, but which may appear to others as improper, as they appear to me necessary.

Congress have continued so thin as to be incompetent to the despatch of the more important business before them. We have

19 MARCH 1787

at present nine States and it is not improbable that something may now be done. The report of Mr. Jay on the mutual violations of the Treaty of peace will be among the first subjects of deliberation.[6] He *favors*[7] *the British claim of interest* but *refers* the *question to the court.* The amount of the *report which is an able one* is that the *treaty should* be *put in force* as a *law and the exposition of it* left like that *of other laws to the ordinary tribunals.*

The *Spanish project sleeps. A* perusal of the *attempt of seven states* to make a *new treaty by repealing* an *essential condition of the old* satisfied me that Mr. *Jay's caution* would *revolt at so irregular a sanction.* A late accidental conversation with *Guardoqui proved to me* that the *negociation is arrested.* It may appear strange that a member of *Congress should be indebted to a foreign minister* for *such information. Yet such* is the *footing on which* the *intemperance* of *party has put the matter* that it rests wholly with *Mr. Jay how far he* will *communicate with Congress* as well as *how far he will negociate with Guardoqui.* But although it appears that the intended *sacrifice of* the *Missisipi will not be made,* the *consequences of the intention* and the *attempt are likely to be very serious.* I have already made known to you the light in which the subject was *taken up by Virginia.* Mr. *Henry's disgust exceeded all measure* and I am not singular in ascribing his refusal to *attend the Convention* to the *policy of keeping himself free* to *combat or espouse the result of it according* to the result *of the Missisipi business among other circumstances. North Carolina also* has given *pointed instructions* to her *delegates. So has New Jersey.* A *proposition* for the *like purpose* was a *few days ago made in the legislature of Pennsylvania* but went off without a *decision on its merits.* Her *delegates in Congress are equally divided* on the subject. The tendency of this *project* to *foment distrusts among the Atlantic states* at a *crisis when harmony* and *confidence ought to have been* studiously *cherished* has not been more *verified than* [by] *its predicted effect* on the *ultramontane settlements.* I have credible information that the people *living on the Western waters are already in great agitation and are* taking *measures, for uniting their consultations.* The *ambition* of *individuals* will *quickly mix itself* with the *original motives of resentment and interest. A communication will gradually* take place *with their British neighbors.* They will be *led to set up for themselves, to seise on the vacant lands, to entice* [emigrants][8] *by bounties,* and an *exemption from federal burdens,* and in all respects to *play the part of Vermont on a larger theatre.* It is *hinted to me*

19 MARCH 1787

that *British partisans* are already *feeling the pulse* of some of the *Western settlements.* Should these *apprehensions not be imaginary Spain may have equal reason* with the *United States to rue the unnatural attempt to shut the Missisipi. Guardoqui has been admonished* of *the danger* and I believe *is not insensible to it tho'* he *affects to be otherwise* and *talks* as if the dependance of *Britain on the commercial favors of his court* would *induce her to play into the hands of Spain.* The eye of *France also can not fail to watch over the Western prospects.* I learn from those who *confer here with Otto and de la forest* that they *favor the opening of the Missisipi* disclaim[ing][8] *at the same time any authority to* speak the *sentiments of their court.* I find that the *Virginia delegates during the Missisipi discussions* last *fall entered into very confidential interviews with these gentlemen.* In one of them the *idea was communicated to Otto* of *opening the Missisipi for exports* but *not for imports* and *of giving to France and Spain* some *exclusive privileges in the trade.* He *promised* to transmit it to *Vergennes to obtain his sentiments* on the *whole matter* and *to communicate them to the delegates.* Not long *since Grayson called on him* and *revived the subject.* He *assured G   that he had recieved no answer* [from][8] *France* and signified his *wish that you might pump the count de Vergennes observing that he would deny to you his having recieved any information from America.*[9] I *discover thro* several *channels that it would be* very *grateful to the French politicians here to see our negociations with Spain shifted into your hands* and *carried on under the mediating auspices of their court.*

Van Berkel has remonstrated against the late *acts of Virginia giving privileges to French wines and brandies in French bottoms,*[10] *contending* that the *Dutch are entitled* by *their treaty to equal exemptions* with the *most favored nation without being subject to a compensation for them.* Mr. *Jay has reported against this construction* but considers the *act of Virginia as violating the treaty.* First *because it appears to be gratuitous*, not *compensatory on the face of it.* Secondly *because the states have no right to form tacit compacts* with *foreign nations.* No decision of Congress has yet taken place on the subject.

The expedition under General Lincoln against the insurgents has effectually succeeded in dispersing them. Whether the calm which he has restored will be durable or not is uncertain. From the precautions taking by the Government of Massts. it would seem as if their apprehensions were not extinguished. Besides disarming and *disfranchising*[11] for a limited time those who have been in arms, as a condition of their pardon, a military corps is to be raised to the amount of 1000, or 1500 men, and to be stationed in the most suspected districts. It is said that notwithstanding these specimens of the temper of the Government, a great proportion of the offenders chuse rather to risk the consequences of their treason, than submit to the conditions annexed to the amnesty, that they not only appear openly on public occasions but distinguish themselves by badges of their character, and that this insolence is in many instances countenanced by no less decisive marks of popular favor than elections to local offices of trust and authority.

A proposition is before the Legislature of this State now sitting for renouncing its pretensions to Vermont, and urging the admission of it into the Confederacy. The different parties are not agreed as to the form in which the renunciation should be made, but are likely to agree as to the substance. Should the offer be made, and Vermont should not reject it altogether I think they will insist on two stipulations at least, 1st. that their becoming parties to the Confederation shall not subject their boundaries, or the rights of their citizens to be questioned under the 9th. art: 2dly. that they shall not be subject to any part of the public debts already contracted.

The Geographer and his assistants have returned surveys on the federal lands to the amount of about 800,000 acres which it is supposed would sell pretty readily for public securities, and some of it lying on the Ohio even for specie. It will be difficult however to *get the*[12] *proper steps taken by Congress, so many of the states having* now *lands of their own at mark*[et]. It is supposed that this consideration had *some share in the zeal for shutting the Missisipi. New Jersey* and some others *having no western land* which *favored this measure* begin now to *penetrate the secret.*

A letter from the Governor of Virga. informs me that the project of paper money is beginning to recover from the blow given it at the last Session of the Legislature. *If Mr. Henry*[13] *espouses it of which* there is *little doubt I think an emission will take place.* The Governor mentioned the death of Col. A. Cary Speaker of the Senate.

This letter will be accompanied by another inclosing a few Peccan nuts. When I sent the latter to the Gentleman who is charged with it, I doubted whether I should be able to finish this in time, and I only succeed by having written to the last moment. Adieu. Yrs. Afy.,   Js. MADISON JR

19 MARCH 1787

RC (DLC: Madison Papers); endorsed; partly in code. Tr (ViU); extract, partly in the hand of N. P. Trist and partly in an unidentified hand; endorsed: "Madison, James N.Y. Mar. 19. 1787. To Thomas Jefferson. Copied from the original at Montpellier, for, and compared by, N. P. Trist Oct. 1. 1834." Recorded in SJL as received 16 June 1787 at Paris.

The LATE ACCIDENTAL CONVERSATION with Gardoqui, as shown by Madison's lengthy memorandum on it, took place on 13 Mch. 1787. Madison wrote: "Called with Mr. Bingham to-day on Mr. Guardoqui, and had a long conversation touching the Western country, the navigation of the Mississippi, and commerce, as these objects relate to Spain and the United States. Mr. Bingham opened the conversation with intimating that there was reason to believe the Western people were exceedingly alarmed at the idea of the projected treaty which was to shut up the Mississippi, and were forming committees of correspondence, &c., for uniting their councils and interests. Mr. Gardoqui, with some perturbation, replied, that . . . they mistook their interest. . . ." (H. D. Gilpin, ed., *Papers of James Madison*, II, 590-1.) The conversation was not only long, but ranged over all aspects of the Mississippi question. Gardoqui regretted the Virginia resolutions, and said that troops and stores would certainly be sent to reinforce New Orleans in consequence; he said that he "had not conferred at all with the Minister of Foreign Affairs since October, and did not expect to confer again." There followed a long discussion of riparian rights under international law, and Gardoqui "was reminded of the doctrine maintained by Spain in 1608, as to the Scheldt." Madison's memorandum concluded: "When we rose to take leave, he begged us to remember what he had said as to the inflexibility of Spain on the point of the Mississippi, and the consequences to America of her adherence to her present pretensions" (same, p. 592-4). If, as Madison endeavored to convey to TJ, it was strange that A MEMBER OF CONGRESS SHOULD BE INDEBTED TO A FOREIGN MINISTER FOR SUCH INFORMATION, his own memorandum of the conversation proves that, if this was a result of THE INTEMPERANCE OF PARTY, so also was the interference of members of Congress in matters properly under the direction of the secretary for foreign affairs. For the conversation with Gardoqui was scarcely ACCIDENTAL, as proved by Madison's memorandum: it was a part of the pattern by which delegates in Congress, particularly those from Virginia, had been for some time carrying on VERY CONFIDENTIAL INTERVIEWS with OTTO AND DE LA FOREST in an effort to enlist Vergennes' protection and influence in the conduct of negotiations with Spain, an object which Madison here supported by transmitting the suggestion that TJ MIGHT PUMP THE COUNT DE VERGENNES. See note to TJ to Ramsay, 27 Oct. 1786, and note to Otto to TJ, 14 Feb. 1787.—On 20 June 1787 TJ acknowledged the receipt of two letters from Madison of 18 and 19 Mch. 1787, which led Gaillard Hunt into the error of supposing that two different extracts from the present letter as printed by Gilpin, *Papers of Madison*, II, 622-7, and in *Letters and Other Writings of James Madison*, I, 284-6, were in fact separate letters; Hunt therefore printed them separately and assigned to the latter (which embraced the first two paragraphs of the present letter) the date of "March 19th [18th], 1787" (Madison, *Writings*, ed. Hunt, II, 324-8, 328-33); the extract published by Gilpin includes almost all of the present text not in *Letters*, but omits the final paragraph in which Madison stated that THIS LETTER WILL BE ACCOMPANIED BY ANOTHER. This other letter, as shown by TJ's acknowledgment and by the entry in SJL under 16 June reading "Madison Jas. N.Y. Mar. 19.—18 (with Paccans)," was actually dated 18 Mch. 1787. It was probably only a note written to accompany the few pecans sealed up in it (see Madison to TJ, 6 June 1787); it has not been found.

[1] At this point Madison deleted the following: "have proceeded to such a degree."

[2] This word in Tr is keyed to a marginal note in Trist's hand, which reads: "That is to say, *Monarchy*. This is the obvious meaning. Moreover, in reading the letter to me to-day, Mr. Madison made a parenthetical remark to that effect. N.P.T. Montpellier Oct. 2. '34."

[3] Madison deleted "somewhere" at this point.

[4] This sentence in Tr is keyed to a marginal note in Trist's hand, which reads: "In reading this Mr. Madison paused here; and said he had subse-

quently satisfied himself that there would be difficulties, perhaps insuperable, in reducing this idea to practice."

[5] Tr ends at this point, begins with the first sentence of this paragraph, and omits all of the passage reading "The first and the last of these States . . . but has not either precluded himself absolutely from stepping into the field if the crisis should demand it," an omission accompanied by the following note in Tr: "(Here follow details about the elections and members)."

[6] At this point Madison deleted a sentence which seems to read: "He favors the claim of interest [. . .]." This was evidently done contemporaneously, for Madison then decided to put the statement in code.

[7] This and the following words in italics, unless otherwise noted, are written in code and most of them were decoded interlineally by TJ. However, TJ occasionally failed to write down the decoding of familiar symbols (for example, he omitted the phrase "in Congress") and Madison, late in life when he had received his letters back from Monticello after TJ's death, supplied the missing words so as to complete the decoding; see the following notes for other changes by Madison.

Their decoding has been verified by the editors, employing Code No. 9.

[8] The text in brackets (supplied) was inserted interlineally by Madison late in life; he had omitted both the text and the corresponding code symbols, though TJ could easily understand from the context what the writer intended. In one instance ("from" before "France") Madison rectified the omission by writing the word above a code symbol as if the two corresponded, whereas they were wholly unrelated.

[9] The preceding fourteen words are underscored in MS; they are also in code and were decoded interlineally by TJ.

[10] The words "in French bottoms" are underscored in MS; they are also in code and were decoded interlineally by TJ.

[11] This word underscored in MS, but not written in code.

[12] Neither TJ nor Madison decoded the symbol for this word, Madison evidently preferring to have the text read as if the article had been intentionally omitted.

[13] Madison wrote only the symbol for "H" and TJ so decoded it, but late in life Madison completed the name "Henry."

To José da Maia

Nismes 19me. Mars

Je profite Monsieur du moment de mon arrivée à Nismes pour vous en faire part. Je resterai ici 3. ou 4. jours, aprés lesquels je partirai pour Avig[non], Mar[seilles], &c. J'en serais enchanté si ce rapprochement de vous me donnera le moyen de vous voir ici. Dans ce cas ayez la bonté de demander seulement le Voyageur etranger qui est arrivé d'aujourdhui. C'est en simple particulier que je m'annonce et qu'on me connoît. Peutetre que vous trouverez commode de vous loger dans le meme hotel. Ce me sera d'autant plus agreable qu'il me mettra plus à portée de m'entretenir avec vous et de vous assurer des sentiments &c.

Dft (ViWC); without indication of addressee or the year; with numerous abbreviations and some deletions; on margin TJ wrote: "que vous trouverez necessaires M. 21.9bre."—a phrase taken from Da Maia's letter to TJ of 21 Nov. 1786. Not recorded in SJL.

In TJ's list of names and addresses of persons he wished to see or consult on his journey (CSmH), there is an entry reading: "Montpelier. M. Maya. chez M. Franc à la petite Ste. Anne." See TJ to Jay, 4 May 1787.

To Madame de Tessé

Nismes. Mar. 20. 1787.

Here I am, Madam, gazing whole hours at the Maison quarrée, like a lover at his mistress. The stocking-weavers and silk spinners around it consider me as an hypochondriac Englishman, about to write with a pistol the last chapter of his history. This is the second time I have been in love since I left Paris. The first was with a Diana at the Chateau de Laye Epinaye in the Beaujolois, a delicious morsel of sculpture, by Michael Angelo Slodtz. This, you will say, was in rule, to fall in love with a fine woman:[1] but, with a house! It is out of all precedent! No, madam, it is not without a precedent in my own history. While at Paris, I was violently smitten with the hotel de Salm, and used to go to the Thuileries almost daily to look at it. The loueuse des chaises, inattentive to my passion, never had the complaisance to place a chair there; so that, sitting on the parapet, and twisting my neck round to see the object of my admiration, I generally left it with a torticollis. From Lyons to Nismes I have been nourished with the remains of Roman grandeur. They have always brought you to my mind, because I know your affection for whatever is Roman and noble. At Vienne I thought of you. But I am glad you were not there; for you would have seen me more angry than I hope you will ever see me. The Pretorian palace, as it is called, comparable for it's fine proportions to the Maison quarrée, totally defaced by the Barbarians who have converted it to it's present purpose; it's beautiful, fluted, Corinthian columns cut out in part to make space for Gothic windows, and hewed down in the residue to the plane of the building. At Orange too I thought of you. I was sure you had seen with rapture[2] the sublime triumphal arch[3] at the entrance into the city. I went then to the Arenas. Would you believe Madam, that in [this 18th. centur]y,[4] in France, und[er the reign of Louis XVI, they] are [at this mo]ment pulling down the circular wall of this superb remain [to pave a ro]ad? And that too from a hill which is itself an entire mass of stone just as fit, and more accessible. A former Intendant, a Monsr. de Baville has rendered his memory dear to travellers and amateurs by the pains he took to preserve and to restore these monuments of antiquity. The present one (I do not know who he is) is demolishing the object to make a good road to it. I thought of you again, and I was then in great good humour, at the Pont du Gard, a sublime antiquity, and [well]

20 MARCH 1787

preserved. But most of all here, where Roman taste, genius, and magnificence excite ideas analogous to yours at every step, I could no longer oppose the inclination to avail myself of your permission to write to you, a permission given with too much complaisance by you, taken advantage of with too much indiscretion by me.[5] Madame de Tott too did me the same honour. But she being only the descendant of some of those puny heroes who boiled their own kettles before the walls of Troy, I shall write to her from a Graecian, rather than a Roman canton; when I shall find myself for example among her Phocean relations at Marseilles. Loving, as you do Madam, the precious remains of antiquity, loving architecture, gardening, a warm sun, and a clear sky, I wonder you have never thought of moving Chaville to Nismes. This is not so impracticable as you may think. The next time a Surintendant des batiments du roi, after the example of M. Colbert, sends persons to Nismes to move the Maison [Car]rée to Paris, that they may not come empty-handed, desire them to bring Chaville with them to replace it. A propos of Paris. I have now been three weeks from there without knowing any thing of what has past. I suppose I shall meet it all [at Aix, where] I have directed my letters to be lodged poste restante. My journey has given me leisure to reflect on this Assemblée des Notables. Under a good and young king as the present, I think good may be m[ade of it.] I would have the deputies then by all means so conduct themselves as [to encorage] him to repeat the calls of this assembly. Their first step should be to get th[emselves] divided into two chambers, instead of seven, the Noblesse and the commons separately. The 2d. to persuade the king, instead of chusing the deputies of the commons himself, to summon those chosen by the people for the Provincial administrations. The 3d. as the Noblesse is too numerous to be all admitted into the assemblée,[6] to obtain permission for that body to chuse it's own deputies. The rest would follow.[7] Two houses so elected would contain a mass of wisdom which would make the people happy, and the king great; would place him in history where no other act can possibly place him. This is my plan Madam; but I wish to know yours, which I am sure is better.[8]

[From a correspondent at N]ismes you will not expect news. Were I [to attempt to give you news, I shoul]d tell you stories a thousand years old. [I should detail to you the intrigue]s of the courts of the Caesars, how they [affect us here, the oppressions of their] Praetors, Praefects &c. I am immersed [in antiquities from morning to night]. For me the city of Rome is actually [existing

[227]

21 MARCH 1787

in all the splendor of it's] empire. I am filled with alarms for [the event of the irruptions dayly m]aking on us by the Goths, Ostrogoths, [Visigoths and Vandals, lest they shoul]d reconquer us to our original bar[barism. If I am sometimes ind]uced to look forward to the eighteenth [century, it is only when recalled] to it by the recollection of your goodness [and friendship, and by those sentiments of] sincere esteem and respect with which [I have the honor to be, Madam, your] most obedient & most humble servant,

TH: JEFFERSON

PrC of first page (MHi). PrC of second and third pages (MoSHi); endorsed by TJ: "Tessé Mar.20.87"; MS is worn and faded, with lower left quarter of third page missing. Tr (DLC); in TJ's hand, differing somewhat in phraseology, as indicated below; words for the missing or illegible parts of PrC have been supplied from Tr. The exact date at which TJ made this copy, or the purpose for which it was made, is not certain; however, it is to be noted that he also made a Tr of the letter to Madame de Tott of 5 Apr. 1787; both of these copies are on very similar paper—probably having been, in fact, parts of the same folio sheet—and, since the paper on which the Tr of the letter to Madame de Tott was written bears the watermark "R BARNARD 1809," both copies were written sometime between 1809 and 1826 and both were evidently written at the same time. From this it is clear that TJ sought to "improve" his text with some particular purpose in mind.

[1] Tr reads instead: "female beauty."
[2] Tr reads instead: "pleasure."
[3] Tr adds at this point: "of Marius."
[4] The text in this and succeeding brackets (supplied) is either illegible or missing from PrC and has been taken from Tr.
[5] Instead of the preceding nine words, Tr reads: "and used by me with too much indiscretion."
[6] Instead of the preceding four words, Tr reads: "of the assemblée."
[7] This sentence is not in Tr.
[8] At this point and in place of this sentence, TJ inserted the following in Tr: "They would thus ⟨place⟩ put themselves in the track of the best guide they can follow, they would soon overtake it, become it's guide in turn, and lead to the wholesome modifications wanting in that model, and necessary to constitute a rational government. Should they attempt more than (not the opinion of the moment but) the established habits of the people are ripe for, they may lose all, and retard indefinitely the ultimate object of their aim. These, madam, are my opinions; but I wish to know yours which I am sure will be better."

From Richard Cary

DR. SIR   Virga. Warwick March 21st. 1787

I received your kind and obliging Letter, by Mr. Le Croix with the Copy of the new, English Edition of Linnæus's System of Vegetables; it got to me in excellent Order sometime in Octr. last, and I now return you best thanks for this Book and your friendly Intention of sending me some of the vegetable Productions of France which I shall most gladly receive.

The Book is valuable and compiled with great Care and with much Pains, and what stil pleases me is that by Advertisements

[228]

21 MARCH 1787

in it I observe the Editors intend to publish English Translations of Linnæus's Genera and Species Plantarum, which will perhaps induce others to publish the whole Works of that learned and ingenous Naturalist in the same Language.

Your Favor of Augt. 12th. 1786 I did not get 'til late in Novr. which put it out of my Power to attempt sending you any Part of the Plants, Shrubs &c. which you have requested, as it woud have been imposible to get 'em to France in Time; Indeed I am apprehensive it will hardly be practicable to send the Trees with any Prospect of Success. Those Gentlemen who I should be proud to please (especially thro' your Medium) must I am affraid be obliged to rest satisfied with the Seeds. The wild trees I have found from Experience, are much more difficult to make live, by transplanting, than what is usually called the domestic trees; and many of the Sorts you want I have planted in an Hour or two after taking them up, to no Purpose. I have seen to the taking up and planting of at least 30 of the Umbrella trees myself, and tho' the greatest Care and Caution were used I have not been able to raise one. Add to this the Inattention of Shippers, the Room they must take up; besides transplanted trees when transported a great Distance seldom or never make either so large, beautiful or thrifty Plants as those raised from Seeds and removed from a Nursery to a moderate Distance.

What further confirms in this Opinion: I have by Means of Mr. Oster the Consul procured for the royal Gardens a Number of different things in this Way and the Gentlemen who wrote for 'em were very particular in requesting that the Seeds should only be sent, for that they had frequently received the Plants, Trees &c. from America but cou'd never succeed that Way.

I have received several things in Return and have entered into a Correspondence with the Ct. Dangivilliers and the Abbé Nolin and shall also be highly pleased to do the same with any Gentlemen you will be so good as to recommend if they should think it worth accepting. One disagreable Circumstance is, I do not understand any thing of the French Language.

Be assured my dear Sir that I shall always esteem it as one [of] the happy Incidents of my Life if I can do any thing that can oblige you or Your Friends, especially those of France, a Country from whom we have received such emminent Assistance and Services, such as ought never to be forgotten but had[1] in perpetual Remembrance.

Some Books directed to me for Mr. Maddison and Mr. Balleni

came safe to Hand and I sent 'em to those Gentlemen. They were the Genl. Chattelux's Journals and a Poem wrote by Colo. Humphreys. As I am unacquainted with the French, I can't have the Pleasure of perusing the General's Work, so can only have it at second Hand. It seems the General's Journal is in some Sort found Fault with, especially the Passages relative to some Military Operations which passed, before the Arrival of the French Troops in America; 'Tis said the General has received bad Information, or has been partial in his Relation of them.

To what I shall send you, I shall subjoin a List with some Remarks as to the Culture &c. which I suppose will be acceptable. Some Articles you wrote for are not to be found or procured in Virga. These I shall also note and endeavour to supply the Deficiency by some others and I again repeat it that I am truly affraid it will be lost Labor to attempt sending Trees except in a very few Instances; but I'll try for the best.

I suppose you have heard of the Insurrection in the Massachusetts. Genl. Lincoln has dispersed the Insurgents and from the last Accounts 'tis said the affair will soon be terminated. By what I can learn tis something like the Matter of the Regulators of No. Carolina, tho' more formidable, but they seem to have no certain Object or System in View.

Mr. Ed. Randolph has resigned his Office of Attorney General and is appointed Governor and Colo. Jas. Innis succeeds Mr. Randolph as Attorney.

Your friends of Mr. Wilson Cary's Family (who are my near Neighbours) are well.

I have the Honor to be Dr. Sir with every Sentiment of Attachment & Respect Yr. most obt. Servt. & Friend,

RICHD. CARY

RC (DLC); endorsed. Recorded in SJL as received 31 May 1787 at Nantes. The subjoined LIST WITH SOME REMARKS, if appended to the letter, has not been found.

[1] Thus in MS; "held" was probably intended.

William Short to the Governor of Virginia

SIR   Paris March 21. 1787

By direction of Mr. Jefferson who is absent, I have the honor of forwarding to your Excellency, the proceedings of the city of Paris on the reception of the Marquis de la fayette's bust presented to them by the State of Virginia. The French Packet which sails

[230]

in a few days furnishes the first opportunity which has been offered, of conveying these proceedings and I make use of it with very great pleasure as it allows me to assure you Sir, of the sentiments of the most profound respect and perfect esteem with which I have long had the honor of being Your Excellency's most obedient & most humble servant, W SHORT

PrC (DLC: Short Papers); endorsed. Enclosure: See note to Le Pelletier to TJ, 1 Feb. 1787, and to De Corny to TJ, 20 Feb. 1787.

William Short to John Jay

SIR   Paris March 21. 1787

Agreeably to Mr: Jefferson's directions on his leaving Paris, I have the honor of forwarding to Your Excellency, the medal engraved for Genl. Greene, under the resolution of Congress. There is one of gold and twenty three of bronze, all of which are committed to the care of Mr. Walton of New York, who sails in the French Packet the 25th. of this month. The medal for Genl. Gates ordered by Congress and contracted for by Colo. Humphries is not yet finished; but will certainly be in time to be sent by the May Packet.

I have the honor of inclosing to your Excellency a letter from Mr. Dumas sent to me some time ago: He gave me reason at the same time to expect others which he purposed sending here to be forwarded by this packet, and which he said would contain information of the greatest importance for Congress on the subject on which he had lately written to them. As yet no such letters have arrived. I hope Your Excellency will be persuaded of the punctuality with which I should have attended to them.

I take the liberty of sending to your Excellency the Speech of the King, and that of the Comptroller-general at the opening of the Assembly as yet sitting at Versailles. I do not presume to obtrude longer on you Sir than to assure you of the sentiments of the most profound respect with which I have the honor to be, Your Excellency's most obedient & most humble Servant,

W: SHORT

RC (DNA: PCC, No. 98, II); endorsed in an unidentified hand. PrC (DLC: Short Papers). Enclosures: (1) Dumas to Jay, 27 Feb. 1787 (see Dumas to Short, 2 Mch. 1787). (2) THE SPEECH OF THE KING, AND THAT OF THE COMPTROLLER-GENERAL are printed in *Procès-Verbal de L'Assemblée de Notables, Tenue à Versailles . . . 1787*, Paris, 1788, p. 52, 56-81.

From William Short

My dear Sir Paris March 22. 1787

Yours of the 15th. from Lyons arrived here on sunday last, and gave great pleasure to all your friends, to me a double portion because it shewed you were pleased with your journey and because it furnished me details on the country you passed through of which I was very desirous to be informed. I hope you will be so good as to continue them. Should I ever be able to make the same trip, they will be to me an useful guide. Should I not, they will be pleasing and useful information. The objects you propose to your attention are precisely those which, in my mind are the most worthy of it. As to manufactures they can be little useful to an American and for cabinets of curiosities he who has seen one complete one, has nothing left to see of the kind since he can have no farther curiosity on the subject.

I went to see the Abbés as you desired. They had heard of you from their friends at Lyons and seemed much pleased, with my communications to them of your gratitude. I waited on Mr. de Laye also agreeably to your request. He desires me to assure you how happy he is that his house has been agreeable to you and how much more happy he shall be if you will revisit it when he shall be there. I prepared a great many civil things to say to him of Mde. de laye, and the satisfaction you had recieved from her civilities, but before I had half finished them he skipped over her to a certain groupe in his salon, executed by a great artist and estimated at 60,000.ᵗᵗ He seems anxious to know what you thought of it, how you liked the arrangement of his estate and his mode of husbandry, to which he seems much attached. I told him you had not had time to enter into any details and that you had seemed perfectly occupied by your gratitude for the *bonté extrême* of Mde. de laye. She had written him a great many civil things about you, and was au desespoir at having a cold during your short stay, which precluded her from procuring you a greater number of pleasures.

I have complied with the other directions of your letter also, in presenting your compliments to your friends and more particularly to Mdes. de Tessé and de Tott. They both expressed the greatest satisfaction at hearing from you, and particularly at seeing that they were remembered by you. Their expressions were wound up to *fortissimo*, reducing them to *forte*, which I take to be the true tone of their friendship, and I think you may rely on the sincerity

22 MARCH 1787

of all they said. Whilst on the subject of Mde. de Tessé, it may be proper to mention to you something of the seeds expected from London. You recollect the letter I wrote to Mr. Ogilvy on that subject, which was solely to desire him to send the box, if in his hands, by the diligence. He acknowleged some time ago the reciept of several of my letters and particularly that, without saying one word of the box of seeds. Before the arrival of his letter Mr. Carnes set out for London. I gave him a memorandum to enquire of Mr. Ogilvy about this box, and if such an one had arrived to have it immediately forwarded by the diligence. Mr. Carnes has only attended to one half of my memorandum, as appears by a letter just recieved from him. He tells me the box has arrived and that he has advised Mr. Ogilvy to look out for a vessel going to Havre, in order to forward it. If one cannot be found soon says he, I shall advise him to forward the box by the diligence, as you seemed very pressing. Was there ever such a bundle of errors one upon another? I have written this morning, being the first post, to beg he will look for no vessel but send the box immediately on here, to your address. I explained all these matters yesterday to Mde. de Tessé. It did not serve, as you may suppose, to heighten her idea of American punctuality.

Since my last the engraver has been busily employed in striking off your maps. He promises the 250 copies shall be delivered without fail the day after to-morrow. His charges are 1. for his work 106^{tt}/, 2. for 250 sheets of paper 60^{tt}/, 3. for striking them off 37^{tt} 10s. I find that Mr. de Crevecoeur thinks himself entitled also to one of these maps. I suppose his claim founded on his possession of one of your books and of course good in the equity of the case. If I mistake not I heard you say that a map was destined for each of the copies you had given, and therefore shall deliver it to him or his order.—His third volume has not yet appeared, but he expects it will in time to let him carry some copies of it to America in May.

Mr. Walton who sat out this morning for Havre took charge of the medals for Congress, that is those of Genl. Greene. I have heard nothing farther from the engraver of Genl. Gates's. I was not certain of my etiquette with respect to Mr. Jay on this occasion. I knew not how to send the medals *tout uniment*, without saying a word on the subject. Nor did I know whether it would not be presumption in me to address him a letter. However I risqued a short one, and as 'I have the honor' 'and your Excellency' are as often repeated as there are lines in the letter, I hope it will not be supposed that I have forgotten the proper distance between him and myself.

Duquesnay was here a few days ago. He says he has put so many engines in motion that he cannot fail of success. Still he is sorry you are not here to countenance his patriotic enterprize. He has begged my *protection*, which I suppose was to counterbalance Mazzei, who he fears will prejudice his schemes in the view of Mr. de l. f. 'comme ils sont trés intimément liés ensemble.' Mazzei has thrown him into some consternation, notwithstanding his certainty of success by demonstrating that there is no geometrical certainty in the case. He has insisted that I should mention to all my friends in America his arrival here, the sensation it has made, notwithstanding the critical moment, as Government was occupied on subjects of a very important nature, and in fine the certain prospect of his succeeding.

Mr. Capitaine's attorney came here some time ago with powers to recieve the bill of exchange you left for him. He left with me his powers and took the bill of exchange.

In my last I mentioned my letter to M. de Colonia. As yet I have recieved no answer. I have taken no further steps, because as yet M. de Crevecoeur and Mr. Barrett have pressed the matter no further.

I mentioned in a former letter the adjournment of the Assembly to the last of this month. The new elections in April had entirely escaped me; a recollection of that circumstance makes me suppose the adjournment to March a thing of course and of form only.

Most of your friends here enquire of me whether you visited the works of Mount Cenis. I have not been able to satisfy their enquiries. As you said nothing of so important an object, I am rather disposed to imagine you did not visit it. And yet I think you would hardly have left it behind you without casting on it *un coup d'oeil*.

I forgot to mention that Mr. Carnes informs me in his letter that Colo. Smith told him he should set out for Paris about the 24th. of this month. He says nothing of the object of his journey.

I inclose you Sir three letters, one of which I have read because it was delivered to me open by Petit on my return here from St. Germains. It was brought here with the objects it mentions by a gentleman from Bordeaux. These objects are here in my care. There is also here a large packet, of the size and shape of the memoire of the Hotel Dieu. It was sent by the Swedish Ambassador.

23 MARCH 1787

I mention its size that you may let me know whether you chuse it should be sent to you by post. I had doubts on the subject but Mr. Petit insists that it would not be proper to send it by post and I subscribe to his opinion, *en attendant cependant vos ordres à cet egard.*

Petit tells me that agreeably to your letter he waited on Miss Jefferson, and that she was and is perfectly well. I communicate this circumstance because I am sure of the pleasure it will give you.

Since your departure I have passed my time alternately two or three days at a time here and at St. Germains: yet in such a manner as to neglect nothing. It has been three days since I have returned from thence and do not purpose going there again before monday next. In the interim I hope to have the pleasure of hearing from you. Be persuaded my dear Sir, of the pleasure it will give Your sincerest friend & servant, W SHORT

RC (DLC); endorsed. PrC (DLC: Short Papers). Recorded in SJL as received 28 Mch. 1787 at Aix-en-Provence. Enclosures: On 28 Mch., according to entries in SJL, TJ received only two letters in addition to Short's: (1) Hopkinson to TJ, 8 Nov. 1786, and (2) McCaul to TJ, 9 Mch. 1787. The third of the THREE LETTERS enclosed by Short must have been the one brought BY A GENTLEMAN FROM BORDEAUX; neither it nor its accompanying objects has been identified.

On the BILL OF EXCHANGE for Capitaine, see TJ to Capitaine, 25 Feb. 1787; to Peters, 26 Feb. 1787. There is in MHi a letter from Capitaine to Short, 23 Mch. 1787, acknowledging the receipt of TJ's letter of 25 Feb. and also "le montant de Cette lettre de Change en une rescription que m'a envoyé M. Gibert mon Notaire," and saying that he was astonished not to have received any letters from Peters, adding: "J'ignore pour mes affaires dont il à bien voulu se charger beaucoup de choses qui me sont essentielles"; there is also in MHi a copy of a power of attorney executed by "Michel Capitaine, Major au Service des Etats unis d'Amerique, chevalier de L'ordre de Cincinatus, demeurant ordinairement a Mezieres en champagne, étant depresent a Paris, Logé rue des prouvaires à l'hotel des Colonies," in which he named Jean Baptiste Le Roux of Paris as his attorney to receive any interest or capital sums due him by the United States and paid through Grand, and to receive from Lafayette and any others the different sums due him. Presumably Le Roux was the ATTORNEY who left HIS POWERS with Short, though this could not have been the copy of the power of attorney just quoted.

It was not in Short's LAST letter (that of 14 Mch.) but in that dated 12 Mch. that he MENTIONED MY LETTER TO M. DE COLONIA. TJ's letter to PETIT was that of 15 Mch. 1787. For a note on the CERTAIN GROUPE at the Chateau de Laye, see TJ to Short, 29 Mch. 1787.

From the Governor of Georgia

SIR 23 March 1787

I am honored with your Excellencys favor of the 22 December 1785 and have taken the earliest Opportunity of laying it before the Hble. House of Assembly of this State, and for your information and the Chevalier de Mezieres inclose you a Resolution of

[235]

that honorable body taken thereon. You may rest assured that the disposition of the Inhabitants of this State to the King of France and his Subjects are founded on the most firm and generous principles, and will always be support[ed] by facts when opportunity offers, and should the Chevalier de Mezieres be able to discover any property of the late General Oglethorp, this State will not be wanting in their aid to forward his right to the Same. It only remains for me to assure you every personal service in my power shall be given to subjects of real merit, of the King of France. I am &c., G[EORGE]. M[ATHEWS].

FC (Governor's Letter Book, 1786-1789, G-Ar). Enclosure missing. On the same date Gov. Mathews wrote to the French consul at Charleston, acknowledging his letter of 20 Dec. 1786 on the same subject and enclosing him a copy of the resolution (same).

From William Carmichael

DEAR SIR Madrid March 25th. 1787

I received somewhat later than I should have expected from its date the Letter you did me the honor to write me the 18th. Ulto. I have forwarded the duplicate of the recall of Mr. Lamb to that Gentleman and have also transmitted to Mr. Barclay the joint confirmation of the Morrocco treaty together with the Letter to Fennish which however is without your signature.

Mr. Barclay writes me from Barcelona, where he is at present, that he chuses to forward it thro' my channel and that he intends to return it me for that purpose. It is not probable that he will meet Mr. Lamb who writes me from Minorca that he means shortly to proceed to N. York. The Latter has occasioned me much chagrin. In the autumn of 1784 Doctor Franklin transmitted me a resolution of Congress relative to a Claim of the State of S. Carolina founded on the aid rendered by a frigate commanded by Commodore Gillon, in taking of the Bahama and Providence Islands, but without any information respecting the amount of the Claim, for in truth I believe he had received none.

In consequence however of this resolution I addressed the Ct. de F. B. and obtained a promise from that Minister to instruct Mr. Gardoqui then going to America to examine and liquidate this claim conjointly with the Ct. de Galves who directed the expedition in question and who was also on his way to the Havanna. I well knew that before any arrangement could take place for the

25 MARCH 1787

Satisfaction of the State of S. Carolina the Latter would be consulted by this Court and As his Absence and distance from this Country must occasion Inevitable delays in a matter which the State seemed to have at heart, I thought it most prudent, uninformed as I was and am still of particular Circumstances, to put it in the train I did.

Not having heard further intelligence on the Subject, I concluded that the affair had been arranged, until by a Letter from Mr. Jay dated the   I was advised that the Claim still subsisted. With this second information however I had no account of the particular services rendered nor of the amount of the claim demanded for those services: I therefore could only speak generally on the subject, and have had no reason, from the Answers I received, to think the aid of *another* particularly in the present *circumstances*, necessary, Had I been possessed of proper documents.

I shall be happy however to cooperate with the Duc de Vauguyon and until his arrival or until I receive the dispatches in question, I must let the Affair remain as it is.

I have been informed of the compliment you paid the New Minister the first Audience he gave the Corps Diplomatique. You will find in the Ct. de Montmorin, unless I am Strangely deceived in my Ideas of him, a much honester Man than Ministers are generally supposed to be. He Appeared to me to have an enlarged liberal and noble Manner of thinking and acting. He is endowed with great penetration and is capable of finesse, but seems to disdain to employ that sort of Talent, unless to combat others with their own weapons, weapons which those who know his Character and Abilities will be unwise to employ. I lately received the portable copying press which you did me the honor to send me. You will see that I make use of the Ink which accompanied it. I dare not express to you how sensible I am of this mark of your notice of me. I hope however I shall never feel remorse, for having from my earliest youth wished to acquire the esteem of those few who possess general esteem.

It seems that G. B. means to negotiate its treaty of commerce here. That court has chosen an able and indefatigable Minister, who can only err from a desire to distinguish himself while at the same time he forms projects, which others like himself must be employed to bring to maturity, and this is not to be expected where system changes but too often with a change of Ministers. I hope your tour will reestablish your health while it will contribute to your Information and amusement. I am constrained to tread the same beaten track. You will, If your hand permits you, think sometimes that my most material Information of American affairs comes from you.

With the highest sentiments of respect & Esteem I have the honor to be Your Excellency's Obliged & Hble. Sevt.,

WM. CARMICHAEL

RC (DLC); endorsed. Recorded in SJL as received 3 May 1787 at Aix-en-Provence.

The LETTER FROM MR. JAY on the South Carolina demands on Spain was that of 1 Dec. 1786 with its various enclosures (printed in *Dipl. Corr.*, *1783-89*, III, 323-47). Unfortunately the compliment that TJ PAID THE NEW MINISTER appears not to have been recorded, but the fact that it was repeated in Madrid indicates that it was perhaps comparable to TJ's famous reply at the French court on succeeding Franklin.

From Martha Jefferson

MY DEAR PAPA March 25th, 1787

Though the knowledge of your health gave me the greatest pleasure, yet I own I was not a little disappointed in not receiving a letter from you. However, I console myself with the thought of having one very soon, as you promised to write to me every week. Until now you have not kept your word the least in the world, but I hope you will make up for your silence by writing me a fine, long letter by the first opportunity. *Titus Livius* puts me out of my wits. I can not read a word by myself, and I read of it very seldom with my master; however, I hope I shall soon be able to take it up again. All my other masters go on much the same—perhaps better. Every body here is very well, particularly Madame L'Abbesse, who has visited almost a quarter of the new building—a thing that she has not done for two or three years before now. I have not heard any thing of my harpsichord, and I am afraid it will not come before your arrival. They make every day some new history on the Assemblée des Notables. I will not tell you any, for fear of taking a trip to the Bastile for my pains, which I am by no means disposed to do at this moment. I go on pretty well with Thucydides, and hope I shall very soon finish it. I expect Mr. Short every instant for my letter, therefore I must leave you. Adieu, my dear papa; be assured you are never a moment absent from my thoughts, and believe me to be, your most affectionate child,

M. JEFFERSON

MS not found; text from the printing in Randolph, *Domestic Life*, p. 114. Recorded in SJL as received 6 Apr. 1787 at Marseilles. Martha, on a dare by one of her schoolmates, gave some sort of playful address to the letter, though its nature is not known; she may have addressed TJ by his official title, knowing that he was travelling as a private citizen and knowing also that the address would be hidden by Short's covering letter (see Short to TJ, 26 Mch. 1787).

From William Short

Dear Sir   Paris March 26. 1787

By my calculation I hoped to recieve your letter from Aix yesterday. Although it has not arrived I shall go into the country to-day, not foreseeing that the delay of one day in recieving it can be attended with any bad consequences. It will come to me at St. Germains in four and twenty hours and perhaps less after its arrival here if that should be before my return. I shall be four or five days absent and then come to Paris in order to do the honors of your house at Longchamp. I mentioned yesterday to Mde. de Tesse with whom I dined, what you had desired me, on this subject. She and Mde. de Tott were both much pleased with your attention. The latter declined it because as she added '*je suis* les offices de cette semaine mais Mamma qui n'en a aucun scrupule peut trés *bien y aller*.' Long debates pour et contre. Mde. de Tesse has never seen Longchamp, which I hardly supposed any Parisian of her age could say. She will come and bring some lady whose name I don't recollect.—She told me it was well I had not made the proposition to Mde. de la fayette; her piety would have been shocked and therefore I shall say nothing to her on the subject. She was a part of the evening at Mde. de Tessé's. When Mazzei arrived he approached her and said whether from *mechanceté* or not I cannot say that he had that moment come from the Hôtel de la fayette where he had been to wait on her but that they told him, Madame la Marquise was gone to *vêpres*.

Mazzei tells me that the men of letters here think very poorly of Mr. Adams book. It is easy to see that these are the disciples of M. Turgot. Mazzei asked me what I thought of it, taking great pains to impress well on my mind that he had not yet read it and of course had not been able to form his opinion. I had just finished it and of course was able to give him mine, which is that it shews Mr. Adams's profound researches on the subject he treats, that there are a great many valuable ideas developped in the work, and that it puts the reader in the plain way of developping others; but

26 MARCH 1787

that it has neither order in its matter or taste in its style.—He desired to know if I thought the translation would *succeed* here. Of that I have my doubts; but should rather suppose it would not as an article of *Librairie*. It is not the kind of work that would be generally read in Paris I should imagine. A few men of learning no doubt would be pleased with it; but most of that class would prefer the original. His translator has read it. I inferred from what Mazzei said that his opinion was not the most favorable. Yet I take it for granted that the translation is going on.

The Maps are all delivered, and I gave notice to the Abbè Morellet two days ago that the plate was at present at his disposal, begging him at the same time to return it as soon as he possibly could as I wished to send it immediately to London.

General Gates's medal is at length advanced to that point at which by the contract the engraver is entitled to recieve 1200^{tt}. I have told him I would write to you on the subject. He promises to finish it, without fail, in time to go by the May Packet. I think the likeness is very good considering the manner in which it has been taken.

On my way to dinner yesterday I called on Miss Patsy to recieve her commands for you. She gave me the inclosed letter; telling me one of her companions had made her a *defi* to put the address as you will observe it. I can join my testimony to her's that she is perfectly well. She seems resigned to *faire ses paques*, and 'suivre les offices' de la semaine sainte *au convent*.

You will see that a packet has arrived and among the letters brought for you I recognise one with the hand and seal of Mr. Wythe. Will you be so good as to let me know Sir, if he mentions the arrival of Majr. Martin, who carried the Arms of Taliaferro. I wrote by him, and therefore am interested in his safe arrival. A bundle of newspapers came addressed to you by post from Mr. Jay. Within it were two letters for you which I inclose, a letter from Congress to His Most Christian Majesty, one for Mr. Dumas and another for M. Carmichael and a third for Mr. Lamb. I will endeavour to find some private hand to whom I can commit a letter for Mr. Carmichael inclosing that for Lamb. With respect to that for the King I shall await your instructions.   Lest Mr. Jay should have omitted particular facts with respect to the eastern disturbances it may be well to mention to you that, from the Papers sent, it appears by Genl. Lincoln's letter to Govr. Bowdoin of the 4th. of Febry. that he had come up by surprize with the main body of the insurgents under Shays, had made 150 prisoners with little or no bloodshed and dispersed the rest so effectually as to advise the Governor to countermand his orders for re-inforcing him with other militia.—Govr. Bowdoin in his speech to the house convened the 3d. of Febry. advises vigorous measures, although there was nothing in fact to be apprehended; he founds his advice on the insurgents having treated with contempt the late mild offer held out to them by the acts of the former session. It appears on the whole that if Government will only be mild and at the same time firm, the whole affair is at an end. I am more certain of their firmness than their mildness. I observe by Genl. Lincoln's letter that Wheeler had desired an interview with Genl. Putnam, that they had accordingly met, that 'Wheeler's principal object seeming to be to provide for his personal safety and no encouragement on this head being given him, he retired.' Would it not have been wise to have given him every encouragement on this head? A letter from Shays to Genl. Lincoln without date also appears in the latest paper that has arrived Febry. 16. It is not published officially. He offers to lay down his arms as well as those of his followers on the condition of a general pardon. He begs Genl. Lincoln to desist from hostilities until an answer can be given by the General Court to their petition for that purpose.

The same papers shew that Pennsylvania and N. Carolina have acceded to the plan of Virginia by appointing commissioners to meet at Philadelphia in May.

I have lately recieved a letter from an American Merchant at Nantes just on his return from Virginia. He tells me the Assembly have annulled the duties on Brandies shipped in American or French bottoms and doubled those on rum and all liquors imported by British Subjects. I suppose it is in consequence of M. de Calonne's letter to you.

The *Assemblee des notables* have not yet put the finishing hand to any of the great works they have begun. This is all that is as yet known with certainty in public of their proceedings. Accept my best & sincerest wishes my dear Sir & believe me your most faithful & affectionate friend, W SHORT

RC (DLC); endorsed. PrC (DLC: Short Papers). Recorded in SJL as received 6 Apr. 1787 at Marseilles. Enclosures: (1) Martha Jefferson to TJ, 25 Mch. 1787. (2) Wythe to TJ, 13 Dec. 1786. (3) Jay to TJ, 9 and 14 Feb. 1787. (4) Otto to TJ, 14 Feb. 1787. (5) Grand to TJ, undated.

TJ did not write Short a LETTER FROM AIX until 27 Mch.; in that from Lyons of 15 Mch. 1787 TJ had said: "You shall hear from me from Aix where I hope to meet letters from you."

From Edward Bancroft

Charlotte Street Rathbone Place.
London March 27th. 1787

DEAR SIR

I have been deprived much longer than I expected of the Pleasure of seeing you in Paris, and I am afraid my business here will not permit my return to that Capital until the middle or latter End of may. It is however at the desire of Mr. Paradise that I now address myself to you, as the present State of his mind (from the recent Elopement and marriage of his eldest Daughter to Count Barziza a Venetian Nobleman) joined to his general ill health renders him unable to write to you himself. Both Mr. and Mrs. Paradise seem convinced from past experience and the present contrariety of their tempers and dispositions that it will be impossible for them to Live happily together; and it is therefore agreed that the Lady shall return to Virginia and be allowed a House in Williamsburgh, and three hundred Pounds sterling ⅌ An. for her Separate maintenance, whilst Mr. Paradise will probably fix himself in some more retired and Cheap situation than his present, perhaps at Oxford, or someplace in France. But as this Plan precludes all probability of his going to America, at least for some years, he is Sollicitous to Commit the Superintendance of his Affairs, and of his Stewards Conduct, to one or two Gentlemen, whose Situations are not too far removed from his Estate, and who are properly qualified, and may be induced, by their Care of his intrests to prevent the ill Consequences which might otherwise arise from his Absence. And as Mr. Paradise has the utmost Confidence in your friendship, as well as in your Judgment of men and things in that Country, he earnestly intreats, as a favour of the highest importance that you will be so kind as to point out one or two Persons to whom he may with Propriety send a Power of Attorney for these Purposes, and that you would at the same time by Letter employ your good offices, to induce these persons to undertake the trust which he wishes to place in them. You are sensible that Mr. Paradise is very much *disinclined* towards the Lee's and those who may be particularly Connected with them, and as Mrs. Paradise is to receive her separate allowance without having any Concern in the Managment of her Husbands affairs, he much wishes that the proposed powers should be sent to persons out of this Connection. Mr. Paradise requests me to assure you of the high esteem and sincere respect which he entertains for you and of his grateful sense of your former favours. Permit me also to join the like assurance respecting myself, and beleive me to be with the greatest truth Dear Sir Your most affectionate & faithful Humble Servant,

EDWD. BANCROFT

RC (DLC); addressed and endorsed. Recorded in SJL as received 3 May 1787 at Aix-en-Provence.

From Buffon

[*Jardin du Roi, Paris, 27 Mch. 1787.* Recorded in SJL as received 3 May 1787 at Aix-en-Provence. Not found.]

To Adrien Petit

[Aix] en Provence. 27me. Mars. 1787.

Je vous ai ecrit, Monsieur Petit, de Lyons pour vous prevenir que j'avois acheté des vins de [Mon]rachet, que le nommé Monsr. Parrain, de la ville de Beaune devoit faire passer à Paris, en vous en avertissant. Comme l'occasion sera bonne pour faire mon approvisionnement de vin en passant à Marseille à Lunel et à Bourdeaux, je vous prie de m'envoyer à Aix tout de suite l'etat actuel de tous les vins que vous avez dans la cave, áfin que je puisse decider de la quantité dont j'aurai besoin. J'ai reçu en arrivant ici votre lettre du 17me. Je me porte bien, mais jusques ici pas mieux pour les eaux, dont j'ai pris onze douches. Faites passer la lettre à ma fille et soyez assuré de mon amitié.   TH: JEFFERSON

PrC (MHi); slightly mutilated. Enclosure: TJ to Martha Jefferson, 28 Mch. 1787.

TJ's letter to Petit from LYONS was evidently that of 15 Mch. which appears to have been sent through MONSR. PARRAIN (see TJ to Parent, 13 Mch. 1787). Petit's LETTRE DU 17ME. has not been found, though it is recorded in SJL.

C. W. F. Dumas to William Short

MONSIEUR   Paris[1] 27e. Mars 1787

Je vous suis bien obligé de la bonté avec laquelle vous avez pris la peine de m'instruire du sort de mes Lettres, et de ma Traite.

Voici une autre Lettre pour le Congrès, qui partira quand elle pourra: ce sera du moins le 10 de May prochain, s'il ne se présente pas d'occasion plus prompte et aussi sure. Vous aurez le

[243]

temps d'en noter à loisir ce que vous jugerez digne de Mr. Jefferson. Le contenu vous fera voir avec combien de raison je dois éviter le passage par l'Angleterre.

Je crois que dorénavant il faudra laisser dormir l'affaire que vous savez, sans en plus parler, jusqu'à la réponse que Mr. Jefferson attend dans 4 mois. Dites-moi, Mon cher Monsieur, si vous devinez le personnage dont je parle à Mr. Jay, qui voudroit qu'on l'envoyât Ministre ici. Si vous l'avez deviné, je compte absolument sur le plus grand secret de votre part. Ce que j'en ai dit, est par devoir indispensable: on m'en a prié fortement. Il ne pourroit être d'aucune utilité aux Etats-Unis ici, et ne donneroit que de l'ombrage à nos républicains et à la France, à cause de ses liaisons eclatantes avec le Chev. H———s; on travailleroit à le faire rappeller, comme on a fait tout recemment quant à un autre Ministre, dont je parle dans cette même Lettre. De mon côté je ne pourrois rien avoir de commun avec lui, sans perdre la confiance de mes meilleurs amis. J'aimerois autant perdre la vie. Ce n'est pas tout; il gâteroit aussi l'affaire de l'Emprunt, par ses liaisons avec une maison de Commerce avec laquelle mes Proposants ne veulent point l'entreprendre par des raisons personnelles, outre que la partie est déjà liée avec d'autres.—Je pourrois en dire bien d'Avantage, si je voulois répéter la Chronique scandaleuse. Mais à Dieu ne plaise. Il seroit vu de très-mauvais oeil: Cela suffit, et rend tout le reste superflu. Je serois bien aise seulement de savoir si vous le devinez. Il vient lui-même de m'écrire une Lettre, et Duplicat, out je vois clairement que mes amis ici sont bien informés de ses desseins. Je suis dans le plus grand embarras que lui répondre. Je ne puis ni lui dire la vérité ni le tromper. On croit ici que c'est sa moitié, à qui les Bals, festins, &c. du Ch. H———s, &c. ont tourné la tête, qui le talonne pour venir s'étaler sur ce théatre diplomatique, où il ne pourroit se soutenir d'une maniere qui fût vraiment honorable et avantageuse à l'Amérique.

Mon Epouse et ma fille, sensibles à votre obligeant souvenir, vous prient d'agréer leurs sinceres complimens.

J'ai l'honneur d'être parfaitement Monsieur Votre très humble et très-obéissant serviteur   C W F Dumas

J'espere que vous avez de bonnes nouvelles de la santé de Mr. Jefferson.

RC (DLC: Short Papers). Enclosure: Dumas to Jay, 23 Mch. 1787 (*Dipl. Corr., 1783-89*, III, 567-70). Dumas may also have enclosed his letter to Jay of 30 Mch. 1787 and its enclosures (same, III, 571-6). Both of these were forwarded by Short in his to Jay of 4 May 1787, q.v.

27 MARCH 1787

LE PERSONNAGE DONT JE PARLE A MR. JAY: This was William Bingham, who Dumas feared would be appointed minister to Holland from the United States (see TJ to Jay, 22 May 1786). In his enclosed letter to Jay, Dumas warned again that Bingham's appointment "would give pleasure neither here nor in France," and in his letter to Jay of 27 Feb.–2 Mch. he had inserted a private "Note, which I beseech you, sir, to keep for yourself alone, without letting any one else see it, or know that I wrote it." In this note he said: "Under the present circumstances, and certainly for a long time to come, as it is my duty to repeat, it is worse than useless to send any one here as Minister, who, by consorting with the *Anglomanes* and idle, sensual, gaming diplomatists, who are always to be found at Sir J—— H——'s, would only give umbrage to the party of the Patriots, and of France, which is fortunately the superior here. I am authorized, nay, entreated, sir, to impress this upon you, and to assure you that the party I have mentioned do not wish Congress to send them a mere Minister of etiquette and ostentation. In the present state of affairs, political as well as financial, *being* is better than *seeming*" (*Dipl. Corr., 1783-89*, III, 567, 570). LE CHEV. H——S was Sir James Harris (1746-1820), British minister to Holland who so well understood the intricacies of parties in that country that he resorted not only to BALS, FESTINS, &C. but also to bribery, intrigue, and all the other arts of diplomacy of which he was master. "Hospitality," he reported to Carmarthen 3 Jan. 1787, "is the life and soul of a party here, and an able cook goes as far, if not further, than an able secretary" (*Diaries and Correspondence of James Harris, First Earl of Malmesbury*, London, 1845, II, 222). Harris' grandson, in a single comprehensive paragraph and without too gross an exaggeration, set forth the important role played by this able diplomat in Holland: "The Bourbons had been and were still playing the blind and desperate game against us in Holland, which they had successfully used in America; and encouraged the Dutch Democrats with money, and promises to establish a pure Republic independent of the Stadtholder. THEY hoped thus to render the States a French province. OUR object was to fortify the national independence of Holland under its ancient constitution, and recover her friendship and alliance. In this trial of skill we were completely victorious, mainly owing to the boldness and ability of Sir J. Harris, who may be said to have created, fostered, and matured a counter-revolution in the States, which restored to the Stadtholder his power, to England her ally, and left nothing for the King of France but the deeper infection of those dangerous doctrines, which his Ministers, in their eagerness to spread them amongst his enemies, received into the vitals of his kingdom, to burst forth for its destruction in 1789. History affords no instance of a political retribution so rapid and so crushing" (same, II, 9). Harris was considerably aided in his plan of an alliance between England and Prussia to support the Stadtholder's party when, in May 1787, the British ministry made available to him £20,000 sterling of secret service money. Even before this Dumas reported that Harris "is employing every means to increase the *Anglomania*. Pleasures, fêtes, play, intrigue, espionage, and corruptions of every kind are set at work, and with but too much success. The representatives of all the other Powers, except France and Spain, have fallen into the snare, and become devoted slaves" (Dumas to Jay, 27 Feb. 1787; *Dipl. Corr., 1783-89*, III, 566). But Harris' success was even more insured by the factor that caused TJ such disturbed reflections—that is, the failure of France to give firm and decisive support to the republican cause. Soon after the signing of the treaty between Prussia and England in 1788 Harris was created Earl of Malmesbury and was invested with the Prussian Order of the Black Eagle. In these interventions by the great powers in Holland's internal struggles it is not likely that either Bingham's appointment or Dumas' continuance would have affected the outcome, though Dumas was undoubtedly correct in thinking that Bingham would have been drawn into the British ambassador's orbit (see TJ to Anne Willing Bingham, 7 Feb. 1787; TJ to Madison, 30 Jan. 1787). For the principal comments by TJ on the civil conflict in Holland, see Autobiography, Ford, I, 101-7; TJ to Jay, 6 Aug., 22 and 24 Sep., and 3 Nov. 1787; 16 Mch. 1788; TJ to Adams, 13 Nov. 1787.

[1] Dumas erroneously wrote "Paris"; this was corrected by Short, who wrote "La Haye" above it.

To William Short

Dear Sir   Aix en Provence March. 27. 1787.

I wrote to you on the 15th. from Lyons, and on my arrival here had the pleasure to find your favors of the 12th. and 14th. with the letters accompanying them. In the hurry of my departure from Paris I omitted to explain myself to you on the subject of the map. The kind of paper on which they are struck is not very material. I had intended 50 on such paper as the proof was, and 200 on a thinner paper, more proper to fold into a book. If the plate is not gone, I would still wish to have the latter parcel struck to give to those who have my book. The 250 which you may have had struck on thick paper will in that case be proper for sale. I would also be glad to have a dozen on bank paper, on account of it's thinness and not breaking on the folds. These may be put conveniently into a traveller's pocket book. But if the plate be gone, no matter, I can have all this done in England. As to the price of the corrections it was impossible for me to settle that, as it would depend on the time employed. A workman of that kind works in England I believe for about two guineas a week, and I conjectured he would be employed two or three weeks: but the real time he was employed, and the value of his time in France, I know not. I will be obliged to you if you will arrange it with him as well as you can, and draw the money on my account from Mr. Grand. You did perfectly right with M. Desmaretz: I will only beg you to present him two copies instead of one, with my compliments and thanks.—The magnets and Lackington's catalogue may await my return to Paris, as I would wish generally all printed papers to do, except where from their nature and importance, you judge it necessary for me to receive them here. Have you ever had an answer from Mr. Ogilvie on the subject of the seeds sent by Mr. Eppes? If not, I will beg of you to write again, as they may be rotting in Mr. Skipwith's magazine. I thank you for the list of Virginia acts. Does not the adjournment to the last of March shew they are not to meet again? That was the day formerly which preceded the expiration of their appointment.— With respect to the ultimate act necessary to enforce the new commercial arrangements promised by M. de Calonnes, you will certainly be received and considered in the bureaux, not as a common messenger, but as speaking in my name; the only difference between yourself and a Secretary of legation, in this particular, being that the latter speaks in the name of his state. But the only bureaux to which we can apply with propriety, or without offence, are those of M. de Calonne, or M. de Montmorin, and applications to these should only be so made as to prevent the object's being forgotten, and not so as to produce any soreness, or to revolt them against us. We have the promise that the regulation shall be retrospective to the date of M. de Calonne's letter to me, and that if any duties are paid in the mean time, they shall be refunded. On a question therefore whether temporary advancements by individuals, or an irritation of the minister, will produce the greatest ill to the public, there can be no hesitation. Mr. Barrett's good sense in particular will relieve you from all difficulty in this matter, and the easiest way to get out of every difficulty, invariably, is to do what is right. The M. de la fayette, seeing M. de Calonnes every day, will be able perhaps to obtain his order for expediting it. I do not know whether to condole with, or to congratulate the Marquis on the death of M. de [Simiane]. The man who shoots himself in the climate of Aix must be a bloody minded fellow indeed.—I am now in the land of corn, wine, oil, and sunshine. What more can man ask of heaven? If I should happen to die at Paris I will beg of you to send me here, and have me exposed to the sun. I am sure it will bring me to life again. It is wonderful to me that every free being who possesses cent ecus de rente, does not remove to the Southward of the Loire. It is true that money will carry to Paris most of the good things of this canton. But it cannot carry thither it's sunshine, nor procure any equivalent for it. This city is one of the cleanest and neatest I have ever seen in any country. The streets are streight, from 20. to 100 feet wide, and as clean as a parlour floor. Where they are of width sufficient they have 1. 2. or 4. rows of elms from 100 to 150 years old, which make delicious walks. There are no portes-cocheres, so that the buildings shew themselves advantageously on the streets. It is in a valley just where it begins to open towards the mouth of the Rhone, forming in that direction a boundless plain which is an entire[1] grove of olive trees, and is moreover in corn, lucerne, or vines, for the happiness of the olive tree is that it interferes with no superficial production. Probably it draws it's nourishment from parts out of the reach of any other plant. It takes well in every soil, but best where it is poorest, or where there is none. Comparing the Beaujolois with Provence, the former is of the richest soil, the latter richest in it's productions. But the climate of Beaujolois cannot be compared with this. I expect to find the situation of Marseilles still pleasanter: business will carry me thither soon, for a

time at least. I can receive there daily the waters from this place, with no other loss than that of their warmth, and this can easily be restored to them. I computed my journey on leaving Paris to be of 1000 leagues. I am now over one fourth of it. My calculation is that I shall conclude it in the earlier half of June. Letters may come to me here till the last day of April, about which time I shall be vibrating by this place Westwardly.—In the long chain of causes and effects, it is droll sometimes to seize two distant links and to present the one as the consequence of the other. Of this nature are these propositions. The want of dung prevents the progress of luxury in Aix. The poverty of the soil makes it's streets clean. These are legitimate consequences from the following chain. The preciousness of the soil prevents it's being employed in grass. Therefore no cattle, no dung. Hence the dung-gatherers (a numerous calling here) hunt it as eagerly in the streets as they would diamonds. Every one therefore can walk cleanly and commodiously. Hence few carriages. Hence few assemblies, routs, and other occasions for the display of dress.—I thank M. Pio for his anxieties on my account. My ostensible purpose of travelling without a servant was only to spare Espagnol the pain of being postponed to another, as I was quite determined to be master of my own secret, and therefore to take a servant who should not know me. At Fontainebleau I could not get one: but at Dijon I got a very excellent one who will probably go through the journey with me. Yet I must say, it is a sacrifice to opinion, and that without answering any one purpose worth a moment's consideration. They only serve to insulate me from the people among whom I am. Present me in the most friendly terms to M. Pio, M. Mazzei and other friends and believe me to be with the most sincere esteem your affectionate friend & servant,
Th: Jefferson

RC (ViW); endorsed: "Jefferson March 27. 87 [received] April 2." PrC (DLC).
[1] These two words interlined in substitution for "a perfect," underlined.

From John Blair

Dear Sir   Wmsburg. March 28th. 1787.

Mrs. Oster, the French consul's lady, leaves this place to morrow to embark for France, in a vessel lying at Portsmouth, in which I am informed your younger daughter is also to go passenger. They will be company for each other, and Mrs. Oster will, I am sure, take pleasure in shewing every attention which can contribute to make the passage more comfortable.—At the request of this lady I am to sollicit your favour, in a matter, which is not in your official line (in that indeed I could have nothing to say to you) but in which, as justice is concerned in it, you probably will think it not an unpleasant business to interfere, only so far as she requests.—This return to her country is designed as a separation from Mr. Oster, being the effect of an inveterate connubial disagreement. She thinks that she has reason to believe, that he has writen to the Minister, to have her confined in a convent, where she might be kept at less cost to him than in any other way. He charges her with extravagance and insanity, of neither of which have I, or those who are more intimate with her than my self, been able to discover the smallest sign. Those who have had the best opportunity of knowing her are impressed with sentiments much in her favour; and altho I am free to confess, that in disputes of this sort I am apt to suspect that there are some faults perhaps on both sides, yet it seems very probable that Mr. Oster's aversion discolours in his eyes her whole conduct, and makes him see faults where others can find none.—It is by no means my wish to raise any prejudice against Mr. Oster; to me he has been uniformly polite, nor am I acquainted with any thing in his character, which can be the subject of reprehension, except in the single instance of his behaviour to his wife. My only wish is to guard *against* prejudice, and to prevent the condemnation of a lady unheard. Mrs. Oster only requests, that [no] measures may be taken against her, without g[iving her a]n oppor[tunity of] producing such satisfactory vouchers res[pecting her character?] as she thinks she can at any time procure.—If [those immediately?] connected with it, were to come on before a public tribunal of justice, it would be proper to leave it there, upon the proofs adduced on each side. But if, as Mrs. Oster fears, the shorter method should be taken, her friends here have no opportunity of informing the mind of the Minister, unless you, Sir, should see nothing amiss in using the access which your public character gives you, to lay before him a caveat in her behalf.—I request the favour that your Excellency would present my very respectful compliments to Mr. Short, and Mr. Mazzei; tell the latter that I have in vain endeavoured to procure some money for him, but I believe Mr. Mattw. Anderson will make him a remitance shortly, if he have not done it already. If I were writing to him now, I would ask him, if he did not think it possible for wives to be less in the wrong than their husbands.—I have the pleasure to acquaint you, that all your friends this way are well, except that Mr. Wythe seems to have much uneasiness on account of his lady's ill state of health. Yet this is not likely to hinder his going to Philadelphia in May, in order to attend the convention, which is to take under consideration the amendments necessary to be made in the American Confederation.

With the greatest respect, I have the honour to be, Your Excellency's most obedient & affectionate servant, JOHN BLAIR

RC (DLC); endorsed. MS is slightly torn at both edges of text; the words in brackets have been supplied conjecturally. Recorded in SJL as received 22 June 1787.
TJ's YOUNGER DAUGHTER (Mary) did not accompany Mrs. Oster (see Banister to TJ, 6 May 1787).

To Martha Jefferson

Aix en Provence March. 28. 1787.

I was happy, my dear Patsy, to receive, on my arrival here, your letter informing me of your health and occupations. I have not written to you sooner because I have been almost constantly on the road. My journey hitherto has been a very pleasing one. It was undertaken with the hope that the mineral waters of this place might restore strength to my wrist. Other considerations also concurred. Instruction, amusement, and abstraction from business, of which I had too much at Paris. I am glad to learn that you are employed in things new and good in your music and drawing. You know what have been my fears for some time past; that you do not employ yourself so closely as I could wish. You have promised me a more assiduous attention, and I have great confidence in what you promise. It is your future happiness which interests me, and nothing can contribute more to it (moral rectitude always excepted) than the contracting a habit of industry and activity. Of all the cankers of human happiness, none corrodes it with so silent, yet so baneful a tooth, as indolence. Body and mind both unemployed, our being becomes a burthen, and every object about us loathsome, even the dearest. Idleness begets ennui, ennui the hypochrondria, and that a diseased body. No laborious person was ever yet hysterical. Exercise and application produce order in our affairs, health of body, chearfulness of mind, and these make us precious to our friends. It is while we are young that the habit of industry is formed. If not then, it never is afterwards. The fortune of our lives therefore depends on employing well the short period of youth. If

28 MARCH 1787

at any moment, my dear, you catch yourself in idleness, start from it as you would from the precipice of a gulph. You are not however to consider yourself as unemployed while taking exercise. That is necessary for your health, and health is the first of all objects. For this reason if you leave your dancing master for the summer, you must increase your other exercise. I do not like your saying that you are unable to read the antient print of your Livy, but with the aid of your master. We are always equal to what we undertake with resolution. A little degree of this will enable you to decypher your Livy. If you always lean on your master, you will never be able to proceed without him. It is a part of the American character to consider nothing as desperate; to surmount every difficulty by resolution and contrivance. In Europe there are shops for every want. It's inhabitants therefore have no idea that their wants can be furnished otherwise. Remote from all other aid, we are obliged to invent and to execute; to find means within ourselves, and not to lean on others. Consider therefore the conquering your Livy as an exercise in the habit of surmounting difficulties, a habit which will be necessary to you in the country where you are to live, and without which you will be thought a very helpless animal, and less esteemed. Music, drawing, books, invention and exercise will be so many resources to you against ennui. But there are others which to this object add that of utility. These are the needle, and domestic oeconomy. The latter you cannot learn here, but the former you may. In the country life of America there are many moments when a woman can have recourse to nothing but her needle for employment. In a dull company and in dull weather for instance. It is ill manners to read; it is ill manners to leave them; no card-playing there among genteel people; that is abandoned to blackguards. The needle is then a valuable resource. Besides without knowing to use it herself, how can the mistress of a family direct the works of her servants? You ask me to write you long letters. I will do it my dear, on condition you will read them from time to time, and practice what they will inculcate. Their precepts will be dictated by experience, by a perfect knowlege of the situation in which you will be placed, and by the fondest love for you. This it is which makes me wish to see you more qualified than common. My expectations from you are high: yet not higher than you may attain. Industry and resolution are all that are wanting. No body in this world can make me so happy, or so miserable as you. Retirement from public life will ere long become necessary for me.

28 MARCH 1787

To your sister and yourself I look to render the evening of my life serene and contented. It's morning has been clouded by loss after loss till I have nothing left but you. I do not doubt either your affection or dispositions. But great exertions are necessary, and you have little time left to make them. Be industrious then, my dear child. Think nothing unsurmountable by resolution and application, and you will be all that I wish you to be. You ask me if it is my desire you should dine at the abbess's table? It is. Propose it as such to Madame de Traubenheim with my respectful compliments and thanks for her care of you. Continue to love me with all the warmth with which you are beloved by, my dear Patsy, yours affectionately, TH: JEFFERSON

RC (NNP). PrC (MHi).

From the Rev. James Madison

DEAR SIR [ca. 28 Mch. 1787]

Mrs. Oster, an agreable and amiable, but unfortunate French Lady will deliver this. And tho' I have Nothing worth communicating, I could not refrain, on so favourable an opportunity, of once more testifying the sincere Wishes I always entertain for your Happiness whilst so remote from your native land, and also Acknowledgments which are due for past Favours.

I sent, some Time past, a small Collection of Marine Productions, which I hope arrived safe. I wish however I had reserved them for this opportunity, as you may probably think them not unworthy of attention.

In this State we enjoy a perfect Tranquility. It could be wished the situation was the same to the North of us. The Beginnings of a civil war there, appear to some as Proofs of the Instability and misery inseperable from a Republican Government. But to others, who I trust judge better, they appear only as the Symptoms of a strong and healthy Constitution, which, after discharging a few peccant Humours, will be restored to new Vigour.

All the States except Connecticut have agreed to send Deputies to the Convention which is to meet at Phila. in May for the Purpose of strengthening the Confederacy. And it is supposed that Connecticut will finally come into the Plan, from which the good Patriots expect permanent Advantages.

Believe me to be, Dr. Sir, with the most sincere Esteem Yr. Friend & Servt., J. MADISON

I have just been honoured by Genl. Chastellux with a Copy of his Travels thro N. America. I find It is but little relished by most here.

RC (DLC); endorsed: "Madison James (Coll[ege])"; without date, but written before 29 Mch. (see Blair to TJ, 28 Mch. 1787; Cary to TJ, 21 Mch. 1787). This is evidently the undated letter from Madison that TJ recorded in SJL as received 22 June 1787, along with Blair's and a (missing) letter from Wilson Miles Cary of 28 Mch. 1787.

To William Short

DEAR SIR   Aix Mar. 29. 1787.

Mine of the 27th. ackowleged the receipt of your favors of the 12th. and 14th. to which I must now add that of the 22d. which came to hand yesterday. Be so good as to give M. de Crevecoeur two maps and a copy of my book which I promised him. I am not certain whether I left the new leaves so that you can find them. If I did, I wish them to accompany the book. I think the engraver's charges reasonable. The packet from the Swedish Ambassador is too large to come on by post and probably not of pressing importance. With respect to the seeds from London, that Mde. de Tessé may not form high expectations from them it is necessary to observe to her that they are only of three or four kinds. There is a great quantity of each, having been written for on the request of M. de Malesherbes, who plants whole forests of every kind. Mde. de Tessé will be so good as to take of each as much as she pleases, and the residue after she is supplied I directed Petit to send to M. de Malesherbe's hotel. It was proper to accompany the medals with a letter to Mr. Jay, and I think it would be of advantage to you to write to him on any other good occasions. With respect to the partition of your time between Paris and St. Germain's, I should suppose it controuled by no circumstance but your own inclination. If you take the trouble once a week to see whether any thing has arisen which you can dispatch yourself, or which would require a communication to me, it will certainly suffice. If Colo. Smith comes to Paris, tell him how much I shall accuse fortune for having so illy timed my absence from thence, and that this is spoken from the sincerity of my heart. I regret the loss of any opportunity of discharging some of the debts of gratitude and inclination which I owe him.—I did not see Mount Cenis. My plan was to have gone to Montbard which was on the left of my road, and then to have crossed again to the right to Mount Cenis. But there were no posts

[253]

29 MARCH 1787

on these roads, the obtaining horses was difficult and precarious, and a constant storm of wind, hail, snow, and rain offered me little occasion of seeing any thing. I referred it therefore to some future excursion from Fontainebleau. The groupe of which M. de Laye spoke to you carries the perfection of the chissel to a degree of which I had no conception. It is the only thing in sculpture which I have seen on my journey worthy of notice. In painting I have seen good things at Lyons only. In Architecture nothing any where except the remains of antiquity. These are more in number, and less injured by time than I expected, and have been to me a great treat. Those at Nismes, both in dignity and preservation, stand first. There is however at Arles an Amphitheatre as large as that of Nismes, the external walls of which from the top of the arches downwards is well preserved. Another circumstance contrary to my expectation is the change of language. I had thought the Provençale only a dialect of the French; on the contrary the French may rather be considered as a dialect of the Provençale. That is to say, the Latin is the original. Tuscan[1] and Spanish are degeneracies in the first degree. Piedmontese (as I suppose) in the 2d. Provençale in the 3d. and Parisian French in the 4th. But the Provençale stands nearer to the Tuscan than it does to the French, and it is my Italian which enables me to understand the people here, more than my French. This language, in different shades occupies all the country South of the Loire. Formerly it took precedence of the French under the name of la langue Romans. The ballads of it's Troubadours were the delight of the several courts of Europe, and it is from thence that the novels of the English are called Romances. Every letter is pronounced, the articulation is distinct, no nasal sounds disfigure it, and on the whole it stands close to the Italian and Spanish in point of beauty. I think it a general misfortune that historical circumstances gave a final prevalence to the French instead of the Provençale language. It loses it's ground slowly, and will ultimately disappear because there are few books written in it, and because it is thought more polite to speak the language of the Capital. Yet those who learn that language here, pronounce it as the Italians do. We were last night treated with Alexis and Justine, and Mazet, in which the most celebrated actress from Marseilles came to bear a part for the advantage of her friend whose benefit night it was. She is in the stile of Mde. Dugazon, has ear, voice, taste and action. She is moreover young and handsome: and has an advantage over Mde. Dugazon and some other of the celebrated ones of Paris, in being clear of that dreadful wheeze or rather whistle in respiration which resembles the agonizing struggles for breath in a dying person.—I thank you for your information of the health of my daughter. My respects to the family of Chaville are always to be understood if not expressed. To Mr. and Mde. de la Fayette also, Messrs. Mazzei, Pio and Crevecoeur, I wish to be presented. Be assured as to yourself that no person can more sincerely wish your prosperity and happiness, nor entertain warmer sentiments of esteem than Dear Sir your affectionate humble servant.

RC (ViW); TJ's signature has been cut away; endorsed: 'Jefferson March 29 [received] April 5 1787."
The GROUPE OF WHICH M. DE LAYE SPOKE (see Short to TJ, 22 Mch. 1787) was the Diana and Endymion "at the Chateau de Laye Epinaye in the Beaujolois, a delicious morsel of sculpture, by Michael Angelo Slodtz" (TJ to Madame de Tessé, 20 Mch. 1787), which evidently has disappeared.

[1] This word interlined in substitution for "Italian," deleted.

From John Bondfield

SIR   Bordeaux 30 March 1787

I have the honor to transmit you inclosed Bill of Loading for Sixty three Cases of Arms shipt on board the Sally Captain Gilkinson for Virginia. The Ship sails to morrow and is a good Vessel and will I hope arrive safe.

By the Ship I transmit the Inspectors Certificate with the Invoices received from the Manufactory and the Bill of Loading to His Excellency the Governor of Virginia. I shall have a reimbursment to make to you as the Duties inward will be repaid me in Virtue of the Passport on their Shipment.

I have been some Days in expectation of seeing you at Bordeaux, Mr. Grand having wrote Mr. feger of your intentions to pay us a Visit. With due Respect I have the honor to be Sir your most obedient Humble servant,   JOHN BONDFIELD

RC (DLC); endorsed. Recorded in SJL as received 3 May 1787 at Aix-en-Provence. The copy of the bill of lading sent to TJ has not been found, but that sent to the governor of Virginia and Bondfield's letter in which it was enclosed are in Vi.

From Francis Eppes

DR. SIR   Eppington March 30. 1787.

I wrote you last fall and sent to the care of Messrs. Fulwer

30 MARCH 1787

Skipwith and Co. a box containing about a bushel of the cones and berries of the Holly. The Ceeder berries accompanies this which will be convey'd in a vessle belonging to Messrs. Shore & McConnico of Petersburg bound to Havedegrass. Every method in my power has been tryd to procure the Murtle berries. Many Gentlemen in the lower country have promis'd to send me about a bushel, however as yet none have arrivd. As soon as they do they shall be forwarded by the first safe opportunity. I was at Monticello in September. It was then too early to determin with certainty what quantity of Tobacco woud be made, however I think the crop will not exceed fifty hhds. including what will be made in Bedford. I have not herd from the plantations or Colo. Lewis since I left them in September for which reason its out of my power to give you any satisfaction respecting them, tho' supose Colo. Lewis has given you every information you wish as well as transmitted you the accounts for the last year, as he at present has the whole management of your affairs. You may assure your self my not acting does not proceed from any disrespect to you or an inclination to save my self trouble but from a thorow conviction that a business like yours can be manag'd to much greater advantage by one person on the spot than by any two men in this country seperated as far as Colo. Lewis and my self. Added to this I know you as well my self have full confidence in Colo. Lewis's integrity and good management.

Polly is very well and will sail by the first good opportunity. We have some expectations that she will go under the protection of the French Consol and his Lady who we hear intend for Europe this Spring. A Friend of Mine has Writen to the Consol on the subject and I expect an answer every moment. She is in high health and I hope will be able to bare the Fatigues of the voyage very well. We are all well and unite in our wishes for your health and happyness. I have inclosd you a letter from Mr. Beall of Wmburg. which will inform you of the fate of the claret you were so obliging as to send us. The two boxes shipped by Mr. Bondfield are arrived. One we have got at home, the other we shall shortly have as its in possession of a Friend of mine. I am Dr. Sir with much esteem Your Friend & Sevt.,

FRANS. EPPES

RC (ViU); addressed and endorsed. Recorded in SJL as received 27 May 1787 at Bordeaux. Enclosure: Samuel Beall to Daniel McCullum, Williamsburg, 3 Dec. 1786, informing him that the "Vessel that is said to have brought the Claret for Mr. Eppes, discharged under the care of Mr. Bonfield, Nephew to Mr. Jno. Bondfield of Bordeaux and the goods were stored with Messrs. Coopers of Portsmouth"; that some of the cargo had been sent from Portsmouth by Bondfield for him to sell; and that he would write at once to obtain information about the claret (MHi).

The FRIEND who wrote to the French

CONSOL (Martin Oster) evidently did not know that Mrs. Oster was going to France alone and that her voyage was an intentional separation from Oster (see Blair to TJ, 28 Mch. 1787; Banister to TJ, 6 May 1787).

From Ferdinand Grand

MONSIEUR [ca. 30 Mch. 1787]

J'ai à répondre aux lettres que vous m'avéz fait l'honneur de m'écrire le 28 du passé et le 15 du courant. J'ai pris notte des dispositions dont vous me chargez par la premiere, en conséquence de laquelle j'ai deja accepté la traitte de £5500. que M. Carmichael a fait sur moi pour compte des Etats unis.

J'ai remboursé Messrs. Finguerlin et Scherer des £1500. que vous en avez recues. Je n'ai pas encore avis du payement de £400 dont vous les avez priés.

Quant à Messrs. Vandenyver freres & Ce. sur la demande que je leur ai faite et de la somme que vous m'aviez chargé de recevoir d'eux et qui est de £17500. à ce qu'ils m'ont dit, ils désirent d'en avoir un ordre de votre part pour me livrer cet argent. Veuillez donc me le transmettre, et j'y joindrai mon reçu de la somme.

Les Séances des Bureaux de la grande assemblée continuent. Ils s'occupent maintenant de la troisieme section qui a pour objet les Domaines et les forests du Roy. La 4e. et derniere concernera l'administration des finances et le crédit. Les Memoires remis de la part du Roy aux Notables seront publiés aujourdhui.

J'espère, Monsieur, que vous êtes toujours également content de votre santé, et que vous le serez des Douches d'Aix, ainsi que du progrès de votre voyage. Si je puis en aucune manière contribuer à son agrément, je vous reitère ma priere de vouloir bien disposer librement de tout ce qui peut dépendre de moi à cet égard.

Je suis avec respect Monsieur Votre très humble et très obéissant-Serviteur, GRAND

RC (DLC); undated; at foot of first page: "Monsieur Th. Jefferson à Marseilles"; endorsed. Recorded in SJL as received 6 Apr. 1787 at Marseilles.

TJ's letter to Grand of LE 15 DU COURANT has not been found, but it was evidently a letter notifying him that he had on that day drawn on Grand in the amount of 1,500 livres in favor of MESSRS. FINGUERLIN ET SCHERER (Account Book under 15 Mch. 1787).

From Madame de Tessé

a Paris ce 30 mars.

Vous m'avés fait parcourir hier bien des siècles, Monsieur, par la peinture des différens mouvemens qui vous agitent à la vue des

[257]

30 MARCH 1787

antiquités Romaines du midi de la France. Elles m'ont semblé décrites pour la première fois parcequ'elles m'inspiroient une impression nouvelle. Je me suis trouvée en Société avec homère, Licurgue et Solon, parcourant les vestiges de la grandeur Egyptienne, j'ai vû Cicéron s'indigner de ce que le tombeau d'archimède étoit ignoré à Syracuse, je me suis élancée dans les siècles à venir, et j'ai distingué la jeunesse américaine lisant avec ardeur et admiration tout ce qu'on aura Recueilli de vos voyages. Lorsque la Richesse de son sol et l'excellence de son gouvernement auront porté l'Amérique Septentrionale au plus haut dégré de Splendeur, que le midi suivra son éxemple, que vous aurés donné des soins à la moitié du globe, on cherchera peutêtre les vestiges de Paris comme on fait aujourd'huy ceux de l'antique Babylone, et les mémoires de Mr. Jefferson conduiront les voyageurs avides des antiquités Romaines et Françoises qui se confondront alors. Telles sont, Monsieur, les pensées qui m'ont remplie toute la soirée d'hier. Mr. Mazzéi m'étant venu voir, je lui ai lu votre lettre comme on lisoit sans doute celle des apôtres dans l'assemblée des premiers chrétiens, pour m'assurer que je sentois la valeur de chacune de vos impressions. Tout ce qui porte une petite empreinte de culte apelle naturellement Mr. Mazzéi.

Mr. Short passe beaucoup de tems à St. Germain, mais il fait des courses à Paris et ne manque pas de me venir voir pour me persuader qu'il y demeure. Je lui ai causé il y a trois jours une plaisante importunité. Il y a à peu près quinze jours que, désirant quelque chose d'angleterre, j'écrivis à Mr. barthelemi, chargé des affaires de France. Le douzième jour après je Reçus par la diligence la chose demandée. Cela me fit naître l'idée de m'adresser à Mr. barthelemi pour vaincre, pardonnés moi l'expression, l'indolence de votre correspondant américain à Londres. Ses yeux toujours fixés sur la Tamise ne peuvent s'en détacher un instant, c'est en vain que Mr. Short l'a prié de mettre à la diligence la caisse de graines arrivées de la Virginie. Cette malheureuse caisse attend toujours qu'on expédie un vaisseau pour le Havre. J'ai demandé à Mr. Short une lettre pour ce digne commerçant et l'ai adressée à Mr. barthelemi qui ira le trouver et le déterminera à prendre la voie de terre. J'espère que vous ne taxerés point ma démarche d'indiscrétion, parcequ'elle est sans inconvénient et qu'en attendant votre Réponse pour la faire, les graines huileuses souffriroient davantage et nous perdrions quinze jours très précieux au printems.

Les discussions continuent dans l'assemblée des Notables, mais il n'y a Rien encore d'arrêté. Les gabelles ont occupé longtems et sérieusement ces messieurs. L'intérêt du peuple, et celui des finances du Roy, est difficile et important à concilier dans un objet qui compose une masse de Revenu aussi considérable. On a proposé hier l'aliénation des domaines et des Réformes sur la Régie des bois appartenant à la couronne. L'impôt territorial et l'examen de l'état Réel des Finances sont Remis à la quatrième section et nous commençons seulement la troisième. Je me Reconnois très incapable de décider quel est le genre d'assemblée le plus propre à discuter les intérêts du Roy et du peuple, mais je prononce hardiment qu'il faudroit que celle c'y prouva au Roy l'identité de ses intérêts, car c'est sans contredit le bien le plus utile qu'on puisse se proposer pour le présent et pour l'avenir. Au Reste, Monsieur, vous m'auriés vue tout à coup désintéressée sur les objets qui fixent l'attention du public si vous étiés Resté à Paris. La poitrine de Mr. de la Fayette a été menacée et l'est encore un peu. J'ai déviné qu'il travailloit trop et je m'en suis assurée. J'ai craint qu'on ne put le soumettre au Régime convenable. J'ai craint que ce printems ne décida en lui une maladie bien dangereuse à son âge. Je suis femme et en conséquence l'intérêt public s'est affaissé, accablé devant l'intérêt particulier. Je n'ai plus vu dans l'assemblée qu'une source de calamités, et pendant huit jours je n'ai formé d'autre voeu que de la voir finir. Mr. de la Fayette a consenti de prendre le sommeil qui lui est nécessaire, il ne maigrit plus, tousse peu et la douleur de poitrine est fort affaiblie. J'ai donc Repris courage et je suis Redevenue citoienne, à mesure que mes allarmes se sont dissipées. L'application que Mr. de la Fayette donne aux affaires lui a fait Retrancher toute correspondence de société. Il ne m'écrit pas même de ses nouvelles. Je n'en Reçois que de son sécretaire. Il est bon que vous en soiés instruit pour ne pas l'accuser d'une négligence dont il sera incapable envers vous dans tous les tems de sa vie. Les marseillois vous rapelleront plustôt les troubadours que les Phocéens, et je doute qu'une seule femme dans cette ville de commerce et de dissipations vous Ramène à l'idée de Me. de Tott. Elle vous a rendu compte de l'impression qu'elle avoit Reçue par le tableau de marius; je n'ai point lu sa lettre, mais je sais qu'elle exprime mal sa pensée si elle ne porte pas l'empreinte d'un attachement sincère et d'une tendre Reconnoissance pour vos bontés. Mr. de Tessé me charge de vous présenter ses hommages. Recevés avec votre bienveillance ordinaire celui de la vénération profonde, de tous les sentimens avec lesquels j'ai l'honneur d'être, Monsieur, votre très humble et très obéissante servante,

NOAILLES DE TESSÉ

31 MARCH 1787

Je soigne moi même dans ma chambre deux *Dionea* qui poussent à merveille. Les autres sont à Châville sous la conduite de mon jardinier.

RC (DLC); endorsed. Recorded in SJL as received 3 May 1787 at Aix-en-Provence.

Almost at the moment Madame de Tessé wrote her amused comment about Short's spending BEAUCOUP DE TEMS A ST. GERMAIN—that is, near the young Duchesse de la Rochefoucauld with whom he had a love affair that became serious around 1790-1792—TJ was telling Short to allow his time between Paris and St. Germain to be "controuled by no circumstance but your own inclination" and he was also anticipating Madame de Tessé about the TROUBADOURS (TJ to Short, 29 Mch. 1787; for a note on Short's love affair, see Malone, *Jefferson and the Rights of Man*, p. 149-50).

From Elizabeth Wayles Eppes

[31 March 1787]

I never was more anxious to hear from you than at present, in hopes of your countermanding your orders with regard to dear Polly. We have made use of every stratagem to prevail on her to consent to visit you without effect. She is more averse to it than I could have supposed; either of my children would with pleasure take her place for the number of good things she is promised. However, Mr. Eppes has two or three different prospects of conveying her, to your satisfaction, I hope, if we do not hear from you.

MS not found; text is from the extract printed in Randolph, *Domestic Life*, p. 124, which is cited there as having been written "Towards the close of the month of March, 1787." This must, however, be a part of the letter from Mrs. Eppes dated 31 Mch. 1787 which TJ recorded in SJL as received 27 May at Bordeaux, along with the letter from her husband of 30 Mch. 1787.

From Mary Jefferson

DEAR PAPA   [ca. 31 Mch. 1787]

I should be very happy to see you, but I can not go to France, and hope that you and sister Patsy are well. Your affectionate daughter. Adieu.

MARY JEFFERSON

MS not found. Text is from Randolph, *Domestic Life*, p. 104, where it is printed as one of three undated letters from Mary Jefferson (see also Mary Jefferson to TJ, ca. 13 Sep. 1785 and ca. 22 May 1786). Though it cannot be proved, it is probable that the present letter is the one which TJ recorded in SJL without date as received 27 May 1787 at Bordeaux with letters from Francis Eppes, 30 Mch. 1787, and Elizabeth Wayles Eppes, 31 Mch. 1787.

From André Limozin

Le Havre, 31 Mch. 1787. Encloses Captain Joshua Oldner's bill of lading for the "twelve Cases Catridge Boxes . . . consigned me for the use of the State of Virginia" and shipped on the *Portsmouth* bound for Norfolk. She is ready to sail with the "very First Fair wind," and Limozin is sending another bill of lading by her to the governor of Virginia. His next letter will bring the note of expenses for these cases. "Captn. Oldner Seems [to] me to be a very cleaver man; he intends to continue Havre de Grace treade." Limozin recommends him to TJ and if he has anything to send to Norfolk, it "must be ready against the month of July. . . . His Ship [is] a good Strong new fast sailing Vessell, which as well as the Master deserves all preference and incouragement." If TJ is surprised because he speaks so much in behalf of a master not consigned to Limozin's house, it is because "it is our duty to do Justice to every Body." Encloses also a letter from Mr. Oster.

RC (MHi); 4 p.; endorsed. Recorded in SJL as received 3 May 1787 at Aix-en-Provence. Enclosures: (1) Bill of lading, dated 31 Mch. 1787 and signed by Joshua Oldner, for "Twelve Cases Merchandize," at the foot of which Oldner wrote: "Contents unKnown" (Vi). (2) The letter from Oster has not been found and is not recorded in SJL among the letters received 3 May at Aix-en-Provence; it may have been only a covering address under Oster's frank for one or more of the letters from Virginia received on that date.

From Adrien Petit

[*Paris, 31 Mch. 1787.* Recorded in SJL as received 3 May 1787 at Aix-en-Provence. Not found.]

To Chastellux

Marseilles Apr. 4. 1787.

I must return you many thanks, my dear friend, for your kind attention in procuring me the acquaintance of Monsr. Bergasse, from whom I have received many civilities, and, what is more precious, abundance of information. To you and to him also I am indebted for an introduction to Monsr. Audibert, in whom I saw enough to make me regret that I could not see more of him. My journey from Paris to this place has been a continued feast of new objects, and new ideas. To make the most of the little time I have for so long a circuit, I have been obliged to keep myself rather out of the way of good dinners and good company. Had they been my objects, I should not have quitted Paris. I have courted the society of gardeners, vignerons, coopers, farmers &c. and have

4 APRIL 1787

devoted every moment of every day almost, to the business of enquiry. M. de Bergasse however united for me all objects, a good dinner, good company, and information. I was unlucky in not having called on you before you went into the country, as I should have derived from you much useful counsel for my journey. I have still a favor to ask of you, which is, a letter to some one good person at Tours in Touraine, where I shall make a short stay of a day or two on my return about the latter part of May or beginning of June. The article Coquilles in the Questions Encyclopediques de Voltaire will inform you what is my object there. I have found the Abbés in general most useful acquaintances. They are unembarrassed with families, uninvolved in form and etiquette, frequently learned, and always obliging. If you know such a one at Tours you will oblige me infinitely by a letter to him: or if you know none yourself, perhaps some of your friends may. I will only beg to be announced but as a voyageur etranger simplement, and that it be addressed à Monsr. Jefferson à Tours, poste restante. This deception keeps me clear of those polite obligations to which I might otherwise be engaged, and leaves me the whole of the little time I have to pursue the objects that always delight me.—I have been concerned with the country I have passed thro hitherto. I could not help comparing it, en passant, with England, and found the comparison much more disadvantageous to the latter than I had expected. I shall have many interrogations to ask of you. These being too many for a letter, they shall therefore be reserved to some future conversation, when I can have the pleasure of returning you thanks in person for the multiplied instances of your goodness and partiality to me, and of assuring you how sincere are those sentiments of esteem and friendship with which I have the honor to be Dear Sir, your affectionate friend & humble servant,

TH: JEFFERSON

PrC (MHi); at foot of first page: "M. le Marq. de Chastellux"; MS faded.
On MONSR. BERGASSE and TJ's interest in COQUILLES, see his journal of his trip through Southern France, printed under date of 10 June 1787.

From Ralph Izard

DEAR SIR　　　　　　　　　　　Charleston 4th. April 1787.

I have lately been favoured with your Letter of 18th. Novr. which went to New York, and from thence came to me here by the Post. You mention the Hague, and are so obliging as to wish me

4 APRIL 1787

there: for this mark of your friendship, be pleased to accept of my thanks. Had the funds of the United States allowed them to make the appointment you allude to last year, I would have accepted of it, and devoted three years of my life to their service. At present I feel much disinclined to it, and most heartily wish that Mr. Madison may be elected whenever the Finances of Congress will admit of it. He is a Member of the Continental Convention which is to meet in Philadelphia next Month for the purpose of revising the articles of Confederation. If the powers of Congress can be so far extended as to give efficacy to the decisions of that body, the measure will assuredly contribute to the security, and happiness, of the Continent. At present our affairs are by no means in a desireable state. I agree with you perfectly in opinion respecting the propriety of our cultivating the closest, and most intimate connexion with France. We have already derived great benefits from her, and much greater may still be expected. We are under considerable obligations to you for your exertions respecting the Commerce of every part of the Continent, and I am confident that very beneficial consequences will result from a continuance of them. The copy of the Letter from M. de Calonne to you, which you enclosed me, shews the good disposition of the Ministry towards us. Much remains however yet to be done; and I am happy to think that whatever extension is given to the Commerce of America may, by good management be made beneficial to France. I should be very glad if their Manufactories could supply us as well, and as cheap as those of England with the coarse articles which are absolutely necessary in this Country. I mean Negro Cloth, Blankets, and implements of Husbandry. When I was in Paris I procured from London a yard of Negro Cloth called there White Plains, and a broad Hoe, and gave them to M. Abeille, who was a Member of a Society for the promotion of Commerce. The Cloth is near a yard wide, perfectly white, very substantial, and comfortable wear for Negroes, and is from 12 to 14½ Pence Sterling pr. Yard by the Piece. The Broad Hoes are from 17 to 18 shillings, and 6 pence a Dozen, and very good. Blankets 4 Shillings, and 3 pence each. I have just copied these articles with their prices from an Invoice lately received from Messrs. Mannings & Vaughan in London, for the use of my Plantations: they were all remarkably good. M. Abeille told me that the Manufacturers of France would soon be able to supply us with the articles I have mentioned, as good, and as cheap. I wish this could be done; and if it could I am persuaded that four fifths of the Planters in this State would deal with France in preference to England. You say that France could consume our whole Crop of Rice. This might easily be done if the matter were put in a proper train. It would give me much pleasure to see it, and returns made entirely in the Manufactures, Wines &c. of France. It is supposed that France contains 24 Millions of Inhabitants. If each of them were to consume two pounds of Rice in a year, the amount would be 96,000 Barrels of 500 ℔., which is more than our annual export of that article since the War. I have seen your Letter to Mr. Jay, in which you mention the comparative goodness of our Rice with that of Italy; and you think ours is not sent to Market in as good order as theirs. In this I am persuaded you are mistaken. When I was in Italy I visited some of the best Rice Plantations in that Country, and was surprized to find how inferior their management of the grain was to ours, after they had got it into the Barn Yard. You may observe how much whiter our Rice is than theirs, which must be owing to that circumstance. Our Rice is more broken than theirs, which is occasioned by two causes: they clean it less than we do, and their grain is thicker in proportion to its length, resembling Barley, which makes it less liable to be broken by the Pestle. I have seen the Grocers in Paris employed in picking out the whole grains from the broken ones. This is a needless trouble as one is just as good as the other. If you have observed the same thing perhaps that may have led you to think that our Rice was not in as good order as the Italian. I am desirous of trying how their Rice would succeed in this Country: and for that reason should be obliged to you if you could procure, and send me any quantity of the seed from one to ten Bushels. It might easily be shipped for this Place from Marseilles; and the best seeds should be chosen. I was in hopes that you might have been able to have induced the Portugueze to receive our Rice on the same terms they did before the War. Lisbon used to take from us annually 20,000 Barrels, and now there is none sent there, which is a considerable disadvantage to us. If Honfleur is made a free Port, with proper management the greatest part of the Rice which would otherwise be sent to Cowes, might be drawn thither. It might be made a Depot for all the goods of Europe consumed by America, and the Ships of this Country, and of France, might return at once with whatever they wanted, without having the trouble of going farther up the Channel. This would be a stroke at the carrying Trade of England, and diminish in a considerable degree the Nursery of their Seamen. France would unquestionably be benefitted by this. In my opinion a proper judgment of her prosperity can never be formed abstractedly. That of England must be her Scale. Upon this Idea my opinion was formed respecting the restrictions on our Trade to the West India Islands. If they were entirely removed from those of France, England would be under the necessity of following the example, and her Seamen would be diminished. Her strength, and prosperity depend entirely on the number of her Seamen; but France has internal resources; and a great Marine is only necessary to her, because her Rival is possessed of one. Mr. Barrett's proposals are not very tempting: any Merchant in France, Holland, or England will receive consignments upon terms more advantageous to the shipper in this Country. I am well acquainted with the character and solidity of Messrs. le Coulteux' House, and think they might be the means of establishing an intercourse very advantageous to the two Countries: but not by such proposals as are contained in Mr. Barrett's letter. Too strict an adherence to immediate profit will not effect a dissolution of old connexions, and long established prejudices. At the same time the present situation of our affairs makes it necessary for an European Merchant to be very circumspect in his dealings with this Country. Though his profits may at first be small, his security ought to be good. The War bore particularly hard upon this State, most of us have been considerably injured, and I have had my share of the public calamity. I find myself about £8,000 Sterlg. in debt, with an Estate which ought not to feel any inconvenience from such a Sum. I wish however to pay it off, and to have but one Creditor. If Messrs. Le Couteulx, or any other substantial House in Paris would pay my Bills to that amount, I would engage to remit them annually 600 Barrels of Rice of 500 French pounds weight neat each, till the whole debt should be paid, and 5 per Cent interest on each Balance. If the Bills could be made payable in London I should prefer it, because they always command a better price. I would give security to three times the amount of the sum borrowed, which should be satisfactory to the Agent of the Lender. I wish not to give you any trouble about this matter; but if you could effect it without much difficulty it would oblige me, and be of service to me.

I am with great regard Dear Sir Your most obt. Servant,

RA. IZARD

Have you received the Laws of this State, and the Newspapers by M. Chatteaufort? The Printer has orders to send the Papers for you regularly to Mr. Jay as you desire, and he tells me it has been done.

RC (DLC): marked "Copy" at head of text; endorsed. Recorded in SJL as received 27 June 1787. A Dupl was enclosed in Lanchon Frères & Cie. to TJ of 4 July 1787 and recorded in SJL as received 8 July 1787 (missing).

From the Papal Nuncio

Paris ce 4 Avril 1787

L'Archevêque de Rhodes a l'honneur de faire part à Monsieur Jefferson qu'il a eu hier ses premieres Audiences du Roi, de la Reine, et de la Famille Royale en qualité de Nonce Apostolique.

RC (DLC); addressed to TJ at "Rue neuve de Berri prés de la Grille de Chaillot en son Hôtel"; endorsed by TJ: "Rome, Nuncio of." Recorded in SJL as received 3 May 1787 at Aix-en-Provence.

To Philip Mazzei

Dear Sir   Marseilles Apr. 4. 1787.

I have had the pleasure of finding your friend Soria alive and one of the most considerable merchants here. I delivered him your letter and he has shewn me all the attentions which the state of his mind would permit. A few days before my arrival his only son had eloped with jewels and money to the value of 40,000 livres, and I believe is not yet heard of. He speaks of you with friendship, and will be happy to see you on your way Southwardly. He has promised to make me acquainted with a well informed gardener whom I expect to find among the most precious of my acquaintances. From men of that class I have derived the most satisfactory information in the course of my journey and have sought their acquaintance with as much industry as I have avoided that of others who would have made me waste my time on good dinners and good society. For these objects one need not leave Paris. I find here several interesting articles of culture: the best figs, the best grape for drying, a smaller one for the same purpose without a seed, from Smyrna, Olives, capers, Pistachio nuts, almonds. All these articles may suceed on, or Southward of the Chesape[ake.] From hence my inclination would lead me no further Eastward as I am to see little more than a rocky coast. But I am encouraged

4 APRIL 1787

here with the hopes of finding something useful in the rice fields of Piedmont, which are said to be but a little way beyond the Alps. It will probably be the middle of June before I get back to Paris. In the mean time I wish to observe [to] you that if this absence, longer than you had calculate[d it], should render an earlier pecuniary supply necessary, lodge a line for me at Aix, poste restante, where I shall find it about the last of this month, and I shall with great pleasure do what may be needful for you. Be so good as to present me respectfully to the Maison de la Rochefoucault, and accept yourself very sincere assurances of esteem and regard from Dear Sir Your affectionate friend & humble servt,

TH: JEFFERSON

PrC (DLC). MS faded; illegible words have been supplied in brackets by the editors.

YOUR FRIEND SORIA: In his list of names and addresses in the rough notes of expenses (CSmH) appears the following name: "Antonio Soria. Negociant a Mars[eilles]." In his of 6 May 1787 TJ enclosed an order on Grand in Mazzei's favor for a PECUNIARY SUPPLY; there is in DLC the following statement of his account:

"Philip Mazzei to Th:J.
Dr.
1785. Aug. 11 To cash   600₶
      Oct. 22. To do.   600₶   1200₶
1786. Mar. 4. To cash   300₶
      June 16. To do.   300₶
      Sep. 21. To do.   36₶   636
1787 Feb. 9. To cash   48₶
      18. To do.   552
Apr. 4. [6 May]
      Order on Grand   600
Cr.
1785. Nov. 15. By cash in full 1200₶
1786. Oct. 4. By cash in full   636₶"

From William Short

MY DEAR SIR   Paris April 4. 1787

I returned from the country the day before yesterday, and the evening of the same day brought here yours of the 27th. ulto. I need not tell you how much pleasure it gave me to see that you were in the midst of constant vivifying sunshine. Although I have little faith in the waters of Aix, I have a great deal in its climate. But provided you receive the benefit you wished for, I will not dispute about the cause which may produce so desirable an effect. I hope you will let me know in your next whether the one or the other has shewn any influence on your wrist.

Your observations respecting Mr. de Calonne's letter, as well as the conduct to be pursued in that and every other case, I am sure are the most just that can be made. To do what is right, is the only means of extricating one's self from every difficulty—but still there is a previous difficulty which sometimes occurs, and that is, to

[267]

know what is right. In the case in question however that difficulty was not immense; and I am very happy to see that my idea of what was proper, corresponded perfectly with yours. I took no further step than writing the letter to M. de Colonia. M. de laf. took up the subject with new zeal. He was aided by M. M. and the Duke of Harcourt—this together with M. de Calonne's dispositions, which are certainly favorable to commerce in general and that of America in particular, have advanced the matter so far, that M. de l.f. told me to day it might be considered as an affair finished.

I shall attend punctually to the several instructions in your letter respecting the map. I have not yet been able to see the person who is striking the maps for the Abbé Morellet, but there will be no difficulty in having the 200 additional struck on thinner paper. It will be necessary however to have two sheets pasted together, the map being too large for any single sheet except of the thick kind which you saw. Should the bank paper be of too small a format, I fear it will be difficult to paste two sheets of that thin kind. Of this however I shall make the proper enquiry.—You desire me to write again to Mr. Ogilvy. You will have seen Sir by my letter of the 22d. in what situation that affair was. Since that Mde. de Tesse, who had lost all confidence in my London correspondent, insisted I should give her a letter for Mr. Ogilvy with an order to deliver the box to the Chargé des affaires of France at London to whom she inclosed it. I have this evening received a letter from Ogilvy which shews that my late letter to Mr. Carnes as well as that for him, were too late. He tells me that he has sent the box of seeds by a vessel bound to Dunkirk addressed to a merchant whose address he forwards to me. I shall write to the merchant on this subject by to-morrow's post.

Mde. de Tesse was here this evening to see the procession. The day was very unfavorable and of course peu de monde. Mde. de Corny wrote me yesterday her intention of coming by your permission les jours de Longchamp. I answered her that it was my intention *d'avoir* passé chez elle de lui faire ma cour, et en même tems de la rapeller qu'elle m'avoit fait esperer que j'aurais le plaisir de la voir ici les jours de Longchamps &c. &c. Yet she did not come, for what reason I cannot say. I shall call on her to morrow to enquire about it.—I received a message from M. de Langeac yesterday evening desiring to know if he might be allowed to come and bring his sister the Marchioness of Chambaraud to see the procession. I was at a loss what answer to make, yet made such an one as authorized his coming. On my return from Mde. de Tesse's, where I dined, I found him in one of the rooms above. His sister was not with him, but there were three other women whom I did not know. He told me his sister had understood there was to be company here to day and therefore did not come but desired she might be permitted to have that pleasure to morrow. Whether she will come or not I cannot say—if she does I shall not know how to send her up stairs, and yet I know not how she and Mde. de Corny may be as to *convenances*.

Mde. de Tessé insisted on my giving her your address that she might send you two pamphlets, which she intended to have countersigned. I told her I would send them to you if she thought proper, but she would not hear of it; urging that she was *dans l'etat de payer 8 ou 9^{lt}* and that the postage would be too considerable, for the value of the things sent.

Lest you should not yet have found out who is President of Congress, it may not be improper to tell you that that body formed itself not till the early part of Febry. and chose Genl. St. Clair their President. I observe that Mr. Madison, and Hawkins of No. Carolina arrived at N. York and took their seats about the same time.

The *Assemblee des notables* have separated for the Easter holidays. The pamphlets which Mde. de Tesse sends you will let you see in what state matters are here, with respect to them. It is thought the result will be that the Controller general will have his 112 millions which he asks in addition, but that the nation at large will be indemnified for this additional burthen by the new regulations which will be established as to 1. provincial assemblies, 2. public oeconomy, 3. more equal distribution of impositions, 4. the liberation of the commerce of grain, and the abolition of the shackles of internal commerce by the *reculement des barrieres*, and 5thly. by other improvements, such as the abolition of the corvee, the checking of abuses in domanial administration &c.—I send you inclosed seven letters being all that have arrived since the last which Petit forwarded to you.—Before this reaches you, you will probably have seen Marseilles. I shall like much to see what you think of it, that I may know whether my predilection for it is well founded. Should you be at Montpelier I hope you will not find it as Rousseau. He says in one of his letters which has just fallen accidentally into my hands, '*on regarde* les etrangers a Montpelier precisément comme une espece d'animaux faits exprès

5 APRIL 1787

pour être pellés, volés, assommés au bout, s'ils avoient l'impertinence de le trouver *mauvais*.'

It is now very late. You are indebted to that circumstance Sir for not receiving a longer and more troublesome letter from Your sincerest friend & servant, W SHORT

RC (DLC). PrC (DLC: Short Papers; endorsed. Recorded in SJL as received 3 May 1787 at Aix-en-Provence. TJ received some thirty-six letters on 3 May at Aix-en-Provence, and it cannot be determined which SEVEN LETTERS were enclosed with the present and which had been sent with Petit's letter of 31 Mch. 1787.

To John Banister

[*Marseilles*, 5 *Apr*. 1787. Recorded in SJL under this date. Not found.]

From Pierre Poinsot des Essarts

St. Germain, 5 *Apr*. 1787. Desires to send to Washington a copy of the writings of one of his relations, and wishes to receive as soon as possible "les armes De cet homme illustre."

RC (DLC); 2 p.; in French; signed: "Des Essarts Cte De Bouville"; endorsed; at foot of text: "Je Demeure Ruë de verneuil faubourg St. germain no. 5." Recorded in SJL as received 3 May 1787 at Aix-en-Provence.

Two days before TJ received this request for a copy of Washington's coat of arms (presumably desired for use in making the binding), Madame des Essarts forwarded to Washington the two-volume edition of the works of her father, C. H. P. de Chamousset, published early in 1787. Washington acknowledged the gift on 8 Jan. 1788 (Washington, *Writings*, ed. Fitzpatrick, XXIX, 362-3; see also *Cat. of Washington Coll. in Boston Athenæum*, p. 483).

To Madame de Tott

Marseilles Apr. 5. 1787.

I thank you sincerely, Madam, for the favour of your letter on the subject of M. Drouay's[1] picture. It has confirmed a part of my own ideas, given some which had escaped me, and corrected others wherein I had been wrong. The strong expression given to the countenance of Marius had absorbed all my attention, and made me overlook the slenderness of his frame, which you justly recall to my mind as faulty in that particular. Give me leave in return to rectify for you an opinion in another kind which I suppose you to entertain, because you have not yet had time to correct all the errors of the [human][2] mind. I presume that you think, as

[270]

5 APRIL 1787

most people think, that a person cannot be in two places at one time. Yet is there no error more palpable than this. You know, for example, that you have been in Paris and it's neighborhood, constantly since I had the pleasure of seeing you there: yet I declare you have been with me above half my journey. I could repeat to you long conversations, word for word, and on a variety of subjects. When I find you fatigued with conversation and sighing for your pallet and pencil, I permit you to return to Paris a while, and[3] amuse myself with philosophizing on the objects which occur. The plan of my journey, as well as of my life, being to take things by the smooth handle, few occur which have not something tolerable[4] to offer me. [The Auberge] for instance in which I am obliged to take refuge at night, presents in the first moment nothing but noise, dirt, and disorder. But the auberge is not to be[5] too much abused. True, it has not the charming gardens of Chaville without, nor it's decorations, nor it's charming society within. I do not seek therefore for the good things which it has not, but those which it has. 'A traveller, sais I, retired at night to his chamber in an Inn, all his effects contained in a single trunk,[6] all his cares circumscribed by the walls of his apartment, unknown to all, unheeded, and undisturbed, writes, reads, thinks, sleeps, just in the moments when nature and the movements of his body and mind require. Charmed with the tranquillity of his little cell,[7] he finds how few are our real wants, how cheap a thing is happiness, how expensive a one pride. He views with pity the wretched rich, whom the laws of the world have submitted to the cumbrous trappings of rank: he sees him labouring through the journey of life like an ass oppressed[8] under ingots of gold, little of which goes to feed, to clothe, or to cover himself; the rest gobbled up by harpies of various description with which he has surrounded himself. These, and not himself, are it's real masters. He wonders that a thinking mind can be so subdued by opinion, and that he does not run away from his own crouded house, and take refuge in the chamber of an Inn.' Indeed I wonder so too, unless he has a Chaville to retire to, and a family composed like that of Chaville, where quiet and friendship can both be indulged.[9] But between the society of real friends, and the tranquillity of solitude the mind finds no middle ground.—Thus reconciled to my Auberge by night, I was still persecuted[10] by day with the cruel whip of the postillion. How to find a smooth handle to this tremendous instrument? At length however I found it in the callous nerves of the horse, to

5 APRIL 1787

which these terrible stripes may afford but a gentle and perhaps a pleasing irritation; like a pinch of[11] snuff to an old snuff-taker.

Sometimes I amuse myself with physical researches. Those enormous boots, for instance, in which the postillion is incased like an Egyptian mummy, have cost me more pondering than the laws of planetary motion did to Newton. I have searched their solution in his physical, and in his moral constitution. I fancied myself in conversation with one of Newton's countrymen, and asked him what he thought could be the reason of their wearing those boots? 'Sir, says he, it is because a Frenchman's heels are so light, that, without this ballast, he would turn keel up.' 'If so, Sir, sais I, it proves at least that he has more *gravity* in his head than your nation is generally willing to allow him.' I should go on, Madam, detailing to you my dreams and speculations; but that my present situation is most unfriendly to speculation. Four thousand three hundred and fifty market-women (I have counted them one by one)[12] brawling, squabbling, and jabbering Patois, three hundred asses braying and bewailing to each other, and to the world, their cruel oppressions, four files of mule-carts passing in constant succession, with as many bells to every mule as can be hung about him, all this in the street under my window, and the weather too hot to shut it. Judge whether in such a situation it is easy to hang one's ideas together. Besides, writing from a colony of your own country, you would rather I should say less of myself and more of that. But, just dropped among them, how can I pretend to judge them with justice?[13] Of beauty, you will say, one may judge on a single coup d'oeil. Of beauty then, Madam, they have a good share, as far as the public walks, the Spectacles, and the assembleé of Mademlle. Conil enable me to decide. But it is not a legitimate Graecian beauty. It is not such as yours. The reason I suppose is that yours is genuine, brought from the spot; [where]as theirs has been made here, and like all fabricated wares is sophisticated with foreign mixture. Perhaps you would rather I should write you news? Les Amandes sont de 22.^{tt}, Cacao 19s, Caffé 31., Cotton 130.^{tt}, huile 22.^{tt}, riz 21.^{tt}, savon 42.^{tt}, terebenthine 17.s &c. &c.[14] This is not in the stile of Paris news; but I write from Marseilles, and it is the news of the place. I could continue it thro' the whole table of prices current; but that I am sure you have enough, and have already in your heart wished an end to my letter. I shall therefore annex but one preliminary condition; which is a permission to express here my respectful attachment to Madame and Monsieur de Tessé, and to assure yourself of those sentiments of perfect[15] friendship & affection with which I have the honor to be sincerely & constantly, Madam, your most obedient & most humble servant,

TH: JEFFERSON

PrC (MHi); MS faded. Tr (DLC); in TJ's hand, differing somewhat in phraseology as indicated below. The exact date at which TJ made this copy, or the purpose for which it was made, is not certain, but it is to be noted that the paper on which Tr is written bears the watermark "R BARNARD 1809" and that this paper is evidently the same as that on which TJ made a similar copy of his letter of 20 Mch. 1787 to Madame de Tessé. Both copies of these letters were therefore made sometime between 1809 and 1826 for an undetermined purpose and both were evidently written at the same time. In both cases also TJ sought to "improve" his text when he came to make the Tr, as the following notes indicate, though the changes here are less extensive than the corresponding alterations in the letter to Madame de Tessé.

[1] This word interlined in Tr in substitution for a deleted name (it appears to read "David's") that TJ had erred in copying from PrC.

[2] MS faded; this and other words in brackets (supplied) have been taken from Tr.
[3] Tr adds at this point: "in the mean time."
[4] Tr reads instead: "good."
[5] Instead of preceding four words, Tr reads: "has been."
[6] Tr reads instead: "portmanteau."
[7] Preceding four words are not in Tr.
[8] The words "labouring through the journey of life like an ass oppressed" are not in Tr.
[9] Tr reads instead: "united."
[10] In making Tr, TJ erred at this point by first writing "persuaded"; he then corrected this to read as above.
[11] Tr reads "Scotch snuff."
[12] Preceding three words are not in Tr.
[13] Tr reads: ". . . to judge the legitimacy of their descent?"
[14] This sentence is altered in Tr to read as follows: "Any thing to obey you— Oil is 10. sols the lb., almonds 2.^{lt} [sic], Cacao 19 s., Caffé. 31.s, rice 21.^{lt} &c."
[15] This word is not in Tr.

From William Macarty

SIR   Lorient 6th. april 1787.

Continual delays and disappointments in my Business and Remittances from america has Involved me in Difficulties with Some of my Creditors who harrass me continually to prevent the bad Consequences, that might attend their pursuit. Messrs. Girardot Haller & Ce. of Paris my principal Creditors, have made application to Monsieur Le Barron de Breteuil for an arret de Surseance for one year.

Permit me, to request you, to represent my unhappy Situation, to the Minister. Your kind influence will be of great Service in obtaining the arret de Surseance which will enable me to do Justice to every one, and preserve me from Ruin. I am with great Respect Sir your most Humble and obedient Servant,

WM. MACARTY

RC (DLC); endorsed. Recorded in SJL as received 3 May 1787 at Aix-en-Provence.

[273]

From Rigoley d'Ogny

MONSIEUR   Paris 6. Avril 1787.

C'est avec grand plaisir, Monsieur, que je vous ai fait remettre en franchise du port maritime et de terre le paquet qui vous avait été adressé de Newyorck par la voye des Paquebots français qui contenait principalement des Gazettes et que vous aviés refusé comme trop taxé. Permettés moi de profiter d'une occasion ou vous Sentés vous même un des inconvéniens qu'il y a que la France n'ait pas encore pû conclure aucun traité relatif à Sa Corrèspondance avec les Etats unis de l'Amérique, pour vous engager à reprendre la Négóciation que j'avais été autorisé à faire avec M. Francklin dès 1784.

Après plusieurs Conférences nous convinmes d'un Projet de traité qu'il se chargea d'envoyer; depuis ce tems là, j'ai cherché inutilement tous les moyens de suivre l'effet de cette négociation sans pouvoir y parvenir.

La régularité du départ des Paquebots français par lesquels s'écoule beaucoup de lettres arrivantes en France des Pays Etrangers, que je laisse passer actuellement franches aux treize Etats unis, doit leur faire sentir la nécessité d'un Traité, parcequ'il ne serait pas juste que la France payât ces Sortes de lettres à l'Etranger sans en être remboursé par les treize Etats unis.

Dans le cas ou vous croiriés pouvoir reprendre cette négociation, j'aurai l'honneur de vous envoyer une Copie de ce Projet de traité et de vous demander un moment de conversation pour en raisonner avec vous. J'en serai d'autant plus flatté que ce sera pour moi une occasion de vous offrir les assurances du Sincère et respectueux attachement avec lequel j'ai l'honneur d'être, Monsieur, Votre très humble et très obéissant serviteur, RIGOLEY D'OGNY

RC (DLC); in a clerk's hand, signed by D'Ogny; endorsed. Tr (DNA: PCC, No. 107, II). Recorded in SJL as received 3 May 1787 at Aix-en-Provence. This letter was forwarded to Jay by TJ on 21 June 1787; see also Short to TJ, 6 Apr. and TJ to D'Ogny, 3 May 1787. Rigoley, Baron d'Ogny, was Intendant Général des Postes aux Lettres.

From William Short

DEAR SIR   Paris April 6. 1787

At length Longchamp is at an end. The company have just left me and I retire from the bustle of the procession to the calmer pleasure of writing to you. My apprehensions as to *convenances* between some of the ladies were without ground. Mde. de Corny and the Marchioness de Chambaraud were previously acquainted. At least they had a great deal of conversation and talked of having met at some supper lately. I waited on Mde. de Corny yesterday. The bad weather prevented her coming the first day, some engagement yesterday, and thus she has only seen the procession to-day, although she seems to enjoy it in an eminent degree. Count Langeac brought only one of the three ladies of the first day, with him yesterday and to-day. It is the Countess de Neuilly and further I know not.—The weather was more favorable yesterday than to-day and of course there was a more numerous concourse. The Alley of the procession was changed this year from the accustomed one to that which leads from Madrid to la Muette. This was occasioned by the advice of a writer in the journal of Paris. The public have been thus informed of the advantage of a change from a narrow sandy path to a wide avenue, and as the public when informed, do what is right, they have not failed in this instance. You see sir that the liberty of the press does good every where. It is true that here the liberty is *quoad hoc*.

I have desired Barrois who superintends the striking of the map for the Abbé Morellet to have struck for you 200, on the same kind of paper with that which he employs for the Abbé Morellet. He thinks there will be difficulty as to the bank paper but will examine into the matter. I have begged him to finish his use of the plate as soon as possible that I may send it to London. At the Abbé Morellet's request I have sent him to-day two of your maps and by your order two to M. Desmarets and two to M. de Crèvecoeur. I should have sent him at the same time a copy of your book as you desire, but have not been able to find where you kept them. Will you be so good as let me know it that I may comply with your request, and thus oblige at the same time M. de Crevecoeur?

I have recieved two letters from Mr. Dumas to be forwarded to Mr. Jay, inclosing a number of Leyden gazettes. He desires me to continue extracting from them such things as may be useful to you on your return. He says the affair at Amsterdam must rest *in statu quo* until you recieve your answer from America which you expected in four months.—He is exceedingly alarmed at the apprehensions of B———'s being sent to the Hague. He goes fully into the matter with Mr. Jay to shew him how impolitic it would be and how disagreeable to France. He declares that he could have nothing in common with him at the Hague, without losing the confidence of his best friends. He does not mention his name in the letter to Mr. Jay, but alludes to what he had said of him on a former occasion. He begs I will let him know if I conjecture who the person is after leaving not the possibility of a doubt on the subject and desires the closest secrecy on my part. It appears clearly that he is really alarmed.

Yours of the 29th. arrived here last evening. I was much pleased to see that you approved of my having written to Mr. Jay; as I had doubts on the subject myself, arising from my perfect unacquaintance with whatever relates to matter of rank or etiquette. I will make use of the medals to be sent by the May packet to write him again.—Colo. Smith has not yet arrived, and I have heard nothing from him lately.

You will recieve Sir with this letter two others, one of which you will be surprized to see opened. I will explain to you the cause of it. When the newspapers arrived by the late packet it was observed that the tax had been altered, but instead of a diminution they had struck out 40.^{lt} and put in its room sixty odd. Petit before recieving them went to enquire into the reason of the augmentation. The Baron D'Oigny (from whom the letter is, which I have opened) with his usual civility and politeness, said he would have the affair regulated and immediately sent me the papers and letters, desiring only that he might retain for some days the enveloppe which had the post mark on it. When his letter arrived to-day Petit was so sure it was nothing but the enveloppe enclosed to you, that he insisted I would open the letter in order to avoid sending you an useless paper. On the contrary I find it is a letter which shews a continuation of those sentiments which the Baron D'Oigny expressed to me previous to your departure last year for England, and which make me regret again the delay with which the instructions from Congress on this subject are attended.

There is also enclosed an announce of the presentation of the Pope's Nuncio. The porter tells me it was brought by his servant.

Mrs. Barrett continues in a low state of health. Her spirits seem much affected. M. de Crevecoeur thinks her certainly in a consumption. I fear that the *ennui* of Paris may at length be attended with serious consequences for her—she never moves out, sees nobody, and in fine leads a life proper to give a consumption were she clear of it. She desired some time ago I would let her know how she could have Miss Jefferson to see her; observing that you had promised to mention to Mde. l'Abbesse, that she had your permission to recieve her. I told her that if you had done that I supposed there would be no difficulty. When I was at the convent some time ago I mentioned this circumstance to Miss Patsy, who told me in answer that you had said nothing about it to the Abbesse. I never see Mr. or Mrs. Barrett without their bringing the affair on the tapis. Although I conjecture your failure to speak to the Abbess was intentional, yet I have supposed it as well not to tell them so.

Blackden is still here—he told me this morning he should stay about six weeks longer. The list of the Americans is as you left it, except Carnes gone to London and Smith to Toulouse. I know of no new ones arrived. A Mr. Garnett who brought some letters and left a card for you two or three weeks past, came here a day previous to his departure for London and left a note for me expressing his mortification at not being able to see me, and desiring if there should be any commands for Mr. Vaughan, that they might be sent to his friend Mr. Milton, still at Paris. Be so good as let me know Sir if your wrist recieves any benefit from the waters or climate of Aix and rest assured of the warmest and sincerest sentiments of friendship with which I am & ever shall be Your, &c.,

W. SHORT

Petit who carried your letter to Miss Jefferson this morning tells me that she was in perfect health.

RC (DLC). PrC (DLC: Short Papers). Recorded in SJL as received 3 May 1787 at Aix-en-Provence. Only two of the enclosures have been identified: (1) D'Ogny to TJ, 6 Apr. 1787 and (2) the Papal Nuncio's note of 4 Apr. 1787. TJ received thirty-six letters at Aix-en-Provence on 3 May 1787, all of them having been forwarded by Short or Petit at various times.

The TWO LETTERS FROM DUMAS TO BE FORWARDED TO JAY were evidently those of 23 Mch. and 30 Mch. 1787 which were sent to Jay by Short on 4 May 1787; the latter may or may not have been enclosed in Dumas to Short, 27 Mch. 1787, q.v. for a note on Dumas' alarm at B———'s (Bingham's) BEING SENT TO FRANCE. In referring to Dumas' going FULLY INTO THE MATTER WITH MR. JAY, Short is alluding to Dumas' letter to Jay of 27 Feb.—2 Mch. 1787 in which Dumas had inserted a private and confidential note concerning the likelihood that a person of Bingham's character would come under the influence of the British minister at The Hague.

To Martha Jefferson

MY DEAR PATSY   Toulon April 7. 1787.

I received yesterday at Marseilles your letter of March 25. and I received it with pleasure because it announced to me that you were well. Experience learns us to be always anxious about the health of those whom we love. I have not been able to write to you so often

[277]

as I expected, because I am generally on the road; and when I stop any where, I am occupied in seeing what is to be seen. It will be some time now, perhaps three weeks before I shall be able to write to you again. But this need not slacken your writing to me, because you have leisure, and your letters come regularly to me. I have received letters which inform me that our dear Polly will certainly come to us this summer. By the time I return it will be time to expect her. When she arrives, she will become a precious charge on your hands. The difference of your age, and your common loss of a mother, will put that office on you. Teach her above all things to be good: because without that we can neither be valued by others, nor set any value on ourselves. Teach her to be always true. No vice is so mean as the want of truth, and at the same time so useless. Teach her never to be angry. Anger only serves to torment ourselves, to divert others, and alienate their esteem. And teach her industry and application to useful pursuits. I will venture to assure you that if you inculcate this in her mind you will make her a happy being in herself, a most inestimable friend to you, and precious to all the world. In teaching her these dispositions of mind, you will be more fixed in them yourself, and render yourself dear to all your acquaintance. Practice them then, my dear, without ceasing. If ever you find yourself in difficulty and doubt how to extricate yourself, do what is right, and you will find it the easiest way of getting out of the difficulty. Do it for the additional incitement of increasing the happiness of him who loves you infinitely, and who is my dear Patsy your's affectionately,

TH: JEFFERSON

RC (NNP). PrC (ViU). The editors are indebted to John Cook Wyllie, Curator of Rare Books of the Alderman Library, University of Virginia, for calling to their attention the fact that the present letter "was still being used as a specimen of letter-writing style in 1876 in J. Willis Westlake's *How to Write Letters*, Philadelphia, Sower, Potts & Co., 1876, pages 95-6" (communication to the editors, 8 July 1953).

From Adrien Petit

[*Paris, 7 Apr. 1787.* Recorded in SJL as received 3 May 1787 at Aix-en-Provence. Not found.]

From David Ramsay

DEAR SIR Charleston April 7th. 1787.

Your favor of October last came to hand last February with the several samples of rice therein referred to. The time of its arrival was opportune. Our house of Assembly was then sitting. I produced the samples of rice on the table of the house for the inspection of the members who were planters. I shewed your letter privately to some of your friends who concurred with me in opinion that it would be beneficial to the public and not indelicate to you to have it inserted in our State gazette. This was accordingly done. If this does not meet your approbation I beg your pardon for making your letter public. It has been serviceable to our planters and I trust will produce no effects to your prejudice. Instead of this it has contributed to impress on our Country Gentlemen a very favorable opinion of you for your particular attention to their interest.

Political necessity has once more compelled the Legislature of this State to enact an instalment law by which all debts contracted before Jany. 1787 (with a few exceptions) are only recoverable by three equal instalments in the years 1788 1789 and 1790. I fear the comments that will be made on this act in Europe. I do not pretend to justify it. I only say that the calamities of the war and the subsequent successive failure of crops for three years in some degree palliate this interference of the legislature.

I hope the Dioneas and the Magnolias arrivd safe. They were lodged in New: York with Mr. Otto. The season was such as Mr. Watson chose but I fear it was too late. If any accident befel them I shall cheerfully replace them this ensuing season.

Our governments in the Southern States are much more quiet than in the northern but much of our quiet arises from the temporising of the legislatures in refusing legal protection to the prosecution of the just rights of creditors. Our eyes now are all fixed on the continental convention to be held in Philada. in May next. Unless they make an efficient federal government I fear that the end of the matter will be an American monarch or rather three or more confederacies. In either case we have not labored in vain in effecting the late revolution for such arrangements might be made as would secure our happiness.

I long to see a French copy of my book. I feel myself much honored by your correspondence and esteem every line from your pen a real favor. With the most exalted sentiments of respect & esteem I am yours most truly, DAVID RAMSAY

RC (DLC). Recorded in SJL as received 6 July 1787.
For a note on Ramsay's publication in the *South Carolina Gazette* of TJ's letter OF OCTOBER LAST, see TJ to Ramsay, 27 Oct. 1786.

To William Short

DEAR SIR Toulon Apr. 7. 1787.

I received yesterday at Marseilles your favor of Mar. 26. I was just then setting out for this place, and therefore deferred answering you till my arrival here. I now inclose you a letter for the Count de Montmorin, which, with that to the King, be pleased to deliver to M. de Montmorin. Is the letter to the king sealed with the seal of Congress? If it is, nothing is necessary to be said on the subject. If it is not, it will be necessary to enter into this explanation: that some time ago I had occasion to deliver to C. de Vergennes a letter from Congress to the king, which was not sealed with the seal of Congress; that C. de Vergennes noticed it to me, and I wrote to Mr. Jay to inform him that hereafter the seal of Congress would be expected to such letters; but that I suppose my letter might not have got to hand when this one came away. The letter to the king is in answer to one he wrote Congress in July last on the birth of the princess. I have apologized in mine to M. de Montmorin for the delay of the answer, Congress not having assembled to do business till the beginning of February. General St. Clair is their president. I inclose you an order on Mr. Grand for 1200 livres for the workman who makes Genl. Gates's medal.—I received a letter from Mr. Wythe as you supposed. It was dated the 13th. Dec. He does not mention Martin's arrival. He had received the Tagliaferro arms; but as I had sent them by two or three opportunities, it does not prove Martin's arrival.

Having taken 40. douches, without any sensible benefit, I thought it useless to continue them. My wrist strengthens slowly: it is to time I look as the surest remedy, and that I believe will restore it at length. I set out tomorrow for Nice. The information received at Marseilles encourages me in my researches on the subject of rice, and that I shall meet with rice fields and the machines for cleaning it just beyond the Alps. Unless they call me into the neighborhood of Turin I shall not go that far, having no object further eastward except the rice. Hitherto my journey has been a continued feast on objects of agriculture, new to me, and, some

9 APRIL 1787

of them at least, susceptible of adoption in America. Nothing can be ruder or more savage than the country I am in, as it must have come from the hands of nature; and nothing more rich and variegated in the productions with which art has covered it. Marseilles is a charming place. All life and activity, and a useful activity like London and Philadelphia. As I shall receive no more of your letters till I get back to Aix you will hear from me less often: probably not at all while beyond the Alps. When I get back to Nice I shall be able to calculate to a day my return to Aix, and of course the term after which it will be proper to send my letters to another stage. Remember me to enquiring friends, and be assured of the sincere esteem with which I am Dear Sir your affectionate friend & servant,

TH: JEFFERSON

P.S. Not being sure of M. de Montmorin's address, I have left it blank. Be so good as to inform yourself of it, and to address the letter.

RC (George W. Glick, New York City, 1948); endorsed: "Jefferson 1787 April 7. [received] 15." PrC (DLC). Enclosures: (1) TJ to Montmorin, Toulon, 6 Apr. 1787 (missing); see note to Jay to TJ, 9 Feb. 1787. (2) Draft on Grand (missing).

I WROTE TO MR. JAY TO INFORM HIM THAT HEREAFTER THE SEAL OF CONGRESS WOULD BE EXPECTED: No such letter has been found, and it is probable that none was written. The only letter from TJ to Jay in the latter part of 1786 that mentions delivery of a document to Vergennes is that of 8 July 1786, q.v., in which TJ discusses the presentation of the report on the Consular Convention. That letter was carried to America by Randall, and TJ may have suggested to Randall that he express to Jay the fact that VERGENNES NOTICED the omission of the seal and that the seal would thenceforth be expected. But TJ knew as early as 6 Dec. 1786 that his letter of 8 July had been received by Jay (see Vol. 10: 455). The inference to be drawn is that TJ's remarks to Short on this matter constitute a diplomatic "explanation" and not necessarily a recital of facts (the letter was actually sealed; see Short to TJ, 24 Apr. 1787).

From Martha Jefferson

MY DEAR PAPA   Panthemont, April 9th, 1787.

I am very glad that the beginning of your voyage has been so pleasing, and I hope that the rest will not be less so, as it is a great consolation for me, being deprived of the pleasure of seeing you, to know at least that you are happy. I hope your resolution of returning in the end of April is always the same. I do not doubt but what Mr. Short has written you word that my sister sets off with Fulwar Skipwith in the month of May, and she will be here in July. Then, indeed, shall I be the happiest of mortals; united to what I have the dearest in the world, nothing more will be requisite

[281]

9 APRIL 1787

to render my happiness complete. I am not so industrious as you or I would wish, but I hope that in taking pains I very soon shall be. I have already begun to study more. I have not heard any news of my harpsichord; it will be really very disagreeable if it is not here before your arrival. I am learning a very pretty thing now, but it is very hard. I have drawn several little flowers, all alone, that the master even has not seen; indeed, he advised me to draw as much alone as possible, for that is of more use than all I could do with him. I shall take up my Livy, as you desire it. I shall begin it again, as I have lost the thread of the history. As for the hysterics, you may be quiet on that head, as I am not lazy enough to fear them. Mrs. Barett has wanted me out, but Mr. Short told her that you had forgotten to tell Madame L'Abbesse to let me go out with her. There was a gentleman, a few days ago, that killed himself because he thought that his wife did not love him. They had been married ten years. I believe that if every husband in Paris was to do as much, there would be nothing but widows left. I shall speak to Madame Thaubeneu about dining at the Abbess's table. As for needlework, the only kind that I could learn here would be embroidery, indeed netting also; but I could not do much of those in America, because of the impossibility of having proper silks; however, they will not be totally useless. You say your expectations for me are high, yet not higher than I can attain. Then be assured, my dear papa, that you shall be satisfied in that, as well as in any thing else that lies in my power; for what I hold most precious is your satisfaction, indeed I should be miserable without it. You wrote me a long letter, as I asked you; however, it would have been much more so without so wide a margin. Adieu, my dear papa. Be assured of the tenderest affection of your loving daughter,

M. JEFFERSON

Pray answer me very soon—a long letter, without a margin. I will try to follow the advice they contain with the most scrupulous exactitude.

MS not found; text is from the printing in Randolph, *Domestic Life*, p. 117-18. Recorded in SJL as received 3 May 1787 at Aix-en-Provence. Patsy's remark about THE HYSTERICS alludes to a sentence of TJ's letter of 28 Mch. 1787.

From Jacques Nicolas Mayeux

Rozoy-sur-Serre, 9 Apr. 1787. States that he had petitioned the Prince of Luxembourg on 15 Apr. 1783 to reimburse him for his services at sea; had no reply; on 15 Mch. last, he again applied to the

Prince, who replied that his claim for services on the ship, *L'Indien*, was not the Prince's responsibility; that he had paid for such services up to the time of sailing; that the ship was chartered by the state of South Carolina, Capt. Gillon being in full charge; that the claim should be presented to TJ; and that he had already urged TJ to pay the soldiers and sailors the wages due them and their shares of the prizes of which Capt. Gillon has given no account. The petitioner claims payment for 300 livres (10s. per day) for pay while he was at sea on the ship, *L'Indien*, having received nothing for twenty months' service during 1781 and 1782, together with his share of the prize money for three ships and their cargoes; begs TJ, in accordance with the King's proclamation of 4 Aug. 1786, to recover for him the money he won by endangering his life.

RC (ViWC); 2 p.; in French; at head of text: "Prises et Captures sur mer." Tr (DNA: PCC, No. 107, II). Not recorded in SJL; copy enclosed in TJ to Jay, 21 June 1787.

From A. E. van Braam Houckgeest

Charleston, S. C., 10 Apr. 1787. In March of 1786, he sent from Charleston, on his brig, *Amitié*, Capt. Peray, among other things, three leather bundles and a small cask of snuff from Brazil which he bought in Charleston, not knowing that it was contraband in France; on arriving at Bordeaux the captain had all of the cargo unloaded, thereby proving that he had no intention of smuggling. The snuff was seized; efforts were made by his agents, without success, to recover it for re-export; but the farmers-general merely cancelled the fine and notified him that he could recover the snuff only through TJ's intervention; applies to TJ to recover the snuff or to see that he is reimbursed for his loss.

RC (DLC); 2 p.; in French; endorsed. Recorded in SJL as received 6 July 1787.
See David Ramsay to TJ, 16 Apr. 1787, in which this letter was enclosed; and TJ to Ramsay, 8 Aug. 1787.

To Lafayette

Nice, April 11, 1787.

Your head, my dear friend, is full of Notable things; and being better employed, therefore, I do not expect letters from you. I am constantly roving about, to see what I have never seen before and shall never see again. In the great cities, I go to see what travellers think alone worthy of being seen; but I make a job of it, and generally gulp it all down in a day. On the other hand, I am never satiated with rambling through the fields and farms, examining the culture and cultivators, with a degree of curiosity which makes some take me to be a fool, and others to be much wiser than I am.

11 APRIL 1787

I have been pleased to find among the people a less degree of physical misery than I had expected. They are generally well clothed, and have a plenty of food, not animal indeed, but vegetable, which is as wholesome. Perhaps they are over worked, the excess of the rent required by the landlord, obliging them to too many hours of labor, in order to produce that, and wherewith to feed and clothe themselves. The soil of Champagne and Burgundy I have found more universally good than I had expected, and as I could not help making a comparison with England, I found that comparison more unfavorable to the latter than is generally admitted. The soil, the climate, and the productions are superior to those of England, and the husbandry as good, except in one point; that of manure. In England, long leases for twenty-one years, or three lives, to wit, that of the farmer, his wife, and son, renewed by the son as soon as he comes to the possession, for his own life, his wife's and eldest child's, and so on, render the farms there almost hereditary, make it worth the farmer's while to manure the lands highly, and give the landlord an opportunity of occasionally making his rent keep pace with the improved state of the lands. Here the leases are either during pleasure, or for three, six, or nine years, which does not give the farmer time to repay himself for the expensive operation of well manuring, and therefore, he manures ill, or not at all. I suppose, that could the practice of leasing for three lives be introduced in the whole kingdom, it would, within the term of your life, increase agricultural productions fifty per cent; or were any one proprietor to do it with his own lands, it would increase his rents fifty per cent, in the course of twenty-five years. But I am told the laws do not permit it. The laws then, in this particular, are unwise and unjust, and ought to give that permission. In the southern provinces, where the soil is poor, the climate hot and dry, and there are few animals, they would learn the art, found so precious in England, of making vegetable manure, and thus improving these provinces in the article in which nature has been least kind to them. Indeed, these provinces afford a singular spectacle. Calculating on the poverty of their soil, and their climate by its latitude only, they should have been the poorest in France. On the contrary, they are the richest, from one fortuitous circumstance. Spurs or ramifications of high mountains, making down from the Alps, and as it were, reticulating these provinces, give to the vallies the protection of a particular inclosure to each, and the benefit of a general stagnation of the northern winds produced by the whole of them, and thus countervail the advantage of several degrees of latitude. From the first olive fields of Pierrelate, to the orangeries of Hieres, has been continued rapture to me. I have often wished for you. I think you have not made this journey. It is a pleasure you have to come, and an improvement to be added to the many you have already made. It will be a great comfort to [you to know, from your own inspection, the condition of all the provinces of your own country, and it will be interesting to them at some future day to be known to you. This is perhaps the only moment of your life in which you can acquire that knolege. And to do it most effectually you must be absolutely incognito, you must ferret the people out of their hovels as I have done, look into their kettles, eat their bread, loll on their beds under pretence of resting yourself, but in fact to find if they are soft. You will feel a sublime pleasure in the course of this investigation, and a sublimer one hereafter when you shall be able to apply your knolege to the softening of their beds, or the throwing a morsel of meat into the kettle of vegetables. You will not wonder at the subjects of my letter: they are the only ones which have been present to my mind for some time past, and the waters must always be what are the fountain from which they flow. According to this indeed I should have intermixed from beginning to end warm expressions of friendship to you: but according to the ideas of our country we do not permit ourselves to speak even truths when they may have the air of flattery. I content myself therefore with saying once for all that I love you, your wife and children. Tell them so and Adieu. Your's affectionately,   TH: JEFFERSON][1]

PrC (DLC); fragment, consisting of last page only, without indication of addressee.
[1] That part of the text within brackets (supplied) represents the whole of the fragmentary PrC; all of the remainder of the text is printed from TJR, II, 104-6.

From Louis Guillaume Otto

MONSIEUR   A Newyork le 11 Avril 1787.

J'ai reçu la lettre que Vous m'avés fait l'honneur de m'ecrire le 14. Janvr. dernier. Je desire plus que personne que le nouveau reglement pour les paquebots se soutienne; il me fournira souvent l'occasion de m'entretenir avec Vous et de recevoir de Vos nouvelles.

Le petit resumé des nouvelles de l'Europe, que Vous voulés bien m'addresser, m'est infiniment precieux. Il sert à fixer mes idées sur plusieurs objets, que les Gazetiers Anglois se plaisent à representer

11 APRIL 1787

sous un faux jour. Je suis egalement reconnoissant des brochures dont Vous avés chargé le Col. Franks; quoique ces sortes de publications n'aient qu'un interêt momentané, elles ont du prix pour un homme qui est loin de sa patrie.

Vos Concitoyens, Monsieur, sont aussi sur le point d'avoir leur *assemblée des notables*. Elle doit se former en May prochain à Philade. Les yeux de toute l'Amerique sont fixés sur ce nouveau Congrès, composé des hommes les plus distingués par leurs connoissances politiques, leur poids et leur integrité. Les observateurs les moins prevenus n'esperent pas cependant de voir finir tous les embarras, mais ils se flattent facilement que cette nouvelle assemblée générale fournira une occasion de discuter à fonds les interêts de l'union et d'examiner jusqu'à quel point les peuples doivent se depouiller de leur liberté. Le sacrifice sera certainement très grand, mais les circonstances le rendent indispensable. Vous connoissés mieux que moi, Monsieur, les avantages et les inconveniens de la confederation actuelle et je me borne à Vous exposer l'opinion du public eclairé.

L'assemblée de Newyork vient d'emanciper les Vermontois et l'on doit s'attendre à voir arriver bientôt en Congrès les representans d'un quatorzieme Etat. Les anciens Proprietaires ont fait leur possible pour faire echouer le Bill qui declare l'independance de Vermont, mais on a cru devoir sacrifier leur interêt au repos public. Vous trouverés à ce sujet dans les gazettes un discours du Col. Hamilton qui a été generalement approuvé.

Le Dr. Ramsay a publié la lettre que Vous lui avés ecrite au sujet des ris de la Caroline. Cette piece a fait beaucoup de sensation; le dernier paragraphe doit en faire surtout dans le coeur d'un François. Vous ne sauriés prendre trop de peine, Monsieur, pour conserver parmi Vos Compatriotes le veritable esprit de l'alliance.

J'ai l'honneur d'être avec un respectueux attachement Monsieur, de Votre Excellence, le très humble et très obeissant serviteur,

OTTO

RC (DLC); endorsed. Recorded in SJL as received 11 June 1787. For a note on Ramsay's publication of TJ's letter AU SUJET DES RIS, see TJ to Ramsay, 27 Oct. 1786.

The DISCOURS DU COL. HAMILTON on the independence of Vermont is to be found in Hamilton, *Works*, ed. H. C. Lodge, VIII, 42-62.

[286]

To William Short

Dear Sir   Nice April 12. 1787.

At Marseilles they told me I should encounter the ricefeilds of Piedmont soon after crossing the Alps. Here they tell me there are none nearer than Vercelli and Novarra, which is carrying me almost to Milan. I fear that this circumstance will occasion me a greater delay than I had calculated on. However I am embarked in the project and shall go through with it. Tomorrow I set out on my passage over the Alps, being to pursue it 93 miles to Coni on mules, as the snows are not yet enough melted to admit carriages to pass. I leave mine here therefore, proposing to return by water from Genoa. I think it will be three weeks before I get back to Nice.— I find this climate quite as superb as it has been represented. Hieres is the only place in France which may be compared with it. The climates are equal. In favor of this place are the circumstances of gay and dissipated society, a handsome city, good accomodations and some commerce. In favor of Hieres are environs of delicious and extensive plains, a society more contracted and therefore more capable of esteem, and the neighborhood of Toulon, Marseilles and other places to which excursions may be made. Placing Marseilles in comparison with Hieres, it has extensive society, a good theatre, freedom from military controul, and the most animated commerce. But it's winter climate far inferior.—I am now in the act of putting my baggage into portable form for my bat-mule; after praying you therefore to let my daughter know I am well and that I shall not be heard of again in three weeks I take my leave of you for that time with assurances of the sincere esteem with which I am Dear Sir your friend & servt.,   Th: Jefferson

RC (ViU); endorsed: "Jefferson April 12 [received] 21 1787." Not recorded in SJL.

To the Abbés Arnoux and Chalut

á Nice ce 12me. Avril 1787.

C'est bien le tems, mes chers Messieurs, de vous faire mes remercimens pour toutes les honnetetés dont je vous suis redevable. Á commencer par Madame de Laye, elle m'a comblé de bontés, de politesses, et de toutes sortes d'attentions. J'ai fait chez elle un sejour de trois jours, qui ont eté remplis d'agremens et d'instructions. Monsieur Tournillon, Monsieur de Pizay, Monsieur le

Prevot d'Ainay se sont empressés de me montrer par toutes les honnetetés possibles combien ils estiment tout ce qui vient de votre part. Monsieur Bernard de Marseilles etoit en campagne. Içi Monsieur Sasserno ne cesse de me donner des preuves de ses dispositions á m'etre utile. Enfin je vois par la que tout le monde vous aime, et que c'est moi qui en profite. Je vous en fais mille et mille remercimens, et c'est du fond de mon coeur que je vous les fais. Mon voyage a eté jusqu'içi on ne peut plus interessant. Demain je partirai pour les rizieres de Piedmont. C'est par elles que je finirai mon voyage de ce coté ci. Je retournerai après par le canal de Languedoc, la Garonne, et la Loire á Paris, ou j'aurai l'honneur de vous revoir aux premiers jours de Juin, de vous dire combien je suis sensible á vos amitiés, combien elles m'ont eté utiles, et de vous prier de vouloir bien agreer tous les sentimens de reconnoissance, d'estime, et de respect, avec lesquels j'ai l'honneur d'etre, mes chers Messieurs, votre trés humble et trés obeissant serviteur,
Th: Jefferson

PrC (DLC); endorsed. This letter, written the day before TJ began his journey across the Alps into Italy, is the last recorded in SJL until those written from Aix-en-Provence on 3 May.

The Abbés Arnoux and Chalut had evidently given TJ letters of introduction to TOURNILLON . . . PIZAY and others named, all of whom appear in TJ's list of names and addresses in his rough notes of expenses (CSmH), as follows: "M. Tournillon l'ainé. Conseiller du roy. Notaire rue de la Barre.—M. l'Abbé Charrier de la Roche, Prevot d'Ainay, vicaire general à Ainay à Lyons.—M. de Pizay. en son hotel rue Sala. à Lyons. . . . M. Bernard de l'Acad. de Marseille, directeur joint de l'Observatoire. à l'Observatoire (de M. l'Abbé Papon). . . . Nice. M. [André] Sasserno. negociant." See TJ to Short, 15 Mch. 1787.

From Francis Hopkinson

Dear Sir   Philada. April 14th. 1787

Your Favour of the 23d. Dec. came to Hand yesterday. I have but just Time to notice the several Articles you mention in the order they stand. The first respects Madame Champes. I have suffered much uneasiness about the first Packet to her, which I delivered to a Gentleman of Bucks County, her near Neighbour, upon his Promise to procure me her Receipt for the Packet. This however hath never been done. It has been often promised and as often forgot. I wrote yesterday to Madame Champes, informing her that I had another Packet for her, which I would deliver only to her written Order, accompanied with her Receipt for the first.— The Manner of preserving the Essence L'Orient is the very method I tried; but I think it changes the Colour. If I had a Day or two's

14 APRIL 1787

Notice more than I have I would send you a Sample—perhaps I shall as it is. I shall have the Experiment of my Spring-Block tried here this Summer and will inform you of the Result.—The Gentleman I spoke to has not sent me the Nuts from Pittsburgh. Now I know that it is the Illinois nut you want, I shall exert myself to procure some for you. I sent you long since a Packet of News-Papers, in which I inclosed the foot and 2 or 3 of the long Feathers of the beautiful Bird I mentioned. I hope they got to hand. I shall soon begin again upon the Harmonica. From the Experiments I have made, I have no Doubt of the Success. I have already applied Keys to the Glasses, furnish'd with artificial Fingers, which answered perfectly, and most delightfully in a great Part of the Scale. Where they did not succeed so well was owing to the Glass not being truly mounted. So that I must, I find, take off the Glasses from the Spindel and mount them anew. The Pedal to the Forte Piano is a good Thought. The Idea is taken from the Pedal Stop of a Church Organ.—The mint is not yet established by Congress. Indeed their Situation is such, that they can establish nothing. The States begin to see the necessity of some alterations in the Terms of Confederation, and a respectable Delegation from most of the States are to meet here next Month to prepare and recommend a new System of Fœderal Union. I am sorry for the Misfortune of your Wrist. I hope it is recovered before this. The next Time you perform this Maneuvre I would recommend your left Wrist for the Experiment. You will find it much more convenient than the Right and it can be every bit as well strain'd. I am glad you approve of our 2d. Volume of Ph. Transactions. A Gentleman lately from London told me that he was present at the Royal Society when our Volume was the Subject of Notice. That particular attention was paid to my Optical Problem, and much Surprise exprest that the Circumstance should have never before been notic'd. The Fact was at first doubted, but Lord Cavendish made the Experiment and declared it was truly stated. It may probably be the Subject of future Discussion.

I cannot forward your News Papers now, they would be too bulky for Mr. Paine's Convenience. I send you however, our Magazines and Monthly Museum. The Proprietors of the Magazine, have engaged me to undertake the Management of the Work, to which they are by no Means Competent themselves. The month of March is my first Exhibition. In the Magazine of this Month, I shall take the Liberty of giving an Extract from your valuable

14 APRIL 1787

Notes on Virginia, respecting the Comparative Size of European and American Animals. I hope this will not displease you. I hope further that you will give me Assistance now and then. I have a very curious Drawing and account of the Remains of an ancient fortified Town on the Muskingum taken by an officer on the Spot. It seems from many Circumstances to be the Vestiges of Art, before this Country was known to Europe. This is an interesting Circumstance in the History of the World. It will be published in the May Magazine. I have invented this Winter a cheap, convenient and useful Appendage to a common Candlestick, which keeps the Flame from being flared by the Wind in Summer or the Fire in Winter, and makes it give a pleasant and steady Light to read or write by. I shall give a Description and Drawing in next month's Magazine.

I have just come from Dr. Franklin. He is well. I saw Mr. Rittenhouse's Family yesterday—all well—Kitty much pleased with her little Book, but lamented that she had no Letter with it. My Mother desires to be affectionately remember'd to Miss Jefferson.

Adieu and believe ever sincerely your's,   F. HOPKINSON

Dr. Griffiths is well, but I have not yet had an opportunity of giving the Enquiries of Monr. Bidon and his able Friends.

RC (DLC); endorsed. Recorded in SJL as received 11 June 1787.

For a discussion of Hopkinson's OPTICAL PROBLEM, see Hastings, *Hopkinson*, p. 361-2. The inscription in Hopkinson's copy of *Notes on Virginia* should have made him more sensitive to TJ's probable attitude toward the publication of an EXTRACT . . . RESPECTING THE COMPARATIVE SIZE OF EUROPEAN AND AMERICAN ANIMALS; that inscription read, in part: "Unwilling to expose them to the public eye, he asks the favor of Mr. Hopkinson to put them into the hands of no person on whose care and fidelity he cannot rely, to guard them against publication." Hopkinson did reprint the Virginia Act for Establishing Religious Freedom, evidently from *Notes on Virginia*, and in the March 1787 issue of the *American Museum*, I, 206-8, he presented "Thoughts on American Genius" in which he stated that "The learned Jefferson, in his excellent 'notes on Virginia,' has refuted this thesis [of Buffon and other naturalists concerning the degeneracy of life in America], with the urbanity of a gentleman, and the accuracy of a scholar, supported by the sound reasoning of a philosopher. His observations, particularly on the writings of the abbé Raynal, and the count de Buffon . . . deserve republication." This same issue contained TJ's letter to Jay, 27 May 1786, and Calonne's letter to TJ, 22 Oct. 1786; same, p. 198-202.

From Francis Hopkinson

Philada. Apr. 14th 1787.

The enclosed Phial contains some of my Essence L'Orient but very imperfectly prepared. I heard only this Morning that Mr.

[290]

14 APRIL 1787

Paine would set off Tomorrow. I had to buy the Fish and prepare the Essence. It should be three or four Days in settling and the water then poured off but I have had only as many Hours for the Purpose, so that great allowances must be made. I have put some volat Spt. Sal Ammoniac and some Spirit of Wine in, which will preserve it, I hope, till it gets to hand. All I want to know is whether the Sample I send is of the right kind. If it should be, I can procure any Quantity of it in the season that is April May and June.

F. HOPKINSON

RC (DLC). This note was probably enclosed in the foregoing. The entry in SJL for 11 June 1787 mentions only one letter of 14 Apr. from Hopkinson.

From Adrien Petit

[*Paris, 14 Apr. 1787.* Recorded in SJL as received 3 May at Aix-en-Provence. Not found.]

From Thomas Mann Randolph, Jr.

DEAR SIR   Edinburgh April 14th. 1787

I received your letter containing advice with respect to my education, which I shall allways feel the advantage of having obtaind and which I shall express my gratitude for by the only method in my power, implicitly following it. I have allready attended a course of lectures on each of the sciences you mentioned except Botany and Anatomy, which are to engross the greater part of my time this summer. It was not without the greatest difficulty and agitation of mind, that I could select one to be the object of my future and allmost sole pursuit. Indeed as on it my success in life hereafter must entirely depend, to determine a matter of such importance without a struggle would argue a stupid carelessness and insensibility. I was long delighted with the charms of Natural History, but found at last that altho it was the most rational and agreeable amusement in which hours of relaxation could be employed, yet it was too trivial to spend a whole life in the prosecution of. Natural Philosophy appeared more deserving of a particular attention, the exalted nature of its objects, and the utility which mankind in general derive from their investigation, seemed to offer a reward equal to the arduous undertaking. The sublime pleasure which the mind feels on the discovery of a Mathematical truth,

14 APRIL 1787

made it still more agreeable from its intimate connection with that delightful tho abstract science Ambition; perhaps I ought to be ashamed to confess it, as it must allways be mixed in some degree with vanity, hindered me from fixing on a knowledge of either of these, as the sole end to which I would wish to attain. Being certain that Politics was a science which would lead to the highest honours in a free state, and the study of which by many of its members would be of the greatest utility to the community in an infant one, I resolved to apply chiefly to it. From this time Montesquieu and Hume have been my principal study. The course of historical reading you advised, I am likewise pursuing. I am conscious that youthful hopes may be too ardent, and that my ideas must be in a great measure visionary, but I am at the same time convinced that Eloquence even in a very middling degree is respectable. My desire to become acquainted with the political constitution and natural productions of my own country, must I am afraid remain some time unsatisfied, as I have yet heard of no author of note who has wrote on its history either natural or civil. I wait with impatience for the publication of the history of the last war by Mr. Gordon of Massachusets. By the perusal of it I hope to have my curiosity in some degree allayed. I must trouble you for your advice on a particular which you did not mention in your letter: I mean the propriety of studying living languages, which has been questioned by so many. The 2 dead languages were all I acquired the least idea of at school, except the French. Having met with many inaccurate translations from there, I began to be afraid that the like mistakes might be committed with respect to the meaning of the original author in others, and to conceive that it was an essential part of education to be qualified for the perusal of books in the principal languages of Europe. With this design I immediately applied to the Italian, encouraged much by the account of the elegance of the poetical compositions in it, I received from those who understood it. Finding even the rudiments of it not so difficult as I expected, I have determined as soon as I shall be capable of reading it with ease, to undertake the Spanish, provided my plan meets with your approbation. This correspondence concerning myself entirely, must be so tedious and uninteresting to you, that was I not certain of your desire for the propagation of knowledge, nothing should induce me to trouble you. I have taken the liberty to procure the seat of an honorary member for you in a society instituted here for the encouragement of the study of

14 APRIL 1787

Natural history among the students at this university. I should not have thought the honor worth your acceptance, was not the list allready adorned wih the names of Black, Priestley and Pennant. Mr. Barton will deliver the Diploma. As my Father is very impatient for my return, I shall probably spend this winter in Paris, and set out the next summer.

Sir your much obliged humble Servt.,

THOMAS M. RANDOLPH

RC (MHi); endorsed: "Randolph Thos. M. junr." Recorded in SJL as received 25 May 1787 at Bordeaux.

The DIPLOMA delivered by MR. BARTON, dated at Edinburgh, 22 Feb. 1787, and signed by the officers of the SOCIETY INSTITUTED HERE [in 1782] FOR THE ENCOURAGEMENT OF THE STUDY OF NATURAL HISTORY AMONG THE STUDENTS, is in MHi; among those who signed were Randolph himself and Benjamin Smith Barton.

From David Rittenhouse

DEAR SIR Philadelphia April 14th. 1787

About the latter end of June last I sent you the 2d. Vol. of our Transactions, directed to Mr. Adams at London. I afterwards found that Mr. Adams was at that time Absent; it is therefore probable that you have not yet recived it. Should it still come to hand it may give you an Opportunity of gratifying some freind. I have some hopes that the Society will publish a Small Volume next winter. I can't however pretend to contribute much towards it as the Business of my Office, continually encreasing, not only occupies my time intirely at present, but is become almost insupportable.—We have abundance of projectors and pretendors to new Discoveries, and many applications to the Legislature for exclusive priviledges, some of them ridiculous enough. The self-moving Boat, the Steam Boat, the Mechanical Miller, the improved Ring Dial for finding the Variations of the Needle. The Surveying Compass to serve 20 other purposes, And a project for finding the Longitude by the Variation of the Magnetical Needle. Of this I shall give you a more particular Account. The Authors first scheme was this. He supposes two invisible Globes, appendages of the Earth, to Govern the Needle and likewise greatly to influence the Tides, one having 70 or 80 Degrees North Declination and the other almost as much South, and he has Assigned the periods of their revolutions. But being told that his Globes would infallibly fall to the Earth unless Supported by an Iron Spike or something of that nature, he has discharged them and contented himself with assigning two points, one near each pole. Thro' the Northern one, he says, pass all the Magnetical Meridians in the Northern Hemisphere, and thro' the other all those of the Southern Hemisphere. He has determined the present situation and periodical revolution of the North point with great precission, of the other he speaks more doubtfully. In a plausible publication he proposes on these principles to find the Longitude Generally and thinks himself intitled to a public reward. I promised myself the pleasure of spending the ensuing Season at home, having been absent three Summers past. My Blessing on Miss Patty. I hope the lameness of your wrist will not long make writing difficult.

I am, dear Sir, with the greatest esteem Your affectionate friend & Humble Servant, DAVD. RITTENHOUSE

RC (DLC); endorsed. Recorded in SJL as received 11 June 1787.
On the PROJECT FOR FINDING THE LONGITUDE, see John Churchman to TJ, 6 June 1787.

From Francis Hopkinson

Philada. April 15th. 1787.

Mr. Paine not setting off to Day, as I expected, gives me an Opportunity of sending another Phial of Essence L'Orient which has had the Advantage of standing all Night to depurate and is richer than that I gave Mr. Paine yesterday. Besides this, I put some Spirit of Wine in the Phial of yesterday, which I observe curdles and discolours the Essence. In this there is nothing but a little Volat. Spirit of Sal Ammoniac. It's Lustre is not abated. It looks at present most beautiful and will, I hope, arrive in good Order to your Hand. I have just heard of the Arrival of Captain Gilpin from some Port of France, and that there is a Packet on board for me. If so it is probably from you. But this is all I yet know about it.

Yours ever, F. HOPKINSON

RC (DLC). Not recorded in SJL, but probably received on 11 June 1787 with Hopkinson's of 14 Apr. 1787.

From St. John de Crèvecoeur

SIR Paris le 16 Avril 1787

As a feeble tho' sincere acknowledgement for your excellent notes on Virginia, as well as for your kindness, Permit me to offer

[294]

you The Second Edition of the Amer: Far. Letters. Spite of all my Care, a great number of Faults are to be found in it, for never before had I seen such Profligate careless Men as the Journeymen Printers I have had to do with. With unfeigned Respect I remain Sir Your most humble Servant, ST. JOHN DE CRÈVECOEUR

RC (DLC); endorsed. Recorded in SJL as received 3 May 1787 at Aix-en-Provence. The three volumes that accompanied this letter (but probably were not forwarded by Short or Petit) were the Paris, 1787, edition of Crèvecoeur's *Les Lettres d'un Cultivateur Américain.*

From David Ramsay

Charleston, S.C., 16 Apr. 1787. Encloses a letter from A. E. Van Braam Houckgeest, formerly of the United Netherlands and now a citizen and "respectable Gentleman of this state." Urges TJ's assistance in his behalf, since he is a "Gentleman of reputation much esteemd by his lately adopted country."

RC (DLC); 2 p.; endorsed. Recorded in SJL as received 6 July 1787. Enclosure: Houckgeest to TJ, 10 Apr. 1787.

From John Sullivan

DEAR SIR   Durham in New Hampshire April 16th. 1787

Upon the receipt of your favor of the 7th. of January 1786 I found that every thing I have done toward procuring for you the Skin and Skeleton of a moose would not answer your Expectations, the bones not being left in the skin or proper Care taken to preserve and dress the skin with the hair on so that no proper resemblance of the Animal could be had. But upon receiving your Letter I immediately applied to Capt. Colborn of Lebanon on Connecticut River to procure me one and Transport him to my House with only the skins opened and the Entrails taken out, and such thick parts of the flesh cut off as would not injure the skin or skeleton. The winter proved extraordinary, much snow but no Crust till the Last of March, at which time a Crust happening he sallied forth with his forces and with Difficulty killed one in Vermont State and transported his Carcass to my House agreable to orders. He was no less than 14 Days with a Team in The Transportation. I send you his Receipt inclosed for the Cash I paid him upon the Arrival of the Animal on the 3d. of this month. The remaining flesh began to be in a state of putrefaction. Every Engine was set at work to preserve the Bones and Cleanse them from the remaining flesh,

16 APRIL 1787

and to preserve the skins with the hair on, with the hoofs on and Bones of Legs and thighs in the skin without putrefaction, and the Jobb was both Expensive and Difficult, and such as was never before attempted, in this Quarter. But it was at Last Accomplished exactly agreable to Your Directions, except that the bones of the head are not Left in the skin agreably to your Directions, as it was not possible to preserve them in that Connection, but the head of the skin being whole and well dresst it may be Drawn on at pleasure. The Horns of the Deer, the Elk and the Caribou I also send. They are not the horns of this Moose but may be fixed on at pleasure. The horns of those animals are not in perfection at this season of the year. The skeleton of the other Animals I have not procured and am much mortifyed and no doubt you will be very greatly surprized at the Expence of what I now send, a particular Account of which will come by Capt. Saml. Pierce by whom I send the articles. I inclose you his note to me which will inform you of the time of his sailing and the manner in which he means to convey them to you, which being the best opportunity that offered I have adopted it. I have been oblidged to make a Draught on you in favor of my brother Judge Sullivan of Boston for forty five pounds sterling to reimburse the money I have advanced and will be the amount of the Expence attending this very troublesome affair. The Skeletons of the other Animals, though they might be procured with Less expence, I could not think of hazarding it without your consent. These animals are generally taken far in the woods and very often, as was the Case with this, Twenty miles from any road. A way must of course be cleared through the wilderness to transport them whole and halled by hand, to some common road. The flesh of them which is considered as of considerable value is mostly Lost. The meat of a moose is generally Esteemed equal in value to that of a Large ox. However if the present Expence is not discouraging I will endeavour to procure the others as Cheap as possible, and although they must fall far short of this will be considerable. I am sorry that one branch of one of the Elks horns has been Cut, but it was the only pair I could procure and as one of them is entire I suppose it cannot be of much consequence. I am most respectfully Dr. Sir yr. very humble Servt.,   JNO. SULLIVAN

RC (DLC). Recorded in SJL as received 26 Sep. 1787. Enclosures: (1) Captain Robert Colburn's receipt to Sullivan, 3 Apr. 1787 (missing). (2) Samuel Pearce to Sullivan, 12 Apr. 1787 (DLC), informing Sullivan that he is not bound for France but will be pleased to ship the box by packet from Southampton to Le Havre, which he thinks is the "readiest and cheapest way"; that he would be glad to accept the bill on TJ but "at present he is

[296]

From Thomas Brand Hollis

DEAR SIR   Chesterfield Street April 17th. 1787.

I request the favor of your benevolent acceptance of the memoirs of the late excellent Thomas Hollis, who was a friend to the rights of America and of mankind in general. How would he have rejoiced to have seen these days "Tyranny defeated and the seeds of freedom planted in another world for which he could scarcely have hoped," tho to which he was in no small degree instrumental by dispersing the best of books on the most interesting subjects.

An encouragement for others to do the like. May they obtain a place in your library which I shall esteem an honor.

A translation of the History of the Hospital of St. Elizabeth just published waits on you, in which are many singular notes and circumstances.

I am Dear Sir with great esteem your most humble Sert.,

T. BRAND HOLLIS

RC (DLC); endorsed. Recorded in SJL as received 25 May 1787 at Bordeaux. The two volumes of *Memoirs of Thomas Hollis*, edited by Francis Blackburne, and privately printed, London, 1780, were not forwarded to Bordeaux by Short (or Petit), but were retained in Paris (see TJ to Hollis, 2 July 1787; Sowerby, No. 389).

From Philip Mazzei

Paris, 17 Apr. 1787. Mazzei here acknowledges TJ's letter of 4 Apr. and thanks him for offering to supply him with money; by exercising rigid economy he can subsist until TJ returns; however, if TJ wishes to give him an order for a small sum he will hold it in reserve and give it back to TJ on his return. The Prince of Condé's cook, during the Prince's absence, took James [Hemings] as a pupil; instructed him for one day in town, five days in the country, and four after their return to town. James says that he learned when they were in the country that the cost, including maintenance, was 12 francs a day; the cook says he told him this before they left town; Mazzei knew nothing of the arrangement until later. Has told James that even if he were informed of the price after they went to the country, he is not to be excused for continuing the four days after their return. The new cook will take James on at 100 francs a month if the arrangement is by the year or

17 APRIL 1787

at 200 francs by the month. The Prince's cook is willing to continue on the old basis when the Prince is in Paris, and will arrange to take him to Burgundy during the session of Parliament there. It is Mazzei's opinion that it would be best to conclude arrangements with the Prince's cook by paying him the five louis for which James' unwariness or indiscretion has obligated him. Asks TJ's decision on the matter. Mazzei went to TJ's house some time ago and, as a result of the conduct of the servants who had been given notice, he ordered them all to be turned out at the end of the month, even though TJ had permitted them to stay until they found other employment; suggests that TJ write Petit to send them away at once if he has not already done so. Is sorry to learn of the knavery of young Soria. Even though TJ finds satisfactory gardeners and farmers in Provence, he will find better ones around Genoa or in Tuscany. They will talk of this in the future. The Marquis (Lafayette) has a chest ailment which causes Mazzei concern; begs TJ to write him seriously not to neglect his health, his life is too precious. Mazzei has finally begun to print; will be satisfied if he is finished in August. Asks for news when time permits.

RC (DLC); 2 p.; in Italian; endorsed. Recorded in SJL as received 3 May 1787 at Aix-en-Provence. See Partout to TJ, Jan. 1787; TJ to Mazzei, 6 May 1787.

From John Sullivan

[*Durham, N.H., 17 Apr. 1787.* Recorded in SJL as received 26 Sep. 1787 (not found); enclosed in Sullivan to TJ, 29 May 1787. See Sullivan to TJ, 16 Apr. 1787; TJ to Sullivan, 5 Oct. 1787.]

From John Adams

DEAR SIR   London 18 Apr. 1787

Mr. Mortimer the Bearer of this Letter, is a Gentleman of Letters, and although little known to me, is recommended by some of my Friends as a worthy, though unfortunate Man. He is represented to be a Friend to Liberty, and Humanity, and as such I beg leave to introduce him to you, and to ask for him any friendly Advice or Aid you may be able to afford him in his Views, of litterary Employment as a Teacher of Languages, or otherwise. With great Regard I am, my dear Sir always yours,

JOHN ADAMS

RC (DLC); endorsed: "Adams John recd. at Nantes." Recorded in SJL as received 31 May 1787.

[298]

From Peter Carr

DEAR UNCLE   Williamsburg, April 18th. '87

Your daughter being about to sail to France gives me an opportunity of informing you of my situation and studies since I wrote last. I am still at the university attending the professors of Nat. and Mor. philosophy, Mathematicks and modern languages; and Mr. Wythe has given me a very friendly invitation to his lectures on law. I have likewise the good fortune to be a private pupil, and am now reading with him, Herodotus, Sophocles, Cicero and some particular parts of Horace. Beside the advantage of his literary instructions he adds advice and lessons of morality, which are not only pleasing and instructive now, but will be (I hope) of real utility in future. He is said to be without religion, but to me he appears to possess the most rational part of it, and fulfills that great command, Do unto all men as thou wouldst they should do unto thee. And now Sir I should be glad of your advice on the subject of religion; as I think it time to be fixed on a point which has had so many advocates and opponents, and still seems to be dubious. I should wish your advice as to the books I should read, and in what order. Mr. Wythe has just put Lucretius into my hands, whose sect and opinions, men generally think dangerous, but under so good a guide I fear not his opinions whatever they be, and hope rather to be benefited, than as some scrupulous people think, contaminated by him. I find nothing as disadvantageous and troublesome as attending too many things at once; I have unfortunately attempted it this year, and am apprehensive I shall have a perfect knowledge of none. I wish for a plan and order of study from you. I have the satisfaction to inform you that my brothers Sam and Dabney are in good situations, the first in Maryland and the second at an accademy in P. Edward under the direction of a Mr. Smith. I was very sorry to hear from Mr. Maury that you thought no American should go to Europe under thirty; I have, and ever had an invincible inclination to see the world, and am perfectly convinced (though my situation is as good as any in this country) that to see something of the world, get the polish of Europe, and mix the knowledge of books with that of men must be infinitely superior to any advantages enjoyed here. My health has been much injured by the air here. I never pass a summer or fall without a severe bilious fever. Present my compliments to my

Cousin Patsy and believe me to be with due respect and affection your nephew, PETER CARR

RC (ViU); endorsed. Recorded in SJL as received 30 June 1787.

From Castries

A Versailles le 19. Avril 1787

Il fut armé à Amsterdam, Monsieur, vers la fin de l'année 1780, une frégate nommée L'Indien commandée par le Capitaine John Joyner au service des Etats de la Caroline du Sud, destinée à coure sur les énemis des Etats Unis de l'Amerique Septentrionale, et sous la conduite du Commodore Gillon. Il paroit que l'Equipage de ce Bâtiment fut engagé à Dunkerque; Il existe en effet au Bureau des classes de ce Port une Liste de 188. hommes entr'autres Matelots, Novices et Volontaires, qui tous obtinrent le 17. Août de ladite année des permissions pour se rendre à Amsterdam et être embarqués sur ladite frégate. On trouve dans ce même Bureau *un avis aux Volontaires* dont je joins ici copie, qui est une espece de convention arrêtée par le Capitaine Joÿner avec ces Volontaires engagés. Il y a tout lieu de croire que l'expédition eût lieu.

Quelques gens de cet Equipage réclament le payement des Salaires qu'ils ont gagnés à bord de ladite frégate L'Indien. Un nommé Nicolas Valentin Fontaine, entr'autres, répete ceux de 21 mois de services sur ce Bâtiment. Je me persuade que si le payement des gens de cet Equipage a été différé jusqu'à présent, ce n'a pû être que par la difficulté de les retrouver, ou peut être parce que ceux cy n'auront pas scû comment et par qui se le procurer. Je vous prie, Monsieur, de vouloir bien faire prendre des renseignemens à ce sujet, à l'effet de faire rendre à ces malheureux la justice qu'ils peuvent avoir droit de réclamer et qu'ils ont tout lieu d'attendre par votre entremise.

J'ai l'honneur d'être très parfaitement, Monsieur, votre très humble et très obéissant serviteur, LE MAL. DE CASTRIES

RC (DLC); in a clerk's hand, signed by Castries; endorsed. Tr (DNA: PCC, No. 107, II). Recorded in SJL as received 3 May 1787 at Aix-en-Provence. Enclosure: "Avis aux Volontaires," undated but evidently issued shortly before or soon after 17 Aug. 1780, by which Captain Joyner of *L'Indien* promised to pay each man his road expenses to Amsterdam where wages would start at £3 sterling per sailor; to give officers and sailors to the number of 500 half the value of prizes taken; and to show good treatment to those behaving as true Americans; in return for which the signatories to the "Avis" acknowledge themselves to be volunteers in the service of South Carolina for twelve months and promise to reach Amsterdam as speedily as possible (DLC: TJ Papers,

13: 2312-3; Tr in DNA: PCC, No. 107, II; containing the names of 24 persons, beginning "Grinnell, Lieutt.—Alexander Moore—James Hogan," &c.). Copies of Castries' letter and its enclosure were forwarded in TJ's to Jay of 21 June 1787.

TJ was never directly concerned with the prolonged negotiations for the settlement of claims against and by the state of South Carolina in connection with the frigate L'INDIEN, renamed the *South Carolina*, but during his residence in France he did at various times, as in this instance, transmit papers relating to the case and answered queries occasioned by the negotiations. In 1778 the state of South Carolina made Alexander Gillon a commodore in the state navy and elected Joseph Joyner, William Robertson, and John McQueen captains of frigates. Gillon, duly authorized by the state to sell products and borrow money abroad for the purchase of three frigates and military and naval stores, arrived in France in 1779. In May 1780 he secured the frigate through the Chevalier de Luxembourg; assembled a crew; bought, on credit for the state, a quantity of clothing and ammunition; and after innumerable delays, which incurred further financial complications, the ship left the Texel in August 1781. Later, Gillon joined the governor of Cuba in an expedition against the Bahamas, for which he never received the sum promised him. In December 1782 the ship was captured by the British. The claims against the state of South Carolina occasioned by this disastrous venture were a matter of litigation until 1854 (DAB, under Gillon; D. E. H. Smith, "Commodore Alexander Gillon and the Frigate South Carolina," *S.C. Hist. and Geneal. Mag.*, IX [1908], 189-219; D. E. H. Smith, "The Luxembourg Claims," same, X [1909], 92-115).

From Benjamin Franklin

DEAR SIR Philada. April 19. 1787

I have lately received your Favour of Dec. 23. The Diplomas I hope are got to hand before this time. I am much oblig'd by your taking care of my Encyclopedie. Mr. Hopkinson will account with you for it.

I am glad to learn that every thing is quiet in Europe, and like to continue so. I hope the same will be the case here; tho' Boutdefeus are not wanting among us, who by inflammatory Writings in the Papers are perpetually endeavouring to set us together by the Ears about Taxes, and Certificates, &c. The Insurgents in the Massachusets are quelled: and I believe a great Majority of that People approve the Measures of Government in reducing them. Yet I see that in the late Election they have left out the late Governor and chosen Mr. Hancock. But he was always more popular than Mr. Bowdoin, had resign'd on Account of his Infirmities, and his Health being mended, his Friends have taken Advantage of the Offence given by Mr. Bowdoin to the Malcontents, to encrease the Number of Votes against him. His refusing the Bill for reducing the Governor's Salary, has also, I imagine hurt his Interest at this Election. So that upon the whole I do not think his not being chosen any Proof of general Dissatisfaction with the Measures taken to suppress the Rebellion, or with the Constitution.

19 APRIL 1787

Our Federal Constitution is generally thought defective and a Convention, first propos'd by Virginia, and since recommended by Congress, is to assemble here next Month, to revise it and propose Amendments. The Delegates generally appointed as far as I have heard of them are Men of Character for Prudence and Ability, so that I hope Good from their Meeting. Indeed, if it does not do Good it must do Harm, as it will show that we have not Wisdom enough among us to govern ourselves; and will strengthen the Opinion of some Political Writers, that popular Governments cannot long support themselves.

I am sorry for the Death of M. Peyronet on Account of Mr. Paine, who would have been pleas'd and instructed by conferring with that ingenious and skilful Artist on the Subject of his Bridge, and it was my Intention to introduce him to Mr. Peyronet's Acquaintance. I have requested the Duke de Rochefoucauld to procure him a Sight of the Models and Drafts in the Repository of the Ponts et Chaussées. You are well acquainted with Mr. Paine's Merit, and need no Request of mine to serve him in his Views, and introduce him where it may be proper, and of Advantage to him.

With great and sincere Esteem I have the honour to be Your Excellency's most obedient & most humble Servant,

B. FRANKLIN

RC (DLC). PrC (DLC: Franklin Papers). Recorded in SJL as received 11 June 1787.

From St. Victour

[*Paris, 19 Apr. 1787.* Recorded in SJL as received 3 May 1787 at Aix-en-Provence. Not found; but see TJ to St. Victour, 6 May 1787.]

From Bellon

Dieppe, 21 Apr. 1787. Encloses a letter just received from Captain Thomson, an Englishman, commanding the *Mercury* "venant de Richmond en Virginie, avec une cargaison de tabac pour la ferme."

RC (DLC); 2 p.; below signature: Interprète Royal, cy devant Employé dans L'armée de Rochambeau, où J'ai Eu L'Honneur de Connoitre Son Excellency à *Baltimore in Maryland*"; endorsed. Recorded in SJL as received 3 May 1787 at Aix-en-Provence. Enclosure not identified, but it was probably one of the Virginia letters received on 3 May—the missing letter from Banister of 25 Dec. 1786, one of Randolph's two letters of 28 Jan. 1787, or one of the letters from Francis and Elizabeth Wayles Eppes or Mary Jefferson (see under 22 and 23 May 1786).

[302]

From the Abbés Arnoux and Chalut

Paris 23. avril 1787.

C'est aux sentiments que vous inspirez Monsieur, que vous devez le bon accuil dont nous remerciez. L'estime et l'attachement que nous avons pour vous nous fera saisir toutes les occasions qui se presenteront pour faire des choses qui vous soient agreables.

Si vous ne connoissiez la france que par les provinces que vous avez parcourues, vous auriez une meilleure opinion des moeurs françoises; vous étes trop eclairé pour attribuer à d'autres causes qu'au Gouvernement les vices qui vous ont choque. Nous sommes ce que les loix nous ont faits. Plaignez notre vieille nation et felicitez-vous de la vertu, de la jeunesse de la vôtre. Nous n'esperons pas de vous ressembler jamais, l'histoire de tous les tems nous ote cet espoir. Nulle nation n'a passé de la corruption a la vertu et à la liberté. Telle est notre destinée.

Nous attendons avec impatience votre retour. Vous viendrez chargé de bien des Connoissances dans les arts utiles, que vous enverrez dans votre patrie comme un hommage de votre amour pour elle. Gardez-vous bien de lui donner le gout des arts agreables. Laissez-nous cet aliment de corruption, et conservez une vertu qui fera seule votre bonheur.

Quand vous serez à Paris nous causerons de La retraite de M. de Calonne, de l'assemblée des notables et nous vous renouvellerons les assurances de notre estime et de notre amitié avec Lesquelles nous avons l'honneur d'être Monsieur vos très humbles et très obeissants Serviteurs,

L'ABBÉ ARNOUX
L'ABBÉ CHALUT

RC (DLC); endorsed. Recorded in SJL as received 3 May 1787 at Aix-en-Provence. In TJ's Alphabetical Index to SJL there is an entry for a letter from the Abbé Arnoux to TJ, dated 3 May 1787. It is possible that Arnoux did write such a letter, but none of that date has been found. The Alphabetical Index, which TJ compiled himself, has an occasional error in it, and the present entry may be one. There is no entry in SJL itself for a letter from Arnoux of 3 May 1787; in the Index TJ probably transposed the date of receipt for the present letter.

From John Banister, Jr.

DEAR SIR New-York Apl. 23d. 1787

Since my arrival here I have been unable to pursue my journey to Virginia on account of a very severe indisposition for which I am in a great measure indebted to the Captn. of the packet. The

[303]

people here like the rest of mankind are discontented with, and cry out against the Government, whilst it only rests with them to form such a one as may render them respectable and happy. No farther powers are as yet given to Congress, nor is their a prospect that they will be granted soon. Many complaints in Virginia of the poverty of the people, and to render the evil still greater they have laid duties on the exportation of those articles which are most likely to bring money into the State. In consequence of this the Tobacco from Carolina no longer comes to Virginia for exportation. There is a heavy tonage on all foreign Shipping. The price of Tobacco is from twenty to twenty two and six pence, the prospects for crops are at present very good.

Colo. Archd. Cary dead, this is all the news I have been able to collect from Virginia. In the course of next month there will be a meeting at Philadelphia of deputies sent by the several states for the purpose of forming some plan by which the chain of Union may be drawn more close and rendered more adequate to the purposes of federal Government. What will be their success cannot as yet be determined, but every person who wishes well to his country must be interested in the occasion. The prospect which lies before us is perhaps the fairest which has been ever spread before any set of men; could they be only persuaded to adapt their ideas to their situation and not think it really worse than it is.

Your seeds have been delivered to the members of Congress, but they have never had it in their power to send them on; they are now under my care and as I set out tomorrow will not be delayed much longer. The seeds being sealed up I shall take none of the Sulla seed but must beg the favor of you to send me some when it will be most convenient to you. Those for South Carolina have been sent to their directions.

I am requested by Mr. Hilegas who lives in the house with me to present you with his best wishes. As soon as I arrive in Virginia I will write you fully on every subject which I think may interest you. In the mean time I am with the greatest respect your obliged friend and humble Servt., JNO. BANISTER Junr.

RC (MHi). Recorded in SJL as received 11 June 1787.

From David S. Franks

Dear Sir   New York 23d. Apl. 1787

After a very disagreable Passage of 50 days we arrived in this City and I take the earliest Opportunity of informing you that I have delivered the Dispatches entrusted to my Care to Mr. Jay and have also acquitted myself of the Little Commissions and orders Your Excellency honored me with at my departure from Paris. The Packages and Letters are all forwarded to their addresses and those recommended to my particular Attention for Philadelphia I sent on by a Colo. Melcher who has promised to deliver them with his own hands.

Our Voyage from Havre was of itself tedious and rendered still more so by the inconvenience of the Ship and the unkind manner with which we were treated; the Provisions of meat were good but the wine was execrable and not a single thing of those refreshments so necessary to People who are sick at Sea, but two loaves of white Sugar and not a drop of white or sweet wines on board. Mr. B. and myself suffered more for the want of them than ever we did for the want of any thing before. Even our eggs, Raisins &c. were expended before we were three weeks out. I mention these things as they appear to me to be impediments to that decided preference which it is wished the French Packets may have over the English; the Lieutenants eat in the Cabin at the first table and think they ought to have the Power of commanding every thing in it, but also over the Persons of the Passengers. This occasions continual disputes and makes the time pass extreamlly irksome to those who are already worn down with fatigue and sickness. There is a second table on Board at which (as on board the french frigates) the Lieutenants might preside and the Captain by that means have it in his Power to furnish his Passengers more abundantly. At present he is only allowed 4 Livres pr. day for his Lieutenants for which he cannot afford to give them such things as he ought to furnish to People who pay him twenty five Louis for the Passage. In short Sir the Affair of living, on board the french packets, is so badly arranged that I am fully convinced that no[1] man who has once crossed the water in the way we have will rather than do it again, give Fifty Louis to go in any other ship. There are two English Packet boats now in this Harbor, and sorry I am to say that they not only merit a Preference but that they will have it too. I wish a change might be effected, and this may be easily done by seperating the Lieutenants from the Passengers.

[305]

23 APRIL 1787

Mr. Banister has been very unwell since his arrival and I am convinced his disorder was chiefly owing to the bad wine he was obliged to drink on board. He will set out in a day or two for Virginia.

I can write you nothing new except the arrival yesterday of an Eastindia Vessell which sail'd from this about 16 months since. She will make a very great Voyage. She brings an Account of the death of the famous Colonel Sears of this City of a fever at Canton. I suppose Mr. Maddesson will write you on the political situation of America. I shall therefore only say that every body here seems much displeased with it, and not much expected from the Convention which is to meet at Philadelphia the 12th. of next month.

I take the Liberty of requesting your Excellency to deliver the inclosed Letter and at the same time to present my most affectionate Regards to all the Passy family and to Mr. Short with my respectful Compliments to Miss Jefferson and to believe me Dear Sir Your most obedient and obliged humble Servt.,

DAVD. S. FRANKS

RC (DLC). Recorded in SJL as received 11 June 1787. Enclosure not identified.

The difficulties that Franks had experienced on embarking at Le Havre (see Franks to TJ, 11 Feb. 1787) were not calculated to soothe his feelings or prepare him for the difficulties of a long voyage. The packet had left Le Havre on 17 Feb. and arrived in New York on Monday morning, 9 Apr. 1787; the *Pa. Journ. and Weekly Adv.* for 28 Apr., quoting a New York paper of 12 Apr., reported on the packet's arrival and added: "Colonel Franks the American consul came passenger in the packet. He informs us of the death of that eminent and patriotic statesman the Count de Vergennes, prime minister of France. America has truly lost a disinterested friend by this sad event."

[1] Thus in MS.

From David Hartley

MY DEAR SIR   Golden Square April 23 1787

By the favour of Coll. Smith I trouble you with this line of which the purpose and contents are only to entitle me to your remembrance. I sincerely regret when I had first the pleasure of your acquaintance that the time allowed me to profit by your friendship was so short. This, for private and personal reasons of respect and friendship to you—and for public reasons, because I know your candour and good dispositions to cultivate friendship and union between our two countries. I beg of you to believe of me the same dispositions and that I shall constantly persevere in them thro all changes and chances. I beg to have the pleasure of hearing from you. I wish very much that I could receive by any channel of communication any sort of news and particular Congress journals from america. Could you be so good as to put [me] into some way of affecting this. I am anxious for the state of public transactions which may interest our two Countries. I am Dear Sir Your much obliged friend & most obedt. Sert., D HARTLEY

RC (DLC); endorsed. Recorded in SJL as received 25 May 1787 at Bordeaux.

From James Madison

DEAR SIR   April 23. 1787.

Since my last which was of March 19. I have had the pleasure of yours of Decr. 16. Jany. 30. and Feby. 7. which were handed to me by Col. Franks. Along with them were received the copying machine and other articles referred to in them. You will accept my warmest thanks for all these favors. The packet for the Governor of Virginia under the same cover with your letter of Feby. 7. has been forwarded. The accident to your wrist was first made known to me by these communications. I learnt with satisfaction from Col. Franks that the pain and weakness was apparently going off, and ardently wish that your projected trip to the South of France may produce a radical cure.

The vigorous measures finally pursued by the Government of Massachusetts against the insurgents, had the intended effect of dispersing them. By some it was feared that they would re-embody on the return of favorable weather. As yet no symptom of such a design has appeared. It would seem that they mean to try their strength in another way; that is, by endeavoring to give the elections such a turn as may promote their views under the auspices of Constitutional forms. How far they may succeed is not yet reducible to certainty. That a great change will be effected in the component members of the government is certain, but the degree of influence imputable to the malcontents can not be well known till some specimen shall be given of the temper of the new rulers. Mr. Hancock takes the place of Mr. Bowdoin. His general character forbids a suspicion of his patriotic principles; but as he is an idolater of popularity, it is to be feared that he may be seduced by this foible into dishonorable compliances. A great proportion of the Senate is also changed, and a greater proportion of the other branch it is expected will be changed. A paper emission at least is apprehended from this revolution in their councils.

23 APRIL 1787

Congress have agreed to Mr. Jays report on the treaty of peace and to an address which accompanies it. Copies of both will no doubt be sent you from his department. The Legislature of this State which was sitting at the time and on whose account the acts of Congress were hurried through, has adjourned till Jany. next without deciding on them. This is an ominous example to the other states, and must weaken much the claim on Great Britain of an execution of the Treaty on her part as promised in case of proper steps being taken on ours. Virginia we foresee will be among the foremost in seizing pretexts for evading the injunctions of Congress. S. Carolina is not less infected with the same spirit. The present deliberations of Congress turn on 1. the sale of the western lands, 2. the Government of the Western settlements within the federal domain, 3. the final settlement of the Accounts between the Union and its members, 4. the *treaty*[1] [with][2] *Spain*.

1. Between six and seven hundred thousand acres have been surveyed in townships under the land ordinance, and are to be sold forthwith. The place where Congress sit is fixed for the sale. Its excentricity and remoteness from the premises will I apprehend give disgust. On the most eligible plan of selling the unsurveyed residue Congress are much divided; the Eastern States being strongly attached to that of townships, nothwithstanding the expence incident to it; the Southern being equally biassed in favor of indiscriminate locations, nothwithstanding the many objections against that mode. The dispute will probably terminate in some kind of compromise, if one can be hit upon.

2. The Government of the settlements on the Illinois and Wabash is a subject very perplexing in itself; and rendered more so by our ignorance of many circumstances on which a right judgment depends. The inhabitants at those places, claim protection against the savages, and some provision for both criminal and Civil justice. It appears also that land jobbers are among them who are likely to multiply litigations among individuals, and by collusive purchases of spurious titles, to defraud the United States.

3. The settlement of the public accounts has long been pursued in varied shapes, and with little prospect of success. The idea which has long been urged by some of us, seems now to be seriously embraced, of establishing a plenipotentiary tribunal for the final adjustment of the mutual claims on the great and simple principle of equity. An ordinance for this purpose has been reported by the Treasury board and has made some progress through Congress.

23 APRIL 1787

It is likely to be much retarded by the thinness of Congress, as indeed is almost every other matter of importance.

4. The *Spanish negociation* is in a very *ticklish situation*. You have been already apprized of the *vote of seven states last fall* for *ceding* the *Mississipi* for a *term of years*. From sundry circumstances it was *inferred that Jay was* not *proceeding under this usurped authority*. A late instruction to *him to lay the state* of the *negociation before Congress* has *discovered* that he has *adjusted* with *Guardoqui* an *article* for *suspending* the *use of the Mississipi* by *the citizens of U.S.* The report however leaves it *somewhat doubtful how far U.S. are commited by this step* and a *subsequent* [Report]² *of* the *secretary* on the *seisure of Spanish property* in the *western country* and on *information of discontents*, touching the *occlusion of the Mississipi* shews that the probable *consequences of the measure perplex him extremely*. It was nevertheless conceived by the *instructed delegations* to be *their duty to press a revocation* of the *step taken* in some *form which would least offend Spain* and *least irritate* the *patrons of* the *vote* [of]² *seven states*. Accordingly a *motion was made* to the *following effect*—that the *present state of the negociation with Spain and of* the *affairs of U.S. rendered it expedient* that *you should proceed under a special commission to Madrid* for the *purpose of making such representations* as *might at once impress* on that *court our friendly disposition* and *induce it to relax* on the *contested points*, and that the *proper communications* and *explanations* should *be made to Guardoqui relative* to this *change in* the *mode of conducting the negociation*. This *motion was referred* to *Mr. Jay* whose *report disapproves of it*. In this state the *matter lies*. Eight *states only being present no effective vote* is to be *expected*. It may notwithstanding be incumbent *on us to try some question* which will at least *mark the paucity of states who abet* the *obnoxious project. Massachusets* and *New York* alone of the present *states are under that* description; and *Connecticut and New Hampshire alone of the absent. Maryland* and *S. Carolina* have heretofore been on the *right side*. Their *future conduct* is somewhat problematical. The opinion of *New Hampshire* is only *conjectured*. The *conversion of Rhode Island* countenances a *hope that she too* may in this instance *desert the New England standard*.

The prospect of a full and respectable convention grows stronger every day. Rho. Island alone has refused to send deputies. Maryland has probably appointed by this time. Of Connecticut alone doubts are entertained. The antifederal party in that State is numerous and persevering. It is said that the elections which are

24 APRIL 1787

now going on, are rather discouraging to the advocates of the Convention. Pennsylvania has added Doctor Franklin to her deputation. There is some ground to calculate on the attendance of Genl. Washington. Our Governor, Mr. Wythe, Mr. Blair, and Col. Mason will pretty certainly attend. The last I am informed is renouncing his errors on the subject of the Confederation, and means to take an active part in the amendment of it. Mr. Henry pretty soon resigned the undertaking. Genl. Nelson was put into his place, who has also declined. He was succeeded by R. H. Lee, who followed his example. Docr. McClurg has been since appointed, and as he was on the spot must have been previously consulted.

Considerable changes are taking place I hear in the County elections in Virginia, and a strong itch beginning to return for paper money. Mr. Henry is said to have the measure in contemplation, and to be laying his train for it already. He will however be powerfully opposed by Col. Mason, if he should be elected and be able to serve, by Monroe and Marshal, and Ludwel Lee (son of R. H. L.) who are already elected, and sundry others of inferior rank. Mr. Harrison the late Governor, has so far regained the favor of Charles City as to be reinstated a representative. The part which he will take is uncertain. From his repeated declarations he ought to be adverse to a paper emission. My next will probably be from Philada. In the mean time with my fervent wishes for your happiness I remain Yr. affecte. friend,   Js. MADISON Jr.

Deaths. Archibald Cary Esqr.
    Jno. Augustine Washington, brother of Genl. W.

RC (DLC: Madison Papers); partly in code; endorsed. Recorded in SJL as received 11 June 1787; entry in SJL has the following notation: "(seems from N.Y.)."

[1] This and subsequent words in italics are written in code and were decoded interlineally by TJ; his text has been verified by the editors, employing Code No. 9.

[2] This word was not in Madison's code or text as originally written, but was interlined by him late in life.

From Edward Carrington

DR. SIR   New York April 24. 1787

I had the honor to receive your favor of the 16th. of Jan. by Colo. Franks, and thank you sincerely as well for the confidence with which you claim my services, as for your friendly communications. The former you may at all times command: the latter will

[310]

not only be gratefully received, but repaid as far as my attempts to do so can go. The letters to your freinds were immediately forwarded under cover to Doctor Curry. The packages are committed to the care of Mr. Banister, who goes off this day by stage to Richmond. No gentleman before him has been travelling thither by this mode since the arrival of the packet, and to have committed them to the stage without the immediate Care of a person who was to go the whole way would have amounted to no more than a consignment to the first stage office in which they might have been deposited for a night, or perhaps to be thrown into the high way by the first traveller who might conceive himself incommoded by them. There is scarsely circumstance of any thing going safely that is casually committed to the stage. Mr. Banister intends to go immediately on, but should he, by any accident be delayed, he will more readily meet with a hand who is going to Richmond further on the way than I shall here, and is apprised of the dispatch which is necessary in the case.

You have doubtless been informed of the measure of a general Convention which was proposed by Virginia in the fall Session, for revising and thoroughly amending the Confederation. Some of the States hesitated upon the adoption of the measure as being unauthorised by Congress, and, of course, improper. To remove every possible difficulty, Congress came to a resolution in February, recommending its adoption; all the states have appointed deputies except Maryland, Connecticut and Rhode Island. Maryland is now in session, and that she will appoint, is not doubted. Connecticut is also in session, and it is believed will appoint. Rhode Island is at all points so anti-federal, and contemptible, that her neglecting the invitation, will probably occasion no demur whatever in the proceedings. The meeting is to take place in Philada. on the second Monday in May. Various are the conjectures as to the issue of this meeting, and still more various are the suggested remedies to the defects of our system. I am rather a zealot in the measure, because it will operate, at least as an alarm, but whether it will be productive of any immediate effects, may be doubtful. Perhaps that experiment has not yet been made of the present system, which could discover its defects, or point to their remedies;—I am certain it is very imperfect, but at the same time there are evident causes for its failure, other than those of defectiveness in the constructure. The best of Governments, like other things, can prosper alone by due attention. America was placed in possession of peace and independence under circumstances which have not only deprived her political systems of the necessary care of her Citizens, but exposed her to the injurious designs of men, whose interest it has been to destroy the efficiency of Government. A great proportion of the people, being loaded with debt, have found an interest in promoting measures directly opposed to good government, and have been solicitous to direct the public affairs, whilst better men have been inactive, or engrossed by the alluring invitation of ease and plenty in our vast western and southern Regions.

The deputies to the convention for Virginia are Genl. Washington, E. Randolph, G. Wythe, John Blair, Geo. Mason, J. Madison and Jas. McClurg. Mr. Henry, Mr. R. H. Lee and Genl. Nelson have declined appointments which were offered them. Genl. Washington it is hoped will attend but there is some reason to apprehend the contrary—his state of health is not a good one.

I am pleased to hear of the impressions which have been received in Europe with respect to the late commotions in Massachusetts. A perfect quiet prevails there now, but it is said the elections for the ensuing year are not free of the influence of the Malcontents.

The Convention will be productive of things worth communicating to you, and I will do myself the pleasure to write by the first opportunity that offers after its commencement.

Be good enough to present me to Mr. Short, to whom I will write by the next packet.

I have the Honour to be with great respect & Esteem Dr. Sir Your Most obt. Servt.,   Ed. Carrington

RC (DLC); endorsed. Recorded in SJL as received 11 June 1787.

For a note on Short's influence in initiating TJ's FRIENDLY COMMUNICATIONS with Carrington, see TJ to Carrington, 16 Jan. 1787.

From John Jay

Dr. Sir   New York 24th. April 1787

Since my last to you of the 9th. February I have been honored with yours of the 27th. October, 12th. November, 31st. December, 9th. January and 1st. and 8th. February last, all of which together with the Papers that accompanied them have been communicated to Congress; but neither on them nor your preceding ones have any Instructions been as yet ordered, so that this Letter like many others will not be very interesting.

It is greatly to be regretted that Communications to Congress are not kept more private. A Variety of Reasons which must be

24 APRIL 1787

obvious to you oppose it; and while the fœderal Sovereignty remains just as it is little Secrecy is to be expected. This Circumstance must undoubtedly be a great Restraint on those public and private Characters from whom you would otherwise obtain useful Hints and Information. I for my part have long experienced the Inconvenience of it, and in some Instances very sensibly.

The Death of Count De Vergennes, of which Major Franks informs us, is to be lamented; and the more so as the Talents, Industry and Disposition towards us of his Successor are uncertain. Who will take his place is an important Question to us as well as to France.

The Convention of which you have been informed will convene next Month at Philadelphia. It is said that General Washington accepts his Appointment to it and will attend. I wish their Counsels may better our Situation; but I am not sanguine in my Expectations. There is Reason to fear that our Errors do not proceed from Want of Knowledge, and therefore that Reason and public Spirit will require the Aid of Calamity to render their Dictates effectual.

The Insurrection in Massachusetts is suppressed, but the Spirit of it exists and has operated powerfully in the late Election. Governor Bowdoin whose Conduct was upright and received the Approbation of the Legislature, is turned out, and Mr. Hancock is elected. Many respectable Characters in both Houses are displaced and Men of other Principles and Views elected. Perhaps the Accounts are exaggerated—perhaps Mr. Hancock will support his former Character, and that the present Legislature will be zealous to maintain the Rights of Government as well as respect the Wish of the People. Time alone can ascertain these Matters—the Language however of such Changes is not pleasant or promising.

For your information I enclose a Copy of certain Resolutions of Congress relative to Infractions of the Treaty of Peace. How they will be received, or what Effect they will have I know not. Some of the States have gone so far in their Deviations from the Treaty, that I fear they will not easily be persuaded to tread back their Steps, especially as the Recommendations of Congress like most other Recommendations are seldom efficient when opposed by Interest. A mere Government of Reason and Persuasion is little adapted to the actual State of human Nature in any Age or Country.

One of our five Indiamen, Vizt. an Albany Sloop, returned a few Days ago in four Months from Canton; and I heard last Evening that one or two Vessels are preparing at Boston for a Voyage to the Isle of France. The Enterprize of our Countrymen is inconceivable,

24 APRIL 1787

and the Number of young Swarms daily going down to settle in the Western Country is a further Proof of it. I fear that Western Country will one Day give us Trouble—to govern them will not be easy, and whether after two or three Generations they will be fit to govern themselves is a Question that merits Consideration. The Progress of Civilization and the Means of Information is very tardy in sparse and separate Settlements. I wish our Differences with Spain in that Quarter were well settled; but the Maxim of *festina lente* does not suit our southern sanguine Politicians.

The English are making some important Settlements on the River St. Lawrence &c. Many of our People go there; and it is said that Vermont is not greatly inclined to be the fourteenth State. Taxes and relaxed Governments agree but ill.

I have the Honor to be &ca.,

JOHN JAY

FC (DNA: PCC, No. 121). Dft (NK-Iselin). Recorded in SJL as received 11 June 1787.

Jay did not enclose merely a copy of CERTAIN RESOLUTIONS OF CONGRESS as they were adopted on 21 Mch. 1787 but the printed circular to the states that Madison had supposed he would send (Madison to TJ, 23 Apr. 1787; TJ to Carmichael, 14 June 1787). The latter, which was an argument calculated to justify the position that "treaties and every Article in them . . . are and ought to be . . . binding on the whole Nation," was submitted to Congress on 6 Apr. and adopted on 13 Apr. (JCC, XXXII, 177-84). An edition of 20 copies of this Address, with the text of the resolutions embedded in Jay's explanatory comment, was printed. On the proposition that treaties were the supreme law of the land, TJ was more closely in agreement with Jay's report than he was with the dictum that A MERE GOVERNMENT OF REASON AND PERSUASION IS LITTLE ADAPTED TO THE ACTUAL STATE OF HUMAN NATURE IN ANY AGE OR COUNTRY. The first of the resolutions reported by Jay faced the constitutional issue squarely. By it Congress declared "That the Legislatures of the several States cannot of right pass any Act or Acts for interpreting, explaining or construing a national treaty or any part or clause of it, nor for restraining, limiting or in any manner impeding, retarding, or counteracting the operation and execution of the same; for that on being constitutionally made, ratified and published they become in virtue of the confederation part of the Law of the Land, and are not only independent of the will and power of such Legislatures, but also binding and obligatory on them" (JCC, XXXII, 124-5, 181). This was a position that TJ and others had consistently supported; in the debate in Congress on 21 Mch., Madison noted that the resolution "declaring the Treaty to have the force of a law and denying the Right of any State to contravene it, was agreed to without dissent and almost without observation" (Madison's "Notes of Debates," JCC, XXXIII, 727). But Congress could only recommend, and Jay's able argument demonstrating the consequences that would ensue if the states continued to construe and contravene treaties by legislation was deprived of its full force by the tide of events: even as he wrote, delegates were preparing to assemble at Philadelphia for the Convention that wrote into the Federal Constitution the clinching words of Article VI which gave permanent force to the validity of his words.

From William Short

My dear Sir Paris April 24. 1787.

Although my two last letters are still at Aix, and although this will arrive there before you I cannot forbear longer the pleasure of writing to you. I will begin by acknowleging the reciept of your two last, one from Toulon and the other from Nice. In consequence of the first I have been to-day to Versailles to see M. de Montmorin, it being the first Versailles-day since its arrival, and I did not suppose I ought to trouble him on any other. As ill fortune would have it M. de Montmorin gave audience at Paris. As it was impossible for me to be acquainted with that circumstance, I suppose I am equally authorized to charge the hire of horses &c. for this trip, and the more so as I had no business at Versailles, *et m'y suis très ennuyé*, during the little time I was obliged to stay there. Of this however I leave you to be the judge at your return. On my way back I passed by M. de Montmorin's hotel in Paris. He was gone out, so that I could not see him, but was told by the Swiss that I could have that honor to-morrow morning.—The letter for the King is sealed with the seal of the United States.

I have recieved and paid the 1200^{tt} you inclosed me, to the engraver of Genl. Gates's medal. I hope to be able to send it by the May packet.

I went to Panthemont yesterday and informed Miss Jefferson of your intended silence for three weeks at least; and I comforted her at the same time by adding that you were well.

Some time ago Mr. Barrett told me that it was desired the Americans who were here should sign a petition to the minister for the rendering Honfleur a free port. I declined it and gave him for reason that although I had in fact no public character, yet as I lived with you and acted under your authority, I was afraid my signing a paper might have some effect in compromitting you in the eyes of those ill-informed, and as I did not suppose you would chuse to be signing petitions, I must beg to be excused from it, notwithstanding my earnest desire to see the success of such a petition. Whether M. de Crevecoeur was acquainted with this circumstance I cannot say, but a few days ago he shewed me as a very meritorious thing, a most humble petition to the Duke d'Harcourt, M. Montmorin &c. which he had drawn and had had signed by all the Americans here, and among the rest he had added, '*W. Short* for *Th. Jefferson.*' I was sincerely mortified at this step of

24 APRIL 1787

M. de Crevecoeur, and observed to him that I did not know how far you would approve of it. He added that there was nothing to be feared and that he had acted entirely by the advice of the Duke D'Harcourt. I did not let him see how much I was displeased with what he had done, for two reasons—first, because it could have produced no change, and secondly because I was sure whatever he did in this affair, was from pure zeal, and with the best intentions in the world. I have thought it necessary to explain this circumstance to you in order that you may direct what you chuse to be done, or let it rest unnoticed as you please.

Mazzei desires me to mention to you that the price of 15.^{lt} which you fixed on Ramsay's history is too high and will prevent the sale. He thinks for Ramsay's interest you had better reduce it to 12.^{lt}

I have forborne saying much to you on the *Assemblée des notables*, for several reasons, and among others because there was so little certainty in any thing I could say on that subject. Yet at present there are circumstances of great importance and of public notoriety, such as the dismission of M. de Calonne and the Garde des sceaux, and the putting in their places M. de Fourqueux, and M. de Lamoignon. The causes of this change are variously reported in public. Many people have foreseen for some time the necessary approach of M. de Calonne's downfall, although there was no apparent loss of esteem in the King's mind towards him. A circumstance which it is believed in Paris, first destroyed the equilibrium of the Comptroller and hastened his precipitation was, the firm conduct of the Bishop of Langres and the Mquis. de la fayette. The latter insisted on an examination into certain abuses which had taken place in the alienation and purchase of the royal domains— the former particularised the abuses and the persons concerned. They were informed the day after by the President of their bureau that if they expected any notice should be taken of their assertions, they must sign them. The Marquis particularized certain facts and signed them to be delivered to the King, by which he estimated these abuses at 45. millions—the bishop asked eight days in order to collect the proofs of what he had advanced and promised to sign them at the expiration of that term. This reduced the Comptroller to bring his matters to a crisis, and either put these gentlemen and others out of the way or yield all hopes of success. In the attempt he fell.—I give you that as the popular opinion of the Parisians, for you know I have no other chanel of learning what passes at Versailles.

The King assembled all the bureaux the day before yesterday

24 APRIL 1787

and made them a speech which does him really infinite honor. You will see it in the public papers, before you get this letter and consequently it is useless that I send it to you: from it you will be able to learn the present situation of affairs in the Assembly.

I shall have a new subject for my letter to Mr. Jay. An Arrêt of the council of February last has just made its appearance here, which raises the duty on foreign stock fish imported into their islands and increases the premium on French importations of that article. I intend to send him the Arrêt; although he will probably first recieve information of it by way of the West Indies.

I recieved a few days ago a letter from Smith, desiring I would give him a bed here for one night—says he shall follow immediately that letter and is on his way to Madrid and Lisbon. I don't know why.

April 25th.—I have been this morning to M. de Montmorin's and delivered him your letter, with that for the King, which he promised to dispose of properly. He told me he had recieved your's from Marseilles, and that he had just recieved a letter also from Mr. Otto. It must have come by a merchant vessel.

I inclose you nine letters, one of which I took the liberty of opening; because being from the Mal. de Castries, I supposed it might contain something relative to commerce which you would chuse should be immediately forwarded to America.

Messrs. Fox and Norris have lately passed through Paris on their way to London and America. Mr. de Crevecoeur sets out for Havre and New York the 7th. of next month. He is accompanied by a young gentleman the son of Mr. Brick of Boston, who was brought from thence to this country under the care of the Mquis. de Vaudreuil. He has been constantly since in a college in Languedoc. I hope you are as much pleased with your transalpine as cisalpine trip, and that you will find on both sides improvements, in the most noble and useful of all arts, capable of being transplanted in America. Adieu, my dear Sir and be assured of the best and most fervent wishes, for your health and happiness, of your friend & servant, W. SHORT

RC (DLC); endorsed. PrC (DLC: Short Papers). Recorded in SJL as received 3 May 1787 at Aix-en-Provence. Of the enclosures, only that of Castries to TJ, 19 Apr. 1787, has been identified.

TJ's letter to Montmorin FROM MARSEILLES was that of 6 Apr. 1787 (missing), which was enclosed in TJ to Short, 7 Apr. 1787; it was evidently only a covering letter for Congress' letter FOR THE KING. The letter FROM OTTO was one of Otto's dispatches to Vergennes, for the news of Vergennes' death only arrived in America with the French packet on 9 Apr. Otto's dispatch No. 80 was dated 17 Feb. and was recieved on 23 Mch. 1787; it discussed

[317]

the "tres secrete" proposal to transfer the American debt to France to a group of Holland bankers. This was probably the dispatch that Montmorin had in mind, for Otto's No. 81 to Vergennes, dated 28 Feb., was not received until 28 May 1787 (Arch. Aff. Etr., Corr. Pol., E.-U., Vol. XXXII; Tr in DLC). MR. BRICK OF BOSTON was Samuel Breck, who had become the protégé of the MQUIS DE VAUDREUIL and who was just completing, under Vaudreuil's patronage, four years of study at the military school for the nobility at Sorèze; in 1792 his father left Boston, partly because of a throat affliction and partly because of his opposition to what he deemed the iniquitous system of taxation of Massachusetts, and took up residence in Philadelphia, where young Breck became a prominent citizen and wrote a highly interesting autobiography (*Recollections of Samuel Breck*, Philadelphia, 1877, ed. H. E. Scudder). The King's SPEECH and the ARRÊT were both enclosed in Short's letter to Jay, 4 May 1787.

From William Hay

SIR Richmond Apl. 26th. 1787

Doctr. Currie our mutual Friend, has been so obliging as to give up to me the new Edition of the Encyclopédie Méthodique of Paris, for which I am to furnish him such standard Books in the English Language, to its Value, as he shall approve of. I have therefore to request you to forward to me the remaining Part of that excellent Work, so soon as the Editors complete it.—The very small Portion of Time, which a Man of Business in this Country, can devote to literary Pursuits, has only enabled me to satisfy my Curiosity, but from what I have read, and from the pleasing Prospect I have of soon being free from the Bustle of active Business, I promise myself much Happiness and Improvement in the perusal of so various and complete a System of the Arts and Sciences. I am also indebted to Doctr. Currie for several Valuable Essays on Air, which you was so obliging as to forward to him. I have read that of M. Sigaud de la Fond on fixed Air, and am extreemly pleased with his accurate Experiments and useful Reflections thereon. The Want of the Apparatus that is necessary to make Experiments in the various Branches of Natural Philosophy Deprives me of that Delight which is derived from a critical Examination of the works of Nature. For the present therefore I must be satisfyed to read the Experiments of others more happily circumstanced than myself.

Your Native Country exibits at present a very gloomy Picture, the most striking Traits of which are a Degeneracy of Manners and an unequal and slow Administration of Justice. The People are greatly in Debt, and the Cry is, *Paper Money*; Punctuality is gone, and all Faith and Credit in Individuals are lost.—The Prudent

26 APRIL 1787

Measures of last Assembly respecting Paper Money and the public Securities, gained them immortal Honour, and had their other Proceedings been dictated by the same wisdom we should ere this Moment have heartily begun a Series of Reformation. The Means, which, since the Peace, have fostered Luxury and Extravagance, are now withheld from the Bulk of the People, the Staple Commodity of the Country is fallen, and Goods are now and will be more and more scarce. Necessity therefore will teach us Frugality and Temperance. Indeed the Culture of Cotton, Flax and Hemp is taken up again, and as if awoke from a Dream, the People wonder how they could lay asside manufacturing the coarse Articles which their Families stood in need of, and of which Experience during the war, taught them the Advantages. Farming and Gardning are more general and the Culture of Grapes is now become fashionable. The Farmer however has seen with Sorrow his Crops of small grain, particularly the wheat and frequently the Corn almost totally destroyed, for some years past, by a pernicious Insect. The Damage is done, while it is yet in its first Stage of Existence; the little Enemy dwells in safety between the outer Leaves which cover the Joints, and the Stalk. In this State they appear not unlike a young Bed Bug and smell exactly as they do, they differ in Colour only by a duskish black Streak across the Neck; when they have acquired wings, they are all over of that dusky Colour, except a very large one which you will find now and then of the same Colour of the Young Brood, whether Male or Female I have not been able to determine. No Remedy has been found out for them. Their Progress is from South to North, and such Havock have they made, that Many Farmers have been obliged to leave off the Culture of wheat, and by that Means, they have left their Farms. The same Bug is known to the Northward and is there denominated the Hessian Fly.

I fear I have intruded too much on your Time, and therefore beg Leave to conclude by recommending to you the Bearer Mr. John Ammonett; he is an honest unsuspicious young Man, and will be obliged to you for your Assistance in the prosecution of a Claim he has in France in Right of his Father who was a Hugenot.

I have the Honour to be very respectfully Sir your most Obt. Sert.,   Wm. Hay

Doctr. Currie wishes in Case an Exchange coulde be made, to have the Dictionary of the Arts & Sciences in English which you esteem the best and the Balance in approved Histories in the English Language. He does not write himself, and requested I would intimate the above to you. WM. HAY

RC (DLC). The postscript has become separated from the text of the letter and is now in MHi. Recorded in SJL as received 30 June 1787.

From John Sullivan, with Account of Expenses for Obtaining Moose Skeleton

DEAR SIR   Durham April 26th. 1787

This Letter comes by my good friend Captain Samuel Pierce on board of whose vessel I send a Large Box containing the Articles mentioned in the Inclosed Account, which will show you the amount of Expences. A copy of my directions to him which I also inclose will show the means used by me to forward those expensive Curiosities to you. Capt. Pierce from motives of friendship for me has engaged to transport it to England and forward it to havre De Grace without any Expence except what may be Demanded for the Conveyance from England to France. And from motives of friendship for you I only Charge for the expences I have paid in Cash without any thing for my own Trouble which has been very considerable. I wish them safe to hand and am very respectfully sir Your most obedt. Servt.,   JNO. SULLIVAN

ENCLOSURE

His Excellency Thos. Jefferson Esqr. To Jno. Sullivan Dr.
1787

	£	s	d
To paid Capt. Robert Colburn for the Skeleton of a moose and Transporting to Durham	28	13	2
To a pair of moose horns and Expence of procuring them		3	15	0
To a pair of Elks horns & expence of procuring	2	10	0
To a pair of Deers horns & expence of procuring	1	10	0
To a pair of Carribous Horns & Expence of procuring	3	15	0
To expence of cleansing the Skeleton from flesh and salting and tending the same to prevent putrefaction	2	14	0
To paid a Tanner for fleshing the Skins		12	0
To paid Expence of Dressing the Skins to preserve it with the hair on, free from worms &c with expence of Allum brick Dust & Tobacco	2	18	0
To paid Expence of a Box and putting up the skeleton &c		16	0
To expence of sending the Box to Portsmouth		12	0

To paid for horns of the Spike hornd Buck		18	0
To paid Expence of 3 times sending to Effingham Connecticut River and the province of Main, to procure the skeleton	12	0	0
To Truckage and Storage paid at Durham and Portsmouth	1	4	0
Errors Excepted Lawful money	61	17	2
Equal in Sterlg. to	46	7	10½

To Jno. Sullivan

RC (DLC). Recorded in SJL as received 1 Sep. 1787 (TJ did not receive Sullivan's letters of 16 and 17 Apr. and 29 May until 26 Sep. 1787). Enclosures: (1) Account of expenses, as above (DLC). (2) Sullivan to Samuel Pearce, 26 Apr. 1787, informing him that the box in his custody "contains the skin, horns and skeleton of a Moose; the horns of the Carribou, Elk, Deer and the spike horn'd Buck"; also requesting him to keep the box right side up as directed; to "preserve it from wet, and give it as much air as possible, without exposing it to heat"; and to send it to the American consul at Le Havre "with my letter to him and the other to Governor Jefferson" (DLC). This letter and enclosure were sent to TJ with Sullivan's of 9 May 1787, q.v.

From John Sullivan

Dear Sir   Durham April 27th. 1787

By my Last I informed you that I had drawn on you for forty five pounds sterling, but Bills on france not having a market here at this time the Bills are returned, and I now Draw on you in favor of Colo. William Smith Secretary to Mr. Adams for forty six pounds seventeen shillings and ten pence being the Ballance of my Account forwarded by Capt. Samuel Pierce, which Draught I doubt not you will honor by payment within the Ten Days Limited in the Bills. The Draught I have made on him is for the same sum at Thirty Days sight which I doubt not he will duly honor upon the Credit of my Draught on you in his favor.

With great respect and Esteem I have the Honor to be sir Yr. Excellencys most obedt. Servt.,   JNO. SULLIVAN

RC (DLC). Recorded in SJL as received 18 July 1787 from "Durham Works." The letter was sent under cover of Sullivan to William Stephens Smith, 27 Apr. 1787 (DLC), which in turn enclosed the draft (see Abigail Adams Smith to TJ, 11 July 1787).

MY LAST: That is, Sullivan's of 17 Apr. 1787, which bore the same relation to the letter of 16 Apr. that the present bears to that of 26 Apr.—that is, to inform that a draft had been drawn.

From Richard O'Bryen

Algiers, 28 Apr. 1787. Is afraid that, unless some speedy measures for redemption are adopted, his crew will be carried off by the plague which "rages so much," because they are "employed on the most laborious work and so much exhausted"; 215 people died in Algiers on the 22nd of April and 200 Christian slaves have died in the last three months. The Spaniards and Neapolitans having redeemed their slaves, there are about 800 slaves belonging to the government and 120 owned privately. Expects his crew to be called to marine duty. One of his crew died of the plague; another suffered from it for fourteen days but has recovered. Allowing the captives to remain in slavery serves no purpose in securing a peace; the redemption of captives and making a peace are separate negotiations. Believes the Dey and his ministers "consider that they made a regular bargain with Mr. Lamb for our ransom"; that it is recorded "on the public books"; and that in any future negotiations the Dey would maintain that the Americans had made a bargain and not fulfilled it. "It seems the Neapolitan Ambassador had obtained a truce with this Regency for three months, and the Ambassador wrote his court of his success, but about the 1st. of April when the cruisers were fitting out, the Ambassador went to the Dey and hoped the Dey would give the necessary orders to the Captains of his cruisers not to take the Neapolitan vessels. The Dey said the meaning of the truce was for not to take the Neapolitan cruisers, but if his chebecs should meet the Neapolitan merchantmen to take them and send them for Algiers. The Ambassador said that the Neapolitan cruisers would not want a pass on those terms. The Dey said if his chebecks should meet either men of war or merchant vessels to take them, so gave orders accordingly. The Algerines sailed the 9th. inst. and are gone I believe off the coast of Italy. This shews there is very little confidence to be put in the royal word. No principal of national honor will bind those people and I believe not much confidence to be put in them in treaties. The Algerines are not inclinable to a peace, with the Neapolitans. I hear of no negociation. When the two frigates arrive with the money for the ransom of the slaves I believe they are done with the Neapolitans."[1] It is not to the advantage of the Algerines to make peace with Naples because that country is situated so nearby that it is easy to capture its vessels; it would be much easier and cheaper for the Americans to make peace because of their distant location. Spain paid 1,200,000 dollars for her peace. When the present Dey dies there will be great changes in the policy of the Regency, "making war on some and making peace on others. It is a great thing in a peace with Algiers to make the treaty with the Dey that has just got the government in his hands as it may be more likely he might keep to the treaty he made himself and they generally do not mind what treaties the former Deys make." No agent of another nation can be trusted to lay the foundation for a peace for the United States because those nations which are at peace with Algiers do not want any others to secure a peace. "Before the war the Americans used to employ 200 sail of merchantmen in the streights trade, and used to reap great advantages by it. But at present our trade is but small being cramped on all quarters." It is best to treat through those who are close to the Dey and money and presents are the only sure approach. "Mr. Woulf," an English merchant, and "Mr. Fauri," watchmaker to the Dey, are proper persons in Algiers to employ for preliminary negotiations.

Tr (DNA: RG 59, Consular Dispatches); in the hand of William Short; endorsed. Tr of extract (same, Misc. Letters Recd.); in a clerk's hand; at head of text, in TJ's hand: "No. 4." PrC of another Tr of extract (DLC); also with "No. 4" in TJ's hand. Tr (DNA: State Dept. Reports); incorporated as document "No. 4" in TJ's report to the House of Representatives on U.S. trade in the Mediterranean, 28 Dec. 1790. Recorded in SJL as received 31 May 1787 at Nantes; copy sent to John Jay in TJ's letter of 21 June 1787. The greater part of this letter is printed in *Barbary Wars*, I, 14-17.

[1] The text enclosed in this set of quotation marks constitutes the whole of the extract used in TJ's 1790 report on Mediterranean trade.

From Charles Thomson

DEAR SIR New York April 28. 1787

On the 30 July 1786 I acknowledged the receipt of your letter of the 10 May, wherein you informed me that a botanical friend of yours had written to Charleston for a number of plants and seeds which were to be sent to me and forwarded to you by the packet. I heard no more of this matter till yesterday when Capt. Lathim delivered me the letter and invoice of which I enclose a copy and informed me the boxes were on board ready to be delivered. I sent immediately to the french Consul to know if the packet was gone. Unfortunately she had sailed the day before.[1] As I was obliged to leave town in a day or two and expect to be some weeks absent I consulted Mr. Otto who was so obliging as to take charge of the boxes and promises to send them by the next packet.[2] And I have requested the favour of him in case the other box by Capt. Tinker arrives before the packet sails to receive and send it also.

I have received your favour of the 17 Decr. last and am very sorry to hear of your misfortune. I hope before this time you have perfectly recovered the use of your wrist.

In referring you to Mr. Whitehurst I did not mean to recommend him as an Author on which you were to build your faith. But I think you will give him credit for solving some of the objections started by other theorists against the universality of the deluge; and for accounting with a great deal of ingenuity for the present appearances and irregularities on the face of our globe. His eruption will tolerably well account for the oblique position of the strata of rocks which is observable in most parts of the world. But what are we to think of their horizontal position in our Western country? Mr. Hutchins the geographer general as well as every other intelligent observer who has been in that country assert this to be the case. Are we to suppose that the surface of the earth in that part of our globe was never broken up?

29 APRIL 1787

A gentleman now in that country lately wrote to me and after mentioning the tradition, which, Doct. Robertson says prevailed among the old Mexicans, that their Ancestors came from the northward about the 10th. century, has endeavoured to shew from relicks still remaining that they went from the country bordering on the Ohio. For want of something more entertaining I send you an extract of his letter and am with sincere esteem & affection Dr. Sir Your most obedient & humble Servt.,   CHAS. THOMSON

The three Boxes 19£. 16s. dollrs. @ 4/8 . . . .   84.85
    freight 1½ dollar 1.50
                                                         ─────
                                                         86.35 Dollars

RC (DLC). Dft (DLC: Thomson Papers). Recorded in SJL as received 1 Sep. 1787. Enclosures: (1) Thomson's phraseology suggests that he enclosed both THE LETTER AND INVOICE, whereas the appended notation of cost and the absence of any record in SJL of receipt of such enclosures on 1 Sep. 1787 suggest that he did neither. (2) Extract of a letter from "a gentleman now in that country": that is, an unsigned Tr (DLC) of a letter from John Cleves Symmes, dated Louisville, 4 Feb. 1787, to Thomson, the whole of which is printed in N.Y. Hist. Soc., *Colls.*, XI (1878), 233-9; the extract consists of all save the opening and closing lines of Symmes' letter.

Thomson wrote to Otto on 28 Apr. 1787 (Dft in DLC: Thomson Papers) saying that the "three Boxes, which you were so obliging as to take charge of are to be forwarded in the first packet that sails for France, to Mr. Jefferson," and asking that the fourth by CAPT. TINKER be forwarded if it arrived in time; he listed the contents of the three boxes as follows:
"N1.   4 Olea Americana

2.   4 Magnolia tripetala
3.   4 Laurus Borbonia
4   4 Prenos glabia
5   4 Cyrella raseimefera
6.   4 Rosa carolina
7   4 Diosperis Verginica
8   4 Cideroxalum tenax
9   4 Lycudamber styraceflua
10   4 Calicarpia Americana
11   4 Andromeda nova species
12   4 Andromeda   do   do
13   4 Larus   do   do
14   4 Rhamnui   do   do
15   4 Planta nova do   do
16   4   do   do   do
17   4 Polyandria moniginia nov. genus
18   4 Yucca   nova species
19   Gordonia lasiarithus
20   Rhamnui pilubile
21   Fothergilla gardini"

[1] Opposite this word is a marginal note in TJ's hand, which reads: "viz Apr. 25."
[2] Opposite this word is the date of its scheduled sailing in TJ's hand: "June 10."

From Chastellux

A Paris le 29 avril 1787

J'ai eté charmé, mon cher et respectable ami, de recevoir de vos nouvelles, et j'ai vu aussi avec la plus grande satisfaction que vous etes content de votre voyage. Tout le patriotisme de mon coeur se réveille quand Monsieur Jefferson visite mon pais. Je voudrois faire comme les meres qui presentent leurs filles dans quelqu'assemblée nombreuse et qui, tenant toujours les yeux fixés sur elles,

les avertissent par leurs regards de veiller sur leur maintien et sur leurs moindres gestes. Vous aurés trouvé, mon cher ami, que nous n'avons pas répondu partout aux bienfaits que la nature nous a prodigué, mais partout où vous aurés reconnu le mal, vous aurés trouvé le remede possible, et même aisé. Qu'il me tarde de causer avec vous de ce que vous aurés vû et remarqué! Mais je crains que Tours ne reponde pas suffisamment à votre attente. Ce pais offre peu de curiosité d'histoire naturelle, et je crois que ce fameux banc de coquille doit sa plus grande celebrité à l'auteur qui en a parlé. Monsieur l'intendant de Tours à qui je me suis adressé pour remplir vos intentions a ecrit ce matin à *Mr. Gentil, premier secretaire de l'intendance* et l'a prévenu que vous desiriés voir beaucoup de choses et très peu d'honneurs, que vous voyagiés comme simple particulier et non comme ministre des etats unis. Vous voudrés bien, mon cher ami, à votre arrivée à Tours, passer chés ce monsieur Gentil. Il vous donnera les personnes les plus propres à vous conduire, suivant les objets que vous désirerés de voir. Un inspecteur vous menera dans les Manufactures, un ingenieur des ponts et chaussés aux [sablières?] et aux autres endroits qui seront dignes d'exciter votre curiosité. Je vous invite à voir Chanteloup en revenant à Paris, car selon toute apparence, vous prendrés le chemin d'Orleans. Vous ferés bien aussi de vous arretter une heure au chateau de Ménars. Vous changerés de chevaux à cet endroit même et vous ne serés pas fâché de voir le chateau qui a appartenu à la celebre Madame de Pompadour.

Comme je ne sais pas à quelle epoque vous recevrés ma lettre, je ne vous dirai pas beaucoup de nouvelles. L'assemblée des notables est occupée à examiner les comptes de recettes et de dépenses que le Roi lui a fait remettre. On discute aussi l'édit pour le *timbre* qui ne sera pas productif en France des mêmes effets qu'il a eus en Amerique. Ce mot de *timbre* n'est jamais prononcé sans exciter une vive émotion dans mon ame; puisque sans lui, l'Amerique n'auroit pas obtenu sa liberté et moi l'amitié de M. Jefferson. Tout est tranquille dans le levant. L'imperatrice de Russie ne sera que 3 jours à chezon [Kerson] et retournera à Petersbourg, sans que son voyage ait troublé d'autres repos que celui des chevaux.

Adieu, mon cher et excellent ami, arrivés comme une abeille qui s'est chargée de butin. Puissiés vous n'avoir trouvé que des fleurs sur votre chemin. L'amitié vous en prepare à votre retour qui sera une veritable fête pour elle.

LE MIS. DE CHASTELLUX

RC (MoSHi); endorsed.

From John Sullivan

Dear Sir   Durham April 30th. 1787

Capt. Pierce having been detained by Contrary winds I took an opportunity of sending to Barstead for a pair of Roe Bucks Horns. This Kind of Deer is very uncommon in America and his horns a very great Curiosity. The horns never grow Larger than those I send nor do those of the spike horned Buck ever exceed in size those I send you. These come free of Charge from your Excellenceys most obedt. servt.,   Jno. Sullivan

RC (DLC). Recorded in SJL as received 1 Sep. 1787; enclosed in Sullivan to TJ, 9 May 1787.

To William Short

Dear Sir   Nice May 1. 1787.

I arrived here this evening, and set out tomorrow morning at day break for Marseilles. From thence I must write to Mr. Jay, and I cannot write till I receive some information at Marseilles. The letter will get to Paris the 8th. or perhaps not till the 9th. and as the packet should sail the 10th. the object of this letter is to pray you to have a trusty Courier ready to start for Havre the moment my letter for Mr. Jay comes to your hand. He should go by the Diligence as far as that goes without stopping, and then by post horses and return by the Diligence. I fear, with all this, there is a possibility of missing the occasion by the packet: however, the wind or other accident may perhaps retard her. If she is gone, he should bring back the letter. Should M. de Crevecoeur be going, I should be very happy to have it put into his hands: otherwise you must be so good as to desire M. Limosin to put it into good hands on board the packet. Does the order against receiving letters after the mail is made up on board the packet still subsist? If it does, it may be necessary to ask a special order from M. Le Couteulx, because if Limozin can not get a trusty hand to take private charge of it, it must go into the mail at Havre.—I have been thus streightened in time by contrary winds which came upon me half way from Genoa here and obliged me to quit my Felucca and take mules, so that I have been 4. days instead of 2. on the way. The 1st. a day of mortal sea-sickness, the last two of great fatigue on the mules and on foot clambering the precipices of the Appennines. This disposes me more to sleep than to write; after

2 MAY 1787

desiring you therefore to let my daughter know I am well and that she shall hear from me at Marseilles, I shall conclude with assurances of the sincere esteem with which I am Dr. Sir your affectionate friend & servant, TH: JEFFERSON

P.S. Be so good as to have my letters henceforth sent to Nantes poste restante. If in the mean time any thing was to arise to call me instantly to Paris, letters lodged with our agents at Bourdeaux, Nantes, L'orient, would find me at one of those places; according to the time at which they should come.

RC (ViW); without indication of addressee; endorsed: "Jefferson May. 1 87 [received] 13." Not recorded in SJL. As Short's endorsement indicates, TJ's fear of MISSING . . . THE PACKET with his important letter of 4 May to Jay was well grounded and his precautions in the present letter were to no avail (see Short to TJ, 14 May 1787).

From James Currie

HBLE. SIR Richmond May 2d. 1787

In the midst of bustle and confusion I take the liberty to write you a few lines, by Mr. John Ammonett a native of Chesterfield County who I understand is come over to France in the Ship Robert, Capt. Ramsay. He is a descendant of French Emigrants here about the year 1700—and is now come to France in quest of an estate, to which he thinks he has a just claim, after the Vouchers of his Authenticity which he will bring over with him. He has been in different Stores here, tho young in business and with one of the best hearts in the World, unequal to the task he has now undertaken without some friendly aid. Any Services you can with propriety render him in investigating this claim with your best advice to him how to act in every respect whatever, and of which he'll stand in need, I shall thank you and it will be obliging a man who will be ever gratefull for the favor conferred upon him. The last letter I had the honor of receiving from your Excellency was dated Paris Jany. 28th. 86. Since which time, I had the pleasure of receiving a Number of Volumes and half Volumes of the Encyclopædia, tho not bound as you once intended I believe, from what your letter says of the binding being cheaper in France than elsewhere. Colo. Munroe's came by same Opportunity which I had care taken of and delivered to him. I thank you likewise for the other Books sent me upon Air &c. &c. My friend Mr. Wm. Hay

[327]

2 MAY 1787

has had their perusal and much delighted with them, as well as the Encyclopædia of which it is probable he has informed you as he writes by this Opportunity. My knowledge in the French has rather diminished than encreased since you left us, being kept in a constant bustle with a variety of attentions to mechanickes of different kinds &c., all of which have vanished into smoke.

The Observations you made upon Messrs. Jay and Little Page were pertinent and too just. Their altercation happened after the date of my letter and after L. P. left this place on his Way to France. His head I thought a good one, his heart I wish I may not have been disapointed in.

I have spoke several times to Archbd. Stuart, concerning the different things he was to procure for you and which I told him I would contrive to you in France. He tells me he has as yet been unable to procure any of them tho in hopes he soon will. I forwarded some time ago a Box from Colo. N. Lewis containing leaves seeds &c. &c., the produce of this Country, by the Way of P. Mouth Virga. to L'Orient. As Neil Jamieson has long left New York and Alexander's Ships are monthly sailing for France, I preferred the nighest Port as the safest. Further I forwarded several Packetts from you sent on by Edwd. Carrington to my care to Colo. N. Lewis, Colo. Banister &c. &c., all of whom have been received before now. Ross and Pleasants had some time ago respectively letters from you and intend themselves the honor of soon writing you; Mr. Wm. Hay I fancy will give you a short sketch of the internal state of this Country at present, in regard to agriculture and manufacture, which have been both shamefully neglected and the last almost entirely laid aside since the return of peace. Your designs for the Capitol arrived long ago and pleased I believe very much, but alas the fund voted by last Assembly is altogether unproductive and I fear exceedingly, and indeed am almost certain, that nothing will be done this year in the matter. We have likewise a French Academy and play house under one roof established by a Mr. Quesnay who I believe is now in France. The[y] stand so near together, that I cant help feeling hurt at 2 such objects of our folly and impotence, as both are unfinished and likely to remain so for some time to come. With much difficulty the Canal from W. Ham here has been kept going on and tho perfectly practicable, I shall be very agreeably dissapointed, if it does not soon stop likewise. We are a Luxurious Voluptuous indolent expensive people without Œconomy or Industry. Our private and publick Virtue you can judge of. Our publick and private faith are much

2 MAY 1787

shaken since you left the American Continent and in short without some speedy and Effectual as well as prudently administred remedy I may venture to say that we are on the Eve of political Damnation. I have just now while writing been informed that Congress have resolved that a payment of British debts is to take place, and it will be communicated to the publick very soon. The Expediency and policy of the Measure, I expect, they have maturely weighed. I wish for the Sake of this Country the Doctrine had been inculcated from the moment peace took place as it would have stimulated to Œconomy and Industry thousands who have been quite the reverse and who unavoidably will and must fall Victims to their extreme imprudence and ill timed show and dissipation of every kind.

Every thing pointed politically respecting this country you hear no doubt from those the best informed, therefore shall not say any thing from my own knowledge, in regard to individualls, or particulars respecting the country at large, but leave that to the Statesmen of our country and your correspondents here; your friends here are all pretty well. Your nephew Mr. P. Kerr I am informed has made considerable progress in his Education. I see him now and then; he was lately here at Mr. Eppes. Miss Polly will inform you of Eppington &c. I believe I before told you Col. R. Randolph Curles died about 12 Months ago. Your old friend Colo. Cary of Ampthill left the stage the 27th. of last Feby. about 2 in the morning and I believe from every one I have heard that no Gentleman of this Country in the memory of man ever left his affairs so distracted. The debts are immense. I had almost said innumerable. His family will be left very bare indeed. The Executions of your friends Eppes and Skipwith and that of Tayloe's Executors are now tearing the Estate to pieces, tho they are blameless, only with much difficulty now getting what they long ago were entitled to. Those of his family he has left have my friendly and most cordial Sympathy.

A Fire broke out in this City the 8 of Jany. 87. about 4 in the morning that destroyed the most flourishing and wealthy part of this small place. I lost an Estate, that was about bringing me in (having just completed my buildings) £700. p. annum. In 2 hours the deed was done. The general opinion is that it was done on purpose; nothing has ever been done by Government or the Corporation to endeavor to discover the perpetrators of the dark deed. Many are wholly ruined and as many more almost irrecoverably injured. Among which class I rank myself. It occasioned, I must confess, a shock from which I am not yet entirely relieved. Time I hope will efface the painfull reflection that I was deprived without any fault of my own of the fruit of many years hard earned industry in the very moment of expected fruition (as no return of rents had ever been made) for disbursements that for me, were immense. It will ever confer much honor and give me real and very sincere pleasure to have a letter from you when ever you please. The Oftner it will be the more agreeable to me; I was sorry to understand by the Governor E. R. Esqr. you had received an Injury in one of your arms or hands. I hope it is well before you read this letter. I should be glad if it is not ill timed or impertinent to be informed confidentially whether you have any views of returning soon (or ever) to your native Country. There never was a time when it was more in want of able statesmen than the present. I'll thank you to tender my very respectfull Compliments to Miss Jefferson, who will receive a letter from Tuckahoe herewith enclosed. And tell Mr. Short I send him sound health and good spirits &c. &c. that is good. In flattering hopes of hearing from you soon and pretty frequently, I have the honor to Subscribe myself Yr. Excellency's most obt. & Very H. Servt.,

JAMES CURRIE

P.S. Mr. Jas. Buchanan has been confined with a dangerous illness 2 Months and will be a considerable time longer. I believe the publick buildings &c. &c. are hurt by his absence.

RC (DLC); endorsed. Recorded in SJL as received 30 June 1787. Enclosure not identified.

From William Fleming

SIR Richmond, 2d. May, 1787.

This will be handed to you by Mr. John Amonat, a native of the Manakin town, of French ancestry, who is going to France in quest of a patrimonial estate. He has lived some time in this city, in the mercantile line, and is a young man of excellent character, but of great simplicity; and, from his inexperience in life, and from his want of knowledge of the French language, I am apprehensive he will find himself much at a loss in the pursuit of his object.

I am persuaded, sir, that you will want no other impulse than your own benign disposition to offer him your advice and countenance in a matter which, to him, will be of great importance and difficulty.

By particular desire of Mr. Eppes, he goes in the ship with Miss Polly Jefferson; and, from his philanthropy, and obliging disposition, I have not a doubt but he will pay her every proper attention that circumstances will admit, to alleviate the irksomeness of the voiage, and to support her spirits, in times of bad weather.—I most sincerely wish her a pleasant passage, and a happy meeting you and her sister.

You have, no doubt sir, been informed that a congress, to be composed of delegates from the several states in the union, elected for the especial purpose of reforming the Confederation, are to meet in Philadelphia, early in this month. The members from this state are General Washington, Geo: Mason, Geo: Wythe, John Blair, Edmd. Randolph, James Madison, and Dr. McClurg, instead of P. Henry, who did not accept his appointment.

Expectations are formed that this convention will lay a foundation for energy and Stability in our federal government, and for rendering us, as a nation, more respected abroad; though I am apprehensive, as there are many different objects and interests to reconcile, it will be a work of time and of difficulty.

We have, for some time, had a cold and dry season, very unfavourable for Tobacco plants, of which there seems to be a general scarcity; but those who were careful to keep their beds closely covered with brush, have great plenty.

I have the honor to be, with great regard, sir, your friend, and obedt. serv., WM. FLEMING

RC (DLC); endorsed. Recorded in SJL as received 30 June 1787.

From Peter J. Bergius

MONSIEUR   Stockholm ce 3 de mai, 1787.

J'ai l'honneur de Vous presenter ma sincere reconnoissance pour Votre bonté avec le diplome de l'illustre Societé litteraire de l'Amerique.

C'est un bonheur pour moi d'être favorablement connu d'un corps si respectable. Je tacherai à mon tour de me faire digne de ce souvenir flateur. Mr. Sparrman, professeur de l'histoire naturelle à Stockholm, et membre de notre Academie des sciences, Vous presentera cette lettre, et en même tems, temoignera le devouëment respectuëux avec lequel j'ai l'honneur d'être Monsieur votre tres humble et tres obeïssant Serviteur, P: J: BERGIUS

Je me prend la liberté de joindre ici un memoire, que j'ai adressé à Votre Societé litteraire illustre.

RC (DLC); endorsed. Recorded in SJL as received 26 July 1787. Enclosure not identified; if received by TJ, it evidently was not forwarded to the American Philosophical Society, for that institution has no record of having received such a memoire by Bergius (communication of Gertrude D. Hess to the editors, 27 Jan. 1955).

To Castries

Aix en Provence. May 3. 1787.

I have received at this place the letter of the 19th. of April which your Excellency did me the honor of writing on the claim of Nicholas Valentin Fontaine for services performed on board the Indian, while employed by the state of South Carolina. I am an entire stranger to the other difficulties which have hitherto retarded the adjustment of those claims. One however has lately become known to me, as the documents were sent thro my hands to our Chargé des affaires at Madrid for the settlement of a very considerable demand against that court, for services rendered by the same vessel. I will immediately transmit, for the Government of South Carolina your Excellency's letter, and may assure you beforehand of the respect with which that and whatever comes from you, will be attended to. I shall with pleasure communicate to the parties interested, in the first possible moment, such resolutions as the government of South Carolina may take for the final liquidation and paiment of their claims: and avail myself of every occasion of offering you the homage of those sentiments of respect and attachment with which I have the honor to be your Excellency's most obedient & most humble servant, TH: JEFFERSON

PrC (DLC).

From William Hay

SIR Richmond May 3d. 1787.

Your favour of the 26th. December inclosing Bill of Lading for the Model of the Capitol came safe to hand, adressed to Mr. Buchanan and myself, and have to appologize for answering it in my private Capacity. There has not been a Meeting of the Directors of the Public Buildings for some considerable Time past and Mr. Buchanan is now confined by a severe spell of Sickness, so that I could neither have the Advice of the Directors nor the Assistance of Mr. Buchanan in the Business. No Delay in the work has been occasioned by the Models not coming to hand, last Summer, and I fear it will stop where it now is for some Time. The pedestal Basement and the principal story were finished by last October, and nothing has been done since. The fund of the 2 p.ct. Additional Duties upon which was charged £5000 to be applied towards completing the public Buildings, has proved unproductive, for the Treasurer assures me, it will not produce the sum which was charged on it in the first Instance for the support of the Members of Congress. The Directors therefore can make no Contract upon this Fund without sacrificing too much to the extravagance of the Times, and when the Assembly meets again I fear no further Assistance will be given on account of the Distress which is universally complained of thro' the State. The Capitol may then remain in its present state for many Years. The Directors themselves have been neglectful, in many things and in none more, than in the want of Acknowledgements to you, for the great Assistance you have given them in this Business. Permit me therefore, to return my sincere thanks, and I am sure they will be those of the Directors in general, for the Interest you have taken in procuring proper Plans and a model for the Ornamenting the Capital of your native Country, and to assure you that I have the Honour to be with Perfect Esteem Sir Your most Obt. Hb. Ser.,   WM. HAY

RC (DLC); endorsed. Recorded in SJL as received 30 June 1787.

From Martha Jefferson

MY DEAR PAPA   Paris May 3 1787

I was very sorry to see by your letter To Mr. Short that your return would be put off, however I hope of not much, as you must be here for the arival of my sister. I wish I was my self all that you tell me to make her, however I will try to be as near like it as I can. I have another landskape since I wrote to you last and began another peice of music. I have not been able to do more having been confined some time to my bed with a violent head ake and a pain in my side which afterwards blistered up and made me

[333]

3 MAY 1787

suffer a great deal. But I am now much better. I have seen a phisician who has just drawn two of my companions out of a most dreadful situation which gave me a great deal of trust in him but the most disagreable is that I have been obliged to discontinue all my masters and am able now to take only some of them, those that are the least fatiguing. However I hope soon to take them all very soon. Mde. L'abesse has just had a fluxion de poitrine and has been at the last extremity but now is better. The *pays bas* have revolted against the emperor who is gone to Prussia to join with the empress and the venitians to war against the turcs. The plague is in spain. A virginia ship comming to spain met with a corser of the same strength. They fought And the battle lasted an hour and a quarter. The Americans gained and boarded the corser where they found chains that had been prepared for them. They took them and made use of them for the algerians them selves. They returned to virginia from whence they are to go back to algers to change the prisoners to which if the algerians will not consent the poor creatures will be sold as slaves. Good god have we not enough? I wish with all my soul that the poor negroes were all freed. It greives my heart when I think that these our fellow creatures should be treated so teribly as they are by many of our country men. A coach and six well shut up was seen to go to the bastille and the baron de Breteuil went two hours before to prepare an apartment. They supose it to be Mde. De Polignac and her sister, however no one knows. The king asked Mr. D'harcourt how much a year was necessary for the Dauphin. M. D'harcourt [af]ter having looked over the accounts told [him] two millions upon which the king could [not] help expressing his astonishement because each of his daughters cost him nine, so Mde. de Polignac has pocketed the rest. Mr. Smith is at Paris. That is all the news I know. They told me a great deal more but I have forgot it. Adieu my dear papa believe me to be for life your most tender and affectionate child,

M JEFFERSON

RC (MHi); addressed and endorsed. Recorded in SJL as received 31 May 1787 at Nantes, being enclosed in Short to TJ, 8 May 1787.

To Rigoley d'Ogny

à Aix en Provence. 3me. Mai. 1787.

Je viens de recevoir içi, Monsieur le Baron, à mon retour d'une petite voiage au-delà des Alpes la lettre, en date 6me. Avril, dont

[334]

vous avez bien voulu m'honorer. Agreez, je vous en prie mes remercimens pour votre bonté en faisant remettre en franchise le paquet de gazettes qui m'avoit eté adressé de New York par la voye des paquebots français. Il y a longtems que j'ai vu avec regret les inconvenients qui resultent de ce qu'il n'y a rien encore de reglé pour la correspondance entre la France et les etats unis. J'ai ecrit là dessus au Congrès, et je suis charmé que votre lettre me donne occasion de rapeller encore cet objet à leur attention. Je saisirai avec empressement le premier moment que leurs ordres me permettront d'entrer en arrangement avec vous sur cet objet, et je me profite de cette occasion de vous donner les assurances les plus sinceres de ces sentimens de respect et d'attachement avec lesquels j'ai l'honneur d'etre, Monsieur le baron, votre très humble et tres obeissant serviteur, TH: JEFFERSON

PrC (MHi); at foot of text: "M. le baron d'Ogny."

From Edmund Randolph

DEAR SIR Richmond May 3 1787

Mr. John Ammonett, who will deliver this letter into your hands, is a descendant from one of the French refugees, patronized and fixed here by King William. He has persuaded himself, upon seeing some publication or other, that restitution is to be made of all the property, which was abandoned by his ancestor. I know not, what testimonies he possesses of his right to inherit, but presume that he is properly provided. He has requested me to recommend him to your protection; to do which I am inclined from the knowledge of his good nature, and of the approbation, which he has received from the merchant, with whom he has lived, as an assistant. But I am convinced, that it would be a sufficient reason with you to befriend him, merely to learn that he is a helpless Virginian and meriting every favor, which integrity and an obliging disposition ought at any time to receive.

I am, dear sir, with great truth yr. friend and serv.

EDM: RANDOLPH

RC (DLC); endorsed. Recorded in SJL as received 30 June 1787.

From American Traders in Guadeloupe

Pointe à Pitre Guadéloupe 3d. May 1787.

MAY IT PLEASE YOUR EXCELLENCY

We the Proprietors, and masters of different Vessels belonging to the united states of America actually at anchor in this harbour take the liberty of addressing to your Excellency our Petition to the Marechal De Castries Secretary of State to his most Christian Majesty. Your Excellency's efforts [in] our favour, and representations to the Ministry shall undoubtedly hinder the inevitable ruin of our Trade in these parts, which the Execution of the King's Edict must naturally occasion.

This harbour is now shut up to Americans, and we are forced to dispose of our Cargoes at Basseterre, the only port where we are allowed to anchor at. This cruel revolution is attended with so many inconveniences that it not only hurts the Colony in general, but puts an absolute stop to our Commercial operations, and ruins the American traders whose speculations prompt them to frequent these Islands for a mutual exchange of their Commodities. We flatter ourselves that your Excellency will exert himself in our favour and obtain from his Majesty the revocation of this fatal Edict. The benefits that will accrue from such a repeal must be advantageous to the Commercial interest of America. We have the honour to remain Your Excellency's most obedient & very humble Servants,

WILLIAM RUSSELL	BENJN. SHILLABER
NAT. WHITMORE	JONA. MASON
PHOENIX FRAZIER	JOS. PEABODY
RICHD. TOPPAN	For twenty three more

RC (ViWC); endorsed by TJ: "Russell et al. on the removal of the free port in Guadeloupe from Pointe à Pitre to Basseterre." Recorded in SJL as received 9 July 1787. Enclosure: Dupl of petition to Castries, dated 3 May 1787, signed by those who signed the present letter to TJ, plus twelve others, all of whom signed "For ten more," setting forth the advantages of Pointe à Pitre over Basse-Terre—a good harbor, a central location near their customers, and facilities for transporting their cargoes on their own craft and taking on rum and molasses safely and quickly, whereas interests of both growers and shippers would be adversely affected by the decree—and requesting that they be allowed to continue using Pointe à Pitre (MS in ViWC; Tr in Short's hand in DLC; Tr in DNA: PCC, No. 107, II, the last being enclosed in TJ to Jay, 6 Aug. 1787).

To Ferdinand Grand

Dear Sir   Marseilles May 4. 1787.

I take the liberty of putting the inclosed letter under your cover to avoid it's being opened. It contains one for Mr. Jay which is to go by the packet sailing from Havre on the 10th. You will perceive therefore at the time of receiving this that there is not a moment to lose. I must therefore beg the favor of you to send a Commissioner instantly with it to my hotel: and, if Mr. Short should happen to be in the country as he may be, to instruct my Maitre d'Hotel to open the letter to Mr. Short, and to do what I have therein desired, which is to dispatch a courier instantly to Havre. Pardon me, Sir, for the trouble I give you which circumstances force me to, and be assured of the sentiments of esteem & respect with which I have the honour to be Sir your most obedient humble servt.,

Th: Jefferson

PrC (DLC). Enclosure: TJ to Short, this date, and its enclosure to Jay.
TJ was correct in supposing that Short might happen to be in the country (see Short to TJ, 14 May 1787).

From Delahais

Monsieur   Paris Ce 4. may 1787.

Permettés que je rappelle à votre Excellence Le payement des pensions de Messieurs Les officiers de L'amerique. Vous avés eu La bonté de me faire Esperer il y a déja du Tems que Ce payement ne Seroit point Eloigné; Cependant il ne se fait point et Monsieur Grand dit n'avoir reçu aucuns ordres à Ce sujet. Voila deux années Echües au premier Janvier Dernier: Je suis Chargé de les recevoir pour Monsieur Le Marquis de La Rouerie, M. Le Major Shaffner et Mon frere, qui m'en demandent Continuellement des Nouvelles et me Chargent de Vous prier de les faire payer. En conséquence J'ose prier Votre Excellence, pour Ces Messieurs de Vouloir bien presser les ordres necessaires pour Ce payement. J'aurois desiré Vous addresser moy même Cette priere de vive Voix, mais La Crainte de Vous être Trop à Charge m'a fait preferer Le party de vous l'addresser par Ecrit.

Je suis avec un profond respect Monsieur Votre Très humble et très Obéissant Serviteur,   Delahais

RC (DLC); endorsed. This is doubtless the letter which TJ incorrectly recorded in SJL as dated 24 May 1787 and received 25 May at Bordeaux.

To John Jay

Sir   Marseilles May 4. 1787.

I had the honour of receiving at Aix your letter of Feb. 9. and immediately wrote to the Count de Montmorin, explaining the delay of the answer of Congress to the king's letter, and desired Mr. Short to deliver that answer with my letter to Monsieur de Montmorin, which he accordingly informs me he has done.

My absence prevented my noting to you in the first moment the revolution which has taken place at Paris in the department of Finance by the substitution of Monsieur de Fourqueux in the place of Monsieur de Calonnes, so that you will have heard of it through other channels before this will have the honour of reaching you.

Having staid at Aix long enough to prove the inefficacy of the waters, I came on to this place for the purpose of informing myself here, as I mean to do at the other sea-port towns, of whatever may be interesting to our commerce. So far as carried on in our own bottoms, I find it almost nothing; and so it must probably remain till something can be done with the Algerines. Tho' severely afflicted with the plague, they have come out within these few days, and shewed themselves in force along the coast of Genoa, cannonading a little town and taking several vessels.

Among other objects of enquiry, this was the place to learn something more certain on the subject of rice, as it is a great emporium for that of the Levant and of Italy. I wished particularly to know whether it was the use of a different machine for cleaning which brought European rice to market less broken than ours, as had been represented to me by those who deal in that article in Paris. I found several persons who had passed thro' the rice country of Italy, but not one who could explain to me the nature of the machine. But I was given to believe that I might see it myself immediately on entering Piedmont. As this would require but about three weeks I determined to go and ascertain this point; as the chance only of placing our rice above all rivalship in quality as it is in colour, by the introduction of a better machine, if a better existed, seemed to justify the application of that much time to it. I found the rice country to be in truth Lombardy, 100 miles further than had been represented, and that tho' called Piedmont rice, not a grain is made in the country of Piedmont. I passed thro the rice feilds of the Vercellese, and Milanese, about 60 miles, and returned from thence last night, having found that the machine is absolutely

4 MAY 1787

the same as ours, and of course that we need not listen more to that suggestion. It is a difference in the species of grain, of which the government of Turin is so sensible, that, as I was informed, they prohibit the exportation of rough rice on pain of death. I have taken measures however for obtaining a quantity of it, which I think will not fail, and I bought on the spot a small parcel which I have with me. As further details on this subject to Congress would be displaced,[1] I propose on my return to Paris to communicate them, and send the rice to the Society at Charlestown for promoting agriculture, supposing that they will be best able to try the experiment of cultivating the rice of this quality: and to communicate the species to the two states of S. Carolina and Georgia if they find it answer. I thought the staple of these two states was entitled to this attention, and that it must be desireable to them to be able to furnish rice of the two qualities demanded in Europe, especially as the greater consumption is in the forms for which the Lombardy quality is preferred. The mass of our countrymen being interested in agriculture, I hope I do not err in supposing that in a time of profound peace as the present, to enable them to adapt their productions to the market, to point out markets for them, and endeavor to obtain favourable terms of reception, is within the line of my duty.

My journey into this part of the country has procured me information which I will take the liberty of communicating to Congress. In October last I received a letter dated Montpelier Octob. 2. 1786. announcing to me that the writer was a foreigner who had a matter of very great consequence to communicate to me, and desired I would indicate the channel thro which it might pass safely. I did so. I received soon after a letter in the following words, omitting only the formal parts. . . .[2] As by this time I had been advised to try the waters of Aix, I [wrote] to the gentleman my design, and that I would go off my road as far as Nismes, under the pretext of seeing the antiquities of that place, if he would meet me there. He met me, and the following is the sum of the information I received from him. 'Brazil contains as many inhabitants as Portugal. They are 1. Portuguese. 2. Native whites. 3. black and mulatto slaves. 4. Indians civilized and savage. 1. The Portuguese are few in number, mostly married there, have lost sight of their native country, as well as the prospect of returning to it, and are disposed to become independant. 2. The native whites form the body of their nation. 3. The slaves are as numerous as the free. 4. The civilized Indians have no energy, and the savage would not meddle. There are 20,000 regular troops. Originally these were Portuguese; but as they died off they were replaced by natives, so that these compose at present the mass of the troops and may be counted on by their native country. The officers are partly Portuguese, partly Brasilians: their bravery is not doubted, and they understand the parade but not the science of their profession. They have no bias for Portugal, but no energy neither for any thing. The Priests are partly Portuguese, partly Brasilians, and will not interest themselves much. The Noblesse are scarcely known as such. They will in no manner be distinguished from the people. The men of letters are those most desirous of a revolution. The people are not much under the influence of their priests, most of them read and write, possess arms, and are in the habit of using them for hunting. The slaves will take the side of their masters. In short, as to the question of revolution, there is but one mind in that country. But there appears no person capable of conducting a revolution, or willing to venture[3] himself at it's head, without the aid of some powerful nation, as the people of their own might fail them. There is no printing press in Brasil. They consider the North American revolution as a precedent for theirs. They look to the United States as most likely to give them honest support, and from a variety of considerations have the strongest prejudices in our favor. This informant is a native and inhabitant of Rio Janeiro the present metropolis, which contains 50,000 inhabitants, knows well St. Salvador the former one, and the Mines d'or which are in the center of the country. These are all for a revolution, and, constituting the body of the nation, the other parts will follow them. The king's fifth of the mines yields annually 13. millions of crusadoes or half dollars. He has the sole right of searching for diamonds and other precious stones, which yields him about half as much. His income alone then from these two resources, is about 10. millions of dollars annually. But the remaining part of the produce of the mines, being 26. millions, might be counted on for effecting a revolution. Besides the arms in the hands of the people, there are public magazines. They have abundance of horses, but only a part of their country would admit the service of horses. They would want cannon, ammunition, ships, sailors, souldiers, and officers, for which they are disposed to look to the U.S., always understood that every service and furniture will be well paid. Corn costs about 20 livres the 100 ℔. They have flesh in the greatest abundance, insomuch that in some parts they kill

4 MAY 1787

beeves for the skin only. The whale fishery is carried on by Brasilians altogether, and not by Portuguese; but in very small vessels, so that the fishermen know nothing of managing a large ship. They would want of us at all times shipping, corn, and salt fish. The latter is a great article, and they are at present supplied with it from Portugal. Portugal being without either army or navy, could not attempt an invasion under a twelvemonth: Considering of what it would be composed it would not be much to be feared, and, if it failed, they would probably never attempt a second. Indeed, this source of their wealth being intercepted, they are scarcely capable of a first effort. The thinking part of the nation are so sensible of this, that they consider an early separation as inevitable. There is an implacable hatred between the Brasilians and Portuguese: to reconcile which a former minister adopted the policy of letting the Brazilians into a participation of public offices; but subsequent administrations have reverted to the antient policy of keeping the administration in the hands of native Portuguese. There is a mixture of natives of the old appointments still remaining in office. If Spain should invade them on their Southern extremities, these are so distant from the body of their settlements that they could not penetrate thence, and Spanish enterprize is not formidable. The Mines d'or are among mountains, inaccessible to any army. And Rio Janeiro is considered as the strongest port in the world after Gibraltar. In case of a succesful revolution, a republican government in a single body, would probably be established.'

I took care to impress on him thro' the whole of our conversation that I had neither instructions nor authority to say a word to any body on this subject, and that I could only give him my own ideas as a single individual: which were that we were not in a condition at present to meddle nationally in any war; that we wished particularly to cultivate the friendship of Portugal, with whom we have an advantageous commerce. That yet a succesful revolution in Brasil could not be uninteresting to us. That prospects of lucre might possibly draw numbers of individuals to their aid, and purer motives our officers, among whom are many excellent. That our citizens, being free to leave their own country individually without the consent of their governments, are equally free to go to any other.

A little before I received the first letter of the Brasilian, a gentleman informed me there was a Mexican in Paris, who wished to have some conversation with me. He accordingly called on me.

4 MAY 1787

The substance of the information I drew from him was as follows. He is himself a native of Mexico, where his relations are principally. He left it at about 17. years of age, and seems now to be about 33. or 34. He classes and characterizes the inhabitants of that country as follows. 1. The natives of old Spain, possessed of most of the offices of government, and firmly attached to it. 2. The clergy equally attached to the government. 3. The natives of Mexico, generally disposed to revolt, but without instruction, without energy, and much under the dominion of their priests. 4. The slaves, mulatto and black, the former enterprising and intelligent, the latter brave, and of very important weight, into whatever scale they throw themselves; but he thinks they will side with their masters. 5. The conquered Indians, cowardly, not likely to take any side, nor important which. 5. The free Indians, brave and formidable, should they interfere, but not likely to do so as being at a great distance. I asked him the numbers of these several classes, but he could not give them. The first he thought very inconsiderable: that the 2d. formed the body of the freemen: the 3d. equal to the two first: the 4th. to all the preceding: and as to the 5th. he could form no idea of their proportion. Indeed it appeared to me that his conjectures as to the others were on loose grounds. He said he knew from good information there were 300,000 inhabitants in the city of Mexico. I was still more cautious with him than with the Brasilian, mentioning it as my private opinion (unauthorised to say a word on the subject otherwise) that a succesful revolution was still at a distance with them; that I feared they must begin by enlightening and emancipating the minds of their people; that as to us, if Spain should give us advantageous terms of commerce, and remove other difficulties, it was not probable that we should relinquish certain and present advantages tho' smaller, to incertain and future ones, however great. I was led into this caution by observing that this gentleman was intimate at the Spanish Ambassador's, and that he was then at Paris, employed by Spain to settle her boundaries with France on the Pyrenees. He had much the air of candour, but that can be borrowed: so that I was not able to decide about him in my own mind.

Led by a unity of subject, and a desire to give Congress as general a view of the dispositions of our Southern countrymen as my information enables me, I will add an article which, old and insulated, I did not think important enough to mention at the time I received it. You will remember, Sir, that during the late war, the British papers often gave details of a rebellion in Peru. The character of those papers discredited the information. But the truth was that the insurrections were so general, that the event was long on the poise. Had Commodore Johnson, then expected on that coast, touched and landed there 2000 men, the dominion of Spain in that country was at an end. They only wanted a point of union which this body would have constituted. Not having this, they acted without concert, and were at length subdued separately. This conflagration was quenched in blood, 200,000 souls on both sides having perished; but the remaining matter is very capable of combustion. I have this information from a person who was on the spot at the time, and whose good faith, understanding, and means of information leave no doubt of the facts. He observed however that the numbers above supposed to have perished were on such conjectures only as he could collect.

I trouble Congress with these details, because, however distant we may be both in condition and dispositions, from taking an active part in any commotions in that country, nature has placed it too near us to make it's movements altogether indifferent to our interests or to our curiosity.

I hear of another Arrêt of this court increasing the duties on foreign stock fish, and the premiums on their own, imported into their islands; but not having yet seen it I can say nothing certain on it. I am in hopes the effect of this policy will be defeated by the practice which I am told takes place on the banks of Newfoundland of putting our fish into the French fishing boats and the parties sharing the premium, instead of ours paying the duty.

I am in hopes Mr. Short will be able to send you the medals of General Gates by this packet. I await a general instruction as to these medals. The academies of Europe will be much pleased to receive each a set.

I propose to set out the day after tomorrow for Bourdeaux (by the canal of Languedoc), Nantes, Lorient and Paris.

I have the honour to be with sentiments of the most perfect esteem & respect, Sir, your most obedient & most humble servant,

TH: JEFFERSON

PrC (DLC); slightly faded. Tr (DNA: PCC, No. 107, II). A few illegible words in PrC have been supplied from Tr. RC (missing) was enclosed in TJ to Short, this date.

TJ's letter to MONTMORIN was written 6 Apr. 1787 (missing). I [WROTE] TO THE GENTLEMAN OF MY DESIGN: TJ probably added a postscript to his letter to José da Maia of 26 Dec. 1786 stating that he would visit Nîmes (see Vol. 10: 637). ANOTHER ARRÊT: See Short to Jay, this date.

[1] Thus in MS, though all editions read "misplaced."

[2] Here TJ inserted all that part of Da Maia's letter of 21 Nov. 1786 embracing the second and third paragraphs ("Je suis Bresilien . . . Vous

trouverez necessaires"), omitting only the first paragraph and the complimentary close and signature. His transcript varied slightly in punctuation, capitalization, and spelling, but was otherwise very exact. In that letter Da Maia had employed the pseudonym "Vendek."

[3] This word interlined in substitution for "expose," deleted.

From Edmund Randolph

SIR   Richmond May 4. 1787.

Being on the point of my departure for Philadelphia, I have only time to inform your excellency, that the information given you by me in my last letter, concerning the bayonets, which were supposed to remain at Havre appears now to be without foundation. I am Sir with the highest respect yr. mo. ob. serv.,

EDM: RANDOLPH

RC (DLC); endorsed. FC (Vi, Executive Letter Book). Not recorded in SJL, and presumably not received until late July or early Aug. 1787, though Randolph's of 3 May 1787 was received as early as 30 June (see TJ to St. Victour, 7 Aug. 1787).

MY LAST LETTER: That is, Randolph's letter of 28 Jan. 1787.

To William Short

DEAR SIR   Marseilles May 4. 1787.

I received last night at Aix your favors of April 4. 6. and 24. by which I perceive that M. de Crevecoeur goes by the present packet and leaves Paris the 7th. I must therefore beg the favor of you to dispatch the inclosed letter to Mr. Jay by a courier in the instant of receiving this to M. de Crevecoeur if he shall have left Paris. The courier must go day and night rather than run any risk of not getting to Havre before the packet sails. Having been just able to finish my letter to Mr. Jay in time for this day's post, I must refer writing to you more lengthily to a future post. I took the liberty in my letter of May 1. from Nice, of desiring you to have future letters sent to me to Nantes, poste restante. I am with sentiments of pure & sincere esteem, Dear Sir your affectionate friend & servant,

TH: JEFFERSON

RC (Vi); endorsed: "[Mr.] Jefferson May 4 [received] 13 1787." PrC (DLC). Enclosure: TJ to Jay, this date. The present letter and its enclosure were enclosed in TJ to Grand, this date.

Since TJ's letter to Jay was concerned principally with the results of his conversations with José da Maia, his urgency in making arrangements for the dispatch to go by the packet of 10 May —to say nothing of his exhausted physical state after an extraordinary trip across the Apennines (see TJ to Short, 1 May, and to Martha Jefferson, 5 May 1787)—tells much of the effect that the secret discussion in Nîmes had upon him. But if TJ expected that Congress, or Jay, might be tempted by his glowing account of the Brazilian mines to undertake the furnishing of "cannon, ammunition, ships, sailors, souldiers, and officers" to support a revolution against Portugal, even on promise that "every service and furniture will be well paid," he was disappointed. Jay transmitted his letter, as Congress received and filed it, without comment. The fact that Short did not receive the letter that was to go by COURIER . . . DAY AND NIGHT until after the packet had sailed was not a disaster in American diplomacy.

William Short to John Jay

SIR Paris May 4. 1787

I have the honor of forwarding to your Excellency by M. de Crevecoeur, the medal for Genl. Gates mentioned in my letter sent by Mr. Walton and accompanying that for Genl. Greene.—M. de Crevecoeur takes charge also of twenty four medals of bronze to be delivered to your Excellency. These have been made agreeably to the contract with Colo. Humphries.

I inclose also sir two arrêts of the King's council, one of which is particularly connected with the commerce of the United States. This is the first opportunity I have had since their publication, of forwarding them, although they were passed in the month of February. But your Exccllency who well knows the impenetrable secrecy of this cabinet will not be surprised at the delay. It is possible you will recieve the first intelligence of these arrêts by the way of the West-Indies; as they must have been sent there long before they were allowed to appear here.

I take the liberty of sending you also Sir, the second speech of the King to the Assembly still sitting at Versailles. It will give your Excellency a proper idea of the progress then made by the Assembly and also of the situation of the finances of this Kingdom. The annual deficit as stated by M. de Calonne in his speech was so alarming that it produced an almost universal discontent of his administration and at length took from him the King's confidence which had been without bounds until a few days before his dismission. He is succeeded by M. de Fourqueux a Counsellor of State, a man far advanced in life, and without any decided character. He has not as yet shewn what his views in general will be, but there is reason to hope that he will not be unfriendly to the commerce of America. Much depends on the dispositions of the Comptroller general.

Your Excellency is well acquainted with the letter which M. de Calonne wrote to Mr. Jefferson on the subject of commerce.

4 MAY 1787

For various reasons he never could be prevailed on during his administration to have his letter registered in council so as to give it its full force. His delay was always supposed to proceed from the confusion and multiplicity of his affairs. He always promised to do it from day to day, and gave uniformly his assurances that when registered, it should have retrospect to the day of its date, so as to indemnify such of the American merchants as had been, and should be, obliged to pay the duties from which his letter promised an exoneration.—This letter has never yet been registered in council and of course remains without effect. M. de Fourqueux has promised however to attend to it the first moment that the multiplicity of his affairs with the Assembly, will admit of it. In this situation remains the letter which is considered here as the basis of the commerce with America. Should it recieve its sanction before the departure of the packet the 10th. of this month, I will not lose a moment in communicating it to your Excellency.

I have delivered to Monsieur de Montmorin, the letter from Congress to the King which came by the last packet.

I inclose for your Excellency two letters from Mr. Dumas. Mr. Jefferson is still absent but may be expected here in a very short time at present, being on his return from the south of France. It is his absence which induced me to take the liberty of troubling your Excellency with this letter. That the interruption may be as slight as possible I have introduced only such circumstances as relate to this country or America, and which I suppose you would wish to be acquainted with. One other however, I hope you will permit me sir to add; that of assuring you that I have the honor to be with sentiments of the most profound respect Your Excellency's most obedient & most humble Servt., W. SHORT

P.S. May 5. At the moment of sealing my letter Sir, I have learned that Mr. de Fourqueux has resigned his office, supposed to be because he was made subordinate to a council of finance of which the Archbishop of Thoulouse is chief. The successor is not yet announced, but the Marquis de la fayette has written to me that he will certainly be M. de Villedeuil, late Intendant of Rouen. As both the Archbishop and M. de Villedeuil are enlightened and virtuous men, and were also of the committee, which met several times last year on the subject of American commerce, and were instrumental in forcing M. de Calonne to write his letter to Mr. Jefferson, there is not the smallest doubt at present that this letter

[346]

5 MAY 1787

will be immediately registered in council and thus have its full effect.

RC (DNA: PCC, No. 87, II); endorsed. Enclosures: (1) Arrêt of 11 Feb. 1787 for extending to "*Eight* Livres the Duty of *five* Livres per Quintal imposed by the arrêt of 25 Septr 1785 on all dried Codfish of the *foreign* fisheries imported into the Windward and Leeward Islands, and extending to *twelve* Livres the *Bounty* of *ten* Livres granted by the Arret of the 18 of the same Month, on every Quintal of dried Codfish of the french Fishery imported into the said islands" (translation made in Jay's office, from accompanying printed text; same, II, 15-6, 21-2). (2) Decree of Louis XVI correcting abuses concerning standard gauges for hogsheads of sugar, barrels, and casks so far as they had arisen from neglect of the regulations of the Arrêt of 1 Mch. 1744 (translation made in Jay's office, from accompanying printed text; same, II, 7-14). (3) Speech of Louis XVI to the Assembly of Notables, 23 Apr. 1787 (clipping from pages 1165-6 of an unidentified French publication; clipping from an English newspaper, both in same, II, 17-9). (4) Dumas to Jay, 23 Mch. 1787, reporting on developments in Holland, and urging again "the necessity of keeping secret the financial operations, on the subject of which Mr. Jefferson has laid a proposition before Congress"; to this Dumas added that no one else should be allowed "to interfere with it except that gentleman and myself, under him. This is absolutely necessary, from the very nature of the business, for its success. The persons who would undertake it, and who will make themselves known in proper time, on the one hand, with France on the other, will be the chief contracting parties; and the United States, if they agree to it, will be only consenting to what will be very advantageous for themselves" (from full text in *Dipl. Corr.*, *1783-89*, III, 567-70; FC in Dumas Letter Book, Rijksarchief, The Hague; photostats in DLC; cf. note to Dumas to Short, 2 Feb. 1787). (5) Dumas to Jay, 30 Mch. 1787, enclosing copy of address of Prince of Orange to the Diet of Overyssel of 13 Mch., together with a copy of the Diet's response of 21 Mch., all printed in *Dipl. Corr.*, *1783-89*, III, 571-6; FC in Dumas Letter Book, Rijksarchief, The Hague; photostats in DLC. See also Dumas to Short, 2 and 27 Mch. 1787.

To Thomas Barclay

Dear Sir   Marseilles May 5. 1787.

After the letter I did myself the honour of writing you to assure you that I would reimburse you the necessary expences for sending young Mercier to his own country, I took occasion in my first to the Governor of Virginia to mention your attention to him, and my undertaking, and to pray that he would endeavor to find out his family. I now receive a letter from the present governor, Mr. Randolph, in which he informs me their enquiries have hitherto been fruitless, but that they will be responsible for the necessary expences. If you will be so good as to furnish me with an account of your disbursements for him, I will replace them.

I proceed from hence the day after tomorrow to Bourdeaux; but as I propose to examine well the canal of Languedoc on my way, I do not expect to leave Bourdeaux till sometime between the 20th. and 25th. of this month. I shall be happy should your return chance

[347]

5 MAY 1787

to place you there before that period, or at Nantes from the 25th. to the 30th. It is two months since I left Paris, so I have no news to offer you. But I can always offer with truth assurances of the sincere esteem with which I have the honour to be Dear Sir Your friend & servt.,
TH: JEFFERSON

RC (DLC). PrC (DLC). The presence of the RC in TJ Papers is unexplained; Barclay acknowledged the letter on 12 June 1787—a fact which suggests that Barclay's letter may have been added to TJ Papers after their acquisition by the federal government.

TJ received Barclay's letter of 26 June 1786 about MERCIER on 13 Aug. 1786 and on that day added a postscript to his FIRST TO THE GOVERNOR OF VIRGINIA of 9 Aug. 1786; no letter from TJ to Barclay offering TO REIMBURSE YOU THE NECESSARY EXPENCES has been found, though it is possible that TJ added a postscript to this effect to his of 31 Aug. 1786 in which he acknowledged, among others, Barclay's of 26 June 1786. The LETTER FROM THE PRESENT GOVERNOR is Randolph's of 28 Jan. 1787.

To Martha Jefferson

MY DEAR PATSY Marseilles May 5. 1787.

I got back to Aix the day before yesterday, and found there your letter of the 9th. of April, from which I presume you to be well tho' you do not say so. In order to exercise your geography I will give you a detail of my journey. You must therefore take your map and trace out the following places. Dijon, Lyons, Pont St. Esprit, Nismes, Arles, St. Remis, Aix, Marseilles, Toulon, Hieres, Frejus, Antibes, Nice, Col de Tende, Coni, Turin, Vercelli, Milan, Pavia, Tortona, Novi, Genoa, by sea to Albenga, by land to Monaco, Nice, Antibes, Frejus, Brignolles, Aix, and Marseille. The day after tomorrow I set out hence for Aix, Avignon, Pont du Gard, Nismes, Montpelier, Narbonne, along the Canal of Languedoc to Toulouse, Bourdeaux, Rochefort, Rochelle, Nantes, Lorient, Nantes, Tours, Orleans and Paris where I shall arrive about the middle of June, after having travelled something upwards of a thousand leagues. From Genoa to Aix was very fatiguing, the first two days having been at sea, and mortally sick, two more clambering the cliffs of the Appennine, sometimes on foot, sometimes on a mule according as the path was more or less difficult, and two others travelling thro' the night as well as day, without sleep. I am not yet rested, and shall therefore shortly give you rest by closing my letter, after mentioning that I have received a letter from your sister, which tho a year old, gave me great pleasure. I inclose it for your perusal, as I think it will be pleasing to you also. But take care of it, and return it to me when I shall get back to Paris, for trifling as it seems, it is precious to me. When I left Paris, I wrote to London to desire that your harpsichord might be sent during the months of April and May, so that I am in hopes it will arrive a little before I shall, and give me an opportunity of judging whether you have got the better of that want of industry which I had began to fear would be the rock on which you would split. Determine never to be idle. No person will have occasion to complain of the want of time, who never loses any. It is wonderful how much may be done, if we are always doing. And that you may be always doing good, my dear, is the ardent prayer of yours affectionately,

TH: JEFFERSON

RC (NNP); endorsed. PrC (MHi). Enclosure: Mary Jefferson to TJ, ca. 22 May 1786, q.v., received by TJ on 3 May 1787.

From André Limozin

Le Havre, 5 May. 1787. Encloses a letter for TJ which "I received yesterday by the English Mail . . . under my Cover." He hopes to hear soon of TJ's safe return to Paris.

RC (MHi); 2 p.; addressed and endorsed. This is probably the letter from Limozin which TJ recorded in SJL as without date and as received 25 May 1787 at Bordeaux. Enclosure not identified.

To William Short

DEAR SIR   Marseilles May 5. 1787.

I wrote you a short letter of the 1st. from Nice, and another of the 4th. from this place. I have now a little more time to go thro' the articles of your several favors of the 4th. 6th. and 24th. With respect to the maps to be struck on bank paper, if there be any difficulty they may be omitted, because I can have them done at London where that operation is familiar.—Nothing can have been more cross-grained than the circumstances of the seeds from London. I fear however, by the trouble Mde. de Tessy[1] has given herself, that she overrates them, and has forgotten what I had mentioned to her on some occasion, that there are only 5. or 6. kinds, and these in great quantity, ordered at the desire of M. de Malesherbes, who plants whole forests. You must be so good as to remind her of this to prevent her being disappointed. I must pray you to return my thanks to Mde. de Tessé for the pamphlets she has been so kind as to send me, for her letter, and all her at-

5 MAY 1787

tentions: nor forget me to Mde. de Tott.—I have not yet been to Montpelier but I can pronounce that Rousseau has done it injury in ascribing to it the character of pillaging strangers, as if it was peculiar to that place. It is the character of every place on the great roads along which many travellers pass. He should also have confined the character to postillions, voituriers, tavern keepers, waiters, and workmen. The other descriptions of people are as good to strangers as any people I have ever met with.—I am unable to tell you where you can find a copy of my book for M. de Crevecoeur. I rather apprehend they are all locked up. No matter now, as I can send one to him by the first packet.—If Colo. Smith shall be passing from Paris to Madrid, he will probably come by Bourdeaux, where I should be happy to meet him. Your right to charge the coach hire to Versailles appears to me perfect: and your ideas just as to the putting either your name or mine to any petition. The thing being done without our knowlege, it will be better to appear to know nothing of it; but if ever it should be mentioned to me, I must disavow it. I shall be glad to avoid this because I know it proceeded from a well meant zeal in the person who did it.— Ramsay's history costs in London 12/ sterling unbound; judge then whether it can be brought from thence to Paris and sold for 12^{tt}.— You enquire kindly the effect of the waters on my wrist. None at all. But time is doing slowly what they cannot do. It strengthens a little.—I am just come from the theatre where I have been much pleased with Mde. de Pontheuil: she has all the excellencies,[1] without any of the faults of Mde. Dugazon. I am sleepy, not yet having had rest enough: so I will bid you Adieu, after giving you sincere assurances of the affection with which I am Dear Sir your friend & servant,

TH: JEFFERSON

P.S. Be so good as to desire Monsr. Frouillé to procure for me the Ephemerides societatis meteorologicae Palatinae, printed at Manheim by C. Fr. Schwan, in 4to. begun in 1781. and consisting by this time of 4. or 5. vols. I shall have occasion for it on my return to Paris. Desire Petit also to notify the servants whom I have dismissed that they must remove by the 25th. of this month, with their effects, and he must see that it be done.

RC (ViW); endorsed: "Jefferson May 5 [received] 13 1787." PrC (DLC).

[1] Thus in Ms.

To Edward Bancroft

Dear Sir Marseilles May 6. 1787.

I recieve your favor of Mar. 27. just as I am setting out for Bourdeaux, Nantes, Lorient and Paris where I shall be about the middle of June. I have hastily scribbled therefore the inclosed letter to Mr. Wythe, which will explain to Mr. Paradise what I suppose best for him to do, without repeating it here which my hurry scarcely admits. If I can do any thing further for him in this or any other matter hereafter, I beg him at all times to command me freely. As he is thinking to retire from London, I cannot help supposing he will find it best to exchange the gloomy climate of England for the genial one of Provence or the riviere of Genes. Be so good as to assure both him and Mrs. Paradise of my constant esteem and accept yourself those sentiments of friendship and respect with which I have the honour to be Dear Sir your most obedt. & most humble servt., Th: Jefferson

P.S. Bring Mr. Paradise with you to Paris and we will there have a consultation on the climate which may best suit him.

PrC (DLC); MS faded. Enclosure: TJ to George Wythe of this date.

From John Banister, Sr., and Anne Blair Banister

Dear Sir May 6th. 1787

This it is very probable will be delivered you by Capt. Ramsay, a very worthy Man who has the Care of your Daughter Miss Polly, in her Voyage to England; and I am confident from my knowledge of him he will be perfectly attentive to her. A few days ago I received your favor inclosing Mr. De Vernon's Paper to whose interest I shall pay the greatest attention and as far as it can now be effected remit to him his monies in the funds here, but I fear Mr. Mark has drawn a great proportion of them, as I see but little, that is only 250£. Virga. due now in this State. I have forbid any further Payment to Mr. Mark. I beg to be informed by the first opportunity in what way Messrs. de Vernon & Dangerard will have the Money as it is received, remitted, whether in Tobacco, or bills. I have every opportunity of selecting Tobacco here, as I know the Planters and in general the lands where it is made.

6 MAY 1787

I find the Wind fair for Capt. Ramsay which allows me no further time at present than to assure you that I am with every Sentiment of esteem and Regard Dr. Sir your Friend & Mo: obedt. Servant,
J BANISTER

Commissioners of this State viz. Edmund Randolph Govr., Geo: Wythe, Genl. Washington, Geo: Mason, J. Blair esquires are gone to Philadelphia to assist in a revision of the Articles of Confederation.

In a few hasty Lines, accept Dear Sir, my Congratulations on the arrival of your Daughter. Captn. Ramsay takes charge of a large Pacquet to you. The contents I hope are not new, as it is only a Duplicate of what I trust has reached your Hands. Mrs. Oster has sail'd for France and will either *see*, or *write* to you on her arrival. I therefore, take the liberty to beg your care of the Letter directed to her, as I know not where to say she is. She is very uneasy to discover (just as she was about to set sail) that Mr. Oster (with his accustom'd ill-nature) prevented her having the charge of your Daughter; a circumstance she had at Heart (which was sufficient Reason for him to disappoint her) as well as Mrs. Eppes. Poor Mr. J. Banister is confined in New York (where he arrived in 50 days from Havre de Grace) with a Cold and Fever caught at Sea. The Letters *must* away. I can no more, than that I am as ever Your Truely Sincere Friend,
A. BANISTER

RC (MHi); Mrs. Banister's note, in her hand, is at foot of text; endorsed: "Bannister, John Senr." Recorded in SJL as received 30 June 1787. See TJ to De Vernon, 12 Aug. 1787.

The LARGE PACQUET sent by Mrs. Banister through Captain Ramsay may have been the DUPLICATE of her letter to TJ concerning Mrs. Oster's difficulties (see Mrs. Banister to TJ, 19 Feb. 1787, note on Dupl).

To Jean Baptiste Guide

SIR   Marseilles May 6. 1787.

A desire of seeing a commerce commenced between the dominions of his majesty the king of Sardinia, and the United States of America, and a direct exchange of their respective productions, without passing thro a third nation, led me into the conversation which I had the honour of having with you on that subject, and afterwards with Monsieur Tallon at Turin, to whom I promised that I would explain to you in writing the substance of what passed between us. The articles of your produce wanted with us are

[352]

6 MAY 1787

brandies, wines, oil, fruits, and manufactured silks: those with which we can furnish you are Indigo, potash, tobacco, flour, salt fish, furs and peltries, ships and materials for building them. The supply of tobacco particularly being in the hands of government solely, appeared to me to offer an article for beginning immediately the experiment of direct commerce. That of the first quality can be had at first hand only from James river in Virginia: those of the second and third from the same place and from Baltimore in Maryland. The first quality is delivered in the ports of France at 38[lt] the quintal, the second at 36.[lt] the third at 34.[lt] weight and money of France, by individuals generally. I send you the copy of a large contract wherein the three qualities are averaged at 36.[lt] They must be delivered at Nice for those prices. Indeed it is my opinion that by making shipments of your own produce to those places and buying the tobaccos on the spot they may be had more advantageously. In this case it would be expedient that merchants of Nice, Turin, and America should form a joint concern for conducting the business in the two countries. Monsr. Tallon desired me to point out proper persons in America who might be addressed for this purpose. The house of the most extensive reputation concerned in the tobacco trade, and on the firmest funds, is that of Messieurs Ross and Pleasants at Richmond in Virginia. If it should be concluded on your part to make any attempt of this kind, and to address yourselves to these gentlemen or to any others, it would be best to write them your ideas, and receive theirs before you make either purchases or shipments. A more hasty conduct might occasion loss, and retard, instead of encouraging the establishment of this commerce. I would undertake to write at the same time to these, or any other merchants whom you should prefer, in order to dispose them favorably, and as disinterestedly as possible for the encouragement of this essay. I must observe to you that our vessels are fearful of coming into the Mediterranean on account of the Algerines: and that if you should freight vessels, those of the French will be most advantageous for you, because received in our ports without paying any duties on some of those articles, and lighter than others on all of them. English vessels on the other hand are distinguished by paying heavier duties than those of any other nation. Should you desire any further information, or to pass letters with certainty to any mercantile house in America, do me the favour to address yourselves to me at Paris, and I shall do whatever depends on me for promoting this object. I have the honour to be with sentiments of high esteem & respect, Sir, your most obedient and most humble servant, TH: JEFFERSON

PrC (DLC). Enclosure: Presumably a copy of Robert Morris' contract with the farmers-general (see Vol. 9: 586-8).

To Philip Mazzei

DEAR SIR Marseilles May 6. 1787.

I found at Aix your favor of the 17th. April, on my return thither the 3d. inst. I now inclose the order you desire. I think I cannot be at Paris before the 15th. of June but shall make a point to be there at that time on account of the approaching Packet. I have made a little tour from Nice across the Alps at the Col de Tende, to Turin, thence thro' the rice country of the Vercellese, Novarese, Milanese, by Milan to Pavia, thence to Genoa, from Genoa about half way by sea, the other half by land to Nice. This will afford us topics for some conversations when I shall have the pleasure of seeing you at Paris. I have received a letter from the Govr. E. R. in which is the following paragraph (date Jan. 28. 1787.) 'Being engaged in preparing for an official visit to the naval offices below I shall for the present only beg you to inform Mr. Mazzei that I have remitted him money—wrote to him in the summer—am settling with Mr. Webb, and shall give him a full detail very soon.'

I inclose you two letters which, being under my cover, have come to me from Paris. I thank you for your attention to James, and will pursue the party you propose of leaving him to the antient cook. With respect to the new one should he not give some reason why he is entitled to more than his master demands? Should he not shew that some person has been fool enough to give him half a guinea a day? Is there any proportion between the annual price of 1200.^{tt} or monthly one of 200.^{tt} and the daily one of 12^{tt}? These however are only my grumblings, for I suppose I must finish by paying. I have desired Mr. Short to give the order relative to the servants. I set out tomorrow morning very early on my Western tour, and it being the hour of bed, I shall bid you Adieu after assurances of the sincere esteem with which I am Dr. Sir your friend & servt., TH: JEFFERSON

PrC (DLC). Tr (DLC); with several minor variations, not noted here. Enclosures: (1) Order on Grand "to pay to Mr. Philip Mazzei or order six hundred livres and charge the same to Sir your very humble servt," dated

Marseilles, 6 May 1787 (PrC on same sheet as PrC of the present letter; see also note to TJ to Mazzei, 4 Apr. 1786). (2) The two enclosed letters for Mazzei have not been identified; very likely they had come under the cover of letters to TJ from Virginia.

To St. Victour & Bettinger

MONSIEUR   Marseilles 6me. Mai. 1787.

Quand le gouvernement de la Virginie nous fit l'honneur, à Monsr. le M. de la Fayette, M. Barclay et moi, de nous charger de la procuration des armes, pour lesquelles nous nous sommes adressés à votre manufacture, il nous donnoit raison de croire qu'il auroit besoin d'encore bien d'autres. Mais jusques ici, il ne s'est expliqué ulterieurement la dessus, et il ne seroit pas sage ni à nous, ni à vous, de prendre aucune demarche pour cet objet qu'après avoir reçu leurs ordres precises. Ils viennent de recevoir les premiers envois de ces armes, et seront bientot en etat de nous informer s'ils en sont contents et pour la qualité et pour le prix. Je me ferai une veritable plaisir de vous communiquer leurs sentiments la dessus au premier moment qu'ils me les feront connoitre. J'ai l'honneur d'etre avec beaucoup de consideration, Monsieur, votre tres humble et tres obeissant serviteur,   TH: JEFFERSON

PrC (ViWC); endorsed.

To George Wythe

DEAR SIR   May 6. 1787.

Mr. Paradise being desirous of placing the conduct of his steward under the controul of some one or two good gentlemen in the neighborhood of his estate, has desired me to recommend his affairs to the persons whom I should think best. But since my departure from Williamsburg things are so much changed that I am incompetent to that nomination. I therefore advise him to execute a power of attorney, leaving a blank for the two names, and that I would ask the favor of you to perform the office, which he had desired of me, of inserting two names. I have been led to take this liberty by a knowlege of your desire to do good, and have it in my power to assure you that you can never render service to a better man. I have mentioned to him Colo. Taliaferro as adjoining his estate, understanding perfectly what a steward should do, and therefore most capable of making one do his duty: but at the same time that I did not know whether Colo. Taliaferro's own affairs would permit him to undertake this office. I remit and recommend therefore Mr. Paradise to your goodness, and beg you to accept th[ose] assurances which both duty and inclination ever prompt me to make of the perfect esteem & respect with which I am Dear Sir Your friend & servant, TH: JEFFERSON

PrC (DLC). Recorded in SJL as written from Marseilles. Enclosed in TJ to Bancroft, this date, unsealed in order that Paradise might see it, thus obviating the need for a separate letter to him.

From Elizabeth Wayles Eppes

[Osborne's, 7 May 1787]

This will, I hope, be handed you by my dear Polly, who I most ardently wish may reach you in the health she is in at present. I shall be truly wretched till I hear of her being safely landed with you. The children will spend a day or two on board the ship with her, which I hope will reconcile her to it. For God's sake give us the earliest intelligence of her arrival.

MS not found; text is taken from Randolph, *Domestic Life*, p. 124-5, where it is printed without date. The letter, of which this extract may be the whole, is certainly that from Mrs. Eppes written 7 May 1787 from Osborne's and recorded in SJL as received 30 June 1787.

From William Short

DEAR SIR   Paris May 8. 1787

My last was of the 24th. and 25th. of April. Yours was from Nice the 12th. Agreeably to your calculation at that time I may now daily expect to hear of your return on this side of the Alps, and I imagine you will certainly be at Aix as soon as this letter. It is the last I shall write you Sir, to that place, unless I find that you will be longer there than I had supposed.

Crevecoeur has gone for Havre, to sail from thence the 10th. He took with him the medals of Genl. Gates. He went from hence in high spirits with respect to the American commerce in consequence of the late revolution in the ministry. The Archbishop of Thoulouse as Chief of the council of finance is considered at present as prime minister. M. de Villedeuil late Intendant of Rouen, Comptroller general, succeeding to M. de Fourqueux after his very short administration. I think there is no doubt that M. de Calonne's letter

8 MAY 1787

will be immediately registered in council. Notwithstanding the enormous deficit at present existing in the finances of this government, France has certainly gained much by the embarassment. The King has become acquainted with the real situation of his affairs, has determined on efficient oeconomies, and acquired a ministry that already possesses the confidence of all the nation, and will very soon, I doubt not, that of all the world. I cannot think the prospects of France were ever more flattering than at this moment. She will certainly be well indemnified for the immense debt—1. by the provincial assemblies, 2. by ameliorations in several departments and 3dly. by learning the necessity of oeconomy and good administration even in times of peace. The Parisians seem in the highest state of exultation at this moment and so general is the satisfaction on the coming into the ministry of the Archbishop that I have heard not one calembour on the occasion. The assembly is proceeding slowly but surely in its views. The late change has occasioned a kind of stand, but they will go on rapidly in future because the Ministry and Assembly will co-operate.

Colo. Smith has been here nine or ten days; he sets off to-morrow without fail for Bourdeaux on his way to Madrid and Lisbon. His business is at the latter place. He was appointed by Congress the first moment of their meeting to go and thank the Queen of Portugal for her civility in desiring her fleet last year to protect the American vessels against the Barbary cruisers. He desires much to see you and desires me to beg you will write to him poste restante at Bordeaux, and tell him where he can join you the nearest in his route. He will be at Bordeaux in a week from this time and will stay there two days; he would willingly make a detour to have an interview with you. Should he not see you he begs you to write to him at Madrid to the care of Mr. Carmichael.

Miss Jefferson has been indisposed but has recovered. I send you a letter from her which will probably mention it. The other letters which are here will be taken by Colo. Smith, who will leave them at Bourdeaux with his banker whose address I shall send you before you arrive there. I wait with great anxiety sir to hear from you and I hope you will be persuaded of the pleasure that your return in good health will give to your sincerest friend & servant,

W Short

RC (DLC). PrC (DLC: Short Papers); endorsed. Recorded in SJL as received 31 May 1787 at Nantes. Enclosure: Martha Jefferson to TJ, 3 May 1787.

From Stephen Cathalan, Jr.

Sir   Marseilles the 9th. May 1787

I hope this Letter will meet your Excellency at Cette, and on that account I direct it to M. Meinadier.

I dare say, you have been pleased in Seing the famous Fontain of Vaucluse, as famous, by the lampid waters Spliting with a great noise against the rocks, as it is by the Loves of Petrarch and Laura.

The Country about L'Isle and avignon is also Charming, tho' by the Cold wheathers we have had lately, you will have Seen the poor Country people in the desolation, by the lost of a great part of their growing Crops.

I remit you here inclosed the Copy, of the general Idea of the trade of Marseilles, by abbé raynal. I will Send one to Thos. Barclay Esqr. as Soon as I will have of his Letters, till now I have received none. If you meet him at Bordeaux, I will be much obliged to you, to tell him that I am in great need of Money, and any remittances he would make to me, as Small as they would be, will be always acceptable. They would be always a proof that he wish much to be able to discharge his Ballance, tho' I doubt not of his Sentiments on that account.

I remit you also the note of one Couffe Levant rice of the Best sort, and of a Bag rice from nice of the Best quality called there *escûma crûvelata*. This cost dearer than the price I Spoke to you; but being for your own use, and free of Bruised grain and Dust, it becomes cheaper than that of 15ᵗᵗ 10s. or 16.ᵗᵗ ₱ ql.

The lombardy rice in Bags of ℔. 350 cost only 13-10 to 14.ᵗᵗ but it is tale and quale.

The amount of this trifling you will be So good as to remit under their receipts either to M. Meinadier, or Sir John Lambert my Bankers at Paris, when Convenient to you.

I have not received yet any answers from the farmers Generals about the Cargo of Tobacco I expect, on the British Ship Minerva; if that I expect from them, is not favorable, I will beg of you to interfer in it, in behalf of Messrs. Willing Morris & Swanwick.

Messrs. Bretoux and me, yesterday gave orders to one of our friends for two Couffes of Levant Rice not milled. They will be here in about 4 Months and I will forward them to you, as Soon as they will be in my power.

The American Capn. harison Came yesterday to my house to tell me, they will discharge him and his Crew, on account of his

Colour, and the algerians; I advised him that he must be forced to it by law, and he must be paid and his crew of all their wages, expences, and Passage, till their arival at new york; in Such transactions an American Consul would be very necessary here.

All my family present you their respects and we wish you an agreable Journey and an happy return to Paris. My wife and me, regret very much that we could not have the pleasure of accompany you. We will be happier Some days or other, in meeting you at Paris.

I beg you to command me in whatever I may be usefull to you, and to continue me the honour of your Friendship. And remain Very respectfully Sir of Your Excellency the most humble obedt. & Devoted Servant, STEPHEN CATHALAN Junr.

M. Meinadier will give you Letters for Some flour Merchants at montauban and Toulouse, if you desire it.

RC (DLC); endorsed. Recorded in SJL as received at "Cette" [Sète] on 13 May 1787; see TJ to Cathalan, 21 July 1787. Enclosures: (1) Raynal's "Idea of the trade of Marseilles" has not been identified. (2) Invoice for one "couffe" of Levant rice and one bag of Piedmont rice, amounting to £85 4s. 6d., shipped on board the *Louise*, Capt. Adrien Thibault (DLC).

From John Sullivan

DEAR SIR   Durham May 9th. 1787

The Box I wrote you of containing the Skin Skeleton and Horns of a moose together with the Horns of the Deer, Elk, Carribou, Roe Buck and Spike horned Buck, was Left by Captain Pierce either through Accident or Design. He sailed the 2d. Instant. I now send it by Capt. Seaward to Boston, who Engages to put it on board some vessel bound to Havre De Grace and in Case of none being ready for Departure to forward it to New York to go by the packet. I enclose you my Letters to Capt. Pierce, and have wrote Monsieur De la Tomb Consul at Boston to assist Capt. Seaward with his advice in forwarding it either by way of New York or Boston, to Havre De Grace, and have wrote the American Consul there to forward it to you and am with great respect Dr. Sir your most obedient servant,   JNO. SULLIVAN

RC (NNP). Recorded in SJL as received 1 Sep. 1787. Enclosures: (1) Sullivan to TJ, 26 and 30 Apr. 1787, with enclosures in the former which included Sullivan's letter of the same date TO CAPT. PIERCE—the only one that has been found.

From John Ammonet

Norfolk, 10 May 1787. Encloses letters of introduction; though he had expected to sail with Capt. Ramsay, the bearer, he postpones his voyage on account of illness. Asks TJ to make inquiries into the matter of his claim to the estate, "perhaps in the Town of Tessey, in lower Normandy," of Jacob Ammonet, who left France for Virginia about 1700. He has credentials proving himself the "legal representative" of Jacob, and encloses a copy of several depositions. TJ's reply should be directed to the care of Edmund Randolph.

RC (DLC); 2 p. Recorded in SJL as received 30 June 1787. Enclosures: (1) Hay to TJ, 26 Apr. 1787. (2) Currie to TJ, 2 May 1787. (3) Fleming to TJ, 2 May 1787. (4) Randolph to TJ, 3 May 1787. (5) Copy in Ammonet's hand of the deposition concerning his identity by John Barnes, Charles Ammonet, and Charlotte J. Chastain before John and Thomas Harris, justices of the peace for Powhatan co., on 9 Aug. 1786. (6) Copy of certification by Edmund Randolph, dated 14 Apr. 1787, that the Harrises were magistrates (both this and foregoing in DLC). See TJ to Randolph, 11 Aug. 1787.

From G. A. Auckler

Monsieur a argenton le 11 may 1787

Pardonnez si je derobe un moment, aux importantes occupations, dont votre place vous a chargé, par des demandes, que vous trouverez peut-être frivoles, mais qui ne sont cependent pas etrangeres à la gloire de l'humanité.

Je soutenois que les nouveaux états de l'amerique Septentrionale, qui viennent de se former, etoient ouverts à tout etranger, qui vouloit s'y établir, et que dès qu'il y avoit acquis quelque possession foncière, il avoit touts droits de cité, et devenoit membre de la republique, et en cette qualité pouvoit exerçer toutes sortes de professions, même les plus nobles, telles que celle d'avocat. C'est ce qui me paroissoit devoir être, du moins, dans un pays nouveau, qui ne demande qu'à se peupler. On me soutenoit le contraire. Je vous supplie, Monsieur, de vouloir bien, si ce n'est pas trop abuser de vos moments, nous decider.

Daignez agreer, Monsieur, que je joigne ici mon profond respect à celui que vous obtenéz de touts ceux, qui vous connoissent.

G. A. Auckler

Mon adresse est Auckler avocat à argenton en berry.

RC (DLC); endorsed. Recorded in SJL as received 31 May 1787 at Nantes.

From the Abbé Guibert

[*14 May 1787. n.p.* Recorded in SJL as received 31 May 1787 at Nantes. Not found.

From William Short

DEAR SIR   Paris Monday 14th. of May 1787

I went into the country on wednesday last, the day of Colo. Smith's departure from this place, and returned here yesterday evening. The Porter who has never failed forwarding me my letters with the greatest punctuality except in this instance, omitted it entirely, so that on my arrival yesterday I recieved in the same instant your three letters of May 1. 4. and 5. The reason of this neglect I cannot learn, or rather there is no reason at all. He says that the letter of May 1 did not arrive until friday. I should suppose he must be mistaken, as that of the 4th. was sent here on thursday by Mr. Grand. That also had its misfortune. Mr. Grand inclosed it to me, and added on the address to be opened by the Maitre d'hotel in case of my absence. This addition escaped notice; so that his letter inclosing yours waited quietly here my arrival. This being the 13th. in the evening, and the packet being to sail the 10th. I deemed it altogether vain to make any effort to send your letter for Mr. Jay by that conveyance. I have written to Mr. Limosin desiring he would let me know if there was any vessel at Havre to sail in a very short time to America, and at the same time I shall look out for an opportunity for England, and forward your letter by one or the other of these chanels as circumstances may direct. I am extremely sorry for the disappointment, but hope you will see clearly that it has been occasioned by ill fortune, and by the porter, rather than any neglect on my part. You expected that your letter would arrive here the 8th. or 9th. but Mr. Grand did not recieve it until the 10th. At least his letter inclosing it to me is of that date and I am persuaded he lost no time in forwarding it. Thus as it arrived here only the evening of the day on which the packet was to sail, the chance against its having been delivered at Havre in time, is very great. At this season of the year it is certainly probable that the packet would sail on the day fixed, and more than probable, before the end of the day after that fixed. It is this Sir which makes me suppose that even had I been in Paris at the arrival of your letter it would not have prevented this inconvenience.

14 MAY 1787

You have acknowleged the reciept of all my letters except my last. It was dated the 8th. inst. and sent to Aix. I am apprehensive you may have passed by that place before its arrival. I hope however you will have left instructions to have your letters sent after you. I am the more desirous you should recieve it because it contains a letter from your daughter. She has been indisposed, but at present perfectly recovered as I learn from Mr. Petit, who carried her your letter this morning. The letters which Colo. Smith took for you from hence will be left with his banker at Bordeaux, in case he should not meet with you himself. You will be therefore so good as send for them on your arrival there at the house of Messrs. N. P. French & Nephew.

At length the fatal box of seeds has arrived. Petit recieved it four days ago and immediately sent it to the hotel de Tessé. He tells me there is only one kind of seeds. I have not since seen Mde. de Tessé so that I know not the kind.

I am very happy your idea respecting Crevecoeur's memoire is the same with that which I had taken up. I am perfectly satisfied it should rest as it is, because I am persuaded if ever you should be obliged to disavow it, you will do me the justice at the same time to exculpate me from the reproach of having acted so inconsiderately.

I went to Frouillé's this morning to desire he would procure you the book you mention. I shall send him to-morrow the title which I forgot to take with me, and he promises to have it here before your return. The Servants you had discharged have all left the place. Espagnol has been and is still very ill.—Your horses are worth the double of what they were when you left them. They want nothing but exercise; of this they never have enough, and perhaps none except when I am in Paris. I use one or the other of them every day in my cabriolet. They both go gently so that I drive them any where that I have occasion to go in Paris. In the beginning Petit gave them exercise, but since the novelty of the thing has gone, he has become tired of it, and exercises only the saddle horse. However on the whole they are well taken care of. On the day of the review Colo. Smith mounted one of your carriage horses, my servant followed us on the other, and I had your sorrel—and your cavalry made really a very good figure. Smith's horse having been in the military line was perfectly trained to the business, and I advise you if ever you go on a like parade to take him in preference to your saddle horse.

The Assembly is still sitting but I know not with precision what

15 MAY 1787

they are doing. The King has determined on a loan, I think of sixty or eighty million. It has been registered in the Parliament, without hesitation, for any thing I have heard to the contrary. It is said that the deficit proves on a further examination to be 180 million instead of 112.

It has been some time since I have seen the Marquis de la fayette. It is said in Paris that M. de Calonne sollicited about the time of his dismission to have him together with the Archbishop of Aix and the Bishop of Langres, and a fourth not known, put in the bastile. This demand with others for the banishment of very respectable and powerful persons served to open the eyes of the King, and very much to his honor. The moment he was disabused, he did not hesitate to sacrifice this minister to the wishes of his people. In this trait there is certainly more real glory, than in the conquest of a kingdom.

This letter will be sent to the care of Mr. Bondfield at Bordeaux, and I hope you will recieve it there. Accept my dear Sir the sincerest wishes for your perfect health and happiness from Your friend & servant, W SHORT

RC (DLC); endorsed. PrC (DLC: Short Papers). Recorded in SJL as received 25 May 1787 at Bordeaux.

From James Madison

DEAR SIR Philada. May 15th. 1787

I am just furnished by Mr. Pollock with a box containing a few Peccan Nuts, which Mr. Jno. Vaughan of this City undertakes to forward by a Vessel just sailing for France.

Monday last was the day for the meeting of the Convention. The number as yet assembled is but small. Among the few is Genl. Washington who arrived on Sunday evening amidst the acclamations of the people, as well as more sober marks of the affection and veneration which continues to be felt for his character. The Governor, Messrs. Wythe and Blair, and Docr. McClurg are also here. Col. Mason is to be here in a day or two. There is a prospect of a pretty full meeting on the whole, though there is less punctuality in the outset than was to be wished. Of this the late bad weather has been the principal cause. I mention these circumstances because it is possible, this may reach you before you hear from me through any other channel, and I add no others because it is merely possible. Adieu. Js. MADISON Jr.

RC (DLC: Madison Papers); endorsed. Recorded in SJL as received 11 July 1787.

John Stockdale to William Short

SIR Piccadilly, London 15th. May, 1787.

I shall esteem it a particular favor if you'll be so good as to send immediately on receipt of this, Mr. Jefferson's plate for the Map of Virginia &c., as I have had his Book printed and waiting for publishing some time. The Season for Sale of Books in London, is now far advanced. Mr. Jefferson in his Letter dated Febry. 27th. inform'd me that I should certainly receive it by the 10th. of March last. I am exceedingly hurt to find that my Man has this Instant inform'd me that he has his doubts wether Mr. Adams's Book was sent to you, agreable to Mr. Jefferson's Order, as we find its not enterd in his Account but I still hope that it was sent. I have sent one this day with the Magazines. There will be very soon another Volume of Mr. Adams's. Should be glad to know if that is wanting.

I am Sir Your obt. hble. Servt., JOHN STOCKDALE

RC (DLC: Short Papers); endorsed: "Stockdale May 15 [received] 19, 87." Short must have erred in docketing this letter as received on the 19th, for on the day after that he wrote Stockdale: "Yours of the 15th is put into my hands at the instant of my setting off into the country, so that I have only one moment to inform you that I shall send immediately to the person who has the plate for the Map and desire him to let me have it in order that it may be forwarded to you. Sh[ould he be] done with it I have left the proper directions here for its being sent without losing a moment. You may be assured that it will not be detained an instant longer than absolutely unavoidable" (Short to Stockdale, 20 May 1787; DLC: Short Papers; in his letter to TJ of 21 May, Short spoke of having received Stockdale's letter "yesterday"). MR. ADAMS'S BOOK had been sent to TJ by Adams himself, but the copy asked for ON MR. JEFFERSON'S ORDER was for Froullé (see Froullé to TJ, 17 Feb. 1787).

From Ferdinand Grand

MONSIEUR Paris le 19 may 1787.

J'ai reçu les lettres que vous m'avez fait l'honneur de m'écrire le 6. du passé et le 4. du courant dattées l'une et l'autre de Marseille. La première me prévenoit du reçu de £600 que vous aviez donné à M. Brethous et m'apportoit votre ordre chez M. Van denyver de £17500 qui m'ont été payées et que j'ai porté au Crédit des Etats Unis. J'ai vu avec bien du regret que vous n'eties pas aussi satisfait des douches que je l'aurois espéré. J'envoyai de suite à M. Short la lettre que renfermoit celle que vous m'avez fait l'honneur de m'ecrire le 4 du courant. J'y joignis un billet pour votre maitre d'hotel pour qu'en l'absence de M. Short il ouvrit la lettre qui lui etoit adressée et se conformat à son contenu. Je lui offris ce qui

[364]

dependoit de moi pour cette prompte éxpedition mais il ne s'en est pas prévalu. C'est le 10. du courant que me parvint votre pacquet.

Je souhaite, Monsieur, que ceci vous trouve encore à Bordeaux avec M. Barclay. Il m'a envoyé une Traitte de £20150. sur les fonds de l'Etat de Virginie qui se trouve réduit par les mandats que vous avez donnés à environ £12000., aux quelles il y aura de plus à ajouter l'intérêt convenu. Ne pouvant outrepasser cette somme, je renvoyé à M. Barclay sa traitte sans mon acceptation, lui faisant part de cette circonstance. Elle etoit destinée au payement d'une partie de poudre à Canon et M. Bonfield devoit la remettre au Vendeur. Je lui écris aussi à ce sujet. J'ai l'honneur d'être avec une considération distinguée Monsieur Vôtre très humble et très obéissant Serviteur, GRAND

RC (DLC); at foot of first page: "Mr. T. Jefferson chez Mrs. feger Gramont & C. à Bordeaux"; endorsed. Recorded in SJL as received 25 May 1787 at Bordeaux.

TJ's letter to Grand LE 6. DU PASSÉ (6 Apr. 1787) has not been found, but is recorded in SJL as having been written from Marseille.

From William Stephens Smith

DR. SIR Bourdeaux May 19th. 1787.

Mr. Short having informed you from Paris of my intention of being here about the 14th. and of the prospect of my remaining 2 or 3 day's, I doubt not but I should have had the pleasure of a line from you had that Letter reached you in time. I shall leave this place in the morning for Madrid, where I should be happy to hear from you. I move by order of Congress to Portugal on temporary business. I shall spend as little time there as possible and think I shall return by the way of Paris to London, and take your Commands to that *polished Island*. Sir Walter Raleigh I immagine will be at your House to receive you, and the Box which Mr. Franks lost. He supposed it was stolen from him, but he left it in the post-chaise which sett him down at Stittenburn.[1] I brought with me a small present of some books from Mr. Hollis and a Play wrote by Mr. Joddrell, which are at your Hotel. The second writing press will I hope arrive before you. Mr. Woodmason had not sent it, he says for want of an oppertunity and promised to forward it by the first that offered.

I have left the Letters which Mr. Short gave me in the care of Messrs. French & Nephew of this place, who will wait on you with them the moment they are informed of your arrival. You will encounter a very disagreable Circumstance at this place—you will find Mr. Barclay confined in the prison at the suit of the above mentioned Gentlemen for a debt of *75.000* Livrs. He has been here about a fortnight and was taken on Wednesday last. When he will get out, I know not. The Creditors expect that Congress will release him. I have put my face against the Idea, as the circumstance arises from Mr. B's negotiations as a merchant and in his private capacity and not as Consul General from the United States. Am I right or wrong? Mr. B on the other hand expects present reliefe from the order of the parliament of Bordeaux, or from the King at Versailles, but I think this cannot be done, for there is no Consular treaty ratified between our Countries. And with respect to his being on his return from his mission to Morrocco, and in that point of light might be considered under the protection of the laws of nation,[2] if it does opperate, it will be but a temporary affair, as on his arriving at Paris the same Game may be played over there. I am very apprehensive that the storm will thicken from all quarters and that he must sink under the accumulated weight. I have been with him and shall see him again to-day. I immagine this will render your stay here very short unless you see a prospect of serving him. Mr. Stephen Sayer is in the same situation in London, and Mr. Lamb is about to embark from Minorca with a load of Jack-asses for America. *Sic transit gloria mundi.* If you should visit England before my return, you will I hope find a young Gentleman there in health and spirits, who I hope will entertain you in the absence of his *Papa.* I had the pleasure of forming some little acquaintance with him before my departure and think him a very decent kind of a lad. His Excellency seems much pleased with him, and expects great things from him hereafter. I must lament that I am so unfortunate as to miss you on my road. I feel a great want of your advice relative to the theatre I am moving towards, and know not how I shall make up for it. I am an entire Stranger to Mr. Carmichael and of course without the introduction of you or Mr. A. shall be obliged to spend two or three day's in endeavouring to gain his confidence, before he will inform me fully how the politicks of his Court stands relative to us all. I believe Mr. A was not in habits of intimacy with him when in france.

    Thus far I had wrote and it was ½ past 2 oClock when Mr. Barclay entered my apartments. I received him as one risen from the dead. The parliament have liberated him upon the principle of his being on his return to Paris, on a public Embassy, and

19 MAY 1787

having the papers relative to it in his possession. You will find him at the Hotel 'Angletere near the palace Gardens. I am Dr. Sir with the greatest respect, W. S. SMITH

RC (MHi); endorsed. Recorded in SJL as received 25 May 1787 at Bordeaux.

SIR WALTER RALEIGH . . . WILL BE AT YOUR HOUSE: See TJ to Smith, 19 Feb. 1787. The PLAY WROTE BY MR. JODDRELL was his tragedy based on an episode in Herodotus, *The Persian Heroine*, which was published in 1786 in octavo and quarto. See Jodrell to TJ, 28 Feb. 1787; the copy sent to TJ was quarto (*Catalogue of the Library of the United States*, Washington, 1815, p. 142). The BOOKS FROM MR. HOLLIS were the two volumes of Blackburne's edition of the *Memoirs of Thomas Hollis* (see Thomas Brand Hollis to TJ, 17 Apr. 1787). For a note on the tangled situation of Barclay and its implications concerning diplomatic relations, see TJ to Jay, 21 June 1787. THE BOX WHICH MR. FRANKS LOST: See TJ to Smith, 19 Feb. 1787.

[1] Thus in MS; it should be Sittingbourne.
[2] Thus in MS; Smith meant to say "law of nations."

From Madame de Tott

A Châville ce 19 may

J'ai été malade assez Longtems après avoir Reçu La Lettre que Vous avez eu La bonté de m'ecrire, Monsieur, et J'ai Crû depuis quelques Jours que Je me porte bien, que celle que je pourrois avoir L'honneur de Vous Ecrire ne Vous parviendroit plus. J'esperois que Votre Retour seroit prochain, mais Mr. Short que j'ai Vû aujourdhui, m'a assurée que ma Lettre Vous parviendroit encore. C'est avec Regret et avec plaisir que je Vous Ecris, Monsieur. Devinez comment cela s'arrange, et quand Vous aurez deviné permettez moi de Vous Remercier de La très Jolie et très aimable Lettre que Vous m'avez Ecrite de Marseille. Je n'aurois Jamais imaginé que J'eusse tant de plaisir à apprendre Le prix des denrées de cette Ville. Je n'aurois Jamais imaginé que je pusse me transporter dans Votre auberge et compter avec Vous les quatre mille trois cent cinquante poissardes qui faisoient Une Vacarme Si Comique sous Vos fenêtres. Enfin Je n'aurois Jamais imaginé trouver un aussi grand interêt à La solution du problème concernant Les postillons de poste, mais il est pourtant très Vrai que j'en ai eu un très grand à Lire et à Relire tous Les tableaux que Vous avez tracés avec Un Crayon digne de Tenieres, et quelquefois digne de Raphael. Ne Vous attendez pas, Monsieur, à Recevoir Le pendant de tous Vos jolis tableaux, sans compter qu'un pauvre petit Barbouilleur comme moi ne doit pas mesurer ses forces avec Les grands hommes dont Je viens de parler. Il y a aussi une Uniformité dans Les tableaux qu'offre La Vie douce et tranquille que

20 MAY 1787

nous menons à Chaville, qui donneroit peut-être un peu de peine au pinceau Sublime du Rédacteur de l'acte d'indépendance; et pour Vous en donner une idée, Je vous dirai seulement que Jupiter pluvieux a été suspendu sur nos têtes pendant près de Six semaines, et que plusieurs fois par Jour, nous allions à La Suite L'un de L'autre donner un petit Coup sur Le baromêttre pour Voir si La colère du Dieu s'étoit enfin apaisée, et ce prophête de malheur nous annoncoit, *Grande pluie*, pour Le Lendemain. Papa et maman ont été infiniment Sensibles à Votre Souvenir. Ils me chargent tous Les deux de Vous dire mille choses tendres en Vous assurant de L'impatience qu'ils ont de Vous Revoir. La mienne est aussi Vive, Monsieur, il me sera bien doux de Vous assurer moi même de Mon attachement et de tous Les Sentiments que je Vous ai Voüés pour La Vie.

RC (MoSHi); endorsed: "Tott Mde de"; without indication of the year, but obviously in reply to TJ's of 5 Apr. 1787 and recorded in SJL as received 31 May 1787 at Nantes.

PAPA ET MAMAN: That is, the Count and Countess de Tessé (see TJ to Madame de Tessé, 20 July 1786).

From John Lamb

Alicante bay May 20th. 1787

I Received your Excellency's letter concerning the Cyphers. The Vessel that I am in here, and bound to America, Doth not take pradick[1] and all papers are so Defaced with Vinager, that it will be Imposible to get the Cypher sound, to hand's where it is ordered. Therefore must Deliver the Same to Congress, whom can Dispose of the Same at their pleasure. I am unhappy that it is so surcomstanced: I hope by this time that your Excellency is fulley persuaded of that Vile Man De Expelley, *whome I have often warned of before this*. His letters have been too freely handed to your Excellency, and to Congress likewise, for the benefit of our peace at Algiers. I most Heartily hope Congress will not be led to thank a man whome was turned out of Algiers for the Most Atrosious crimes, and Sum cay Confined at present, and I make no Doubt of the Truth of the same. If your Excellency can come at the Truth from Madrid, I am of opinion that you will think as I Do on the matter; I add that we have not had a wors Enemy than the above mention De Expelley. How far he Deceived Mr. Carmichael whilst he was holding him up to Our Publick's Vew I cannot pretend to say. But if Mr. Carmichael was not Deceive in the Man, he had a Desine to baffle my efforts whilst on my Late Mission

[368]

21 MAY 1787

to make room for a more favourite plan. With news I can give your Excelency no lite at present, but that the number of our wretched people in Algiers are reduced by the Plague. Unhappy mess indeed. I have had a Verey Disagreable winter. But am Sumpthing Recruted. I hope to be at Congress by the beginning August nex. I am Exceedingly sorrey that Mr. Barkley missed me. That he had Authority to Settle my accounts he writes me. I Am Your Excellincys Most Hmle. Servt., JOHN LAMB

RC (DLC); splotched in places by some liquid, perhaps "Vinager." Tr (DNA: PCC, No. 107, II). Enclosed in TJ to Jay, 21 June 1787, and printed in *Dipl. Corr., 1783-89*, II, 59-60, with some polishing of Lamb's spelling and grammar. Enclosed in Robert Montgomery to TJ, 22 May 1787, which was recorded in SJL as received in Paris 16 June.

TJ's LETTER CONCERNING THE CYPHERS (missing) may have suggested that they be turned over to Carmichael; if so, this gives point to Lamb's remark that CONGRESS . . . CAN DISPOSE OF THE SAME AT THEIR PLEASURE. (See TJ to Carmichael, 26 Dec. 1786.)

[1] In Tr this word is given as "prodick," but "pratique" is inserted above it in an unidentified hand, perhaps by Weaver who printed it thus in *Dipl. Corr., 1783-89*, II, 59. *Pratique*, a maritime term signifying permission to communicate with a port after a vessel had been given a bill of health or had performed quarantine, was certainly what Lamb meant. If so, Lamb's reason loses some of its force in view of the fact that, while being in quarantine and himself unable to go ashore, he nevertheless sent ashore the very letter in which the reason was offered (Montgomery to TJ, 22 May 1787). If he could do this, it is not clear why he could not also have dispatched the codes.

To Martha Jefferson

May 21. 1787.

I write to you, my dear Patsy, from the Canal of Languedoc, on which I am at present sailing, as I have been for a week past, cloudless skies above, limpid waters below, and on each hand a row of nightingales in full chorus. This delightful bird had given me a rich treat before at the fountain of Vaucluse. After visiting the tomb of Laura at Avignon, I went to see this fountain, a noble one of itself, and rendered for ever famous by the songs of Petrarch who lived near it. I arrived there somewhat fatigued, and sat down by the fountain to repose myself. It gushes, of the size of a river, from a secluded valley of the mountain, the ruins of Petrarch's chateau being perched on a rock 200 feet perpendicular above. To add to the enchantment of the scene, every tree and bush was filled with nightingales in full song. I think you told me you had not yet noticed this bird. As you have trees in the garden of the convent, there must be nightingales in them, and this is the season of their song. Endeavor, my dear, to make yourself acquainted with the music of this bird, that when you return to your own country you may be able to estimate it's merit in comparison with that of the mocking bird. The latter has the advantage of singing thro' a great part of the year, whereas the nightingale sings but 5. or 6. weeks in the spring, and a still shorter term and with a more feeble voice in the fall. I expect to be at Paris about the middle of next month. By that time we may begin to expect our dear Polly. It will be a circumstance of inexpressible comfort to me to have you both with me once more. The object most interesting to me for the residue of my life, will be to see you both developing daily those principles of virtue and goodness which will make you valuable to others and happy in yourselves, and acquiring those talents and that degree of science which will guard you at all times against ennui, the most dangerous poison of life. A mind always employed is always happy. This is the true secret, the grand recipe for felicity. The idle are the only wretched. In a world which furnishes so many emploiments which are useful, and so many which are amusing, it is our own fault if we ever know what ennui is, or if we are ever driven to the miserable resource of gaming, which corrupts our dispositions, and teaches us a habit of hostility against all mankind.—We are now entering the port of Toulouse, where I quit my bark; and of course must conclude my letter. Be good and be industrious, and you will be what I shall most love in this world. Adieu my dear child. Yours affectionately,

Th: Jefferson

RC (NNP); endorsed. PrC (MHi). Recorded in SJL under this date as written "near Toulouse." Enclosed in TJ to Short, this date.

From James Maury

Dear Sir   Liverpool 21 May 1787

I had the Honor of your favor of the 24 December. Previous to this I Had been informed of the favorable Alterations you had procured in the Tobaccoe Contract, for which our Countrymen in particular are much indebted to you: as it has certainly been the Means of the Article's maintaining, not only in Virginia, a better price than it otherwise would have done, but here also. For, as the Manufacturers in this Kingdom no longer have the picking and Culling of the Intire Crops of America at there Markets as formerly, the value of such as is suitable to their purposes, has increased accordingly. But, Sir, a late occurrence has very much alarmed every Wellwisher to our Staple. Mr. Morris's Bills in payment of his purchases for the Farmers are protested to a great amount; and, I learn, Mr. Rucker, the person whom he placed in London for the purpose of negociating, after having accepted largely and no remittances coming from France to enable him to pay, has gone over to know the occasion of it. Now as this disappointment, in its Consequences, affects more or less all who are concerned in the American Trade, I beg the favor, if no Impropriety, of your Information on the Cause of this disaster, assuring you no improper use shall be made of your Confidence.

In February I sent a Vessell to James river and by it an order to my agent at Richmond to purchase your and a few other Choice S W Mountain Crops for a Manufacturer here. What I have recieved of this Kind of Tobaccoe has generally rendered at least as well as what you mention.

I am much obliged to you for your mention of me to Mr. Adams, whom I waited on about the Time your Letter was dated.

I have had no very late accounts from Virginia.

I have the Honor to be with particular Esteem & Regard Dr. Sir your most obt. Servt., JAMES MAURY

RC (MHi). Recorded in SJL as received 11 June 1787.

To William Short

DEAR SIR

On the Canal of Languedoc, approaching Toulouse. May 21. 1787.

The only incalculable part of my journey now drawing to a close, I am able to give you a state of my future motions from which there will probably be no considerable variation, unless any considerable accident happen. I expect to arrive on the days following at the several places named.

May 23. Bourdeaux
31. Nantes
June 4. Lorient
7. Rennes
8. Nantes
11. Tours
13. Orleans
15. Paris

As there is a possibility that I may vary my route a little from Lorient, so as to avoid the repassage by Nantes, it will be adviseable to retain at Paris all letters which may arrive there after the 25th. of this month. I have passed through the Canal from it's entrance into the mediterranean at Cette to this place, and shall be immediately at Toulouse, in the whole 200 American miles, by water; having employed in examining all it's details nine days, one of which was spent in making a tour of 40 miles on horseback, among the Montagnes noires, to see the manner in which water has been collected to supply the canal; the other eight on the canal itself. I dismounted my carriage from it's wheels, placed it on the deck of a light bark, and was thus towed on the canal instead of the post road. That I might be perfectly master of all the delays necessary, I hired a bark to myself by the day, and have made from 20. to 35 miles a day, according to circumstances, always sleeping ashore. Of all the methods of travelling I have ever tried this is the pleasantest. I walk the greater part of the way along the banks of the canal, level, and lined with a double row of trees which furnish shade. When fatigued I take seat in my carriage where, as much at ease as if in my study, I read, write, or observe. My carriage being of glass all round, admits a full view of all the varying scenes thro' which I am shifted, olives, figs, mulberries, vines, corn and pasture, villages and farms. I have had some days of superb weather, enjoying two parts of the Indian's wish, cloudless skies and limpid waters: I have had another luxury which he could not wish, since we have driven him from the country of Mockingbirds, a double row of nightingales along the banks of the canal, in full song. This delicious bird gave me another rich treat at Vaucluse. Arriving there a little fatigued I sat down to repose myself at the fountain, which, in a retired hollow of the mountain, gushes out in a stream sufficient to turn 300 mills, the ruins of Petrarch's chateau perched on a rock 200 feet perpendicular over the fountain, and every tree and bush filled with nightingales in full chorus. I find Mazzei's observation just that their song is more varied, their tone fuller and stronger here than on the banks of the Seine. It explains to me another circumstance, why there never was a poet North of the Alps, and why there never will be one. A poet is as much the creature of climate as an orange or palm tree. What a bird the nightingale would be in the climates of America! We must colonize him thither. You should not think of returning to America without taking the tour which I have taken, extending it only further South. I intend to propose to Colo. T M Randolph the permitting his eldest son to take it the next spring, and suppose it would be an agreeable and oeconomical circumstance to you both to go together. You should not stop short of the country of Monsr. Pio, to whom be pleased to present me in the most friendly terms, as also to M. Mazzei, the M. de la fayette and Chastellux, maison de

Chaville, two Abbés &c. Desire Frouillé to procure for me immediately le Recueil alphabetique des droits de traites uniformes 4. v. 8vo. printed in 1786, and, as is said, at Lyons. Petit should immediately make them plant the vacant space of the garden in Indian corn in rows 3. feet apart, the plants a foot apart in the row. I finish my page with assurances of the sincere esteem and attachment with which I am dear Sir your affectionate friend & servant, TH: JEFFERSON

RC (ViW); endorsed: "Jefferson May 21, [received] 28 1787." PrC (DLC). Enclosure: TJ to Martha Jefferson, this date.

From William Short

DEAR SIR Paris May 21. 1787

A letter I recieved yesterday from Mr. Limosin shews that your letter would have been much too late for the packet had it been forwarded on immediately on its arrival. The Packet sailed from the road of Havre at 5. o'clock in the morning of the 10th. Your letter arrived at Paris the evening of the same day.—Mr. Limosin tells me there is only an English ship at Havre, to sail soon for Alexandria. I have therefore preferred giving your letter to Colo. Blackden who sets out without fail for London the day after tomorrow. I think there is no danger of his remaining here after that day. He promises to be punctual in forwarding it by the first vessel which sails for America. I have desired him not to let it go through the English post-office.

My last to you was of the 14th. Sir and sent to the care of Mr. Bondfield at Bordeaux. I hope you have recieved it as well as the letters which Colo. Smith took with him. Paul Jones after going as far as Brussels on his way to Denmark *rebroussoit chemin* and set sail in the last Packet from Havre for America. Rucker also took a sudden departure from London, and embarked on the same vessel with his lady and sister. It is said the cause of it is the protest of £50,000 sterling of Morris's bills of exchange on London. Besides these there were many other Passengers on board, mostly Americans. Five of them came from London on purpose to go in that packet. This is the beginning of the triumph of that port.

The seeds for Madame de Tessé are the Magnolia glauca. Had she had her choice in the whole vegetable kingdom, it is what she would have chosen. Hitherto she has been accustomed in Europe to recieve it in small handfulls. It is the first instance of a box

22 MAY 1787

coming charged with that alone. She says that M. de Malesherbes has been obliged to say enough, though more insatiable than herself. In fine she is charmed with this example of Virginian profusion. It seems to have compensated for Virginian inattention.—Among the letters I here inclose you, is one from Mde. de Tott, who will tell you probably a great many fine things on the part of Mde. de Tesse. I leave the article of compliments &c. to her.

I recieved yesterday a letter from Stockdale begging I would send him without delay the plate. I despatched instantly a messenger to Barrois, the Abbé de Morellet's bookseller, whom I have been hurrying from the moment of his having the plate in his possession. His answer was that he did not know if the striker of the maps was done with it but would send to know, and give me an answer this morning, yesterday being sunday. I have heard nothing yet from him. I have desired Petit not to let him rest as Stockdale seems very intent on having the plate immediately.

The Assembly it is said will rise on Thursday, and a bed of justice is talked of but I believe without foundation. The American credit has been treated very contemptuously in the Count D'Artois bureau, and the American debt affected by some, to be considered as *doubtful*. On enquiry into this debt I find I have been mistaken in supposing that the interest of the 24. millions had been hitherto paid. The arrears are much greater both of principal and interest than I had imagined. Would to Heaven America would determine to pay off the whole both due and to become due, at one blow.—During the month of May we have had incessant rains until three or four days past; the wind is now north and promises fair weather. I hope it will soon bring you here. Be assured my dear Sir of the sincerest attachment of Your friend & servant,

W Short

RC (DLC); endorsed. PrC (DLC: Short Papers). Recorded in SJL as received 31 May 1787 at Nantes. In addition to the letter from Madame de Tott of 19 May 1787, the following that TJ also received at Nantes at the same time were probably enclosed by Short: From Adams, 18 Apr. 1787; from Cary, 21 Mch. 1787; from Eppes, 23 Oct. 1786; from Martha Jefferson, 3 May 1787; and from Wythe, Jan. 1787.

From William Drayton

Sir   Charleston, May 22d. 1787.

I had the Honour to receive your Excellency's Letter of the 6th. of February with the Box of Cork-Oak Acorns. Your former Letter

[374]

miscarried; but the Parcel of Spanish St. Foin seed reach'd me, tho' very lately; and I am afraid it is so much injur'd by the Delay, (being extremely mouldy), that it will not vegetate: at least there is no appearance of it yet, where I planted it, in my Garden. I return your Excellency many thanks in the Name of our Society for your condescending to be a Member, and being so attentive to the Designs of it's Institution.

There has been lately discovered among us a Grain, which if it does not prove an advantageous Article for Exportation, may still be extremely useful for domestic Purposes. The Discovery has been so lately communicated to the Society, that altho' the Plant is very common, and generaly known to most of us, it has not yet been investigated sufficiently for me to give a botanical description of it. The Grain is like a large Oat; when clear'd of the Husk, it resembles Rice, except that it is rounder and longer; some plain Bread made of it was perfectly sweet and palatable. The Stalk is a kind of Cane; it grows luxuriantly in our richest swamps, is very productive, and is perennial. I take it to be, what Carver in his Description of the western Parts of this Continent calls the wild Rice.

We shall be extremely oblig'd to your Excellency for any farther Communications, which your Leisure and Residence in Europe shall enable you to make tending to the Improvement of Agriculture in these States.

I have the Honour to be, with the greatest Respect, Your Excellency's most obedient humble Servant, WM. DRAYTON

RC (DLC); endorsed. Recorded in SJL as received 16 Dec. 1787.

From André Limozin

Le Havre, 22 May 1787. Transmits account of expenses "for the 12 large Boxes Cartouch Boxes" shipped on the *Portsmouth*, Captain Oldner, for Norfolk. The whole amounts to £ 588-17-6, which has been debited against TJ's account. "Mr. Rucker, residing in London, of the House Constable, Rucker & Co. of New York, hath found himself in the most cruel Situation to leave London because he could not honor Robt. Morris's drafts which he had accepted for a very important sum of money. That unexpected Circumstance hurts prodigiously Mr. Robt. Morris's Credit."

RC (Vi); 2 p.; endorsed. Recorded in SJL as received at Paris 11 June 1787. Enclosed statement of account not identified.

From Robert Montgomery

Sir   Alicante 22. May 1787

The inclosed for Your Excellency was deliverd me by John Lamb Esqr. who calling in here on his way from Mahon to N. York, was obliged to remain in Quarantine on Account of Some appearance of Contagion among the Spanish Slaves from Algeirs now on the Island of Minorca, and as he Could not come on shore desired I would be Very perticular in forwarding his letter, of which you will please do me the Honor of acknowledgeing the receipt.

I had the Honour of Establishing the first American House of Commerce that ever appeard in Spain, and Since that time in 1776 have contributed to the Extent of my Power to the welfare of our Countrey, which is Known to Mr. Jay, and when in Spain I requested he would recommend me to Congress for the apointment of Consul at this place, in Consequence of which I had the inclosed letter, which you will be so kind as to return and Excuse the trouble as I only Send it as an Introduction not presuming to write you without one.

I believe that Congress have not yet appointed any Consuls for Spain, and as they will be Necessary in the Great Tradeing Towns, my pretention, for that place at Alicant still Remains as at the begining, 'tho I have Served in that line for Eleven years past with as Scrupulous an attention to the Intrest of the Countrey as if I had had the Commission.

The Algerin Corsairs are now all at Sea, four small Vessels Saild the begining of last Month with orders to Cruise in the Medeterranian and Streights Mouth and the rest of them about two Weeks after for the Western Ocean. My last letters from Algeirs are of the 4 March. They Mention that one of our unhappy Wretches there was dead of the plague, the Sailors are at work with the Slaves of Other Nations in the ship Yard, the Mates and Captains had orders to retire to the Countrey where they would be less exposed to danger of the infection.

Should you Honor me with any Commands you may Depend on my Zeal And attachment being with very Sincere Respect Sir Your Excellencys Most obedt. Huml. Servant,

ROBT. MONTGOMERY

RC (DLC); endorsed. Recorded in SJL as received 16 June 1787. Enclosures: (1) Lamb to TJ, 20 May 1787. (2) Jay to Montgomery, of unknown date and not found.

From Ferdinand Grand

Monsieur   Paris ce 23 may 1787.

Je prens la liberté de vous confirmer la lettre que j'ai eu l'honneur de vous ecrire le 19 de ce mois; qui avoit pour un principal objet la traitte de Mr. Barclay pour les Etats de Virginie de £20150. Et comme en réflechissant sur cette affaire, il seroit possible que vous eussiés pu avoir l'idée de faire porter cette somme au compte des Etats unis; ce qui n'est pourtant pas très probable, puisque vous aurés pû être à même de juger d'après les derniers comptes que j'ai eu l'honneur de vous fournir, que ce compte ne devoit pas non plus présenter des fonds libres. J'ai cependant cru devoir, Monsieur, faire jetter un coup d'oeuil sur sa situation, et je remarque que les Etats unis y sont débiteurs d'environ £11/000 à 12/000 au moins. Je ne doute pas que vous n'ayez jugé convenable d'ecrire préssamment et depuis longtems sur ces affaires au Congrès.

Je vous renouvelle l'assur[ance] des obeissances de ma famille et des sentimens respectueux avec [les]quels j'ai l'honneur d'être, Monsieur, Votre très humble et très obeissant serviteur,

                                                     Grand

RC (DLC); at foot of text: "Mr. Jefferson chez. Mrs. feger Gramont Ce Bordeaux"; endorsed. Recorded in SJL as received at Paris 11 June 1787.

From the Abbé Gaubert

[*Before 25 May 1787*. At Bordeaux, according to an entry in SJL of this date, TJ received a letter from "Gaubert Abbé." No place or date of writing was given, and letter has not been found; see entry for TJ to Gaubert, 13 June 1787.]

From Wilt, Delmestre & Cie.

[*L'Orient, 25 May 1787*. Recorded in SJL as received at Paris 11 June 1787. Not found.]

To John Banister, Jr.

                                    Bourdeaux May 26. 1787

Th: Jefferson's compliments to Mr. Bannister. Meeting at this place with Capt. Gregory, just sailing for Virginia he takes the occasion of inclosing to him two letters received in the course of his journey. The hurry in which he is leaves him time at present only to reiterate his prayers for the health and happiness of Mr. Bannister and assurances of his esteem, as well as of that he bears to Mr. Bannister the father, and Mrs. Bannister.

PrC (DLC). Enclosures not identified.

To William Carmichael

Dear Sir   Bourdeaux May 26. 1787.

Being thus far on my tour through the seaports, I find here a letter from Colo. Smith, informing me of his having passed this place on his way to Madrid. As I believe you are not acquainted with each other, give me leave to recommend him to your attentions, not as a matter of formality but with all the warmth which his uncommon merit deserves. His good sense you will immediately perceive, but the virtues of the heart re[quir]e time and trial. I have had occasion to see them in him, and can assure you that his candor [and] honour may be [re]lied on under every possible circumstance [sh]ould there be occasion for confidential communications between [you]. I shall moreover acknolege as a debt any civilities you will be so good as to shew him. I expect to be at Paris by the [middle] of the next month and from thence again to resume the thread of our correspondence which my journey has for a while interrupted. I have the honour to be with sentiments of the highest esteem & respect Dear Sir Your most obedient & most humble servt.,   Th: Jefferson

PrC (MHi); considerably faded (in general copies made by the portable copying press, being executed under varying conditions, were inferior to those made by TJ's large press); some words supplied conjecturally. Enclosure: TJ to Smith, 26 May 1787.

To Francis Eppes

Dear Sir   Bourdeaux May 26. 1787.

Making a tour round the sea-ports of this country on matters of business, and meeting at this place with Capt. Gregory, just sailing for Portsmouth, I cannot deny myself the pleasure of asking you to participate of a parcel of wine I have been chusing for myself. I do it the rather as it will furnish you a specimen of what is the very best Bourdeaux wine. It is of the vineyard of Obrion, one of the four established as the very best, and it is of the vintage of 1784. the only very fine one since the year 1779. Six dozen bottles of it will be packed separately addressed to you and delivered to Capt. Gregory, who will take care to send it to you, and perhaps call on you himself. If he does you will find him a good humoured agreeable man. Much hurried by my departure hence, I cannot enter into details of news &c. I must beg you however to deliver my love to Jack, to tell him that his letter which he wrote near a year ago, came to my hands but a few days ago at Marseilles, and that it shall be among the first I answer on my arrival at Paris, which will not be till the middle of next month. He will have more claims to every service of mine than I can possibly find opportunities of rendering them. Recall me to the affectionate remembrance of Mrs. Eppes and the family. I say nothing of my dear Poll, hoping she is on her passage, yet fearing to think of it. Adieu my dear Sir and be assured of the warmest esteem of your affectionate friend & servant, TH: JEFFERSON

PrC (MHi); endorsed by TJ, by mistake: "Smith Wm." According to the entry in SJL, the letter from JACK—that of John Wayles Eppes of 22 May 1786—was received at Aix on 3 May 1787, not at Marseilles.

From Robert Montgomery

Alicante, 26 May 1787. Wrote by the last post and enclosed a letter from Lamb, "who is Yet in Quarantine." A vessel arrived at Carthagena from Algiers last week brought news of the Dey's death and the continuance of the plague. Has no other news except that he has been told that "the Cecession of hostillities with Napoles has not been Very Strictly attended to on the Side of the Pirates."

RC (DLC); 2 p.; endorsed. Recorded in SJL as received 11 June 1787.

From G. Pin

MONSIEUR   Toullouse le 26 may 1787

Des affaires pressantes m'ont Empeché de vous faire parvenir Plutot l'itineraire du Canal que vous desiries recevoir. Je l'insere icy. S'il y a quelque autre Eclaircissement qui puisse vous plaire, veuillés me donner Vos ordres. Personne ne sera plus Exact que moy à les Executer et à vous donner des preuves du Zele qui m'anime pour tout Ce qui peut vous Interresser.

Je suis avec respect Monsieur Votre tres humble et tres obeissant Serviteur, G PIN

RC (DLC); endorsed. Recorded in SJL as received 31 May 1787 at Nantes. Enclosure: Report on the construction and commercial advantages of the Languedoc Canal, its route, the distances between locks, and junctions with other trade routes (DLC; in French; undated; at head of text: "Canal des Mers de Languedoc"; 7 p.; in an unidentified hand).

To William Stephens Smith

DEAR SIR   Bourdeaux May 26. 1787.

I find here the letter you were so kind as to leave for me and am truly sorry I did not arrive in time to have the pleasure of meeting with you here. I hope however you will take Paris in your way back, and indemnify my loss. I am to thank you as usual for favors, attention to the press, the mathematical instrument, books, letters &c. This done I will pass to a more pleasing subject still, that of congratulation on the birth of the young son. May his days be many, and brighten all yours. This goes under cover to Mr. Carmichael, whom it will reach before you will, and it's envelope will have prepared him to meet you with all the confidence you may wish. My letters from Paris attending me at Nantes, I am not able to give you details of any occurrences since you left that place; and the hurry with which I am pursuing the objects which brought me here in order that I may get on the road again, oblige me to conclude with wishes for your happiness always repeated, yet always sincere, and assurances of the esteem with which I am Dear Sir your friend & servt.,   TH: JEFFERSON

RC (MHi: DeWindt Collection); addressed: "A Monsieur—Monsieur le Colonel W. S. Smith Secretaire de legation des E. U. d'Amerique à la cour de Londres chez Monsieur Carmichael à Madrid"; endorsed. PrC (MHi). TJ to Carmichael, 26 May 1787 was IT's ENVELOPE.

From Martha Jefferson

MY DEAR PAPA   Paris, May 27th, 1787.

I was very glad to see by your letter that you were on your return, and I hope that I shall very soon have the pleasure of seeing you. My sister's letter gave me a great deal of happiness. I wish she would write to me; but as I shall enjoy her presence very soon, it will make up for a neglect that I own gives me the greatest pain. I still remember enough of geography to know where the places marked in your letter are. I intend to copy over my extracts and learn them by heart. I have learnt several new pieces on the harpsichord, drawn five landscapes and three flowers, and hope to have done something more by the time you come. I go on pretty well with my history, and as for *Tite Live* I have begun it three or four times, and go on so slowly with it that I believe I never shall finish it. It was in vain that I took courage; it serves to little good in the execution of a thing almost impossible. I read a little of it with my master who tells me almost all the words, and, in fine, it makes me lose my time. I begin to have really great difficulty to write English; I wish I had some pretty letters to form my style. Pray tell me if it is certain that my sister comes in the month of July, because if it is, Madame de Taubenheim will keep a bed for her. My harpsichord is not come yet. Madame L'Abbesse is better, but she still keeps her bed. Madame de Taubenheim sends her compliments to you. Pray how does your arm go? I am very well now. Adieu, my dear papa; as I do not know any news, I must finish in assuring you of the sincerest affection of your loving child, M. JEFFERSON

MS not found; text from Randolph, *Domestic Life*, p. 121-2. Recorded in SJL as received at Paris 16 June 1787, and given the date of 26 May 1787.

Enclosed in Short to TJ, 29 May 1787. YOUR LETTER: TJ to Martha, 5 May 1787. MY SISTER'S LETTER: Mary to TJ, 22 May 1786.

From William Short

DEAR SIR   Paris May 29. 1787

I recieved yesterday evening your favor of the 21st. from the canal of Languedoc and in consequence of the route which you trace I send this to L'Orient to the care of the American Agent there. I percieve by your letter that mine of the 8th. must necessarily have missed you at Aix. I hope that of the 14th. sent to the care of Mr. Bondfield at Bordeaux, and that of the 21st. sent to Nantes post restante, have been more fortunate. I see also that you must have been too late to have found Smith at Bordeaux.

Your several letters have pushed forth a germ that has been long existing in my breast and made me determine I think unchangeably on a tour through France and Italy. Your letter of yesterday makes me hope there will be no obstacle in the only circumstance which could be one. I mean your leave of absence from Paris during a sufficient time for that purpose. I should desire much a companion for several reasons. The only possible objection to him you propose arises from the idea with which his name inspires me, of the impossibility of his conforming to so oeconomical a plan as I should propose. However prudent his determinations might be I should have little faith in his perseverance. The season that would be most agreeable to me is also different from that you mention. The plan I have thought of would be to set out from Paris in the winter, push forward in a right line to the southermost point of my journey and from thence return gradually to Paris *cum prima hirundine*. I am far from supposing the winter more agreeable than the spring for travelling, but my plan has the advantage of absence from Paris during a part of the winter, which is so much clear gain.—I saw M. de Pio yesterday evening and the Abbés this morning. I discharged your commissions to them all, and they are all very thankful for your remembrance. I saw also the Marquis de la fayette yesterday morning but it was before recieving your letter. His stay is at present at Paris, the assembly having risen on the 25th. The prospects of the present moment are certainly still very flattering. The Archbishop has at length many calumniators. They think his principles are changed since his coming into the ministry. The Marquis de la f—— says it is not true and I believe him.—Nothing as yet done for Mr. de Calonne's letter to you, the delay unaccountable except on the principle of the multiplicity and importance of the affairs of the present moment. However I have no doubt matters will be put right by time.—Mr. Grand wrote you a letter last week and sent it to Bordeaux to the care of his correspondent there. I think from the view of your march that you will necessarily have recieved it there. It will give you I believe an unexpected view of the funds of Congress here. It affects me the more particularly at present, because, having recieved remittances some time ago from America, and having, as I supposed, in Mr. Grand's hands one years salary with which I had not meddled, it happened that an increase of wealth, as is generally the case, brought with it an increase of avarice. I determined therefore to blend together my late remittances from America and the year's salary in arrear, and place the whole with Mr. Grand who was to employ it so as to derive a considerable interest. I purposed making use of the salary as it should become due in future for my future support, leaving the rest to grow in Mr. Grand's hands. Before we perfected this plan he discovered the state of the American funds to be what he states them to you, so away went my scheme of becoming rich for that moment; yet I hope I shall not be obliged to abandon it altogether.

29 MAY 1787

The Packet in which Franks and Banister sailed, has returned and the letters it brought arrived here yesterday together with New-York Papers as late as the 24th. of April. There are four letters for you two of which are public. From the papers I collect that New York has passed an act confirming the independance of Vermont, and has also named commissioners for the convention in Philadelphia. At the election for Governor of Massachusetts, Mr. Hancock had a small majority above Mr. Bowdoin in Boston. How the election has been in the other parts of the state does not appear.—Congress have diminished all the salaries of their officers in America, the President inclusive.—Rhode Island seems at present under an administration that does it no honor—however although by no means foederally disposed, I do not observe that they have made any change in their grant of the impost to Congress. Petit desires me to mention to you that it would be well for you whilst at L'Orient to purchase three or four dozen of china plates. He has some time ago planted corn, but not so much as you seem to desire. He says it is too late to plant the grain at present and therefore intends filling up the deficiency by plants which he will purchase, and thus gain the time lost.

Barrois has sent me word that he cannot part with the plate before the last of this week. I do not think it certain that he will do it even then. Should he delay would you chuse that I should insist on having it to forward to Stockdale?

I am ashamed to tell you, but it is true, that Blackden is still in Paris. I was persuaded from what I knew of his circumstances that he would not remain longer than the day he fixed, but I was decieved. He has still your letter for Mr. Jay. What shall I do with it? The English ship bound to Alexandria of which Limosin wrote to me is probably gone before this. I am out of all patience with Blackden. I think it is the last time he will decieve me.

In consequence of your desire the letters which arrive are detained here for you, except one from Miss Jefferson which I inclose you, because I am persuaded of the pleasure it will give you to hear from her. It was written before the reciept of that which came inclosed to me for her yesterday, and which I sent her immediately on opening my letter. Petit who saw her tells me she was perfectly well. Be assured my dear Sir of the sentiments of the most sincere attachment with which I am your friend & servant,

W Short

RC (DLC); endorsed. PrC (DLC: Short Papers). Recorded in SJL as received in Paris on 16 June 1787. Enclosure: Martha Jefferson to TJ, 27 May 1787.

From John Sullivan

Dear Sir   Durham in New Hampshire May 29th. 1787

Before your Moose and other Articles were on their way I found myself under the Necessity of Drawing on you for forty five pounds Sterling, not exactly knowing the amount of Expences attending or that might attend the Business. Capt. Pierce was to have carried them but unfortunately Left them. I afterward sent the Box to Boston to the Care of Mr. De la Tombe and am informed that it is now on its way for havre de grace. The Bills for forty five pounds are returned, as Bills on france will not sell at this time, and have Drawn for the full Ballance being forty six pounds seven shillings and ten pence Sterling and Inclosed the Account in my Letter of advice. The Bills are in favor of William Smith Esqr. Secretary to Mr. Adams in London, upon whom I have taken the Liberty to Draw for that Sum and inclosed the Bills on you to reimburse him. I now do myself the honor to inclose you the Letters and papers which were to have accompanied the first Bills as they are more particular than the Last. I wish them all safe to hand and have the honor to be with the highest Esteem and respect Dr. Sir your most obedient Servant,   Jno. Sullivan

RC (DLC). Recorded in SJL as received 26 Sep. 1787. Not all of the enclosed "Letters and papers" have been identified with certainty, but they are known to have included Sullivan's two earlier letters to TJ, and enclosures, of 16 Apr. and 17 Apr. 1787, which were received at the same time as the present letter.

From Miguel de Lardizábel y Uribe

Madrid, 30 May 1787. Since he has received no reply to the letter he wrote on his arrival in Spain, he writes again to inquire about TJ's health, and to express appreciation for his many courtesies. His earlier letter mentioned that he had put the copying press into Carmichael's hands; has been almost constantly at court, and so unable to procure the books TJ desired, but promises to do his utmost. Sends compliments to Short, and gives Madrid as address.

RC (MHi); 2 p.; in French; endorsed. Recorded in SJL as received 23 June 1787. Lardizábel's previous letter has not been found.

From George Washington

Dear Sir   Philadelphia 30th. May 1787.

It has so happened, that the letter which you did me the honor of writing to me the 14th. of November last, did not come to my hands till the first of the present month; and at a time when I was about to set off for the Convention of the States appointed to be holden in this City the 14th. Instt. Consequently, it has not been in my power, at an earlier period, to reply to the important matters which are the subjects thereof. This, possibly, may be to be regretted if the house of de Coulteaux should, in the meantime, have directed its enquiries to Philadelphia, Baltimore, or New York without having had the advantages which are to be derived from the extension of the inland navigations of the Rivers Potomack and James, delineated to them. Silence on this head may be construed into inferiority, when the fact (in my judgment) is, that Alexandria or Richmond, provided the communication with the latter can be conducted by the Greenbrier and Great Kanhawa (as some aver and others doubt), has infinite advantages over either of the Towns just mentioned. With respect to James River, I am not able to speak with so much precision as of the former, with which (having had opportunities to be so) I am much better acquainted. —To this therefore I shall chiefly confine my observations.

In investigating the advantages of Alexandria as the most proper place for a principal deposit in the Fur Trade, I have thought it necessary to leave as little room for partiality, and prejudice to operate as possible, by concealing, as far as may be, the object of the investigation.—Tho' the result has been favourable to Alexandria, I trust it will be found to have arisen from such weighty considerations, as must be felt by every mind; particularly that of the Merchant whose interests on this subject must alone determine the scale. With a very superficial knowledge of the relative Geography of the places* in contemplation by Monsr. Coulteaux to establish a concern in the Fur Trade to the Country yielding this article, a meer glance at the Map must decide Alexandria in point of distance to be the most convenient spot.—Hence, a considerable saving would accrue in the article of Land-carriage; an object of so much importance in the communication between places[1] seperated by immense wildernesses, and rugged roads, as to render any comment on it to a Merchant, superfluous.—But the difficulty

---

* Alexandra.   Baltimore,   Philada.   New York.

30 MAY 1787

arising from this source (tho' already less) will soon, in a great measure, be obviated with respect to Alexandria, by the extension of the Navigation of Potomack.—The progress already made in this great National work, not only justifies this opinion, but the most sanguine expectations which have been formed of its success. —Granting therefore that the advantages of a greater proximity to the Fur Country, was not on the side of Alexandria, still the immense superiority which a communication almost by water, would give it, must be obvious to all who consider the ease with which the distant produce of the different, and opposite parts of the earth are mutually exchanged, by means of this element. As neither of the other places can ever enjoy this singular benefit to so great a degree, Alexandria must, of course, be the place to which the Inhabitants of the Western Country must resort with all their Commodities (unless by the other channel mentioned, Richmond should be found equal to it); and from whence they will take back their returns in foreign products with the least expence. The Act for opening a road from the highest point to which the Navigation of Potomack can be extended, to the Cheat river, must also be considered as an important circumstance in favour of Alexandria; and in the same light the act of the last Session for opening a road to the mouth of the Little Kanhawa, from the road last mentioned, must be considered.—Besides these, leave has been obtained from Pensylvania by the States of Virginia and Maryld., to open another road from Wills Creek to the Yohiogani, by the nearest and best rout. By these acts, great part of the Trade which has been accustomed to flow through Pittsburgh to Philadelphia must be derived[2] in rich streams to the Potomack; for I believe it to be as true in commerce as in every thing else, that nature, however she may be opposed for a while, will soon resume her regular course—neither therefore the attractive power of Wealth, nor the exertions of industry, will long, it is presumed, withhold from Alexandria the advantages which nature has bestowed on her.

If the great extent of territory adjacent to the Fur Country, which Virginia possesses, in comparison with the States to which the other Towns belong, be viewed, Alexandria must still be considered as the most proper place.—The Country about the Illinois and Wabash (Rivers which nearly reach the Lakes in their Course) has been long considered as the most abundant in Furs; and the completion of the Navigation of James River must, without doubt, render Richmond the most convenient for *these* of any other; if, as I have once or twice before observed, the Navigation

30 MAY 1787

of the Kanhawa can be improved to any good account. By those however who are not acquainted with the nature of the western waters, and the short portages between them, it may be objected that the Rivers abovementioned are too far South to meet with good Furs; but it may not be amiss to observe here, that the Rivers of lake Erie &c. communicate so nearly, and with such ease, with those of the Ohio, as to afford the shortest and best transportation from Detroit; by which all the Furs of the upper lakes must pass; whether they go to Canada, New York, Philadelphia, Baltimore, Alexandria or Richmond; and that the Routs from thence to the two latter are thro' the territory of the United States; whereas the one to New York passes along the line, and is, besides, subject to interruptions by Ice when these are entirely free from it. These objections, particularly the latter, apply in a degree both to Philadelphia and Baltimore; because if either can avail itself of water transportation, it must be by the more Northerly streams of the Ohio, with the waters of the Susquehanna, considerably above the Monongahela, and still more so above the Great Kanhawa, the first of which communicates with the River Potomack, and the latter with that of James.

The last advantage which occurs to me in favor of Alexandria, is, that the business would be carried on there without any competition: No one having yet engaged so deeply in it, as to hold out any encouragement. I have even been informed that Waggons loaded with Furs, have sometimes passed through Alexandria to Baltimore in search of a Market; and from Winchester it is their common practice to go there with this commodity; tho' Alexandria is much more convenient to them.—On the side of New York, the most eligable Posts for this trade are in the possession of the British; and whenever they are ceded it will, I expect, be found, that the Merchants of that Nation, from their Wealth, long establishment, and consequent knowledge of the Country, will be such formidable competitors, as to draw the greater part of the Furs into Canada.

I shall now proceed to mention a person in whose skill and integrity, Monsr. Coulteaux may, I think, have the fullest confidence; and tho' I am precluded in some measure from so doing by being told that it is required that he should be an American born; I shall still venture to name a Gentleman who is a native of Ireland—Colo. John Fitzgerald. The active Services of this Gentleman during the War, his long residence in the Country and intermarriage in it (with one of the most respectable families, Digges of Maryland) all entitle him to be considered as an American.—The laws of this Country know no difference between him and a native of America. He has besides been bred to trade, is esteemed a man of property and is at present engaged in the former in Alexandria. Lest however this should be considered as an insuperable obstacle, I shall name a second—Robert Townshend Hooe Esqr., who has every desired requisite.—I shall just observe, that if the business is carried on extensively, it would probably require the various acquaintance and combined activity of each of those Gentlemen.

I come now to the other part of your letter, which concerns the Cincinnati, and here indeed I scarcely know what to say.[3] It is a delicate, it is a perplexing subject.—Not having the extract from the Encyclopedia before me, I cannot now undertake to enter into the merits of the publication.—It may therefore perhaps be as much as will be expected from me, to observe that the Author appears in general to have detailed very candidly and ingenuously the motives, and inducements which gave birth to the Society. Some of the subsequent facts, which I cannot, however, from memory pretend to discuss with precision, are thought by Gentlemen who have seen the publication to be mistated; in so much that it is commonly said, truth and falsehood are so intimately[4] blended, that it will be[5] difficult to sever them. For myself, I only recollect two or three circumstances, in the narration, of which palpable mistakes seem to have insinuated themselves.—Majr. L'Enfant did not arrive and bring the Eagles during the Session of the General meeting, but sometime before that Convention. The Legislature of Rhode Island never passed any Act whatever on the subject (that ever came to my knowledge)[6] notwithstanding what Mirabeau and others had previously advanced.—Nothing can be more ridiculous than the supposition of the author that the Society was instituted partly because the Country could not then pay the Army, except the assertion that the United States have now made full and compleat provision for paying not only the arrearages due to the officers, but the half pay or commutation, at their option. From whence the Author deduces an argument for its dissolution. Though I conceive this never had any thing to do with the Institution; yet, the officers, in most of the States, who never have, nor I believe[7] ever expect to receive one farthing of the principal or interest on their final settlement securities, would doubtless be much obliged to the Author to convince them how, and when they received a compensation for their Services. No foreigner, nor Amer-

30 MAY 1787

ican who has been absent some time, will easily comprehend how tender those concerned are on this point.—I am sorry to say a great many of the officers consider me as having in a degree committed myself by inducing them to trust too much in the justice of their Country.—They heartily wish no settlement had been made, because it has rendered them obnoxious to their fellow Citizens, without affording the least emolument.

For the reason I have mentioned,[8] I cannot think it expedient for me to go into an investigation of the writers deductions. I shall accordingly content myself with giving you some idea of the part I have acted, posterior to the first formation of the Association.

When I found that you and many of the most respectable characters in the Country would entirely acquiesce with the Institution as altered and amended in the first General Meeting of 1784, and that the objections against the[9] obnoxious parts were wholly done away, I was prevailed upon to accept the Presidency. Happy in finding (so far as I could learn by assiduous enquiries) that all the clamours and jealousies which had been excited against the original association, had ceased; I judged it a proper time in the last Autumn, to withdraw myself from any farther Agency in the business, and to make my retirement compleat agreably to my original plan. I wrote circular letters to all the State Societies, announcing my wishes, informing that I did not propose to be at[10] the triennial meeting, and requesting not to be re-elected President.—This was the last step of a public nature I expected ever to have taken. But having since been appointed by my Native State to attend the National Convention, and having been pressed to a compliance in a manner which it hardly becomes me to describe; I have in a measure, been obliged to sacrifice my own Sentiments, and to be present in Philadela. at the very time of the General Meeting of the Cincinnati, after which I was not at liberty to decline the Presidency without placing myself in an extremely disagreeable situation with relation to that brave and faithful class of men, whose persevering[11] friendship I had experienced on so many trying occasions.[12]

The business of this Convention is as yet too much in embryo to form any opinion of the result. Much is expected from it by some, but little by others, and nothing by a few.—That something is necessary, all will agree; for the situation of the General Government (if it can be called a government) is shaken to its foundation and liable to be overset by every blast.—In a word, it is at an end, and unless a remedy is soon applied, anarchy and confusion

30 MAY 1787

will inevitably ensue. But having greatly exceeded the bounds of a letter already I will only add assurances of that esteem, regard, and respect with which I have the honor to be Dear Sir Yr. most obed. & Very Hble. Serv., G: WASHINGTON

RC (DLC); endorsed. Dft of that part concerning the Society of the Cincinnati (DLC: Washington Papers); in the hand of David Humphreys, with two corrections in Washington's hand; at head of text: "Sketch in Answer to Mr. Jefferson's letter." FC (DLC; Washington Papers); in an unidentified hand, with corrections by another. Recorded in SJL as received 20 Aug. 1787. Some of the variations between texts are noted below.

See note to TJ to Washington, 14 Nov. 1786, which Washington received about 25 Apr. 1787, not THE FIRST OF THE PRESENT MONTH. Humphreys saw Washington in Philadelphia at the general meeting of the Cincinnati and then or soon after drew up the form of a reply to TJ's comments on the Cincinnati that Washington incorporated with two slight modifications in the present letter. On returning home Humphreys wrote Washington on 28 May 1787: "I intended fully when I left Philadelphia, to have written to you from New York, but on my arrival there my Servant (who was a German) ran away, and I was so occupied in procuring another, that I have not been able to take up the pen until the present moment.—Recollecting imperfectly, as I do, the purport of Mr. Jefferson's letter, as well as of the Extract from the Encyclopedia; I have found myself embarrassed in attempting to say any thing on so delicate a subject—especially considering it a subject on whose merits Posterity is to judge, and concerning which every word that may be drawn from you, will probably hereafter be brought into question and scrutinised. —Under this view I have thought, the less that could with decency be said, the better" (DLC: Washington Papers). The phrasing of this letter would seem to indicate that Humphreys enclosed the Dft in it (see Humphreys, *Humphreys*, I, 415), but the date of the letter evidently would have made it impossible for its enclosure to arrive in Philadelphia in time to be incorporated in Washington's letter. Several explanations occur: (1) Humphreys had written the statement before he left Philadelphia and intended his letter, which had no enclosure and which arrived after Washington had fully utilized Humphreys' statement, as nothing more than an expression of his own misgivings that he had perhaps said too much in the Dft. (2) He enclosed the Dft but misdated his letter. (3) Washington received Humphreys' letter with the enclosed Dft but misdated his own. (4) Washington began his letter on 30 May but held it open until he received Humphreys' letter and the promised statement. The last of these seems the most likely explanation. Washington had promised Dr. David Stuart that he would write to TJ as soon as he arrived in Philadelphia. He, Stuart, COLO. JOHN FITZGERALD, and Dr. James Craik had dined together at Mount Vernon on Sunday, 6 May, when they no doubt discussed the matter that enlisted Washington's keen interest and caused him to want to reply to TJ at the earliest moment—that is, the overture of Messrs. Le Couteulx concerning the fur trade. On 30 Apr. Dr. Stuart had written Washington giving data on this that would be useful in drafting a reply to TJ. These, Washington replied, "are all clear and self-evident and in some instances may be enlarged. Did you communicate the plan to Cols. Fitzgerald and Hoes [ROBERT TOWNSHEND HOOE]? and how far did you give either, or both, reason to believe they would be recommended to Mr. Jefferson . . . ? I wish to be fully informed of this that I may govern myself accordingly" (Washington to Stuart, 5 May 1787; *Writings*, ed. Fitzpatrick, XXIX, 211).

[1] This word repeated.
[2] In FC this word deleted and "drawn" substituted.
[3] Text of Dft begins at this point, but its opening remarks read: "I scarcely know what to say respecting that part of your communication which concerns the Cincinnati. It is a delicate, it is a perplexing subject."
[4] In Dft this word written in substitution for "dexterously and," deleted.
[5] Dft and FC both read: "will become very difficult."
[6] The clause in parentheses is interlined in Dft in Washington's hand.

⁷ Preceding two words interlined in Dft in Washington's hand.
⁸ Both Dft and FC read, instead: "I first mentioned."
⁹ Both Dft and FC read at this point: "hereditary and other."

¹⁰ Dft reads at this point: "at Philadelphia at the triennial meeting"; in FC "triennial" is deleted and "General" interlined in substitution.
¹¹ FC reads: "patriotism and."
¹² Text of Dft ends at this point.

From Jeudy de l'Hommande

Votre Excellence

De L'hotel des armes De L'empire
Rue dauphine Ce 31 mai 1787

Le Commerce des Farines, étant une branche de la plus grande importance pour Les Treize Etats unis, Votre Patrie, et le défaut qu'elles ont de ne pas se Conserver dans les Colonies Françoises, Angloises et Espagnolles, étant on ne peut plus prejuciable aux habitans ou Négocians qui en font Commerce: Pourois–Je avoir L'honneur de vous demander, Si vous seriez dans le cas de traiter avec moi du secret et des Moyens de ne fabriquer à l'avenir que des Farines de bonne qualité dans votre Pays, dont Je suis Libre et certain de vous en démontrer toutes les causes, et les Moyens qui S'y opposent, pour en instruire les Fabriquans?

Ne veuillez pas croire, Votre Excellence, que je vous propose un Projet en L'air, et sans avoir une Connoissance exacte des causes qui font que Les farines de France sont superieures aux Votres, de même que de Celles qui font qu'elles ne Se Conservent pas la plupart du temps en mer dans les Vaisseaux, avec les Moyens *Physiques* d'empêcher à l'avenir qu'elles ne s'y gatent aussi frequemment? Je ne vous parle, Votre Excellence, qu'avec pleine connoissance de cause, et une étude de la Nature dans tous ses Phénomènes depuis trente ans, à qui Je dois ces Lumieres; et vous allez en Juger.

Ayant voyagé en France dans les Pyrenées, La Gascogne, à Bordeaux, et dans tous les lieux de Fabrique D'où on exporte des farines de ce Royaume; ensuite en Angleterre, en Hollande et dans les Colonies françoises, particulierement à St. Domingue où J'ai été dans le Cas d'observer la difference des Climats, et les effets que La Chaleur pouvoit faire sur ce Comestible; Il m'a fallu avoir fait tous ces voyages, vu et observé tous ces differens endroits, en Naturaliste et en Physicien, pour être dans le cas de revéler toutes les Causes qui peuvent nuire à ce genre de fabrication, par L'analogie qu'il y a entre tous les Climats sous les mêmes Latitudes, et la difference qu'il peut y avoir entre un Climat chaud et temperé, et Plus ou moins temperé.

1 JUNE 1787

Ainsi, Votre Excellence, Vous pouvez Juger maintenant, Si J'ai L'honneur de vous parler en homme qui n'est pas certain de son fait.

Ne croyez pas cependant que J'en veuille priver ma Patrie. Dieu me preserve de pareils sentimens, mais Comme chaque Pays à ses instructions particulieres à recevoir, Je puis rendre service à toutes les Puissances Maritimes sans Nuire à L'autre en quelque sorte; et d'ailleurs, comme mes Connoissances interessent trop L'humanité pour ne pas les divulguer autant qu'elles le méritent, il est Naturel que J'en tire tout l'avantage possible, pour me dédommager des frais Considerables que mes Voyages m'ont Couté, parce qu'il n'y en a aucune qui voudroit me rembourser toutes les depenses et sacrifices que j'ai faits à ce sujet.

Je suis et serai Prêt d'avoir L'honneur de vous rendre mon respect quand il vous plaira.

Dans cette intention, J'ai L'honneur d'etre avec les Sentimens Les plus distingués, Votre Excellence, Votre très humble et très obéissant Serviteur,   JEUDY DE LHOMMANDE

RC (DLC); endorsed: "de l'Hommande." Recorded in SJL as received in Paris 11 June 1787.

From Anne Willing Bingham

[Philadelphia, 1 June 1787]

I am too much flattered by the Honor of your letter from Paris, not to acknowledge it by the earliest opportunity, and to assure you that I am very sensible of your attentions. The Candor with which you express your sentiments, merits a sincere declaration of mine.

I agree with you that many of the fashionable pursuits of the Parisian Ladies are rather frivolous, and become uninteresting to a reflective Mind; but the Picture you have exhibited, is rather overcharged. You have thrown a strong light upon all that is ridiculous in their Characters, and you have buried their good Qualities in the Shade. It shall be my Task to bring them forward, or at least to attempt it. The state of Society in different Countries requires corresponding Manners and Qualifications; those of the french Women are by no means calculated for the Meridian of America, neither are they adapted to render the Sex so amiable or agreable in the English acceptation, of those words. But you must confess, that they are more accomplished, and understand the Intercourse of society better than in any other Country. We

1 JUNE 1787

are irresistibly pleased with them, because they possess the happy Art of making us pleased with ourselves; their education is of a higher Cast, and by great cultivation they procure a happy variety of Genius, which forms their Conversation, to please either the Fop, or the Philosopher.

In what other Country can be found a Marquise de Coigny, who, young and handsome, takes a lead in all the fashionable Dissipation of Life, and at more serious moments collects at her House an assembly of the Literati, whom she charms with her Knowledge and her bel Esprit. The Women of France interfere in the politics of the Country, and often give a decided Turn to the Fate of Empires. Either by the gentle Arts of persuasion, or by the commanding force of superior Attractions and Address, they have obtained that Rank and Consideration in society, which the Sex are intitled to, and which they in vain contend for in other Countries. We are therefore bound in Gratitude to admire and revere them, for asserting our Privileges, as much as the Friends of the Liberties of Mankind reverence the successfull Struggles of the American Patriots.

The agreable resources of Paris must certainly please and instruct every Class of Characters. The Arts of Elegance are there considered essential, and are carried to a state of Perfection; the Mind is continually gratified with the admiration of Works of Taste. I have the pleasure of knowing you too well, to doubt of your subscribing to this opinion. With respect to my native Country, I assure you that I am fervently attached to it, as well as to my Friends and Connections in it; there is possibly more sincerity in Professions and a stronger desire of rendering real services, and when the Mouth expresses, the Heart speaks.

I am sensible that I shall tire you to Death from the length of this Letter, and had almost forgot that you are in Paris, and that every instant of your Time is valuable, and might be much better employed than I can possibly do it. However, I shall reserve a further examination of this subject to the Period, when I can have the happiness of meeting you, when we will again resume it. I feel myself under many obligations for your kind present of les Modes de Paris; they have furnished our Ladies with many Hints, for the decoration of their Persons, and I have informed them to whom they are indebted. I shall benefit by your obliging offer of service, whenever I shall have occasion for a fresh Importation of Fashions; at present I am well stocked having lately received a variety of Articles from Paris.

1 JUNE 1787

Be so kind as to remember me with affection to Miss Jefferson—tell her she is the envy of all the young Ladies in America, and that I should wish nothing so much as to place my little Girl, under her inspection and protection, should she not leave Paris before I re-visit it. I shall hope for the pleasure of hearing from you, and if you accompany another book of fashions, with any new Opera's or Comedies, you will infinitely oblige me. It is quite time I bad you adieu, but remember that this first of June I am constant to my former opinion, nor can I believe that any length of time will change it. I am determined to have some merit in your eyes, if not for taste and judgment, at least for consistency.

Allow me my dear Sir to assure you that I am sincerely & respectfully yours &c., A BINGHAM

RC (MHi); without date, which has been supplied from that in the final paragraph and which, in view of the remarks in TJ to Mrs. Bingham of 7 Feb. 1787, need not be taken as literally exact; the same may be said of her statement that she had answered that letter "by the earliest opportunity." Recorded in SJL as received, without date, on 27 Aug. 1787.

From J. P. P. Derieux

Collé, Albemarle co., 1 June 1787. Although unknown to TJ, he hopes TJ will forgive his presumption in enclosing some letters to be posted, for the province and for Paris. He asks that if necessary the letter for Philip Mazzei, his father-in-law, be forwarded or put into the hands of Favi, chargé d'affaires for Tuscany, who is generally in communication with him; that TJ deliver himself those for his relatives, Mde. Plumard de Bellanger and M. Viel (attorney for the King's Council, whose letter contains a power of attorney), in order that on TJ's return Derieux may have first-hand news of them; and that any letters for Derieux be sent under the cover of Col. Nicholas Lewis of Charlottesville.

RC (DLC); 2 p.; in French; endorsed. Recorded in SJL as received 7 Aug. 1787. Enclosures not found, but see Madame Plumard de Bellanger to TJ, 16 Sep. 1787; TJ to J. P. P. Derieux, 16 Sep. 1787.

To Martha Jefferson

MY DEAR PATSY   Nantes June 1. 1787.

Your letter of May 3. came to me at this place. Since this I hear nothing from you; but I hope your health is reestablished. I have received letters from America as late as March assuring me that your sister shall be sent this summer. At that time however they

[394]

did not know certainly by what occasion she could come. There was a hope of getting her under care of the French Consul and his lady, who thought of coming to France. The moment and place of her arrival therefore are still incertain. I forgot in my last letter to desire you to learn all your old tunes over again perfectly, that I may hear them on your harpsichord on it's arrival. I have no news of it however since I left Paris, tho' presume it will arrive immediately as I had ordered. Learn some slow movements of simple melody, for the Celestini stop, as it suits such only. I am just setting out for Lorient, and shall have the happiness of seeing you at Paris about the 12th. or 15th. of this month, and of assuring you in person of the sincere love of your's affectionately,

TH: JEFFERSON

RC (NNP).

To William Short

DEAR SIR　　　　　　　　　　　　　　　Nantes June 1. 1787.

Your favor of May 8. which had arrived at Aix after I had passed that place, followed me here where I have received it, as also that of May 21. The one by Colo. Smith I received at Bourdeaux. He had left that place a week before I reached it. I wrote to him to the care of Mr. Carmichael. I left Mr. Barclay at Bourdeaux. He waited only the post of the day before yesterday to set out for Paris. But I have betted him a bottle of Burgundy on being there before him. Mr. Cairnes being absent from this place, and Mr. Loreilhe from Lorient will probably shorten my stay at both, so that I may be at Paris three or four days sooner than I had expected, say from the 11th. to the 15th. Your's of the 8th. of May, and my daughter's inclosed in it mention her illness and that she was recovering. You last saying nothing of her, proceeds I hope from her being well: but it would be a relief to me to know that this is the case as soon as possible. The first place at which I could meet a line from you will be Tours, and perhaps not till Orleans. Will you be so good as write me a line simply saying if she is well and send it by duplicate to each of these places poste restante. It had better contain nothing but a sentence relative to her as I may miss the one at Tours. You may add if you please a word of Espagnol's health. Pray tell him that I enquire after his health. It may serve to reestablish his confidence in my dispositions towards him, if that has

been weakened by my not taking him on my journey, and having actually carried another thro' the whole of it. Adieu my dear Sir & be assured of the sincere wishes for your happiness of your affectionate friend and servt.,
TH: JEFFERSON

RC (ViW); endorsed: "Jefferson June 1 recd. at St. Germain [June] 9 1787." PrC (DLC); endorsed through error by TJ, and so catalogued: "Bannister J."; a question mark, perhaps later and probably not by TJ, was added to this endorsement.

YOUR LAST: That is, Short's of 21 May 1787. TJ was wrong in supposing that he received a letter from Short BY COLO. SMITH . . . AT BOURDEAUX; the one he received there was dated 14 May, after Smith had left Paris, and was sent in care of Bondfield.

From Feger, Gramont & Cie.

MONSIEUR Bordeaux Le 2 Juin 1787

Nous sommes bien impatients d'apprendre vôtre heureux retour dans la capitale, et nous vous renouvellons bien sincèrement nos regrets de n'avoir pas eu le bonheur de vous posseder plus longtems.

Il nous est venu, depuis votre départ, une lettre pour vous que nous adressons aujourdhui à Mr. Grand en le remerciant de son attention à nous procurer votre Connoissance.

Nous avons chargé, suivant vos Ordres, Six dousaines de bouteilles de vin de Chateaux Margaux, en trois caisses, sur le Navire le Comte d'artois, et nous les adressons à Mr. *Frances Eppes* à *Eppington* à qui nous en remettons le connoissement.

Et nous adressons aujourdhui le restant de la Barique de vin, en quatre caisses de 45 Bouteilles, à Mr. Garovey à Rouen, avec priere de vous les faire passer et nous lui en remettons également le connoissement.

Voici la facture du tout montant à £.747.11s., que nous portons au Compte de Mr. Grand avec qui vous voudrés bien vous en entendre.

Nous vous renouvellons les assurances des Sentiments de zèle et de Respect avec lesquels nous avons l'honneur D'être Monsieur Vos trés humbles et trés obeissants serviteurs,

FEGER GRAMONT & CIE

RC (MHi); endorsed. Enclosure (MHi): Invoice from Feger, Gramont & Cie. covering two shipments of Chateau Margaux 1784: the first, shipped in *Le Comte d'Artois*, marked FEP, and addressed to "M.frances Eppes Esqr à Epington in chesterfield en Virginie," consisted of three cases containing 24 bottles each; the second, shipped in *Le Vendangeur*, marked JEF, and consigned to Garvey at Rouen consisted of four cases of 45 bottles each—or a total of 252 bottles @ 55 sols each, amounting in all to 693 livres; to this were added commission, fees, and other charges, bringing the total cost to 747 livres 11 sols (actually, due to an error in calculating the costs of cases, fees, &c., the total should have been 748 livres 11 sols).

The letter that arrived at Bordeaux after TJ's departure and was returned to MR. GRAND was probably Grand's own letter to TJ of 23 May 1787.

From C. W. F. Dumas

The Hague, 5 June 1787. Short's last letter causes him to hope that TJ has returned to Paris in good health and particularly that he has recovered "la libre usage d'une main si bien faisante et si utile à la patrie et à l'humanité." In Holland everyone lives in readiness, and in anxiety too, for a civil war. The crisis is to come this month: "Il est question de tout sauver ou de tout perdre." Has two other dispatches to send to Congress, one from Sweden, the other for the Department of War. Will send them by the two next regular posts, and would be obliged to hear from TJ or Short whether these two and the present arrive safely.

RC (DLC); 2 p.; in French. FC (Dumas Letter Book, Rijksarchief, The Hague; photostats in DLC). Recorded in SJL as received at Paris 11 June 1787. Enclosure: Dumas to Jay, 5 June 1787, which in turn encloses a "Note" signed Feronce de Rosencrantz, dated Brunswick, 16 May 1787, concerning the forwarding of a letter notifying George Charles Frederic Hartmann, formerly of the Brunswick troops and now a resident of Virginia, to appear before 1 Feb. 1788 to establish his claim to an estate in Brunswick (both in same and both printed in *Dipl. Corr., 1783-89*, III, 577-8, though the letter to Jay is there dated 7 June, and the "Note" is dated 15 May 1787).

From John Churchman, with a Memorial on Magnetic Declinations

DEAR FRIEND   Philadelphia 6th mo. June 6th. 1787.

I take the liberty of Writing on a subject which as it is interesting to Society I hope will require but little apology. And yet I must be ingenious enough to confess that in my pursuits of this subject I have not been without a view to my own emolument, in which I have done nothing more than to accept of the invitation held out by many Governments of Europe to engage in the public service with promises of Generous reward. I must beg it as a favour that the enclosed paper may be presented to the Royal Academy of Sciences at Paris, altho I had sent it by another conveyance, but as I had not a Friend at Court the receipt of which may be uncertain, concern[ing] which I would wish to renew the old contract "no purchase no pay." If it should meet with success I shall hold myself in duty bound to make ample satisfaction for the trouble: whether or no I shall be under many obligations to a

[397]

6 JUNE 1787

person who is generally esteemed the best judge of business of this Nature by the Inhabitants of the States which he represents. I would wish it to be delivered whether there is a prospect of reward or not. The Secretary of Congress has been obliging enough to propose writing a Line on my behalf. I remain with the greatest sentiments of respect &ca. &ca., JOHN CHURCHMAN

P.S. I shall be glad to receive a Line enclosing an account of the present variation at Paris.

ENCLOSURE

Philada. 4th Mo. april 10th. 1787

The Memorial of John Churchman respectfully represents

That the Variation of the Compass and its hitherto imagined uncertain Laws have long engaged the attention of Philosophers And Mathematicians. Why it should move at one Time slow, at another Time quick, now become stationary and then retrograde, has puzzled the Enquirer, and although these varieties have been continually Subjects of observation, Yet I have never heard that any Regular System hath hitherto been published to account for or foretel upon any rational plan, what will be the future Movements of this wonderful Phenomenon, the Magnetic Influence. Whether My attempts to reconcile all these Difficulties and of consequence to build on them a certain System of Longitude will prove true or false must be left to the world to judge.

From a variety of observations, Reflections and Deductions, the following Conclusions are assumed.

1st. That the Magnetic Needle hath a Direction to two Points at certain Distances, one from the North, the other from the South Pole of the Earth.

2ly. That these Points, to which it hath a Direction are properly called Magnetic Poles.

3ly. That the Magnetic Poles perform Revolutions in certain given Times from West to East.

4ly. That by a Variety of Deductions, and by laying down Many observations of the variation of the Magnetic Needle, one of these Poles is found to be at a certain Distance from the North Pole of the Earth, which for distinction May be called the North Magnetic Pole.

5ly. That the orbit in which the South Magnetic Pole moves, is larger than the Northern orbit.

6ly. That the angle between a Meridian of the Earth and the Magnetic Meridian is the Variation of the Compass.

7ly. That the Northern Magnetic Pole in 1779 was in Latitude 76.° 4′ and Longitude 85.° 12′ west from London and its period of Revolution is 463 years 344 days.

8ly. That the Situation of the Southern Magnetic Pole for want of a sufficient Number of observations, I have not yet so accurately determined, but in the Year 1777 I calculate it to have been in 72 degrees

[398]

South Latitude and 140 degrees East Longitude from London or Greenwich.

That from hence the Longitude of either Pole is easily determined, and I have formed a Sett of Tables of their Annual Situations from the Year 1657 (when a Line of no variation passed over London) to the Year 1888, when a Line of no Variation will again pass the same Place.

That having the Latitude of the Magnetic Poles and by ascertaining the Longitude of the same from the Tables for any given Time, we are able to determine the Longitude of any Place with the greatest Precision from a combined observation of the Latitude of the Place and the Variation of the Magnetic Needle.

It may be necessary to observe that a Magnetic Meridian for any part of this Globe is a circle drawn through the two Magnetic Poles and the place of observation. If the Magnetic Poles were diametrically opposite to each other, the Line of no Variation would coincide with the Meridian of the Earth, and all the Magnetic Meridians would of consequence be great Circles; but though this is not the case, the Longitude is determined by a Method full as simple as if they were great Circles; that the Magnetic Meridians meet in the two Magnetic Poles, and that these Poles are in certain parts of their orbits in certain Times. There is sufficient Proof, by laying down on a Globe the observations of the Variation Made by the late celebrated Cap. Cook in his last Voyage round the world as well as those made by other able Navigators.

JOHN CHURCHMAN

RC (MiU-C); addressed; endorsed, and beneath endorsement is a notation in TJ's hand: "varian. at Paris 21° W." Enclosure (MiU-C). Thomson's letter of this date may have been enclosed also.

From Lafayette

MY DEAR FRIEND   Paris June the 6th. 1787

It would Be almost as easy to shoot one of the flying Geniuses of the Arabian Nights as to direct a letter to the place where it Has the Best chance to Hit You. I Have Been dilatory in My Answer, which must be imputed to the public Hurry of National Affairs. But as I Now Hope for Your Speedy Return, I shall Make this letter the Shorter Because I Have thousand things to tell you. Our Assembly Has ended with. Advantages Have Been obtained—dearly paid—But Not inconsiderable in their present State, and future prospects. This new administration is very able and Virtuous, and in the Arch Bishop you will find a Man truly Great and Good. You will not be displeased to Hear that Count d'artois's Bureau Have adressed the king in favor of the protestants and for a Revisal of our jurisprudence. Indeed I Hope our french affairs will take a good turn. I Had letters from America by the last

6 JUNE 1787

packet. Rhode island seems to be averse to the New Convention. But it can go on without Her delegates. New york Has not immediately adopted the Measures proposed by Congress for the Execution of the treaty with G.B. From those intelligences, the Ennemies of America never fail to Conclude, and the ignorant part of the people, which, with Respect to America, includes almost Every European, Never fail to Repeat that every thing there is in Confusion. For my part, I know as well as You, and our American friends, that Every thing will come to Rights, and that in the Mean While that Government is not Be[ing] so much abused, where the far Greater proportion of the people are Happier than Any where else on the Globe. Adieu, My good friend, Most affectionately Yours, LAFAYETTE

You will Be glad to hear that our Respected friend M. de Males Herbes is called Again to the Council of State. I Rejoice for my Country in the Acquisition of this good, and Enlightened Minister, and Consider this choice as a good omen for the Administration that is Newly set on foot. The duke of nivernois, a very Honest and sensible man is also called to the Council. I want You to know the Arch Bishop of Toulouse, Because I am sure You will find that He is the Very Man to Manage the affairs of a Great Empire.

RC (DLC); endorsed: "Fayette M. de la." Recorded in SJL as received 11 June 1787 at Paris.

From James Madison

DEAR SIR Philada. June 6th. 1787.

The day fixed for the meeting of the Convention was the 14th. ult: on the 25th. and not before seven States were assembled. General Washington was placed unâ voce in the chair. The Secretaryship was given to Major Jackson. The members present are from Massachusetts Mr. Gherry, Mr. Ghorum, Mr. King, Mr. Strong. From Connecticut Mr. Sherman, Doct. S. Johnson, Mr. Elseworth. From N. York Judge Yates, Mr. Lansing, Col. Hamilton. N. Jersey, Governour Livingston, Judge Brearly, Mr. Patterson Attorney Genl. [Mr. Houston and Mr. Clarke are absent members.] From Pennsylvania Doctr. Franklyn, Mr. Morris, Mr. Wilson, Mr. Fitzimmons, Mr. G. Clymer, Genl. Mifflin, Mr. Governeur Morris, Mr. Ingersoll. From Delaware Mr. Jno. Dickenson, Mr. Read, Mr. Bedford, Mr. Broom, Mr. Bassett. From Maryland Majr. Jenifer only. Mr. McHenry, Mr. Danl. Carrol, Mr. Jno. Mercer,

6 JUNE 1787

Mr. Luther Martin are absent members. The three last have supplied the resignations of Mr. Stone, Mr. Carrol of Carolton, and Mr. T. Johnson as I have understood the case. From Virginia Genl. Washington, Governor Randolph, Mr. Blair, Col. Mason, Docr. McClurg, J. Madison. Mr. Wythe left us yesterday, being called home by the serious declension of his lady's health. From N. Carolina, Col. Martin late Governor, Docr. Williamson, Mr. Spaight, Col. Davy.—Col. Blount is another member but is detained by indisposition at N. York. From S. Carolina Mr. John Rutledge, General Pinkney, Mr. Charles Pinkney, Majr. Pierce Butler. Mr. Laurens is in the Commission from that State, but will be kept away by the want of health. From Georgia Col. Few, Majr. Pierce, formerly of Williamsbg. and aid to Genl. Greene, Mr. Houston.— Mr. Baldwin will be added to them in a few days. Walton and Pendleton are also in the deputation. N. Hamshire has appointed Deputies but they are not expected; the State treasury being empty it is said, and a substitution of private resources being inconvenient or impracticable. I mention this circumstance to take off the appearance of backwardness, which that State is not in the least chargeable with, if we are rightly informed of her disposition. Rhode Island has not yet acceded to the measure. As their Legislature meet very frequently, and can at any time be got together in a week, it is possible that caprice if no other motive may yet produce a unanimity of the States in this experiment.

In furnishing you with this list of names, I have exhausted all the means which I can make use of for gratifying your curiosity. It was thought expedient in order to secure unbiassed discussion within doors, and to prevent misconceptions and misconstructions without, to establish some rules of caution which will for no short time restrain even a confidential communication of our proceedings. The names of the members will satisfy you that the States have been serious in this business. The attendance of Genl. Washington is a proof of the light in which he regards it. The whole Community is big with expectation. And there can be no doubt but that the result will in some way or other have a powerful effect on our destiny.

Mr. Adams' Book which has been in your hands of course, has excited a good deal of attention. An edition has come out here and another is on the press at N. York. It will probably be much read, particularly in the Eastern States, and contribute with other circumstances to revive the predilections of this Country for the British Constitution. Men of learning find nothing new in it, Men

6 JUNE 1787

of taste many things to criticize. And men without either, not a few things, which they will not understand. It will nevertheless be read, and praised, and become a powerful engine in forming the public opinion. The name and character of the Author, with the critical situation of our affairs, naturally account for such an effect. The book also has merit, and I wish many of the remarks in it, which are unfriendly to republicanism, may not receive fresh weight from the operations of our Governments.

I learn from Virginia that the appetite for paper money grows stronger every day. Mr. H—n—y is an avowed patron of the scheme, and will not fail I think to carry it through unless the County[1] which he is to represent shall bind him hand and foot by instructions. I am told that this is in contemplation. He is also said to be unfriendly to an acceleration of Justice. There is good reason to believe *too*[2] *that* he is[3] *hostile* to *the object of the convention* and that *he wishes either a partition or total dissolution of the confederacy.*

I sent you a few days ago by a Vessel going to France a box with peccan nuts planted in it. Mr. Jno. Vaughn was so good as to make the arrangements with the Capt: both for their preservation during the voyage and the conveyance of them afterwards. I had before sent you via England a few nuts sealed up in a letter.

Mr. Wythe gave me favorable accounts of your Nephew in Williamsburg. And from the Presidt. of Hampden Sidney who was here a few days ago I received information equally pleasing as to the genius, progress, and character of your younger nephew.

I must beg you to communicate my affectionate respects to our friend Mazzei, and to let him know that I have taken every step for securing his claim on Dorhman, which I judged most likely to succeed. There is little doubt that Congress will allow him more, than he owes Mr. Mazzei, and I have got from him such a draught on the Treasury board as I think will ensure him the chance of that fund. Dorman is at present in Virga. where he has also some claims and expectations, but they are not in a transferrable situation. I intended to have written to Mazzei and must beg his pardon for not doing it. It is really out of my power at this time. Adieu. Yrs. affy.,

J M

RC (DLC: Madison Papers); endorsed; partly in code. Recorded in SJL as received 14 July 1787.

[1] Late in life Madison interlined at this point: "[Prince Edward]."

[2] This and subsequent words in italics are written in code and were decoded interlineally by TJ; his decoding has been verified by the editors, employing Code No. 9.

[3] These two words were omitted by Madison when writing the letter and were supplied by him late in life.

From Charles Thomson

Dear Sir   Philadelphia June 6. 1787

Having come to this place on account of some private business, I have been waited on by Mr. J. Churchman, a native of this commonwealth, who flatters himself that he has made a discovery which will be of great public utility, in short nothing less than an easy and certain mode of ascertaining the longitude by what is commonly called the variation of the compass. He offered to explain to me the principles of his discovery; but as disquisitions of this nature are out of my line, and as the business on which I have come here would not admit of my paying attention to the Subject I have referred him to others more conversant than I am in matters of this kind.

Wishing to submit the matter to your consideration he has requested me to accompany the letter and piece, he means to send you, with a few lines recommending his scheme to your attentive perusal and if you shall find his principles well founded, his deductions justly drawn and the result such as he flatters himself it is, that you will as far as you shall judge proper favour him with your countenance in perfecting his system and endeavouring to obtain the rewards promised for the discovery. With great esteem and regard I have the honor to be Dear Sir Your most obedt. and most humble servt.,   Chas. Thomson

RC (DLC). This letter may have been enclosed in Churchman to TJ, 6 June 1787.

From Eliza House Trist

Dr. Sir   Philadelphia June 6th. 1787

I with much pleasure acknowledge the receipt of your very kind favors of Dec. 86. and Feby. 87. Tho the dates were at distant periods, they were presented to me nearly at the same time. However great the satisfaction which I ever experience when honord by such testimonials of friendship, I wou'd not wish to purchase it at the expence which I find it has cost you. The pain with which you wrote renders indeed the proof of your condecending goodness the more flattering to me; but I could not wish for it untill you recover strength eno' to perform those offices without inconvenience. No one can feel more interested in so desireable an event then my self because no one can esteem you more. If my prayers cou'd avail,

6 JUNE 1787

your happiness wou'd be without alloy. But as humanity can not furnish a single instance of real happiness I can only wish your health and preservation. I shou'd have been well pleased to have visited my friends in Richmond; and to cultivate an acquaintance with your amiable friend Mr. Eppes wou'd have been a sufficient inducement for me to have undertaken the journey had my Brother fulfilld his engagement with me. But circumstanced as I was a perfect noun substantive, the viset might have been considerd by my acquaintances as a project of enterprise which tho laudable where necessity urges, is not an admirable trait in the character of a female. Such has long been my defenceless situation, but I look forward for the happiness of a protector in my Son. He is now allmost of stature sufficient to perform the duty of a gallant.—I thank you, my heart thanks you for the trouble you have been at to promote the interest of my self and Son. I received a letter from Mrs. Champernowne dated the 3d. of last March acquainting me with the sudden Death of her Eldest Brother; the only surviveing one she says, he means to write to me him self and inform me what I may draw for. She desires me to get a certificate of Browses birth taken from the register on oth and attested by several reputable housekeepers who have allways known him. I dont know whether there will be any difficulty in proving the truth. Gov. Randolph who is now with us, is so obligeing as to promise me his advise upon the occasion. She further informs me of receiving a letter from you and expresses great satisfaction at the pleasing account you gave of her Nephew. Mr. Trist of London I fancy has not adverted to the time that the invitation was given for our going to England. While the old Lady lived there appeard a desire in the family for the child to be sent to them, and indeed Mr. Trist and my self were solicited to abandon the scheme of setling on the Mississippi and go to England, but since his death they have never mention'd any thing on that subject to me. I wrote two letters to Mr. Trist of London but never received any from him. I shall take your advise and write him again. I am under great obligations to Mr. Trumbull for the pains he has taken in my affairs. I shou'd have no objection to undertake a voyage if the interest of my Son shou'd require it but circumstanced as I am it wou'd be impossible. I fear if the family know I have caused an enquiery into the situation of their family affairs, they may be offended, as Mrs. Champernowne seems to be willing to give me the information I ask. My letter being spun out to a tiresome length allready, I leave to those who are more capable of knowing than my self what is going forward in the political world to inform you.—The murmer of poverty still prevails but to appearence are as great as ever. Our family is much enlarged by the meeting of the convention of the States. Gov. Randolph, Dr. McClurg, Mr. Madison and Mr. Beckley all of your State make a part. Mrs. Randolph did not accompany her Husband. She has lately presented Mr. Randolph another little one, but is now so well recoverd as to undertake the journey and in a short time I hope to have the happiness of seeing her in this city. My Mother and Brother accept your kind remembrance with pleasure and in return present their respects and best Wishes, my son is well, and my health thank God is much improved. I am Dr. Sir your much obliged friend and Hume. Servt.,

E. Trist

RC (MHi); endorsed: "Trist Mrs." Recorded in SJL as received 14 July 1787.

The ELDEST BROTHER (semicolon added editorially after this phrase to clarify the text) was Hore Browse Trist, for whom Mrs. Trist's son was named; THE ONLY SURVIVEING brother was the Rev. Browse Trist (Mrs. Trist to TJ, 24 July 1786).

From C. W. F. Dumas

The Hague, 7 June 1787. Encloses the dispatch relating to Sweden mentioned in his last; has nothing to add that TJ will not find in it. "L'apostume ici n'est pas crevé encore. Leurs Hautes Puissances ou plutôt celui dont elles sont les Marionettes et les pantins, témoignent un grand appétit d'être les Despotes de l'armée de la République, et de chaque Province. On met bon ordre à cela dans celle-ci au moins."

RC (DLC); 2 p.; in French; endorsed. FC (Dumas Letter Book, Rijksarchief, The Hague; photostats in DLC); varies slightly in phraseology. Recorded in SJL as received 11 June 1787. Enclosure: Dumas to Jay, 7 June 1787, which in turn enclosed a letter from Baron Schultz d'Ascheraden, Swedish envoy at The Hague, requesting Dumas' good offices in the matter of the recovery of a vessel belonging to a subject of Sweden, concerning which D'Ascheraden enclosed a "Note" describing Captain Adolph F. Dahlberg, who was suspected of having run away with the vessel and of operating her under false pretences; the vessel was described in the note, attested by Dumas, as "painted black when she left Calmar, had a figure of a little girl at her head, and was called the Mary Elizabeth" (letter and enclosures printed in *Dipl. Corr., 1783-89*, III, 578-90; FC in Dumas Letter Book, Rijksarchief, The Hague; photostats in DLC; Tr in DNA: PCC, No. 93, III; see JCC, XXXIII, 535n.).

From John Rutledge

DEAR SIR   Philadelphia June 7th. 1787

I take the Liberty of recommending to Your Countenance and Protection, my eldest son, who will have the Honour of presenting this Letter.

8 JUNE 1787

It is my Wish, that he remain till december in France, then to go to England to attend the Courts and Houses of Parliament in Winter. I would have him to go also to Holland to visit the Hague, and some of the German Courts, and to bend his thoughts and Attentions to those Places and Objects which may be most worthy of them during his Absence from Carolina. That Time I compute will be two Years and a half. I request that you will do me the Honour to favour him with your Advice from Time to Time, and to afford him such Recommendations and Introductions as may be advantageous to him, in the Countries to which he will repair. My Brother Edward on my lately coming from Charleston requested that I would not fail to remember him very particularly to you. I have the Honour to be, with great Respect and Esteem, Dr. Sir yr. most obed. servt., J: RUTLEDGE

P.S. Should my son have occasion for more Money whilst in France, than he carries and than he has an order for, from Mr. Ross of this City on Le Couteulx & Co., be pleased to have him supplied by them with what further sums he may want. I shall make Arrangements for Remittances to reimburse as soon as I return to Charleston, which will be as soon as the Convention now sitting here rise.

RC (DLC); endorsed. Recorded in SJL as received 13 July 1787.

From C. W. F. Dumas

Note de la Haie le 8e. Juin 1787

Le soussigné croit devoir adresser l'incluse directement au Département militaire des Et. Unis, sans en embarrasser celui des affaires Etrangeres, et ajouter seulement ici, pour que S. E. Mr. Jefferson sache de quoi il s'agit, que l'on m'apprend que Mr. Fred. Werneck, Capitaine Prussien, s'étoit rendu en 1776 en Amérique, et y avoit débuté par servir les Et. Unis comme Ingénieur volontaire; puis en 1779 comme Lieutenant Colonel en Virginie, où il dirigeoit les fortifications de l'Etat; et qu'il mourut en 1783 "Colonel Ingénieur à Richmont; et que la Régence y a pris sous garde et protection son hoirie en argent et terres. Qu'il a un frere, Lieutenant Colonel au service de France, incapable d'écrire par de grieves blessures; et un autre à Nassau Idstein," à qui j'avois fait tenir la Lettre pour lui du Département militaire, et qui m'adresse les incluses en réponse.

9 JUNE 1787

Son Excellence Mr. Jefferson, ou Mr. Short, voudront bien avoir la bonté de m'accuser par un mot la reception de celle-ci et de mes deux précédentes, et agréer mes respects et ceux de ma famille.

Leur très humble et très obeissant serviteur,

C W F DUMAS

RC (DLC). FC (Dumas Letter Book, Rijksarchief, The Hague; photostats in DLC). Enclosure: Dumas to Henry Knox, secretary at war, 8 June 1787, informing him in response to previous inquiries that he had succeeded in locating Werneck and enclosing two letters from him for the War Department that he now sends under TJ's cover (same).

From Edward Carrington

DEAR SIR   New York June 9. 1787

I did myself the honor to address you by favor of Mr. Payne, in answer to yours of the 16th. January.

The proposed scheme of a convention has taken more general effect, and promises more solid advantages than was at first hoped for. All the States have elected representatives except Rhode Island, whose apostasy from every moral, as well as political, obligation, has placed her perfectly without the views of her confederates; nor will her absence, or nonconcurrence, occasion the least impediment in any stage of the intended business. On friday the 25th. Ult. seven States having assembled at Philadelphia, the Convention was formed by the election of General Washington President, and Major W. Jackson Secretary. The numbers have since encreased to 11 States—N. Hampshire has not yet arrived, but is daily expected.

The Commissions of these Gentlemen go to a thorough reform of our confederation. Some of the States, at first, restricted their deputies to commercial objects, but have since liberated them. The latitude thus given, together with the generality of the Commission from the States, have doubtless operated to bring Genl. Washington forward, contrary to his more early determination. His conduct in both instances indicate a deep impression upon his mind, of the necessity of some material change. It belongs to his wisdom and weight of character to be averse to meddling in a fruitless attempt; and this must have been the case upon a confined ground, or a very partial representation of the States: it would have been equally inconsistent with his situation to come forward upon any occasion, except in the extremity of public necessity. In every public act he hazards, without a possibility of gaining, reputation. He already

[407]

9 JUNE 1787

possesses everything to be derived from the love or confidence of a free people, yet it seems that it remained for himself to add a lustre to his character, by this patriotic adventure of all, for his countries good alone.

The importance of this event is every day growing in the public mind, and it will, in all probability, produce an happy era in our political existence; taking a view of the circumstances which have occasioned our calamities, and the present state of things and opinions, I am flattered with this prospect. Public events in the United States since the peace have given a cast to the American character, which is by no means its true countenance. Delinquencies of the States in their fœderal obligations; acts of their legislatures violating public Treaties and private Contracts, and an universal imbecility in the public administrations, it is true, form the great features of our political conduct; but these have resulted rather from constitutional defects, and accidental causes than the natural dispositions of the people. Destitute as the fœderal sovereignty is of coercive principle, backwardness in the component parts to comply with its recommendations, is natural and inevitable. Coercion in Government produces a double effect—while it compels the obedience of the refractory, it redoubles the alertness of the virtuous by inspiring a confidence in the impartiality of its burthens. From defect of penalty, ideas of delinquency are inseparable. States, as well as individuals, will contemplate both together, and apprehensions of unequal performance, produce disgust and apathy throughout.

The nefarious Acts of State Governments have proceeded not from the will of the people. Peace once obtained, men whose abilities and integrity had gained the intire popular confidence, whose zeal or indolence in the public affairs alike moved or lulled the people, retired from the busy scene, or at least acted with indifference. The news papers ceased to circulate with public information. Demagogues of desperate fortunes, mere adventurers in fraud, were left to act unopposed. Their measures, of course, either obtained the consent of the multitude by misrepresentation, or assumed the countenance of popularity because none said nay. Hence have proceeded paper money, breaches of Treaty &c. The ductility of the Multitude is fully evidenced in the case of the late tumults in Massachusetts. Men who were of good property and owed not a shilling, were involved in the train of desperado's to suppress the courts. A full representation of the public affairs from the General Court through the Clergy has reclaimed so great a proportion of

9 JUNE 1787

the deluded, that a Rebellion which a few months ago threatened the subversion of the Government is, by measures scarcely deserving the name of exertion, suppressed, and one decided act of authority would eradicate it forever. In this experiment it is proved that full intelligence of the public affairs not only would keep the people right, but will set them so after they have got wrong.

Civil Liberty, in my opinion, never before took up her residence in a country so likely to afford her a long and grateful protection as the United States.—A people more generally enlightened than any other under the sun, and in the habits of owning, instead of being mere tenants in, the Soil, must be proportionably alive to her sacred rights, and qualified to guard them; and I am persuaded that the time is fast approaching when all these advantages will have their fullest influence. Our tendency to anarchy and consequent despotism is felt, and the alarm is spreading. Men are brought into action who had consigned themselves to an eve of rest, and the Convention, as a Beacon, is rousing the attention of the Empire.

The prevailing impression as well in as out of Convention is that a fœderal Government adapted to the permanent circumstances of the Country, without respect to the habits of the day, be formed, whose efficiency shall pervade the whole Empire: it may, and probably will, at first be viewed with hesitation, but derived and patronised as it will be, its influence must extend into a general adoption as the present fabric gives way. That the people are disposed to be governed is evinced in their turning out to support the shadows under which they now live, and if a work of wisdom is prepared for them, they will not reject it to commit themselves to the dubious issue of anarchy.

The debates and proceedings of the Convention are kept in profound secrecy. Opinions of the probable result of their deliberations can only be formed from the prevailing impressions of men of reflection and understanding.—These are reducible to two schemes—the first, a consolidation of the whole Empire into one republic, leaving in the states nothing more than subordinate courts for facilitating the administration of the Laws.—The second an investiture of a fœderal sovereignty with full and independant authority as to the Trade, Revenues, and forces of the Union, and the rights of peace and War, together with a Negative upon all the Acts of the State legislatures. The first idea, I apprehend, would be impracticable, and therefore do not suppose it can be adopted. General Laws through a Country embracing so many climates, productions, and manners as the United States would operate many oppressions, and a general legislature would be found incompetent to the formation of local ones, as a majority would in every instance be ignorant of, and unaffected by, the objects of legislation. The essential rights as well as advantages of representation would be lost, and obedience to the public decrees could only be ensured by the exercise of powers different from those derivable from a free constitution. Such an experiment must therefore terminate in a despotism, or the same inconveniencies we are now deliberating to remove. Something like the second will probably be formed; indeed I am certain that nothing less than what will give the fœderal sovereignty a compleat controul over the state Governments will be thought worthy of discussion. Such a scheme constructed upon well adjusted principles would certainly give us stability and importance as a nation, and if the Executive powers can be sufficiently checked, must be eligible. Unless the whole has a decided influence over the parts, the constant effort will be to resume the delegated powers, and these cannot be an inducement in the fœderal sovereignty to refuse its assent to an innocent act of a State. The negative which the King of England had upon our Laws was never found to be materially inconvenient.

The Ideas here suggested are far removed from those which prevailed when you was amongst us, and as they have arisen with the most able, from an actual view of events, it is probable you may not be prepared to expect them. They are however the most moderate of any which obtain in any general form amongst reflective and intelligent Men. The Eastern opinions are for a total surrender of the state sovereignties, and indeed some amongst them go to a monarchy at once. They have verged to anarchy, while to the southward we have only felt an inconvenience, and their proportionate disposition to an opposite extreme is a natural consequence.

I have encroached on your patience by a long letter, nor could I compress the information which I wished to convey into a smaller compass. Disquisition has been avoided except where it became necessary to compleat my ideas, because, being possessed of facts and circumstances your own reflections will furnish better, and it will afford me pleasure, as well as improvement, to receive them from you.

Mr. Rutledge son of Governor Rutledge will be the bearer of this and I beg leave to introduce him to your attentions. He has been some time at Phila. and will be able to give you some information upon our public affairs. Be good enough to present me to Mr. Short, and assure yourself that it is with the greatest esteem and respect that I have the honor to subscribe myself, Your Most obt. Servt., ED. CARRINGTON

RC (DLC); endorsed. Recorded in SJL as received 14 July 1787.

SOME AMONGST THEM GO TO A MONARCHY AT ONCE: Others at this time were reporting such views among some of the conservative leaders of New England. Otto, in February, reported on the political situation in Massachusetts, where the conflict between Bowdoin, "tout devoué au parti des hommes riches," and Hancock, leader of the popular party, had left the aristocratic element so angry that its adherents began to look with longing upon "la douce securité et le calme d'un Etat monarchique"; several persons, Otto stated to Vergennes, had assured him that they would have no objection to the setting up of a monarchy in Massachusetts (Otto to Vergennes, 28 Feb. 1787; Arch. Aff. Etr., Corr. Pol., E.-U., XXXII; Tr in DLC; Otto added that the political revolution in Massachusetts was gratifying "puisque le parti de M. Bowdoin est sous l'influence de M. John Adams et par consequence contraire à la France").

From Richard Claiborne, with Enclosure

DEAR SIR   London No. 14 King Street Cheapside 9. June 1787.

I beg leave to trouble your Excellency on a subject which is of material consequence to me. Colonel Blackden, no doubt, informed you of my being the proprietor of Lands in the western country of Virginia; of which he had some for sale while he was in France, tho they turned out short of my expectations. I have therefore applied my thoughts to another system, which there is a greater certainty of deriving benefits from, namely, that of settling the property with Inhabitants, and the particulars are now under consideration by a Gentleman of this city. In the mean time, should any one be disposed to purchase, I shall have it in my power to accommodate them independant of those Lands which I have reserved for settlements, and for no other purpose. They are a large body, dissected into Tracts of 1000 Acres each, situate on Cheat river, through which the road runs that has been cut from Potomack River to Monongalia River; and are spoken of in the highest terms by Gentlemen who have seen them. The opening of the Potomack is a very leading consideration to their cultivation, and I have determined to spare no pains in promoting the business with all the means I can raise. Whether therefore, in case of sale or any other mode of disposal, I shall be happy in a few sentiments from your Excellency of the fertility of that part of the Country which I have mentioned, and the advantages flowing to it from the improvement of the Potomack.—Also that you will favor the subject with an opinion, at what price Good Lands might be estimated in the Counties of Harrison and Monongalia. How far your Excellency

9 JUNE 1787

will be pleased to go as to this latter point, I leave altogether to yourself. I would only observe that I wish nothing more than to deal candidly with all mankind, and the better my sentiments are corroborated by respectable authority, the more apt I shall be to meet with success. As to the quality of the Lands, it will be my province to make them such as I shall discribe them to be, and as I shall deal in none but those that are good, I hope that taking this and the other advantages into consideration, your Excellency will find it not disagreable to give an opinion; which if still not pointedly, will serve to promote a price. I have uniformly impressed my mind with the sum of 5/. pr. acre as a price which might be exceedingly elegible for purchasers, but this I do not mean to advance as a principle towards your opinion.

Having possessed your Excellency fully of the object I have in view, I hope that the materials with which you will be able to furnish me, will be a means of effecting a matter which promises such solid advantages. If I can obtain my wishes, I mean to return to Virginia, and superintend the business myself, in which case, an additional happy reflection springs in my mind, that it will be the means of promoting the Interest of my Country. In the mean time, and at all times, I shall be happy to serve your Excellency as far as it lies in my power.

I take the liberty to inclose, by way of news, some extracts of Letters which I have received from Mr. Henry Banks who is my corrispondent in Richmond Virginia, and hope they will prove acceptable to you.

I am, Dear Sir, with much respect your Excellency's Most obedient & most humble Servant, RD. CLAIBORNE

ENCLOSURE

Henry Banks to Richard Claiborne
Richmond Feby. 25. 87.

"The last advices which were forwarded to you from this quarter were from my Brother Ferard, since which I have performed a very long tour to our Frontiers, not a little exposed to hardship, bad fare and cold weather, in which I have become fully satisfied of the possibility of drawing the furr Trade from the channels in which it has been so long runing, to wit, Canada, to this place. Every assembly do more and more increase the value of western property by the encouragement given to the settlers by opening roads, and palliating Taxes. The last have sanctioned and authorised a new road from Staunton to Kentuckie, which will save 200 miles from the former route, to which 5000£ was voted, the deficiency to be made up by subscriptions. I was made one of the Commissioners, upon the duties of which, of Five,

9 JUNE 1787

I immediately entered, and taking the event upon myself without consultation, have employed therein a large number of hands. This road intersects the great Kenhaway below the Rapids at the distance of 300 miles from Richmond—the road all the way good from that place to any of the Kentuckie settlements. There is an easy and certain communication by water, which even in the greatest flood, is practicable. The clearing of James River will open the communication to be easy, even for the bringing of hemp &c from the Kenhaway. This all being done, proper posts established, and a store on the Ohio at the mouth of the Kenhaway, the furs must find their way to Richmond. A stock of 10,000£ could be well engaged herein, and from that to any larger sum. It must be evident that while we hold 600 miles upon the Ohio and while we supply that Country with Goods on liberal terms, the Trade must have a tendency to this place and to Alexandria, whose advantages are nearly equal. I shall in a few days make a second tour to Greenbrier, where the people have universally offered to elect me for the House of Assembly."

March 18th. 1787.

"You can have no idea of the scarcity of money and the general distresses which pervade this Country. Scarcely a man who is not a defendant in some suit or other, and a great proportion subject to executions. Some of the first characters in confinement. All these things strongly indicate that the next assembly must make some new regulations in the internal police of this Country.

I have written often to you of the ease with which a furr trade could be drawn to this place from the waters of the Ohio and Mississipi. Nature has made the communications much more easy and they would have been used but for the Indians, who are now made quiet by over awe. There are great advantages arising to some company who shall first properly engage. A stock of 10,000£ is sufficient to begin the business, and a much larger sum may be employed profitably. The channel is now receiving a proper establishment. The roads are opening. When completed, I shall commit the whole to print, with my observations. I shall use every exertion in my power to have the business perfected, which the office of a Commissioner for that purpose will enable me to do.

RC (CSmH); endorsed. Recorded in SJL as received 17 June 1787. Enclosures: Extracts of letters from Henry Banks to Claiborne, printed above (DLC; in Claiborne's hand).

From Benjamin Hawkins

Dear Sir   New York the 9th June 1787

By the june Packet I have the happiness of complying in a great measure with my promise of the eighth of march. Finding that I had lost most of my plants through the inattention or ignorance of the Captain who had the care of them from North Carolina although

[413]

I made repeated trials and the last with giving particular directions on the proper method of treating them. And fearing that similar inattention might prevent your receiving of them, I have taken the liberty of addressing the whole to M. le Comte de Buffon intendant du Jardin du Roi au Jardin du Roi a Paris. And in return for this liberty I have requested the favor of the Comte to divide the plants equally between you and himself.

Mr. de la Forest dos not go to France as I expected but he nevertheless interests himself in the safety of the plants and has written to Monsieur de Mistral commissarie general de la Mazine au ordonnateur au Havre, to forward with great care the box and four earthen pots in which they are contained. As soon as I can procure any of the seeds, I will send them as you have directed. The largest of the pots and the broken one is filled with the native soil. In the box and the other pots I laid a clay foundation, not having a sufficiency of the Native soil to fill them. You know I believe that they grow low down in North Carolina where the soil is generally moist.

I expected to have had the pleasure of communicating to you the part of the information on Indian Queres which I had allotted to Mr. McGillivray but my letters are not yet come to hand, tho' I have reason to believe that he wrot to me some time in march by our Superintendant of Indian affairs and as he is on his way hither probably I shall get them within this month.

Our friend Colonel Carrington promises me to give you a long narrative of our Politics, and therefore it would be superfluous if not presumptuous in me to do it. I will only add that every citizen of the United States is looking up with eager anxious hopes to the convention for an efficient Government: that the proceedings of the Convention are under such an injunction of Secrecy as that confidential communications are inconsistent with the rules established as necessary to preserve the fullest freedom of discussion and to prevent misconceptions and misconstructions without doors.

Adieu Dear Sir, and believe me sincerely and truly your faithful friend and Most obedient humble Servt,

BENJAMIN HAWKINS

Enclosed is a duplicate of the letter to the Count.

RC (DLC); endorsed. Recorded in SJL as received 14 July 1787. Enclosure not found.

"Ecu de Calonne," 1786. (See p. xxxi.)

Marius at Minturnes, by Jean Germain Drouais. (See p. xxxi.)

Paris in 1787. (See p. xxxi.)

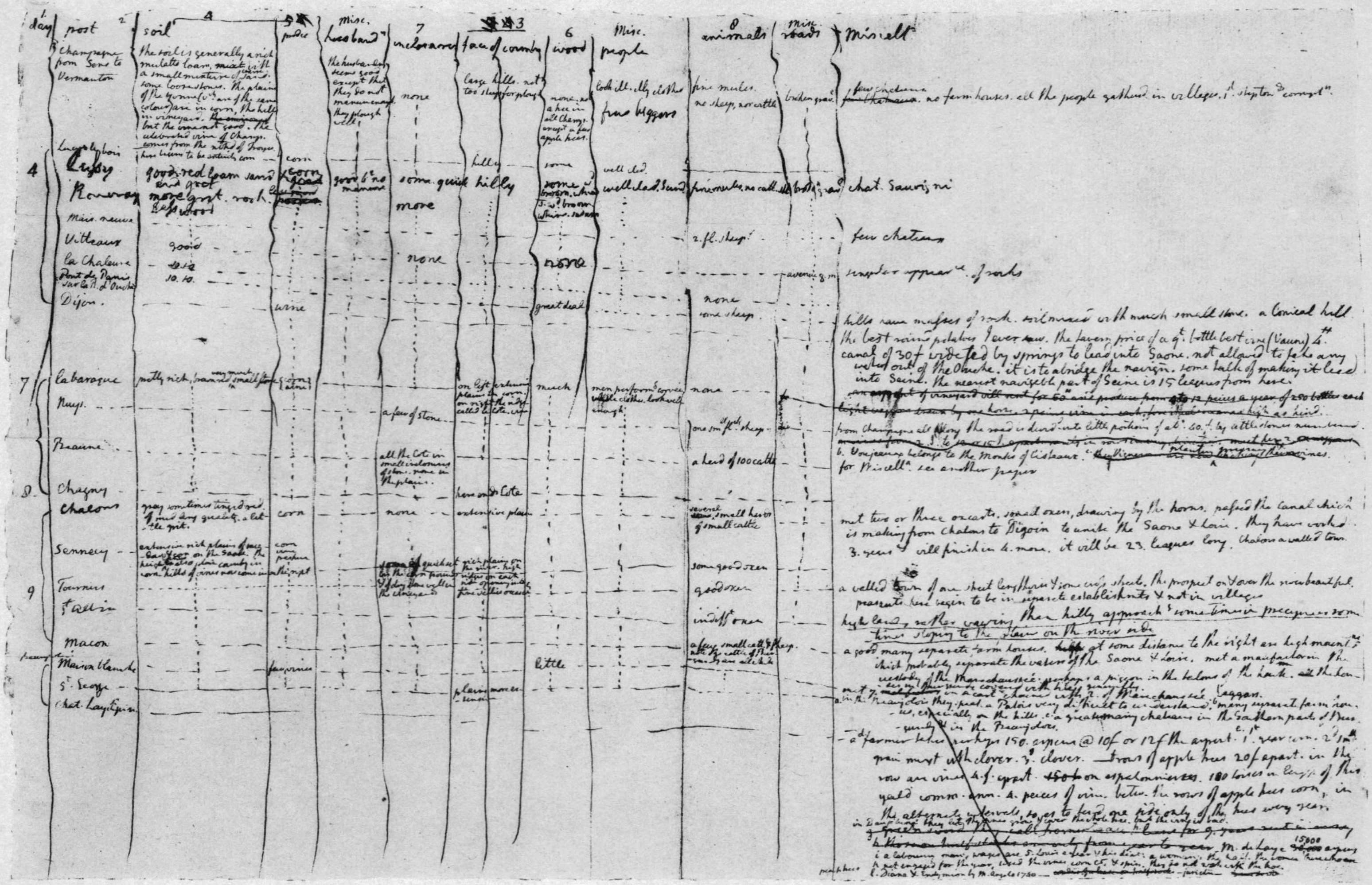

Château de Vermanton, near Auxerre. (See p. xxxii.)

Château de Chagny, between Beaune and Chalons. (See p. xxxii.)

Macon. (See p. xxxii.)

Pont du Gard. (See p. xxxii.)

Aix-en-Provence. (See p. xxxii.)

Fountain of Vaucluse and environs. (See p. xxxii.)

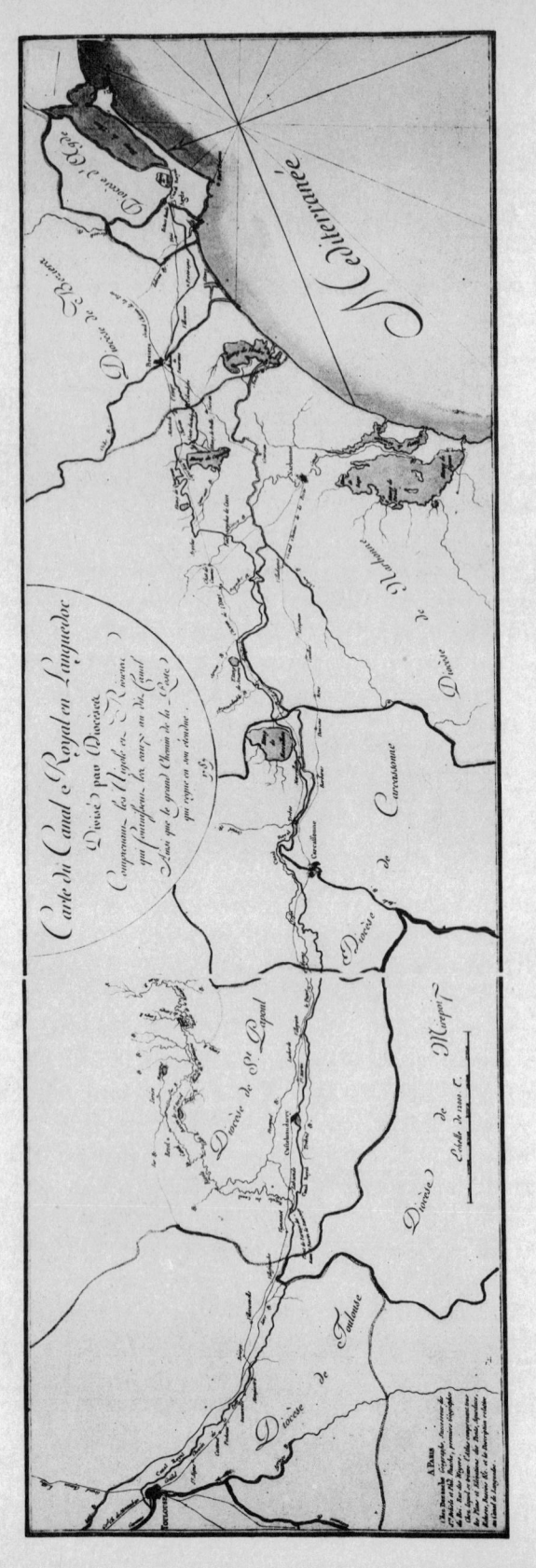

Map of the Canal of Languedoc. (See p. xxxiii.)

Notes of a Tour into the Southern Parts of France, &c.

Memorandums taken on a journey from Paris into the Southern parts of France and Northern of Italy, in the year 1787.

CHAMPAGNE. March 3. SENS to VERMANTON. The face of the country is in large hills, not too steep for the plough, somewhat resembling the Elk hill and Beverdam hills of Virginia. The soil is generally a rich mulatto loam, with a mixture of coarse sand and some loose stone. The plains of Yonne are of the same colour. The plains are in corn, the hills in vineyard, but the wine not good. There are a few apple trees but none of any other kind, and no inclosures. No cattle, sheep, or swine. Fine mules.

Few chateaux. No farm houses, all the people being gathered in villages. Are they thus collected by that dogma of their religion which makes them believe that, to keep the Creator in good humor with his own works, they must mumble a mass every day? Certain it is that they are less happy and less virtuous in villages than they would be insulated with their families on the grounds they cultivate. The people are illy clothed. Perhaps they have put on their worst clothes at this moment as it is raining. But I observe women and children carrying heavy burthens, and labouring with the hough. This is an unequivocal indication of extreme poverty. Men, in a civilised country, never expose their wives and children to labour above their force or sex, as long as their own labour can protect them from it. I see few beggars. Probably this is the effect of a police.[1]

BURGUNDY. Mar. 4. Lucy le bois. Cussy les forges. Rouvray. Maison-neuve. Vitteaux. La Chaleure. Pont de Panis. Dijon. The hills are higher and more abrupt. The soil a good red loam and sand, mixed with more or less grit, small stone, and sometimes rock. All in corn. Some forest wood here and there, broom, whins and holly, and a few inclosures of quick hedge. Now and then a flock of sheep.

The people are well clothed, but it is Sunday. They have the appearance of being well fed. The Chateau de Sevigny, near Cussy les forges is in a charming situation. Between Maison neuve and Vitteaux the road leads through an avenue of trees 8. American miles long in a right line. It is impossible to paint the ennui of this avenue. On the summits of the hills which border the valley in which Vitteaux is, there is a parapet of rock, 20. 30. or 40. feet perpendicular, which crowns the hills. The tops are nearly level and appear to be covered with earth. Very singular. Great masses of rock in the hills between la Chaleure and Pont de Panis, and a conical hill in the approach to the last place.

DIJON. The tavern price of a bottle of the best wine (e.g. of Vaune) is 4.ᵗᵗ The best round potatoes here I ever saw. They have begun a canal 30. feet wide, which is to lead into the Saone at   . It is fed by springs. They are not allowed to take any water out of the riviere d'Ouche, which runs through this place on account of the mills on that river. They talk of making a canal to the Seine, the nearest navigable part of which at present is 15. leagues from hence. They have very light waggons here for the transportation of their wine. They are long and narrow, the fore wheels as high as the hind. Two peices of wine are drawn by one horse in one of these waggons. The road, in this part of the country, is divided into portions of 40. or 50. feet by stones, numbered, which mark the task of the labourers.

March 7. 8. From LA BARAQUE to CHAGNY. On the left are plains which extend to the Saone, on the right the ridge of mountains called the Cote. The plains are of a reddish-brown, rich loam, mixed with much small stone. The Cote has for it's basis a solid rock on which is about a foot of soil, and small stone in equal quantities, the soil red and of midling quality.[2] The plains are in corn, the Cote in vines. The former has no inclosures, the latter is in small ones of dry stone wall. There is a good deal of forest. Some small herds of small cattle and sheep. Fine mules which come from Provence and cost 20. Louis. They break them at 2. years old, and they last to 30.

The corn lands here rent for about 15ᵗᵗ the arpent. They are now planting, pruning, and sticking their vines. When a new vineyard is made they plant the vines in gutters about 4. feet apart. As the vines advance they lay them down. They put out new shoots, and fill all the intermediate space till all trace of order is lost. They have ultimately about 1. foot square to each vine. They begin to yeild good profit at 5. or 6. years old and last 100. or 150. years. A vigneron at Voulenay carried me into his vineyard, which was of about 10. arpents. He told me that some years it produced him 60. peices of wine, and some not more than 3. peices. The latter is the most advantageous produce, because the wine is better in

[416]

quality and higher in price in proportion as less is made: and the expences at the same time diminish in the same proportion. Whereas when much is made, the expences are increased, while the quality and price become less. In very plentiful years they often give one half the wine for casks to contain the other half. The cask for 250. bottles costs 6^{tt} in scarce years and 10^{tt} in plentiful. The FEUILLETTE is of 125. bottles, the PIECE of 250., and the QUEUE, or BOTTE of 500. An arpent rents for from 20.^{tt} to 60.^{tt} A farmer of 10. arpents has about three labourers engaged by the year. He pais 4. Louis to a man, and half as much to a woman, and feeds them. He kills one hog, and salts it, which is all the meat used in the family during the year. Their ordinary food is bread and vegetables. At Pommard and Voulenay I observed them eating good wheat bread; at Meursault, rye. I asked the reason of the difference. They told me that the white wines fail in quality much oftener than the red, and remain on hand. The farmer therefore cannot afford to feed his labourers so well. At Meursault, only white wines are made, because there is too much stone for the red. On such slight circumstances depends the condition of man!— The wines which have given such celebrity to Burgundy grow only on the Cote, an extent of about 5 leagues long, and half a league wide. They begin at Chambertin, and go on through Vougeau, Romanie, Veaune, Nuys, Beaune, Pommard, Voulenay, Meursault, and end at Monrachet.[3] The two last are white; the others red. Chambertin, Voujeau, and Veaune are strongest, and will bear transportation and keeping. They sell therefore on the spot for 1200.^{tt} the Queue, which is 48. sous the bottle. Voulenaye is the best of the other reds, equal in flavor to Chambertin &c. but being lighter, will not keep, and therefore sells for not more than 300^{tt} the Queue, which is 12. sous the bottle. It ripens sooner than they do and consequently is better for those who wish to broach at a year old. In like manner of the White wines, and for the same reason, Monrachet sells at 1200^{tt} the Queue (48s. the bottle) and Meursault of the best quality, viz. the Goutte d'or, at only 150^{tt} (6s. the bottle). It is remarkeable that the best of each kind, that is, of the Red and White, is made at the extremities of the line, to wit, at Chambertin and Monrachet. It is pretended that the adjoining vineyards produce the same qualities, but that, belonging to obscure individuals, they have not obtained a name, and therefore sell as other wines. The aspect of the Cote is a little South of the East. The Western side is also covered with vines, is apparently of the same soil; yet the wines are only of the coarsest kinds. Such too are those which are produced in the Plains: but there the soil is richer and less stony. Vougeau is the property of the monks of Citeaux, and produces about 200 pieces. Monrachet contains about 50 arpents, and produces one year with another about 120 peices. It belongs to two proprietors only, Monsr. de Clermont, who leases to some wine merchants, and the Marquis de Sarsnet of Dijon, whose part is farmed to a Monsr. de la Tour whose family, for many generations, have had the farm. The best wines are carried to Paris by land. The transportation costs 36^{tt} the peice. The more indifferent go by water. Bottles cost 4½ sous each.

March 9. CHALONS. SENNECY. TOURNUS. ST. ALBIN. MACON. On the left are the fine plains of the Saone; on the right, high lands, rather waving than hilly, sometimes sloping gently to the plains, sometimes dropping down in precipices, and occasionally broken into beautiful vallies by the streams which run into the Saone. The Plains are a dark rich loam, in pasture and corn; the heights more or less red or reddish, always gritty, of midling quality only; their sides in vines, and their summits in corn. The vineyards are inclosed with dry stone walls, and there are some quickhedges in the corn grounds. The cattle are few and indifferent. There are some good oxen however. They draw by the head. Few sheep, and small. A good deal of wood lands.

I passed three times the canal called le Charollois, which they are opening from Chalons on the Saone to Digoïn on the Loire. It passes near Chagny, and will be 23. leagues long. They have worked on it 3. years, and will finish it in 4. more. It will reanimate the languishing commerce of Champagne and Burgundy, by furnishing a water transportation for their wines to Nantes, which also will receive new consequence by becoming the emporium of that commerce. At some distance on the right are high mountains, which probably form the separation between the waters of the Saone and Loire.—Met a malefactor in the hands of one of the Marechaussée; perhaps a dove in the talons of the hawk. The people begin now to be in separate establishments, and not in villages. Houses are mostly covered with tile.

BEAUJOLOIS. Maison blanche. St. George. Chateau de Laye Epinaye. The face of the country is like that from Chalons to Macon. The Plains are a dark rich loam, the hills a red loam, of midling quality, mixed generally with more or less coarse sand

and grit, and a great deal of small stone. Very little forest. The vineyards are mostly inclosed with dry stone wall. A few small cattle and sheep. Here, as in Burgundy, the cattle are all white.

This is the richest country I ever beheld. It is about 10. or 12. leagues in length, and 3. 4. or 5. in breadth; at least that part of it which is under the eye of the traveller. It extends from the top of a ridge of mountains running parallel with the Saone, and sloping down to the plains of that river scarcely any where too steep for the plough. The whole is thick sown with farm houses, chateaux, and the Bastides of the inhabitants of Lyons. The people live separately, and not in villages. The hillsides are in wine[4] and corn: the plains in corn and pasture. The lands are farmed either for money, or on half-stocks. The rents of the corn lands farmed for money are about 10. or 12.*t* the arpent. A farmer takes perhaps about 150. arpents for 3. 6. or 9. years. The 1st. year they are in corn, the 2d. in other small grain, with which he sows red clover; the 3d. is for the clover. The spontaneous pasturage is of greenswerd, which they call fromenteau. When lands are rented on half stocks, the cattle, sheep &c. are furnished by the landlord. They are valued and must be left of equal value. The increase of these, as well as the produce of the farm, are divided equally. These leases are only from year to year. They have a method of mixing beautifully the culture of vines, trees and corn. Rows of fruit trees are planted about 20. feet apart. Between the trees, in the row, they plant vines 4. feet apart and espalier them. The intervals are sowed alternately in corn, so as to be one year in corn the next in pasture, the 3d. in corn, the 4th in pasture &c. 100. toises of vines in length yeild generally about 4. peices of wine. In Dauphiné, I am told, they plant vines only at the roots of the trees and let them cover the whole trees. But this spoils both the wine and the fruit. Their wine, when distilled, yeilds but one third it's quantity in brandy. The wages of a labouring man here are 5. Louis, of a woman one half. The women do not work with the hough: they only weed the vines, the corn, &c. and spin. They speak a Patois very difficult to understand. I passed some time at the chateau de Laye epinaye. Monsieur de Laye has a seignory of about 15,000 arpents, in pasture, corn, vines, and wood. He has over this, as is usual, a certain jurisdiction both criminal and civil. But this extends only to the first crude examination, which is before his judges. The subject is referred for final examination and decision to the regular judicatures of the country. The Seigneur is keeper of the peace on his domains. He is therefore subject to the expences of maintaining it. A criminal prosecuted to sentence and execution, costs M. de Laye about 5000.ʰᵗ This is so burthensome to the Seigneurs, that they are slack in criminal prosecutions. A good effect from a bad cause. Thro' all Champagne, Burgundy and the Beaujolois, the husbandry seems good, except that they manure too little. This proceeds from the shortness of their leases. The people of Burgundy and Beaujolois are well clothed, and have the appearance of being well fed. But they experience all the oppressions which result from the nature of the general government, and from that of their particular tenures, and of the Seignorial government to which they are subject. What a cruel reflection that a rich country cannot long be a free one.—M. de Laye has a Diana and Endymion, a very superior morsel of sculpture by Michael Angelo Slodtz, done in 1740. The wild gooseberry is in leaf, the wild pear and sweet briar in bud.

LYONS. There are some feeble remains here of an amphitheatre of 200. feet diameter and of an aqueduct in brick. The Pont d'Ainay has 9. arches of 40. feet from center to center. The piers are of 6. feet.—The Almond is in bloom.

DAUPHINE. From St. Fond to Mornas. March 15. 16. 17. 18. The Rhone makes extensive plains, which lie chiefly on the Eastern side, and are often in two stages. Those of Montelimart are 3. or 4. miles wide, and rather good. Sometimes, as in the neighborhood of Vienne, the hills come in precipices to the river, resembling then very much our Susquehanna and it's hills, except that the Susquehanna is ten times as wide as the Rhone. The high lands are often very level.—The soil, both of hill and plain, where there is soil, is generally tinged, more or less, with red. The hills are sometimes mere masses of rock, sometimes a mixture of loose stone and earth. The plains are always stony and, as often as otherwise, covered perfectly with a coat of round stones of the size of the fist so as to resemble the remains of inundations from which all the soil has been carried away. Sometimes they are midling good, sometimes barren. In the neighborhood of Lyons there is more corn than wine, towards Tains more wine than corn. From thence the Plains, where best, are in corn, clover, almonds, mulberries, walnuts. Where there is still some earth they are in corn, almonds, and oaks; the hills are in vines.—There is a good deal of forest wood near Lyons, but not much afterwards. Scarcely any inclosures. There are a few small sheep before we reach Tains; there the number increases.

Nature never formed a country of more savage aspect than that on both sides the Rhone. A huge torrent, rushing like an arrow between high precipices often of massive rock, at other times of loose stone with but little earth. Yet has the hand of man subdued this savage scene, by planting corn where there is a little fertility, trees where there is still less, and vines where there is none. On the whole, it assumes a romantic, picturesque and pleasing air. The hills on the opposite side of the river, being high, steep, and laid up in terrasses, are of a singular appearance. Where the hills are quite in waste, they are covered with broom, whins, box, and some clusters of small pines. The high mountains of Dauphiné and Languedoc are now covered with snow. The Almond is in general bloom, and the willow putting out it's leaf. There were formerly OLIVES at Tains: but a great cold some years ago killed them, and they have not been replanted. I am told at Montelimart that an Almond tree yeilds about 3. livres profit a year. Supposing them 3. toises apart there will be 100 to the Arpent, which give 300.^{tt} a year, besides the corn growing in the same ground.—A league below Vienne, on the opposite side of the river is COTE ROTIE. It is a string of broken hills, extending a league on the river from the village of Ampuys to the town of Condrieux. The soil is white, tinged a little, sometimes with yellow, sometimes with red, stony, poor and laid up in terrasses. Those parts of the hills only which look to the sun at Mid-day or the earlier hours of the afternoon produce wines of the first quality. 700 vines 3 feet apart, yeild a feuillette, which is about 2½ peices to the arpent. The best red wine is produced at the upper end in the neighborhood of Ampuys; the best white next to Condrieux. They sell of the first quality and last vintage at 150^{tt} the Piece, equal to 12.s the bottle. Transportation to Paris is 60.^{tt} and the bottle 4.s so it may be delivered at Paris in bottles at 20s. When old it costs 10. or 11. Louis the Piece. There is a quality which keeps well, bears transportation, and cannot be drunk under 4. years. Another must be drunk at a year old. They are equal in flavor and price. The best vintages of red wine are of Monsieur de la Condamine seigneur d'Ampuys, dans son fief de Monlis, le Marquis de Leusse dans son grand tupin, M. de Montjoli, M. du Vivier, and M. du Prunel. The best of white are at Chateau grillé by Madame la veuve Peyrouse.

The wine called HERMITAGE is made on the hills impending over the village of Tains; on one of which is the hermitage which gives name to the hills for about two miles, and to the wine made on them. There are but three of those hills which produce wine of the 1st. quality, and of these the middle regions only. They are about 300 feet perpendicular height, ¾ of a mile in length and have a Southern aspect. The soil is scarcely tinged red, consists of small rotten stone, and, in it's most precious parts, without any perceptible mixture of earth. It is in sloping terrasses. They use a little dung. An Homme de vignes, which consist of 700 plants 3. feet apart, yeilds generally about ¾ of a peice, which is nearly 4 peices to the arpent. When new the Peice is sold at about 225,₶ old at 300.₶ It cannot be drunk under 4. years, and improves fastest in a hot situation. There is so little White made in proportion to the red, that it is difficult to buy it separate. They make the White sell the Red. If bought separately it is from 15. to 18. Louis the peice, new, and 3₶ the bottle old. To give quality to the Red, they mix ⅛ of white grapes. Portage to Paris is 72₶ the peice, weighing 600 lb. There are but about 1000. peices of both red and white of the 1st. quality made annually. They are made by M. Meus, seigneur of the place, M. de Loche avocat, M. Berger avocat, M. Chanoine Monron, M. Gaillet, M. de Beausace, M. Deure, M. Chalamelle, M. Monnet and two or three others. Vineyards are never rented here, nor are labourers in the vineyard hired by the year. They leave buds proportioned to the strength of the vine: sometimes as much as 15. inches. The last Hermit died in 1751.

In the neighborhood of Montelimart and below that they plant vines in rows 6. 8. or 10. feet apart, and 2. feet asunder in the row, filling the intervals with corn. Sometimes the vines are in double rows 2. feet apart. I saw single asses in ploughs proportioned to their strength. The plough formed of three peices, thus
a. is the beam, to which the share is fixed,
b. a crooked bough of a tree sometimes single, sometimes forked, c. a crooked bough also
to which the swingletree was fastened. Asses or mules, working in pairs, are coupled by square yokes in this form   the side peices only sliding out to disengage the animal.
There are few chateaux in this province. The people too are mostly gathered into villages. There are however some scattering farm houses. These are made either of mud or of round stone and mud. They make inclosures also in both those ways. Day laborers receive 16.s or 18.s the day, and feed themselves. Those by the year receive, men 3. Louis and women half that, and are fed. They rarely eat meat; a single hog salted being the year's stock for a family. But they have plenty of cheese, eggs, potatoes and other vegetables, and walnut oil with their sallad. It is a trade

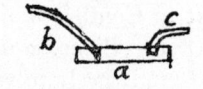

here to gather dung along the road for their vines. This proves they have few cattle. I have seen neither hares nor partridges since I left Paris, nor wild fowl on any of the rivers. The roads from Lyons to St. Rambert are neither paved nor gravelled. After that they are coated with broken flint. The ferry boats on the Rhone, and the Isere, are moved by the stream, and very rapidly. On each side of the river is a moveable stage, one end of which is on an axle and two wheels, which, according to the tide, can be advanced or withdrawn so as to apply to the gunwale of the boat. The Pretorian palace at Vienne is 44. feet wide, of the Corinthian order, 4. columns in front, and 4. in flank. It was begun in the year 400. and finished by Charlemagne. The Sepulchral pyramid, a little way out of the town, has an order for it's basement, the pedestal of which from point to point of it's cap is 24f. 1.I. At each angle is a column, engaged one fourth in the wall. The circumference of the three fourths disengaged is 4.f. 4.I. Consequently the diameter is 23.I. The base of the column indicates it to be Ionic, but the capitals are not formed. The Cornice too is a bastard Ionic without modillions or dentils. Between the columns on each side is an arch of 8.f. 4.I. opening, with a pilaster on each side of it. On the top of the basement is a zocle, in the plane of the frieze below. On that is the pyramid, it's base in the plane of the collanno of the pilaster below. The pyramid is a little truncated on it's top. This monument is inedited.

Mar. 18. Principality of ORANGE. The plains on the Rhone here are 2. or 3. leagues wide, reddish, good, in corn, clover, almonds, olives. No forest. Here begins the country of olives, there being very few till we enter this principality. They are the only tree which I see planted among vines. Thyme growing wild here on the hills. Asses very small, sell here for 2. or 3. Louis. The high hills in Dauphiné are covered with snow. The remains of the Roman aqueduct are of brick. A fine peice of Mosaic, still on it's bed, forming the floor of a cellar. 20 feet of it still visible. They are taking down the circular wall of the Amphitheatre to pave a road.

March 19. to 23. LANGUEDOC. Pont St. Esprit. Bagnols. Connault. Valignieres. Remoulins. St. Gervasy. Nismes. Pont d'Arles. To Remoulins there is a mixture of hill and dale. Thence to Nismes, hills on the right, on the left plains extending to the Rhone and the sea. The hills are rocky. Where there is soil it is reddish and poor. The plains generally reddish and good, but stony. When you approach the Rhone, going to Arles, the soil becomes a dark grey loam, with some sand, and very good. The culture is

TOUR THROUGH SOUTHERN FRANCE 1787

corn, clover, St. foin, olives, vines, mulberries, willow, and some almonds. There is no forest. The hills are inclosed in dry stone wall. Many sheep.

From the summit of the first hill after leaving Pont St. Esprit, there is a beautiful view of the bridge at about 2. miles distance, and a fine landscape of the country both ways. From thence an excellent road, judiciously conducted, thro very romantic scenes. In one part, descending the face of a hill, it is laid out in Serpentine, and not zig-zag, to ease the descent. In others it passes thro' a winding meadow, from 50. to 100. yards wide, walled as it were on both sides by hills of rock; and at length issues into plane country. The waste hills are covered with thyme, box, and chenevert. Where the body of the mountains has a surface of soil, the summit has sometimes a crown of rock, as observed in Champagne. At Nismes the earth is full of limestone. They use square yokes as in Dauphiné. The horses are shorn. They are now pruning the olive. A very good tree produces 60. ℔. of olives, which yield 15 ℔. of oil: the best quality selling at 12.s the ℔. retail, and 10.s wholesale. The high hills of Languedoc still covered with snow. The horse chesnut and mulberry are leafing; appletrees and peas blossoming. The first butterfly I have seen. After the vernal equinox they are often 6. or 8. months without any rain. Many separate farmhouses, numbers of people in rags, and abundance of beggars. The Mine of wheat, weighing 30. ℔. costs 4^{tt} 10.s, wheat bread 3.s the pound. Vin ordinaire, good and of a strong body 2.s or 3.s the bottle. Oranges 1.s apeice. They are nearly finishing at Nismes a grist mill worked by a steam engine, which pumps water from a lower into an upper cistern, from whence two overshot wheels are supplied, each of which turns two pair of stones. The upper cistern being once filled with water, it passes thro the wheels into the lower one from whence it is returned into the upper by the pumps. A stream of water of ¼ or ½ inch diameter supplies the waste of evaporation, absorption, &c. This is furnished from a well by a horse. The arches of the pont St. Esprit are of 88. feet. Wild figs, very flourishing, grow out of the joints of the Pont du Gard. The fountain of Nismes is so deep, that a stone was 13″ descending from the surface to the bottom.

March 24. From Nismes to Arles. The plains extending from Nismes to the Rhone in the direction of Arles is broken in one place by a skirt of low hills. They are red and stony at first, but as you approach the Rhone they are of a dark grey mould, with a little sand, and very good. They are in corn and clover, vines, olives, almonds, mulberries, and willow. There are some sheep, no wood, no inclosures.

The high hills of Languedoc are covered with snow. At an antient church in the suburbs of Arles are perhaps some hundreds of antient stone coffins along the road side. The ground is thence called les champs elysées. In a vault in the church are some preciously wrought, and in a back yard are many antient statues, inscriptions &c. Within the town are a part of two Corinthian columns, and of the pediment with which they were crowned, very rich, having belonged to the antient Capitol of the place. But the principal monument here is an Amphitheatre, the external portico of which is tolerably compleat. How many of these porticoes there were, cannot be seen: but at one of the principal gates there are still 5. measuring from out to in 78f. 10 I., the vault diminishing inwards. There are 64. arches, each of which is from center to center 20.f. 6.I. Of course the diameter is of 438. feet, or of 450. feet if we suppose the 4. principal arches a little larger than the rest. The ground floor is supported on innumerable vaults. The first story, externally, has a tall pedestal, like a pilaster, between every two arches: the upper story a column, the base of which would indicate it Corinthian. Every column is truncated as low as the impost of the arch, but the arches are all entire. The whole of the upper entablature is gone, and of the Attic, if there was one. Not a single seat of the internal is visible. The whole of the inside, and nearly the whole of the outside is masked by buildings. It is supposed there are 1000. inhabitants within the Amphitheatre. The walls are more entire and firm than those of the Amphitheatre at Nismes. I suspect it's plan and distribution to have been very different from that.

TERRASSON. The plains of the Rhone from Arles to this place are a league or two wide: the mould is of a dark grey, good, in corn and lucern. Neither wood, nor inclosures. Many sheep.

ST. REMIS. From Terrasson to St. Remis is a plain of a league or two wide, bordered by broken hills of massive rock. It is grey and stony, mostly in olives. Some almonds, mulberries, willows, vines, corn and lucern. Many sheep. No forest, nor inclosures.

A labouring man's wages here are 150^{tt}, a woman's the half, and fed. 280. ℔. of wheat sells for 42.^{tt} They make no butter here. It costs, when brought, 15.s the ℔. Oil is 10.s the ℔. Tolerable good olive trees yeild one with another, about 20. ℔ of oil. An olive tree must be 20 years old before it has paid it's own expences. It lasts for ever. In 1765. it was so cold that the Rhone was frozen over at Arles for 2. months. In 1767. there was a cold spell of a week which killed all the olive trees. From being fine weather in one hour there was ice hard enough to bear a horse. It killed people on the road. The old roots of the olive trees put out again. Olive grounds sell at 24.ᵗᵗ a tree, and lease at 24 sous the tree. The trees are 15. pieds apart. But Lucerne is a more profitable culture. An arpent yeilds 100. quintals of hay a year, worth 3ᵗᵗ a quintal. It is cut 4. or 5. times a year. It is sowed in the broad cast and lasts 5. or 6. years. An arpent of ground for corn rents at 30.ᵗᵗ to 36.ᵗᵗ Their leases are for 6. or 9. years. They plant willow for fire wood, and for hoops to their casks. It seldom rains here in summer. There are some chateaux, many separate farm houses, good and ornamented in the small way, so as to shew that the tenant's whole time is not occupied in procuring physical necessaries.

March 25. Orgon. Pontroyal. St. Cannat. From Orgon to Pontroyal, after quitting the plains of the Rhone, the country seems still to be a plain cut into compartments, by chains of mountains of massive rock running thro it in various directions. From Pontroyal to St. Cannat the land lies rather in basons. The soil is very various. Grey and clay, grey and stony, red and stony; sometimes good, sometimes midling, often barren. We find some golden willows. Towards Pontroyal the hills begin to be in vines, and afterwards is some pasture of green swerd and clover. About Orgon are some inclosures of quickset, others of conical yews planted close. Towards St. Cannat they begin to be of stone.

The high mountains are covered with snow. Some separate farm houses of mud. Near Pontroyal is a canal for watering the country. One branch goes to Terrasson, the other to Arles. At St. Cannat a hill covered with pines. There is no forest; many sheep.

March. 25. 26. 27. 28. AIX. The country is waving, in vines, pasture of green swerd and clover, much inclosed with stone, and abounding with sheep.

On approaching Aix the valley which opens from thence towards the mouth of the Rhone and the sea is rich and beautiful: a perfect grove of olive trees, mixt among which is corn, lucerne and vines. The waste grounds throw out thyme and lavender. Wheat-bread is 3s. the ℔., cow's milk 16s. the quart, sheep's milk 6s., butter of sheep's milk 20s. the ℔., oil of the best quality 12s. the ℔., and 16s. if it be virgin oil. This is what runs from the olive when put into the press, spontaneously: afterwards they are forced by the press and by hot water. Dung costs 10s. the 100 ℔. Their fire wood is chene-vert and willow. The latter is lopped every three years. An ass sells for from 1. to 3. Louis; the best mules for 30. Louis. The best asses will carry 200. ℔., the best horses 300 ℔., the best mules 600 ℔. The temperature of the mineral waters of Aix is 90.° of Farenheit's thermometer at the spout. A mule eats half as much as a horse. The allowance to an ass for the day is a handful of bran mixed with straw. The price of mutton and beef about 6½s the ℔. The beef comes from Auvergne, is poor and bad. The mutton is small but of excellent flavor. The wages of a labouring man are 150^{tt} the year, a woman's 60^{tt} to 66^{tt} and fed. Their bread is half wheat, half rye, made once in 3. or 4. weeks to prevent too great a consumption. In the morning they eat bread with an anchovy, or an onion. Their dinner in the middle of the day is bread, soupe, and vegetables. Their supper the same. With their vegetables they have always oil and vinegar. The oil costs about 8s. the ℔. They drink what is called Piquette. This is made after the grapes are pressed, by pouring hot water on the pumice. On Sunday they have meat and wine. Their wood for building comes mostly from the Alps down the Durance and Rhone. A stick of pine 50. feet long, girting 6.f. 3.I. at one end, and 2.f. 3.I. at the other costs delivered here 54.^{tt} to 60.^{tt} 60 lb. of wheat cost 7.^{tt} One of their little asses will travel with his burthen about 5. or 6. leagues a day, and day by day: a mule from 6. to 8. leagues. (Note it is 20. American miles from Aix to Marseilles, and they call it 5. leagues. Their league then is of 4. American miles.)

Mar. 29. MARSEILLES. The country is hilly, intersected by chains of hills and mountains of massive rock. The soil is reddish, stony and indifferent where best. Whenever there is any soil it is covered with olives. Among these are vines, corn, some lucerne, mulberry, some almonds and willow. Neither inclosures, nor forest. A very few sheep.

On the road I saw one of those little whirlwinds which we have in Virginia. Also some gullied hill-sides. The people are in separate establishments. 10 morning observations of the thermometer, from the 20th. to the 31st. of March inclusive, made at Nismes, St. Remy, Aix and Marseilles give me an average of 52½° and 46° and 61° for the greatest and least morning heats. 9. afternoon observations yeild an average of 62⅔° and 57.° and 66.° the greatest and least. The longest day here from sunrise to sunset is 15H. 14.′ The shortest is 8H.-46.′ The latitude being   . There are no tides in the Mediterranean. It is observed to me that the olive tree grows no where more than 30 leagues distant from that sea. I suppose however that both Spain and Portugal furnish proofs to the contrary, and doubt it's truth as to Asia, Africa and America. There are 6. or 8. months at a time here without rain. The most delicate figs known in Europe are those growing about this place, called figues Marcelloises, or les veritables Marcelloises, to distinguish them from others of inferior quality growing here. These keep any length of time. All others exude a sugar in the spring of the year and become sour. The only process for preserving them is drying them in the sun, without putting any thing to them whatever. They sell at 15s. the lb. while there are others as cheap as   the ℔. I meet here a small dried grape from Smyrna without a seed. There are a few of the plants growing in this neighborhood. The best grape for drying known here is called des Panses. They are very large, with a thick skin and much juice. They are best against a wall of Southern aspect, as their abundance of juice requires a great deal of sun to dry it. Pretty good fig trees are about the size of the Apricot tree and yeild about 20. ℔. of figs when dry, each. But the largest will yeild the value of a Louis. They are sometimes 15.I. diameter. It is said that the Marseilles fig degenerates when transplanted into another part of the country. The leaves of a Mulberry tree will sell for about 3,^{tt} the purchaser gathering them. The CAPER is a creeping plant. It is killed to the roots every winter. In the spring it puts out branches which creep to the distance of 3.f. from the center. The fruit forms on the stem as that extends itself, and must be gathered every day as it forms. This is the work of women. The pistache grows in this neighborhood also, but not very good. They eat them in their milky state. Monsieur de BERGASSE has a wine-cellar 240. pieds long, in which are 120. tons of from 50. to 100 peices each. These tons are 12. pieds diameter; the staves 4.I. thick, the heading 2½ pouces thick. The temperature of his cellar is of 9½° of Reaumur. The best method of packing wine, when bottled, is to lay the bottles on their side, and cover them with sand. The 2d. of April the young figs are formed: the 4th. we have Windsor beans. They have had Asparagus ever since the middle of March. The 5th. I see strawberries and the Guelder rose in blossom. To preserve the raisin, it is first dipped into lye and then dried in the sun. The Aloe grows in the open ground. I measure a mule, not the largest, 5f. 2.I. high. Marseilles is in an amphitheatre, at the mouth of the Vaune, surrounded by high mountains of naked rock, distant 2. or 3. leagues. The country within that amphitheatre is a mixture of small hills, vallies and plains. The latter are naturally rich. The hills and vallies are forced into production. Looking from the chateau de Notre dame de la garde, it would seem as if there was a Bastide for every arpent. The plain lands sell for 100. Louis the Carterelle which is less than an acre. The ground of the arsenal in Marseilles sold for from 15. to 40. Louis the square verge, being nearly the square yard English. In the feilds open to the sea they are obliged to plant rows of canes every here and there to break the force of the wind. Saw at the Chateau Borelli pumps worked by the wind; the axis of the vanes vertical, the house open thus the radius 12.f. 5.I, external circumference 103. feet. 16 windows. The sails 4. feet wide and 12 feet high.

April 6. from MARSEILLES to AUBAGNE. A valley on the Vaune bordered on each side by high mountains of massive rock, on which are only some small pines. The interjacent valley is of small hills, vallies and plains, reddish, gravelly, and originally poor, but fertilised by art, and covered with corn, vines, olives, figs, almonds, mulberries, lucerne and clover. The river is 12. or 15. feet wide, 1. or 2. feet deep and rapid.

From Aubagne to Cuges, Beausset, Toulon. The road quitting the Vaune and it's wealthy valley, a little after Aubagne, enters those mountains of rock and is engaged with them about a dozen miles. Then it passes 6. or 8. miles thro' a country, still very hilly and stony, but laid up in terrasses, covered with olives, vines and corn. It then follows for 2. and 3. miles a hollow between two of those high mountains which has been found or made by a small stream. The mountains then reclining a little from their perpendicular and presenting a coat of soil, reddish and tolerably good has given place to the little village of Olioules, in the gardens of which are Oranges in the open ground. It continues hilly till we enter the plain of Toulon. On different parts of this road there are figs in the open fields. At Cuges is a plain of about ¾ mile diameter, surrounded by high mountains of rock. In this the CAPER is principally cultivated. The soil is mulatto, gravelly, and of midling quality, or rather indifferent. The plants are set in quincunx about 8.f. apart. They have been covered during winter by a hill of earth a foot high. They are now uncovering, pruning and ploughing them.

TOULON. From Olioules to Toulon the figs are in the open fields. Some of them have stems of 15.I. diameter. They generally fork near the ground, but sometimes have a single stem of 5.f. long. They are as large as Apricot trees. The Olive trees of this day's journey are about the size of large apple trees. The people are in separate establishments. Toulon is in a valley at the mouth of the Goutier, a little river of the size of the Vaune; surrounded by high mountains of naked rock leaving some space between them and the sea. This space is hilly, reddish, gravelly, and of midling quality, in olives, vines, corn, almonds, figs, and capers. The capers are planted 8.f. apart. A bush yeilds, one year with another, 2. ℔. worth 12s. the ℔. Every plant then yeilds 24s.-1. sterling. An acre containing 676. plants would yeild 33£. 16s sterl. The fruit is gathered by women who can gather about 12. ℔. a day. They begin to gather about the last of June and end about the middle of October. Each plant must be picked every other day. These plants grow equally well in the best or worst soil, or even in walls where there is no soil. They will last the life of a man or longer. The heat is so great at Toulon in summer as to occasion very great cracks in the earth. Where the caper is in a soil that will admit it, they plough it. They have peas here through the winter, sheltering them occasionally and they have had them ever since the 25 March without shelter.

April 6. HIERES. This is a plain of two or three miles diameter, bounded by the sea on one side and mountains of rock on the other. The soil is reddish, gravelly, tolerably good and well watered. It is in olives, mulberries, vines, figs, corn and some flax. There are also some cherry trees. From Hieres to the sea, which is 2. or 3. miles, is a grove of orange trees, olives, and mulberries. The largest orange tree is of 2.f. diameter one way and 1.f. the other (for the section of all the large ones would be an oval, not a round) and about 20.f. high. Such a tree will yeild about 6000. oranges a year. The garden of M. Fille has 15600 orange trees. Some years they yeild 40,000[tt], some only 10000[tt], but generally about 25,000.[tt] The trees are from 8. to 10.f. apart. They are blossoming and bearing all the year, flowers and fruit, in every stage, at the same time, but the best fruit is that which is gathered in April and May. Hieres is a village of about 5000 inhabitants, at the foot of a mountain which covers it from the North and from which extends a plain of 2. or 3. miles to the sea shore. It has no port. Here are Palm trees 20. or 30.f. high, but they bear no fruit. There is also a botanical garden kept by the king. Considerable salt ponds here. Hieres is 6 miles from the public road. It is built on a narrow spur of the mountain. The streets in every direction are steep, or steps of stairs, and about 8 feet wide. No carriage of any kind can enter it. The wealthier inhabitants use chaises á porteurs. But there are few wealthy, the bulk of the inhabitants being labourers of the earth. At a league distance in the sea is an island, on which is the Chateau de Geans belonging to the Marquis de Pontoives. There is a causeway leading to it. The cold of the last November killed the leaves of a great number of the orange trees and some of the trees themselves.

From Hieres to CUERS, PIGNANS, LUC is mostly a plain with mountains on each hand at a mile or two distance. The soil is generally reddish, and the latter part very red and good. The growth is olives, figs, vines, mulberries, corn, clover and lucerne. The olive trees are from 3. to 4. diameter. There are hedges of pomegranates, sweetbriar and broom. A great deal of thyme growing wild. There are some enclosures of stone, some sheep and goats.

April 9. From Luc to VIDAUBAN, MUY, FREJUS the road leads thro vallies, and crosses occasionally the mountains which separate them. The vallies are tolerably good, always red, and stony, gravelly or gritty. Their produce as before. The mountains are barren.

LESTERELLE, NAPOULE. 18 miles of ascent and descent of a very high mountain. It's growth, where capable of any, two leaved pine, very small, and some chene-verte.

ANTIBES, NICE. From Napoule the road is generally near the sea, passing over little hills or strings of vallies, the soil stony and much below mediocrity in it's quality. Here and there is a good plain.

There is snow on the high mountains. The first frogs I have heard are of this day (the 9th). At Antibes are oranges in the open ground, but in small inclosures: palm trees also. From thence to the Var are the largest fig trees and olive trees I have seen. The fig trees are 18.I. diameter and 6.f. stem, the Olives sometimes 6.f. diameter and as large heads as the largest low ground apple trees. This tree was but a shrub where I first fell in with it, and has become larger and larger to this place. The people are mostly in villages.—The several provinces, and even cantons are distinguished by the form of the women's hats, so that one may know of what canton a woman is by her hat. From Antibes to the Var it is shaped thus ⋀ of straw, light and cool.

NICE. The pine bur is used here for kindling fires. The people are in separate establishments. With respect to the Orange there seems to be no climate on this side of the Alps sufficiently mild in itself to preserve it without shelter. At Olioules they are between 2. high mountains: at Hieres, covered on the North by a very high mountain, at Antibes and Nice covered by mountains, and also within small high inclosures. Qu. to trace the true line from East to West which forms the Northern and natural limit of that fruit? Saw an Elder tree (Sambucus) near Nice, 15.I. diameter and 8.f. stem. The wine made in this neighborhood is good, tho' not of the first quality. There are 1000 mules, loaded with merchandize, which pass every week between Nice and Turin, counting those coming as well as going.

April 13. SCARENA, SOSPELLO. There are no Orange trees after we leave the environs of Nice. We lose the Olive after rising a little above the village of Scarena on Mount Braus, and find it again on the other side a little before we get down to Sospello. But wherever there is soil enough, it is terrassed and in corn. The waste parts are either in two leaved pine and thyme, or of absolutely naked rock. Sospello is on a little torrent called Bevera which runs into the river Roia, at the mouth of which is Ventimiglia. The olive trees on the mountain are now loaded with fruit; while some at Sospella are in blossom. Fire wood here and at Scarena costs 15s. the quintal.

April 14. CIANDOLA. TENDE. In crossing Mount Brois we lose the Olive tree after getting to a certain height, and find it again on the other side at the village of Breglio. Here we come to the river Roia which, after receiving the branch on which is Sospello, leads to the sea at Ventimiglia. The Roia is about 12. yards wide and abounds with speckled trout. Were a road made from Breglio, along the side of the Roia, to Ventimiglia, it might turn the commerce of Turin to this last place instead of Nice; because it would avoid the mountains of Braus and Brois, leaving only that of Tende; that is to say it would avoid more than half the difficulties of the passage. Further on, we come to the Chateau di Saorgio, where a scene is presented, the most singular and picturesque I ever saw. The castle and village seem hanging to a cloud in front. On the right is a mountain cloven through to let pass a gurgling stream; on the left a river over which is thrown a magnificent bridge. The whole forms a bason, the sides of which are shagged with rocks, olive trees, vines, herds &c. Near here I saw a tub-wheel without a ream; the trunk descended from the top of the water fall to the wheel in a direct line, but with the usual inclination. The produce along this passage is most generally olives except on the heights as before observed, also corn, vines, mulberry, figs, cherries and walnuts. They have cows, goats and sheep. In passing on towards Tende, olives fail us ultimately at the village of Fontan, and there the chesnut trees begin in good quantity. Ciandola consists of only two houses, both taverns. Tende is a very inconsiderable village, in which they have not yet the luxury of glass windows: nor in any of the villages on this passage have they yet the fashion of powdering the hair. Common stone and limestone are so abundant that the apartments of every story are vaulted with stone to save wood.

April 15. LIMONE. CONI. I see abundance of limestone as far as the earth is uncovered with snow, i.e. to within half or three quarters of an hour's walk of the top. The snows descend much lower on the Eastern than Western side. Wherever there is soil there is corn, quite to the commencement of the snows, and I suppose under them also. The waste parts are in two leaved pine, lavender and thyme. From the foot of the mountain to Coni the road follows a branch of the Po, the plains of which begin narrow, and widen at length into a general plain country bounded on one side by the Alps. They are good, dark-coloured, sometimes tinged with red, and in pasture, corn, mulberries and some almonds. The hillsides bordering these plains are reddish, and, where they admit of it, are in corn, but this is seldom. They are mostly in chesnut, and often absolutely barren. The whole of the plains are plentifully watered from the river, as is much of the hill side. A great deal of Golden willow all along the rivers on the whole of this passage thro' the Alps. The Southern parts of France, but still more the passage thro' the Alps, enables one to form a scale of the tenderer plants, arranging them according to their several powers of resisting cold. Ascending three different mountains, Braus, Brois, and Tendé, they disappear one after another; and, descending on the other side, they shew themselves again one after another. This is their order, from the tenderest to the hardiest. Caper. orange. palm. aloe. olive. pomegranate. walnut. fig. almond. But this must be understood of the plant: for as to the fruit, the order is somewhat different. The caper, for example, is the tenderest plant; yet being so easily protected, it is the most certain in it's fruit. The almond, the hardiest plant, loses it's fruit the oftenest, on account of it's forwardness. The palm, hardier than the caper and the orange, never produces perfect fruit in these parts.—Coni is a considerable town, and pretty well built. It is walled.

April 16. CENTALE. SAVIGLIANO. RACCONIGI. POERINO. TURIN. The Alps, as far as they are in view from North to South, shew the gradation of climate by the line which terminates the snows lying on them. This line begins at their foot Northwardly, and rises, as they pass on to the South, so as to be half way up their sides on the most Southern undulations of the mountain, now in view. From the mountain to Turin we see no tree tenderer than the walnut. Of these, as well as of almonds and mulberries there are a few: somewhat more of vines, but most generally willows and poplars. Corn is sowed with all these. They mix with them also clover and small grass. The country is a general plain; the soil dark, sometimes, tho' rarely, reddish. It is rich. Much infested with wild onions. At Racconigi I see the tops and shucks of Maise, which prove it is cultivated here: but it can be in small quantities only, because I observe very little ground but what has already something else in it. Here and there are small patches prepared I suppose for maize. They have a method of planting the vine which I have not seen before. At intervals of about 8.f. they plant from 2. to 6. plants of vine in a cluster. At each cluster they fix a forked staff, the plane of the prongs of the fork at a right angle with the row of vines. Athwart these prongs they lash another staff, like a handspike, about 8.f. long, horizontally, 7. or 8. feet from the ground. Of course it crosses the rows at right angles. The vines are brought from the foot of the fork up to this cross peice, turned over it, and conducted along over the next, the next, and so on as far as they will extend, the whole forming an arbour 8.f. wide and high, and of the whole length of the row, little interrupted by the stems of the vines, which being close round the fork, pass up thro' hoops, so as to occupy a space only of small diameter. All the buildings in this country are of brick, sometimes covered with plaister, sometimes not. There is a very large and very handsome bridge of 7. arches over the torrent of Sangone. We cross the Po in swinging batteaux. Two are placed side by side, and kept together by a plank floor, common to both, and lying on their gunwales. The carriage drives on this, without taking out any of the horses. About 150 yards up the river is a fixed stake, and a rope tied to it, the other end of which is made fast to one side of the batteaux so as to throw them oblique to the current. The stream then acting on them, as on an inclined plain, forces them across the current in the portion of a circle of which the rope is the radius. To support the rope in it's whole length, there are 2. intermediate canoes, about 50. yards apart, in the head of which is a short mast. To the top of this the rope is lashed, the canoes being free otherwise to concur with the general vibration in their smaller arks of circles. The Po is, there, about 50. yards wide, and about 100. in the neighborhood of Turin.

TOUR THROUGH SOUTHERN FRANCE 1787

April 17. 18. *Turin.* I observe them carrying very long beams on two pairs of wheels, which the beam connects together. The wheels with their hounds are placed thus and the beam is lashed from the hind to the fore axle. The first nightingale I have heard this year is to-day, (18th.). There is a red wine of Nebiule made in this neighborhood which is very singular. It is about as sweet as the silky Madeira, as astringent on the palate as Bordeaux, and as brisk as Champagne. It is a pleasing wine. At Moncaglieri, about 6 miles from Turin, on the right side the Po begins a ridge of mountains, which following the Po by Turin, after some distance, spreads wide and forms the dutchy of Montferrat. The soil is mostly red and in vines, affording a wine called Montferrat, which is thick and strong.

April 19. SETTIMO. CHIVASCO. CILIANO. S. GERMANO. VERCELLI. The country continues plain and rich, the soil black. The culture corn, pasture, maise, vines, mulberries, walnuts, some willow and poplar. The maize bears a very small proportion to the small grain. The earth is formed into ridges from 3. to 4.f. wide, and the maize sowed in the broad cast, on the higher parts of the ridge, so as to cover a third or half of the whole surface. It is sowed late in May. This country is plentifully and beautifully watered at present. Much of it is by torrents which are dry in summer. These torrents make a great deal of waste ground, covering it with sand and stones. These wastes are sometimes planted in trees, sometimes quite unemployed. They make hedges of willow, by setting the plants from 1. to 3.f. apart. When they are grown to the height of 8. or 10.f. they bend them down and interlace them one with another. I do not see any of these however which are become old. Probably therefore they soon die. The women here smite on the anvil, work with the mawl and the spade. The people of this country are ill dressed in comparison with those of France, and there are more spots of uncultivated ground. The plough here is made with a single handle, which is a beam 12.f. long, 6.I. diameter, below, and tapered to about 2.I. at the upper end. They use goads for the oxen, not whips. The first SWALLOWS I have seen are to-day. There is a wine called Gatina made in the neighborhood of Vercelli, both red and white. The latter resembles Calcavallo. There is also a red wine of Salusola which is esteemed. It is very light. In the neighborhood of Vercelli begin the RICE fields. The water with which they are watered is very dear. They do not permit rice to be sown within 2. miles of the cities on account of the insalubrity. Notwithstanding this, when the water is drawn off the fields in August, the whole country is subject to agues and fevers. They estimate that the same measure of ground yields three times as much rice as wheat, and with half the labour. They are now sowing. As soon as sowed, they let on the water, 2. or 3.I. deep. After 6. weeks or 2. months they draw it off to weed: then let it on again, and it remains till August, when it is drawn off about 3. or 4. weeks before the grain is ripe. In September they cut it. It is first threshed: then beaten in the mortar to separate the husk; then by different siftings it is separated into 3. qualities. 12 rupes = 300. ℔. of 12. oz. each, sell for 16.ᵗᵗ money of Piedmont, where the livre is exactly the shilling of England. 12. rupes of maize sell for 9.ᵗᵗ The machine for separating the husk is thus made. In the axis of a water wheel are a number of arms inserted, which, as they revolve, catch the cog of a pestle, lift it to a certain height, and let it fall again. These pestles are 5¼I. square, 10.f. long, and at their lower end formed into a truncated cone of 3.I. diameter where cut off. The conical part is covered with iron. The pestles are 10½ apart in the clear. They pass through two horizontal beams, which string them, as it were, together, and while the mortises in the beams are so loose as to let the pestle work vertically it restrains it to that motion. There is a mortar of wood, 12. or 15I. deep under each pestle, covered with a board, the hole of which is only large enough to let the pestle pass freely. There are two arms in the axis, for every pestil, so that the pestle gives two strokes for every revolution of the wheel. Poggio, a muletier, who passes every week between Vercelli and Genoa will smuggle a sack of rough rice for me to Genoa; it being death to export it in that form. They have good cattle in good number, mostly cream coloured, and some middle sized sheep. The streams furnish speckled trout.

April 20. NOVARA. BUFFALORA. SEDRIANO. MILAN. From Vercelli to Novara the fields are all in rice, and now mostly under water. The dams separating the several water plats, or ponds, are set in willow. At Novara there are some figs in the gardens, in situations well protected. From Novara to the Ticino it is mostly stony and waste, grown up in broom. From the Ticino to Milan it is all in corn. Among the corn are willows principally, a good many mulberries, some walnuts, and here and there an almond.

The country still a plain, the soil black and rich, except between Novara and the Ticino as before mentioned. There is very fine pasture round Vercelli and Novara to the distance of 2. miles within which rice is not permitted. We cross the Sisto on the same kind of vibrating or pendulum boat as on the Po. The river is 80. or 90. yards wide; the rope fastened to an island 200. yards above, and supported by 5. intermediate canoes. It is about 1½ I. in diameter. On these rivers they use a short oar of 12f. long, the flat end of which is hooped with iron shooting out a prong at each corner, so that it may be used occasionally as a setting pole. There is snow on the Appenines near Genoa. They have still another method here of planting the vine. Along rows of trees they lash poles from tree to tree. Between the trees are set vines which passing over the pole, are carried on to the pole of the next row, whose vines are in like manner brought to this, and twined together; thus forming the intervals between the rows of trees alternately into arbors, and open space. Another method also of making quickset hedges. Willows are planted from one to two feet apart, and thus interlaced so that every one is crossed by 3. or 4. others.

April 21. 22. MILAN. Figs and pomegranates grow here unsheltered, as I am told. I saw none, and therefore suppose them rare. They had formerly olives; but a great cold in 1709 killed them, and they have not been replanted.—Among a great many houses painted al fresco, the Casa Roma and Casa Candiani by Appiani, and casa Belgioiosa by Martin are superior. In the second is a small cabinet, the cieling of which is in small hexagons, within which are Cameos and heads painted alternately, no two the same. The salon of the casa Belgioiosa is superior to any thing I have seen. The mixture called Scaiola, of which they make their walls and floors, is so like the finest marble as to be scarcely distinguishable from it. The nights of the 20. and 21st. inst. the rice ponds freezed half an inch thick. Drowths of 2. or 3. months are not uncommon here in summer. About 5. years ago there was such a hail as to kill cats. The Count del Verme tells me of a pendulum Odometer for the wheel of a carriage. Leases here are mostly for 9. years. Wheat costs a Louis d'or the 140. ℔. A labouring man receives 60.ᵗᵗ and is fed and lodged. The trade of this country is principally rice, raw silk, and cheese.

April 23. CASINO. 5. miles from Milan. I examined another rice-beater of 6. pestles. They are 8f. 9.I. long. Their ends, instead of being a truncated cone, have 9. teeth of iron, bound closely together thus ▦ Each tooth is a double pyramid, joined at the base. When ▦ put together they stand thus, ▦ the upper ends placed in contact so as to form them into ▦ one great cone, and the lower end diverging. The upper are socketed into the end of the pestle, and the lower, when a little blunted by use, are not unlike the jaw-teeth of the Mammoth, with their studs. They say here that pestles armed with these teeth, clean the rice faster and break it less. The mortar too is of stone, which is supposed as good as wood, and more durable. One half of these pestles are always up. They rise about 21.I. Each makes 38. strokes in a minute. 100. ℔. of rough rice is put into the 6. mortars and beaten somewhat less than a quarter of an hour. It is then taken out, put into a sifter of 4.f. diameter suspended horizontally; sifted there; shifted into another of the same size, sifted there, returned to the mortars, beaten a little more than a quarter of an hour, sifted again, and it is finished. The 6. pestles will clean 4000 ℔. in 24 hours. The pound here is of 28. oz., the ounce equal to that of Paris. The best rice requires half an hour's boiling; a more indifferent kind somewhat less. To sow the rice, they first plough the ground, then level it with a drag harrow, let on the water; when the earth is become soft they smooth it with a shovel under the water, and then sow the rice in the water.

ROZZANO.[5] PARMESAN CHEESE. It is supposed this was formerly made at Parma, and took it's name thence, but none is made there now. It is made thro all the country extending from Milan 150. miles. The most is made about Lodi. The making of butter being connected with the making cheese, both must be described together. There are, in the stables I saw, 85. cows, fed on hay and grass, not on grain. They are milked twice in the 24. hours, 10 cows yeilding at the two milkings a brenta of milk, which is 24. of our gallons. The night's milk is scummed in the morning at day break, when the cows are milked again and the new milk mixed with the old. In 3. hours the whole mass is scummed a second time, the milk remaining in a kettle for cheese, and the cream being put into a cylindrical churn, shaped like a grindstone, 18.I. radius and 14.I. thick. In this churn there are three staves pointing inwardly endwise to break the current of the milk. Thro it's center passes an iron axis with a handle at each end. It is turned about an hour and an half by two men till the butter is produced. Then they pour off the buttermilk and put in some water which they agitate backwards and forwards about a minute, and pour it off. They take out the butter, press it with their hands into loaves, and stamp it. It has no other washing. 16 American gallons of milk yield 15 ℔. of butter, which sells at 24 sous the ℔.

The milk which after being scummed as before had been put into a copper kettle receives it's due quantity of rennet and is gently warmed if the season requires it. In about 4. hours it becomes a slip. Then the whey begins to separate. A little of it is taken out. The curd is then thoroughly broken by a machine like a chocolate mill. A quarter of an ounce of saffron is put to 7. brenta of milk to give colour to the cheese. The kettle is then moved over the hearth, and heated by a quick fire till the curd is hard enough, being broken into small lumps by continual stirring. It is moved off the fire, most of the whey taken out, the curd compressed into a globe by the hand, a linen cloth slipped under it, and it is drawn out in that. A loose hoop is then laid on a bench and the curd, as wrapped in the linen is put into the hoop. It is a little pressed by the hand, the hoop drawn tight, and made fast. A board 2.I. thick is laid on it, and a stone on that of about 20 lb. weight. In an hour the whey is run off and the cheese finished. They sprinkle a little salt on it every other day in summer and every day in winter for 6. weeks. 7. brentas of milk make a cheese of 50. ℔., which requires 6. months to ripen, and is then dried to 45 ℔. It sells on the spot for 88^{tt} the 100. ℔. There are now 150. cheeses in this dairy. They are 19.I. diameter and 6.I. thick. They make a cheese a day in summer, and 2. in 3. days, or 1. in 2. days in winter.

The whey is put back into the kettle, the butter milk poured into it, and of this they make a poor cheese for the country people. The whey of this is given to the hogs. 8. men suffice to keep the cows and do all the business of this dairy. Mascarponi, a[6] kind of curd, is made by pouring some butter milk into cream, which is thereby curdled, and is then pressed in a linen cloth.[7]

The ICE-HOUSES at Rozzano are dug about 15.f. deep, and 20.f. diameter and poles are driven down all round. A conical thatched roof is then put over them 15f. high. Pieces of wood are laid at bottom to keep the ice out of the water which drips from it, and goes off by a sink. Straw is laid on this wood, and then the house filled with ice always putting straw between the ice and the walls, and covering ultimately with straw. About a third is lost by melting. Snow gives the most delicate flavor to creams; but ice is the most powerful congealer, and lasts longest. A tuft of trees surrounds these ice houses.[8]

Round Milan, to the distance of 5. miles, is corn, pasture, gardens, mulberries, willows and vines, for in this state, rice-ponds are not permitted within 5. miles of the cities.

BINASCO. PAVIA. Near Cassino the rice ponds begin and continue to within 5. miles of Pavia, the whole ground being in rice, pasture, and willows. The pasture is in the rice grounds which are resting. In the neighborhood of Pavia again is corn, pasture &c. as round Milan. They gave me green peas at Pavia.

April 24. VOGHERA. TORTONA. NOVI. From Pavia to Novi corn, pasture, vines, mulberries, willows, but no rice. The country continues plain, except that the Appenines are approaching on the left. The soil, always good, is dark till we approach Novi, and then red. We cross the Po where it is 300 yards wide, on a pendulum boat. The rope is fastened to one side of the river 300 yards above, and supported by 8. intermediate canoes, with little masts in them to give a greater elevation to the rope. We pass in 11 minutes. Women, girls, and boys are working with the hoe, and breaking the clods with mauls.

Apr. 25. VOLTAGGIO. CAMPO MARONE. GENOA. At Novi the Appenines begin to rise. Their growth of timber is oak, tall, small, and knotty, and chesnut. We soon lose the walnut ascending, and find it again about one fourth of the way down on the South side. About half way down we find figs and vines, which continue fine and in great abundance. The Appenines are mostly covered with soil, and are in corn, pasture, mulberries and figs, in the parts before indicated. About half way from their foot at Campo marone to Genoa we find again the olive tree. Hence the produce becomes mixed of all the kinds before mentioned. The method of sowing the Indian corn at Campo-marone is as follows. With a hoe shaped like the blade of a trowel 2f. long and 6.I. broad at it's upper end, pointed below and a little curved, they make a trench. In that they drop the grains 6.I. apart. Then 2.f. from that they make another trench, throwing the earth they take out of that on the grain of the last one with a singular slight and quickness: and so through the whole peice. The last trench is filled with the earth adjoining.

Apr. 26. GENOA. Strawberries at Genoa. Scaffold poles for the upper parts of a wall, as for the 3d. story, rest on the window sills of the story below. Slate is used here for paving, for steps, for stairs (the rise as well as tread) and for fixed Venetian blinds. At the Palazzo Marcello Durazzo benches with strait legs, and bottoms of cane. At the Palazzo del prencipe Lomellino at Sestri a phaeton with a canopy. At the former, tables folding into one

TOUR THROUGH SOUTHERN FRANCE 1787

plane. At Nervi they have peas, strawberries &c. all the year round. The gardens of the Count Durazzo at Nervi exhibit as rich a mixture of the Utile dulci as I ever saw. All the environs of Genoa are in olives, figs, oranges, mulberries, corn and garden stuff. Aloes in many places, but they never flower.

April 28. NOLI. The Appenine and Alps appear to me to be one and the same continued ridge of mountains, separating every where the waters of the Adriatic gulph from those of the Mediterranean. Where it forms an elbow touching the Mediterranean, as a smaller circle touches a larger within which it is inscribed in the manner of a tangent, the name changes from Alps to Appenine. It is the beginning of the Appenine which constitutes the state of Genoa, the mountains there generally falling down in barren naked precipices into the sea. Wherever there is soil on the lower parts it is principally in olives and figs, in vines also, mulberries and corn. Where there are hollows well protected there are oranges. This is the case at Golfo de Laspeze, Sestri, Bugiasco, Nervi, Genoa,[9] Pegli, Savona, Finale, Oneglia (where there are abundance), St. Remo, Ventimiglia, Mantone, and Monaco. Noli, into which I was obliged to put by a change of wind is 40. miles from Genoa. There are 1200 inhabitants in the village, and many separate houses round about. One of the precipices hanging over the sea is covered with Aloes. But neither here, nor anywhere else where I have been, could I procure satisfactory information that they ever flower. The current of testimony is to the contrary. Noli furnishes many fishermen. Paths penetrate up into the mountains in several directions about ¾ of a mile; but these are practicable only for asses and mules. I saw no cattle nor sheep in the settlement. The wine they make is white and indifferent. A curious cruet for oil and vinegar in one piece, and in this form ⚯ . A bishop resides here whose revenue is 2000.[lt] = 66 guineas. I heard a nightingale here.

April 29. ALBENGA. In walking along the shore from Louano to this place I saw no appearance of shells. The tops of the mountains are covered with snow, while there are olive trees &c. on their lower parts. I do not remember to have seen assigned any where the cause of the apparent colour of the sea. It's water is generally clear and colourless if taken up and viewed in a glass. That of the Mediterranean is remarkeably so. Yet in the mass, it assumes *by reflection* the colour of the sky or atmosphere, black, green, blue, according to the state of the weather.—If any person wished to retire from their acquaintance, to live absolutely unknown, and

TOUR THROUGH SOUTHERN FRANCE 1787

yet in the midst of physical enjoiments, it should be in some of the little villages of this coast, where air, earth and water concur to offer what each has most precious. Here are nightingales, beccaficas, ortolans, pheasants, partridges, quails, a superb climate, and the power of changing it from summer to winter at any moment, by ascending the mountains. The earth furnishes wine, oil, figs, oranges, and every production of the garden in every season. The sea yeilds lobsters, crabs, oysters, thunny, sardines, anchovies &c. Ortolans sell at this time at 30s = 1/ sterling the dozen. At this season they must be fattened. Through the whole of my route from Marseilles I observe they plant a great deal of cane or reed, which is convenient while growing as a cover from the cold and boisterous winds, and, when cut, it serves for espaliers to vines, peas &c. Thro' Piedmont, Lombardy, the Milanese and Genoese, the garden bean is a great article of culture, almost as much so as corn. At Albenga is a rich plain opening from between two ridges of mountains triangularly to the sea, and of several miles extent. It's growth is olives, figs, mulberries, vines, corn, beans and pasture. A bishop resides here whose revenue is 40,000.^{tt} This place is said to be rendered unhealthy in summer by the river which passes thro the valley.

April 30. ONEGLIA. The wind continuing contrary, I took mules at Albenga for Oneglia. Along this tract are many of the tree called Carroubier, being a species of Locust. It is the Ceratonia siliqua of Linnaeus. It's pods furnish food for horses and even for the poor in times of scarcity. It abounds in Naples and Spain. Oneglia and Port Maurice, which are within a mile of each other are considerable places and in a rich country. At St. Remo are abundance of oranges and lemons and some palm trees.

May 1. VENTIMIGLIA. MENTON. MONACO. NICE. At Bordighera between Ventimiglia and Menton are extensive plantations of palms on the hill as well as in the plain. They bring fruit but it does not ripen. Some thing is made of the midrib which is in great demand at Rome on the Palm sunday, and which renders this tree profitable here. From Menton to Monaco there is more good land, and extensive groves of oranges and lemons. Orange water sells here at 40s = 16d. sterling the american quart. The distances on this coast are from Laspeze, at the Eastern end of the territories of Genoa to Genoa 55. miles geometrical, to Savona 30. Albenga 30. Oneglia 20. Ventimiglia 25. Monaco 10. Nice 10. = 180. A superb road might be made along the margin of the sea from Laspeze where the champaign country of Italy opens, to Nice where the

TOUR THROUGH SOUTHERN FRANCE 1787

Alps go off Northwardly and the post roads of France begin, and it might even follow the margin of the sea quite to Cette. By this road travellers would enter Italy without crossing the Alps, and all the little insulated villages of the Genoese would communicate together, and in time form one continued village along that road.

May 3. LUC. BRIGNOLLES. TOURVES. POURCIEUX. LA GALINIERE. Long small mountains very rocky, the soil reddish from bad to midling, in olives, grapes, mulberries, vines and corn. Brignolles is in an extensive plain, between two ridges of mountains and along a water course which continues to Tourves. Thence to Pourcieux we cross a mountain, low and easy. The country is rocky and poor. To la Galiniere are waving grounds bounded by mountains of rock at a little distance. There are some inclosures of dry wall from Luc to la Galiniere. Sheep and hogs. There is snow on the high mountains. I see no plumbs in the vicinities of Brignolles; which makes me conjecture that the celebrated plumb of that name is not derived from this place.

May 8. ORGON. AVIGNON. VAUCLUSE. AVIGNON. Orgon is on the Durance. From thence it's plain opens till it becomes common with that of the Rhone, so that from Orgon to Avignon is entirely a plain of rich dark loam, which is in willows, mulberries, vines, corn and pasture. A very few figs. I see no olives in this plain. Probably the cold winds have too much power here. From the Bac de Novo (where we cross the Durance) to Avignon is about 9. American miles; and from the same Bac to Vaucluse, 11. miles. In the valley of Vaucluse and on the hills impending over it are Olive trees. The stream issuing from the fountain of Vaucluse is about 20. yards wide, 4. or 5.f. deep and of such rapidity that it could not be stemmed by a canoe. They are now mowing hay, and gathering mulberry leaves. The high mountains, just back of Vaucluse, are covered with snow. Fine trout in the stream of Vaucluse, and the valley abounds peculiarly with nightingales. The vin blanc de M. de Rochegude of Avignon resembles dry Lisbon. He sells it at 6. years old for 22s. the bottle, the price of the bottle &c. included.

AVIGNON. REMOULINS. Some good plains, but generally hills, stony and poor, in olives, mulberries, vines and corn. Where it is waste the growth is chenevert, box, furze, thyme and rosemary.

May 10. NISMES. LUNEL. Hills on the right, plains on the left. The soil reddish, a little stony and of midling quality. The produce olives, mulberries, vines, corn, St. foin. No wood and few inclosures. *Lunel* is famous for it's vin de muscat blanc, thence called

Lunel, or vin Muscat de Lunel. It is made from the raisin muscat, without fermenting the grape in the hopper. When fermented, it makes a red Muscat, taking that tinge from the dissolution of the skin of the grape, which injures the quality. When a red Muscat is required, they prefer colouring it with a little Alicant wine. But the white is best. The price of 240. bottles, after being properly drawn off from it's lees, and ready for bottling costs from 120. to 200.^{tt} of the 1st. quality and last vintage. It cannot be bought old, the demand being sufficient to take it all the first year. There are not more than from 50. to 100. pieces a year made of the first quality. A setterie yields about one piece, and my informer supposes there are about two setteries in an arpent. Portage to Paris by land is 15.^{tt} the quintal. The best recoltes are those of M. Bouquet and M. Tremoulet. The vines are in rows 4.f. apart every way.

May 11. MONTPELIER. Snow on the Cevennes, N.W. from hence. With respect to the Muscat grape, of which the wine is made, there are two kinds, the red and the white. The first has a red skin, but white juice. If it be fermented in the cuve, the colouring matter which resides in the skin, is imparted to the wine. If not fermented in the cuve, the wine is white. Of the white grape, only a white wine can be made.—The species of St. foin cultivated here by the name of SPARSETTE is the Hedysarum Onobryches. They cultivate a great deal of Madder (Garance) Rubia tinctorum here, which is said to be immensely profitable. M. de Gouan tells me that the pine, of which they use the burs for fuel, is the Pinus sativus, being two leaved. They use for an edging to the borders of their gardens the Santolina, which they call Garderobe. I find the yellow clover here in a garden: and the large pigeon succeeding well confined in a house.

May 12. FRONTIGNAN. Some tolerable good plains in olives, vines, corn, St. foin, and Luzerne. A great proportion of the hills are waste. There are some inclosures of stone, and some sheep.— The first four years of MADDER are unproductive. The 5th. and 6th. yields the whole value of the land. Then it must be renewed. The Sparsette is the common, or true St. foin. It lasts about 5. years. In the best land it is cut twice, in May and September, and yields 3000 ℔. of dry hay to the Setterie the first cutting, and 500. ℔. the second. The Setterie is of 75. dextres en tout sens, supposed about 2. arpens. Luzerne is the best of all forage. It is sowed here in the broad cast, and lasts about 12. or 14. years. It is cut 4. times a year and yeilds 6000 ℔. of dry hay at the 4.

cuttings to the Setterie.—The territory in which the vin muscat de FRONTIGNAN is made is about a league of 3000 toises long, and ¼ of a league broad. The soil is reddish and stony, often as much stone as soil. On the left it is a plain, on the right hills. There are made about 1000 pieces (of 250 bottles each) annually, of which 600 are of the first quality made on the coteaux. Of these Madame Soubeinan makes 200., M. Reboulle 90., M. Lambert, medecin de la faculté de Monpelier 60. M. Thomas notaire 50. M. Argilliers 50. M. Audibert 40. = 490. and there are some small proprietors who make small quantities. The 1st. quality is sold, brut, for 120.^{tt} the piece. But it is then thick, must have a winter and the fouet to render it potable and brilliant. The fouet is like a chocolate mill, the handle of iron, the brush of stiff hair. In bottles this wine costs 24.s the bottle &c. included. It is potable the April after it is made, is best that year, and after 10. years begins to have a pitchy taste resembling it to Malaga. It is not permitted to ferment more than half a day, because it would not be so liquorish. The best colour, and it's natural one, is the amber. By force of whipping it is made white but loses flavor. There are but 2. or 3. peices a year, of red Muscat, made, there being but one vineyard of the red grape, which belongs to a baker called Pascal. This sells in bottles at 30.s the bottle included. Rondette, negociant en vin, Porte St. Bernard fauxbourg St. Germain à Paris, buys 300. pieces of the 1st. quality, every year. The coteaux yeild about half a piece to the Setterie, the plains a whole piece. The inferior quality is not at all esteemed. It is bought by the merchants of Cette, as is also the wine of Bezieres, and sold by them for Frontignan of 1st. quality. They sell 30,000 pieces a year under that name. The town of Frontignan marks it's casks with a hot iron. An individual of that place, having two casks emptied, was offered 40.^{tt} for the empty cask by a merchant of Cette. The town of Frontignan contains about 2000 inhabitants. It is almost on the level of the ocean. Transportation to Paris is 15.^{tt} the quintal, and is 15 days going. The price of packages is about 8^{tt}–8 the 100 bottles. A setterie of good vineyard sells for from 350.^{tt} to 500.^{tt} and rents for 50.^{tt} A labouring man hires at 150.^{tt} the year, and is fed and lodged: a woman at half as much. Wheat sells at 10.^{tt} the settier, which weighs 100. ℔s. poids de table. They make some Indian corn here which is eaten by the poor. The olives do not extend Northward of this into the country above 12. or 15. leagues. In general the Olive country in Languedoc is about 15. leagues broad. More of the waste lands between Frontignan and Mirval are capable of culture: but it is a marshy country very subject to fever and ague, and generally unhealthy. Thence arises, as is said, a want of hands.

CETTE. There are in this town about 10,000 inhabitants. It's principal commerce is wine. It furnishes great quantities of grape pomice for making verdigriese. They have a very growing commerce, but it is kept under by the privileges of Marseilles.

May 13. AGDE. On the right of the Etang de Tau are plains of some width, then hills, in olives, vines, mulberry, corn and pasture. On the left a narrow sand bar separating the etang from the sea along which it is proposed to make a road from Cette to Agde. In this case the post would lead from Monpelier, by Cette and Agde to Bezieres, being leveller, and an hour, or an hour and a half nearer. Agde contains 6. or 8,000 inhabitants.

May 14. BEZIERES. Rich plains in corn, St. foin and pasture; hills at a little distance to the right in olives, the soil both of hill and plain is red, going from Agde to Bezieres. But at Bezieres the country becomes hilly, and is in olives, corn, St. foin, pasture, some vines and mulberries.

May 15. BEZIERES. ARGILIES. LE SAUMAL. From Argilies to Saumal are considerable plantations of vines. Those on the red hills to the right are said to produce good wine. No wood, no inclosures. There are sheep and good cattle. The Pyrenees are covered with snow. I am told they are so in certain parts all the year. [The Canal of Languedoc along which I now travel is 6. toises wide at bottom, and 10 toises at the surface of the water, which is 1. toise deep. The barks which navigate it are 70. and 80. feet long, and 17. or 18. f. wide. They are drawn by one horse, and worked by 2. hands, one of which is generally a woman. The locks are mostly kept by women, but the necessary operations are much too laborious for them.][10] The encroachments by the men on the offices proper for the women is a great derangement in the order of things. Men are shoemakers, tailors, upholsterers, staymakers, mantua makers, cooks, door-keepers, housekeepers, housecleaners, bedmakers. They coëffe the ladies, and bring them to bed: the women therefore, to live are obliged to undertake the offices which they abandon. They become porters, carters, reapers, wood cutters, sailors, lock keepers, smiters on the anvil, cultivators of the earth &c. Can we wonder if such of them as have a little beauty prefer easier courses to get their livelihood, as long as that beauty lasts? Ladies who employ men in the offices which should be reserved for their sex, are they not bawds in effect? For every man whom they thus employ, some girl, whose place he has taken, is driven to whoredom.—[The passage of the eight locks at Bezieres, that is from the opening of the 1st. to the last gate, took 1. Hour 33′. The bark in which I go is about 35.f. long, drawn by one horse, and goes from 2. to 3. geographical miles an hour.] The canal yeilds abundance of carp and eel. I see also small fish resembling our perch and chub. Some plants of white clover, and some of yellow on the banks of the canal near Capestan; Santolina also and a great deal of a yellow Iris. [Met a raft of about 350 beams 40.f. long, and 12. or 15.I. diameter, formed into 14. rafts tacked together.] The extensive and numerous fields of St. foin, in general bloom, are beautiful.

May 16. LE SAUMAL. MARSEILLETTE. May 17. Marseillette. CARCASSONNE. [From Saumal to Carcassonne we have always the river Aube close on our left. This river runs in the valley between the Cevennes and Pyrenees, serving as the common receptacle for both their waters. It is from 50. to 150. yards wide, always rapid, rocky, and insusceptible of navigation. The canal passes in the side of the hills made by that river, overlooks the river itself, and it's plains, and has it's prospect ultimately terminated, on one side by mountains of rock overtopped by the Pyrenees, on the other by small mountains, sometimes of rock, sometimes of soil overtopped by the Cevennes. Marseillette is on a ridge which separates the river Aube[11] from the etang de Marseillette. The canal, in it's approach to this village, passes the ridge, and rides along the front overlooking the etang and the plains on it's border; and having passed the village recrosses the ridge and resumes it's general ground in front of the Aube.[11]] The growth is corn, St. foin, pasture, vines, mulberries, willows, and olives.

May 18. CARCASSONNE. CASTELNAUDARI. [Opposite to Carcassonne the canal receives the river Fresquel, about 30. yards wide, which is it's substantial supply of water from hence to Beziers. From Beziers to Agde the river Orb furnishes it, and the Eraut from Agde to the etang de Thau. By means of the ecluse ronde at Agde the waters of the Eraut can be thrown towards Bezieres to aid those of the Orb as far as the ecluse de Porcaraigne, 9 geometrical miles. Where the Fresquel enters the canal there is, on the opposite side, a waste, to let off the superfluous waters. The horse-way is continued over this waste by a bridge of stone of 18 arches.] I observe them fishing in the canal with a skimming net of about 15. feet diameter, with which they tell me they catch carp. Flax in blossom. Neither strawberries nor peas yet at Carcassonne. The Windsor bean just come to table. From the ecluse de la Lande we see the last olive trees near a metairée or farmhouse called la Lande. On a review of what I have seen and heard of this tree, the following seem to be it's Northern limits. Beginning on the Atlantic, at the Pyrenees, and along them to the meridian of la Lande, or of Carcassonne: up that Meridian to the Cevennes, as they begin just there to raise themselves high enough to afford it shelter. Along the Cevennes to the parallel of 45.° latitude, and along that parallel (crossing the Rhone near the mouth of the Isere) to the Alps, thence along the Alps and Appenines to what parallel of latitude I know not. Yet here the tracing of the line becomes the most interesting. For from the Atlantic so far, we see this production the effect of shelter and latitude combined. But where does it venture to launch forth, unprotected by shelter, and by the mere force of latitude alone? Where for instance does it's northern limit cross the Adriatic?*—I learn that the olive tree resists cold to 8.° of Reaumur below the freezing point, which corresponds to 14.° above zero, of Farenheit: and that the orange† resists to 4.° below freezing of Reaumur, which is 23.° above zero of Farenheit.

May 19. CASTELNAUDARI. ST. FERIOL. ESCAMAZE. LAMPY. Some sheep and cattle. No inclosures. St. Feriol, Escamaze and Lampy are in the montagnes noires. The country almost entirely waste, some of it in shrubbery. The voute d'Escarmaze is of 135 yards. Round about Castelnaudari the country is hilly, as it has been constantly from Beziers. It is very rich. Where it is plain, or nearly plain, the soil is black: in general however it is hilly and reddish, and in corn. They cultivate a great deal of Indian corn here, which they call Millet. It is planted, but not yet up.

May 20. CASTELNAUDARI. NAUROUZE. VILLEFRANCHE. BAZIEGE. [At Naurouze is the highest ground which the canal had to pass between the two seas. It became necessary then to find water still higher, and to bring it here. The river Fresquel heading by it's two principal branches in the Montagnes noires, a considerable distance off to the Eastward, the springs of the most western one were brought together, and conducted to Naurouze, where it's waters are divided, part furnishing the canal towards the ocean, the rest towards the Mediterranean, as far as the ecluse de Fresquel where, as has been before noted, the Lampy[12] branch, and the Alzau, under the name of the Fresquel, enter.

* It is a principal produce of the island of Cherso, in lat. 45¼.° 3.Fortis.c.8.
† Les orangers et les Amandiers ne resistent point à un froid de 5° audessous de la glace lorsqu'il survient aprés la pluie ou le degel. Journ. Par. 1789. Jan. 6.

They have found that a lock of 6. pieds is best. However, 8 pieds is well enough. Beyond this it is bad. Monsr. Pin tells me of a lock of 30. pieds made in Sweden, of which it was impossible to open the gates. They therefore divided it into 4. locks. The small gates of the locks of this canal have six square pieds of surface. They tried the machinery of the jack for opening them. They were more easily opened, but very subject to be deranged, however strongly made. They returned therefore to the original wooden screw, which is excessively slow and laborious. I calculate that 5. minutes are lost at every bason by this screw, which on the whole number of basons is one eighth of the time necessary to navigate the canal: and of course, if a method of lifting the gate at one stroke could be found, it would reduce the passage from 8. to 7. days, and the freight equally. I suggested to Monsr. Pin and others a quadrantal gate turning on a pivot, and lifted by a lever like a pump handle, aided by a windlass and cord, if necessary. He will try it and inform me of the success. The price of transportation from Cette to Bordeaux thro' the canal and Garonne is   the quintal: round by the streights of Gibraltar is   . 240. barks, the largest of 2200 quintals (or say in general of 100 tons) suffice to perform the business of this canal, which is stationary, having neither increased nor diminished for many years. When pressed, they can pass and repass between Thoulouse and Beziers in 14. days: but 16. is the common period. The canal is navigated 10½ months of the year; the other month and a half being necessary to lay it dry, cleanse it, and repair the works. This is done in July and August, when there would perhaps be a want of water.]

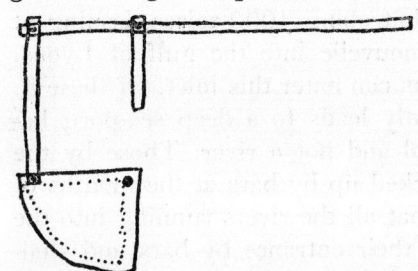

May 21. BAZIEGE. TOULOUSE. The country continues hilly, but very rich. It is in mulberries, willows, some vines, corn, maize, pasture, beans, flax. A great number of chateaux and good houses in the neighborhood of the canal. The people partly in farm houses, partly in villages. I suspect that the farm houses are occupied by the farmer, while the labourers (who are mostly by the day) reside in the villages. Neither strawberries nor peas yet at Baziege or Toulouse. Near the latter are some feilds of yellow clover.

[At Toulouse the canal ends. It has four communications with the Mediterranean. 1. Through the ponds of Thau, Frontignan,

Palavas, Maguelone, and Manyo, the canal de la Radele aiguesmortes, le canal des salines de Pecair, and the arm of the Rhone called Bras de fer, which ends at Fourquet, opposite to Arles, and thence down the Rhone. 2. At Cette by a canal of a few hundred toises leading out of the etang de Thau into the sea. The vessels pass the etang, through a length of 9000 toises, with sails. 3. At Agde, by the river Eraut, 2500 toises. It has but 5. or 6. pieds of water at it's mouth. It is joined to the canal at the upper part of this communication by a branch of a canal 270 toises long. 4. At Narbonne by a canal they are now opening, which leads from the great canal near the Aquaeduct of the river Cesse, 2600 toises, into the Aude. This new canal will have 5 lock-basons of about 12. pieds fall each. Then you are to cross the Aude very obliquely, and descend a branch of it 6000. toises through 4. lock basons to Narbonne, and from Narbonne down the same branch 1200. toises into the etang de Sigen, across that etang 4000 toises, issuing at an inlet, called the Grau de la nouvelle into the gulf of Lyons. But only vessels of 30. or 40. tons can enter this inlet. Of these 4. communications, that of Cette only leads to a deep sea-port, because the exit is there by a canal and not a river. Those by the Rhone, Eraut, and Aude are blocked up by bars at the mouths of those rivers.] It is remarkeable that all the rivers running into the Mediterranean are obstructed at their entrance by bars and shallows, which often change their position. This is the case with the Nile, the Tyber, the Po, the Lez, le Lyvron, the Orbe, the Gly, the Tech, the Tet &c. Indeed the formation of these bars seems not confined to the mouths of the rivers, tho' it takes place at them more certainly. Along almost the whole of the coast, from Marseilles towards the Pyrenees, banks of sand are thrown up, parallel with the coast, which have insulated portions of the sea, that is, formed them into etangs, ponds, or sounds, through which here and there, narrow and shallow inlets only are preserved by the currents of the rivers. These sounds fill up in time with the mud and sand deposited in them by the rivers. Thus the etang de Vendres, navigated formerly by vessels of 60 tons, is now nearly filled up by the mud and sand of the Aude. The Vistre and Vidourle which formerly emptied themselves into the Gulf of Lyons, are now received by the etangs de Manjo and Aiguesmortes, that is to say, the part of the gulf of Lyons which formerly received, and still receives, those rivers; is now cut off from the sea by a bar of sand which has been thrown up in it, and has formed it into sounds. Other proofs that the land gains there on the sea are that

TOUR THROUGH SOUTHERN FRANCE 1787

the towns of St. Gilles and Notre dame d'aspoets, formerly seaports, are now far from the sea, and that Aiguesmortes, where are still to be seen the iron rings to which vessels were formerly moored, and where St. Louis embarked for Palestine, has now in it's vicinities only ponds which cannot be navigated, and communicates with the sea by an inlet, called Grau du roy, through which only fishing barks can pass. It is pretty well established that all the Delta of Egypt has been formed by the depositions of the Nile and the alluvions of the sea, and probable that that operation is still going on. Has this peculiarity of the Mediterranean any connection with the scantiness of it's tides, which even at the Equinoxes, are of 2. or 3. feet only?

[An accurate state of the locks, of their distances from each other, of their fall of water, and of the number of basons to each.

	Distance toises	Fall pi. po. li.[13]	Basons
From Cette to the mouth of the canal at the Western end of the etang de Thau 9000 toises.			
From the said mouth of the canal to the lock of Bagnat (the fall of which is 6 pi. 11 po.)	2533	....	1
to the river Eraut	1530		
along the river to the entrance of the canal called Cassalet haut	603		
to the Round lock	199		
Note. The Round lock forms a center between 3. branches of canal of different levels. 1. The Cassalet haut beforementioned, which is the highest. 2. The canal leading to Bezieres, which is 1 pi. 6 po. lower than the Cassalet haut. 3. The canal called Cassalet bas, leading to the port of Agde, 270 toises long, & 5 pi. 3 po. lower than the canal of Bezieres. At Agde, the waters of the river having shot over the bishop's mill dam are almost in the level of the Mediterranean. It is from this fall they begin to calculate the height of the point of partition above the mediterannean. The ascent into the canal of Bezieres, as before mentioned is		.. 5 3	

[451]

TOUR THROUGH SOUTHERN FRANCE 1787

	Distance toises	Fall pi. po. li.[13]	Ba- sons
From the Round lock to that of Porti- ragnes	6614	6 10	1.
lock of Villeneuve	2297	6 6 3	1.
Arieges	727	3	1.
to the entrance into the river Orb	2151	. . . . . .	1.
along the river and across it to the canal on the Western side	446		
to the lock of Notre-dame	113	13 8	1.
Fonceranes	459	64 0 9	8
Argent	27,532	6 4 6	1
Pelaurier	1,321	15 2 0	2
Ognon	1,408	17 5 4	2.
Ons	344	9 11 3	1
Jouars	1893	10 6 0	1
Picherie	3267	13 8 1	2.
l'Aiguille	1552	18 0 6	2
St. Martin	919	17 9 11	2
Fonfile	638	26 11 1	3
Marseilette	1622	11 5 5	1.
Trebes	4802	23 11 4	3
Ville du Bert	2356	8 0 4	1.
l'Eveque	410	9 5 6	1
Fresquel	1958	4 3 7	1.
Villody	1736	14 9 9	2.
Foucaut	1800	19 5 3	3
la Douce	792	9 3 0	1
L'harmenis	708	12 0 0	1
la Lande	158	16 2 3	2
Ville seque	2544	6 7 7	1
Beteil	3832	6 5 6	1
Bram	2868	7 3 7	1
Sauzens	633	7 11 10	1
Villepinte	864	9 10 0	1
Treboul	1958	9 9 5	1
la Criminelle	715	10 3 0	1
la Perrugue	257	6 2 0	1
la Guerre	562	7 5 1	1
St. Sernin	482	7 3 6	1
Guillermin	306	8 10 9	1
Vivier	247	22 9 7	3
Gaye	837	16 6 0	2
St. Roch pres le bassin de Castel- naudari	829	29 8 0	4
la Planque	2238	8 0 3	1
la Domergue	633	7 7 4	1
Laurens	628	20	3
Roc	641	16 8 0	2

[452]

TOUR THROUGH SOUTHERN FRANCE 1787

	Distance toises	Fall pi. po. li.[13]	Ba-sons
Medecis, where the canal attains it's whole height, or point of partition	378	7 10 6	1
Sum of Distance, height, and number of basons from the beginning of the canal, at W. end of Thau ..	93,340	581 3	74
The canal then passes level by Naurouse to the lock of Montferran, where is the first descent	2516	7 2 1	1
From Montferran to Vignonet	2151	9 8 0	1
Encassan	786	14 6 0	2
Reneville	1498	8 3 9	1
Gardouche ...	2102	6 0 0	1
Laval	729	16 5 0	2
Negra	2169	12 5 0	1
Sanglier	1883	12 10 10	2
Aiguevives ...	784	13 0 0	2
Mongiscar ...	1638	12 8 8	2
Vic	3864	7 6 0	1
Castanet	864	15 1 0	2
Bayard	6261	14 2 4	2
Matabiore	166	6 7 4	1
Roquets	640	14 9 7	2
Biarnois	505	7 3 8	1
de la Garronne at Toulouse .	486	15 3 9	2
to the Garonne, on a level ..	64		
Sum of Distance, height and number of basons from lock of Monferran, point of partition	26,590	193 11 0	26

RECAPITULATION

From the Etang de thau to the middle point of the highest water of the canal	94,598	581 3 0	74
From the same middle point to the Garonne	27,848	193 11 0	26
Sum, from the Western end of the etang de Thau to the Garonne .	122,446		100

[453]

TOUR THROUGH SOUTHERN FRANCE 1787

The communication from the Western end of the canal to the ocean is by the river Garonne. This is navigated by flat boats of 800. quintals when the water is well but when it is scanty these boats can carry only 200. quintals till they get to the mouth of the Tarn. It has been proposed to open a canal that far from Toulouse along the right side of the river.]

May 22. TOULOUSE. 23. Agen. 24. Castres. Bordeaux. The Garonne and rivers emptying into it make extensive and rich plains, which are in mulberries, willows, corn, maize, pasture, beans and flax. The hills are in corn, maize, beans and a considerable proportion of vines. There seems to be as much maize as corn in this country. Of the latter there is more rye than wheat. The maize is now up, and about 3.I. high. It is sowed in rows 2f. or 2½f. apart, and is pretty thick in the row. Doubtless they mean to thin it. There is a great deal of a forage they call Farouche. It is a species of red trefoil, with few leaves, a very coarse stalk, and a cylindrical blossom of 2.I. length and ¾ I. diameter, consisting of floscul[e]s exactly as does that of the red clover. It seems to be a coarse food, but very plentiful. They say it is for their oxen. These are very fine, large and cream coloured. The services of the farm and of transportation are performed chiefly by them. A few horses and asses, but no mules. Even in the city of Bordeaux we see scarcely any beasts of draught but oxen. When we cross the Garonne at Langon we find the plains entirely of sand and gravel, and they continue so to Bordeaux. Where they are capable of any thing they are in vines, which are in rows 4. 5. or 6. feet apart, and sometimes more. Near Langon is Sauterne, where the best white wines of Bordeaux are made. The waste lands are in fern, furze, shrubbery and dwarf trees. The farmers live on their farms at Agen, Castres, Bordeaux. Strawberries and peas are come to table; so that the country on the canal of Languedoc seems to have later seasons than that East and West of it. What can be the cause? To the Eastward the protection of the Cevennes makes the warm season advance sooner. Does the neighborhood of the Mediterranean cooperate? And does that of the Ocean mollify and advance the season to the Westward? There are Ortolans at Agen, but none at Bordeaux. The buildings on the Canal and the Garonne are mostly of brick; the size of the bricks the same with that of the antient Roman brick as seen in the remains of their buildings in this country. In those of a circus at Bordeaux, considerable portions of which are standing, I measured the bricks and found them 19. or 20. inches long, 11. or 12. inches wide, and from 1½ to 2 inches thick. Their texture as fine, compact and solid as that of porcelaine. The bricks now made, tho' of the same dimensions, are not so fine. They are burnt in a kind of furnace, and make excellent work. The elm tree shews itself at Bordeaux peculiarly proper for being spread flat for arbours. Many are done in this way on the quay des Charterons. Strawberries, peas, and cherries at Bordeaux.

May 24. 25. 26. 27. 28. BORDEAUX. The cantons in which the most celebrated wines of Bordeaux are made are MEDOC down the river, GRAVE adjoining the city and the parishes next above; all on the same side of the river. In the first is made red wine principally, in the two last, white. In Medoc they plant the vines in cross rows of 3½ pieds. They keep them so low that poles extended along the rows one way, horizontally, about 15. or 18.I. above the ground, serve to tye the vines to, and leave the cross row open to the plough. In Grave they set the plants in quincunx, i.e. in equilateral triangles of 3½ pieds every side; and they stick a pole of 6. or 8. feet high to every vine separately. The vine stock is sometimes 3. or 4.f. high. They find these two methods equal in culture, duration, quantity and quality. The former however admits the alternative of tending by hand or with the plough. The grafting of the vine, tho a critical operation, is practised with success. When the graft has taken, they bend it into the earth and let it take root above the scar. They begin to yeild an indifferent wine at 3. years old, but not a good one till 25. years, nor after 80, when they begin to yield less, and worse, and must be renewed. They give three or four workings in the year, each worth 70.tt or 75.tt, the journal, which is of 840. square toises, and contains about 3000 plants. They dung a little in Medoc and Grave, because of the poverty of the soil; but very little; as more would affect the wine. The journal yeilds, communibus annis, about 3. pieces of 240. or 250 bottles each. The vineyards of first quality are all worked by their proprietors. Those of the 2d. rent for 300.tt the journal: those of the 3d. at 200.tt They employ a kind of overseer at four or five hundred livres the year, finding him lodging and drink; but he feeds himself. He superintends and directs, but is expected to work but little. If the proprietor has a garden the overseer tends that. They never hire labourers by the year. The day wages for a man are 30. sous, a woman's 15. sous, feeding themselves. The women make the bundles of sarment, weed, pull off the snails, tie the vines, gather the grapes. During the vintage they are paid high and fed well.

Of RED WINES, there are 4. vineyards of first quality, viz. 1. Chateau Margau, belonging to the Marquis d'Agicourt, who makes about 150. tonneaux of 1000 bottles each. He has engaged to Jernon a merchant. 2. La Tour de Segur, en Saint Lambert, belonging to Monsieur Mirosmenil, who makes 125. tonneaux. 3. Hautbrion, belonging ⅔ to M. le comte de Femelle, who has engaged to Barton a merchant, the other third to the Comte de Toulouse at Toulouse. The whole is 75. tonneaux. 4. Chateau de la Fite, belonging to the President Pichard at Bordeaux, who makes 175 tonneaux. The wines of the three first are not in perfection till 4 years old. Those [of] de la Fite, being somewhat lighter, are good at 3 years, that is, the crop of 1786 is good in the spring of 1789. These growths, of the year 1783 sell now at 2000.^{tt} the tonneau, those of 1784, on account of the superior quality of that vintage, sell at 2400,^{tt} those of 1785 at 1800,^{tt} those of 1786 at 1800,^{tt} tho they sold at first for only 1500.^{tt} RED WINES of the 2d. quality are ROZAN belonging to Madame de Rozan, Dabbadie, ou Lionville, la Rose, Quirouen, Durfort; in all 800 tonneaux, which sell at 1000.^{tt} new. The 3d. class are Calons, Mouton, Gassie, Arboete, Pontette, de Terme, Candale; in all, 2000 tonneaux at 8 or 900.^{tt} After these they are reckoned common wines and sell from 500.^{tt} down to 120.^{tt} the ton. All red wines decline after a certain age, losing colour, flavour, and body. Those of Bordeaux begin to decline at about 7. years old.

Of WHITE WINES, those made in the canton of Grave are most esteemed at Bordeaux. The best crops are 1. PONTAC, which formerly belonged to M. de Pontac, but now to M. de Lamont. He makes 40. tonneaux which sell at 400.^{tt} new. 2. ST. BRISE, belonging to M. de Pontac, 30 tonneaux at 350.^{tt} 3. DE CARBONIUS, belonging to the Benedictine monks, who make 50 tonneaux, and never selling till 3. or 4. years old, get 800.^{tt} the tonneau. Those made in the three parishes next above Grave, and more esteemed at Paris are 1. SAUTERNE. The best crop belongs to M. Diquem at Bordeaux, or to M. de Salus his son in law. 150. tonneaux at 300.^{tt} new and 600.^{tt} old. The next best crop is M. de Fillotte's 100. tonneaux sold at the same price. 2. PRIGNAC. The best is the President du Roy's at Bordeaux. He makes 175 tonneaux, which sell at 300.^{tt} new, and 600.^{tt} old. Those of 1784, for their extraordinary quality sell at 800.^{tt} 3. Barsac. The best belongs to the President Pichard, who makes 150. tonneaux at 280.^{tt} new and 600.^{tt} old. Sauterne is the pleasantest; next Prignac, and lastly Barsac; but Barsac is the strongest; next Prignac, and lastly Sauterne; and all stronger than Grave. There are other good crops made on the same paroisses of Sauterne, Prignac, and Barsac; but none as good as these. There is a Virgin wine, which tho' made of a red grape, is of a light rose colour, because, being made without pressure the colouring matter of the skin does not mix with the juice. There are other white wines from the preceding prices down to 75.^{tt} In general the white wines keep longest. They will be in perfection till 15. or 20. years of age. The best vintage now to be bought is of 1784, both of red and white. There has been no other good year since 1779.

The celebrated vineyards beforementioned are plains, as is generally the canton of Medoc, and that of Grave. The soil of Hautbrion particularly, which I examined, is a sand, in which is near as much round gravel or small stone, and a very little loam: and this is the general soil of Medoc. That of Pontac, which I examined also, is a little different. It is clayey, with a fourth or fifth of fine rotten stone; and of 2. feet depth it becomes all a rotten stone. M. de Lamont tells me he has a kind of grape without seeds, which I did not formerly suppose to exist, but I saw at Marseilles dried raisins from Smyrna, without seeds. I see in his farm at Pontac some plants of white clover and a good deal of yellow; also some small peach trees in the open ground. The principal English wine merchants at Bordeaux are Jernon, Barton, Johnston, Foster, Skinner, Copinger and McCartey. The chief French wine merchants are Feger, Nerac, Brunneau, Jauge, and du Verget. Desgrands, a wine broker, tells me they never mix the wines of first quality: but that they mix the inferior ones to improve them. The smallest wines make the best brandy. They yield about a fifth or sixth.

May 28. 29. From Bordeaux to BLAYE the country near the river is hilly, chiefly in vines, some corn some pasture. Further out are plains, boggy and waste. The soil in both cases clay and grit. Some sheep on the waste. To ETAULIERE we have sometimes boggy plains, sometimes waving grounds and sandy, always poor, generally waste in fern and furze, with some corn however interspersed. To MIRAMBEAU and ST. GENIS it is hilly, poor and mostly waste. There is some corn and maize however, and better trees than usual. Towards Pons it becomes a little red, mostly rotten stone. There are vines, corn, and maize, which is up. At PONS we approach the Charenton: the country becomes better, a blackish mould mixed with a rotten chalky stone, a great many vines, corn, maize and farouche. From LAJART to SAINTES and ROCHEFORT the soil is reddish, it's foundation a chalky rock at about a foot depth, in vines, corn, maize, clover, lucerne and pasture. There are more and better trees than I have seen in all my journey; a great many apple and cherry trees. Fine cattle, and many sheep.

May 30. From Rochefort to LE ROCHER it is sometimes hilly and red with a chalky foundation, midling good in corn, pasture, and some waste. Sometimes it is reclaimed marsh in clover and corn, except the parts accessible to the tide which are in wild grass. About ROCHELLE it is a low plain. Towards USSEAU and half way to Marans level highlands, red, mixed with an equal quantity of broken chalk, mostly in vines, some corn and pasture: then to MARANS and half way to St. Hermines it is reclaimed marsh, dark, tolerably good and all in pasture: there we rise to plains a little higher, red, with a chalky foundation boundless to the eye and altogether in corn and maize. May 31. At ST. HERMINES the country becomes very hilly, a red clay mixed with chalky stone, generally waste in furze and broom, with some patches of corn and maize and so it continues to CHANTENAY, and ST. FULGENT. Thro the whole of this road from Bordeaux are frequent hedge rows and small patches of forest wood, not good, yet better than I had seen in the preceding part of my journey. Towards Montaigu the soil mends a little, the cultivated parts in corn and pasture, the uncultivated in broom. It is in very small inclosures of ditch and quickset. On approaching the Loire to NANTES the country is leveller, the soil from Rochelle to this place may be said to have been sometimes red, but oftener grey and always on a chalky foundation. The last census, of about 1770. made 120,000 inhabitants at Nantes. They conjecture there are now 150,000 which equals it to Bordeaux.

June 1. 2. The country from Nantes to LORIENT is very hilly and poor, the soil grey. Nearly half is waste, in furze and broom, among which is some poor grass. The cultivated parts are in corn, some maize, a good many apple trees, no vines. All is in small inclosures of quick hedge and ditch. There are patches and hedgerows of forest wood, not quite deserving the name of timber. The people are mostly in villages, they eat rye bread and are ragged. The villages announce a general poverty as does every other appearance. Women smite on the anvil, and work with the hoe, and cows are yoked to labour. There are great numbers of cattle, insomuch that butter is their staple. Neither asses nor mules, yet it is said that the fine mules I have met with on my journey are raised in Poictou. There are but few chateaux here. I observe mill ponds, and hoes with long handles. Have they not, in common with us, derived these from England, of which Bretagne is probably a colony? Lorient is supposed to contain 25,000 inhabitants. They tell me here that to make a reasonable profit on potash and pearl ash, as bought in America, the former should sell at 30.̃ the latter 36.̃ the quintal. Of turpentine they make no use in their vessels. Bayonne furnishes pitch enough. But tar is in demand, and ours sells well. The tower of Lorient is 65. pi. above the level of the sea, 120. pi. high, 25. pi. diameter; the stairs 4. feet radius, and cost 30,000.̃ besides the materials of the old tower.

June 3. 4. 5. The country and productions from Lorient to RENNES, and Rennes to Nantes, are precisely similar to those from Nantes to Lorient. About Rennes it is somewhat leveller, perhaps less poor, and almost entirely in pasture. The soil always grey. Some small separate houses which seem to be the residence of labourers, or very small farmers; the walls frequently of mud, and the roofs generally covoured with slate. Great plantations of walnut, and frequent of pine. Some apple trees and sweet briar still in bloom, and broom generally so. I have heard no nightingale since the last day of May. There are gates in this country made in the form here represented. The top rail of the gate overshoots backwards the hind post so as to counterpoise the gate and prevent it's swagging.

NANTES. Vessels of 8.f. draught only can come to Nantes. Those which are larger lie at Point boeuf, 10 leagues below Nantes, and 5. leagues above the mouth of the river. There is a continued navigation from Nantes to Paris thro' the Loire, the canal de Briare and the Seine. Carolina rice is preferred to that of Lombardy for the Guinea trade because it requires less water to boil it.

June 6. 7. 8. NANTES. ANCENIS. ANGERS. TOURS. Ascending the Loire from Nantes, the road, as far as Angers, leads over the hills, which are grey, oftener below than above mediocrity, and in corn, pasture, vines, some maise, flax and hemp. There are no waste lands. About the limits of Bretagne and Anjou, which are between Loriottiere and St. George, the lands change for the better. Here and there we get views of the plains on the Loire, of some extent and good appearance, in corn and pasture. After passing Angers, the road is raised out of the reach of inundations, so as at the same time to ward them off from the interior plains. It passes generally along the river side; but sometimes leads thro' the plains, which, after we pass Angers, become extensive and good, in corn, pasture, some maize, hemp, flax, peas and beans; many willows also, poplars and walnuts. The flax is near ripe. Sweetbriar in general bloom. Some broom here still, on which the cattle and sheep browze in winter and spring when they have no other green food: and the hogs eat the blossoms and pods in spring and summer. This blossom, tho' disagreeable when smelt in a small quantity, is of delicious fragrance when there is a whole field of it. There are some considerable vineyards in the river plains, just before we reach les trois volées, (which is at the 136th. mile stone) and after that, where the hills on the left come into view, they are mostly in vines. Their soil is clayey and stoney, a little reddish and of Southern aspect. The hills on the other side of the river, looking to the North, are not in vines. There is very good wine made on these hills; not equal, indeed to the Bordeaux of best quality, but to that of good quality, and like it. It is a great article of exportation from Anjou and Touraine, and probably is sold abroad under the name of Bordeaux. They are now mowing the first crop of hay. All along both hills of the Loire is a mass of white stone, not durable, growing black with time, and so soft that the people cut their houses out of the solid with all the partitions, chimnies, doors &c. The hill sides resemble coney burrows, full of inhabitants. The borders of the Loire are almost a continued village. There are many chateaux, many cattle, sheep, and horses; some asses.

TOURS is at the 119th. mile stone. Being desirous of enquiring here into a fact stated by Voltaire in his Questions encyclopediques. art. Coquilles, relative to the growth of shells unconnected with animal bodies at the chateau of Monsr. de la Sauvagiere near Tours, I called on M. Gentil premier Secretaire de l'Intendance, to whom the Intendant had written on my behalf at the request of the Marquis de Chastellux. I stated to him the fact as advanced by Voltaire and found he was, of all men, the best to whom I could have addressed myself. He told me he had been in correspondence with Voltaire on that very subject, and was perfectly acquainted with M. de la Sauvagiere, and the Faluniere where the fact is said to have taken place. It is at the Chateau de Grille mont, 6. leagues from Tours on the road to Bordeaux, belonging now to M. d'Orçai. He sais that de la Sauvagiere was a man of truth, and might be relied on for whatever facts he stated as of his own observation: but that he was overcharged with imagination, which, in matters of opinion and theory, often led him beyond his facts: that this feature in his character had appeared principally in what he wrote on the antiquities of Touraine: but that as to the fact in question he believed him. That he himself indeed had not watched the same identical shells, as Sauvagiere had done, growing from small to great: but that he had often seen such masses of those shells of all sizes, from a point to full size, as to carry conviction to his mind that they were in the act of growing: that he had once made a collection of shells for the Emperor's cabinet, reserving duplicates of them for himself; and that these afforded proofs of the same fact: that he afterwards gave those duplicates to a M. du Verget, a physician of Tours of great science and candour, who was collecting on a larger scale, and who was perfectly in sentiment with M. de la Sauvagiere: that not only the Faluniere, but many other places about Tours, would convince any unbiassed observer that shells are a fruit of the earth, spontaneously produced: and he gave me a copy of de la Sauvagiere's Recueil de dissertations, presented him by the author, wherein is one Sur la vegetation spontanée des coquilles du chateau des Places. So far I repeat from him. What are we to conclude? That we have not materials enough yet to form any conclusion. The fact stated by Sauvagiere is not against any law of nature, and is therefore possible: but it is so little analogous to her habitual processes that, if true, it would be extraordinary: that, to command our belief therefore, there should be such a suite of observations as that their untruth would be more extraordinary than the existence of the fact they affirm. The bark of trees, the skin of fruits and animals, the feathers of birds receive their growth and nutriment from the internal circulation of a juice thro' the vessels of the individual they cover. We conclude from analogy then that the shells of the testaceous tribe receive also their growth from a like internal circulation. If it be urged that this does not exclude the possibility of a like shell being produced by the passage of a fluid thro the pores of the circumjacent body, whether of earth, stone, or water; I answer that it is not within the usual oeconomy of nature to use two processes for one species of production. While I withold my assent however from this hypothesis, I must deny it to every other I have ever seen by which their authors pretend to account for the origin of shells in high places. Some of these are against the laws of nature and therefore impossible: and others are built on positions more difficult to assent to than that of de la Sauvagiere. They all suppose these shells to have covered submarine animals, and have then to answer the question How came they 15,000 feet above the level of the sea? and they answer it by demanding what cannot be conceded. One therefore who had rather have no opinion, than a false one, will suppose this question one of those beyond the investigation of human sagacity;

or wait till further and fuller observations enable him to decide it.

CHANTELOUP. I heard a nightingale to-day at Chanteloup. The gardener sais it is the male, who alone sings, while the female sits; and that when the young are hatched, he also ceases. In the Boudoir at Chanteloup is an ingenious contrivance to hide the projecting steps of a stair-case. 3 steps were of necessity to project into the Boudoir. They are therefore made triangular steps; and instead of being rested on the floor as usual, they are made fast at their broad end to the stair door, swinging out and in with that. When it shuts, it runs them under the other steps; when open, it brings them out to their proper place. In the kitchen garden are three pumps worked by one horse. The pumps are placed in an equilateral triangle, each side of which is about 35.f. In the center is a post 10. or 12.f. high and 1.f. diameter. In the top of this enters the bent end of a lever thus   of about 12. or 15.f. long with a swingle tree at the other   end. About 3.f. from the bent end it receives, on a pin, three horizontal bars of iron, which at their other end lay hold of one corner of a quadrantal crank (like a bell crank) moving in a vertical plane, to the other corner of which is hooked the vertical handle of the pump: thus This crank turns on it's point as a center, by a pin or pivot passing thro' it at (a), the horse moving the lever horizontally in a circle; every point in the lever describes a horizontal circle. That which receives the three bars at (b) in the diagram, describes a circle of 6.f. diameter. It gives a stroke then of 6.f. to the handle of each pump, at each revolution.

BLOIS. ORLEANS. June 9. 10. At Blois the road leaves the river, and traverses the hills, which are mostly reddish, sometimes grey, good enough, in vines, corn, St. foin. From Orleans to the river Juines at ESTAMPES, it is a continued plain of corn and St. foin, tolerably good, sometimes grey, sometimes red. From Estampes to ESTRECHY the country is mountainous and rocky, resembling that of Fontainebleau. Qu. if it may not be the same vein?

MS (DLC); 44 p.; in TJ's hand. N (MHi); fragment, consisting of two pages joined to form a single sheet, on which TJ arranged vertical columns for tabulating rough notes day by day; endorsed: "Rough notes of journey through Champagne, Burgundy, Beaujolois." These notes cover the period from 1 to 14 Mch. 1787, and their twelve columns bear the following captions: "day," "post," "soil," "produce," "husbandry," "inclosure," "face of country," "wood," "people," "animals," "roads," and "miscellaneous." These columns were subsequently numbered by TJ in order to consolidate them and (with the exception of the first two) to rearrange their order for the succeeding tabulation of rough notes, of which another single sheet, also fragmentary, exists in CSmH and

[462]

covers the period from 15 to 23 Mch. 1787, wherein the columns are reduced from twelve to nine and those labelled "husbandry," "people," and "roads" in N (MHi) are included under "miscellaneous." See facsimile reproduction of the former sheet in this volume, wherein TJ's economy of space and words is clearly illustrated in the compilation of the rough notes from which (with letters written by him on his journey) the expanded fair copy of his "Memorandums taken on a journey" was later executed. Tr of extract of MS concerning the making of Parmesan cheese (The Rosenbach Company, Philadelphia, 1946); in TJ's hand; with one significant sentence that is unique with this text (see note 7 below); enclosed in TJ to Charles Clay, 12 Oct. 1799. Another extract on the same subject (printed in *The American Farmer*, I [1820], 410-11); enclosed in TJ to John Skinner, 24 Feb. 1820. Another extract containing portions of the MS covering the Canal of Languedoc (DLC: Washington Papers); in William Short's hand; with caption reading: "Extract from notes made on a journey through the south of France 1787"; accompanied by an engraved map of the canal (Paris, 1787; see illustration in this volume); both Tr and map were enclosed in TJ to Washington, 2 May 1788, from which it is evident that TJ had compiled the MS between 10 June 1787 and 2 May 1788. (It is also evident that, in expanding N (MHi) and N (CSmH) and their missing counterparts, TJ utilized the press copies of some of his letters to Short and others describing and commenting upon the scenes through which he travelled.) The portions of the MS covered by the foregoing three extracts are indicated in the notes below, where these are referred to respectively as the Clay extract, the Skinner extract, and the Washington extract.

The modern spellings of some of the place names given by TJ are inserted here in parentheses: VAUNE, VEAUNE (Vosne); VOULENAY (Volnay); VOUGEAU (Vougeot); ROMANIE (Romanée); CONNAULT (Connaux); VALIGNIERES (Valliguières); TERRASSON (not certainly identifiable, but probably Tarascon); VAUNE river (Huveaune); GOUTIER (Eygoutier); GEANS (Giens); MANTONE (Menton); BEZIERES (Beziers); ARGILIES (Argeliers); LE SAUMAL (Le Sommail); ERAUT (Herault); PORCARAIGNE (Portiragnes); CHANTENAY (Chantonnay); POINT BOEUF (Paim Bœuf). TJ's reference to PUMICE is to *pomice*, the pulp left after the pressing of the grapes. THE MARQUIS DE SARSNET OF DIJON was evidently the Marquis de Sassenay of Châlons-sur-Saône, near Dijon. On MONSIEUR DE BERGASSE, see TJ to Chastellux, 4 Apr. 1787. The information about the Canal of Languedoc was furnished to TJ by G. Pin (see his letter of 26 May 1787). In N (CSmH) TJ listed the names of persons whom he wished to see on his journey, including some to whom he had been given letters of introduction. This list, recorded in two different places in N (CSmH), reads:

"Monsr. Parent Maitre Tonnelier à Beaune fxbrgs Bretonniere

Mde. de Laye en son chateau de Laye Epinaye prés Villefranch en Beaujolois.

M. de Mot. M. le Prieur.

Mm. Finguerlin et Scherer. banquiers à Lyons.

M. Tournillon l'ainé. Conseiller du roy. Notaire rue de la Barre

M. l'Abbe Charrier de la Roche, Prevot d'Ainay, vicaire general à Ainay à Lyons

M. de Pizay, en son hotel rue Sala. à Lyon.

M. Bugnet. Architecte a Lyons.

Nismes

Montpelier. M. Burnet Durand et de la Marche. banquiers.

Montpelier. M. Maya. chez M. Franc a la petite Ste. Anne.

M. Bernard de l'Acad. de Marseille, directeur joint de l'Observatoire. à l'Observatoire. (de M. l'Abbé Papon)

Le revd. Dom Bruzatin, Prieur des religieux feuillants (de M. Dupoux de Lyon)

Antonio Soria. Negociant-a Mars.

J. L. Brethoul

M. Bergasse

M. Audibert.

Nice.

M. Sasserno. negociant.

M. Tourneri Directeur de la manufacture royale de tabac.

M. Jn. Bste. Guide

M. le Comte de St. André Lt. Genl. des armées du roi, Commandant de la Comté et ville de Nice.

Le Clerc & co. banquiers.

Bourdeaux. M. feger Gramont & co. banquiers.

Nismes. Dor. José Joaquim Maya Barbalho &c. Rio de Janr. ou.

[463]

11 JUNE 1787

Docteur Joseph Joachim Maya Barbalho. Rio Janeiro.
Turin.
M. l'Abbe Deleuze professeur à l'academie royale de M. Sasserno.
MM. Donaud pere et fils et Tallon. (de M. Guide)
MM. Tollot pere et fils, banquiers. (du Baron Le Clerc et co.)
Milan. L'Abbé de Regibus.
Genoa.
Son Excelle. Mons. le Marq. Jean Luc-Durazzo. (de M. le Marq. de Spinoia.)
Messrs. Bertrand Ricard et Bramerel Banquiers (le Baron le Clerc de Nice)
Messrs. Aimé Regny pere et fils et compe. (de M. Guide de Nice)."
To this TJ added the following title of a book: "Ephemerides societatis meteorolgicae Palatinae. Manheimii. Apud C. Fr. Schwan. Commencee en 1781. 4to." (see TJ to Short, 5 May 1787; Sowerby No. 654). For TJ's ENQUIRING . . . INTO A FACT STATED BY VOLTAIRE and the writings of DE LA SAUVAGIERE on the subject, see TJ to Chastellux, 4 Apr. 1787; Chastellux to TJ, 29 Apr. 1787; and Sowerby No. 647.

[1] Compare the foregoing with the entry in N (MHi), wherein the present paragraph is elaborated from the brief entry: ". . . no farm houses: all the people gathered in villages. 1st step to[war]ds corrupt[io]n." Compare also TJ to Short, 15 Mch. 1787.
[2] In margin of MS at this point TJ wrote "Aussay"; there is an entry under 8 Mch. in his rough expense account notes of his journey (CSmH) which reads: "Aussay. Paid Parent, guide to this place which is the depot of the wines of Monrachet 6f."

[3] In margin at this point TJ drew the following diagram:

```
                     o    la baraque
"Chambertin o        r.
Vougeau         o    r.
         r. r.
Romanie   o o        Veaune
              r o    Nuys
Beaune          o    r.
Pommard       o      r.
Voulenaye     o      r.
Meursault     o      w.
Montrachet    o      w.
              o      Chagny"
```

The dotted vertical lines indicate the main route; the locations of villages with respect to it are designated by "o." Red and white wines are shown by "r" and "w."
[4] Thus in MS; TJ's "w" and "v" are at times almost impossible to distinguish, but he sometimes used "wine" in the sense here employed.
[5] Clay extract and Skinner extract both begin at this point and the latter is preceded by the date "1787. Apr. 23."
[6] In Clay extract TJ inserted at this point "delicious."
[7] Clay extract ends here, except for the following important and revealing sentence, not published heretofore: "I attended in a dairy from sunrise to sunset, and wrote down the preceding process as it was executed under my view."
[8] Skinner extract ends at this point.
[9] TJ repeated "Sestri" at this point.
[10] This and subsequent passages in square brackets (supplied) comprise the whole of the Washington extract.
[11] Thus in MS; an error for "Aude."
[12] Washington extract reads "Lampry."
[13] That is: "pi[eds] po[uces] li[gnes]."

From Dr. Lambert

MONSEIGNEUR   Frontignan bas-Languedoc 11. juin 1787.

L'ignorance où j'ai été, jusqu'au moment de votre Depart, de L'honneur que vous me faisiés, et du bonheur que j'avois de vous posséder chez moi, a peutêtre été Cause de mon trop de Liberté, et de franchise à votre Egard. Daignez en aggréer mes très humbles Excuses, et Les sentiments de la plus Vive et de la plus Re-

[464]

spectueuse Reconnoissance. Sans sçavoir avec qui j'avois l'honneur de me trouver et de Converser, j'ai bien fait avec plaisir tout ce que j'ai pû, mais je n'ai peutêtre pas fait tout Ce que j'aurois Deu. Si ayant Le malheur que cela soit à vos yeux, vous Daignez m'en accorder Le pardon, je compterai toute ma Vie, Le jour où vous honoriez ma maison et ma Table de votre presence, Le Premier de mes jours; je me Le Rapellerai à tout instant, j'aurai un plaisir infini à Le nommer à mes Enfants, je leur Repeterai sans Cesse L'heure, Le moment où La Providence me procura L'avantage, l'honneur et Le plaisir D'etre Connû de Vous.

J'ai Rempli avec La plus Severe Exactitude, L'ordre que vous me donnattes de vous adresser Deux Cents Cinquante Bouteilles Muscat de mon Crû, du Même que vous avez choisi; j'y ai ajoutté tout Le muscat Rouge qui est sorti Brillant du petit Barril que vous avez vû dans mon magazin, ainsi que vous L'avez Desiré. Je n'ai pû en Remplir que trente trois Bouteilles. Il vous arrivera dans Six Caisses marquées J.M.P. et des No. 96. 97. 98. 99. 100. 101., Dont facture est Cy jointe et se porte à £:374.ᶦᵗ14s.

Ce vin, que j'ai Eu l'honneur de vous adresser Ces jours Derniers par La Messagerie Royalle, et au quel vous avez donné La preference, est extremement Liquoreux; C'est L'effet de la Secheresse qui a Regné ici pendant tout L'Eté dernier; et Comme nous Receuillons Rarement du Vin Si parfait, et si parfumé, il vous sera agreable de Le metre en Cave, pour Le Laisser Viellir.

Si, satisfait de mon Exactitude, et de ma bonne Volonté, vous m'honorez de vos Commissions, Les années à Venir, comme vous m'avez fait la grace de me Le promettre, vous m'obligerez sensiblement de Le faire au plus tard en Septembre où Octobre, afin que je puisse mettre en Reserve, tout Ce que j'aurai de plus parfait, et que je puisse me preparer à vous en faire L'expedition sous La forme, et de La maniere qui vous seront Le plus agreables.

Je suis avec un très profond Respect Monseigneur Votre très humble et très obeissant Serviteur,   LAMBÊRT D.M.

RC (MHi); endorsed. Recorded in SJL as received 21 June 1787. Enclosure not found, but there are in DLC the following documents (all being printed forms, filled in) concerning the shipment of this wine: (1) Statement of the carrier, Jean Coste, indicating that the wine weighed 1,215 lbs. and that TJ was to pay the driver 16ᶦᵗ per hundredweight plus the various duties, all of which amounted to 212ᶦᵗ 19s. according to a notation on verso; dated 2 June 1787. (2) Receipt for duties paid at Gannat (in Auvergne) by the driver, Jean Tapon, dated 21 June 1787. (3) *Laissez-passer* issued to the driver, Tapon, by the *Commis des Aides* at Paris, 1 July 1787.

From Thomas Barclay

Dear Sir Bordeaux 12 June 1787

After you left this place My Fever Encreased upon me and Confined me two Days to my Bed. I am Now pretty well and I think I shall proceed home tomorrow, But I have Not given Mrs. Barclay any hopes of seeing me soon lest I shou'd Disapoint her. I Never stood so much in Need of your advice as I Do at this Moment. The House of French & Nephew have Refused Every accommodation that I have had in My Power to offer, and all the attempts that I Cou'd make to satisfy them have produced nothing But the Most Malignant and Malicious answers that Nothing but the Money or security in this City wou'd be Received, with the strongest asseverations that wherever I Go, thither will they Pursue me. Under these Circumstances I Confess I am Very ill at Ease, and indeed somewhat Bewilderd. The Idea of another attack being Made on my Person, perhaps in the Moment of my Joining my Family, is a Very unpleasing object for Contemplation, and it seems in some Degree Necessary that I shoud get among my Papers before I proceed to America. My Embarrassments arise from a Very unfortunate Connection that I Formed at L'orient with a Mr. Moylan there, who Dying suddenly left me a Great Debt to strugle with, and after paying about Two thirds of it, I was on the point of proceeding to America, from whence in Eighteen Months I have Not Received a livre but Fifty Pounds. And I think had not Mess. French & Nephew in the Most Treacherous Manner thrown this Dificulty in my way, In twelve or fifteen Months I shou'd have Discharged the Remainder of my Engagements. Wou'd you Beleive that those People in the last letter which they wrote to me at Madrid, said that I was, in going to America, proceeding as Any honest good man in my Circumstances ought to do. It is a very Common thing for the Minister at Versailles to give to People in my situation a safe Conduct for six or twelve Months, and I wrote to the Marquis De la Fayette, upon this subject from the Prison, and twice afterwards, but to none of those letters have I Received any answer whatever. Nor do I Pretend to form any Conjecture from this silence. All I Can say is that it will be Utterly Impossible for me to Pay Mess. French or any Body Else without going to America, and that Every attempt made to Prevent me will answer no End but that of Injuring all Parties Concerned. If my Person is at Risk I Cannot attend to the settlement of my affairs. I

Propose leaving My family behind me, and Mr. Zachriah Loreilhe, who is Equally Bound with me in all the Engagements, will stay at Lorient untill they are liquidated.

After having thus stated to you my Condition, any appology for the Trouble I give you will be Unnecessary. If my office of Consul is sufficient to Protect my Person, a safe Conduct will be Unnecessary. But then one will be wanted for M. Loreilhe. If this security Can be obtained Even for Six Months, it will Give time to look about and make some Exertions, But in seven Years of the Present situation, nothing of Consequence Cou'd be Effected. I Beg you will take such steps as you shall Judge necessary to Releive me from the shocking situation in which I am placed, and if you Judge proper Communicate with the Marquis De La Fayette. I hardly think I shall leave Bordeaux until there is time for a line from you in answer to this. Therefore please to put one under Cover to Mr. Bondfield. Some of my Friends hold forth the Danger that I may Run as soon as I get out of the Jurisdiction of the Parliament of Bordeaux. You will wonder perhaps at my undecidedness on the point of going from hence. I Cannot help it, I have so much to Risk, and the Issue is so uncertain. I am Ever Dear Sir Your Most Obed & Obliged THOS. BARCLAY

I received a letter from you last Post written from Marseilles.

RC (DLC); endorsed. Recorded in SJL as received 16 June 1787.

From Thomas Barclay

DEAR SIR Bordeaux 12 June 1787

I wrote you by this Post, and am Now to Inform you that Mess. French & Co. have Employ'd the Mare-chaussee at all the Passes out of the Jurisdiction of the Parliament of Bordeaux to stop me on the Road. A suspicion of such a proceeding made me Alter my Intention of setting out, and I have Now Certain Information that it is so.

I see Nothing for Me to Do, but to Remain where I am, untill you have seen the Minister, and untill I learn the Extent of My hopes. I am Dear Sir Your Very obed THOS. BARCLAY

RC (DLC); endorsed. Recorded in SJL as received 19 June 1787.

From Motture

Paris, rue du Cherche midy, 12 June 1787. Though unacquainted with TJ, he asks him to forward two sets of the memoirs of the Royal Academy of Sciences at Turin (in 2 vols., quarto), one to Benjamin Franklin, and the other to the American Philosophical Society. "I am sure that Science now a days meets everywhere with friends and protectors, and that my request will not fail of success."

RC (DLC); 2 p.; signed: "Motture Secretary to the Sardinian ambassador." Not recorded in SJL.

To Cassini

[*Paris 13 June 1787.* Entry in SJL under this date reads: "Cassini. le comte de à l'Observatoire royal." Not found.]

To Champion

[*Paris, 13 June 1787.* Entry in SJL reads: "Champion. le Comte de. à l'Abbaye St. Germains des prés, r. Colombier." Not found.]

From Richard Claiborne

DEAR SIR   London No. 14 King St. Cheapside 13. June 87.

I went this morning to a Book-binder to purchase the notes of Your Excellency on the State of Virginia, but was informed by the Gentleman, that the Book was not published, as it was waiting for a map which was to be prefixed to it, and I am to call in the course of a fortnight or 3 weeks.

I have taken the liberty to avail myself of the early part of this interval to mention a circumstance which occured to me some time since, that I hope your Excellency will now be able to obviate. A Gentleman who made an offer to purchase Lands of me, that lie in the State of Virginia, was detered because he could neither see the lines of the County, or the river on which they were situated, mentioned in the Map. He purchased "Jefferson's" for the purpose of inspecting it, and tho I told him that that was composed long before the new Counties, Viz. Monongalia, Harrison &c. &c. &c. were made, and that the author did not go so interiorly into the Country as to examine the smaller branches of the Rivers, he would not be satisfied. The County and River which I particularly allude to is Harrison and Hughs's. All the rest however, I hope to see deliniated, as I am interested in and on many of them, even to those in Kentuckie. I hope your Excellency will pardon the liberty I have taken, as it is a matter which concerns me much, as the Gentleman has still an inclination towards the purchase, and I have reason to believe that it will take place as soon as things can be properly pointed out. As far back as Jany. last, I wrote Colo. Blackden, to make application to your Excellency on this subject, and whether he did or did not, I never got information.

I am with the sincerest re[spect] Yr. Excellency's Most obedient Humble Servant, R. CLAIBORNE

I hope your Excellency will excuse my Rasures.

RC (CSmH). Recorded in SJL as received 19 June 1787.

To the Abbé Gaubert

[*Paris, 13 June 1787.* Entry in SJL reads: "Gaubert l'Abbé. r. de l'eveque butte St. Roche. No. 34." Not found.]

To William Carmichael

DEAR SIR   Paris June 14. 1787.

Having got back to Paris three days ago, I resume immediately the correspondence with which you have been pleased to honour me. I wish I could have begun it with more agreeable information than that furnished me by Mr. Grand, that the funds of the United states here are exhausted and himself considerably in advance, and by the Board of treasury at New York that they have no immediate prospect of furnishing us supplies. We are thus left to shift for ourselves without previous warning. As soon as they shall replenish Mr. Grand's hands, I will give you notice, that you may recommence your usual draughts on him, unless the Board should provide a separate fund for you, dependant on yourself alone, which I have strongly and repeatedly pressed on them in order to remove the indecency of suffering your draugh[ts] to pass thro' any intermediate hand for paiments.

My letters from America come down to the 24th. of April. The disturbances in the Eastern states were entirely settled. I do not learn that the government had made any examples. Hancock's

[469]

14 JUNE 1787

health being re-established, the want of which had occasioned him to resign the government of Massachusets, he has been re-elected to the exclusion of Govr. Bowdoin. New York still refuses to pass the impost in any form and were she to pass it, Pennsylvania will not uncouple it from the Supplementory funds. These two states and Virginia are the only ones, my letters say, which have paid any thing into the Continental treasury for a twelvemonth past. I send you a copy of a circular letter from Congress to the several states insisting on their removing all obstructions to the recovery of British debts. This was hurried that it might be delivered to the assembly of New York before they rose. It was delivered, but they did nothing in consequence of it. The Convention to be assembled at Philadelphia will be an able one. Ten states were known to have appointed. Maryland was about to appoint. Connecticut was doubtful: and Rhode island had refused. We are sure however of eleven states. South Carolina has prohibited the importation of slaves for three years; which is a step towards a perpetual prohibition. Between six and seven hundred thousand acres of land are actually surveied into townships and the sale to begin immediately. They are not to be sold for less than a dollar the acre in public certificates. I wrote you from Bourdeaux, on the subject of Colo. Smith. I was sorry I missed him there, for other reasons as well as from a curiosity to know his errand.—The Notables have laid the foundation of mu[ch] good here; you have seen it detailed in the public papers. The Prince of Wales is likely to recover from his illness, which was very threatening. It is feared that three powers have combined to lift the Prince of Orange out of his difficulties. Have you yet the cypher of which I formerly wrote to you, or any copy of it? I am with sincere esteem Dr. Sir your most obedient & most humble servant, TH: JEFFERSON

PrC (DLC). Enclosure: Copy of Congress' circular letter to the states, 23 Apr. 1787, recommending repeal of all state legislation which in any way tended to obstruct or negate the operation of the Treaty of Peace (JCC, XXXII, 177-84). Jay's letter of 24 Apr. 1787, which had enclosed a copy of this resolution, was received at Paris by TJ on his arrival on 11 June and was one of two letters that brought his American news down to 24 Apr.; the other was from Edward Carrington.

TJ wrote the first three lines of this letter in code in his letter to Carmichael of 15 Dec. 1787 in order to check the accuracy of Carmichael's copy of the code.

To C. W. F. Dumas

SIR   Paris June. 14. 1787.

I arrived at this place three days ago, and avail myself of the first possible moment of acknowleging the receipt of your favors of the 5th. and 7th. of June. The letters they accompanied for Mr. Jay shall be sent by the packet which sails the 25th. instant, and by a passenger. My letters from America are none later than the 24th. of April. The disturbances in the Eastern states were entirely settled. I do not learn that the government required any capital punishments. We promise ourselves good from the Convention holding at Philadelphia. It consists of the ablest men in America. It will surely be the instrument of referring to Congress the regulation of our trade. This may enable them to carry into effect a general impost which one or two obstinate states have so long prevented. Between six and seven hundred thousand acres of land are now surveied into townships, and will be immediately sold. The backwardness of the states to bring money into the public treasury has increased rather than diminished. This has prevented the Treasury board from remitting any money to this place for some time past, and Mr. Grand has given me notice that their funds in his hands are exhausted, and himself considerably in advance. This renders it necessary for us to suspend all draughts on him until he shall receive supplies from the Board of treasury, to whom I write to press remittances. The moment we shall have wherewithal to answer your accustomary draughts I will exercise the pleasing office of giving you notice of it. Indeed, [as] I perceive by the papers that Mr. Adams is gone over to Holland [I] am not without hopes that his object may be to procure supplies of money, and that your exertions joined with his may give relief to us all. I have no answer from Congress on the subject which has been thought of between us. I am afraid we may consider the refusal of the impost as an answer. I am exceedingly anxious to see the turn the affairs of your country may take. It will surely be seen soon whether for the better or worse. I wish nothing may be gathering in the horizon to obscure the prospects of the patriotic party. My prayers for their prosperity are warm, as are the sentiments of personal esteem and respect with which I have the honour to be Sir your most obedient & most humble servant,   TH: JEFFERSON

PrC (DLC). Not recorded in SJL.

To Martha Jefferson

Paris June 14. 1787.

I send you, my dear Patsy, the 15 livres you desired. You propose this to me as an anticipation of five weeks allowance. But do you not see my dear how imprudent it is to lay out in one moment what should accomodate you for five weeks? That this is a departure from that rule which I wish to see you governed by, thro' your whole life, of never buying any thing which you have not money in your pocket to pay for? Be assured that it gives much more pain to the mind to be in debt, than to do without any article whatever which we may seem to want. The purchase you have made is one of those I am always ready to make for you, because it is my wish to see you dressed always cleanly and a little more than decently. But apply to me first for the money before you make a purchase, were it only to avoid breaking thro' your rule. Learn yourself the habit of adhering vigorously to the rules you lay down for yourself. I will come for you about eleven o'clock on Saturday. Hurry the making your gown, and also your reding-cote. You will go with me some day next week to dine at the Marquis Fayette's. Adieu my dear daughter. Your's affectionately,

Th: Jefferson

RC (Mrs. David Haas, New York City, 1944). PrC (MHi). A later Tr, with apparently a tracing of TJ's signature, is in NNP, followed by a facsimile of RC; on the verso of Tr is a note which reads: "The original of this letter was given to Mr. Henry S. Randall of New York, March 1853." Not recorded in SJL.

To Parent

à Paris ce 14me. Juin 1787.

Si vous croyez, Monsieur, que le vin de Voulenayé et le vin de Meursault de la qualité nommée Goutte d'or peuvent etre transportés à Paris pendant les chaleurs actuelles, je vous prierai de m'envoyer une feuillette de chacune de ces deux especes, en bouteilles, des meilleures crues, et de la recolte qui est la meilleure pour etre bu le moment actuel. Vous aurez la bonté de m'indiquer la personne auquel je pourrai faire toucher le montant, ce que je ferai le moment que vous me la ferez connoitre. Il faudra m'avertir un peu en avance de l'arrivée des vins, afin que je peux faire prendre les arrangemens necessaires au bureau de la douane de

Paris. Je vous prierai de faire cette expedition sans perte de tems, les vins etant destinés pour le moment actuel. Il n'y a que trois jours que je suis de retour de ma voyage. J'ai l'honneur d'etre avec des sentimens d'estime tres distingués, Monsieur, votre très humble et très obeissant serviteur,
& emsp;TH: JEFFERSON

P.S. Mettez sur toutes les lettres de voiture &c. que ce sont des Vins ordinaires, et si le voiturier consentiroit d'entrer Paris par la grille des champs elysées, ce me donneroit moins d'embarras, parce que ma maison touche à cette grille-la. C'est la partie de Paris la plus eloignée de vous, ainsi vous aurez la bonté d'arranger avec le voiturier combien il faudra lui payer d'extraordinaire pour ça.

PrC (MHi).

From Joel Barlow

SIR & emsp; Hartford Connecticut June 15 1787

Your character in the literary as well as political world has induced me to request your acceptance of the Poem herewith forwarded to the care of the Marquis de la Fayette. What is said in it of the french king and nation may perhaps occasion it to be translated into that language. Should this ever be done, I would wish it might be in a manner that the work may not appear to disgrace that illustrious personage who condescended to recieve the dedication.

Your Notes on Virginia are getting into the Gazetts in different States, notwithstanding your request that they should not be published here. We are flattered with the idea of seeing ourselves vindicated from those despicable aspersions which have long been thrown upon us and echoed from one ignorant Scribbler to another in all the languages in Europe.

With the greatest respect I have the honour to be, Sir, your very obet. Servt., & emsp;JOEL BARLOW

RC (MHi); endorsed: "Barlow Joel (author of the Vision of Columbus)." Enclosure: Copy of *The Vision of Columbus*, Hartford, 1787. Not recorded in SJL.

The ILLUSTRIOUS PERSON WHO CONDESCENDED TO RECIEVE THE DEDICATION was Louis XVI.

From Wilt, Delmestre & Cie.

Monsieur L'orient le 15. Juin 1787.

Un de nos Amis ayant bien voulu nous partager une Balle de Caffé Moka, nous lui en avons pris 50 ℔ pour vous, d'apres les ordres qu'il vous a plu nous donner pendant votre Sejour ici, et les avons chargé ce jour à la Messagerie à votre addresse; nous souhaitons que vous le trouviez aussi bon que vous pouvez le desirer. Comme la Balle entamée restera peutetre long tems en cet état entre les mains de notre ami, si vous en voulez davantage nous vous en expedierons ce qu'il vous en fera plaisir, cet ami en ayant une partie de 80 Balles.

Vous en avez cy joint la facture montant à £138.ᵗᵗ 19s. que nous prendrons la liberté de tirer Sur vous à l'occasion, si vous voulez bien le permetre.

Nous avons l'honneur d'etre avec une respectueuse Consideration Monsieur Vos tres humbles serviteurs,

Wilt Delmestre & Cie.

RC (DLC). Recorded in SJL as received 19 June 1787. Enclosure (DLC): Invoice of Wilt, Delmestre & Cie., 15 June 1787, covering 50 ℔s. net of Mocha coffee @ 46 sols per lb., or 115ᵗᵗ, plus duty, carriage, packing, and other costs which brought the total to 138ᵗᵗ 19s.

To the Commissioners of the Treasury

Gentlemen Paris June 17. 1787.

Your favor of Feb. 16. has duly come to hand. I will beg leave to repeat an explanation, which I think I had the honor of giving you in a former letter, of the reason why the bills of Mr. Dumas have been paid for some time past by Mr. Grand. Soon after the departure of Dr. Franklin a bill drawn by Mr. Dumas on me was presented for a quarter's salary. I went to Mr. Grand and asked him if he knew the meaning of it. He told me that Mr. Dumas's salary had always been paid here by draughts on Dr. Franklin. I supposed it had been in consequence of some instruction from the office of finance to Dr. Franklin, and therefore have continued to accept Mr. Dumas's bills for his salary, and to direct their paiment by Mr. Grand. Very soon also after I came into office Mr. Grand sent me a bill drawn *on him* for a quarter's salary by Mr. Carmichael, and asked me if he must pay it. I wished to decline medling with his paiments in general, and to leave him free to apply

17 JUNE 1787

any monies in his hands according to the instructions he should receive from your board. He told me he had never paid money till first approved by Doctr. Franklin, and could not venture to do it now without my approbation. He told me particularly that Mr. Carmicha[el's] salary had always been paid here by order from Dr. Frankl[in]. I therefore found it necessary to continue things on their former plan till I could have the honor of your answer to a letter I immediately wrote you on the subject, but to which I am not able to refer you particularly, because having been written before I had either a secretary or copying press, I retained no copy. It is particularly disagreeable to me to have any thing to do with the paiment of those gentlemen's salaries, because tho they stand on an equal line with myself it seems to subject their demands to my controul. It exposes us too to misunderstandings, which might be extremely injurious to the public good, and should therefore be guarded against by removing all occasions which might induce them. A continual and confidential correspondence among us is necessary. Permit me therefore to pray that you will so good as to place their funds so as that my interposition may not be necessary. I have just written to both the information which it is my duty to communicate to you that Mr. Grand has notified me the monies in his hands are exhausted and that he is considerably in advance. Public creditors, in their own country, are surrounded by their own resources, or can obtain a credit, on failure to receive their regular appointments. Our situation is different. But I am sure nothing is necessary to be urged on this head.

I saw Mr. Dobrée at Nantes, and examined the condition of the stores attached by him. I found it much better than had been represented, and him so reasonable that I trust we shall be able to settle his claim amicably. He is to send me an exact state of these stores which I will do myself the honor of forwarding to you. I have that of being with sentiments of the most perfect esteem & respect Gentlemen your most obedient & most humble servt.,

TH: JEFFERSON

P.S. I should have observed in answer also to an article of your letter that Mr. Barclay has settled Mr. Grand's account and doubtless will furnish you a copy of it.

PrC (DLC).

In stating that he had RETAINED NO COPY of the letter written before he HAD EITHER A SECRETARY OR COPYING PRESS, TJ erred. He had had both a secretary and a copying press for some time when he wrote Osgood "as a friend" on 5 Oct. 1785 setting forth the suggestion that he advanced officially and formally in his later letter of 26 Jan. 1786 to the Commissioners of the Treasury. In their reply to the present letter on 10 Nov. 1787, the Commissioners finally, after almost two years, agreed that TJ's suggestion that no foreign agent should be dependent upon another for his salary was "perfectly consonant" with their views.

To Du Pin d'Assarts

SIR Paris June 18. 1787.

I learn with sincere concern the distressed situation in which you find yourself. However unqualified as a stranger to decide in general on the various cases of misfortune which present themselves, I am still persuaded your's is real. I therefore feel the more regret on being obliged to assure you that it is out of my power to relieve you from your situation. The king is in disposition, as well as in duty, the common father to all his people: and we cannot but hope that your birth, your services, and your misfortunes will give success to the supplications you have addressed to him for relief. In this hope I can only add assurances of the sentiments of respect with which I have the honour to be Sir, your most obedient & most humble servant, TH: JEFFERSON

PrC (DLC). Recorded in SJL as addressed to: "du Pin d'Assarts. r. traversiere St. Honoré No. 32."

To John Banister, Jr.

DEAR SIR Paris June 19. 1787.

I have received your favor of April 23. from New York and am sorry to find you have had a relapse. Time and temperance however will cure you, to which add exercise. I hope you have long ago had a happy meeting with your friends, with whom a few hours would be to me an ineffable feast. The face of Europe appears a little turbid, but all will subside. The Empress has endeavored to bully the Turk, who laught at her and she is going back. The Emperor's reformations have occasioned the appearance of insurrection in Flanders, and he, according to character, will probably tread back his steps. A change of system here with respect to the Dutch, is suspected: because the kings of Prussia and England openly espouse the cause of the Stadholder, and that of the Patriots is likely to fall. The American acquaintances whom you left here, not being stationary, you will hardly expect news of them. Mrs. Barrett, lately dead, was I think known to you. I had a letter from Lediard lately dated at St. Petersburg. He had but two shirts, and yet more shirts than shillings. Still he was determined to obtain the palm of being the first circum-ambulator of the earth. He sais that having no money they kick him from place to place and thus he expects to be kicked round the globe. Are you become a great walker? You know I preach up that kind of exercise. Shall I send you a Conte-pas? It will cost you a dozen Louis, but be a great stimulus to walking, as it will record your steps. I finished my tour a week or ten days ago. I went as far as Turin, Milan, Genoa, and never passed three months and a half more delightfully. I returned thro' the canal of Languedoc, by Bourdeaux, Nantes, Lorient, and Rennes, then return to Nantes and came up the Loire to Orleans. I was alone thro the whole, and think one travels more usefully when they travel alone, because they reflect more.

Present me in the most friendly terms to Mrs. Bannister and to your father and be assured of the sincere esteem of Dear Sir your friend & servt., TH: JEFFERSON

P.S. Do not suppose, because I say nothing of the plants, that I have forgotten them. I send you to the care of Mr. Madison the Mercure de France from the time of your departure, as you desired, and shall continue it. Send me in return the two best Viriginia newspapers which will be about the price of the Mercure and save the trouble of keeping an account. Sending them to Mr. Madison at New York, they may come clear of postage, as I shall endeavor to pass the Mercure to you.

PrC (DLC).
John Ledyard's LETTER FROM . . . ST. PETERSBURG was that of 19 Mch. 1787, received at Bordeaux 25 May 1787.

To Thomas Barclay

DEAR SIR Paris June 19. 1787.

Your favor of the 12th. came to hand two days ago. Your adversary had been busy here in endeavoring to have your privilege examined and withdrawn. They had, as I think, interested Mr. Eden, the British minister, and thro' that or some other channel conveied a story to the ear of some of the ministers, very unfavorable to you. They had particularly represented some circumstance attending the original contracting of the debt as contrary to good faith: that it was for wines (I believe) sold and to be paid for by a particular cargo of tobacco; that the wines being received, the cargo was otherwise applied. I mention these circumstances which

I have heard vaguely, meerly to suggest to you the propriety of sending me a short state of the real transaction. I am this moment returned from the Count de Montmorin, to whom I have spoken on the subject of your letter of safe conduct. I told him I knew nothing of the original transaction which I knew to have been represented to your disadvantage, but that from my personal knowlege of you I would pledge my own honour, either that nothing wrong had attended that transaction, or that you had no hand in it. We proceeded then to speak on the subject of your privilege. He said it was a settled point that the character of Consul does not privilege any person in this country against their creditors: that as to your character to the court of Marocco, 1. it might admit of question whether it could be a protection at all as it was not derived from Congress immediately: 2. that it would only have been a protection back to the place where you had received it had you come thither immediately; but that the long stay you had made at Bourdeaux seemed to have terminated it there. I told him you were arrested immediately almost on your arrival at Bourdeaux. But, says he, that arrest was annulled in a few days: yes, I replied, but the same creditors threatened to arrest you again the moment you should go out of the jurisdiction of Bourdeaux, and that tho' the second arrest might be anulled also, yet it was not a pleasant thing to be imprisoned and remain till a parliament could order the doors open. This seemed to make an impression, and we spoke of the safe conduct. He said he thought he could obtain a letter of safe conduct which should protect you till you should get to Paris, but that you would be liable to arrest the moment you should arrive. I asked if a Safe conduct could not be obtained to bring you to Paris, back again to Bourdeaux, and even to America. He thought it would be very doubtful and difficult: that you must in that case obtain the consent of the principal mass of your creditors, and furnish me with it: that tho he could not be sanguine as to the success, he would do what should depend on him: but he doubted the issue. You will be so good therefore as to decide on this view of the subject. The dates of your arrival at Bourdeaux, arrest, and discharge will be material. Be assured that no endeavors shall be spared on my part, if you conclude to ask a Safe-conduct. If you should find it more eligible to proceed from Bourdeaux to Congress directly, I know of nothing relative to your office which need prevent it. I have the pleasure to inform you that Mrs. Barclay and your family are well; and pray you to accept assurances of the

sincere esteem & respect with which I have the honor to be Dear Sir Your friend & servant,
            Th: Jefferson

P.S. I could wish a state of the treacherous conduct of French & co. of their letter to you advising you to go to America, &c. in case it should be necessary for me to apply to the minister.

PrC (DLC). Enclosed in TJ to Feger, Gramont & Cie., this date.

To Feger, Gramont & Cie.

Gentlemen   Paris June 19. 1787.

I am honoured with your letter of the 2d. instant together with the state of the wine therein inclosed, for which Mr. Grand will take care to reimburse you. It would have given me great pleasure to have been able to remain longer at Bourdeaux, which among other gratifications would have presented me that of cultivating longer your acquaintance; but I was not master of my own time. I take the liberty of putting under your cover a letter to Mr. Barclay, which be so good as to have delivered him thro' a confidential hand. Accept here my thanks for the civilities and attentions you were pleased to shew me at Bourdeaux and assurances of the sentiments of esteem & respect with which I have the honor to be Gentlemen your most obedient & most humble servant,
            Th: Jefferson

PrC (MHi). Enclosure: TJ to Barclay, this date.

From the Abbés Arnoux and Chalut

Paris, 20 June [1787]. Decline TJ's invitation for Saturday next because of a previous engagement.

RC (MHi); 1 p.; in French; dated only; "Paris mercredi matin 20 Juin"; 1787 was the only year during TJ's stay in France that 20 June fell on a Wednesday.

To William Macarty

              June 20. 1787.

12 plats d'entrée d'environ 11. pouces
12 plats d'entremets d'environ 11. pouces
6. douzaines d'assiettes plates

2. douzaine d'assiettes à soupe
8. Compotiers moiens
4. plats de releve, 2 longues, et 2 ronds
2. Soupieres
2. Saladiers
2. jattes ronds.

Mr. Jefferson will be obliged to Mr. McCarty to send him the above articles from Lorient, by land. His bill for the amount shall be paid on sight by his very humble servant,

TH: JEFFERSON

PrC (DLC). In DLC: TJ Papers, 37:6314 there is a memorandum in Petit's hand which lists the number of pieces to be ordered, with several changes in TJ's hand and endorsed by him: "McCarty Wm. note for china June 20. 1787."

To James Madison

DEAR SIR   Paris June 20. 1787.

I wrote you last on the 30th. of Jan. with a postscript of Feb. 5. Having set out the last day of that month to try the waters of Aix, and been journeying since till the 10th. inst. I have been unable to continue my correspondence with you. In the mean time I have received your several favors of Feb. 15. Mar. 18. 19. and Apr. 23. The last arrived here about the 25th. of May, while those of Mar. 18. and 19. tho' written five weeks earlier arrived three weeks later. I mention this to shew you how incertain is the conveyance thro' England.

The idea of separating the executive business of the confederacy from Congress, as the judiciary is already in some degree, is just and necessary. I had frequently pressed on the members individually, while in Congress, the doing this by a resolution of Congress for appointing an Executive committee to act during the sessions of Congress, as the Committee of the states was to act during their vacations. But the referring to this Committee all executive business as it should present itself, would require a more persevering self-denial than I supposed Congress to possess. It will be much better to make that separation by a federal act. The negative proposed to be given them on all the acts of the several legislatures is now for the first time suggested to my mind. Primâ facie I do not like it. It fails in an essential character, that the hole and the patch should be commensurate. But this proposes to mend a small hole by covering the whole garment. Not more than 1. out of 100.

state-acts concern the confederacy. This proposition then, in order to give them 1. degree of power which they ought to have, gives them 99. more which they ought not to have, upon a presumption that they will not exercise the 99. But upon every act there will be a preliminary question. Does this act concern the confederacy? And was there ever a proposition so plain as to pass Congress without a debate? Their decisions are almost always wise: they are like pure metal. But you know of how much dross this is the result. Would not an appeal from the state judicatures to a federal court, in all cases where the act of Confederation controuled the question, be as effectual a remedy, and exactly commensurate to the defect. A British creditor, e.g. sues for his debt in Virginia; the defendant pleads an act of the state excluding him from their courts; the plaintiff urges the Confederation and the treaty made under that, as controuling the state law; the judges are weak enough to decide according to the views of their legislature. An appeal to a federal court sets all to rights. It will be said that this court may encroach on the jurisdiction of the state courts. It may. But there will be a power, to wit Congress, to watch and restrain them. But place the same authority in Congress itself, and there will be no power above them to perform the same office. They will restrain within due bounds a jurisdiction exercised by others much more rigorously than if exercised by themselves.—I am uneasy at seeing that the sale of our Western lands is not yet commenced. That precious fund for the immediate extinction of our debt will I fear be suffered to slip thro' our fingers. Every delay exposes it to events which no human foresight can guard against. When we consider the temper of the people of that country, derived from the circumstances which surround them, we must suppose their *separation*[1] *possible* at every moment. If they can be *retained til* their governments *become* settled and wise, they will *remain* with us always, and be a precious part of our strength and of our virtue. *But* this affair of *the Missisipi* by shewing that *Congress is capable* of hesitating on a question which proposes a *clear sacrifice* of the *western* to the *maritime states* will with difficulty be *obliterated.* The proposition of *my going to Madrid* to *try* to *recover* there the ground which has been *lost* at *New York* by the *concession* of the vote of *seven states* I should think desperate. With respect to *myself*, weighing the pleasure of *the journey* and bare possibility of *success* in one scale, and the strong *probability* of *failure* and the public *disappointment directed* on *me* in the other, the latter preponderates. Add to this that *jealousy* might be *excited* in the *breast* of a *person* who could find occasions of making *me uneasy*.

The late changes in the ministry here excite considerable hopes. I think we *gain in them all*. I am particularly happy at the *reentry* of *Malsherbes* into the *council*. His knolege, his integrity render his value inappreciable, and the greater *to me* because while he had no *view* of *office we* had established together the most unreserved *intimacy*. So far too *I am pleased* with *Montmorin*. His honesty proceeds from *the heart* as well as *the head* and therefore may be more surely *counted on*. *The king* loves *business*, *oeconomy*, *order* and *justice*. *He* wishes sincerely the good of *his people*. *He* is *irascible*, *rude* and very *limited in his understanding*, *religious* bordering only on *bigotry*. *He* has no *mistress*, *loves his queen* and is too much *governed by her*. *She is capricious* like *her brother and governed* by *him*, devoted to *pleasure and expence*, *not remarkable* for any other *vices or virtues*. *Unhappily the king* shews a propensity for the *pleasures* of the *table*. That for *drink* has *increased lately* or at least it is *become more known*. For European news in general I will refer you to my letter to Mr. Jay. Is it not possible that the occurrences in Holland may excite a desire in many of leaving that country and transferring their effects out of it? May make an opening for shifting into their hands the debts due to this country, to it's officers and farmers? It would be surely eligible. I believe Dumas, if put on the watch, might alone suffice: but surely if Mr. Adams should go when the moment offers. *Dumas* has been in the habit of sending his *letters open* to *me* to be *forwarded* to Mr. *Jay*. During my absence they passed through Mr. *Short's* hands who made *extracts* from them by which I see he has been recommending himself and *me* for the *money negociations in Holland*. It might be thought perhaps that *I have* encouraged *him in* this. Be assured, my dear Sir, that no such idea ever entered my head. On the contrary it is a *business* which would be the most *disagreeable to me* of all others, and for which *I am* the most *unfit person living*. *I do* not understand *bargaining* nor possess the *dexterity* requisite to *make* them. On the other hand Mr. *A.* whom I expressly and sincerely recommended, stands already on ground for that business which *I* could not gain in years. Pray set *me* to rights in the minds of those who may have supposed *me privy* to this proposition. En passant, I will observe with respect to *Mr. Dumas* that the death of the *C. de V.* places Congress more at *their* ease how to dispose of *him*. Our credit here has been ill treated here in public debate, and our *debt* deemed *apocryphal*. We should try to transfer this *debt* elsewhere, and leave nothing

20 JUNE 1787

capable of exciting ill thoughts between us. I shall mention in my letter to Mr. Jay a disagreeable affair in which *Mr. Barclay* has been thrown into[2] at *Bordeaux*. An honester man cannot be found, nor a *slower* nor more *indecisive one. His affairs* too are so *embarrassed and desperate* that the *public reputation* is every moment in danger of being *compromitted* with *him*. He is perfectly amiable and honest with all *this*.

By the next packet I shall be able to send you some books as also your watch and pedometer. The two last are not yet done. To search for books and forward them to Havre will require more time than I had between my return and the departure of this packet. You did perfectly right as to the paiment by the Mr. Fitzhughs.— Having been a witness heretofore to the divisions in Congress on the subject of their foreign ministers, it would be a weakness in me to suppose none with respect to myself, or to count with any confidence on the renewal of my commission, which expires on the 10th. day of March next: and the more so as, instead of requiring the disapprobation[3] of 7. states as formerly, that of one suffices for a recall when Congress consists of only 7. states, 2 when of 8. &c. which I suppose to be habitually their numbers at present. Whenever I leave this place, it will be necessary to begin my arrangements 6. months before my departure: and these, once fairly begun and under way, and my mind set homewards, a change of purpose could hardly take place. If it should be the desire of Congress that I should continue still longer, I could wish to know it at farthest by the packet which will sail from New York in September. Because were I to put off longer the quitting my house, selling my furniture &c. I should not have time left to wind up my affairs: and having once quitted, and sold off my furniture, I could not think of establishing myself here again. I take the liberty of mentioning this matter to you not with a desire to change the purpose of Congress, but to know it in time. I have never fixed in my own mind the epoch of my return so far as shall depend on myself, but I never suppose it very distant. Probably I shall not risk a second vote on this subject. Such trifling things may draw on one the displeasure of one or two states, and thus submit one to the disgrace of a recall.

I thank you for the Paccan nuts which accompanied your letter of March. Could you procure me a copy of the bill for proportioning crimes and punishments in the form in which it was ultimately rejected by the house of delegates? Young Mr. Bannister desired me to send him regularly the Mercure de France. I will ask leave

20 JUNE 1787

to do this thro' you, and that you will adopt such method of forwarding them to him as will save him from being submitted to postage, which they would not be worth. As a compensation for your trouble you will be free to keep them till you shall have read them.

I am with sentiments of the most sincere esteem Dear Sir Your friend & servt., TH: JEFFERSON

RC (DLC: Madison Papers); partly in code. PrC (DLC: TJ Papers, 30: 5123-6, 5128-30). MS (DLC: TJ Papers, 30: 5127); consisting of one page *en clair* of the words and phrases to be encoded, but including one word not encoded and omitting another that was.

The PERSON WHO COULD FIND OCCASIONS OF MAKING ME UNEASY was John Jay, whose negotiations with Gardoqui had so aroused some of the Southern delegates in Congress, including Madison, as to cause them to propose the measure for carrying the negotiations on the matter of the navigation of the Mississippi to Madrid, a proposal that TJ, viewing the issue with his customary realism, regarded as DESPERATE. It may have been in 1787 that TJ employed his own PEDOMETER to make the calculations of the length of his stride and rate of walking in winter and summer that are recorded in two undated memoranda in DLC: TJ Papers, 234: 41941. The first memorandum records TJ's "winter" pace and reads as follows:

	double steps
"Grille [de Chaillot] to the stone No. 3	1174.
Grille to Neuilly	2430
Grille round the ⊓ of the Roule & grand chemin	2394
Grille to Statue Louis XV	820
Statue Lou. XV. to Chat. Thuilleries	475
Grille to Chateau des Tuileries	1295

I step a French mile of 1000 toises = 6408 Eng.f. in 1053 double steps. This yields 3 f. & ½ I. English to the step and 1735 steps to the mile.

I walk a French mile in 17½ minutes. A French mile is = 1.21 or 1¼ Eng. miles. I walk then at the rate of 4³⁄₂₀ miles or 4.mi.264 yards an hour."

The second memorandum, on a smaller scrap of paper, records TJ's "summer" pace and reads as follows:

"Walking moderately in the summer I walked a Fr. mile of 1000 T = 6408 f. in 1254. steps and in 26.¹ That gives 2.55 f. to the step and
2066½ steps to the Eng. mile
1735. the brisk walk of winter
331. difference."

¹ This and subsequent words in italics are written in code and have been decoded by the Editors, employing the MS *en clair* and Code No. 9.
² TJ omitted the word "jail" in both the letter and the MS *en clair*.
³ This word interlined in substitution for "votes," deleted.

From Parent

MONSIEUR   A Beaune ce 20 juin 1787

J'ay Recue votre lettre du 14 du Courant par laquelle vous me marque de vous achette deux feuillette de vin. J'en a fait l'achet, l'une de la goute d'or provenant de Mr. Bachey de Meurseault de 84, et l'autre en Rouge des meilleur Elemant qui se nommé la Comarenné en 85, que j'ay collé sur le Champ pour estre mis en bouteille Dans douze ou quatorze jours Pour Estre bien Cler fin; et à l'egard des Chaleur quand il seron Dans le panier bien Enballé

21 JUNE 1787

il n'y auroit Rien à Craindre, et puis jusqu'à present les Chaleur, ce ne sont point forte.

J'ay Recüe, Monsieur, pour la feuillette de Montrachet de Mr. Latour 339tt de Messieurs Finguerlin et Scherer De lion [Lyons]: Sçavoir la feuïllette 279,tt Pour les bouteille 30,tt Pour les Panier 6,tt Pour l'emballagé 8,tt pour mettre en bouteille 4,tt pour la fisselle et les bouchon Et la paille 3,tt et pour faire Conduire les Bouteille auxey [au chai] et les Ramené à Beaune Pleine 3tt—le tout monte à la Somme de trois cent trente Neuf livres. Et à l'egard des Ceps de vignes que vous aves Demandé, je fut sur le Champ aux clos de veougeot et aux Chambertin pour vous en procuré, mais il estoit toute Coupé, mais j'en ait Des assure pour la fin d'octobre, et on m'a promis meme De Chevollés qui [. . . .][1]

Monsieur, les Deux feuillette que je vous Enverré, je Crois que vous auré lieux d'estre Comptent pour la qualité, j'ay choisy ce qu'il y a de Mieux dans Nos Climas. Le Rouge tout Compris vous Reviendra vingt Deux Sols la bouteille, et le blanc Ne vous Reviendra que vingt un Sols. Monsieur Bachey en a Encorre quatre feuillettes. J'ay eu Six livres pour moy de la feuillette, surquoy je vous fere Passé les Cepts de vigne sans aucune interrest. Je suis tres Sincèrement, Monsieur, Votre tres humble et tres obeissant Serviteur,

PARENT

RC (MHi); endorsed; MS slightly mutilated. Recorded in SJL as received 23 June 1787. At bottom of text, in TJ's hand, there is the following tabulation of costs and estimate of cost-per-bottle:

"124. bottles Monrachet.
en futailles		274tt
bouteilles	30tt	
panier	6	
emballage	8	
tirage	4	
ficelle, bouchons, paille	3	
voiturage á Beaune	3	65

Voiturage á Paris	34—10
	373—10
It costs then by the bottle en futaille	2tt—4 s
the bottle, cork, bottling, package, &c.	11
transportation to Paris	5
	3—."

[1] MS torn; four or five words missing.

From Richard Claiborne

DEAR SIR   London No. 14 King Street 21. June 1787.

I am sorry to Give your Excellency trouble, which I have done in one or two late instances, and particularly so now, as it is on an occasion of a peculiar nature. I write in a confidential manner, meaning nothing further for the present than a private communication; as it relates to a subject in which my interest is materially involved, and yet I mean no further promulgation of the matter than it really requires.

Your Excellency already knows that Colo. Saml. Blackden was in Paris on the subject of the sales of my property. From others I obtained information that he had disposed of a quantity, and by himself, when he returned to London, but he neither gave me the particulars, or in what manner the monies arising therefrom had been appropriated, and in this inexplicit manner, took his departure, as he informed he, for Amsterdam, having stayed with me only one Evening and the next day. He also took with him his Lady, and all their Baggage that were of material consequence, promising to write to me and give me an account of his transactions in Paris, as soon as he reached his papers, which he had left on the verge of France, or some place by which he was to take his Rout to Amsterdam. Being of an unsuspecting nature myself, and having the highest opinion of the rectitude and good management of the Colonel, I let an opportunity pass in which it might have been more proper for me to obtain an explicit account. Reflecting therefore on this, as well as that I have received no letter from him since his departure which is now 15 days, as well as that he is in possession of a valuable quantity of my property, under absolute powers of sale, and the whole dependant alone on his integrity, I have become very solicitous that the business should be explained so far as it has taken effect on his part, and the rest placed on a satisfactory footing. I would pray of Your Excellency therefore to acquaint me if you know any thing of the Colonel at present, and his transactions and conduct in Paris? I am aware that this question involves a matter of a serious nature, namely the Gentlemans reputation, inasmuch as that I hope he stands fair with Your Excellency, the Marquis De La Fayette, and other characters of distinction and respectability, but when the substance of what I have written, as well as that I have received of him only the amount of 51£ for my own use, are considered, and that my enquiries are meant for nothing further than what I hope his merit will stand the best of, I shall be acquited of any thing improper or ungenteel: I will further observe, for the satisfaction of Your Excellency, that whatever communications you are pleased to transmit me, I shall make no further use of than as materials to direct me in the course it will be requisite to pursue. And I sincerely hope, for the honor of human nature, as well as for Colonel Blackden in particular that the Investigation will terminate to his credit.

21 JUNE 1787

I am, with the sincerest respect, and Esteem, Your Excellency's Most obedient Humble Servant   R. CLAIBORNE

RC (MoSHi); endorsed. Recorded in SJL as received 26 June 1787.

To George Rogers Clark

DEAR SIR   Paris June 21. 1787.

The bearers hereof Doctor Sangrain and Monsieur Picque purposing to go to Kentucky to establish themselves, I take the liberty of recommending them to your notice and civilities. The former is recommended to me by a very good friend of mine, as a gentleman of skill in his profession, of general science and merit. The latter is associated with him in the design of procuring a considerable establishment in our new country. I beg leave to recommend them particularly to your counsel and protection against imposition in their purchases to which as strangers they will be exposed. The services and attentions you will be so good as to shew them will be deemed obligations to him who has the honour to be with sentiments of high esteem and respect Dear Sir Your friend & servant,

TH: JEFFERSON

PrC (DLC); at foot of text: "General Clarke."

To John Jay

SIR   Paris June 21. 1787.

I had the honour of addressing you in a letter of May 4. from Marseilles which was to have gone by the last packet; but it arrived a few hours too late for that conveiance, and has been committed to a private one passing thro' England, with a promise that it should go thro' no post office.

I was desirous, while at the seaports, to obtain a list of the American vessels which have come to them since the peace, in order to estimate their comparative importance to us, as well as the general amount of our commerce with this country, so far as carried on in our own bottoms. At Marseilles I found there had been 32. since that period; at Cette not a single one; at Bayonne, one of our free ports, only one. This last article I learnt from other information, not having visited that place; as it would have been a deviation, from my route, too considerable for the importance of the object.

[487]

21 JUNE 1787

At Bordeaux, Nantes and Lorient I could not obtain lists in the moment, but am in hopes I shall be able to get them ere long. Tho' more important to us, they will probably be more imperfect than that of Marseilles. At Nantes I began with Mr. Dobrée an arrangement of his claims. I visited the military stores which have been detained there so long, opened some boxes of each kind, and found the state of their contents much better than had been represented. An exact list of the articles is to be sent me. In the mean time the following is near the truth.

- 24. casks of gunlocks
- 6. cases of gun barrels
- 65. cases of old bayonets
- locks and furniture of 3100 fire arms of various kinds taken from the peasants of Bordeaux when they were deprived of the droit de chasse, and purchased by Mr. Dean.

The above are broken, eaten up with rust and worth nothing.

- 15,000 peices of walnut for gun stocks, very good.
- 30. cases of muskets from Holland; about 27. in each chest: say about 700 muskets with their bayonets: good of their form but not of the best form. In such condition that they will need only such a cleaning as the souldier himself can give.
- 21. cases of sabres from Holland, about 63. in each case. Say about 1300 in good condition.
- 18. hogsheads of gunflints.
- 10. anchors weighing in the whole about 21,500 lb.

But we must deduct about a fifth from the muskets and sabres; because there are in the warehouse five tier of cases, the bottom one of which having been partly under water during an inundation of the Loire, that whole tier may be considered as lost. Another deduction will be warehouse rent 600ᵗᵗ a year from the year 1782. Still they remain an object of too much value to be abandoned, if they can be withdrawn by mutual consent, without any notice of their having been in the hands of justice. Mr. Dobrée appears to be so reasonable that I am in hopes this may be done. The importations into Lorient of other fish oils, besides those of the whale, brought to my notice there a defect in the letter of Monsieur de Calonnes of Oct. 22. which letter was formerly communicated to you. In that *whale oil* only was named. The other fish oils therefore have continued to pay the old duties. In a conference with Monsr. de Villedeuil, the present Comptroller general, since my return, I proposed the extending the exemption to all *fish-oils*, according to the letter of the Hanseatic treaty, which had formed the basis of the regulations respecting us. I think this will be agreed to. The delays of office first, then the illness of M. de Calonnes, and lastly his removal and the throng of business occasioned by the assemblée des Notables, have prevented the reducing the substance of the letter into the form of an Arret as yet; tho' I continued solliciting it as much as circumstances would bear. I am now promised that it shall be done immediately, and that it shall be so far retrospective to the date of the letter as that all duties paid since that shall be refunded.

Tho' we are too little interested in the proceedings of the Assemblées des Notables to render minute details of them desireable to Congress, yet I suppose a general view, now that the assembly is closed and their measures fixed, may be acceptable.

The deficiency of the public revenues, compared with the public expences was become so considerable, that it was evident some of the wheels of government must stop, unless they could be relieved. Continual borrowings, in time of profound peace, could not be proposed and a new tax under the same circumstances might crush the minister, unless he could procure a powerful support. He proposed therefore the calling an assemblée des Notables. He proffered them an universal redress of grievances; laid open those grievances fully, pointed out sound remedies, and covering his canvas with objects of this magnitude, the demand of money became a little accessory scarcely attracting attention. The persons chosen were the most able and independant characters in the kingdom; and their support, if it could be obtained, would be enough for him. They improved the occasion of redressing their grievances, and agreed that the public wants should be relieved; but went into an examination of the causes of them. It is supposed Monsr. de Calonnes was conscious his accounts could not bear examination; and it is said and believed that he asked of the king to send 4. members to the bastile, of whom the M. de la Fayette was one, to banish 20. others, and two of his ministers. The king found it shorter to banish him. His successor went on in full concert with the assembly. The result has been an augmentation in the revenue, a promise of oeconomies in it's expenditure; of an annual settlement of the public accounts, before a council, which the Comptroller, having been heretofore obliged to settle only with the king in person, of course never settled at all; of the abolition of the Corvées; reformation of the Gabelles; suppression of the interior custom houses; free commerce of grain internal and external; and the establishment of Provincial assemblies: which, all together, constitute a vast mass of improvement in the condition of this nation. The establishment of the Provincial assemblies is a fundamental improvement. They will be of the choice of the people; one third renewed every year; in those provinces where there are no states, that is to say, over about three fourths of the kingdom. They will be partly an Executive themselves, partly an executive Council to the Intendant to whom the Executive power in his province has been heretofore entirely delegated. Chosen by the people, they will soften the execution of hard laws: and, having a right of representation to the king, they will censure bad laws, suggest good ones, expose abuses; and their representations, when united, will command respect. To the other advantages may be added the precedent itself of calling the assembly of Notables, which may perhaps grow into habit. The hope is that the improvements thus promised will be carried into effect, that they will be maintained during the present reign; and that that will be long enough for them to take some root in the constitution, so that they may come to be considered as a part of that, and be protected by time and the attachment of the nation.   The new accessions to the ministry are valued here. Good is hoped from the Archbishop of Toulouse who succeeds the Count de Vergennes as Chef du conseil de finance. Monsieur de Ville-deuil the Comptroller general has been approved by the public in the offices he has heretofore exercised. The Duke de Nivernois, called to the Council, is reckoned a good and able man: and Monsieur de Malesherbes, called also to the council, is unquestionably the first character in the kingdom for integrity, patriotism, knowlege, and experience in business. There is a fear that the Marechal de Castries is disposed to retire.

The face of things in Europe is a little turbid at present: but probably all will subside. The Empress of Russia, it is supposed, will not push her pretensions against the Turks to actual war. Weighing the fondness of the Emperor for innovation against his want of perseverance, it is difficult to calculate what he will do with his discontented subjects in Brabant and Flanders. If those provinces alone were concerned, he would probably give back: but this would induce an opposition to his plans in all his other dominions. Perhaps he may be able to find a compromise. The cause of the Patriots in Holland is a little clouded at present. England and Prussia seem disposed to interpose effectually. The former has actually ordered a fleet of 6. sail of the line, Northwardly, under Gore; and the latter threatens to put his troops into motion. The danger of losing such a weight in their scale, as that of Prussia, would occasion this court to prefer conciliation to war. Add to this the distress of their finances, and perhaps not so warm a zeal in the new ministry for the innovations in Holland. I hardly believe they will think it worth while to purchase the change of constitution proposed there at the expence of a war. But of these things you will recieve more particular and more certain details from Mr. Dumas, to whom they belong.

Mr. Eden is appointed Ambassador from England to Madrid. To the hatred borne us by his court and country, is added a recollection of the circumstances of the unsuccesful embassy to America, of which he made a part. So that I think he will carry to Madrid dispositions to do us all the ill he can.

The late change in the ministry is very favorable to the prospects of the Chevalier de la Luzerne. The Count de Montmorin, Monsr. de Malesherbes, and Monsr. de Lamoignon the garde des sceaux, are his near relations. Probably something will be done for him, and without delay. The promise of the former administration to the Count de Moutier to succeed to this vacancy, should it take place, will probably be performed by the present one.

Mr. Barclay has probably informed you of his having been arrested in Bordeaux for a debt contracted in the way of his commerce. He immediately applied to the parliament of that place who ordered his discharge. This took place after five days actual imprisonment. I arrived at Bordeaux a few days after his liberation. As the Procureur general of the king had interested himself to obtain it with uncommon zeal, and that too on public principles, I thought it my duty to wait on him and return him my thanks. I did the same to the President of the parliament for the body over which he presided, what would have been an insult in America being an indispensable duty here. You will see by the inclosed printed paper on what grounds the Procureur insisted on Mr. Barclay's liberation. Those on which the parliament ordered it are not expressed. On my arrival here I spoke with the Minister on the subject. He observed that the character of Consul is no protection in this country against process for debt: that as to the character with which Mr. Barclay had been invested at the court of Marocco, [it was ques]tionable whether it could be placed on the diplomatic line, as it had not been derived immediately from Congress; that if it were, it would have covered him to Paris only, where he had received his commission, had he proceeded directly thither, but that his long stay at Bordeaux must be considered as terminating it there. I observed to him that Mr. Barclay had been arrested almost immediately on his arrival at Bordeaux. But sais he the arrest was made void by the parliament, and still he has continued there several weeks. True, I replied, but his adversaries declared they would arrest him again the moment he should be out of the jurisdiction of the parliament of Bourdeaux, and have actually engaged the Marechaussée on the road to do it. This seemed to impress him. He [said] he could obtain a letter of sauf conduit which would protect him to Paris, but that immediately on his arrival here he would be liable to arrest. I asked him if such a letter could not be obtained to protect him to Paris, and back to Bordeaux and even to America? He said that for that, the consent of the greater part of his creditors would be necessary, and even with this it was very doubtful whether it could be obtained. Still if I would furnish him with that consent, he would do what should depend on him. I am persuaded he will, and have written to Mr. Barclay to obtain the consent of his creditors. This is the footing on which this matter stands at present. I have stated it thus particularly that you may know the truth, which will probably be misrepresented in the English papers, to the prejudice of Mr. Barclay. This matter has been a great affliction to him, but no dishonour where it's true state is known. Indeed he is incapable of doing any thing not strictly honourable.

In a letter of Aug. 30. 1785. I had the honour of mentioning to you what had past here on the subject of a convention for the regulation of the two post offices. I now inclose you a letter from the Baron D'Ogny who is at the head of that department, which shews that he still expects some arrangement. I have heard it said that M. de Creve-coeur is authorized to treat on this subject. You doubtless know if this be true. The articles may certainly be better adjusted there than here. This letter from the Baron d'Ogny was in consequence of an application from a servant of mine during my absence, which would not have been made had I been here. Nor will it be repeated; it being my opinion and practice to pay small sums of money rather than to ask favors.

I have the honor to inclose you also copies of a letter and papers from the Marechal de Castries on the claim of an individual against the state of South Carolina for services performed on board the Indian; and the petition of another on a like claim. Also copies of letters received from Obryan at Algiers, and from Mr. Lambe. A letter of the 26th. of May from Mr. Montgomery at Alicant informs me that, by a vessel arrived at Carthagena from Algiers, they learn the death of the Dey of that republic. Yet as we hear

21 JUNE 1787

nothing of it thro' any other channel it may be doubted. It escaped me at the time of my departure to Aix to make arrangements for sending you the gazettes regularly by the packets. The whole are now sent, tho' a great part of them are so old as to be not worth perusal. Your favor of April 24. has been duly received. I have the honour to be with sentiments of the most perfect esteem & respect, Sir, your most obedient & most humble servant,

TH: JEFFERSON

PrC (DLC); one page of MS faded; illegible words in brackets (supplied) are drawn from Tr. (DNA: PCC, No. 107, II). Enclosures: (1) Printed copy of the order of 19 May 1787 of the court of the parliament of Bordeaux ending the imprisonment of Thomas Barclay (Arch. Aff. Etr., Paris, Corr. Pol., E.-U., XXXII; Tr in DLC; another in DNA: PCC, No. 107, II). (2) D'Ogny to TJ, 6 Apr. 1787. (3) Castries to TJ, 19 Apr. 1787, and its enclosure. (4) Mayeux to TJ, 9 Apr. 1787. (5) O'Bryen to TJ, 28 Apr. 1787. (6) Lamb to TJ, 20 May 1787.

The incident of Barclay's ARREST, imprisonment, release, and flight from Bordeaux deserves particular comment for several reasons: in this and other instances he has been confused with another who bore the same name; his plight was due, in some measure at least, to the fact that his country was inexcusably dilatory in rendering him compensation for services performed; and this episode involved TJ in discussions with Montmorin concerning the question of diplomatic immunity under the law of nations.

Thomas Barclay of Philadelphia (1728-1793), who negotiated the treaty with Morocco, is at times confused with the much younger Thomas Barclay of New York (1753-1830), who became a Loyalist, served in the British army, and later became consul-general for Great Britain in the northeastern part of the United States (a sketch of the latter, but not of the former, is in DAB; see Sowerby, No. 2305, note). Thomas Barclay of Philadelphia was a merchant and an active patriot during the Revolution. He was a member of the Committee of Correspondence of Philadelphia, 1774-1775, and it is possible that TJ met him while attending the second Continental Congress. Barclay's country seat, "Somerset," stood in a grove of pines on a bluff opposite Trenton, New Jersey, and it was there that Generals Stirling and Wayne had their headquarters in 1781 when the two British spies, John Mason and James Ogden, were handed over by the Board of Sergeants of the mutinied Pennsylvania Line and were tried and executed (PMHB, XXXVIII [1914], 47, note; Carl Van Doren, *Mutiny in January*, New York, 1943, p. 152, 154-6). Shortly after this, Barclay's commercial activities carried him to France. According to the memorial presented to Congress by his widow some two decades after the Bordeaux incident—it was drafted by TJ himself while president—and the report of the committee of claims of the House of Representatives to whom the memorial had been referred, Barclay performed between 1781 and 1787 "a variety of necessary and important services for the United States" in Europe and Africa. He was appointed vice-consul in France on 26 June 1781 at a salary of $1,000 per annum, and on 5 Oct. 1781 he was appointed consul. On 18 Nov. 1782 Congress designated him as commissioner with full powers to settle the accounts of the United States in Europe; his commission stated that Congress would "hereafter make adequate provision for the said commission, according to the nature and extent of the services performed" (*American State Papers*, IX, *Claims*, p. 347-54). On 31 Mch. 1791 he was appointed consul for Morocco by TJ, a fact which manifests the latter's continuing confidence in Barclay's probity. Barclay departed to assume these new duties, but died suddenly at Lisbon on 19 Jan. 1793. Some time afterwards his house in Philadelphia was destroyed by fire and all of his papers and effects were lost (PMHB, XXXVIII [1914], 47, note; Robert Barclay to TJ, 28 July 1806; TJ to Robert Barclay, 4 Nov. 1806).

"I have no more Doubts of the Justice of Congress than I have of my Existence," wrote the aging and troubled Barclay on his way to Morocco (Barclay

[493]

to TJ, 24 Jan. 1787). His confidence was justified, but the promise by Congress in 1782 to compensate him "hereafter" carried no time limit. Such an adventurer as Steuben, vigorously pressing his claims for compensation and basing them upon flimsy if not fraudulent grounds, met with fairly speedy attention through the assistance of Alexander Hamilton and others (see Vol. 7:100-1); indeed, in the opinion of some, generosity was added to promptness, for though the Baron had "received little money, and less Flattery" in Europe, Congress had "added bounty to the exact Justice and possessed him of real monies exceeding in amount the life aggregate of the revenues of a prince of the German Empire" (Rufus King to Elbridge Gerry, 5 Nov. 1786; Burnett, *Letters of Members*, VIII, No. 539). This was exaggerated, but the treatment given by Congress to the flamboyant, pushing, and not wholly trustworthy Steuben stands in marked contrast to that accorded the more diffident, more faithful, and more deserving Barclay. The salary that might have enabled him to adjust his affairs properly was never granted during his lifetime. Fifteen years after his death, Congress came to the relief of his widow by compensating her for his services between 1781 and 1787 at the rate of $1,000 per annum for his duties as vice-consul and $3,333⅓ per annum for his offices of consul, commissioner of accounts, and agent (report of committee of claims, 8 Jan. 1808; *American State Papers*, IX, *Claims*, p. 347-54). This was, of course, exclusive of his expenses. On setting out on the Moroccan mission Barclay had been given a letter of credit not to exceed $20,000 and against this he had issued drafts totalling £4,545 (or 109,080₶). The balance was against him when he settled the accounts for the mission at L'Orient on 12 July 1787: "Upon this Account," he wrote TJ and Adams, "I shall remain Indebted to the United States, (untill I make a Settlement with them, and untill I know what I am to charge for my Voyage) 13901₶ 10s." (see Vol. 8:614, 622-3; Barclay to Commissioners, 13 July 1787). But this was a small debit compared with the amount of salary due for more than six years' services. To this neglect must be added another injury: Virginia funds that were to be drawn upon by Barclay in his capacity as agent for that state in the purchase of arms had necessarily been used by TJ to replenish the dwindling reserves of the United States in Paris. In consequence, Barclay's draft on Grand had been protested at the very moment of his incarceration at Bordeaux (see Grand to TJ, 19 and 23 May 1787; TJ to Governor of Virginia, 3 Aug. 1787).

TJ had long known about the involved state of Barclay's commercial transactions. These had evidently embarrassed both men at the very outset of the Moroccan mission. In 1785 TJ, writing to Vergennes to inform him of the missions of Lamb and Barclay, had asked the minister for "Letters of protection for their persons, effects, vessels and attendants during their passage to and from Africa," and these, along with passports, had been granted promptly (TJ to Vergennes, 12 Oct. 1785; Vergennes to TJ, 27 Oct. 1785). He had applied to the Spanish ambassador, Count d'Aranda, for similar protection for Barclay. At that point TJ expected that Barclay would set out from Paris at once and that Lamb would follow, but, soon after D'Aranda replied that he was not authorized to grant such protection and that application would have to be made to the court at Madrid, TJ wrote Carmichael that "an important matter detains Mr. Barclay some days longer" (TJ to D'Aranda, 22 Oct. 1785; D'Aranda to TJ, 22 Oct. 1785; TJ to Carmichael, 4 Nov. 1785). It is very likely that this important matter was a promissory note for 10,000₶ given early in 1785 by Barclay to John van Heukelom & Son that fell due about the time that Barclay was scheduled to depart and "was not Paid, Without great difficulty" (Van Heukelom & Son to TJ, 1 Mch. 1786). TJ was well aware that the public interest had been seriously affected by the claims of importunate creditors during the Revolution—a considerable amount of arms and military stores belonging to the United States had been detained at Nantes by judicial decree on a claim of Schweighauser & Dobrée that Franklin had refused as unfounded—and he certainly would have taken every precaution against a similar injury to the public interest when Barclay, harassed by creditors, was travelling abroad with about a thousand guineas worth of gold watches, snuff boxes, and other valuable property; it is significant that he had asked for a Spanish passport for Bar-

[494]

clay but not for Lamb, though he stated that the latter carried no presents of value. It may also be significant that Barclay took a circuitous route to Madrid. An interruption of his mission did occur at that city when another creditor, Veuve Samuel Joly of St. Quentin, caused him to be confined to the limits of the capital until he had discharged his indebtedness, which he did with a draft that was protested—an incident that TJ evidently learned about neither from Barclay nor from Carmichael, but from the French *commissionaire du commerce* (Boyetet to TJ, 24 July 1786; TJ to Boyetet, 28 July 1786). But these embarrassments, though disturbing, never affected TJ's belief in Barclay's honesty. To Jay, TJ wrote that Barclay was "incapable of doing any thing not strictly honourable" and to Madison he declared: "an honester man cannot be found, nor a slower nor more indecisive one" (TJ to Jay, 21 June 1787; TJ to Madison, 20 June 1787; on Barclay's slowness, it may be noted that he had taken seven months to reach Morocco and even longer to return). Over the years TJ demonstrated his belief that Barclay was "perfectly amiable and honest," but in 1787 he knew, as he reported confidentially to Madison (not to Jay), that Barclay's affairs had become "so embarrassed and desperate that the public reputation is every moment in danger of being compromitted with him" (TJ to Madison, 20 June 1787). Though feelings of friendship and a desire for justice entered into the balance, the controlling factor in TJ's vigorous interposition in the Bordeaux incident was his deep concern for the reputation of the United States. Barclay may have been perfectly honest, he may have been injured by the dilatoriness of Congress, and he may have suffered at the hands of his partner Moylan, but TJ could scarcely succeed in his great object of promoting the growth of cordial commercial relations between the two countries if American public agents, for whatever cause, aroused hostile feelings within the business community in France.

Barclay arrived in Bordeaux on 5 May 1787 and called that night on his creditors, French & Nephew. He found them cordially disposed, as they had been when in correspondence with him in Madrid some fourteen months earlier; ten days later he was, on their complaint, "arrested by five Ruffians" (Barclay to TJ, 29 June and ca. 3 July 1787). Four days after this he was released through the energetic action of Dudon fils, *Procureur Général du Roi*. Dudon rested his argument on Barclay's petition for release squarely on the law of nations: "quand le droit des gens est intéressé, ce n'est pas par les formes consacrées pour les actions civiles, et purement judiciaires, qu'il peut être défendu et vengé." Barclay, he pointed out, was clothed in the dual character of consul-general of the United States and "de leur Agent extraordinaire auprès de l'Empereur de Maroc." "Il vient de remplir en cette qualité la mission dont il étoit chargé par sa République," Dudon declared; "il a joui chez cette nation, si récemment sortie des ténebres de la barbarie, de la plénitude du droit des gens. Il revenoit en France, joignant à la foi des traités, les passeports particuliers de sa majesté, et il a été emprisonné à Bordeaux à la requête des sieurs French Neveu & Compagnie, en vertu d'une condamnation obtenue contre lui devant les juges et Consuls de Paris." Dudon declined to discuss the nature of the debt or the commercial operations which produced it. Instead, he addressed himself to what he considered a "violation la plus révoltante du droit des Nations." The publicists were unanimous in their view of the sanctity of the persons of envoys from one nation to another "sous quelque titre que ce puisse être; et l'histoire venant a l'appui de leurs principes, nous voyons d'âge en âge jusque dans les siecles les plus reculés, ce caractere d'Ambassadeur, d'Envoyé ou de Représentant, respecté chez tous les peuples, des flots de sang répandus pour venger l'injure faite a quelqu'un de ces hommes revêtus d'un ministere national." Grotius, Bodin, Montesquieu, and Vattel were appealed to in support of the view that the ambassador, representing his sovereign in a foreign state, must be free; that to injure him would be to injure his master and his nation; that to arrest him or do him violence would be to wound "le droit d'Ambassade, qui appartient à tous les souverains." Dudon then cited an instance in which this principle was violated: "L'Angleterre, absorbée par l'esprit de commerce, osa s'écarter un instant de ces principes de droit public. L'Ambassadeur de Pierre-le-Grand fut arrêté, pour dettes, dans les rues de Londres; mais, l'Europe entiere réclama, et le Parle-

[495]

ment d'Angleterre fit un acte, par lequel la capture de l'Ambassadeur fut déclarée contraire au droit des gens, en vertu duquel les personnes des Ambassadeurs et autres ministres publics, ont toujours été considerées comme des personnes sacrées." Barclay, he pointed out, had been arrested and "tous les papiers relatifs à sa mission, sequestrés par un Huissier, avec eux tous les titres qui peuvent justifier de son caractere et de ses droits"—an act that might justify penalties for the guard and for the complainant. "Mais," he concluded, "une nation nouvelle, qui doit son existence à la protection de sa majesté et au puissant secours des armes francaises, éprouvant en France, dans la personne de son Representant, un genre d'outrage dont toutes les puissances sont solidairement intéressées à se plaindre, a droit d'attendre de vous une satisfaction éclatante." He therefore urged that Barclay's arrest and imprisonment be annulled; that the papers and effects that had been seized to his prejudice be restored to him; and that an Arrêt to this effect be printed and published. President de Pichard of the parliament of Bordeaux signed the Arrêt on 19 May 1787 (*Arrêt de la Cour de Parlement, qui casse l'emprisonnement de sieur Thomas Barklai* [Bordeaux, 1787]; Sowerby, No. 2305; Tr of the Arrêt is in DNA: PCC, No. 107, II, 26-31; printed text in Arch. Aff. Etr., Paris, Corr. Pol., E.-U., XXXII). Dudon's effort was indeed carried out with UNCOMMON ZEAL, AND THAT TOO ON PUBLIC PRINCIPLES. Aside from resting his case on the law of nations, Dudon seems to have been inspired by friendship for the United States and also for Barclay. Had he not pressed the argument so vigorously, the Barclay affair might very well have endangered Franco-American relations in much the same way as had the Marbois affair of 1784 (see Vol. 7:306-8; also, Alfred Rosenthal, "The Marbois-Longchamps Affair," PMHB, LXIII [1939], 294-301). Charles Thomson had suspected that the attack on Marbois by Longchamps, who may have been a British spy during the Revolution, was a premeditated incident planned by those who sought to disturb American relations with France; it is conceivable, particularly in the light of the British ambassador's intervention in the case (see below) and of the suddenness and violence of French & Nephew's effort to avenge themselves, that the Barclay incident was in part the result of a similar motivation. Perhaps it was with this in mind that TJ, performing an act which in America WOULD HAVE BEEN AN INSULT, called on Dudon and also on THE PRESIDENT OF THE PARLIAMENT (Pichard) to express his gratitude when he arrived in Bordeaux five days after Barclay's release.

Dudon evidently thought French & Nephew would try to have the Arrêt annulled, for he sent a copy of it to Montmorin as soon as it was printed, asking for approval. The assumption was well founded, for the Bordeaux merchants brought pressure to bear upon Montmorin from all sides. They wrote to him on 26 May appealing for protection against Barclay, who, they said, "invoque le Droit des Gens qu'il a violé lui même de la maniere la plus formelle." They stated that a purchase of goods had been made by them in 1783 for the account of Barclay, Moylan, and Company of L'Orient to the extent of 67,206^{lt} 5s. 11d. which that firm had promised to pay out of a consignment of 500 hhds. of tobacco already shipped to Louis Alexandre of Bordeaux; that, after more than two years of vexatious delays and protested drafts from Barclay, they had obtained judgment against him; and that, if the king protected the representative of another nation, such an envoy should not be permitted to vex his subjects. They therefore requested orders to the commandant of Bordeaux to compel Barclay to discharge his debt. This statement of their case French & Nephew sent under cover to G. Woulfe, a Paris banker, who, in forwarding it to Montmorin, described them as "des braves et honnetes gens, et des Citoyens distingués et utiles" who had been tricked out of a great part of their fortune by the "conduite insidieuse et malhonnête" of Barclay. The Bordeaux merchants sent similar statements to Breteuil, to Lamoignon, and to Fumel, who in turn forwarded them to Montmorin. On 15 June the minister wrote to Dudon formally approving the position that he had taken; on the same day he wrote to Fumel, stating that Barclay's rank as consul offered him no protection, but that he had gone to Morocco in the character of minister of the United States to negotiate a treaty; that the king had both recognized him in this character and had furnished him with passports; and that the immunity thus provided would cease only "à l'instant ou ce Caractère s'est evanoui par son retour aux fonctions de Consul general ou par sa rentrée dans la classe des simples Particuliers." Thus Barclay had not been legitimately arrested. "Mais," Montmorin advised Fumel, "vous verrés aussi d'un côté que rien n'empeche les Sr. French de reprendre leurs poursuites contre lui par devant les juges de la Capitale, qu'aucune raison tirée du code des Nations ne pourra plus le soustraire aux condamnations que ces juges ont prononcées, ou qu'ils prononceront encore contre lui, et que si le Sr. Barclay quittoit Paris dans ce moment cy rien ne les empecheroit de le faire arreter par tout ou ils pourroient l'aprehender." Furthermore, French & Nephew would have had the same right at Bordeaux, despite the immunity attached to Barclay in his character as minister, if he had attempted to return to America, "parce que ces franchises n'ont eu pour objet que de le mettre en etat de vaquer aux fonctions publiques que ses souverains lui avoient commises et que ces fonctions auroient cessé à notre egard au moment ou il se seroit preparé a quitter le Royaume." Montmorin sent copies of this letter to Breteuil and replied to Woulfe and French & Nephew. But scarcely had these letters been despatched before he had cause to regret the position that he had taken, for the next day Lord Dorset took the matter up with the minister (Dudon fils to Montmorin, 22 May 1787; French & Nephew to Montmorin, 26 May 1787; G. Woulfe to Montmorin, 2 June 1787; Montmorin to Fumel, 15 June 1787; Lamoignon to Montmorin, 15 June 1787; Montmorin to Breteuil, 15 June 1787; Montmorin to French & Nephew, 19 June 1787; Montmorin to Woulfe, 19 June 1787; Breteuil to Montmorin, 20 June 1787, acknowledging Montmorin's letter to Fumel and stating: "Je la trouve parfaitement conforme aux vraix principes du droit des gens"; all in Arch. Aff. Etr., Paris, Corr. Pol., E.-U., XXXII; Tr in DLC; see Barclay to TJ, 29 June 1787, for his account of the shipment of tobacco that he was accused of diverting from its promised object).

It is not clear what motives lay back of Dorset's intervention, but the fact that he did so indicates the powerful influences set in motion by Barclay's determined creditors. It is also certain that Dorset's interest was decisive in causing Montmorin to reverse himself. The British ambassador was in full possession of the facts of the case as stated by French & Nephew; he also suggested that some of Barclay's debts had been incurred before he became consul and were accompanied by fraudulent circumstances. He hinted that there might be doubt as to whether Barclay really was clothed with the pretended character of "agent extraordinaire." Without pursuing this last, Dorset declared however: "il est notoire qu'il est parti de Maroc depuis plusieurs mois, qu'il a resté quelque temps à Cadiz; on m'assure qu'il a même été ici a Paris, le lieu de son prétendu domicile; et l'on voit qu'actuellement il demeure à Bordeaux et nullement comme un voyageur qui se rend au lieu de sa demeure.—Sur ces faits je m'en rapporte à Votre Excellence pour prendre telles mesures que vous jugerez convenables, soit en ordonnant la cassation immédiate de l'arrêt qui met le Sr. Barklay en liberté de refuser le payement de sa dette, ou en l'obligeant de donner les suretés necessaires pour que les Sr. French & Nephew ne soient point abusivement frustrés du payement d'une dette legitime" (Dorset to Montmorin, 16 June 1787; same). It is not certain who reported so accurately on Barclay's movements, but TJ believed that French & Nephew had interested Eden in their behalf (TJ to Barclay, 19 June 1787). It is possible that this was the case: Eden's long connection with the British intelligence service would have made it easy for him to find out all about Barclay's slow journey to and from Morocco. It is also significant that TJ esteemed the mild and urbane Dorset, but that he believed Eden was disposed TO DO US ALL THE ILL HE CAN. Whether Dorset's extraordinary interposition was undertaken on his own initiative or at Eden's suggestion is not known, but, on its surface, the Bordeaux incident would appear to have been of no concern to the British ambassador or to his nation, except in the general question of diplomatic immunity.

On the day following Dorset's appeal, TJ called at the Foreign Office to request the safe conduct that Barclay had asked for. Montmorin's responses voiced the opinions that Dorset had expressed —the hint of duplicity on Barclay's part, the doubt of his diplomatic rank since he had not been deputed by Congress, the tardiness of his journey, &c. This differed materially from what Montmorin had given Fumel and Dudon two days earlier, but TJ was scarcely in a position to argue that Barclay was anything more than an agent. In his letter of commendation to Barclay of 3 Aug. 1787 he referred to him as "minister to Marocco," but this was written after the Bordeaux incident: when he had applied for a passport in 1785 it was for "Thomas Barclay, Esqr., agent to the court of Morocco" (Commissioners to Vergennes, 1-11 Oct. 1785) and Vergennes had issued it as such. Though he could not have known it, TJ was on still shakier ground when he asked if a safe conduct could be issued to enable Barclay to go to America, for Montmorin's position as expressed to Fumel had already ruled out any possibility of immunity for Barclay, even as minister, if he showed any inclination to depart for America. Thus Montmorin could only reply to this inquiry that it was "doubtful" (TJ to Barclay, 19 June 1787). He promised to do what he could. There can scarcely be any doubt that, as TJ reported to Barclay on 4 July, Montmorin was cordially disposed, but he was also sorely troubled. (A rough, undated aide-mémoire of TJ's request, probably made by Rayneval, is in Arch. Aff. Etr., Paris, Corr. Pol., E.-U., XXXII; Tr in DLC.)

On the very day that TJ reported to Barclay about his interview at the Foreign Office, Montmorin wrote to Dudon reversing the position that he had taken on 15 June: "j'étois dans la ferme persuasion," he declared, "que ce Consul général revenoit directement du Havre, et qu'il n'etait que de passage à Bordeaux pour retourner à son domicile qui est à Paris. Comme je suis informé du contraire, et comme la qualité de Consul Général dont est revetu le Sr Barklay ne le soustrait pas a la jurisdiction ordinaire surtout pour des faits de commerce, rien ne sauroit empêcher les Srs French de le poursuivre par toutes les voyes de droit pour recouvrement de la créance qu'ils ont sur lui. Je m'impresse, M[onsieur], de vous faire part de ces principes, afin de rectifier ce qu'une erreur de fait m'avoit engagé a vous mander. Je suis persuadé d'avance . . . que vous ne ferez pas intervenir votre Ministere pour mettre obstacle aux nouvelles poursuites des Srs. French." Montmorin forwarded a copy of this letter to President de Pichard; the drafts for both letters were prepared by Rayneval (Montmorin to Dudon, 19 June 1787; Montmorin to Pichard, 21 June 1787; Arch. Aff. Etr., Paris, Corr. Pol., E.-U., XXXII; Tr in DLC).

Dudon, who must have received this letter around 25 June, did not reply until Saturday the 30th, when he entered a vigorous protest. The "Protecteurs des Sieurs French," he declared, had somehow obtained copies of Montmorin's letter and had made it public. He thought, nevertheless, that it was not too late to bring before Montmorin "quelques reflections que votre justice, et votre profonde Sagesse approuveront Certainement." The application of the principles of the law of nations to Barclay's case was not so erroneous as his adversaries had tried to persuade the minister: Barclay was indeed on his way through Bordeaux to Paris to complete his mission, as Dudon thought he could prove by information he had obtained from "un portefeuille contenant en original le traité d'entre l'empereur de Maroc et les etats unis de l'Amerique, et une lettre de l'empereur a ces memes Etats. J'ai eu trois jours ce portefeuille en mon pouvoir. Plusieurs Magistrats ont vu avec moi ces pieces authentiques." Dudon concluded from this that the mission of an ambassador or an envoy could be considered at an end only when he had delivered up to the power he represented the letters and treaties that he had been authorized to negotiate. These documents, he reported, had not been introduced in evidence before the parliament when the Arrêt was issued; Barclay had only shown his passports at that time, since his papers had been seized at the moment of his arrest. But the first use Barclay had made of his liberty was to justify his public character by showing the treaty of which he was the bearer. "Sans doute," Dudon declared, "si le Sieur Barklai n'etoit que Consul Général, il Seroit soumis a touttes les Loix du Commerce qu'il exerce mais jugés vous meme Monsieur le Comte d'après l'exposé que j'ai l'honneur de vous faire, s'il n'est pas encore Aujourdhuy revetu d'un Caractere national, qui le met sous la Sauvegarde du droit Public. Je ne dois pas d'ailleurs oublier de vous dire que M. de Jefferson passant à Bordeaux est venu lui meme chez moi, attester par les remerciements qu'il m'a faits,

21 JUNE 1787

la qualite qu'il reconnoissoit dans la personne du Sieur Barklay.—Les Sieurs French meritent . . . toutte votre protection pour leur procurer le payement d'une dette aussi legitime que Considérable. Je me permettrai meme de vous dire qu'il semble que les Etats unis ne pourroient mieux reconnoitre les egards que l'on a eu pour leur délégué, qu'en assurant l'acquittement de cette dette: mais que je m'egare ou non, je vous demande votre protection en faveur des Sieurs French pour l'epoque a laquelle leur debiteur cessera d'etre sous la protection du droit des gens. Dans ce moment ci je vous supplie Monsieur le Comte, de vous tenir en garde contre des sollicitations que peuvent facilement se procurer des Negotiants qui achettent beaucoup de vin dans un pays ou les personnages les plus Considérables n'ont d'autre fortune que cette espèce de denrée, qui met tous les Etats presque a la merci du Commerce" (Dudon to Montmorin, 30 June 1787; same). The *Procureur du Roi* was not only steadfast in support of the public principles that he had originally argued so zealously, but he also pointedly described the means by which those who opposed his position were able to bring influence to bear on the minister. The chief difficulty with his new evidence was that the "originals" of the Treaty with Morocco had been sent to America some months earlier and TJ himself had already told Barclay: "If you should find it more eligible to proceed from Bourdeaux to Congress directly, I know of nothing *relative to your office* which need prevent it" (TJ to Barclay, 19 June 1787; italics supplied).

Dudon may have realized that his appeal was too late. The matter was to be taken up by the Parliament of Bordeaux on Monday, 2 July, and Barclay was almost certain to undergo another arrest, with the danger of years of imprisonment. What Dudon did in the face of this threat was to send a secret messenger to Barclay, warn him of his danger, and thus give Bondfield time to engage the boat that spirited the "cruelly agitated" Barclay and his partner Loreilhe away from Bordeaux on Sunday night (Bondfield to TJ, 3 July 1787). Two days later Dudon wrote Montmorin that French & Nephew had requested of the parliament that Barclay be arrested again and that "votre facon de penser sur l'etendue et le terme des privileges attaches a la mission dont cet Etranger Etoit chargé" would determine the outcome. Dudon had reason to voice this opinion; on the same day he declared before the parliament: "Vu la requête, ensemble les pieces. Vu aussi la Lettre écrite, par Monsieur le Comte de Montmorin, aux Suppliants, le 19 Juin dernier; et autre Lettre, à nous adressée par le même Ministre, portant que ledit Barklay n'est plus revêtu d'aucun caractere public.—Requérons; attendu ce qui resulte desdites Lettres, que la Commission dud. Sr. Barklay a pris fin, faisant droit de l'opposition que nous déclarons formée envers l'Arrêt de la Cour, dud. jour 19 Mai der., remettre les Parties au même et semblable état qu'elles étoient auparavant; en conséquence, être permis aux Supplians de faire de nouveau arrêter ledit Barklay, en vertu des condamnations, portant contre lui contrainte par corps; moyennant ce, être déclaré n'y avoir lieu de prononcer sur l'opposition formée, par les Supplians, envers l'Arrêt de la Cour du 19 Mai dernier, ni sur les autres conclusions de la présente Requête." Accordingly, on 4 July 1787, the Arrêt of 19 May was revoked and a new one, calling for Barclay's arrest and declaring that he was no longer clothed with a public character, was issued. French & Nephew, expressing their great gratitude to Montmorin for his part in this new turn in the affair, nevertheless had reason to complain: "mais notre debiteur en a été averti à tems et il a disparu." Protesting against their great loss, they declared: "C'est donc à vous, Monseigneur, que nous en devons toute la reconnaissance et nous Solicitons de Votre grandeur de Nouveau de representer notre Situation on ne peut plus malheureuse auprès du Congrès ou auprès de Mr. Jefferson leur representant à Paris et de les obliger a nous Cautionner du Moins en France afin d'Eviter des poursuites Ulterieures de notre part Contre le Sieur Barclay à Paris. Il est d'ailleurs de toute Justice puisque notre debiteur a eté Enlargi des prisons par Egard au Congrès." Montmorin, who had not replied to Lamoignon's appeal of 15 June in behalf of French & Nephew and who evidently did not reply to Dudon's letter of 3 July, closed the matter by informing Lamoignon that the creditors were armed with new powers, but that he had been informed Barclay had departed for America (Dudon to Montmorin, 3 July 1787; French & Nephew to Montmorin, 21 July 1787; Montmorin to Lamoignon, 6 Aug. 1787; all in Arch. Aff. Etr., Paris, Corr. Pol., E.-U., XXXII; Tr. in DLC; the Arrêt of 4 July 1787 is in *Journal de Guienne*, 17 July 1787, enclosed in Bondfield to TJ, 17 July 1787, q.v.; see also TJ to Jay, 6 Aug. 1787).

Thus Barclay had escaped the very real danger of a long, harrowing, and disgraceful imprisonment; the consequent threat to Franco-American relations was avoided; Dudon had maintained his "public principles" steadfastly in the face of the minister's about-face; French & Nephew had received all of the legal weapons that would be needed against their adversary once he reentered French jurisdiction; TJ was no longer obliged to press for a safe conduct at the very moment when he was bending every effort to have the regulations favoring American commerce enforced; and Montmorin was released from the mounting pressures that had troubled him so greatly in this affair. In view of this practical denouement, it is difficult to avoid the surmise that the person in "high office" who was ultimately responsible for the secret warning sent to Barclay on Sunday, 1 July, may have been one occupying a much higher office than that of *Procureur Général du Roi* for Bordeaux. Such a surmise may be unfounded, and may even be unjust, but so effective a solution to the problem posed by a small incident that had potential influence on much larger issues would not very likely have escaped the notice of so skilled and so cordially disposed a diplomat as Montmorin.

To Barrois

a Paris ce 22me. Juin 1787.

Au moment, Monsieur, où vous avez reçu la planche, vous avez eté averti qu'elle ne pouvoit pas rester chez vous que le tems necessaire pour tirer le nombre de cartes que vous croyiez vous etre necessaire. Ce pourroit être l'affaire d'une semaine ou de deux semaines. Vous l'avez gardé plus de deux mois, je vous ai fait avertir moimeme le 11me. du courant que je me croyois obligé de l'envoyer à Londres par la Diligence qui devoit partir le 16me. et en la demandant aujourdhui 22me. vous me repondez que vous allez avoir soin que votre Imprimeur ne la quitte pas. Mettez vous, Monsieur, à la place du libraire de Londres, qui aprés avoir fini l'impression de son edition en 3. semaines, l'a gardé dejà deux mois sans pouvoir la mettre en vente, manque de la planche, et jugez s'il doit etre laissé plus long temps en sacrifice à des delais où il a nul part. C'est de toute necessité donc Monsieur que vous remettiez la planche dans l'instant meme à la personne qui se presente avec cette lettre à fin que je l'envoye à Londres par la Diligence de demain. J'ai l'honneur d'etre Monsieur votre tres humble et trés obeissant serviteur, TH: JEFFERSON

PrC (MHi). JE VOUS AI FAIT AVERTIR MOIMEME LE 11 ME.: This was probably done by letter, but no such communication has been found (see TJ to Morellet, 2 July 1787).

From John and Lucy Ludwell Paradise

London, 22 June 1787. They plan to leave for Virginia within a week or two; thank TJ for his valuable help and offer to perform any services for him there. Their eldest daughter was married on 4 Apr. to "His Excellency Count Antonio Barziza a Patrician of the Republick of Venice and a Gentleman with a good Character, and fortune," whose estates are at Bergamo. They have given Count and Countess Barziza a letter of introduction to TJ at Paris, and if he should ever go to Italy, "you should be sure to meet with persons that would shew you all the attention that such merit as yours deserves." The Countess' address is: "à Son Excellence Madame la Comtess Paradise Barziza à Bergamo Venise Italy." Their friend, Dr. Bancroft, has been most helpful to them, and they would appreciate any service TJ might render this "truly Good and Honest Gentelman."

RC (DLC); 4 p.; in Mrs. Paradise's hand; addressed and endorsed. Recorded in SJL as received 26 June 1787.

To R. & A. Garvey

GENTLEMEN   Paris June 24. 1787.

I have taken the liberty of desiring Messieurs Féger and Gramont of Bourdeaux to send me a parcel of wine addressed to your care. I will ask the favor of you to forward it by land, as the conveiance by water is very slow and incertain. I expect that a harpsichord will be sent me from England, addressed also to your care. This I will pray you to order up by water, as it would be ruined coming by land. I will always replace your expences on demand, either to your correspondent here, or to any person in whose favor you will be pleased to draw. I have the honor to be gentlemen your most obedient & most humble servt.,   TH: JEFFERSON

PrC (DLC).

From Abigail Adams

MY DEAR SIR   London june 26 1787

I have to congratulate you upon the safe arrival of your Little Daughter, whom I have only a few moments ago received. She is in fine Health and a Lovely little Girl I am sure from her countanance, but at present every thing is strange to her, and she was very loth to try New Friends for old. She was so much attachd to the Captain and he to her, that it was with no small regret that I

27 JUNE 1787

seperated her from him, but I dare say I shall reconcile her in a day or two. I tell her that I did not see her sister cry once. She replies that her sister was older and ought to do better, besides she had pappa with her. I shew her your picture. She says she cannot know it, how should she when she should not know you. A few hours acquaintance and we shall be quite Friends I dare say. I hope we may expect the pleasure of an other visit from you now I have so strong an inducement to tempt you. If you could bring Miss Jefferson with you, it would reconcile her little Sister to the thoughts of taking a journey. It would be proper that some person should be accustomed to her. The old Nurse whom you expected to have attended her, was sick and unable to come. She has a Girl about 15 or 16 with her, the Sister of the Servant you have with you. As I presume you have but just returnd from your late excursion, you will not put yourself to any inconvenience or Hurry in comeing or sending for her. You may rely upon every attention towards her and every care in my power. I have just endeavourd to amuse her by telling her that I would carry her to Sadlers Wells. After describing the amusement to her with an honest simplicity, I had rather says she see captain Ramsey one moment, than all the fun in the World.

I have only time before the post goes, to present my compliments to Mr. Short. Mr. Adams and Mrs. Smith desire to be rememberd to you. Captain Ramsey has brought a Number of Letters. As they may be of importance to you to receive them we have forwarded them by the post. Miss Polly sends her duty to you and Love to her Sister and says she will try to be good and not cry. So she has wiped her eyes and layd down to sleep.

Believe me dear Sir affectionately yours &c &c,

A ADAMS

RC (DLC); endorsed. Recorded in SJL as received 30 June 1787.
The GIRL ... WITH HER was Sally Hemings, who was only fourteen at the time, having been born in 1773 (Edwin M. Betts, *Thomas Jefferson's Farm Book*, 1953, p. 128).

From Abigail Adams

DEAR SIR   London june 27 1787

I had the Honour of addressing you yesterday and informing you of the safe arrival of your daughter. She was but just come when I sent of my letter by the post, and the poor little Girl was very unhappy being wholy left to strangers. This however lasted only a few Hours, and Miss is as contented to day as she was misirable yesterday. She is indeed a fine child. I have taken her out to day and purchased her a few articles which she could not well do without and I hope they will meet your approbation. The Girl who is with her is quite a child, and Captain Ramsey is of opinion will be of so little Service that he had better carry her back with him. But of this you will be a judge. She seems fond of the child and appears good naturd.

I sent by yesterdays post a Number of Letters which Captain Ramsey brought with him not knowing of any private hand, but Mr. Trumble has just calld to let me know that a Gentleman sets off for paris tomorrow morning. I have deliverd him two Letters this afternoon received, and requested him to wait that I might inform you how successfull a rival I have been to Captain Ramsey, and you will find it I imagine as difficult to seperate Miss Polly from me as I did to get her from the Captain. She stands by me while I write and asks if I write every day to her pappa? But as I have never had so interesting a subject to him to write upon [. . .] I hope he will excuse the hasty scrips for the [scanty?] intelligence they contain, and be assured Dear Sir that I am with sentiments of sincere esteem your Humble Servant,   A ADAMS

RC (DLC); endorsed; MS slightly mutilated. Recorded in SJL as received 6 July 1787.

To Martha Jefferson

MY DEAR PATSY   Thursday June 28.

Madame de Traubenheim wrote me word yesterday you were unwell. I shall come to Panthemont to-day to pay her a visit, and to bring you to dine, if well enough. Let me know by the bearer if you are well enough to come out. Make it a rule hereafter to come dressed otherwise than in your uniform. Our dear Polly was to sail certainly the 1st. of May. She must therefore be arrived in England now. Adieu, my Dear, Yours affectionately,

                                              TH: J.

MS not found; text is from a photostat in NcU; without indication of the year; addressed: "A Mademoiselle Mademoiselle Jefferson à l'Abbaye royale de Panthemont." Not recorded in SJL.

The letter from MADAME DE TRAUBENHEIM has not been found, and is not recorded in SJL.

From Thomas Barclay

Dear Sir   Bordeaux 29 June 1787

I Received with the greatest pleasure your letter of the 19th. I Cannot Express my Gratitude to you for your Declaration to the Count de Montmorin, and it is with much satisfaction to my own heart that I Can assure You, You went not an Inch too far. The Breach of faith which they alude to, was occasiond by the following Circumstance. M. Moylan of Lorient when passing through this Town to the Waters of Bareges, Expected a Vessel from America with some Tobacco, and he put into the hands of Mess: French & Nephew a letter to the Super Cargo of the Vessel, advising him to Value himself on that House, and Desiring him to pay into their hands the Amount of the Tobacco belonging to Barclay Moylan & Co. of Lorient. The ship in place of Coming to Bordeaux, went to Londonderry in Ireland, from whence some Remittances were made to me on account of the Tobacco, all of which I paid away on account of the House at Lorient, without paying any part to Mess: French & Co. Nor Did I ever know that any such letter was ever written until the 14th. of last Month, when Mess. French & Co. mentiond it to me for the First time. Nor have I Ever to this hour heard it Read, or read it my self, and the Reason why I Did Not pay them any part of that Money was because they had Drawn Bills of Exchange on Me for the whole of their Demand, which were not become due—and their Doing so Certainly shew'd they Renounced all pretentions to any Claim on the Tobacco which they Did not Even Mention to me when we settled in this Town our whole Account. They say the Destination of the ship was alterd, but I say it was Not Done by orders of any Person in Europe. No person in this Quarter of the Globe had a Right or Cou'd alter it. When M. Moylan Died I wrote to these people requesting they wou'd accept of an order on our Friends at Philadelphia to account with them for the Effects which they had shipped, and that if any loss happen'd, I wou'd make it Good to them, but they preferd making the Arrangements with my self, and assured me I shou'd have what time I pleased for the Payment if I wou'd assume it, as at first I Refused to do, for there were some Very Disputable points between Us.

When I was last at Madrid I wrote to Mess. French & Nephew that I thought it advisable to get out to America in order to Ease my self of the Embarrassments into which I had been led by M. Moylan, and their answer was that I was going to Do what Every

29 JUNE 1787

good man in My Circumstances ought to do. They complimented me on my Honor and honesty, and Concluded with a hope that I wou'd pay them the Amount of their account, before I went agreeable to my Promises. I answerd that if I staid seven years in France I saw No likely-hood of Paying any Body, for that since I left France in My Journey to Morocco I had Received No more than one thousand livres from that Country.—Unluckilly I Tore the letter which they wrote to me Not thinking it of any Consequence, but I did not wish that the young man who lived with Me shou'd see it. But they Do not know that I have it not, nor Do they Deny having written it. I arrived here the 5th. of last Month, and that Night waited upon French & Co. They pressed me to sleep at their House and received me with the greatest kindness, Even kissing me in the most Cordial manner. On Monday I Dined with them, and proposed having a Meeting to talk over our affairs. They had some Engagements which induced them to appoint sunday for that purpose, upon which I Proposed Monday the following Day, and on Friday I again Dined with them, and on My Beginning a Conversation about our Matters, two of the Partners, begged I wou'd make myself Easy, for that on Monday all matters shou'd be settled to the Mutual satisfaction of all Parties. We met on Monday Morning, when Mr. Lynch the person who waited on you here, appologised for the freedom with which he woud ask me some Questions and I Begged he woud speak freely of Every thing that Dwelt on his Mind. He made several Demands all of which I answerd with the strictest Veracity, and Informed him that I had paid to several other people Considerable sums of money without having given his House any, because I thought they Did not so much want it, and Because they had given me such assurances of their Friendship and attachment, Mr. Lynch having himself some time before told me I shou'd always find them the same. We concluded by my saying that I wou'd Reflect upon what passed, and Endeavor to satisfie them, and we parted with the Utmost Appearance of Regard, shook hands, and Mr. Lynch said he wou'd Call on me at my lodging, and appoint a Time for a second Meeting.

On the same day some letters were put [into] my hands from America, one of which Containd some Circumstances Concerning a landed property of mine in Pennsylvania, which shewd Clearly that I have an Undoubted right to the Disposal of it. I had purchased it of the state of Pennsylvania a little before I left America, but I had not got the Deed for it. In the morning I put with great joy those letters into my Pocket, and on my way to Mess: Frenches

[505]

was arrested by five Ruffians, who absolutely (and literaly) Dragged me to Prison, Drawing three large knives upon me. I mention this Circumstance Because when two of the Partners heard it they applauded the Conduct of the fellows, said Every thing was done to their satisfaction, and they paid 25 Guineas for the apprehending me. A Gentleman of this Town waited on French & Co. when I was in Prison with offers of what ever was in my power. And the answer which was given, was, that any farther applications without an absolute payment of the Money wou'd be look'd upon as an Insult.

I shall have occasion to Trouble you again on the subject and will have Done at Present. To Justify myself in Your Eyes I will next post send you a note of the Proposals which I have made to these Savages, with the Brutal answers which they Returned, answers that wou'd add Disgrace to a Shylock. I am always Dear Sir Your Ever obliged   THOS. BARCLAY

I have not had the heart to write a line to Mr. Adams on this shocking affair.

RC (DLC); endorsed. Recorded in SJL as received 4 July 1787.

From R. & A. Garvey

Rouen, 29 June 1787. Acknowledge TJ's letter of 24 June; they will forward the four cases of wine by land and the harpsichord from England by water, as soon as they arrive. They have also received from "a Mr. Js. Woodman [Woodmason] of London" a bill of lading for "a Patent copying Machine," shipped on board the *Adventure*, Captain Damon, and will advise TJ when the three items are sent off.

RC (MHi); 2 p.; endorsed. Recorded in SJL as received 30 June 1787.

From Pierre Bon

EXCELLENCE   De Lyon le 30e. Juin 1787.

Quoique je n'aye pas l'avantage d'etre connu de vous, je viens vous supplier de vouloir bien vous interesser dans l'affaire le plus juste qui parut jamais: Divers membres de la Regence du Canton de Berne en Suisse ont exercé envers moi des violences inouïes, je n'ai pu en avoir justice depuis audelà de cinq ans que je la sollicite, et ce qu'il y a d'etrange, c'est que plus j'ai de droit, plus j'ai de difficultés à le faire percer. Je demande avis aux Jurisconsultes sur trois questions, je desire d'avoir aussi celui des ameriquains; à cet effet je prends la liberté de m'addresser à vôtre Excellence. Par la voye du Carosse de cette Ville je vous ai addressé Vingt exemplaires de mon Memoire à Consulter, je prie Vôtre Excellence de les recevoir et de vouloir bien me faire avoir la Consultation des Jurisconsultes les plus distingués des Etats-Unis; Elle aura dans ma Patrie la consideration qu'elle merite. Pour ma part j'ai en singuliere estime les principes de vos bons compatriotes. Je supplie votre Excellence de croire que mon langage est sincère, ce n'est point celui de la flaterie aujourdhui si usité; le Très honnorable Docteur Franklin que votre Excellence remplace connoit mes sentimens; on les voit dans un petit Ouvrage que je fis en 1780 en faveur de la liberté ameriquaine, j'en ai joint quelques exemplaires au paquet.

Depouillé, je suis actuellement hors d'etat de payer la Consultation que j'implore autrement que par la plus vive gratitude, mais ce ne sera pas je pense un obstacle pour l'obtenir, surtout si Vôtre Excellence daigne appuyer ma Demande et la recommander comme je l'en supplie: Etant redigée dans la langue du Paÿs en Anglois, je voudrois quelle me fut expediée sous le couvert de *Mr. le Receveur Matthey à Neufchatel en Suisse.*

Je saisis cette occasion pour vous faire mes hommages et me dire, avec un profond respect, de votre Excellence Le très humble et très obeïssant Serviteur, PIERRE BON

<small>RC (DLC); endorsed. Recorded in SJL as received 3 July 1787. Bon's MEMOIRE, of which he sent twenty copies to TJ, has not been identified. There appears to be no evidence that TJ acknowledged the present letter or the publication.</small>

From Stephen Cathalan, Sr.

Marseilles, 30 June 1787. Hopes this letter will find TJ at Paris, pleased with his journey; "the Season is now too far advanced to travel, but nothing is difficult when Inspired as you are, by the desire to render the result of your observations usefull to your Country." The ship, *Minerva*, Captain Dill, arrived on 14 June with a cargo of tobacco and Carolina rice. It was with great difficulty he received 36.ᵗᵗ 5s per quintal for the tobacco, except for two small shipments from Cap François and Wilmington, N.C., of which the farmers-general had had previous notice and which brought only 36.ᵗᵗ He apprehends "that in a very short time, they will notice and pay it no more here than 35.ᵗᵗ They pay no attention to the treaty of Berny in these ports, and I don't know if they do the same in the Northern Ports." The 15 per cent tare allowed here exceeds that in some other ports, where "it is nett tare, and at L'orient 101 ℔. pr. each one." Believes that with the expiration this year of Robert Morris' contract, a new agreement for 1788 and following years should be made: (1) that the farmers-general would equalize prices, conditions of payment, and tares in all French ports—or at least at Marseilles and Sète, where "on account of Insurances, Freight &ca. this article ought to be paid here at Least 20s. more than in the northern Ports"; (2) that they would buy at fixed prices certain quantities of Virginia and other quality tobaccoes to be imported at Le Havre, Dieppe, Morlaix, Bordeaux, and Marseilles for Sète; (3) that should the importations exceed those specified for a certain port, "then they will be Free to treat at a Lower Price for the Parcels exceeding, or not buy them at all." The farmers-general would then be certain of supplies, and the merchants of their engagements; "otherwise the Farmers are at Liberty to lower from a day to another the prices because they are the only Purchasers.—Nobody but Your Excellency can make such application at Court for that affair, if you find it proper and advantageous to the trade of your Country; and beg you to tell me your Sentiments on that Point for my government." If the farmers-general treat with merchants for a specific quantity, Cathalan will undertake a share for Marseilles or Sète. He suggests that the farmers-general also make snuff and rolled tobacco at prices low enough for the large demand abroad; "that would become a new Branch of Trade, which could be extended to large Sums, and open new channels very advantageous to america and France. . . . There is no doubt that the Consumption of Tobacco would encrease, and I could treat for a quantity of Tobacco manufactured at Cette for some years, if they would engage to Sale to any other; it would be a good affair if by your Credit you could obtain it, the Best way would be to apply to the Countrolleur Genl. or Monsr. de Toulouse; your Excellency make only *ouverture* and if such thing meet not with too high difficulties, I would on your answer make a memorandum on that subject, or go to Paris if necessary." He was very surprised to read in the *Journal de Provence* of Barclay's imprisonment for debts due V. & P. French & Neveu of Bordeaux and of his release; "I am so much Surprised of it that in many occasions these Gentlemens have wrotte to me, that they and I would rest assured that with Patience we shall be paid of him." Cathalan hopes that other creditors will not be satisfied to his exclusion and, though he will take no action against Barclay, he must ensure "at least that I may receive by repartitions as much as they will receive." Since TJ was in Bordeaux at that time, Cathalan asks his view of the affair and information of Barclay's whereabouts and plans. The carpenter of the American ship *Sally*, discharged with the crew upon the sale of the vessel in Marseilles, "has turned mad. . . . It is a pity, but he became so furious that the Magistrates sended to me to put him at Bedlam," where he has been for fifteen days. His trunks were inventoried and the 15 louis and 3 crowns found therein may not cover the costs of an extended stay, which costs a foreigner 12s. a day. He is now goodill better, he takes Baths and the doctor hopes that he will be cured." Cathalan asks TJ's advice and how payment will be made "in case he was [confined] for more time than he has money."

Encloses bill of lading for the rice; has sold the 20 tierces of Carolina rice at 16.ᵗᵗ per quintal. He has seen the "analize" of TJ's *Notes on*

Virginia in the *Mercure de France*; "I cannot procure that Book here, it would be a new obligation if you would send it to me."

RC (DLC); 4 p.; signed "Stephen Cathalan Jun" for Stephen Cathalan, Sr. (see TJ to Cathalan, 21 July 1787). Enclosure (printed form, DLC): Bill of lading dated 7 May 1787 for two bags containing 386 pounds of Levant and Piedmont rice, shipped by Cathalan on board the *Louise*, Captain Adrien Thibault, consigned to Rouen for TJ.

The date of the bill of lading shows that TJ's arrangements for smuggling out of Italy a larger quantity of rough rice than the "small parcel" that he himself carried out had been promptly and successfully executed, despite his misgivings (see TJ to Jay, 4 May 1787).

To Madame de Corny

Paris June 30. 1787.

On my return to Paris, it was among my first attentions to go to the rue Chaussée d'Antin No. 17. and enquire after my friends whom I had left there. I was told they were in England. And how do you like England, madam? I know your taste for the works of art gives you a little disposition to Anglomany. Their mechanics certainly excel all others in some lines. But be just to your own nation. They have not patience, it is true, to sit rubbing a peice of steel from morning to night as a lethargic Englishman will do, full charged with porter. But does not their benevolence, their chearfulness, their amability, when compared with the growling temper and manners of the people among whom you are, compensate their want of patience? I am in hopes that when the splendor of their shops, which is all that is worth seeing in London, shall have lost the charm of novelty, you will turn a wishful eye to the good people of Paris, and find that you cannot be so happy with any others. The Bois de Boulogne invites you earnestly to come and survey it's beautiful verdure, to retire to it's umbrage from the heats of the season. I was through it to-day, as I am every day. Every tree charged me with this invitation to you. Passing by la Muette, it wished for you as a mistress. You want a country house. This is for sale, and in the Bois de Boulogne, wh[ich] I have always insisted to be most worthy of your preference. Come then and buy it.   If I had had confidence in your speedy return, I should have embarrassed you in earnest with my little daughter. But an impatience to have her with me after her separation from her friends, added to a respect for your ease, have induced me to send a servant for her.

I tell you no news, because you have correspondents infinitely more au fait of the details of Paris than I am. And I offer you no services, because I hope you will come as soon as the letter could which should command them. Be assured however that no body is more disposed to render them, nor entertains for you a more sincere and respectful attachment than him who, after charging you with his compliments to Monsieur de Corny, has the honour of offering you the homage of those sentiments of distinguished esteem & regard with which he is, dear Madam, your most obedient & most humble servant. TH: JEFFERSON

PrC (DLC).

From C. W. F. Dumas

The Hague, 30 June 1787. Encloses a letter to be sealed and forwarded to Jay; acknowledges TJ's of 14 June 1787, to which he will reply by the next post.

RC (DLC); 2 p.; in French; endorsed. FC (Dumas Letter Book, Rijksarchief, The Hague; photostats in DLC). Enclosure: Dumas to Jay, 30 June 1787, informing him that "the Netherlands are now a prey to a most horrible and monstrous coalition between a detestable oligarchy and a vile rabble, ready to destroy and pillage whatever it can lay its hands on"; that the Stadtholder has thrown off the mask and remains inactive at the head of the troops with which he invaded Utrecht; that the princess has just been arrested as she was passing the frontiers of Holland and prevented from continuing her journey to The Hague, "where she wished to arrive in haste, under pretence of '*negotiating the restoration of tranquillity according to the true interests of the nation, and under certain conditions*' (these were her expressions when she was stopped in her march by a body of armed citizens); but in reality intending to take advantage of the frightful disorders for which the mob here were already prepared. They should have made her return to Guelderland; but a degree of respect (perhaps extravagant) for her sex and birth caused them to allow her to remain at Schoonhoven . . . until the resolution of the States of Holland had been taken on a letter which she wrote to them about her said pretended negotiation, although she has no right nor title to meddle with affairs of state at all"; and that Dumas' distress is extreme, for which reason he urges that the United States bankers at Amsterdam pay him both his arrears and his salary as it becomes due, this being "the most rational and least expensive way" (*Dipl. Corr., 1783-89*, III, 581-2; FC in Dumas Letter Book, Rijksarchief, The Hague, photostats in DLC, varying in phraseology and having some names and phrases heavily obliterated).

From Feger, Gramont & Cie.

Bordeaux Le 30 Juin 1787

Nous avons Reçu, Monsieur, la Lettre que vous nous aves fait L'honneur de nous Ecrire Le 19 Courant. Celle qu'elle renfermoit Pour Mr. Barclay luy fut apportee dans L'instant Par Mr. Bonfield qui se Trouva avec nous au moment ou nous venions de decacheter la Vôtre et qui voulut bien se charger de la Luy remettre afin

[510]

30 JUNE 1787

d'Eviter un Plus Long Retardement. Nous ne douttons point qu'il ne vous En ait deja accusé La reception.

Nous avons prié Mr. Grand de vous Prevenir que nous allions Retirer d'un navire arrivé de la nouvelle angleterre une Caisse de Graines de Jardin qu'on nous avoit dit Etre à votre adresse et de vous demander vos ordres pour vous La faire parvenir. Veuilles nous faire Connoitre vos Intentions à Cet Egard. Vous nous Trouveres toujours prets à Saizir les occasions à vous donner des preuves de notre Devouement. Nous Prennons, Monsieur, la Liberte de renfermer inclus un Pacquet qui vient de nous Etre adresse de Philadelphie Pour Mr. Nathaniel Barret Esqr. que nous supposons Etre Connu de vous. Nous prennons ce party attendu qu'on nous dit que ce Pacquet Contient des Papiers de Consequence et qu'il Courroit beaucoup de Risque d'Etre Egaré, si ce Mr. Barret n'est pas Generallement Connu, n'y ayant Rien sur l'adresse qui indique sa demeure.

Vous Connoisses, Monsieur, touts nos Regrets de n'avoir Pas pu vous Posseder plus Long temps icy. Mettes nous à meme de Vous Prouver notre Devouement et Le Respect avec Lequel nous avons L'honneur d'Etre, Monsieur, Vos tres humbles et tres obeissants Serviteurs, FEGER GRAMONT & CIE.

RC (MHi); endorsed. Recorded in SJL as received 4 July 1787. Enclosure not identified.

From William Stephens Smith

DEAR SIR Madrid June 30th. 1787.

I must most pointedly express my obligation for the Letter of introduction which you forwarded for me to Mr. Carmichael. He has done every thing in his power to make my time pass agreable here. It is with pleasure I observe him perfectly well received in the first Circles of the Court, and think him fully accomplished for a political career. I have been detained here much longer than I expected in consequence of the indisposition of my servant, but he is now recovered and I shall proceed on Tuesday next for Lisbon. After complying with the wishes of Congress at that Court I shall return with all possible expedition to London. For reasons too obvious to need a particular detail, I think it more than probable I shall have the honor of paying my respects to you at Paris on my way, as hinted in my last letter from Bourdeaux. I have once more to thank you for a Lesson. It was contained in your

[511]

30 JUNE 1787

letter from that place. You wrote as if you had not noticed the disagreable parts of my Letter. I should learn a great deal of prudence if it was possible for me to be near you for any length of time.—Mr. Carmichael will inform you that our unfortunate Countrymen were well at Algiers on the 12th. inst. tho' the pest rages there to a great degree, it has already carryed off near 20,000 in and about the Capital. The algerines have taken 2 (certain) some say 4. Spanish vessels, condemned and sold them and sent their Crews into Slavery. The ostensible reason for this is, that they had not the proper passes. It produces no small sensation here, and its consequences are expected to be serious unless ample satisfaction is made. The Neapolitan and Portuguese Ministers are retired from Algiers without concluding a peace, and matters seem to be again getting afloat for more blows and further negotiation, but a few weeks will fully decide this point. You have such regular information and so good from Mr. Carmichael that it is superfluous for me to say any thing about the Death of Galvez the late Minister of the Indies, or the expected changes which are looked for in the administration of the affairs of that Country So. A[merica]. A packet has arrived at Corunna from New York with dispatches to Government as late as the 18th. of May. The Commercial convention were to meet on the 21st. and Congress have once more in contemplation to return to Philadelphia. Colo. Franks had arrived and the Letters which you sent me to Bath the last autumn were safely deliverd by the Gentleman to whom I entrusted them. You express a wish in your last to Mr. Carmichael that you had met me at Bourdeaux &c &c. I should have waited your arrival if my situation there had not been rendered painful by the Circumstance that took place on the day of *my* arrival. Mr. Short will in a few words inform you of my ostensible object at the court of Lisbon and Mr. Jay say's 562. 163. 449. 350. 92. 213. 479. 609. 57. 189. 547. 407. 407. 642. 186. 48. 449. 186. 72. 290. 136. 92. 368. 38. 582. 518. 48. 186. 149. 327. 48. 186. 92. 547. 324. 290. 82. 518. 72. 393. 525. 371. 407. 82. 570. 189. 339. 380. With my best respects to Mr. Short and the Marquis I am Dr. Sir Your obliged Humble Servt.   W. S. SMITH

RC (DLC); endorsed; partly in code. Recorded in SJL as received 14 July 1787.

The code that Smith employed here was one used by Adams and Jay to which TJ did not have access. On 31 Aug. 1787 TJ wrote Smith: "I have four cyphers, two of which it was possible you might have copies of, and two impossible. I tried both the possible and impossible; but none would explain it." To this Smith replied on 18 Sep. 1787: "The Cypher which put you to so much trouble I copied from Mr. Jay's Letter to Mr. Adams which I had with me and was intended to convey this

[512]

Idea—that Congress expected that the polite manner in which they appear to have intended forwarding their Letter of thanks to her most faithful majesty might produce agreable effects relative to the conclusion of the pending treaty." The letter from Jay to Adams is that of 6 Feb. 1787, but the passage in code was not taken from that letter, but from its enclosure, which was a copy of Jay's report to Congress of 25 Jan. 1787 on Adams' letter of 27 June 1786 expressing the thanks of Congress for the action of the Queen of Portugal in ordering her squadron in the straits to protect vessels of the United States equally with those of Portugal. In the following passage of this report the sentence in italics (supplied) represents the passage encoded by Smith: "As this communication was made by the [Portuguese] Envoy in London to Mr. Adams, your secretary thinks this letter should be transmitted to him; and that the compliment would be more delicate if his Secretary was commissioned to carry and deliver it. *Perhaps, too, so striking a proof of respect might, among other consequences, promote the conclusion of the treaty*" (*Dipl. Corr., 1783-89*, II, 680-1, where both Jay's letter to Adams of 6 Feb. 1787 and its enclosure are printed). Adams instructed Smith to proceed by way of Paris and Madrid, to pay his "respects to the Ministers of the United States residing at those Courts, and to the Ministers of Foreign Affairs of those sovereigns; and endeavor to collect intelligence of any kind, commercial and political, in which the United States may be interested"; to gather information concerning the Barbary powers and the relations of Portugal and other states to them; to inform himself "particularly of the state of the commerce between the United States and Portugal, and by what means it might be extended, improved, and increased, to the mutual advantage of both nations"; and to inquire "whether the treaty which was signed last May between the American Ministers and the Chevalier del Pinto has been agreed to by his Court, and, if not, what are the objections, and whether there is a prospect of a renewal of the negotiation" (Adams to Smith, 11 Apr. 1787; same, III, 79-81). TJ understood very well that the OSTENSIBLE OBJECT AT THE COURT OF LISBON was not the real or sole purpose of Smith's mission, but neither Adams nor Jay had kept him informed of the other objects in view and the present letter from Smith was evidently the first inkling he had of their nature. For Smith's full report to Jay (which Adams caused him to make directly to the secretary for foreign affairs) see same, II, 69-84. The gist of his report on the status of the proposed treaty with Portugal was that a counter-projet would be drawn up and sent to Adams, but that "a Minister on the spot would save a great deal of trouble; and on this subject . . . her Majesty was not much pleased that she had not been noticed by Congress in the same way that her friends and neighboring nations had been" (same, II, 76).

From Vernes

MONSIEUR

Paris samedi 30 Juin 1787. hôtel de la compagnie des Indes rüe de Grammont

J'ai l'honneur d'envoyer à Vôtre Excellence un précis fort éxact de ce qui s'est passé sur les tabacs. Si vous voulez bien accorder un rendez vous à M. Berard et à moi pour demain matin, nous pourrons vous donner les éclaircissements que, d'après la lecture de ce précis, vous pourrez croire nécessaires rélativement à la démarche que vous allez faire. M. Berard désirant aller à Versailles, s'il étoit indifférent à Vôtre Excellence de nous assigner ce rendez vous un peu de bonne heure, à huit heures par exemple, nous vous en aurions beaucoup d'obligations.

1 JULY 1787

Il est vrai que souvent les Navires pour la côte d'or et la côte d'Angole relachent à Lisbonne pour y prendre du tabac de Brésil dont la qualité est preferée par les noirs. Cependant cette qualité n'est pas exclusive. Quelques Navires relachent à Guernesey pour y prendre du tabac d'Amérique. C'est un bon article d'assortiment, mais qui ne va pas à 50 Boucauds par Navire.

L'on n'obtiendroit pas l'entrepôt pour cet objet dans les ports qui ne sont pas francs. Mais, comme cet entrepôt èxiste déjà dans les ports francs, il me semble plus simple de demander et plus aisé à obtenir, qu'il soit permis aux Negriers françois de prendre dans les ports francs les tabacs dont ils auront besoin pour leur traite.

Je suis avec respect Monsieur Vôtre très humble & très obeissant serviteur,

VERNES

RC (DLC); endorsed by TJ: "Vernet" [sic]. Recorded in SJL as received 30 June 1787.

The enclosed PRECIS FORT EXACT DE CE QUI S'EST PASSE SUR LES TABACS may have been an early draft of Bérard's Observations on the tobacco trade between the United States and France, printed under 3 Sep. 1787, q.v. for a note on Bérard's letter to the farmers-general of 14 July 1787 and other documents involved in the efforts being made by TJ, Lafayette, Bérard, and their coadjutors in the summer of 1787 to force compliance with the regulations adopted at Berni in May 1786 (see Bérard to TJ, 6 May 1786, note). Vernes may also have enclosed the "Résultat du Commerce des Etats unis de L'Amerique avec le Port de L'Orient depuis le 1er. Mai 1786, jusquau 1er. Juillet 1787" (DLC: TJ Papers, 30: 5174; in a clerk's hand, endorsed by TJ: "Berard"). This summary showed that for the department of L'Orient during 14 months, 89 American vessels had entered (all save one, which entered the port of Brest, had entered at L'Orient); the aggregate value of their cargoes of tobacco was 4,372,241.℔ Their exportations were valued at 1,386,763,℔ of which 792,424℔ were accounted for in French manufactures and the remainder in products of French trade with the Orient, foreign manufactures, &c. Deducting the value of these exports, together with "la dépense occasionnée par le sejour des Bâtiments américains et les Pacotilles des Equipages," &c., from the value of their imports of tobacco, there remained an estimated "Balance au désavantage de la france" of 2,021,478.℔ "Mais," the estimate concluded, "ce résultat prouve que le contrat avec M. Moris qui se paye en Lettres de change est encore bien plus désavantageux, puisque la moitié de l'importation faite dans un seul Port et par le Commerce particulier a été payé par des Denrées et objets de notre industrie, ou par une réexportation à l'étranger toujours utile à L'industrie de la nation." (Cf. TJ's argument in his letter to Vergennes, 15 Aug. 1785 and also in that to Montmorin, 23 July 1787.)

To Abigail Adams

Paris July 1. 1787.

A thousand thanks to you, my dear Madam, for your kind attention to my little daughter. Her distresses I am sure must have been troublesome to you: but I know your goodness will forgive her, and forgive me too for having brought them on you. Petit now comes for her. By this time she will have learned again to love the hand that feeds and comforts her, and have formed an attachment to you. She will think I am made only to tear her from all her affections. I wish I could have come myself. The pleasure of a visit to yourself and Mr. Adams would have been a great additional inducement. But, just returned from my journey, I have the arrearages of 3. or 4. months all crouded on me at once. I do not presume to write you news from America, because you have it so much fresher and frequenter than I have. I hope all the disturbances of your country are quieted and with little bloodshed. What think you of present appearances in Europe? The Emperor and his subjects? The Dutch and their half king, who would be a whole one? in fine the French and the English? These new friends and allies have hardly had time to sign that treaty which was to cement their love and union like man and wife, before they are shewing their teeth at each other. We are told a fleet of 6. or 12. ships is arming on your side the channel; here they talk of 12 or 20, and a camp of 15,000 men. But I do not think either party in earnest. Both are more laudably intent on arranging their affairs.—Should you have incurred any little expences on account of my daughter or her maid, Petit will be in a condition to repay them. If considerable, he will probably be obliged to refer you to me, and I shall make it my duty to send you a bill immediately for the money. Count Sarsfeild sets out for London four days hence. At dinner the other day at M. de Malesherbe's he was sadly abusing an English dish called Gooseberry tart. I asked him if he had ever tasted the cranberry. He said, no. So I invited him to go and eat cranberries with you. He said that on his arrival in London he would send to you and demander á diner. I hope Mrs. Smith and the little grandson are well. Be so good as to present me respectfully to her. I have desired Colo. Smith to take a bed here on his return. I will take good care of him for her, and keep him out of all harm. I have the honour to be with sentiments of sincere esteem & respect Dear Madam your most obedient & most humble servt.,

TH: JEFFERSON

RC (MHi: AMT). PrC (DLC).

To John Adams

DEAR SIR   Paris July 1. 1787.

I returned about three weeks ago from a very useless voiage. Useless, I mean, as to the object which first suggested it, that of

1 JULY 1787

trying the effect of the mineral waters of Aix en Provence on my hand. I tried these because recommended among six or eight others as equally beneficial, and because they would place me at the beginning of a tour to the seaports of Marseilles, Bourdeaux, Nantes and Lorient which I had long meditated, in hopes that a knowlege of the places and persons concerned in our commerce and the information to be got from them might enable me sometimes to be useful. I had expected to satisfy myself at Marseilles of the causes of the difference of quality between the rice of Carolina and that of Piedmont which is brought in quantities to Marseilles. Not being able to do it, I made an excursion of three weeks into the rice country beyond the Alps, going through it from Vercelli to Pavia about 60 miles. I found the difference to be, not in the management as had been supposed both here and in Carolina, but in the species of rice, and I hope to enable them in Carolina to begin the Cultivation of the Piedmont rice and carry it on hand in hand with their own that they may supply both qualities, which is absolutely necessary at this market. I had before endeavored to lead the depot of rice from Cowes to Honfleur and hope to get it received there on such terms as may draw that branch of commerce from England to this country. It is an object of 250,000 guineas a year. While passing thro' the towns of Turin, Milan and Genoa, I satisfied myself of the practicability of introducing our whale oil for their consumption and I suppose it would be equally so in the other great cities of that country. I was sorry that I was not authorized to set the matter on foot. The merchants with whom I chose to ask conferences, met me freely, and communicated fully, knowing I was in a public character. I could however only prepare a disposition to meet our oil merchants. On the article of tobacco I was more in possession of my ground, and put matters into a train for inducing their government to draw their tobaccos directly from the U.S. and not as heretofore from G.B. I am now occupied with the new ministry here to put the concluding hand to the new regulations for our commerce with this country, announced in the letter of M. de Calonnes which I sent you last fall. I am in hopes in addition to those, to obtain a suppression of the duties on Tar, pitch, and turpentine, and an extension of the privileges of American *whale* oil, to their *fish* oils in general. I find that the quantity of Codfish oil brought to Lorient is considerable. This being got off hand (which will be in a few days) the chicaneries and vexations of the farmers on the article of tobacco, and their elusions of the order of Bernis, call for the next attention. I have reason to hope good dispositions in the new ministry towards our commerce with this country. Besides endeavoring on all occasions to multiply the points of contact and connection with this country, which I consider as our surest main-stay under every event, I have had it much at heart to remove from between us every subject of misunderstanding or irritation. Our debts to the king, to the officers, and the farmers are of this description. The having complied with no part of our engagements in these draws on us a great deal of censure, and occasioned a language in the Assemblées des notables very likely to produce dissatisfaction between us. Dumas being on the spot in Holland, I had asked of him some time ago, in confidence, his opinion on the practicability of transferring these debts from France to Holland, and communicated his answer to Congress, pressing them to get you to go over to Holland and try to effect this business. Your knowlege of the ground and former successes occasioned me to take this liberty without consulting you, because I was sure you would not weigh your personal trouble against public good. I have had no answer from Congress, but hearing of your journey to Holland have hoped that some money operation had led you there. If it related to the debts of this country I would ask a communication of what you think yourself at liberty to communicate, as it might change the form of my answers to the eternal applications I receive. The debt to the officers of France carries an interest of about 2000 guineas, so we may suppose it's principal is between 30. and 40,000. This makes more noise against [us] than all our other debts put together.

I send you the arrets which begin the reformation here, and some other publications respecting America: together with copies of letters received from Obryon and Lambe. It is believed that a naval armament has been ordered at Brest in correspondence with that of England. We know certainly that orders are given to form a camp in the neighborhood of Brabant, and that Count Rochambeau has the command of it. It's amount I cannot assert. Report says 15,000 men. This will derange the plans of oeconomy. I take the liberty of putting under your cover a letter for Mrs. Kinloch of South Carolina, with a packet, and will trouble you to enquire for her and have them delivered. The packet is of great consequence, and therefore referred to her care, as she will know the safe opportunities of conveying it. Should you not be able to find her, and can forward the packet to it's address by any very safe conveiance I will beg you to do it. I have the honour to be with sentiments of the most perfect friendship & esteem Dear Sir your most obedient & most humble servant, TH: JEFFERSON

RC (MHi: AMT). PrC (DLC). Enclosures: (1) All of the "arrets which begin the reformation here" have not been certainly identified, but they must have included copies of the regulations for the formation of the royal council on finances and commerce and for the administration of these matters; and the edict authorizing the creation of provincial and municipal parliaments (*Recueil général des anciennes lois françaises*, XXVIII, 354-74). (2) O'Bryen to TJ, 28 Apr. 1787. (3) Lamb to TJ, 20 May 1787. (4) TJ to Anne Cleland Kinloch, 1 July 1787, with its enclosure.

To Matthew Boulton

[SIR] Paris July 1. 1787.

I had the honour of putting into your hands, when at Pa[ris a list] of some plated ware, of which I wished to know the cost before I should d[ecide] on the purchase. You were so good as to charge yourself with giving me that information on your arrival in London. Supposing that either you may have mislaid my note, or that your answer may have miscarried I take the liberty of troubling you again with the list and of asking information on the subject. We were in hopes before this to have seen you again in Paris, commencing establishments of your works in this country. I have the honour to be Sir your most obedt. & most humble servt.,
TH: JEFFERSON

2. Soup terreens middlesized, say 11. inches long.
2. dishes for the terreens to stand in.
10. dishes, round, of 10½ I. diameter.
2. dishes, oval, 16 I. long, 10½ I. wide.
4. dishes, oval, 12 I. long, 9 I. wide.
   plated in the best manner, with a plain bead.

P.S. My servant is the bearer of this, and leaves London Monday morning the 9th. inst.

PrC (DLC); MS slightly torn.

To Richard Claiborne

SIR Paris July 1. 1787.

Just returned from a journey of 3. or 4. months I have been immersed in such a mass of writing that it has been impossible for me sooner to acknolege your favors of June 9. 13. and 21. With

[518]

respect to the quality of lands in general in the counties of Monongalia and Harrison, it is impossible for me to give any opinion, because I never was in that part of the country at all, nor nearer it than Winchester. I of course am as little able to say any thing of the prices. I have often heard of lands on the great Kanhaway and Ohio selling for 20/ the acre. If yours therefore are good I should suppose they must be cheap enough at the price of 5/ mentioned in your letter. The plate for my map comes by this conveyance to Mr. Stockdale. It goes no further Westward than the mouth of the Kanhaway, nor does it contain any thing Eastward of that but what was to be found in Scull's, Hutchins's, and Fry & Jefferson's maps.

With respect to Colo. Blackden my information will be very imperfect, having been absent from this place the 3 months and a half preceding his departure. I know only that he conveyed to a Monsieur de Lormerie a large tract of land: I was witness to the deed; but do not remember the quantity precisely. I have heard that he received five hundred guineas of the money, but I do not know this myself, nor how much remains yet to be received, nor yet any thing of his conduct in your affairs. The persons most likely to give you a good account would be a Mr. Appleton, or a Mr. Barrett, if you know either of them. On writing to them yourself they will be much more likely to give a satisfactory account to you than to me. The being in a public character renders gentlemen uncommunicative and reserved in cases of this kind. If I can be otherwise useful to you I shall be so with real pleasure, being with much esteem & respect Sir your most obedient & most humble servt.,
TH: JEFFERSON

PrC (CSmH); endorsed.

To Maria Cosway

Paris July 1. 1787.

You conclude, Madam, from my long silence that I am gone to the other world. Nothing else would have prevented my writing to you so long. I have not thought of you the less. But I took a peep only into Elysium. I entered it at one door, and came out at another, having seen, as I past, only Turin, Milan, and Genoa. I calculated the hours it would have taken to carry me on to Rome. But they were exactly so many more than I had to spare. Was not this provoking? In thirty hours from Milan I could have been at the espousals of the Doge and Adriatic. But I am born to lose every thing I love. Why were you not with me? So many enchanting scenes which only wanted your pencil to consecrate them to fame. Whenever you go to Italy you must pass at the Col de Tende. You may go in your chariot in full trot from Nice to Turin, as if there were no mountain. But have your pallet and pencil ready: for you will be sure to stop in the passage, at the chateau de Saorgio. Imagine to yourself, madam, a castle and village hanging to a cloud in front. On one hand a mountain cloven through to let pass a gurgling stream; on the other a river, over which is thrown a magnificent bridge; the whole formed into a bason, it's sides shagged with rocks, olive trees, vines, herds, &c. I insist on your painting it.

How do you do? How have you done? and when are you coming here? If not at all, what did you ever come for? Only to make people miserable at losing you. Consider that you are but 4. days from Paris. If you come by the way of St. Omers, which is but two posts further, you will see a new and beautiful country. Come then, my dear Madam, and we will breakfast every day á l'Angloise, hie away to the Desert, dine under the bowers of Marly, and forget that we are ever to part again. I received, in the moment of my departure your favor of Feb. 15. and long to receive another: but lengthy, warm, and flowing from the heart, as do the sentiments of friendship & esteem with which I have the honor to be, dear Madam, your affectionate friend & servant,

TH: JEFFERSON

PrC (ViU); endorsed.

To Anne Cleland Kinloch

DEAR MADAM   Paris July 1. 1787.

Having no acquaintance from South Carolina in London since the departure of Mr. Blake, which I suppose to have taken place, I take the liberty of sending to your care a small parcel of Piedmont rice, addressed to Mr. Drayton chairman of the committee of the South Carolina society for promoting and improving agriculture. It is of a different quality from that of South Carolina: better for some purposes, but not so good for others. It is however rather more in demand and sells somewhat higher. Thinking it desireable for the state to furnish the market with both qualities, I have taken measures to obtain a considerable quantity. These however may fail, as it's exportation rough, from Piedmont, is prohibited. I am therefore anxious that the little I brought away may pass safely to South Carolina. It will serve to possess them of the seed.

Being in England the last year, I took a tour Northwardly as far as Birmingham, and returned by the way of Worcester. On my getting back to London I was much mortified to hear that I had passed you in that town without knowing it. Certainly it would have been a great gratification to me to have presented my respects personally to yourself and Mrs. Huger. Mr. McQueen by whom I was honoured with a letter from you, flattered us for a while with the hope of your visiting Paris. But we suspected afterwards that he threw cold water on the proposition. Should you not have abandoned the thought altogether, I should charge myself with your commands very chearfully to provide apartments for you either in Paris or it's neighborhood, exactly such as you should be pleased to describe. The post would offer opportunities of proposing to you beforehand the several situations offered, that you might take your choice among them. A residence in town or country in France, is I fancy as oeconomical as an equal one in town or country in England. If Mrs. Huger's son is with her, it might be an additional inducement to place him in a situation where he might learn to speak the language of the country. This becomes daily more and more necessary for us, and at his age is not more than the work of six months. I pray you to command my services freely, to present me respectfully to your daughter Mrs. Huger, and to accept yourself assurances of the esteem & respect with which I have the honor to be Madam your most obedient and most humble servant, TH: JEFFERSON

RC (MHi: AMT). PrC (MHi). The presence of the RC in the Adams papers indicates that, as TJ had supposed might be the case, Adams was unable to find Mrs. Kinloch; however, the "small parcel" of Lombardy rice, addressed by TJ and enclosed in a teacanister, was forwarded to South Carolina safely (see TJ to Adams, 1 July 1787; Adams to TJ, 10 July 1787; and Drayton to TJ, 25 Nov. 1787). This "small parcel" was the one that TJ personally brought out of Italy; the measures taken to procure "a considerable quantity" were similarly successful (see Cathalan to TJ, 30 June 1787; TJ to Cathalan, 21 July 1787).

To John Stockdale, with Orders for Books

SIR Paris July 1. 1787.

Finding on my return to this place that the bookseller to whom I had committed the plate of my map, instead of keeping it only

1 JULY 1787

a fortnight, had not yet delivered it to be forwarded to you, I demanded an instantaneous delivery of it. A thousand evasions have led me through three weeks, so that it was not till yesterday that I could obtain it, threatening on the return of my messenger without it, that I would apply to the police. He thereon sent it, having yet 350. less than his number struck off. I now forward it to you in the care of a servant whom I send to London on other business, and I will pray you, as soon as you can possibly have your number struck off, to give me notice that I may take measures either for striking off in London the number still wanted here or for having the plate brought back, which will probably be the measure. I must get you to send me the books herein named. Besides this I wish to receive from Lackington, Chiswell street, those stated on the next leaf, as far as they remain unsold. As my friend Colo. Smith is absent from London and Lackington gives no credit, will you be so good as to procure from him the books, send them with the others, and pay him for them, for which I will duly account with you. My servant comes back in the Diligence which leaves London on Monday the 9th. inst. and will take care of them if you can have them all packed and delivered to him in time. If Lackington has the whole of those books still on hand, which is not probable, they will be under 5£. I am with much esteem Sir your very humble servt., TH: JEFFERSON

The Reviews[1]
Remarks on Chastellux travels. 1787. G. and T. Wilkie.
Ludlam's introduction and notes on Bird's method of dividing astronomical instruments.[2] Sewel, 1786.
Evelyn's terra by Hunter.[3] Dodsley 1787. 5/
Retrospect of the portraits in the Short review. Stockdale.[4]
Adair's[5] Sketch of the natural history of the human body and mind.[6] Dilly.
Adair's medical cautions for the consideration of invalids.
Trusler's London adviser and guide.[7] Baldwin.
Tarleton's history of the campaigns in 1780 and 1781.[8]
Abercrombie's gardener's pocket dict. 3. v. 8vo.[9] Davis.
Kirwan's estimate of the temperature of different climates.[10] Elmesley.
Sylva. or the wood. 8vo. 5/. Payne & son.
Bell's Shakespeare. I have the first 32. Nos. Send me what is since published.

1 JULY 1787

Hargrave's Coke Littleton. I have as far as page 330. Send me what has since come out.

If you can procure for me a copy of all Tacitus's works in Latin, in usum Delphini and in 8vo. send them: and in that case send also from Lackington No. 1529. Tacitus's works by Gordon 5 v. 8vo. 14ƒ6. But if you cannot find the precise Latin edition above indicated, do not send the English one.[11]

P.S. I send a map coloured, as a model for the colouring.

ENCLOSURE

Second part of Lackington's catalogue for 1787.

[22]	Marshall's Chronological [&c] h.b. fair. fol. 2/
[3]47.	American traveller. 4to. 2/6
519.	Alfred's Anglo-Saxon version of Orosius. 8vo. 6/.
	If this is sold send any one of Nos. 523. 518. 522. 520.
600.	Colden's history of the 5. nations. 4/
870.	Petty's Political arithmetic 1/
1781	Creech's Lucretius. 2. v. 8vo. h. b. neat. 3/3
1789.	Evans's old ballads. 4. v. 8vo. 15/9
1980.	Moore's fables. 12mo. 1/3
2632.	Hargrave's argument in the Negro's case. 8vo. 1/
2644.	Molloy de jure maritimo. 1/
2657.	Wentworth's office of executors. 8vo. 2/6
3906.	Sterling's Ovidii tristia 1/6
3907.	Sterling's Phaedrus. 1/6 Catonis 9d.
3912.	Sterling's Florus 1/6 his Persius 6d.
3916.	Sterling's Pomey's Pantheon. 9d.
4294.	Septuagint and New testament. Greek 7/6 fol.
4323.	Justiniani historia Veneta. fair, gilt. fol. 3/
4362.	Arriani expeditio Alex. Gr. Lat. fol. neat. 8/6 Steph. 1575.
4588.	Sophoclis tragoediae. Gr. Lat. cum scholiis 8vo. 2/9
4623.	Q. Curtius Delphini. 8vo. 1/6
4632.	Horace Delphini. 1/
4794.	Ciceronis Tusculanerum disput. neat gilt. 2/ Foulis 1744.
4923.	Relation del Cardinal Bentivoglio. 12mo. 1/
6522.	Julian's works by Gibbon. 2. v. 10/6 8vo.
6532.	Lucretius. Lat & Eng. prose. 2. vol. neat. 4/6 8vo.
1529.	Tacitus's works by Gordon. 5. v. 8vo. 14/6[12]

PrC (DLC). Dft of appended list (MHi); undated. Enclosure: List from Lackington's catalogue (Dft in MHi; undated; PrC in DLC as "stated on the next leaf" is much more abbreviated and signed "Th:Jefferson Paris. July 1.1787"; variations between Dft and PrC of both lists are indicated in notes below).

[1] This title not in Dft.
[2] Dft reads: "4to. 2/."
[3] Dft reads: "4to."
[4] Dft reads: ". . . portraits delineated

in a Short Review of the Political State. 8 vo. 1/. Stockdale."

[5] Dft reads: "Philosophical and Medical."

[6] Dft reads: "8vo. 4/."

[7] Dft reads: "12mo. 3/."

[8] Dft reads: "in N.America. 26/."

[9] Dft reads: "10/6."

[10] Dft reads: "3/."

[11] Dft, instead of the preceding three paragraphs, reads only: "Shakesp. Co. Lit.Tacit."

[12] This title is not in PrC, but it is covered by the last paragraph of the appended list.

To John Bondfield

Dr. Sir   Paris July 2. 1787.

Revising the letters and notes in my possession on the subject of our commerce, I observe you say in your letter of Dec. 12. that we pay Alien duties in the ports of France, supposed the double of what we ought to pay. If by this you mean that we are not on as favourable a footing as Spain, it would be vain to remonstrate on that subject. The family compact expressly excluded all other nations from the advantages the two parties ceded to each other but if there be any other nation which enjoys greater advantages in the ports of France than we do, I should wish to know it, because, if it be not in consequence of a particular compensation, I should hope to remove it. Will you be so good as to explain this matter? And shall I ask the further favor of you to forward the inclosed letter by the first vessel going from your port to Virginia. I wish to hear from Mr. Barclay who I suppose is still with you, and whose service and comfort I have sincerely at heart. I am with much esteem & respect Dr. Sir Your most obedt. humble servt.,

Th: Jefferson

PrC (DLC). Enclosure: Evidently TJ to Francis Eppes, this date.

To Francis Eppes

Dear Sir   Paris, July 2d, 1787.

The present is merely to inform you of the safe arrival of Polly in London, in good health. I have this moment dispatched a servant for her. Mr. Ammonit did not come, but she was in the best hands possible, those of Captain Ramsay. Mrs. Adams writes me she was so much attached to him that her separation from him was a terrible operation. She has now to go through the same with Mrs. Adams. I hope that in ten days she will join those from whom she is no more to be separated. As this is to pass through post-offices, I send it merely to relieve the anxieties which Mrs. Eppes and

2 JULY 1787

yourself are so good as to feel on her account, reserving myself to answer both your favors by the next packet. I am, with very sincere esteem, dear Sir, your affectionate friend and servant,

TH. JEFFERSON

MS not found; text from Randolph, *Domestic Life*, p. 125. Recorded in SJL. This is evidently the letter that TJ enclosed in his letters of this date to Bondfield at Bordeaux and to Wilt, Delmestre & Cie. at L'Orient, a fact which perhaps explains the absence of a PrC in TJ Papers.

To William Gordon

SIR   Paris July 2. 1787.

Being just returned from a tour through the Southern parts of France and Northern of Italy, I could not till this moment acknolege the receipt of your obliging letter with the papers accompanying it. It happened unluckily also that those addressed to the Marquis de la Fayette were under my cover. I put them into his hands the moment of my return. From the opportunities you have had of coming at facts known as yet to no other historian, from your dispositions to relate them fairly, and from your known talents, I have sanguine expectations that your work will be a valuable addition to historical science: and the more so, as we have little yet on the subject of our war which merits respect. I fear however that this is not the feild from which you are to expect profit. The translation will sell here: but few read English. Be assured that nothing shall be wanting on my part to encourage a preference of the original to a translation: but it will not be till the fall that either will be called for, because during summer the readers are in the country. I got from a bookseller here about forty guineas for a first copy of Dr. Ramsay's work, which he had translated. If this would be an object with you I offer you my service. I have the honour to be with sentiments of great esteem Sir your most obedient & most humble servant,   TH: JEFFERSON

RC (James F. Drake, Inc., New York City, 1946); addressed: "Doctr. William Gordon London"; endorsed in part: "an[swere]d. Sepr. 6." PrC (DLC).

To David Hartley

DEAR SIR   Paris July 2. 1787.

I received lately your favor of April 23, on my return from a journey of 3. or 4. months, and am always happy in an occasion

2 JULY 1787

of recalling myself to your memory. The most interesting intelligence from America is that respecting the late insurrection in Massachusets. The cause of this has not been developed to me to my perfect satisfaction. The most probable is that those individuals were of the imprudent number of those who have involved themselves in debt beyond their abilities to pay, and that a vigorous effort in that government to compel the paiment of private debts and raise money for public ones, produced the resistance. I believe you may be assured that an idea or desire of returning to any thing like their antient government never entered into their heads. I am not discouraged by this. For thus I calculate. An insurrection in one of 13. states in the course of 11. years that they have subsisted amounts to one in any particular state in 143 years, say a century and a half. This would not be near as many as has happened in every other government that has ever existed: so that we still have the difference between a light and a heavy government as clear gain. I have no fear that the result of our experiment will be that men may be trusted to govern themselves without a master. Could the contrary of this be proved, I should conclude either that there is no god, or that he is a malevolent being. You have heard of the federal convention now sitting at Philadelphia for the amendment of the Confederation. Eleven states appointed certainly, it was expected that Connecticut would also appoint the moment it's assembly met. Rhode island had refused. I expect they will propose several amendments, that that relative to our commerce will probably be adopted immediately, but that the others must await to be adopted one after another in proportion as the minds of the states ripen for them. Dr. Franklin enjoys good health. I shall always be happy to hear from you, being with sentiments of very sincere esteem & respect Dr. Sir Your most obedient & most humble servt.,

TH: JEFFERSON

P.S. I forgot to observe that to have American intelligence regularly, you had better have a newspaper from New-York, and two from Philadelphia, that is to say, one of each party. Dr. Franklin could indicate the best, and they would come regularly once a month by your packets.

RC (CtY); endorsed. PrC (DLC).

To Thomas Brand Hollis

SIR   Paris July 2. 1787.

On my return from a tour through the Southern parts of France and Northern of Italy, I found here the present of books you had been so kind as to send me. I should value them highly for their intrinsic merit, but much more as coming from you. You will have seen that at length one of our republics has experienced those commotions which the newspapers have been always ascribing to all of them. I am not satisfied what has been the cause of this, but the most probable account is that these individuals were of those who have so imprudently involved themselves in debt, and that a vigorous exertion in their government to enforce the paiment of private debts and raise money for the public ones, occasioned the insurrection. One insurrection in thirteen states in the course of eleven years that they have existed, amounts to one in any individual state in 143. years, say a century and a half. This will not weigh against the inconveniencies of a government of force, such as are monarchies, and aristocracies. You see I am not discouraged by this little difficulty, nor have I any doubt that the result of our experiment will be that men are capable of governing themselves without a master. I have the honor to be with sentiments of the highest esteem & respect Sir your most obedient and most humble servt.,   TH: JEFFERSON

PrC (DLC).

To Richard Paul Jodrell

Paris July 2. 1787.

Mr. Jefferson's compliments to Mr. Joddrell and thanks him for the copy of the Persian Heroine which he was so good as to send him, and which he finds here on his return from a journey of 3. or 4. months. Not having yet had a moment to look into a book of any kind he has still to come the pleasure of reading this, which he is persuaded from it's reputation, and that of it's author, will be great.

PrC (DLC).

From Lormerie

MONSIEUR Paris 2. Juillet. 1787 rüe Basse St Denis. No 7.

Vous avés bien voulu me Promettre une Réponse sur le mémoire que j'ai Eu L'honneur de vous remettre il ÿ a plusieurs jours relativement aux *moÿens d'opérer la sureté publique dans les états unis.*

Je vous serai fort obligé, Monsieur, de vouloir bien par la même occasion me faire savoir *le nom des deux personnes* que vous m'avés dit etre partïes par le dernier paquébot pour acheter des terres en *Kentucké, à quelle compagnie* ils sont liés en Françe, et *si ç'est sur les bords de L'ohio,* ou ailleurs qu'ils veulent acquerir.

Permettés moi Encore, Monsieur, de vous demander quelle confiançe je puis avoir en un ouvrâge nouveau intitulé *De la françe et des Etats unis* par *Etienne De Clavière et J. P. Brissot de Warville. 1787.* Je ne Doute point que cet ouvrâge ne vous soit fort connu, même avant d'avoir eté imprimé.

Il me reste à vous supplier, Monsieur, de vouloir bien me dire votre sentiment avec toute la franchise qui vous est naturelle tant sur cet ouvrâge que sur le mien. Je scais que je suis un très jeune écrivain Politique et je Cherche à m'eclairer par les lumières des hommes instruits, surtout par les vôtres. Si les bonnes intentions peuvent inspirer de bonnes idées je ne suis pas sans espoir absolument et j'Espère au moins profiter de mes fautes pour mieux faire.

J'aÿ L'honneur d'Etre avec la plus Respectueuse et tres sincère considération, Monsieur, Votre très humble et très obeissant Serviteur, DE LORMERIE

P.S. Vous me ferés le plus sensible Plaisir, Monsieur, de m'instruire dans les occasions, de ce qui pouroit arriver d'intèressant pour Les ètats unis, et particulièrement pour *la Virginie* et *L'Etat de Kentucké.* Je m'intéresse bien cordialement à la Prosperité d'un Paÿs que je considère, comme L'azile de la Sagesse, des moeurs, et de la liberté, l'exemple et l'admiration des deux mondes, et *dont L'idée* (pour me servir des expressions d'un ecrivain très moderne) *ne peut être rèveillée sans exçiter un Saint Enthousiasme!*

RC (DLC); endorsed.
The MEMOIRE that Lormerie sent to TJ some days earlier has not been identified.

To James Maury

DEAR SIR Paris July 2. 1787.

The reason why the receipt of your favor of May 21. has been thus long unacknoleged was my absence on a tour round the seaport towns from which I am just returned. In the mean time the occasion of your enquiry relative to Mr. Morris's bills has passed. Nor could I now explain the reason of their protest. I understand however that they are since honoured. The effect therefore will only be to shew that there is a limit even to his credit.

Present appearances in Europe would seem to threaten war. On one side England sending a navy of observation to hover over Holland, and Prussia an army. This country sending a navy and army to hover over the other side of the same country. Yet it is morally sure that all these powers desire peace most ardently. It remains to see then whether they mean any more than to arrange a kind of constitution which shall be merely neutral and to force it on the United Netherlands as was done in the case of Geneva. I need not write you American news. You have it of later date than I have. I shall therefore only add assurances of the esteem and respect with which I am Dr. Sir Your friend & servt.,

TH: JEFFERSON

PrC (DLC).

To the Abbé Morellet

Paris July 2. 1787.

I am sorry, my dear Sir, that your interest should be affected by the ill behavior of Barrois. But when you consider the facts you will be sensible that I could not have indulged his indolence further without increasing the injury to a more punctual workman. Stockdale of London had asked leave to print my Notes. I agreed to it, and promised he should have the plate of the map as soon as it should be corrected, and the copies struck off for you and myself. He thereupon printed his edition completely in three weeks. The printer, who was to strike off 250 maps for me, kept the plate but 5. days. It was then delivered to Barrois with notice that it could not be left longer with him than should suffice to strike off his number. Repeated applications for it by Mr. Short and my servant were only answered by repeated promises, and times of delivery fixed, no one of which was performed. When I returned he had been possessed of the plate upwards of two months. I was astonished and confounded to be told that it had not been sent to Stockdale and that his edition had been lying dead on his hands three months. I sent to Barrois the very day of my return to let him know

2 JULY 1787

that justice to Stockdale did not permit me to defer sending him the plate any longer: yet I would wait 5. days, at the end of which he must deliver me the plate whether his maps were done or not. I received no answer, but waited 10. days. I then sent for the plate. The answer was he was not at home. I sent again the next day. Answer he was not at home. I sent the third day. Not at home. I then ordered the messenger to go back and wait till he should come home. This produced an answer of two lines 'qu'il alloit soigner son ouvrier.' I wrote him word in return to deliver the plate instantly. This I think was on a Saturday or Sunday. He told the messenger he would let me have it the thursday following. I took patience, and sent on the Friday, but telling the messenger if he refused to deliver it, to inform him I would be plagued no more with sending messages, but would apply to the police. He then delivered it and I sent it off immediately to London. He had kept it three months, of which three weeks was after my return. I think Sir you will be satisfied that justice to Stockdale, justice to myself who had passed my word for sending on the plate, and sensibility to the shuffling conduct of Barrois, permitted me to act no otherwise.—But no matter. Let his ill behavior make no odds between you and me. It will affect your interest, and that suffices to determine me to order back the plate as soon as Stockdale has done with it. He will not require more days than Barrois months. So that it will be here before you can want it. But it must never go into Barrois' hands again nor of any person depending on him or under his orders. The workman who struck off the 250 for me seems to have been diligent enough. Either he or any other workman you please of that description shall have it to strike what number you wish. I forgot to observe in it's proper place, that when I was in the midst of my difficulties I did myself the honor of calling on you, as well to have that of asking after your health on my return, as of asking your assistance to obtain the plate. Unluckily you were gone to Versailles, so I was obliged to proceed as well as I could. It is no excuse for Barrois to say he could not get his Imprimeur to proceed. He should have applied to another, but as to you it shall be set to rights in the manner I have before stated. Accept my regret that you were in the hands of so undeserving a workman, and one who placed me under the necessity of interrupting a work which interested you. Be assured at the same time of the sincerity of those sentiments of esteem & respect with which I have the honor to be Dear Sir your most obedient & most humble servant, TH: JEFFERSON

PrC (DLC).

TJ's letter TO BARROIS THE VERY DAY OF MY RETURN (11 June), if the message was in fact put in writing, has not been found. The chronology here given needs clarification. TJ wrote or sent to Barrois on 11 June, promising to wait until the 16th. He then SENT FOR THE PLATE on Friday, 22 June, after having WAITED 10 DAYS (see TJ to Barrois, 22 June 1787). On Saturday and Sunday, 23 and 24 June, TJ made his repeated appeals, and it was evidently on the latter date that Barrois sent his ANSWER OF TWO LINES (missing) and that TJ WROTE HIM WORD IN RETURN (also missing). TJ's communication on the FOLLOWING . . . FRIDAY was probably an oral message; if in writing, it has not been found. From this chronology it appears that the plate was received on 29 June, slightly less than THREE WEEKS after TJ's return (see TJ to Stockdale, 1 July 1787). The present letter was probably in reply to one written by Morellet stating that his edition of *Notes on Virginia* was being obstructed by the withdrawal of the plate; if so, that letter has not been found. In stating to Morellet that Barrois' printer had kept the plate UPWARDS OF TWO MONTHS, TJ either erred or else Morellet did not act promptly when Short advised him on 24 Mch. that the plate was available; for if he acted promptly on getting this notice, then Barrois' printer must have had possession of the plate for about two and a half months (see Short to TJ, 12, 14, 22 and 26 Mch. 1787).

Jefferson's Instructions to Adrien Petit

[ca. 2 July 1787]

Le moment de votre arrivée à Londres, allez chez M. Adams et donnez lui les lettres à son adresse.

Allez aussi chez Monsr. Stockdale libraire, donnez lui la lettre à son adresse et la planche et la carte, et avertissez-le du moment de votre depart de Londres. Il vous chargera des livres pour moi.

Allez aussi chez M. Beckett pour commander le bois de lit. Il tient magazin de malles, bois de lit &c. Vous le trouverez dans le Haymarket, ou Pall-Mall. John, qui etoit mon domestique, peut bien le vous indiquer. Demandez à M. Beckett son adresse, áfin que je puisse m'adresser à lui ci-apres pour des choses de son genre.

Tout-ça le soir de votre arrivée.

Remettez les lettres à Monsr. Boulton, et à Madme. Cosway.

Achetez moi 4. etuis de cure-dents selon le modele et 6. paires de bas de coton, de la grandeur et qualité de celui que je vous donne. Je les ai payé 5/ la paire. Demandez à Madame Smith ou à Madame Adams si elles connoissent les ordres que M. Smith pourroit avoir donné relativement au clavecin. Allez aussi chez M. Kirkman qui l'a fait. Il demeure No. 19, Broad Street, Carnaby Market, et demandez lui si le clavecin est expedie, et quand et par quelle occasion. Si elle n'est pas expedié, prenez des mesures pour la faire expedier à Rouen à l'adresse de M. Garvey.

M. Smith devoit m'envoyer les portraits de Sr. Walter Raleigh, de M. Adams et la mien qui est chez M. Brown. Vous pouvez les apporter dans la diligence.

PrC (MHi); undated and unsigned; in TJ's hand, at foot of text: "Petit." Date has been assigned from internal evidence and from TJ's entry in Account Book under 2 July 1787 which reads: "advanced him [Petit] 35 Louis—840 [livres] for journey to London"; see also TJ to Eppes, this date.

To Sir John Sinclair

DEAR SIR   Paris July 2. 1787.

I avail myself of the earliest moment possible after my return to thank you for the sketch of your last year's journey which has come duly to hand. I send you through the medium of Count Sarsfeild a late publication on the connections between France and the United states which is said to be well written. I have not yet read it, and indeed I wonder how any body finds time to read any thing in Europe. I have had a most agreeable and interesting journey. My route was Lyons, Aix, Marseilles, Toulons, Nice, Turin, Milan, Genoa, Nice, Aix, Nismes, Montpelier, the Canal de Languedoc, Bourdeaux, Nantes, Lorient, Rennes, Nantes, Tours and Orleans. It was cruel, when at Milan, not to be able to take the step to Rome. But there are Moral slaveries as absolute as the Physical ones. I shall always be happy to hear of your welfare, and will sometimes take the liberty of obtruding on your leisure moments. I am with much sincerity Dear Sir Your most obedient & most humble servt.,   TH: JEFFERSON

PrC (DLC).
The LATE PUBLICATION that TJ sent was evidently *De la France et des Etats-Unis, ou de l'importance de la révolution d'Amérique pour le bonheur de la France*, by Brissot de Warville and Etienne Clavière.

To Benjamin Vaughan

DEAR SIR   Paris July 2. 1787.

Your favor of Feb. 16. came to my hands in the moment I was setting out on a tour through the Southern parts of France and Northern of Italy, from which I am but just now returned. I avail myself of the earliest moment to acknolege it's receipt and to thank you for the box of magnets which I find here. Tho I do not know certainly by or from whom they come, I presume they came by Colo. Smith who was here in my absence, and from Messrs. Nairne and Blunt thro' your good offices. I think your letter of Feb. 16. flatters me with the expectation of another with observations on the hygrometers I had proposed. I value what comes from you too

[532]

much not to remind you of it. Your favour by Mr. Garnett also came during my absence. I presume he has left Paris, as I can hear nothing of him. I have lost the opportunity therefore of seeing his method of relieving friction, as well as of shewing by attentions to him respect for yourself and your recommendations. Mr. Payne (Common sense) is here on his way to England. He has brought the model of an iron bridge, with which he supposes a single arch of 400 feet may be made. It is not yet arrived in Paris. Among other projects with which we begin to abound in America, is [that] for finding the Longitude by the Variation of the magnetic needle. The author supposes two points, one near each pole, thro' the Northern of which passes all the Magnetic meridians of the Northern hemisphere, and thro the Southern those of the Southern hemisphere. He determines their present position and periodical revolution. It is said his publication is plausible. I have not seen it.

What are you going to do with your naval armament on your side the channel? Perhaps you will ask me what they are about to do here? A British navy and Prussian army hanging over Holland on one side, a French navy and army hanging over it on the other, looks as if they thought of fighting. Yet I think both parties too wise for that, too laudably intent on oeconomising rather than on further embarrassing their finances. May they not propose to have a force on the spot to establish some neutral form of a constitution which these powers will cook up among themselves?, without consulting the parties for whom it is intended? The affair of Geneva shews such combinations possible. Wretched indeed is the nation in whose affairs foreign powers are once permitted to intermeddle!—Ld. Wycombe is with us at present. His good sense, information and discretion are much beyond his years, and promise good things for your country. I beg you to accept assurances of the esteem & respect with which I have the honor to be Dr. Sir your most obedt. & most humble servt., TH: JEFFERSON

PrC (DLC).

From Villedeuil

Paris Le 2. Juillet 1787.

Je viens, Monsieur, de me faire rendre compte des motifs qui ont empêché les fermiers généraux d'exécuter les dispositions contenües dans la lettre que M. de Calonne vous a adressée le 22. 8bre. dernier.

J'ai été informé, Monsieur, que les fermiers généraux qui n'avoient pas eu connoissance dans le principe des dispositions de cette lettre, avoient reçu le premier Avril dernier l'ordre de s'y conformer et que le 5 du même mois ils avoient adressé à leurs directeurs et autres Employés dans les Ports du royaume des instructions pour ne percevoir sur les huiles et autres produits de la pêche américainne que les droits mentionnés dans la lettre de M. de Calonne.

J'aurai soin, Monsieur, de maintenir ces dispositions et de faire rendre justice aux Négociants de qui la ferme générale auroit pu éxiger de plus forts droits.

J'ai l'honneur d'être avec un très Sincère attachement, Monsieur, Votre très humble et très obéissant Serviteur,

DE VILLEDEUIL

RC (DLC); a clerk's hand, signed by Villedeuil. Tr (MHi); in an unidentified hand; at foot of text: "(Test Wm. Short Secry.)." Tr (DNA: PCC, No. 107, II); enclosed in TJ to Jay, 6 Aug. 1787. Recorded in SJL as received 5 July 1787.

To Wilt, Delmestre & Cie.

GENTLEMEN   Paris July 2. 1787.

Your favor of June 15. is come duly to hand, as well as the coffee therein announced, the quantity of which suffices for some time. Your draught on me for the amount shall be duly honoured with thanks for the trouble you have taken. May I ask the favor of you to send the inclosed letter by the first vessel going from your port to Virginia. I have the honour to be with great esteem & respect Gentlemen your most obedient & most humble servt.,

TH: JEFFERSON

PrC (DLC). Enclosure: Probably a copy (perhaps the PrC) of TJ to Francis Eppes, 2 July 1787, another copy of which was enclosed in TJ to John Bondfield of this date.

From Thomas Barclay

DEAR SIR   [ca. 3 July 1787]

My last Containd a pretty long state of the affair Between the House of French & Nephew, and myself, of which I had not time to make any Copy, to put an End to your Trouble in this Disagreeable subject. I shall Conclude it, by informing you as Breifly

3 JULY 1787

as I Can of what has passed since the time of my Enlargement, observing that Before I applied to the Parliament I offerd by the mediation of a Gentleman at Bordeaux, a Bond Payable in 12 Months with a Mortgage on some landed property in America, which I Believe to be of the full Value of all the sum which they say is Due to them, and to which they Replied, that they Knew their own business, and if any Person again applied to them they wou'd look upon it as an Insult, for Nothing but an absolute payment of the Money wou'd be accepted. And Mr. Valentine French with the Bitterest Curses which he Called down upon self if he did not persever, Declared that while a Drop of Blood flowd in his Veins, I shou'd remain where I was, Nay that I shou'd Rot was his horrid word, untill he was paid and as the law orders provision to be made for Confined Debtors by the Persons who put them in Prison, the Worthy Gentlemen paid Seven livres ten sols for my Months Maintanence, and Fever which Confined me to my Bed after you went away, and an Expectation of a letter from the Marquis De lay Fayette, who Expecting my Return to Paris, Did Not write untill he was Undeceived by a second letter from me, prevented my going to Paris for some time, when I Received a letter from a Friend of mine Informing me that Mess. French & Co. had told him that they had procured an order for the Marechaussee to follow and Capture me as soon as I shou'd get out of the District of the Parliament of Bordeaux, and he added that they Desired I shou'd have Notice of what was Intended if I left that City.

Prior to, and after this declaration, several offers were Made by me of which here follows a note.

1. To Invest all the Property I have in the world, in the Hands of Trustees untill all Demands for which I am Accountable are Discharged, to Pursue the Recovery of the Debts Due to me and to attend to the settlement of the Affairs, on being allowd 5 ₱ Cent on the Recoveries for the Mantainance of my self and Family.

2. That my wife wou'd Join me in assigning over all her Right as well as mine to all my Property, to be placed in the Hands of Trustees for the Payment of all Engagements in which I am Concerned, upon being Discharged from farther Trouble, and Intitled to resume the Remainder of my property, when these Engagements are fulfilled.

Note if Mess. French & Nephew were Even to Drive me to an act of Bankruptcy, Mrs. Barclay wou'd be Intitled to the First Demand of between seventy and Eighty thousand livres. But this

3 JULY 1787

is a sacrafice that I am sure she wou'd gladly make to secure my Peace of mind.

3. I Desired to Know who their Agent at Paris was, that I might if possible arrange matters some way to his satisfaction.

This I Did at the Desire of one of the Most Respectable Characters in Bordeaux* to whom Mess: French & Nephew had often applied Concerning my affairs, and who advised me to Content my self with this, and not to leave the City untill I Did it.

4. Mess: French & Nephew often said that I must have a great Deal of Money Due to me from a Particular Quarter† which they Named, adding that I ought to give them a Bill on that Quarter.

I offerd them a Bill agreeable to their Desire, which wou'd have been paid out of the First Monies Coming to me from thence.

5. I Renew'd my proposal of a Bond and Mortgage on landed property, and offerd to prove by letters the Right I had to that property.

To these overtures, all of which were in writing, the following Verbal answers were Returned. That my Existence depended on their being paid, they wou'd meet me in Evry part of the Globe, if I went to India their friend General Conway wou'd pursue me. If they were not paid I shou'd never enjoy any office under Congress. If I had made a Fortune it was owing to them. My wife and Children shou'd not have a livre to Buy Bread untill they were paid. If I had any Property in America to Mortgage I shou'd write to Congress, and get that Body to Certify it, for I shou'd not leave Bordeaux untill they were paid, and they Desired M. Mitchell to tell me to make no more applications to them, for they had given me a plain, decisive and final answer. This last message was Couched in such Indecent language that I Cannot Commit it to paper.

I informed you in my last letter upon what pretences Mess. French & Nephew have grounded their Complaint of my Duplicity, and how Ignorant I was of the Transaction. I am Informed those Gentlemen have Circulated Copies of the letter which M. Moylan wrote to them when he was at Bordeaux, and which I never heard of untill the 12th. of May when they produced it, and as it is signed with the Names of Barclay, Moylan & Co. and the Explanation attending it, it passes with some people as a letter from me, who they say alterd the Destination afterwards of the Vessel, which undoubtedly must give a Very unfavorable Impression of the

---

* *The Pro[cu]re[ur].*[1]
† *Congress.*

Transaction. And to this I have Nothing to oppose but the Most solemn asseveration that I was Innocent and Ignorant of both, nor had any person in Europe a right to Change the vessels voyage. But to Convince you that Mess. French & Nephew themselves did not think there was any thing wrong in this alteration, I subjoin an Extract of a letter which I Received from them a little before I left Paris on my Journey to Morocco. It was written not only after the Vessel in question arrived in Londonderry, but after she went out from thence to America and returned to L'orient all of which they were well acquainted with, and they Never once Complaind of any Breach of promise. I found this letter among my Papers some days ago, and You will perceive it to be in a Very Different style from what any House wou'd write to a Person who had Committed an act of Treachery to them.

I shall not lengthen my letter by any appology, But Conclude with great Esteem and Respect Dear Sir Your Very much Obliged and obed Servant, THOS. BARCLAY

RC (DLC); undated; partly in code. This is clearly the undated letter from Barclay whose receipt TJ recorded in SJL on 13 July 1787, along with two other letters of 6 and 8 July from L'Orient. Barclay had escaped from Bordeaux on Sunday, 1 July, with the help of John Bondfield (see Bondfield to TJ, 3 July 1787), and arrived at L'Orient shortly afterward, where he wrote the present letter and later enclosed it in his to TJ of 6 July 1787. Enclosures: (1) Extract of a letter from French & Nephew to Barclay, 13 Dec. 1785, saying that they had written several times without hearing; that they feared his illness might be the cause; and asking "when we may expect the pleasure of seeing you here, a pleasure you may be persuaded we shall Rejoice at, Especially our N.F[rench] who Wishes to make a personal acquaintance with you." (2) J. H. Delap to Barclay, Bordeaux, "Tuesday morning," 12 June 1787, saying that Anthony Lynch had called upon him to say that French & Nephew understood he was about to leave Bordeaux "this Evening or Tomorrow" and that they had obtained an order "for the Marechaussee to Follow and to Capture you as soon as you got out of the District of the Parliament of Bordeaux"; from this it is clear that Delap's letter was received after Barclay's first letter to TJ of 12 June 1787 and was the cause of his second (both enclosures are in Barclay's hand and are attached to his letter).

LAFAYETTE did intercede with the ministry in response to a letter from Barclay, but it is not correct to say that the latter's arrest was a violation of his "consular immunity" or that, as a result of Lafayette's intercession, the "local courts quickly released him, and Lafayette successfully interceded with the ministers to defend him from further molestation" (Gottschalk, *Lafayette, 1783-1789*, p. 330, citing Lafayette to Short, 31 May [1787], DLC: Short Papers, and referring to Myrna Boyce, "The Diplomatic Career of William Short," *Journal of Modern History*, XV [1943], 98). It was the vigorous effort of Dudon fils, *Procureur Général du Roi* for Bordeaux, that resulted in Barclay's release even before Lafayette had heard of his imprisonment, and it was a secret message from Dudon that kept Barclay from being imprisoned a second time. When Montmorin reversed his position on the case, Barclay was not safe from arrest anywhere in France. He probably remained in hiding from 1 July, when he fled from Bordeaux at night, to 2 Aug. 1787, when he sailed for America. See note to TJ to Jay, 21 June 1787.

[1] That is, the *Procureur Général du Roi* for Bordeaux, Dudon fils (see above). The two footnotes in this let-

ter marked by an asterisk and a dagger (in MS) were written in code by Barclay, and have been decoded by the editors, employing a partially reconstructed key to Code No. 11 that has been made up from various passages in the correspondence between TJ and Barclay and TJ and Carmichael, and pieced together from other evidence. The matter in brackets (supplied) is conjectured, but there can be no doubt that Dudon is the individual referred to. See also TJ to Barclay, 4 July 1787.

From John Bondfield

Sir Bordeaux 3 July 1787

Mr. Barclay wore down by the inflexable obstinacy of his cruel persecutors who cease not to raise interest to excecute their inhuman projects, flatter'd himself to receive thro your interest a *safe Conduct* for himself and his partner Mr. Loreille. This engaged his remaining here from Poste to Poste. He communicated to me your letter to him under cover to Mess. Feger. From the contents I perseived Arguments started by Monsr. De montmorin that render'd his situation very precarious and the obtaining a protection for his person and of his Partners very doubtful. In an undecided state he rested suspended to Sunday last. Having dined with me he return'd to his Hotel. A Gentleman unknown to him called upon him and desired that I might be sent for. Having to communicate some thing of consiquence as that it was nessessary I should be present, Mr. Barclay came back to my House. I emediately accompanied him, and the Gentleman soon after came up. He then inform'd us that he was deputed by a Person in high office (the P—d—R—) to inform him M.B. that it was indispensible to his safety that he should leave town that night and not delay an instant longer than nessessity required, that the next morning in virtue of instructions receiv'd a Parlementary hearing would take place which would be attended with disagreable consiquences. Mr. Barclays safety being thus drawn to an instant I emediately engaged a Craft to carry Mr. Barclay and Mr. Loreille down the River. They left this on Sunday Evening. Mr. Barclay will probably write you so soon as he shall have got where he can recover strength and Calm. He was cruelly agitated when he left me. His adversarys were yesterday very Buissy but I have not yet seen my reporter to learn the fruit of their labour.

Many Ships are come in from America. The Farmers Agent has inform'd the private Importers that their supplies are compleated. If true, we must expect a considerable fall in the prices. I am advised many Cargoes are on the way and many preparing for France.

[538]

3 JULY 1787

A ship of Seven hundred hogsheds arrived this Instant from Virginia. The ship belongs to London. The Americans who are here murmer that strangers should be employed in a branch where markt privalidges have been in View to favor the Navigation of America and France and that these strangers, who are many, pertake and in some measure reap all the advantages.

I have not yet obtained Answers to my Letters from Lisbon that I wrote to have further information of the Consular regulations at that residence. So soon as I can procure the returns of the Imports at this City from America since the peace I shall transmit them. With due Respect I have the honor to be Sir your most Obedient Humble Servant, JOHN BONDFIELD

RC (DLC); addressed; endorsed. Recorded in SJL as received 7 July 1787. P—D—R—: Dudon fils, *Procureur Général du Roi.* See note to TJ to Jay, 21 June 1787.

Jefferson's Observations on Calonne's Letter Concerning American Trade

Observations on the letter of Monsieur de Calonnes to Monsieur Jefferson, dated Fontainebleau Octob. 22. 1786.

A committee was appointed, in the course of the last year, to take a view of the subjects of commerce which might be brought from the United states of America, in exchange for those of France, and to consider what advantages and facilities might be offered to encourage that Commerce. The letter of Monsieur de Calonnes was founded on their[1] report. It was conclusive as to the articles on which satisfactory information had been then obtained, and reserved for future consideration certain others needing further enquiry. It is proposed now to review those unfinished articles, that they also may be comprehended in the Arret, and the regulations on this branch of commerce be rendered complete.

1. The letter promises to diminish the Droits du roi et d'amirauté, paiable[2] by an American vessel entering into a port of France, and to reduce what should remain into a single duty, which shall be regulated by the draught of the vessel, or her number of masts. It is doubted whether it will be expedient to regulate the duty in either of these ways. If by the draught of water, it will fall unequally on us as a Nation; because we build our vessels sharp-bottomed, for swift sailing, so that they draw more water than those of other nations, of the same burthen; if by the number of

[539]

masts, it will fall unequally on individuals, because we often see ships of 180 tons, and brigs of 360. This then would produce[3] an inequality among individuals of 6. to 1. The present principle is the most just, to regulate by the burthen.

It is certainly desireable that these duties should be reduced to a single one. Their names and numbers perplex and harrass the merchant more than their amount, subject him to imposition, and to the suspicion of it where there is none. An intention of general reformation in this article has been accordingly* announced with the augmentation as to foreigners. We are in hopes that this augmentation is not to respect[5] us; because it is proposed as a measure of reciprocity; whereas in some of our states no such duties exist, and in others they are extremely light; because we have been made to hope a diminution instead of augmentation; and because this distinction can not draw on France any just claims from other nations, the *Jura gentis amicissimae* conferred by her late treaties having reference expressly to the nations of *Europe* only, and those conferred by the more antient ones not being susceptible of any other interpretation, nor admitting a pretension of reference to a nation which did not then exist, and which has come into existence under circumstances distinguishing it's commerce from that of all other nations. Merchandize received from them take emploiment from the poor of France; ours give it: theirs is brought in the last stage of manufacture, ours in the first: we bring our tobaccoes to be manufactured into snuff, our flax and hemp into linen and cordage, our furs into hats, skins into sadlery, shoes and clothing: we take nothing till it has received the last hand.

2. Fish-oils. The Hanseatic treaty was the basis on which the diminution of duty on this article was asked and granted. It is expressly referred to as such in the letter of Monsieur de Calonnes. Instead however of the expression 'huile et graisse de baleine et d'autres poissons' used in that treaty, the letter uses the terms 'huiles de baleine, Spermaceti, et tout ce qui est compris sous ces denominations.' And the farmers have availed themselves of this variation to refuse the diminution of duty on the oils of the Vache marine, chien de mer, esturgeon and other fish. It is proposed therefore to re-establish in the arrêt the expressions of the Hanseatic treaty, and to add from the same treaty the articles 'baleine coupée et fanon de baleine.'

The letter states these regulations as finally made by the king. The merchants on this supposition entered into speculations. But they found themselves called on for the old duties, not only on other

*Memoires presentées à l'Assemblée des Notables pa. 534

3 JULY 1787

fish oils, but on the whale oil. Monsieur de Calonnes always promised that the Arrêt should be retrospective to the date of the letter, so as to refund to them the duties they had thus been obliged to pay. To this attention is prayed in forming the arrêt. His majesty having been pleased, as an encouragement to the importation of our fish oils, to abolish the Droits de fabrication, it is presumed that the purpose* announced of continuing those duties on foreign oils will not be extended to us.

* Memoires presentées &c. pa. 51. 52.

3. Rice. The duty on this is only 7½ deniers the Quintal, or about one quarter per cent on it's first cost. While this serves to inform government of the quantities imported, it cannot discourage that importation. Nothing further therefore is necessary on this article.

4. Pot-asse. This article is of principal utility to France in her bleacheries of linen, glass works, and soap-works; and the Potash of America, being made of green wood, is known to be the best in the world. All duty on it was therefore abolished by the king. But the city of Rouen levies on it a duty of 20. sols the Quintal, which is very sensible in it's price, brings it dearer to the bleacheries near Paris, to those of Beauvais, Laval &c. and to the glassworks, and encourages them to give a preference to the potash or soude of other nations. This is a counteraction of the views of the king expressed in the letter which it is hoped will be prevented.

5. Turpentine, tar, and pitch, were not decided on the former occasion.[6] Turpentine (Terebenthine) pays 10. sols the Quintal and 10 sols the livre, making 15. sols the Quintal; which is 10. percent on it's prime cost. Tar, (goudron, brai gras) pays 8 livres the leth[7] of 12. barrels, and 10 sols the livre, amounting to 20 sols the barrel, which is 12½ per cent on it's prime cost. Pitch (brai sec) pays 10. sols the Quintal and 10. sols the livre, making 15. sols the Quintal, which is 20. per cent on it's prime cost. Duties of from 10. to 20. per cent on articles of heavy carriage, prevent their importation. They eat up all the profits of the merchant, and often subject him to loss. This has been much the case with respect to turpentine, tar and pitch, which are a principal article of remittance for the state of North Carolina. It is hoped that it will coincide with the views of government in making the present regulations, to suppress the duties on these articles, which of all others can bear them least.

MS (ViWC): in TJ's hand; endorsed by him: "Commerce with France. Observations on M. de Calonne's letter of Oct. 22. 1786. Given in to the C. de Montmorin July 4. 1787"; undated. PrC of foregoing (DLC). RC (Arch. Aff. Etr., Paris, Corr. Pol., E.-U., XXXII, 111-12); in Short's hand; in French; at head of text: "Envoyé copie à M. de Villedeuil le 25 Juillet 1787." PrC of foregoing (DLC). Tr (Arch. Aff. Etr., Paris, Mémoires et Documents, E.-U., IX, 168, 171). Tr (DNA: PCC, No. 107, II); incomplete, since this volume ends with p. 59. PrC of Tr (DLC); in Short's hand; in English. Recorded in SJL under 3 July 1787. See TJ to Jay, 6 Aug. 1787.

¹ Tr reads "this."
² Tr reads "paid."
³ Tr reads "introduce."
⁴ Tr reads "52."
⁵ Tr ends at this point.
⁶ This sentence not in Short's PrC of Tr. RC reads: "Il n'a rien été décidé sur ces articles dans le premier rapport du Comité."
⁷ This word—for which no satisfactory explanation has been found in any of the English, Scottish, or American dictionaries of dialects or colloquialisms —was translated by Short as *tonneau* ("Le goudron . . . paye 8.ᵗᵗ par tonneau de douze barrils"), thus indicating that TJ employed it in the same sense that *ton* (OE. *tunne*, OF. *tonne*) came to be used in the latter part of the 17th century: that is, as a unit for measuring the carrying capacity or burden of a ship, the amount of cargo, &c. In 1655, for example, the Parliament of Scotland stipulated that "Two Buts, two Pipes, Four Hogsheads, six Tierces, three Punchions . . . and eight Quarter-Casks shall be accounted for a Tun" (OED).

From the Abbé Morellet

MONSIEUR mardi [3 July 1787]

Le detail dans lequel vous aves l'extrême complaisance d'entrer me demontre avec la derniere evidence que vous aves poussé la patience et la bonté jusqu'où elles pouvoient aller, et que Barrois est coupable non seulement d'une negligence et d'une paresse impardonnable mais d'une injustice dont je suis fort blessé en se plaignant lorsqu'il n'a que des excuses à faire lui même et des torts les plus graves du monde. Je suis moi même bien honteux d'avoir pensé un moment d'après lui que votre domestique l'avoit traité durement et de vous avoir présenté cette espece de plainte si injuste et si mal placée. Je vous prie d'oublier la foiblesse que j'ai eüe de croire aux propos du libraire, qui est d'ailleurs un honnête homme mais qui est aussi l'homme le plus negligent. Si j'avois eu la moindre notion de ce qui se passoit et des delais qu'on mettoit à vous satisfaire, soyes sur que la planche vous eut été rendüe et envoyée à londres il y a six semaines. Mais un billet de Barois a eté pour moi la premiere nouvelle de tout cela. Si vous aves la bonté de nous faire ravoir la planche après que Mr. Stockdale en aura fait usage, je la remettrai moi même à un imprimeur et elle ne rentrera jamais dans les mains d'un homme si horriblement negligent. Je suis vraiment au desespoir du desagrement et de l'embarras que je vous ai causé bien malgré moi. Agreës mes très humbles excuses et conserves moi la bienveillance dont vous m'honores et que je merite par les sentimens respectueux avec lesquels j'ai l'honneur d'etre Monsieur Votre très humble et très obeissant Serviteur,

L'ABBE MORELLET

RC (DLC); endorsed. Date is established by entry in SJL for 3 July 1787 for receipt of an undated letter from Morellet, which clearly is the present one since it is in reply to TJ's of the day preceding.

From André Pepin

Paris le mardy 3. jllet. 1787 hotel Dauphin
Monseigneur rue de Seine FauxB. St. Gain.

André Pepin, Lieuttenant dans les armées des Etats unis, a L'honneur de vous Exposer qu'à son arrivée En cette ville Vous avez eu la bonté de lui donner le 26. aout der. un passeport pour aller En piemont sa patrie où Ses affaires l'appellaient. Il pensait vendre-là le peu de fortune qui devait lui Etre laissée par ses parents, il a trouvé tous les biens substitués: de sorte qu'il a fait un très long voyage En pure perte; Et il est obligé de remmener une de ses filles qui Est passée en France depuis deux ans avec sa soeur qui a Epousé un français. Son Embaras extreme avec sa fille est de payer son passage. Il ne demande pas qu'on lui En fasse la remise, mais seulement que l'on permette qu'il ne paye qu'en amérique, Et la derniere Table est celle qu'il veut.

À qui faut-il recours dans son malheur? Il ne peut recourir qu'à vous, Monseigneur: il s'est présenté plusieurs fois En votre hotel, mais inutilement. Il ose donc attendre de vous au moins L'honneur d'une audience. Son passeport d'ailleurs aurait besoin d'être rafraîchi. N'abandonnez pas, Monseigneur, un Etranger et un de vos sujets. Il ne peut se dispenser d'attendre que vous l'honoriez d'une réponse.

Il vous présente son plus profond respect, Et Est pour la vie, Monseigneur, Votre très humble et très obéissant Serviteur,

André Pepin

RC (DLC); endorsed. Recorded in SJL as received the same day.

To André Pepin

A Paris 3me. Juillet 1787.

Je suis extremement faché, Monsieur, de l'embarras où vous vous trouvez pour votre passage en Amerique: et d'autant plus que je n'y peux pas remedier. De payer votre passage moimeme me seroit là chose impossible: et de demander au ministre qu'on vous dispense du reglement qui en demande le paiment d'avance, par un ordre superieur, seroit une indiscretion pour laquelle je ne pourrois pas repondre. La seule mesure seroit, à ce qui me semble, que vous vous appliquiez au capitaine du Paquet boat qui doit partir de Havre le 10me. du mois prochain, et que vous l'assuriez que vous serez dans le cas, à votre arrivée en Amerique, de lui payer la passage. Je ne connois pas le nom du capitaine ni du Paquet boat, ou j'aurais l'honneur de vous les indiquer, mais vous pouvez les connoitre en vous presentant au bureau de M. Le Coulteulx qui en a la direction. C'est probable que le Capitaine se trouve à Paris, ou peut être à Havre. J'ai l'honneur de vous envoyer le passeport que vous me demandez et d'etre Monsieur votre très humble et très obeissant serviteur,   TH: JEFFERSON

PrC (DLC). Neither the passport enclosed in this letter nor that issued on 26 Aug. 1786 (see Pepin to TJ, this date) has been found.

To Thomas Barclay

DEAR SIR   Paris July 4. 1787.

I wrote you a fortnight ago an account of what had passed on your subject that day. Yesterday I had a long conference with M. de [Rayneval].[1] It is impossible for a person to be more cordially disposed than M. de Montmorin but opposition from another quarter of the [sea] and the difficulty of the case [trouble] him. [Rayneval] observed to me that there was no country in Europe but France which took any notice of the character of a minister en passage between two other nations: but France doing it for other nations, I observed, and he agreed she should do it for us. But he repeated the objection of your long stay at Bourdeaux, and I the answer which I had before given on that subject, and which admits no reply. He added what I had never heard before: that France does not permit even a minister to her own court to depart without paying his debts, or giving either private or public security for them. I denied that this could be justified by the law of nations. He said he would send me a copy of the memoir on that subject which his court had sent to all the courts of Europe in the case of the Landgrave of Hesse, and ended by pressing the distress in which M. de Montmorin found himself, and how much they should be relieved by an amicable arrangement. I am afraid they are pressing on the other side a reversal of the decision of Bordeaux. I always suppose that the most honest way of acting for another is to give a true state of things without disguise. I therefore told you in the first moment at Bordeaux what I thought

4 JULY 1787

of it. As soon as I found that the practice of this country relative to a minister en passage allowed an opening in your favor, I pushed it and still push it on that point. But they oppose their practice as to the debts even of a minister to their court. I make it a point to remove from the minds of those with whom I speak all doubts as to your conduct, and I believe I satisfy them, as I am satisfied myself of it's perfect rectitude. I shall not fail to urge for you whatever their usage will admit; but acknolege that I apprehend for the event, and that an amicable arrangement should be pressed on your part. It is some days since I heard from your family. They were then well. I am in daily hopes of receiving a letter from you in answer to my last, and beg you to count on any service I can render you in this or any other matter as well as on the sentiments of esteem and friendship with which I have the honour to be Dear Sir Your most obedient & most humble servt.,

TH: JEFFERSON

PrC (DLC); partly in code.

[1] This and succeeding words in italics are written in code. The editors have only partially reconstructed this code (Code No. 11), for which no key has been found. The words in brackets supplied) are conjectured. See notes to Barclay to TJ, ca. 3 July 1787, and TJ to Jay, 21 June 1787.

From Clesle

[*N.p., 4 July 1787.* Recorded in SJL as received 4 July 1787. Not found.]

To Feger, Gramont & Cie.

GENTLEMEN   Paris July 4. 1787.

Monsieur Grand has just informed me that there is arrived at Bourdeaux to your address a box of seeds for me. I will beg the favor of you to forward them by land, either by the Fourgon, Messagerie or Diligence as you shall think best. If it be small it might come better by the Diligence. Any expences occurring herein you will be so good as to notify to Mr. Grand who will pay them. I have the honor to be with much esteem & respect Gentlemen Your most obedient & most humble servt,

TH: JEFFERSON

PrC (MHi).

From Lanchon Frères & Cie.

L'Orient, 4 July 1787. Enclose a letter for TJ brought from Charlestown, S.C., by Capt. Jacobs of the *Union*. They and Richard Harrison of Alexandria were sorry to have missed TJ when he was in L'Orient; offer their services for themselves and their house at Le Havre, "Mangon La Forest & Compy. . . . in receiving or Conveying packetts or any thing you may think proper from or to America."

RC (MHi); 2 p.; endorsed. Recorded in SJL as received 8 July 1787. Enclosure: After TJ's entry in SJL of receipt of the present letter is an entry reading: "Izard Ralph. dupl. of June 27," an evident reference to Izard's of 4 Apr. 1787, the original of which TJ had received on 27 June.

To André Limozin

Sir   Paris July 4. 1787.

Your favors of the 31st. March, 5th and 22d of May coming while I was absent on a voiage of 3. or 4. months, have for that reason remained thus long unanswered. Your bill for the amount of your advances for me shall be duly answered: I will ask the favor of you at the same time to send me a state of the articles that I may transfer them to the account of the United states, or of the state of Virginia or to my own private account, according to their nature. I shall very soon trouble you with some boxes of books which I shall pray you to forward by the next packet.

A letter from a friend in Virginia informs me he sent a package of seeds addressed to me by a ship belonging to Shore, McConnico and Ritson merchants of Petersburg in Virginia, which sailed in the month of March, bound for Havre. Would you be so good as to make some enquiry for them?

I am charged to enquire for possessions supposed to be in or about a town called Tessey in Lower Normandy, and to have belonged to Jacob Ammonet a refugee who left France in 1700. If you can aid me in finding out either the town, family, or possessions it will confer an obligation on Sir your most obedient & most humble servant,   Th: Jefferson

PrC (MHi).

From Parent

[*Beaune, 4 July 1787.* Recorded in SJL as received 7 July 1787. Not found.]

To Hérault

July 5. 1787.

A person who would wish to have a good general idea of the laws of England, should read the following books.

	£	s	d	
Blackstone's Analysis 8vo.	0	4	6	
Dalrymple on feudal property 8vo.		3	0	
Blackstone's commentaries. 4 v. 8vo.	1	10	0	
Gilbert's law of Evidence 8vo.		5	0	
[every thing he wrote is excellent]				
Cuningham's law of bills. 8vo. [1778]		7	0	
Molloy de jure maritime 2. v. 8vo.		12	0	
Gilbert's history and practice of Chancery 8vo. [1758]		5	0	
Kaim's Principles of Equity. 2. v. 8vo.		10	0	3 16 6

A foreign lawyer, who might have occasion sometimes to discuss particular points more in detail, should add to his library the following.

	£	s	d
Coutumes Anglo-Normands de Houard. 4. v. 4to. [Paris] 56ᵗ	2	6	8
Finch's law. fol. [1613.]		4	0
Cuningham's Law dictionary. 2. v. fol. [latest edition]	3	16	0
Hale's history and Analysis of the law. 1716. [an author of high authority]		3	0
Rastall's collection of statutes. 2. v. fol. [1618.]	1	11	6
Statutes at large by Hawkins & Cay. 9. v. fol.	2	2	0
Ruffhead's index to the statutes. 8vo.		7	0
Hawkins's Pleas of the crown. fol. [1771.]	1	10	0
Hale's Pleas of the crown. 2. v. fol. [1739.]		18	0
Burn's justice 4. v. 8vo. [1780.]	1	8	0
Gilbert's law of devises 8vo. [1773]		5	0
Gilbert's law of Uses 8vo.		5	0
Gilbert's law of tenures. 8vo.		5	0
Sayer's law of costs. 8vo.		4	0
Cuningham's Merchant's lawyer. 2. v. 8vo. [1768]		12	0

5 JULY 1787

Swinburne on Wills. 4 to [1677]	4 0	
Burne's Ecclesiastical law. 4. v. 8vo. [1781.]	1 4 0	
Abridgment of cases in Equity. 2. v. fol. [1756 & 1769.]	2 13 0	19 18 2

The following books added to the preceding constitutes such a law library as suffices for lawyers of the ordinary class in England or America.

	£ s d	
Coke's institutes 3. v. fol. [1st. vol. 2d. edition 7/6. 2d. & 3d. vols. of the 5th. edition 1671. but with the tables 30/.]	1 17 6	
Gilbert's history & practice of civil actions. 8vo. [1779]	5 0	
Coke's reports. French. fol. 13. parts.	11 0	
Croke's reports. 3. v. fol. [1669.]	1 8 0	
Vaughan's reports. fol. [1677.]	12 0	
Salkeld's reports by Wilson. 3 parts in 1. vol. [1773.]	1 16 0	
Lord Raymond's reports [1743.] 2. v. fol.	2 10 0	
Strange's reports. [2. v. fol. £3. or 2. v. 8vo. 21/]	1 1 0	
Burrow's reports. [5. v. fol. £7—1. or 5. v. 8vo. £2—12s—6d]	2 12 6	
Beawe's lex mercatoria. fol.	1 11 6	
Harrison's practice in Chancery. 2. v. 8vo. [1779.]	12 0	
Francis's maxims in equity fol.	6 0	
Vernon's reports. 2. v. fol.	1 16 0	
Peere-Williams' reports. 3. v. fo. [1740-1746.]	3 3 0	
Cases tempore Talbot. fol.	10 0	
Atkyns's reports. [3. v. fol. £3—3. or 3. v. 8vo. 27/]	1 7 0	21 18 6

£45 13 2

After these, succeeds a croud of authors of inferior authority, which however the lawyers provide themselves with in proportion to their wealth and eminence. A catalogue of these may be extended to thousands of pounds.

PrC (DLC). Square brackets are in MS.

This list was probably addressed to Marie Jean Hérault de Séchelles (1759-1794), a young lawyer and public figure who was counsel to the Parliament of Paris (1785), member of the Legislative Assembly (1791), member of the National Convention (1792), and assisted in drafting the new constitution (1793). He was guillotined at Paris on 5 Apr. 1794.

John Jay to William Short

SIR   New York 5th: July 1787.

Mr. Walton delivered to me immediately on His arrival, your Letter of the 21 March with the Medals, &c. mentioned in it; and I was last week favored with your subsequent one of the 4th: May last, with the other Medals and the Papers sent with it. Accept my Thanks for your Attention in transmitting the Speeches of the King of France and his minister to the notables. Such Intelligence is interesting. It seems from the arret respecting the Bounty and Duty on Fish, that the absolute Prohibition of foreign Fish is in Contemplation—a Circumstance of much Importance to the United States. "*Local Circumstances*" will however always operate in our Favor, and if wisely improved must in Time more than rival any Fishery not so circumstanced even tho' aided by Bounties.

The Business of Finance appears to occupy the attention of France and Britain as well as America; and doubtless with much Reason. I wish we made more progress in it; but among other Reasons, the sitting of the Convention at Phila. has called so many members from Congress, that a sufficient number of States are not represented to enable them to advance in that or any other Business which requires the Presence of nine States. Hence it happened that I have not yet been enabled to write to Mr. Jefferson on a certain Subject mentioned in his Letters, and on which I reported agreeably to his Ideas. I regret this Delay especially as it is uncertain how much longer it may continue.

The Letter of Mr: Calonne should certainly be registred. The Honor of Government appears to dictate it; and it would not be wise to disappoint Expectations so excited. From these and particularly from the other Considerations which you suggest, there is Reason doubtless to expect that the Letter will take Effect. So soon as a proper number of States shall be represented in Congress, I hope they will take up my Report respecting the number of medals to be struck, and how distributed. I concur in Sentiment with Mr. Jefferson on this Subject. I have the Honor to be Sir, your mo. obt. & very huble Servant,   JOHN JAY

Dft (NK-Iselin); at foot of text: "Wm. Short Esqr. Secy. to the ⟨Honble Thos. Jefferson⟩ am: Legation at the Court of France"; endorsed. FC (DNA: PCC, No. 121).

The CERTAIN SUBJECT on which Jay reported to Congress was the proposal to transfer the American debt to France to a group of Holland bankers. Jay's remark that he had reported AGREEABLY TO HIS IDEAS is not to be taken to mean that Jay's opinion or report coincided with TJ's, but merely that he had transmitted TJ's letter of 26 Sep. 1786 as TJ desired. This was done on 18 Jan. and on 2 Feb. Congress referred TJ's letter to the Commissioners of the Treasury to report; their report, submitted 19 Feb., recommended for a variety of reasons that "it would be proper without delay to instruct the Minister of the United States at the Court of France not to give any sanction to any negociation which may be proposed for transferring the debt due from the United States, to any State or company of Individuals who may be disposed to purchase the same." This was approved by Congress, but not until 2 Oct. 1787 (JCC, XXXII, 12; XXXIII, 589-92).

To Villedeuil

SIR   Paris July 5. 1787

In the moment that I recieved Your Excellency's letter of the 2d. inst. I was doing myself the honor of enclosing to you a copy of some observations on the letter of M. de Calonne which I had put into the hands of His Excellency Count de Montmorin on Tuesday last. Their object being to throw further light on the several subjects of that letter, some of which were left incomplete for want of information, I take the liberty of submitting them to your inspection and of praying that they may be considered when the regulations announced in the letter shall recieve their final and more solemn form. You will perceive that they include, among others, the alterations proposed in the conversation with which you were pleased to honor me some days ago.

I beg you to accept assurances of those sentiments of perfect esteem and respect with which I have the honor to be Your Excellency's most obedient and humble servant,

TH: JEFFERSON

PrC (MHi); in Short's hand, signed by TJ. PrC of Tr (DLC); French translation; in Short's hand; at head of text: "Traduction de la lettre precedente." Enclosure: Observations on Calonne's letter of 22 Oct. 1786, printed above under 3 July 1787, and handed by TJ to Montmorin on that day.

From Abigail Adams

MY DEAR SIR   London july 6 1787

If I had thought you would so soon have sent for your dear little Girl, I should have been tempted to have kept her arrival here,

6 JULY 1787

from you a secret. I am really loth to part with her, and she last evening upon Petit's arrival, was thrown into all her former distresses, and bursting into Tears, told me it would be as hard to leave me as it was her Aunt Epps. She has been so often deceived that she will not quit me a moment least she should be carried away. Nor can I scarcly prevail upon her to see Petit. Tho she says she does not remember you, yet she has been taught to consider you with affection and fondness, and depended upon your comeing for her. She told me this morning, that as she had left all her Friends in virginia to come over the ocean to see you, she did think you would have taken the pains to have come here for her, and not have sent a man whom she cannot understand. I express her own words. I expostulated with her upon the long journey you had been, and the difficulty you had to come and upon the care kindness and attention of Petit, whom I so well knew. But she cannot yet hear me. She is a child of the quickest sensibility, and the maturest understanding, that I have ever met with for her years. She had been 5 weeks at sea, and with men only, so that on the first day of her arrival, she was as rough as a little sailor, and then she been decoyed from the ship, which made her very angry, and no one having any Authority over her; I was apprehensive I should meet with some trouble. But where there are such materials to work upon as I have found in her, there is no danger. She listend to my admonitions, and attended to my advice and in two days, was restored to the amiable lovely Child which her Aunt had formed her. In short she is the favorite of every creature in the House, and I cannot but feel Sir, how many pleasures you must lose by committing her to a convent. Yet situated as you are, you cannot keep her with you. The Girl she has with her, wants more care than the child, and is wholy incapable of looking properly after her, without some superiour to direct her.

As both Miss Jefferson and the maid had cloaths only proper for the sea, I have purchased and made up for them, such things as I should have done had they been my own, to the amount of Eleven or 12 Guineys. The particulars I will send by Petit.

Captain Ramsey has said that he would accompany your daughter to Paris provided she would not go without him, but this would be putting you to an expence that may perhaps be avoided by Petits staying a few days longer. The greatest difficulty in familiarizing her to him, is on account of the language. I have not the Heart to force her into a Carriage against her will and send her from me almost in a Frenzy; as I know will be the case, unless I

[551]

can reconcile her to the thoughts of going and I have given her my word that Petit shall stay untill I can hear again from you. Books are her delight, and I have furnished her out a little library, and she reads to me by the hour with great distinctness, and comments on what she reads with much propriety.

Mrs. Smith desires to be remembered to you, and the little Boy his Grandmama thinks is as fine a Boy as any in the Kingdom. I am my dear sir with Sentiments of Esteem Your Friend and Humble Servant, A ADAMS

RC (DLC); addressed; endorsed. Recorded in SJL as received 10 July 1787.

From Thomas Barclay

L'Orient, 6 July 1787. Encloses a letter written since his arrival there. "It relates intirely to my affair with French & Nephew, and Do's not Call on you for any Immediate attention. I trouble you with it to shew you that I Did all that I thought my Duty towards these Men." Lynch, whom TJ saw at Bordeaux, called on Barclay, and they parted "on such terms as made me Expect an accommodation wou'd have Immediately follow'd"; supposes however he was overruled, "for the next day he was as Rancorous as Ever." Sunday evening Barclay was informed that, at French's request, on Monday the parliament of Bordeaux would send for him; that firm had prevented his leaving for Paris and "they were Representing to the Parliament, that I availed myself of my Public Character, and was making unnecessary Delays there to screen my self from them. As I Did not wish to be any longer troublesome to the Parliament, I reach'd Nantes in about 60 hours." Hopes to leave L'Orient soon and to write to TJ from America. The vessel will stop at Tercera; his health and spirits are good. He needs money, and though he knows TJ has "no power to order me any," has drawn on TJ for 1200 livres at eleven days' sight in favor of Zachariah Loreilhe (dated Bordeaux, 30 June), "which you will please to order Mr. Grand to Pay, and Place to the Public account." He will write again.

RC (DLC); 3 p.; endorsed: "Barclay Thos. French & nephew." Recorded in SJL as received 13 July 1787. Enclosure: Barclay's undated letter to TJ, printed above under 3 July.

To Dr. Lambert

à Paris ce 6me. Juillet 1787.

J'ai reçu, Monsieur la lettre que vous m'avez fait l'honneur de m'adresser le 11me. Juin, et aussi les 283. bouteilles de vin que vous m'avez expedié par la messagerie royale. Je leur trouve toutes les bonnes qualités pour lesquelles vos vins sont si renommés et j'en suis parfaitement content. Je me ferai un devoir et un plaisir d'en payer le montant 374.₶14s à telle personne que vous aurez la bonté de m'indiquer. Toutes les fois que j'en aurai besoin d'une provision ulterieure j'aurai l'honneur de vous la demander. Je ne crois pas que ca sera plutot que l'automne de l'annee prochaine et je vous demanderai d'en faire les expeditions futures par voie de la mer, le transport par la messagerie, et les droits en chemin, augmentant le prix 15. sous par bouteille. Les choses obligeantes dont votre lettre est remplie, Monsieur, sont l'effet de votre bonté. Je vous dois mille remercimens, et je vous les rends de tout mon coeur, de la reception hospitaliere et honnete que vous avez bien voulu me faire chez vous. Je vous etois très redevable de la bonne chere que vous m'avez fait faire, et, cherchant de m'instruire de tout ce qui concernoit les vins de Frontignan, j'etois bien heureux de me trouver dans les mains d'une personne si capable de m'en donner les meilleurs renseignements. J'en etois très sensible dans le moment, je le suis encore, et je le serai toujours. Je vous prie Monsieur d'en agreer tous mes remerciments et l'assurance de la sinceritè des sentiments d'estime et d'attachement avec lesquelles j'ai l'honneur d'etre Mons. votre tres humble et tres obeissant serviteur,

Th: Jefferson

PrC (MHi); at foot of text: "Monsr. Lambert D.M."

To Miguel de Lardizábel y Uribe, with Enclosure

Sir   Paris July 6. 1787.

I have duly received the letter you did me the honor to write me from Madrid the 30th. of May. But that which you mention to have written before has never come to my hands. I had known of your safe arrival in Madrid by a letter from Mr. Carmichael informing me he had received the copying press. I hope yours also has answered your expectations. I have had a journey of between three and four months through the Southern parts of France and Northern of Italy. It has been very agreeable but the effect of the waters of Aix were not sensible on my wrist which reestablishes itself slowly. I took the liberty of putting into your hands a catalogue of the Spanish books on the subject of America which I wished to acquire. I now send that of the books of the same kind

6 JULY 1787

which I already possess, as it may be a further guide in the execution of the commission you are so kind as to undertake for me. I shall always be happy to receive news of your health and welfare, being with sentiments of very sincere attachment and esteem Sir Your most obedient & most humble servt.,   TH: JEFFERSON

ENCLOSURE

Spanish books on the subject of America, already possessed by Th: J.

Notitia de la California por Miguel Venegas.
Noticias Americanas de Don Antonio de Ulloa.
Historia de las Indias por Frances Lopez de Gomora, 12 mo.
Historia general de las islas y tierra firma del Mar oceano di Herrera.
Historia de la conquista de Mexico por De Solis.
El Orinoco ilustrado por Gumilla.
Historia natural y moral de las Indias por Acosta.
Viage à la America meridional por Juan de Ulloa. 4. vol. fol.
Observaciones Astronomicas y Phisicas por Juan de Ulloa.
Comentarios reales de los Incas del Peru por Garcilasso de la Vega.
la Florida por Garcilasso de la Vega.
Historia general de la Florida por de Cardenas y Caro.
La Monarquia Indiana por De Torquemada.

PrC (DLC). Enclosure (PrC in DLC).

To Lormerie

SIR   Paris July 6. 1787.

The load of business which has accumulated during my absence has put it out of my power to answer sooner the letter and observations with which you were pleased to honour me. I have perused those observations with attention, and think them judicious, and well calculated to remedy the evil of public robbers and unsafe highroads. But it is a happy truth for us, Sir, that these evils do not exist, and never did exist in our part of America. The Sieur de Perponcher has suffered himself to be misled probably by the English papers. I attended the bar of the Supreme court of Virginia ten years as a student, and as a practitioner. There never was during that time a trial for robbery on the highroad, nor do I remember ever to have heard of one in that or any other of the states: except in the cities of New York and Philadelphia immediately after the departure of the British army. Some deserters from that army infested those cities for a while; but as I have heard nothing of them for some time past, I suppose the vigilance of the civil magistrate has suppressed the evil.

Mr. Warville was so good as to give me a copy of the book written by himself and M. Claviere on France and the United States, but I have not yet had time to read it. The talents and information of those gentlemen leave me without doubt that it is well written. I have the honour of inclosing you your observations with thanks for their perusal and assurances of the sentiments of

PrC (DLC); lacks final part of complimentary close (see Vol. 9: 217, note 1); MS faded, and someone later (probably Henry A. Washington) attempted to clarify the text by overwriting, an effort that produced the erroneous reading "M. Claivierie" at the foot of the text in place of the original "M. de Lormerie" (see Vol. 10: 288, note 1), as shown by the fact that this is a reply to Lormerie's of 2 July 1787 and by the entry in SJL for such a letter under 6 July 1787. Enclosure: Lormerie's "memoire . . . relativement *aux moÿens d'opérer la sureté publique dans les états unis*" (not found, but see Lormerie to TJ, 2 July 1787).

To Robert Montgomery

Sir   Paris July 6. 1787.

I duly received your favor of the 22d. May, with the letter from Mr. Lamb, and that from Mr. Jay which I now return you. I am happy that you have so good a place in the dispositions of a person, through whom the Consular appointments will probably pass. Congress have yet done nothing on that subject. Whenever they shall take it up I have no doubt they [will] do justice to the considerations which present themselves in your favor. You mentioned in a former letter the death of the Dey of Algiers. Having heard nothing further of this, I have supposed it might want confirmation. Having communicated it to Congress, if you should have received later information on the subject I will thank you to enable me to confirm or contradict it in my next letters. I have the honour to be Sir your most obedient humble servt.,   TH: JEFFERSON

PrC (DLC); at foot of text: "Mr. Robert Montgomery Alicant." Enclosure not found, but see Montgomery to TJ, 22 May 1787.

To G. Pin

à Paris ce 6me. Juillet 1787

Je me profite, Monsieur, du premier moment de mon arrivée pour vous accuser la reception de la lettre que vous avez eu la bonté de m'adresser de Toulouse le 26me. Mai, avec les renseignements sur le canal de Languedoc. Ces renseignements sont exacts, bien detaillés, et precieux, comme on devoit en attendre d'une personne de vos connoissances. Ils remplissent parfaitement l'objet que je m'avois propose en prenant la liberté de vous les demander, et j'espere que ma patrie en sera profitée. Je vous prie Monsieur d'en agreer touts mes remerciments aussi bien pour cette nouvelle marque de votre attention, que pour celles dont vous avez bien voulu m'honorer à Toulouse, et l'assurance de la sinceritè des sentiments de reconnoissance et d'attachement avec lesquelles j'ai l'honneur d'etre Monsieur Votre tres humble et tres obeissant serviteur, TH: JEFFERSON

PrC (MHi).

From Andrew Ramsay

SIR London July 6th. 1787

I was this morning honoured with your letter of the 2d. and am happy any Attentions I have paid Miss Jefferson meets with your Approbation. Indeed any person whose care she was put Under must have been void of feeling if they neglected her.

Her sweet disposition and good nature demanded every attention; and her Vexation and the Affliction she underwent on leaving her Aunt, made it nesseray to be attentive at first for I was afraid of her getting sick but she soon got over it and got so fond of me that she seldom parts with me without tears, and indeed I am almost the same way with her. Every expence of her passage was paid in Virginia and I engaged to see her safe home to Paris if you had not left some particular Orders with Mr. Adams. I shall not be busy in another weeks time and if no person comes from you to Convey her over and it meets with your Approbation I shall do myself that honor. I have the honor to be Sir your most hble. Ser.,
ANDW. RAMSAY

RC (MHi); endorsed. Recorded in SJL as received 10 July from "Ramsay capt." TJ's LETTER OF THE 2D. has not been found.

To Thomas Mann Randolph, Jr.

SIR Paris July 6. 1787.

Your favor of April 14. came here during my absence on a journey through the Southern parts of France and Northern of Italy, from which I am but lately returned: this cause alone has

6 JULY 1787

prevented your receiving a more early answer to it. I am glad to find that among the various branches of science presenting themselves to your mind you have fixed on that of Politics as your principal pursuit. Your country will derive from this a more immediate and sensible benefit. She has much for you to do. For tho' we may say with confidence that the worst of the American constitutions is better than the best which ever existed before in any other country, and that they are wonderfully perfect for a first essay, yet every human essay must have defects. It will remain therefore to those now coming on the stage of public affairs to perfect what has been so well begun by those going off it. Mathematics, Natural philosophy, Natural history, Anatomy, Chemistry, Botany, will become amusements for your hours of relaxation, and auxiliaries to your principal studies. Precious and delightful ones they will be. As soon as such a foundation is laid in them as you may build on as you please hereafter, I suppose you will proceed to your main objects, Politics, Law, Rhetoric and History. As to these, the place where you study them is absolutely indifferent. I should except Rhetoric, a very essential member of them, and which I suppose must be taught to advantage where you are: you would do well therefore to attend the public exercises in this branch also, and to do it with very particular diligence. This being done, the question arises, where you shall fix yourself for studying Politics, Law, and History? I should not hesitate to decide in favor of France, because you will at the same time be learning to speak the language of that country, become absolutely essential under our present circumstances. The best method of doing this would be to fix yourself in some family where there are women and children, in Passy, Auteuil or some other of the little towns in reach of Paris. The principal hours of the day you will attend to your studies, and in those of relaxation associate with the family. You will learn to speak better from women and children in three months, than from men in a year. Such a situation too will render more easy a due attention to oeconomy of time and money. Having pursued your main studies here about two years, and acquired a facility in speaking French, take a tour of 4. or 5. months through this country and Italy, return then to Virginia and pass a year in Williamsburg under the care of Mr. Wythe, and you will be ready to enter on the public stage, with superior advantages. I have proposed to you to carry on the study of the law, with that of Politics and History. Every political measure will for ever have an intimate connection with the laws of the land; and he who knows nothing of these will

[557]

6 JULY 1787

always be perplexed and often foiled by adversaries having the advantage of that knolege over him. Besides it is a source of infinite comfort to reflect that under every change of fortune we have a resource in ourselves from which we may be able to derive an honourable subsistence. I would therefore propose not only the study, but the practice of the law for some time, to possess yourself of the habit of public speaking. With respect to modern languages, French, as I have before observed, is indispensible. Next to this the Spanish is most important to an American. Our connection with Spain is already important and will become daily more so. Besides this the antient part of American history is written chiefly in Spanish. To a person who would make a point of reading and speaking French and Spanish, I should doubt the utility of learning Italian. These three languages, being all degeneracies from the Latin, resemble one another so much that I doubt the possibility of keeping in the head a distinct knowlege of them all. I suppose that he who learns them all will speak a compound of the three, and neither perfectly.—The journey which I propose to you need not be expensive, and would be very useful. With your talents and industry, with science, and that stedfast honesty which eternally pursues right, regardless of consequences, you may promise yourself every thing—but health, without which there is no happiness. An attention to health then should take place of every other object. The time necessary to secure this by active exercises, should be devoted to it in preference to every other pursuit. I know the difficulty with which a studious man tears himself from his studies at any given moment of the day. But his happiness and that of his family depends on it. The most uninformed mind with a healthy body, is happier than the wisest valetudinarian.—I need not tell you that if I can be useful to you in any part of this or any other plan you shall adopt, you will make me happy by commanding my services.

Will you be so good, Sir, as to return my most respectful thanks for the diploma with which I am honored by the society instituted with you for the encouragement of the study of Natural history. I am afraid it will never be in my power to contribute any thing to the object of the institution. Circumstances have thrown me into a very different line of life; and not choice, [as] I am happy to find is your case.—In the year 1781. while confined to my room by a fall from my horse, I wrote some Notes in answer to the enquiries of M. de Marbois as to the Natural and Political state of Virginia. They were hasty and indigested: yet as some of these touch slightly on some objects of it's natural history, I will take the liberty of asking the society to accept a copy of them. For the same reason, and because too they touch on the political condition of our country, I will beg leave to present you with a copy, and ask the favor of you to find a conveyance for them from London to Edinburgh. They are printing by Stockdale, bookseller Piccadilly, and will be ready in 3. or 4. weeks from this time. I will direct him to deliver two copies to your order. Repeating constantly the proffer of my services, I shall only add assurances of the esteem and attachment with which I am Dear Sir Your friend & servt.,

TH: JEFFERSON

PrC (DLC).

To G. A. Auckler

MONSIEUR Paris 7me. Juillet 1787.

Je voyageois en Italie au moment où vous m'avez fait l'honneur de m'adresser votre lettre de l'11me. Mai. Je profite du premier moment libre depuis mon retour pour y faire reponse. Les etats de l'Amerique ne sont touts egalement favorables à l'etranger qui s'y domicile. Il y en a qui ne leur permettent pas d'exercer les premieres charges des corps Executifs ou Judiciaires, ni d'etre du corps legislatif. Il y en a d'autres, comme la Virginie par exemple, ou l'etranger, faisant declaration qu'il va s'y domicilier, et qu'il sera fidele à l'etat, rentre dans touts les droits de citoyen née, sans aucune exception. Je ne connois pas assez les loix des differents etats pour vous detailler le plus ou le moins de liberté que chacun donne à l'etranger domicilié. J'ai l'honneur d'etre avec les egards les plus distingués Monsieur votre très humble et très obeissant serviteur, TH: JEFFERSON

PrC (DLC); at foot of text: "M. Auckler, avocat à Argenton en Berry."

To Guillaume Delahaye

[*Paris, 7 July 1787.* Recorded in SJL under this date. Not found.]

To Pierre Poinsot des Essarts

à Paris 7me. Juillet.

J'etois absent, Monsieur, sur une voiage de trois à quatre mois

8 JULY 1787

quand vous m'avez fait l'honneur de m'adresser votre lettre du 5me. Avril. Je profite du premier moment libre depuis mon retour pour vous informer que je ne me souviens pas du tout des armes du General Washington, et qu'etant dans l'habitude de detruire les enveloppes des lettres qui me sont adressées, je n'ai plus cette ressource pour les chercher et vous en donner l'empreinte. Peutetre que M. le Marquis de la Fayette, qui reçoit souvent des lettres du General, pourroit en avoir conservé les envelopes avec l'empreint de son cachet. J'ai l'honneur d'etre, Monsieur, avec une consideration distinguée, votre très humble et très obeissant serviteur,

TH: JEFFERSON

PrC (DLC); MS torn along bottom edge, where TJ wrote: "M. Des Essarts [Conte] de [Bouvi]lle ru[e] de Verneuil [faubourg] St. G[erm]ai[n] N[o. 5]."

TJ's HABITUDE DE DETRUIRE LES ENVELOPPES DES LETTRES QUI ME SONT ADRESSEES was evidently a long-established one, to judge from this first reference to it, and it continued throughout life. He "destroyed" the address-covers of letters sent to him by utilizing their blank spaces for rough drafts, drawings, calculations, &c.

From Thomas Barclay

L'Orient, 8 July 1787. Encloses a sight draft in favor of TJ on Grand for 2,370 livres dated "the 31st. past" which balances his account current with the state of Virginia, also enclosed. Before this was opened, he was engaged by the Governor and Council of Virginia in other business; after its completion he was sent funds with instructions for their disbursement. "I was desired to accept of the remainder, which I did, and as near as I recollect it paid some necessary Expences . . . incurred in the pursuit of the object." From this he paid Houdon in advance 1,200 livres toward the price of 1,000 crowns set for the first bust of Lafayette, and, shortly before his trip to Morocco, the 1,800 livres for the second bust by an order on Ferdinand Grand to be charged to Virginia. The account, stated from memory, should be correct, "for by my giving the State credit for this sum, I pay for the whole of the Busts agreeable to my Instructions." Any errors result from the inaccessibility of his vouchers before he leaves for America; however, he will rectify them as soon as they become evident. He also encloses a "sort of a State" of TJ's account with him. "Perhaps the articles left open on both sides will nearly balance each other. From the second part a Balance appears due to me of 519 livres. Please to put the whole right and whatever the Balance may be, pay it to Mrs. Barclay."

RC (Vi); 2 p.; in an unidentified hand, with complimentary close and signature in Barclay's hand; endorsed. Recorded in SJL as received 13 July 1787. Enclosures: (1) Sight draft on Grand in favor of TJ, at Bordeaux, dated "31" June 1787 (Vi). (2) Account with Virginia dated at L'Orient, 8 July 1787 (Vi); a note at foot of text in TJ's hand reads: "See Mr. Barclay's letter of July 27. 1787. that he has omitted in this account to charge the state of Virginia 3. muskets made at Liege, which (filling up the blank of transportation from

[560]

Paris to Lorient with 21ᵗᵗ 4) amounts to 108ᵗᵗ 8s. I will therefore pay that sum to Mrs. Barclay and charge it in my account against the state of Virginia, viz 2370ᵗᵗ + 108—8s = 2478ᵗᵗ 8." (For an explanation of the phrase "filling up the blank," see Barclay to TJ, 27 July 1787, note 1.) (3) The enclosed "sort of a State" of Barclay's account with TJ has not been found. TJ's copy of it, with additions to 24 Jan. 1788, is in DLC.

From Francis Hopkinson

DEAR SIR   Philada. July 8th. 1787

I take the Opportunity of a Vessel going to Havre de Grace to send you a large Packet of News Papers, Magazines, *Museums* &c. to which I have added some Publications of our Literati and Politicians. To save any Postage from Havre to Paris I have address'd the Packet to Mr. Andrew Lamouzine, and requested him either to forward it to you, or keep it till sent for. I have got some Illinois Nuts for you, but Mr. Madison tells me he has sent you a Parcel.

As to Politics—The Papers will inform you that the Government of Masachusetts has been exceedingly disturbed and even endanger'd by Insurgents whose Numbers alone made them worthy of Notice. Rhode Island is at present govern'd by Miscreants void of even the external appearances of Honour or Justice. She has in Effect, tho' not expresly, withdrawn herself from the Union. A serious Storm seems to be brewing in the South West about the Navigation of the Mississipi. A Convention of Delegates from all the States, except Rhode Island, is now setting in this City. General Washington President. Their Business is to revise the Confederation, and propose Amendments. It will be very difficult to frame such a System of Union and Government for America as shall suit all Opinions and reconcile clashing Interests. Their Deliberations are kept inviolably secret, so that they set without Censure or Remark, but no sooner will the Chicken be hatch'd but every one will be for plucking a Feather. But the Papers I send should excuse me from taking up my Paper with Politics.

As to Philosophy—We abound with Schemers and Projectors. There is one *Fitch* who has been this Twelve month endeavouring to make a Boat go forward with Oars, worked by a Steam Engine. He has made several unsuccessful attempts, and spent much Money in the Project and has heated his Imagination so as to be himself a Steam Engine. I have no Doubt but that a Boat may be urged forward by such Means, but the enormous Expence and Complexity of the Machine must prevent its coming into common use. We have also a *Mr. Churchman*, who has found out the Longitude by means of the Variation of the Needle. All he asks to be allowed him is that there are two invisible Moons, one revolving round the North and the other round the South Pole, in small Circles, and in Times of his own contriving. These Moons by their attraction occasion the Phenomenon called Magnatism, and their periodical Revolutions form the magnetic Meridian and cause the Variations of the Compass. This learned Man understands as much of Philosophy as can be acquired by practical Surveying; and as much of Navigation as can be obtain'd from padling in a Canoe. A Mr. Workman, one of the Teachers in our University, has also made a Machine for discovering Longitude which is nothing more than a convenient application of the *Ring Dial*, which finds the true solar Meridian; underneath this is the magnetic Needle, and a graduated Circle designates the Degrees and Minutes of Difference between the solar and magnetic Meridians. But amongst these semi-lunatic Projectors, I must not omit myself. I have sent in to the philosophical Society a Contrivance for the perfect Measurement of Time, and I see no Reason *in Theory* why it should not answer. I am now making Experiments to ascertain *the Fact*. My Device consists of a small glass Syphon, the shorter Leg of which is fixed in a Float of Cork or light Wood, which is to rest on the Surface of a Small Bason of Spirit, the longer Leg of the Syphon to come over the Edge of the Bason and to be drawn out to an exceeding fine Point so that the Liquor may fall in Drops only. Directly under the discharging Leg of the Syphon is a long glass Tube, such as one used for Barometers, which receives the falling Drops, and the Rise of the Liquor in the Tube is to designate the Hours and Parts of an Hour on a Scale pasted along Side of it for that Purpose. As the receiving Orifice of the Syphon must always be at the same Distance below the Surface of the Liquor, it must always be prest by the same Weight, and my Expectation is that equal Quantities of the Fluid will be discharged in equal Times. I succeeded in making the Harmonica to be played with Kees, as far as I believe the Instrument is capable; but it required too much Address in the manner of wetting the Cushions, for common Use. In the Course of my Experiments I discover'd a method of drawing the Tone from Metal Bells by Friction, to an amazing Perfection, without the necessity of Water or any Fluid. I am getting a Set of Bells cast, and expect to introduce a new musical Instrument to be called the *Bellarmonic*. I have only Room to assure you that I am as ever Your affectionate   F. HOPKINSON

If you can conveniently (very conveniently) send me 3 (or 6 Bottles if cheap) of the french Vingar such as we used to have at the Chevr. de la Luzerne's I shall be much obliged to you. I am very fond of it and it is not to be had here, for money. I meet with the same kind at Mr. Morris's.

Dr. Franklin is well. Mr. Rittenhouse has been indisposed, is gone into the Country back of New York State, to run public Lines. I long to receive more of the Encyclopedia and Phys-Œconomi. I have nothing more to do with our magazine. I only conducted it for March, April and May. Mr. Bartram gave me the enclosed long since. I know not whether the Box of Seeds mentioned were ever forwarded. It was left with his Brother, waiting for Conveyance. I will enquire about it Tomorrow.

RC (DLC); endorsed. The MS containing the postscript has in the course of time become separated from the present letter and attached instead to that from Hopkinson of 9 Dec. 1786; but "the enclosed" which Hopkinson states he had received "long since" was Bartram's letter to TJ of 14 Dec. 1786, which, as indicated in SJL, was received the same day as the present letter, 26 Aug. 1787. It is therefore certain that the postscript belongs to the present letter. The other enclosures have not been further identified.

From William Macarty

L'Orient, 8 July 1787. The plates he had mentioned are 36 livres a dozen; there are also two tureens at 36 livres, but none of the other items TJ listed. If TJ wishes them at that price, he will forward the plates and tureens. Fears TJ has not succeeded in obtaining a safe conduct for him; "however necessary the arret de Surseance may be for me, I would not wish for it, unless consider'd as an act of Justice as well as a favour."

RC (DLC); 2 p.; endorsed: "McCarty Wm." Recorded in SJL as received 13 July 1787.

To the Abbé de Arnal

Sir Paris July 9. 1787.

I had the honour of informing you when at Nismes that we had adopted in America a method of hanging the upper stone of a grist mill which had been found so much more convenient than the antient as to have brought it into general use. Whether we derive the invention from Europe, or have made it ourselves, I am unable to say. The difference consists only in the Spindle and horns. On the former plan, the horns were of a single peice of iron in

9 JULY 1787

the form of a cross, with a square hole in the middle, thus which square hole fitted on the upper end of the spindle. The horns were then fixed in cross grooves in the bottom of the upper stone, which was to be laid on the spindle so that the plane of it's grinding surface should be perfectly perpendicular to the spindle. This was a difficult and tedious operation, and was to be repeated every time the stones were dressed. According to the present method, two distinct peices of iron are substituted for the horns: the one in this form   of such breadth and thickness as to support the whole weight of the stone. It's streight ends are to be firmly fixed in one of the cross grooves of the stone, the circular part should rise through the hole in the center of the stone so as to be near it's upper surface. In the middle of this semicircular part, and on it's under surface (at a) should be a dimple to which the upper end of the spindle should be adjusted, by giving it a convexity fitted to the concavity of the dimple. The other peice of iron is only a streight bar, to be firmly fixed in the other of the cross grooves of the stone, and to have a square hole in it's center thus   . The corresponding part of the spindle must be squared to fit this hole. The office of the first peice of iron is to suspend the stone, that of the last is to give and continue it's motion. The stones [bein]g dressed, and these peices firmly fixed in it, it is turned over on the spindle so that the point of the spindle may enter the dimple of the semicircular iron, and the stone be suspended on it freely. It will probably not take at first it's true position which is that of the plane of it's grinding surface being truly perpendicular to the spindle. The workman must therefore chip it at top, with a chissel, till it hangs in that just position. This being once done, is done for ever: for whenever they dress the stones afterwards they have only to return the upper one to it's pivot and it will resume it's equilibrium. It sometimes happens that one side of the stone, being softer than the other, wears faster, and so the equilibrium is lost in time. Experience has shewn that a small departure from the equilibrium will be rectified by the bedstone, which serves as a guide to the running stone till it assumes it's motion in a true plane, which it will afterwards keep. But should a defect of the stone render this [depar]ture from the equilibrium too considerable, it may be necessary to set it to rights, at certain periods, by chipping it again on the top. I had promised, when I had the honour of seeing you at Nismes, to send you a model of this manner of fixing the mill-stone: but the expence of sending

9 JULY 1787

a model by post, the danger of it's being lost or destroyed by the Messagerie, and the hope that I could render it intelligible by a description and figures, have induced me to prefer the latter method. I shall with great pleasure give any further explanations which may be necessary for your perfect comprehension of it, and the more so as it will furnish me with new occasions of assuring you of those sentiments of respect and esteem with which I have the honor to be Sir your most obedient & most humble servant,

TH: JEFFERSON

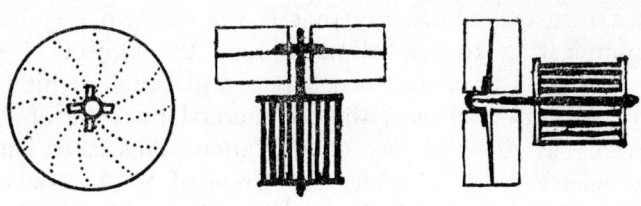

PrC (DLC); at foot of first page: "M. l'Abbé D'Arnal, ancien chanoine d'Alais à Nimes."

From William Carmichael

DEAR SIR   Madrid 9th. July 1787

I had the honor to receive in course of post your favors of the 26th. of May from Bourdeaux and of June the 14th. from Paris. Colonel Smith having himself expressed a desire to acquaint you with the Object of his mission from motives which you will feel, I left that task to him, and of course deferd doing myself the honor of writing to you until I might have it in my power to communicate something worthy your Attention. Mr. Grand had anticipated the disagreable Information you give me of the State of our funds in Europe and will have communicated to you my situation in consequence thereof. I have taken the proper precautions to extricate myself as well as I can, but permit me to remark, that it is painful to submit to obligations which I have endeavoured to avoid since my residence in this Country. As I know not the Amount of the Sums due by the United States to Mr. Grand, I cannot be a judge of his reasons to despair of their Credit. But I know that his Banking house was what the french call mesquin until it first had the good Fortune to become known to the French Ministry by its Connection with us and until it acquired a degree of reputation by the payment made on our account. Of this I can assure you that I have many proofs in my possession.

[565]

9 JULY 1787

Colonel Smith left me the fourth Inst. I find that Gentleman in every respect such as you describe him to me. Agreable to his desire I presented him to the Ct. de Florida Blanca by whom he was very well received and from whom he had a Letter recommending him in his Majestys name to the Frendly offices of the Spanish Chargé des Affaires at the Court of Portugal. I also procured him an unlimited credit with the first commercial house at Lisbon and letters of Introduction which I hope will prove agreable and useful to him.

I must own to you frankly that I was somewhat embarrassed in communicating to the Minister here the Object of Colonel Smiths Voyage. I have obtained here a declaration of his Catholic Majestys resolution to treat the commercial Interests of America as favorably as those of any other Nation. This court interested itself to releive from Captivity the Crew of an American vessel carried into Morrocco and obtained the Restoration of the vessel Captured. Not content with this Interference, it procured an offer from the Emperor to make a treaty with the United States thro the Mediation of his Catholic Majesty. Congress hath been Advised of all these Circumstances and yet no notice has yet been taken by that Body of the good offices of this Court except by some Insinuations which Mr. Jay in a Letter to me desired me to make of the future steps that Congress would take to manifest their sense of his Catholic Majestys good offices. I had in some measure fulfilled Mr. Jays injunctions. On the Arrival of Colonel Smith I was constrained to hackney (if I may be permitted the expression) the same trite declaration. It succeeded—But I must pray you, if the Subject Strikes you as it doth me, to represent to Congress the necessity of these Little Attentions. For what hath Portugal done to merit the marked thanks of Congress. An offer to protect our Commerce as that of its own subjects! That is to say, that her faithful Majestys Ships of war will not permit an Algerine or Barbary corsair, with which Portugal is at war to take any of our vessels in their view, or to retake them if captured. I must own I see no great merit in this communication of her faithful Majestys Intentions. I have looked upon it rather as an advance of the Treaty which has been so long on the Carpet and in Consequence have mentioned to Colonel Smith my Ideas of bringing it forward, that is of giving the portuguese Ministry the opportunity of Explaining their Sentiments on this point.

I have nothing from Algiers that can Induce me to beleive the Treaty with this country is in a way of being concluded to the

9 JULY 1787

Satisfaction of Both parties. On the contrary either this Country must submit to the extortion and even caprice of the Dey and Regency or run a risque of losing the great sums it has already expended for this object of pacification. I have Letters from our Captives in a complaining Stile. I have received accounts from the Ct. D'Expilly of the Advances he has made for their sustenance, until the 1st. of April. The vouchers and receipts are good and there is near 800 Dollars to pay him, but as Mr. Lamb has left a private account against D'Expilly in the hands of Mr. Montgomery of Alicant, I shall endeavour to pay the public Debt by the private account of Mr. Lamb. At All Events I wish to know how I may in case of Exigency reimburse the sum abovementioned.

The Death of the Minister of Indies (the Marquis de Senera) will occasion many changes here. In fact the Spanish possessions in America are in a critical Situation. By force it is impossible to preserve their dependance on this Government. But I am persuaded that the Cte. de Florida Blanca will pursue every measure of conciliation to lose nothing by the Death of Galvez. He had too many fits of phrensy and folly to Listen to reason. I enter into no details of the Politics of this Court. In the present situation of Europe, you are at the fountain head and can better develop than myself the Catastrophe. I own I cannot plunge thro' the chaos. I have the cypher you mention and you may make use of it when you think proper. By your manner of employing it I shall judge of what I ought to do. I shall never be more happy than in having an opportunity of assuring you of the great regard and Esteem with which I have the honor to be Your Excellencys Most Obedt. & Hble. Sert., WM. CARMICHAEL

Dupl (DLC); at head of text: "Copy." Recorded in SJL as received 29 Aug. 1787. This Dupl was enclosed in Carmichael to TJ, 22 Aug. 1787, which TJ acknowledged on 25 Sep. 1787 and stated that he had never received the original.

From Maria Cosway

London 9 July 1787

Do you deserve a long letter, My dear friend? No, certainly not, and to avoid temptation, I take a small sheet of paper; Conversing with you, would break on Any resolution. I am determind to prevent it. How long you like to keep your friends in anxiety!—How Many Months was you without writing to Me? And you felt no remorse?—I was glad to know you was well, sure of your being much engaged and diverted, and had only to lament I was not a Castle hanging to cloud, a stream, a village, a stone on the pavement of Turin, Milan, and Genoa &c. &c. No! I enter'd in the Calculation of hours that prevented you from visiting Rome. I am not sure if I had any share in the *provoking part*; oh! if I had been a shadow of this *Elysium* of yours! how you would have been tormented! I must excuse you a little, since you tell me you thought of me, and Italy was your Object. You advise me to go this beautifful tour, do you forget, che fu la Mia Cuna, che sull' limpido Corrente del' Arno ricevei la Vita? Che all Tevere fu il mio primo viaggio. Che Turino M'arrestò Nella Mia strada a Londra? Con-tutto ciò vorrei che M'avesse dato una pià lunga relazione dell' Suo Viaggio; le Sue osservazioni mi piacciono, il Suo gusto e buono, le Sue lettere m'interessano, ed aspettavo quasi in dritto, che mi avrebbe scritte tante pagine, quanti giorni fu assente. Specialmente avendo tanti suggetti, se pure qualcosa può Mancare per ajutare la Sua immaginazione, Ma renderebbeli lo Scrivermi più piacevole, Mentre, ripass[er]ebbe con la penna quei luoghi che gli dettero tanto piacere. Sono veramente Mortificata, nientte potrebbe pacificarmi, che queste linee sono Sue, ed allora, Non Misuro la scarsezza delle linee Ma il piacere che M'apporttano.

Non so se verremo a Parigi quest' anno, temo di No, Mio Marito Comincia a dubitarne, giusto al tempo che dovrebbe prepararsi per partire; Non puol credere quanto Mi dispiace quest' incertezza, ò tutto da temere contro il Mio desiderio. Perche promettere? Perche lusingarmi? Mi par Un sogno d' esservi stato, e lo desidero adesso realizzato, per l' impressione che mi lasciò. Almeno dia la Consolazione di ricevere nuove di un luogo che tanto M'interessa. Mi dica che Comedie ci sono nuove e buone, che Opere, che produzioni d'arti &c. &c. tutto quelche può indurlo a scrivermi delle lunghe lettere. Mi guastò sull' principio della nostra corrispondenza, glielo dissi, non a piu seguitato.

Ho avuto il piacere finalmente di vedere Madme. de Corny Mi piace assai, e molto amabile, e graziosa. Mi rincresce non averla Conosciuta prima.

Non. Mi dice niente ne della Sua Salute, ne del Suo braccio, bravo bravissimo.

Mi dispiace che non o occasione di vedere la Sua Figlia che mi dicono e qui presentemente. Non Conosco Mrs. Adams, e mi lusingo che se lei avessi creduto che io potessi esserle utile in qualsiasi Cosa, avrebbe reso giustizia all' Mio desiderio di Mostrarli in ogni oc-

9 JULY 1787

casione quanto son riconoscente della Sua amicizia per la Sua piu Aff.ma ed Ob.ma Serva, MARIA COSWAY

Mio Marito à l'onore di presentarli i Suoi ossequi.

Will you excuse the liberty I take in troubling you with these letters and a parcel. I shall be much obliged to you if you will be so good to send them. I dont know where the Duchess of Kingston leaves [lives] as I used to send to her at Calais and have been told she has removed from her House in Paris.

RC (ViU); endorsed. Recorded in SJL as received 15 July 1787. Accompanying "letters and a parcel" not further identified.

Translation of that part of the text in Italian: [do you forget] that it was my cradle, that on the limpid current of the Arno I received life! That my first voyage was to the Tiber. That Turin stopped me on my way to London! With all that I wish you had given me a longer account of your voyage; your observations pleased me, your taste is good, your letters interest me, and I expected almost by right, that you would write me as many pages as you were days absent. Especially having so many subjects to aid what was lacking in your imagination, it would render writing to me more pleasant for you while you reviewed with your pen those places which gave you so much pleasure. I am truly mortified. Nothing could pacify me, except that these lines are yours, and then I do not measure the sparseness of the lines but the pleasure which they bring me.

I do not know that we shall come to Paris this year. I fear not. My husband begins to doubt it, just at the time when one should begin to prepare to leave; You cannot believe how much this uncertainty displeases me, when I have everything to fear against my desire. Why promise? Why lead me to hope? It seems a dream to have been there and I now wish it to be real, because of the impression it left upon me. At least console me by receiving news of a place which so much interests me. Tell me what comedies there are that are new and good, what operas, what works of art &c. &c. everything that can induce you to write me long letters. You spoiled me in the beginning of our correspondence, I told you, you have not continued.

I have finally had the pleasure of seeing Mdme. de Corny. I like her very much, she is amiable and gracious. I regret not having known her earlier.

You do not tell me anything either of your health or of your arm, bravo bravissimo.

I am sorry I have not had occasion to see your daughter who they say is presently here. I do not know Mrs. Adams, and I flatter myself that if you had believed that I might have been useful to her in any way at all, you would have gratified my desire to show you on every occasion how grateful I am for your friendship for your most affectionate and obedient servant, MARIA COSWAY—My husband has the honor to present his respects.

From Madame de Corny

a down place le 9 juillet 1787.

Je suis dautant plus flattée de votre Souvenir, monsieur, que j'ay euë vraiment a me plaindre de vous, ayant decouvert, par hasard, que vous aviez differer votre depart pour les provinces meridionales sans avoir ete assez bon pour men avertir mais le present doit effacer le passe. Je suis fort aise davoir la certitude de vous trouver a paris. Je ne scais rien de ma marche, jusqu'a present elle a ete bien contrariee. Je part ce Soir pour bath, dela j'irai a bristol, oxford, bleinheim, stow. Ma sante a bien souffert, je nay passe que huit jours a Londres. Ma fatigue etoit extrême jay recherché du repos a la campagne mais la fievre et un rhume des plus considerables mont rendu incapable de toute chose. Jespere que le voyage projette me sera utille, sans quoi je serois authorisee a dire que langleterre a un climat bien nuisible a mon temperament.

Je nay point fait usage de votre lettre pour Mde. Adam. Jen ai fait de même pour les autres dont jetois chargée, mais si javois Scu que votre enfant etoit chez elle je naurois pas differe dun moment a laller voir. Je regrette que vous mayez privé dun moyen de vous être utille. Je suis dans une telle ignorance sur toute les beautees de langleterre que vous devez trouver bien simple mon desir de retourner a paris mais jay encor si present les agonies du passage de la mer que je ne me trouve pas encor assez forte pour me comdamner de nouveau a ce vrai suplice.

Jay l'honneur monsieur de vous renouveller les assurances de mon attachement.

RC (DLC); unsigned. This letter was not posted but enclosed in Madame de Corny's of 4 Aug. 1787 after she had returned to London from her trip into the country. Both letters were recorded in SJL as received 21 Aug. 1787.

TJ's letter of introduction POUR MDE. ADAM is that to Abigail Adams, printed above at the end of Nov. 1786 from the press copy; Mrs. Adams probably never saw the original.

To Jan Ingenhousz

SIR   Paris July 9. 1787.

An absence of three or four months on a journey through the Southern parts of France and Northern of Italy, has prevented my acknowleging earlier the receipt of your favor of Dec. 28. together with the pamphlet received through Barrois, for which I beg the author to accept my sincere thanks. Any letters or parcels from yourself to Doctr. Franklin, if you will do me the honor of addressing them to my care, can be forwarded regularly and safely every six weeks by the packet boats of this country which ply between Havre and New York. In like manner any letters, newspapers or other things from Dr. Franklin to yourself shall be duly forwarded through the Imperial Ambassador. A letter from Dr. Franklin about the last of April informs me he is in as good health as when he left Passy. I shall embrace with great pleasure every occasion of being useful to you, as well as of assuring you of the high respect and esteem with which I have the honour of being Sir Your most obedient & most humble servt.,

TH: JEFFERSON

RC (PPAP); addressed: "A Monsieur Monsieur Ingenhausz Medecin de la cour &c. à Vienne"; endorsed. PrC (DLC).

To Lanchon Frères & Cie

GENTLEMEN   Paris July 9. 1787.

Your favor of the 4th. instant came to hand yesterday together with the letter which it covered. Accept my thanks for your kind attention on this occasion and friendly offers in future. I learn with much regret that Mr. Harrison was in Lorient while I was there without my knowing it; and the more so as he would probably have furnished me occasion of procuring the honor of your acquaintance. My visit to Lorient having been meerly with a view to become acquainted with the circumstances of our commerce there, I should have embraced with pleasure every occasion of making acquaintance with those who could have given me informations thereon. As occasions may still arise of my revisiting that place I shall certainly do myself the pleasure of seeing you in that case. I have the honor to be with great regard Gentlemen your most obedient & most humble servant,   TH: JEFFERSON

PrC (DLC).

From Wilt, Delmestre & Cie

L'Orient, 9 July 1787. Acknowledge TJ's letter of 2 July; have drawn on him this date, for the coffee they sent, for 138ᵗᵗ 19s. payable to the order of Messrs. Delaville, Le Roulx & Carié. They have received on their brig, *La Sophie*, arrived there from Philadelphia 28 June, a box "Sans dessus, remplie de terre avec une addresse PACAN *or Illinois nuts, for Mr. Jefferson a Paris.*" Since there were no instructions, the captain did not know whether they should be watered, but decided against it, "et la terre nous en parait très seche." If he wishes them to forward the box, he should direct them whether or not to water the earth and to leave the box uncovered.

RC (DLC); 2 p.; in French; endorsed. Recorded in SJL as received 13 July 1787.

The draft by Wilt, Delmestre & Cie., dated at L'Orient, 9 July 1787, payable at one day from date to "Messieurs Laville Leroux & Carier" for the amount stated, endorsed over to La Buissiere Carié Fils & Cie., and bearing on its face the following in TJ's hand: "July 21. 1787. Accepted. Th: Jefferson" is in DLC. The PACAN OR ILLINOIS NUTS were those sent by Madison (see Madison to TJ, 15 May 1787).

To Abigail Adams

Dear Madam   Paris July 10. 1787.

This being the day on which, according to my calculation, my daughter would be crossing the channel, I had calculated the course from Dover to Calais and was watching the wind when your favour of the 6th. was put into my hands. That of June 27. had been received four days ago. I perceived that that had happened which I had apprehended, that your goodness had so attached her to you that her separation would become difficult. I had been in hopes that Petit would find means to rival you, and I still hope he will have done it so as that they may be on their way here at present. If she were to stay till she should be willing to come, she would stay till you cease to be kind to her, and that, Madam, is a term for which I cannot wait. Her distress will be in the moment of parting and I am in hopes Petit will soon be able to lessen it.—We are impatient to hear what our federal convention are doing. I have no news from America later than the 27th. of April. Nor is there any thing here worth mentioning. The death of Mr. Saint James and flight of M. de Calonnes are perhaps known to you. A letter of M. de Mirabeau to the K. of Prussia is handed about by the Colporteurs. I will endeavor to find an opportunity of sending it to Mr. Adams.—Your kind advances for my daughter shall be remitted you by Colo. Smith when he returns or some other good opportunity. I have the honor to be with sentiments of gratitude for your goodness and with those of perfect esteem Dr. Madam your most obedt. humble servt.,   Th: Jefferson

RC (MHi: AMT); addressed: "Mrs. Adams London." PrC (DLC).

From Abigail Adams, with List of Purchases for Mary Jefferson

Dear Sir   London july 10th. 1787

When I wrote you last I did not know that petit had taken places in the Stage and paid for them. This being the case I have represented it to your little daughter and endeavourd to prevail with her to consent to going at the time appointed. She says if I must go I will, but I cannot help crying so pray dont ask me to. I should have taken great pleasure in presenting her to you here, as you would then have seen her with her most engageing countanance.

10 JULY 1787

Several lines of an old song frequently occur to me as different objects affect her.

> What she thinks in her Heart
> You may read in her Eyes
> For knowing no art
> She needs no disguise.

I never saw so intelligent a countanance in a child before, and the pleasure she has given me is an ample compensation for any little services I have been able to render her. I can easily conceive the earnest desire you must have to embrace so lovely a child after so long a seperation from her. That motive, and my own intention of setting out next week upon a journey into the County of Devonshire, has prevaild with me to consent to parting with her so soon, but most reluctantly I assure you. Her temper, her disposition, her sensibility are all formed to delight. Yet perhaps at your first interview you may find a little roughness but it all subsides in a very little time, and she is soon attached by kindness. I inclose a memorandum of the articles purchased [I have? be]en a little particular, that you might know how I [have dispose]d of the money. If at any time I can be of service in this [respec]t it will give me pleasure. I have desired petit to Buy me 12 Ells of black lace at 8 Livres pr. Ell and 1 dozen of white and one of coulourd Gloves. You will be so good as to place them to my account and Col. Smith will take them when he returns.

As to politicks, to avoid touching so disagreeable a subject, I send you the Boston news papers received by the last vessels.

Mrs. Paridise has just left me and desires to be rememberd to you. She is just upon the eve of departure for virginia. Whether he can be prevaild upon to go on Board altho their passage is taken, and every thing in readiness, is very uncertain. She is determined at all Hazards. He most assuredly will get a Seat in Kings Bench if he stays behind. His affairs are daily worse and worse. Mr. Adams will write you. He has not a portrait that he likes to send you. Mr. Trumble talks of taking one. If he succeeds better than his Brethren, Mr. Adams will ask your acceptance of it. You will be so good as to let me hear from my dear little Girl by the first post after her arrival. My Love to her sister whom I congratulate upon such an acquisition.

I have not been able to find Mrs. Kinlock yet, but hope too. If I should not, Mr. Heyward is going to carolina in a few days and

10 JULY 1787

I will send the package by him. All your other Letters were deliverd as directed.

With Sentiments of the highest Esteem I am dear sir your Humble Servant,   A ADAMS

I have received of petit six Louis d'ors. [I do not know] what the exchange is. But the remainder you wi[ll be so good] as to let him purchase me some lace and Gloves with the remainder.

ENCLOSURE

Memorandum of articles by Mrs. Adams for Miss Jefferson & Maid

	£	s	d
Paid for bringing the Trunks from Tower Hill		5	6
Four fine Irish Holland frocks	3	10	
5 yd. white dimity for shirts		15	
4 yd. checked muslin for a frock	1	10	
3 yd. lace Edging to trim it		6	6
To making the frock		5	
3 yd. flannel for under coats		7	6
A Brown Bever Hat & feathers		13	
2 pr. leather Gloves		2	4
5 yd. diaper for arm Cloths		5	10
6 pr. cotton Stockings		13	6
3 yd. blue sash Ribbon		3	
To diaper for pockets linning tape cloth for night caps &c		5	6
To a comb & case, comb Brush, tooth Brush		1	6

For the Maid Servant

	£	s	d
12 yds. calico for 2 short Gowns & coats	1	5	6
4 yd half Irish linen for Aprons		7	4
3 pr Stockings		6	
2 yd linning		2	
1 Shawl handkerchief		4	6
paid for washing		6	8
Sterling	10	15	8
	11	16	2[1]

Received Six Louis d'ors of petit.   A ADAMS

RC (DLC); addressed and endorsed; MS mutilated, and some words supplied conjecturally. Recorded in SJL as received 15 July 1787. Enclosure (DLC) in Mrs. Adams' hand.

[1] This correction of Mrs. Adams' total is in TJ's hand.

[574]

From John Adams

Dear Sir   Grosvenor Square July 10, 1787

I received with great Pleasure your favour of the first.—Your Excursion I dare answer for it, will be advantageous in many respects to our Country.—The object of mine to Holland was to procure Money, and I had the good fortune to obtain as much as was necessary for the then present Purpose: but it was not in Consequence of any orders from Congress, and therefore I am under some Apprehension for fear my Loan should not be ratified with so much Promptitude as I wish. If Congress ratify my Loan they will be able to pay the 2000 Guineas to the officers you mention, and to pay the Principal Sum too, if they please.—I have no doubt that Congress might borrow Money in Holland to pay off the Debt to France, if the States would lay on a Duty, to pay the Interest.—If you will venture to draw upon Willinks and Van Staphorsts, I Suppose you may have the Money to pay the French officers their Interest. But perhaps you would choose to have a previous order of Congress or the Board of Treasury.

I am extreamly sorry, that you could not come for your Daughter in Person, and that we are obliged to part with her so soon. In my Life I never saw a more charming Child. Accept of my Thanks, for the Pamphlets and Arrets.—Tell Mazzei, he cannot conceive what an Italian I am become.—I read nothing else, and if he writes to me it must be in that Language: but he must remember to make his Letters, so plain, that I can see them. In writing English he is obliged to write so slow that his Characters are visible; but in Italian such is the Rapidity of his Eloquence, that I must get a Solar Microscope, if he is not upon his guard. You too, write Italian, and if you like it, you will oblige me: but I am not yet presumptuous enough to write a Line in any Thing but rugged American. I am, my dear Sir with perfect Friendship yours,

John Adams

RC (DLC). FC (MHi: AMT); in Abigail Adams Smith's hand. Recorded in SJL as received 15 July 1787.

From Blumendorf

[Paris], 10 July 1787. He will forward TJ's letter to Ingenhousz and will be happy to be of any further service.

RC (MHi); 1 p.; in French.

From C. W. F. Dumas

Monsieur   Lahaie 10e. Juillet 1787

En réponse à la Lettre dont Votre Excellence m'a favorisé en date du 14e. Juin dernier, l'Extrait ci-joint fera connoître à Votre Excellence la démarche que j'ai dû faire aujourd'hui en conséquence auprès de Mr. Adams. Il me paroît nécessaire que Votre Excellence veuille bien lui confirmer de son côté promptement, ce que je lui mande de l'incertitude où Votre Excellence est, que la Caisse de Paris puisse payer mon semestre courant. J'ai lieu de croire que Mr. Adams a réussi dans l'objet de son voyage à Amsterdam. Il a passé très-rapidement ici, s'est arrêté peu à Amsterdam, et est retourné par une autre route à Londres. Ainsi je ne sais rien par lui de ses opérations.

Nous vivons ici dans les anxiétés journalieres que nous causent, outre la guerre civile, les séditions d'une canaille excitée, d'une partie des troupes corrompue, et d'une mauvaise Justice et Police entre autres à Lahaie. On s'occupe avec succès à purger et rétablir les troupes. Les deux autres maux sont invétérés, et leur cure très-difficiles. Ces deux monstres sont nourris par la politique infernale d'une des regences oligarchiques, pour ronger la république dès son origine.

Il n'y a rien du tout d'exagéré, ni qui ne soit vrai à la Lettre dans l'exposé de ma situation à Mr. Adams. J'ai même, pour qu'il ne s'imaginât pas qu'il y a de l'affectation de ma part, omis des circonstances qui l'agravent: par exemple que je suis malade avec mon Epouse et ma fille, et que le produit de ma petite ferme est si mauvais cette année qu'il ne vaut pas les fraix de l'entretien nécessaire et des Impôts.

Je suis avec grand respect, De Votre Excellence le très-humble et très-obeissant serviteur,   C W F Dumas

RC (DLC); endorsed. Recorded in SJL as received 14 July 1787. Dumas omitted the "Extrait ci-joint" and sent it with his later letter of 12 July 1787 (see note there).

From John Stockdale

Sir   Piccadilly London 10th. July 1787

I received your favor of July the 1st. together with the plate, safe, by your Messenger; it has been a great disappointment to me, not receiving it, at the time promised, and I am afraid a detriment

10 JULY 1787

to the sale of the Book, London now being nearly empty of Book buyers. And I am sorry to inform you that the plate is so much wore, that the Impressions which I want will not be quite leidgeable. By the appearance of the plate there must have been about 1,500 taken off so that I may truly say that it has lessened the Value of it to me and the purchasers, for which reason you will probably have no objections to make me a less charge, than you alluded to in a former Letter. I have sent one Copy of the Book and Map, for your Inspection, and should you wish to have 50 or 100 more in boards they are at your service, without being charg'd to Account. But as I hinted before in a former Letter, I beg not to be misunderstood, as I will pay freely whatever you may think Just, after you have weighed it in your mind. By the advice of a friend I have put at the Corner "Published as the Act directs" and enter'd the Book at Stationers hall, for no other reason but to prevent any other spurious Editions. At the same time I hereby acknowledge, that I have no right, or title, in the work, except what I print at my own expence. I have printed 1,000 and shall print the same number of the Maps, which I suppose will be nearly completed by the time that I can receive a Letter from you. The Book I believe you will find, very correct and neatly printed. I have added "Illustrated with a Map &c." in the Title Page, which was absolutely necessary, otherways the Booksellers would frequently sell the Book without the Map, the necessity of which, I hope will be a sufficient apology for the liberty I have taken. I have taken great pains to procure Smith's Map of Virginia, but without Success, therefore was absolutely obliged to give up the Idea. I met with three different Copies of the Work, but without the Map, nor does any of our Gentlemen even remember to have seen a Map to the Book.

I have Inclosed a Copy of your Advertisement, that I shall this week send to every Paper in England and Scotland, to be inserted, which I believe are between 70 and 80 in Number, and which will cost me upwards of £30, but I hope the Book will repay me. Tacittus's Works in Latin is not to be got in 8vo.

Inclos'd is Lackington's Bill which I have Paid; and I will at any time execute any of your Commands with Pleasure. All the other Articles you were so good as to order, you will find in the Parcell.

Should there be any thing published that has great merit for the Instruction or entertainment of Youth, I shall esteem it a particular favor, if you will be so good as to order it to be sent to me and at the same time I return you my sincere thanks for continuing to

10 JULY 1787

send Mr. Berquin's Works which you will be so good as to pay for, and I will when ever I am informed, give you Credit in your Account for the same. I am with great Respect, Sir, Your much oblig'd and very humble Servant, JOHN STOCKDALE

RC (MHi). Recorded in SJL as received 15 July 1787. Enclosures not found.

From John Trumbull

DEAR SIR London 10th. July 1787.

I have long been ashamd of having not yet given you a decisive answer to your enquiries about the Will of Mr. Trist, and have indeed defer'd writing to this time hoping to be fully informd at last: but tho' I gave your letter to a Proctor in the Commons immediately, who undertook to get the necessary information, and have frequently calld upon him, yet I have not even this morning been able to learn any thing to the purpose.

I do not wish to call a second time on the Mr. R. Trist of Arundel Street, as I thought from his reception of me, that enquiries on this subject were not very agreeable to him. At least He was very far from Civil but if I cannot obtain the necessary knowledge from the commons, I will venture him again.

Your little girl who is here, is a charming little creature. She goes with some reluctance, but the sight of you and her sister will soon put her in spirits. I hope Miss Jefferson enjoys perfect health.

I am not yet decided when I shall be able to have the honor of seeing you at Paris. But it will be the first moment of convenient leisure, and I hope in September during the Salon.

Mrs. Cosway desires me to close my letter—dinner is on table and She half starv'd. I must therefore bid you Adieu & am your most grateful JNO. TRUMBULL

RC (DLC); endorsed. Recorded in SJL as received 15 July 1787.

From Nathaniel Barrett

SIR Paris 11th. July 1787

The Letter which you did me the honour to communicate to me, from Mr. de Villedeul, I have attentively perused, and beg the Liberty of making the following remarks.

Mr. de Villedeul advises you that the Farmers General received

[578]

on the 1st. of April last an order from Monsr. de Calonne to comply with the Contents of his Letter to you of the 22d. October last and that on the fifth of the same Month they issued their Orders to the different Bureaux to comply therewith. But it appears that this was not done. For on the Cargo of the Sally, Capt. Coffin from Nantucket loaded with Oil, which arrived at Rouen in December consign'd to Messrs. Le Couteulx & Co., the Strangers' Duty was demanded and paid the 10th. March last, instead of the duties mentioned in Mr. De Calonnes Letter to you of 7^{tt} 10s. ₩ Ce. and 10s. ₩ Livre, altho this Cargo was imported in an American Ship, and directly from America, which are the only proofs requisite to claim the Alleviation of the Duties promised to the Americans. And when Messrs. Le Couteulx represented the Case and requested a return of the surplus Duties they were answerd that they had no Orders, and to this day the Money has not been refunded, as appears by certificates in the hands of Messrs. Le Couteulx & Co. amounting to 12,831. 8. 6., instead of the duty of 7^{tt} 10s. ₩ 520 and 10s. ₩ Le. which would have amounted to 4126 Ls.

Please Sir, then to communicate this Letter to Monsr. de Villedeul, that he may give Directions to the Farmers General to have this Matter rectifyed and the surplus money repaid to Mess. Le Couteulx & Co.

I have the honour to be with the greatest respect Sir Your mo. Obedt. Servt., NAT BARRETT

RC (DLC); endorsed. Recorded in SJL as received 12 July 1787. This letter was enclosed in TJ to La Boullaye, 17 July 1787.

From Richard Claiborne

DEAR SIR   London No. 15 Bartlets
                     Buildings. 11. July 1787

I am honored with your Excellency's favor of the 1. Inst. for which I thank you with much sincerity.

I am in Corrispondence with Colonel Blackden, who is in Amsterdam, so that I hope to trouble your Excellency no more on that score. I have no doubt it will be considered that I meant no injury to the Colonel, but only acted in the exigency as others would have done. I trust that things will be set right immediately; if not I shall corrispond with the Characters you have mentioned, observing a proper line of Delicacy with respect to your Excellency.

I take the liberty to mention that I am in treaty with a Gentleman

[579]

for the settlement of some of my property in the State of Virginia, and to beg, that Your Excellency will favor me with a few sentiments, about those sort of people who would probably make the most elegible Tenants; whether Americans, or Europeans? Sometimes, I have thoughts, that Families collected from different parts of America, might answer best, being inured to the Country, acquainted with its regulations, and not inclined to any other, but whether the easy acquirement of property would not induce them to procure Fee Simple rights, and improve for themselves, and the expence I might be at in endeavoring to confine them to their engagements, would not be greater than the object would amount to, is another querie. Then again, I have thoughts of Palatines from Germany, and other Europeans as I can procure them, and bind them for so many years, at the end of which time, Farms would be improved, and they would prefer to become Tenants. I will thank your Excellency for your thoughts on these heads, when it is perfectly convenient to your leisure.

I am, Dear Sir, with the greatest respect your Excellency's Most obedient and most humble Servant, R: CLAIBORNE

RC (MoSHi); addressed and endorsed. Recorded in SJL as received 21 July 1787.

From Abigail Adams Smith

SIR Grosvenor Square July 11th. 1787

I received last week the enclosed Letter addressed to you under Cover to Mr. Smith, and from the Contents of Mr. Smiths Letter (of which I enclose you a Copy), I concluded to keep it till his return. But this Morning the Bill of which the enclosed is a Copy was presented by the House of Smith, Bright, and Gray, for acceptance, which induces me to forward your Excellencys Letter and Copies of the other Papers.

My Father accepted the Bill and will at the expiration of the thirty days pay the Money, if Mr. Smith should not return before, unless you should give other orders. I am Sir with great respect your Humble Servt., A SMITH

RC (MHi); endorsed. Recorded in SJL as received 18 July 1787. Enclosures (DLC): (1) Sullivan to TJ, 27 Apr. 1787. (2) Copy by Mrs. Smith of Sullivan to Smith, 27 Apr. 1787, enclosing Sullivan's draft of that date payable at ten days on TJ in favor of Smith for £46 17s 10d, and informing Smith that he had drawn on him at thirty days because "Bills on France will not sell here at this time without great Loss, and having advanced Cash for Governor Jefferson to amount of the Contents and forwarded the Articles by

Capt. Pierce, have taken the Liberty to trouble you to negotiate the Affair for me." (3) "Copy of the Bill presented by the House of Smith, Wright, and Gray," in Abigail Smith's hand, drawn on Smith and payable at thirty days' sight in favor of James Sullivan, with an acceptance by John Adams reading: "July 11th 1787 for the Honour of Colln. Smith in his absence in Portugall Accepted by John Adams."

The draft by Sullivan on TJ at ten days' sight is in DLC: TJ Papers, 29: 4982.

From C. W. F. Dumas

MONSIEUR La Haie 12e. Juillet 1787

Les maux multipliés dont je me vois assailli et menacé, en affectant ce qui me reste de force de corps et d'ame, ont fait échapper à mon attention fatiguée le papier essentiel ci-joint, mentionné dans la Lettre que j'eus l'honneur d'écrire avanthier à Votre Excellence. Je lui en demande pardon.

Les Etats d'Overyssel viennent de suspendre pareillement le Prince comme Capitaine-Général. De son côté, il a fait ravager quelques Jardins et Fermes appartenants à des Bourgeois de Déventer en deçà de l'Yssel en Gueldre. Le reste de notre situation peut se connoître assez bien dans la Gazette de Leide, la seule véridique. Avec tout cela, la seule Province d'Hollande, pourroit mettre à la raison en 15 jours de tems le Stadhouder et son odieuse cabale dans la pluralité des Députés aux Etats-Generaux ici, sans une autre Cabale, bien plus odieuse encore, d'une damnable et parricide Oligarchie, qui ne pouvant se résoudre à dépendre de la masse honnête et seule estimable de leurs Concitoyens, mettent toutes les entraves qu'ils peuvent au mouvement de la machine.

Je suis avec grand respect, De Votre Excellence, Le très-humble et très-obéissant serviteur, CWF. DUMAS

RC (DLC). Recorded in SJL as received 16 July 1787. Enclosure: "Extrait de ma Lettre de ce jour 9 Juillet 1787 à S.E.Mr. Adams Min. Pl. des Et. Unis d'Amerique à Londres," stating that TJ had informed him that the state of American funds at Paris might not enable him to honor Dumas' draft for the current half-year payment on salary due 19 Oct. 1787; that, as this was something he depended upon for daily subsistence, he had discussed with the bankers of the United States at Amsterdam the possibility of receiving his salary in future at their hands as the easiest, most convenient, and least expensive mode; that, in order to avoid damaging the credit of the United States, he had nevertheless not shown them TJ's letter; and that they had agreed, provided this course met with the approval of Adams, which Dumas urgently requested since the interruption of his salary would deprive him of his last source of income, for "je ne pourrois pas même me réfugier dans ma petite ferme en Gueldre, où la force militaire vient de désarmer tout le peuple, et où l'on est à tout moment exposé au pillage et au meurtre" (DLC).

In the retained copy of Dumas' letter to Adams of which an extract was here enclosed, the date is given as 6 July 1787 (Dumas Letter Book, Rijksarchief, The Hague; photostats in DLC). That letter in turn enclosed a copy of TJ's letter to Dumas of 14 June 1787. But Dumas was not being entirely candid in saying that he had not revealed the state of things as set forth in TJ's letter, for on the day that he wrote Adams he also wrote Messrs. Hubbard of Amsterdam, enclosing his letter to Adams which he asked them to read and which he said he was leaving unsealed for the benefit of Messrs. Willink & Van Staphorst (same). No one was confused by this, or enlightened, for the Amsterdam bankers were well aware of the state of American funds in Paris.

From Ladevese

Le Vigan, 12 July 1787. Mr. [James] Laurens, brother of the former president of Congress, died in January 1784; in his will he made a legacy "aux pauvres protestans de cette ville." The widow and niece of the deceased wrote him, when they left for London, that the money would be paid "immédiatement après l'ouverture du testament"; has had no news from the Laurens family and does not know whether they are in England or America; asks TJ to forward the enclosed to Miss Laurens or to Henry Laurens, former president of Congress; by this act he will render "service à nos pauvres qui sont en grande nombre et les moyens de mon Eglise ne sont pas considerables."

RC (DLC); 2 p.; in French; at foot of text: "Mon adresse: à Mr. Ladevese au vigan en Sevenes"; endorsed. Recorded in SJL as received 22 July 1787 from Ladevese at "Nismes." For an account of James Laurens and his legacy pertaining to indigent protestants of Le Vigan, near Nîmes, see D. D. Wallace, *Life of Henry Laurens*, N.Y., 1915, p. 427.

Thomas Barclay to the American Commissioners

GENTLEMEN   L'Orient 13th. July 1787

I do myself the Honor to inclose you two Books of 82 Pages containing all my Accounts respecting my Mission to Morocco, by which you will see that the amount of the Expences attending the Negociation Including the Presents and all the Travelling Charges of Mr. Franks and myself amount to 95,179.10 which Sum I shall place to the Debit of the United States. The particulars of the Purchases made, and of the Appropriation of all the Presents, together with an Account of the Articles remaining on Hand make a part of these Accounts, and I do not know that any thing whatever is left unexplained, when I have told you that my reason for leaving the Lawns and Cambricks in the Hands of Mr. Champion of this place for Sale, was because the Farmers General wou'd not permit me to carry them out of the Town by Land. Mr. Champion Died suddenly in April last, and at present nothing is done or can be done in his Affairs, which are all sealed up by the Judges, and are

13 JULY 1787

likely to remain so some time. I shall direct the Account of the Goods to be lodged in the Hands of Mr. Loreilhe here in order that he may claim them.

I annex an account of Bills drawn on Mr. Adams amounting to £4645. Sterg., one Hundred pounds of which in favor of Mr. Grand, he writes to me, was never sent forward for acceptance, in which case, I have promised to account with him for it, and then the Amount will be £4545. Stg. which, supposing the Exchange to be on an average 24 Livres the pound Sterling clear of Negociating fees in Paris the sum will be in Livres 109,080, so that upon this Account I shall remain Indebted to the United States, (untill I make a settlement with them, and untill I know what I am to charge for my Voyage) 13901^{tt} 10s. I have also some suspicion that I must have drawn a Bill not included in this Account, but I am not certain, as most of my Papers are at St. Germains. Mr. Adams will be so kind as to procure from the Banker, who paid the Draughts, an account of the particulars, and transmit it to me under Cover to Mr. Jay at New York, assuring himself that a final settlement shall be made to the intire satisfaction of Congress, and to that of you, Gentlemen.

The necessity I am under of hastening out to America shou'd not have prevented my waiting on Mr. Adams in London for his commands, had not Mr. Jefferson given me a full dispensation on that Head, and therefore I know Mr. Adams will excuse me.

Before I take leave, permit me to thank you both for the many marks of Esteem, and attention with which you have honor'd me, and to request most earnestly a continuance of that regard, which I sincerely assure you is very presious to Gentlemen Your most obt. and obliged Servant, THOS. BARCLAY

P.S. The precise Exchange of the Bills cannot be adjusted, untill I receive Mr. Grand's accounts.

RC (DLC); in clerk's hand, signed by Barclay and with this notation at foot of text in his hand: "This Copy for Mr. Jefferson having sent one to Mr. Adams in London." Recorded in SJL as received with Barclay's letters of 12 (missing), 14, and 16 July on 20 July 1787. RC (MHi: AMT); in clerk's hand, signed by Barclay and with corresponding notation. Tr (DNA: PCC, No. 91). Tr (DNA: PCC, No. 107). Enclosures: (1) The "two books of 82 Pages containing all my Accounts" did not accompany this letter or its duplicate to Adams, for reasons explained in Barclay to TJ, 14 July 1787; these "two books" may indeed have been carried by Barclay to America; they are now in DNA: PCC, No. 91, II, 346-91, 392-435. (2) Copies of the list of drafts made by Barclay on Adams are to be found with all texts of the present letter in DLC, MHi: AMT, and DNA: PCC.

Barclay evidently spoke the truth when he said that he did not think ANY THING WHATEVER IS LEFT UNEXPLAINED in his accounts. The TWO BOOKS OF 82 PAGES included some interesting and revealing details in their fullness: "powder and pomatum," "a box and tickets at the play House at Barcelona," a gratuity to "the Doorkeeper of the Cathedral [at Murcia] for shewing the Church steeple," and other similar expenses were included along with the usual costs incident to 18th century travel (even among the latter are many that strike an unfamiliar note, such as the charge for paying a servant to carry a light for the American agents on their way home after a dinner in Morocco). The listing of gifts for the Emperor of Morocco and his officials reveals both Parisian and Moroccan taste in the late 18th century. The gifts included many gold and silver watches, a pair of pistols inlaid with gold, "an alarum silver watch," a blue enamelled gold snuff box, three boxes of perfume, "a Sword with the Arms of the United States on the Handle," eight dozen silver spoons and six dozen forks, "50½ dozen Phosphorus Matches," tea, sugar, cambrics, silks, muslins, &c. At the first audience with the Emperor, Barclay presented "A large Elegant Umbrella of Crimson Silk, lined with White, the seams Coverd with Rich Gold lace, and the Border of Gold Fringe and Tassels"; there was also "A Clock in the Bottom of a Cage, with an Artificial bird, that sings every hour, or when a string is pulled, and sings Six Tunes"; another "Clock in the Form of the Temple of Diana, with five Pillars and Pedestals of Elegant Marble"; gold watches, a gold box, phosphorus matches, and many other gifts—all these were wrapped in great silk handkerchiefs and "were carried [to the audience] by Thirty Six Jews, and Five Servants." Taher Fennish, whose services were so indispensable in negotiating the treaty, was given a silver watch, fine cloths, tea, sugar, and other gifts wrapped in five handkerchiefs; in addition, $600 was paid on 30 July 1786 to "Taher Fennish who made the Treaty and who escorted us to Mogadore from Morocco." The accounts also include such entries as the following: "for papers of a particular kind to write the Treaty," "for Copying the Treaty in Arabic 2d time," "for putting the Kings Seal to the Treaty and Letters," "for binding the Book with the Treaty," &c. David Franks' "Accounts of Expences from Paris to Morocco, and Back to Madrid" are included in the total of 95,179.₶—10 and were "Settled at the Escurial 16th Nov. 1786, when Col. Franks Returned to France." Barclay's accounts, as "Settled at L'Orient the 12th of July 1787," actually totalled 97,030.₶—11, but there was a deduction of 1,851₶—1 for books bought at Alicante, Valencia, and elsewhere—at least part of which were for TJ.

From John Stockdale

[London, 13 July 1787. Recorded in SJL as received 18 July 1787. Not found.]

From Thomas Barclay

[L'Orient, 14 July 1787]

Since writing the letter which accompanies this I found the Following Memorandums in a Book of mine. It will Enable you to fill up one of the Blanks in the little Account I sent you.

Mr. Jefferson 2 Dozens Madiera wine	30 livs. ℔ Doz.	60
1½ Doz. Frontignan	24	36
1½ of Muscat	18	27
2 Pounds of tea		16
		139
Received Twenty four livres		24
	livs.	115

Expence of China at Rouen

[584]

14 JULY 1787

I Do not know why the 24 livres are Deducted. Possibly you paid them to me for the Expences of the China, at Rouen. But the above is an Exact Copy of the memorandum.

Thos. Barclay

The First safe Conveyance to Paris by a private person shall Carry to you and Mr. Adams all my Accounts of Any sort Respecting my Journey to Morocco. They are too voluminous to send by post, and are Contain in 82 folio pages. I Believe they are free from Error, and that Every thing is properly Accounted for.

Whatever letters you favor me with to your friends in America, with your other Commands put them as soon as Convenient under Cover for me to Mr. Jay. The wind is still obstinate this 14th.

RC (DLC); without date, except the reference in Barclay's final sentence. Recorded in SJL as dated 14 July and received 20 July, along with Barclay's letters of 12 (missing), 13, and 16 July 1787; in his reply of 3 Aug. TJ refers to this letter as being undated. Though no enclosure is mentioned, it is almost certain that Barclay enclosed an "Extract of a Letter from Bordeaux dated 9 July 1787" from John Bondfield which reads: "Your Persecutors are uncertain the route you have taken. The day you left this they were busy, but since I do not find they have gone on all has been suspended. I have seen your Friend in high Office. He informed me that orders were received to reexamin your Powers, that he had doubts, and believed you subject to the courts, your mission being expired. It is fortunate you had a friend otherways you might have again had the repetition of Frenches lenity. Your Bill of five hundred Livres is not accepted. Grand gave for answer he had not any funds of the Drawers nor of the State of Virginia. This comes very unseasonably having need to assist a Friend, whose wants are urgent, and which I may possibly be obliged to reimburse" (DLC; in clerk's hand). To this Barclay added at the foot of the text: "Mr. Jefferson will if possible procure Payment to the Bill on Mr. Grand in Favor of Mr. Bondfield 500 livres on account of the State of Virginia." Barclay's "Friend in high Office" was Dudon fils; see note to TJ to Jay, 21 June 1787.

From Gaudenzio Clerici

Honble. Sir

Dalla Campagna Milanese nelle vicinanze di Ticino li. 14. Luglio 1787

I had the honor of sending to You, Sir, a letter by the Post shortly after my arrival to Italy. Altho it contained nothing interesting, I wish it had come to its destiny: for at the peril of being thought either too vain or too affected, or even too presumptuous, I would act in a manner that it should not be entirely blotted out of Your memory the name of a Young man for whom You have been pleased, Sir, to shew so kind and so benevolent a disposition to do him good. Some days after the writing of that letter, I was favored by the Marquis de Cacciapiatti with a letter that was recommended from

[585]

14 JULY 1787

America to Your Care; for which I give my most humble thanks.

The same Marquis de Cacciapiatti and his Brother the Chevalier told me on that occasion of either having seen or heard that Monsr. de Jefferson was, at the time of their coming thro' Turin, quietly philosofizing in that Capital. I could not hesitate much to believe it: for I really thought it would have been very difficult for a person so laudably curious to know of the world and of worldly affairs to resist the temptation of seeing Italy! being so near it, and in so favorable a season. In effect sometimes after, passing this way the Comte Del Verme *figlio*, who being very fond of renewing the idea of Your native Land, as often as he makes these excursions is pleased to call upon me to entertain himself upon America, and told me that he had truly the pleasure of a personal acquaintance with Mr. Jefferson at Milan, who introduced himself to him knowing of his having been an American visitor. He said, then, and doubt not, but said it sincerely, that he never had occasion in his life to regret the loss of an acquaintance of two days so sensibly as that of Mr. Jefferson. *O quanto avvei desiderato che fossero Stati*, said he to me, *due mesi! Almeno due mesi!*—He would have written to You, Sir, as he said that You had promised to him a book upon America, of which he now forgot the title. But something preventing him that pleasure desired me that having occasion to write to You, Sir, I would present You with his most respectful compliments and would express his desire to know whether you had returned safely and in good health to the place of Your residence.

I do not know, but one more letter for me may come to importune Your goodness from America. In that case I would humbly request of You the favor to inclose it to Monsr. Le *Comte Francois del Verme fils*, Milan, in case You have any occasion to write to him.— If the shortness of the time did not permit You, Sir, to make the remarks You wished upon the method of making our Cheeses, give me leave, Sir, to offer You my humble services not only in that particular but in whatever You may think me capable of. You may imagine, Sir, how much and how greatly I would think myself honored by Your commands, and how particularly I should be pleased with such an opportunity, when with the most unaffected sincerity I tell You, that there is not a person in the world to whom I more zealously and respectfully subscribe my name in quality of a Very Humbl. and very Obedt. Servt.,

GAUDENZIO CLERICI

RC (DLC); endorsed. Recorded in SJL as received 24 July 1787.

From Feger, Gramont & Cie.

Bordeaux, 14 July 1787. Acknowledge TJ's letter of 4 July and inform him that they have forwarded to his address the box of seeds from Norfolk; enclose statement of their charges, amounting to 7.ᵗᵗ17s.6d.

RC (MHi); 4 p.; in French; endorsed. Recorded in SJL as received 18 July 1787. Enclosure (MHi).

To Edward Rutledge

Dear Sir   Paris July 14. 1787.

I received your favor of the 14th. of October in the moment I was setting out on a tour of the seaport towns of this country, from which I have been not long returned. I received it too with that kind of heart felt pleasure which always attends the recollection of antient affections. I was glad to find that the adaption of your rice to this market was considered worth attention as I had supposed it. I set out from hence impressed with the idea the rice-dealers here had given me, that the difference between your rice and that of Piedmont proceeded from a difference in the machine for cleaning it. At Marseilles I hoped to know what the Piedmont machine was: but I could find nobody who knew any thing of it. I determined therefore to sift the matter to the bottom by crossing the Alps into the rice country. I found the machine exactly such a one as you had described to me in Congress in the year 1775. There was but one conclusion then to be drawn, to wit, that the rice was of a different species, and I determined to take enough to put you in seed: they informed me however that it's exportation in the husk was prohibited: so I could only bring off as much as my coat and surtout pockets would hold. I took measures with a muletier to run a couple of sacks across the Appenines to Genoa, but have not great dependance on it's success. The little therefore which I brought myself must be relied on for fear we should get no more; and because also it is genuine from Vercelli where the best is made of all the Sardinian Lombardy, the whole of which is considered as producing a better rice than the Milanese. This is assigned as the reason of the strict prohibition. Piedmont rice sells at Nice (the port of it's exportation) when I was there at 17 livres French, the French hundred weight. It varies from time to time as the price of wheat does with us. The price of Carolina rice at Bordeaux, Nantes, Lorient and Havre varies from 16ᵗᵗ to 24.ᵗᵗ the French quintal which is equal to 109 ℔. our weight. The best ports to send it to are Bordeaux and Havre (or Rouen which is the same thing as Havre) but it is essential that it arrive here a month before the commencement of Lent, when the principal demand is made for it. Carolina rice after being sorted here into several qualities, sells from 6 sols to 10 sols the French pound, retail, according to the quality. Unsorted and wholesale about 30.ᵗᵗ the French quintal. Piedmont rice is but of one quality, which sells retail at 10. sous the Fr. pound, and wholesale is about 3 or 4ᵗᵗ dearer than yours. In order to induce your countrymen to ship their rice here directly, I have proposed to some merchants here to receive consignments allowing the consignor to draw in the moment of shipping for as much as he could sell for on the spot, and the balance when it should be sold. But they say that is impossible. They are to consider and inform me what are the most favorable terms on which they can receive it. I am told that freight, insurance and commission are about 4.ᵗᵗ the Fr. quintal, to a seaport town. I have written so long a letter on the subject of rice to Mr. Drayton for the society of agriculture, that I will trouble you with no further particulars but refer you to that. Indeed I am sensible I have written too much on the subject. Being absolutely ignorant of it myself, it was impossible for me to know what particulars merited communication. I thought it best therefore to communicate every thing. After writing that letter, I received one from Mr. Izard, by which I found that he had examined the rice-process in Lombardy. He was so much more capable than myself of giving the details that I had at one moment determined to suppress my letter. However observing that he considered the rice of Piedmont to be of the same species with yours, and suspecting myself certainly that it is not, I determined to hazard my letter and all those criticisms which fall justly on an ignorant person writing on a subject to those much more learned in it than himself. A part of my letter too related to the olive tree and caper, the first of which would surely succeed in your country and would be an infinite blessing after some 15. or 20. years: the caper would also probably succeed and would offer a very great and immediate profit.—I thank you for your obliging mention of my worthless Notes on Virginia. Worthless and bad as they are they have been rendered more so, as I am told, by a translation into French. That I may have neither merit nor demerit not my own, I have consented to their publication in England. I advised the bookseller to send 200 copies to Philadelphia and 200 to Richmond, supposing that number might be sold in the United

14 JULY 1787

states: but I do not know whether he will do it. If you give me leave I will send you a copy of the original impression.—I congratulate you, my dear friend, on the law of your state for suspending the importation of slaves, and for the glory you have justly acquired by endeavoring to prevent it for ever. This abomination must have an end, and there is a superior bench reserved in heaven for those who hasten it.—The distractions of Holland thicken apace. They begin to cut one anothers throats heartily. I apprehend the neighboring powers will interfere: but it is not yet clear whether in concert, or by taking opposite sides. It is a poor contest, whether they shall have one, or many, masters. Your nephew is arrived here in good health. My first interview with him has impressed me much in his favor. Present me very respectfully to Mrs. Rutledge, as well as to your brother and his house. Accept yourself assurances of the sincere esteem and respect with which I am Dear Sir your most obedient & most humble servt., TH: JEFFERSON

P.S. I inclose you propositions on the subject of rice, received since writing this letter.

RC (PHi); endorsed. PrC (DLC); lacks postscript. Enclosure: Bérard's notes on the rice trade, 15 July 1787.

From Frederick Soffer

Bordeaux, 14 July 1787. Is unknown to TJ, but aware of his "Uniform and Steady Attachment to the Interests of the United States and the Citizens thereof." Has just arrived from Charleston in the ship *Maryland*, of Baltimore, of which he is master and part owner; She is a fine ship of 300 tons, but there is little "Business . . . for her in these Seas"; is "meditating a Voyage to the Isle of France"; makes inquiries concerning the reception of American ships in that colony—whether they may carry freight from France to that place; whether they would be subject to duties in addition to those paid by French ships; whether they could carry flour and other products from America to the colony and be "Freely Received."

RC (DLC); 2 p.; endorsed. Recorded in SJL as received 20 July 1787.

To Wilt, Delmestre & Cie.

GENTLEMEN   Paris July 14. 1787.

I am honoured with your letter of the 9th. instant, announcing your draught for 138ᵗᵗ 19s which shall be paid on sight. It has not yet been presented. I thank you for your attention to the Paccan nuts, and will pray you to have a top nailed on the box and to forward it by the Diligence. I am always apprehensive of things being stopped on the road in shifting from one carriage to another, or at the barrieres where some duty is to be paid, when the parcel is not in the care of some one who accompanies it. But I imagine there are precautions to be taken to prevent this. I will be obliged to you to have this attention for me. If it can be so arranged as that all the expences shall be paiable here on delivery, it will be most convenient. The earth in the box should not be watered. I beg your pardon for this trouble and am with much esteem and regard gentlemen your most obedient & most humble servant,

Th: Jefferson

PrC (DLC).

Notes on the Rice Trade Supplied by Jean Jacques Bérard & Cie.

Nottes pour Son Excellence Monsieur de Jefferson sur le Commerce du Riz

D'après les nottes que Monsieur de Jefferson a bien voulu communiquer sur la Consommation en France du Riz de Caroline, et le désir qu'il montre de donner de la consistence à ce commerce, Les Srs. Jean Jaques Berard & Compe. de Lorient sont disposés à faire tout ce qui dépendra d'eux pour concourir à ses vües et étendre les liaisons entre les deux nations.

Les avances considérables demandées par les planteurs de Caroline deviennent assez gênantes et éxigent des moyens étendus. Ce n'est que l'activité que les Américains donneront à ce commerce, et la certitude de leurs opérations périodiques et bien concertées qui pourront les rendre moins onéreuses à la maison qui voudra y employer sa fortune et son crédit.

Si Son Excellence désire réellement de former ces liaisons et veut un peu patroniser cette branche et y donner des encouragements, on consentiroit, si cela est nécessaire, à avancer aux planteurs, dès l'arrivée de leurs riz, nouveaux et marchands, dans le port de décharge, la somme de douze à quinze Livres Tournois par quintal, que Monsieur de Jefferson croit nécessaire et qui équivaut au coût du Riz dans la Caroline.

Si ce commerce s'étendoit, les Srs. Berard & Compe. feroient ces avances également sur les chargements qu'ils enverroient vendre dans d'autres ports de France pour Compte des propriétaires, toujours à leur consignation et Direction, parce qu'ils les y feroient gérer par leurs agents ou par les maisons qu'ils pourroient y établir si l'objet en valoit la peine. Et de cette manière on soutiendroit mieux le prix en diminuant la concurrence des vendeurs.

Il seroit même nécessaire pour le bien de cette branche de commerce que les Navires fussent toujours fretés pour L'orient et un autre port indistinctément de la baye de Biscaye, de la Manche ou de la Mer du Nord jusqu'à Hambourg, ayant ordre de mouiller en dehors de L'orient pour y prendre celui de leur destination qui leur seroit porté en deux heures. Là, Messrs. Bérard, toujours avisés de l'Etat et des besoins de tous les marchés, feroient rendre le Navire dans le port le plus convenable. Pour cela, il faudroit qu'on leur eut envoyé d'avance des Etats Unis les ordres et les détails nécessaires pour les assurances, de manière à ce qu'elles pussent être faites solidement.

En leur donnant d'avance leurs ordres pour des marchandises en retour des Riz expediés, les planteurs seroient assurés que leurs Navires les trouveroient à Lorient toutes prêtes à être embarquées pour le retour de ceux des Navires de Riz qui se destineroient pour les Carolines.

La Situation de Lorient sur les deux mers au centre des divers ports de consommation de Riz, et la franchise dont on y jouit, le rendent très propre à être ainsi le Centre de ce commerce, et à y former un Entrepôt. Et si l'on pouvoit obtenir la liberté d'y charger du tabac en feuilles sur les Navires François pour la Côte de Guinée, les Négriers de tous nos ports, y trouvant la réunion de ces deux articles, viendroient s'y en approvisionner régulièrement.

Il seroit nécessaire que Monsieur de Jefferson s'occupât promptement d'obtenir du Gouvernement une prime sur la sortie des *White plains* que l'on peut fabriquer en France, d'après des échantillons et la comparaison des prix et qualités d'Angleterre avec celles de France. En attendant l'on pourroit avoir à Lorient des *White plains* anglois à peu près aux mêmes prix, et peut être absolument aux mêmes prix qu'à Londres: la franchise de Lorient les y faisant recevoir librement et ressortir, ainsi que toute autre marchandise Angloise ou étrangère sans aucuns droits.

On prieroit Son Excellence d'avoir la bonté de faire faire le plustôt possible ces ouvertures en Caroline et demander les dispositions des planteurs, les Srs. Jn.Js. Berard & Cie. devant être

16 JULY 1787

prévenus de bonne heure des envoys préparés pour prendre leurs mesures en conséquence.

MS (DLC); without signature or date; in the hand of Vernes; assigned to this date from the following entry under 15 July in SJL: "Vernes. Paris. July 15"; and the postscript to TJ's letter to Edward Rutledge, 14 July, which indicates that these notes were received after he had completed the letter but before it was posted. See also Vernes to TJ, 30 June 1787; TJ to Izard, 1 Aug. 1787; TJ to Drayton, 30 July 1787.

To Abigail Adams

Dear Madam   Paris July 16. 1787.

I had the happiness of receiving yesterday my daughter in perfect health. Among the first things she informed me of was her promise to you, that after she should have been here a little while she would go back to pay you a visit of four or five days. She had taken nothing into her calculation but the feelings of her own heart which beat warmly with gratitude to you. She had fared very well on the road, having got into favor with gentlemen and ladies so as to be sometimes on the knee of one sometimes of another. She had totally forgotten her sister, but thought, on seeing me, that she recollected something of me. I am glad to hear that Mr. and Mrs. Paradise are gone or going to America. I should have written to them, but supposed them actually gone. I imagined Mr. Hayward gone long ago. He will be a very excellent opportunity for sending the packet to Mr. Drayton. Petit will execute your commissions this morning, and I will get Mr. Appleton to take charge of them. He sets out for London the day after tomorrow. The king and parliament are at extremities about the stamp act, the latter refusing to register it without seeing accounts &c. M. de Calonne has fled to the Hague. I had a letter from Colo. Smith dated Madrid June 30. He had been detained by the illness of his servant, but he was about setting out for Lisbon. My respects attend his lady and Mr. Adams, and eternal thanks yourself with every sentiment of esteem and regard from Dear Madam your most obedient & most humble servt,   Th: Jefferson

RC (MHi: AMT); addressed and endorsed; postmarked: "JY 19." PrC (DLC); lacks part of complimentary close (see Vol. 9: 217, note 1).

From Thomas Barclay

Sir   L'Orient 16th. July 1787

Permit me to trouble you once more before my departure on the subject of two Affairs in which the Interest of the United States has been for some years engaged.

In 1783 Messrs. LaVayse and Puchelberg of this Town made some Purchases at Public Auction of sundry Prize Goods brought in here by Captain John Barry of the Alliance Frigate on which a balance of 72263.15.6 Livres is still due, and which these Gentlemen have refused to pay, because the Money has been attached in their Hands by Messrs. Fosters freres of Bordeaux, who alledge that a large Sum is due to them by the United States for Damages which they sustained by the Capture of a Vessel of theirs by Captain Landois, which Vessel was sent into this Port, and afterwards discharged, her cargo of Wines intended for the Dublin Market was sold here, it is said to a considerable loss, which composes the demand made by the Fosters.—Doctor Franklin was always of opinion that these Gentlemen had no proper demand on the United States for this loss. The Vessel was given up out of a compliment to the Court of France, having had a Passport from the King, desiring *his Subjects* not to molest or hinder her in her Voyage and Doctor Franklin was clearly of opinion that this Passport had been used on a former occasion and that it cou'd afford her, at the time she was taken, no protection whatever.— I have made many Representations on this Subject to the late Minister M. De Vergennes which were supported by all the Influence of Doctor Franklin, but I never was able to procure any Decission, nor even to get the Money lodged in the Hands of some indifferent Person untill it wou'd be adjusted. And so long as we decline bringing it into the common Courts of the Kingdom, they holding the Property in the mean time, if the Minister will not interfer the matter must remain as it has done. I flatter myself that by an application from you to M. Montmorin, the money might at least be drawn out of the Hands of LaVayse and Puchelberg and placed in those of some solid Banker at Paris, if not paid to you for the use of the United States.

The other matter which I beg leave to mention to you, is an Insurance which I made at Amsterdam for account of the United States. On this occasion I shall refer you to a Declaration made by Mr. Loreilhe of this Town, which with some Papers lying in my

16 JULY 1787

Office at St. Germain, are all the Vouchers that belong to it. The Gentlemen at Amsterdam have in my opinion behaved very badly, and I shou'd have commenced a Suit against them long ago but I waited the return of M. Loreilhe from America, and his leisure to go to Holland to pursue it. I flatter myself he will be able to undertake it in the course of this Summer in which case he will write to you, and if you approve of it, you will furnish him with Money for his Expences, and leave to me the settlement with him for his Trouble when he has taken it. I think he may prove a usefull Evidence if a Suit is commenced. If Mr. Gruels accounts from Nantes cou'd be procured it wou'd be a very desireable Object to Sir Your most obt. and obliged Servant, THOS BARCLAY

RC (DLC); in a clerk's hand, signed by Barclay; addressed on verso of enclosure; endorsed by TJ: "Barclay Thos. LaVayse & Puchelberg's affair Geraud & Roland's do." Recorded in SJL as received 20 July 1787. Enclosure (DLC): Deposition of Zachariah Loreilhe, dated 16 July 1787, stating that he was present when, in July 1782, Thomas Barclay negotiated with the firm of Geraud & Rolland, of Amsterdam, to have the latter insure a quantity of goods shipped to Philadelphia on the brigantine *Elizabeth* for the account of the United States; that Geraud & Rolland agreed to underwrite the whole risk; and that Barclay paid the premium for the insurance by a bill on Dr. Franklin.

From Joseph Fenwick

Bordeaux, 16 July 1787. Asks whether there will be any regulations on the tobacco trade between France and the United States after Mr. Morris' contract expires. Since 1 May 7,100 hhds. of tobacco have arrived of which 6,000 hhds. are for Mr. Morris' account; the farmers general have refused to purchase "from Adventurers at the stipulated prices under the pretext of having bought their quantity"; believes they have also refused at L'Orient, Marseilles, and every other port, and that they will have it in their power to reduce the price considerably. He expects a large cargo from the Potomac and is at a loss to know whether to sell it for what the farmers will pay or hold it for a better price; since he is young and "just venturing into the mercantile line," his future will depend on "the first essay"; hopes TJ will give his opinion on these questions.

RC (DLC); 2 p.; endorsed. Recorded in SJL as received 21 July 1787.

To John Trumbull

DEAR SIR   Paris July 16. 1787.

I am favoured with your letter of the 10th. and happened just then to have received one from Mrs. Trist. She informs me that she has received a very friendly letter from Mrs. Champernoone who seems disposed to give her full information. She would not

[594]

wish a further application to Mr. Trist of London, nor that the family should know she has been enquiring into their affairs. Notwithstanding however her confidence in Mrs. Champernoon, I would wish we could get the will desired formerly, only not letting it be known.—We shall be happy to see you here whenever you come. Your bed and plate will attend you. My love to Mrs. Cosway. Tell her I will send her a supply of larger paper. The moment of the post approaching prevents my troubling you with a commission relative to a harpsichord I have in London, and which shall be the subject of another letter. I am Dear Sir with much esteem & respect Your most obedient & most humble servt, TH: JEFFERSON

PrC (DLC). The letter from Mrs. Trist that TJ had just received was hers of 6 June, which arrived on 14 July 1787.

To John Adams

DEAR SIR   Paris July 17. 1787.

I have been duly honoured with your's of the 10th. inst. and am happy to hear of the success of your journey to Amsterdam. There can be no doubt of it's ratification by Congress. Would to heaven they would authorize you to take measures for transferring the debt of this country to Holland before you leave Europe. Most especially is it necessary to get rid of the debt to the officers. Their connections at court are such as to excite very unfavorable feelings there against us, and some very hard things have been said (particularly in the Assemblée des Notables) on the prospects relative to our debts. The paiment of the interest to the officers would have kept them quiet: but there are two years now due to them. I dare not draw for it without instructions, because in the instances in which I have hitherto ventured to act uninstructed, I have never been able to know whether they have been approved in the private sentiments of the members of Congress, much less by any vote. I have pressed on them the expediency of transferring the French debts to Holland, in order to remove every thing which may excite irritations between us and this nation. I wish it may be done before this ministry may receive ill impressions of us. They are at present very well disposed. I send you by Mr. Appleton some pamphlets and have the honour to be with sentiments of very cordial esteem & respect Dear Sir your affectionate humble servant,

TH: JEFFERSON

RC (MHi: AMT); endorsed in part: "ansd. Aug. 25. 1787." PrC (DLC).

From John Bondfield

Bordeaux, 17 July 1787. Encloses an arrêt concerning Thomas Barclay which is "couched in terms so offensive to the parties interested" that it throws "a heavy imputation" on all who interested themselves in his behalf "in his Official capacity." Bondfield is especially pointed out as having misled the authorities. Although Barclay's Moroccan mission is at an end, his person is still protected under the "Convention of the 29 July 1784" as consul.

RC (DLC); endorsed. Recorded in SJL as received 24 July 1787. Enclosure (DLC): Two pages of the issue of *Journal de Guienne* for 17 July 1787, in which is printed an Arrêt in favor of French & Nephew against Barclay; see note to TJ to Jay, 21 June 1787.

To La Boullaye

Sir   Paris July 17. 1787.

I have the honour of now inclosing to you a letter from the American merchant who claims the reimbursement of duties on whale oil which he has been obliged to pay, contrary to the tenor of the letter of M. de Calonne. This merchant established himself here for the particular purpose of carrying into execution the orders relative to the 800,000 ℔. weight of oil mentioned in that letter. Notwithstanding this, he has been obliged by the farms to pay, not only the Hanseatic duties, but those also paid by the least favoured nations. I beg leave to recommend him, Sir, to your good offices to obtain his reimbursement. He resides in the Rue Clery, and is connected with the house of Messrs. Le Coulteux.

My letter to M. de Vergennes is now in the hands of a person to be translated and copied. I shall not be able to send it to you till tomorrow, when I shall be sure to do myself that honour. I have now that of assuring you of those sentiments of esteem and attachment with which I have the honour to be Sir your most obedient & most humble servant,   Th: Jefferson

PrC (DLC). Enclosure: Nathaniel Barrett to TJ, 11 July 1787.

From Dr. Lambert

Frontignan, 17 July 1787. Acknowledges TJ's letter of 6 July; will ask M. Cabanis, his banker in Paris, to collect the 374.ᵗᵗ14 which TJ owes him; will always execute orders promptly and with care.

RC (MHi); 2 p.; in French; endorsed. Recorded in SJL as received 26 July 1787. There is also in MHi a receipt dated at Paris 3 Sep. 1787, signed by J. Cabanis, for payment by TJ of 374.ᵗᵗ 14 for Muscat wine received from Lambert; endorsed by TJ: "Lambert."

[596]

To André Limozin

Sir   Paris July 17. 1787.

I did not know till last night that my bookseller had sent off the three boxes of books which I had mentioned in a former letter that I should take the liberty of addressing to your care. I will beg the favor of you to send them all by the next packet to New-York, ordering them all to be delivered to Mr. Madison, whose address is on the box marked I.M. No. 4. and who will take charge of the other two for Doctor Franklin and Mr. Hay. It is indifferent to me whether the freight is paid here or at New York. I will ask the favor of you to add these to the state of your other disbursements for me, to send me a note of them, and either to draw on me for them or tell me into whose hands I may pay them here. I am desirous of inserting them into the accounts I shall transmit by the next packet. I have the honour to be with great esteem Sir Your most obedient & most humble servant,

             Th: Jefferson

PrC (MHi).

To John Stockdale

Sir   Paris July 17. 1787.

According to the desire expressed in your last letter I send you a book which has just appeared, of the instructive kind and fit for children. It is entitled 'a complete course of instructions and anecdotes by Father Berenger,' 2.v. 12 mo. Having little time to read I have been able to peruse only about 30. or 40. pages, and so far it appears to me to be one of the best things I have ever seen of the kind. If it does not correspond with your view you will easily get this single copy off your hands. You will receive at the same time another volume of the former work. With respect to my map as I never desired any thing more than to make it pay for engraving, transporting backwards and forwards, duties &c., pay what you think it's worth. The translater here gives a livre a copy. I had thought a shilling in England proportioned to this, as books are dearer there. Pay therefore 10d. a peice, [or] whatever sum you please. I thank you for your offer of 100. copies, but I would not desire them. A dozen may enable me to oblige some friends as they are probably better printed than those done here. Desire your correspondent at Edinburgh, if you please, to deliver two of the dozen copies to Mr. Thos. Mann Randolph student at the college of Edinburgh, and to seek him out for that purpose. I think 20. or 30. copies might be sold here. If you have no correspondent, my Bookseller Frouillé, Quai des Augustins, an extremely honest man, will dispose of them for you. I am Sir your most obedt. humble servt, TH: JEFFERSON

P.S. I inclose you a note for some books.

PrC (DLC). The enclosed note for books has not been found.

To John Trumbull

DEAR SIR   Paris July 17. 1787.

In a letter of yesterday I threatened you with a commission on the subject of a harpsichord. This has been made for me by Kirkman and paid for by Colo. Smith. It was then carried to the shop of Mr. Walker to have the Celestini stop put to it, which is done and the instrument there now ready to be delivered. I wish it therefore to be well packed and forwarded by water to Rouen to the care of Mr. Garvey merchant at that place. I suppose Mr. Kirkman would be willing, and would chuse indeed to pack it: and I think it would be well to wrap the instrument in woollen before it is put into it's box, in order to guard it against the damps of the sea and the ships hould. As I could find a use here for 3. or 4. striped blankets (sometimes called Dutch blankets) they might be used for wrapping as far as they would go, and their deficiency supplied by green bays which will also be useful to me. A little expence should not be spared in packing an instrument which has cost so much and which will be irreparably ruined if the damp gets to it. Whatever be the expences of package &c. paiable in London shall be replaced to you the moment you will be so good as to inform me of them. Mr. Garvey will pay the freight to Rouen. Be so good as to take a bill of lading from the Captain who receives the instrument, and forward it to me by the first post after it is shipped that I may send it with proper direction to Mr. Garvey before the arrival of the vessel. I am with much esteem Dr. Sir your friend & servt., TH: JEFFERSON

P.S. Mrs. Adams or Mrs. Smith could perhaps tell whether Colo. Smith may have paid for packing as it is possible that may have been put into the bill by the furnisher, in expectation that he should pack it.

PrC (DLC).

To Adam Walker

Sir Paris July 17. 1787.

A servant of mine who was lately in London, informing me that he had seen my Harpsichord in your shop, finished, and ready to be delivered on my sending an order for it, I write the present to desire you to deliver it to Mr. John Trumbull or order. I do not know what arrangements Colo. Smith took for the having it packed. He is now absent. Probably it should be packed by Mr. Kirkman the maker. Mr. Trumbul will be so good as to settle this either with you or him, and to pay any thing which remains unpaid by Colo. Smith. Your further attention, where necessary will oblige Sir Your very humble servant, Th: Jefferson

PrC (DLC). Recorded in SJL under this date as follows: "Walker (of London. Celestini)."

To La Boullaye

Sir Paris July 18. 1787.

I have now the honour of inclosing you a translation of my letter to the Count de Vergennes on the subject of tobacco. I took the materials for my calculation from the new Encyclopedie. I was informed that article was written by the Abbé Baudeau, and that he was well acquainted with the subject. However you will be able to set them right. It was objected that the expence of manufacturing was stated too low by me, because the farmers pretend that there is a waste of one third or one fourth. I enquired very particularly in London from the manufacturers themselves what they reckoned the waste. They told me, nothing at all, because they sell their snuff wetter than the tobacco is which they buy. This difference of moisture more than makes good the waste. They find that they sell more pounds of snuff than they buy pounds of tobacco.

I shall hope that before the expiration of the order of Bernis, his majesty's ministers will be able to find some effectual and stable relief to this important branch of commerce: and that in the mean time the execution of that order will be strictly required by them. I propose to ask of his Excellency the count de Montmorin that the Farmers be required to report their purchases of the last year, stating particularly 1. the quantities purchased, 2. the prices paid, 3. the times of the purchase and paiment, 4. the flag of the vessel in

18 JULY 1787

which the tobacco was imported, 5. her name, and 6. the port to which she came. The first four articles make part of the conditions required by the order: the 5th. and 6th. are necessary to correct any errors which may be in their report. The 3d. article is necessary to shew that they have made as prompt paiment to the merchants as to Mr. Morris.

This business involving the interests of France as well as of the United states, I sollicit the favor of your attentions to get it through, and have the honour to be with sentiments of the most perfect esteem and regard Sir your most obedient & most humble servt., TH: JEFFERSON

PrC (DLC). Enclosure (PrC in DLC): Translation of TJ to Vergennes, 15 Aug. 1785.

From James Madison

DEAR SIR   Philada. July 18. 1787.

I lately received and forwarded to Mr. Jno. Banister Jr. a packet which came from you under cover to me. I had an opportunity which avoided the charge of postage.

The Convention continue to sit, and have been closely employed since the Commencement of the Session. I am still under the mortification of being restrained from disclosing any part of their proceedings. As soon as I am at liberty I will endeavor to make amends for my silence, and if I ever have the pleasure of seeing you shall be able to give you pretty full gratification. I have taken lengthy notes of every thing that has yet passed, and mean to go on with the drudgery, if no indisposition obliges me to discontinue it. It is not possible to form any judgment of the future duration of the Session. I am led by sundry circumstances to guess that the residue of the work will not be very quickly dispatched. The public mind is very impatient for the event, and various reports are circulating which tend to inflame curiosity. I do not learn however that any discontent is expressed at the concealment; and have little doubt that the people will be as ready to receive, as we shall be able to propose, a Government that will secure their liberties and happiness.

I am not able to give you any account of what is doing at N. York. Your correspondents there will no doubt supply the omission. The paper money here ceased to circulate very suddenly a few days ago. It had been for some time vibrating between a depreciation of

[600]

12. and of 20 Per Ct. The entire stagnation is said to have proceeded from a combination of a few people with whom the Country people deal on market days against receiving it. The consequence was that it was refused in the market, and great distress brought on the poorer Citizens. Some of the latter began in turn to form combinations of a more serious nature in order to take revenge on the supposed authors of the stagnation. The timely interposition of some influencial characters prevented a riot, and prevailed on the persons who were opposed to the paper, to publish their willingness to receive it. This has stifled the popular rage, and got the paper into circulation again. It is however still considerably below par, and must have received a wound which will not easily be healed. Nothing but evil springs from this imaginary money wherever it is tried, and yet the appetite for it, when it has not been tried, continues to be felt. There is good reason to fear that the bitterness of the evil must be tasted in Virga. before the appetite there will be at an end.

The Wheat harvest throughout the Continent has been uncommonly fine both in point of quantity and quality. The crops of corn and Tobacco on the ground in Virginia are very different in different places. I rather fear that in general they are both bad: particularly the former. I have just received a letter from Orange which complains much of appearances in that neighbourhood; but says nothing of them in the parts adjacent. Present my best respects to Mr. Short and Mr. Mazzei. Nothing has been done since my last to the latter with regard to his affair with Dorhman. Wishing you all happiness, I am Dr. Sir Yr. affec. friend & servt.,

Js. MADISON Jr.

RC (DLC: Madison Papers); endorsed. Recorded in SJL as received 19 Dec. 1787.

From Burrill Carnes

SIR Nantes 19th July 1787

I arrived here five days past after a most agreeable journey via Champagne and Burgundy.

I saw your Wine Cooper at Beaune who I believe is a perfect honest man. I really hope in the Course of business it will be in my power to throw some Commissions in his way. Immediately after my arrival here I call'd upon Mr. Dobrée and examined such a part of the Accounts of Mr. Schweighauser's disbursements for

19 JULY 1787

the different ships &c. to his consignment as he had in his possession, all which I found in the most perfect order and conformable to those he furnished; but there still remains accounts of several prizes sold at L'Orient and Brest, accounts of disbursements for the Arsenal, Ships Boston, Ranger, and Spy, and advances made to American officers and seamen in distress and prisoners of war to be examin'd, which can not be effected till the original Vouchers come on from Brest and L'Orient. So soon as possible you may rely upon it Sir I will compleat this business, and at same time I have the honor to advise you of it, I hope I shall also be able to hand you List of the Different American Vessels that have arrived here since the year 1782 with the outlines of their Cargo's &c. Mr. Dobrée appears very anxious about their disbursements on Account of the Ship Alliance, the Vouchers of which I have examin'd and found perfectly right, so far as respects the money being paid for that Ship. I find Sir there has been but one American Ship for eight months past to this place, which surprises me much considering the favorable situation for American business, one of the best I think in the Kingdom, for many reasons. A proof it is is that, beyond any doubt the greatest part of the American produce that arrives at L'Orient is sent here for sale, which occasions a very considerable expence and delay, and I believe that the Goods ship'd from L'Orient to America go from hence in the same proportion, so that the American Merchant at least pays a double Commission, besides expences, delay, and the very great disadvantage of not having his goods laid out agreeable to orders by his friend at L'Orient.

Foreseeing these disadvantages, Sir it is a long time since I determin'd to establish myself in this City and indeed Sir here is a Circular letter I take the Liberty to enclose, a number of which I sent to my friends in America in '85, but to no effect. I am now about forming a new establishment under the firm of Burrill Carnes & Co. I therefore hope Sir you will indulge me with permission, in the most respectful manner, of solliciting your friendship with those of your friends in America that may have business this way, at same time to offer my assurances that whatever property may be intrusted to my care shall be dispos'd of with most perfect obedience to orders, and while in my possession in as perfect security to the proprietor. Pray Sir excuse the freedom I have taken thus far of asking your attention from matters of greater consequence, but Sir it proceeds from a contiousness that very advantageous business may be done between America and this place, which may in some measure benefit our Country, and on all occasions where that can be the case I shall always consider myself the happiest of my Countrymen to be able to contribute.

I have the honor to be most respectfully Sir Your most Obedient & very Humble Servant, BURRILL CARNES

RC (DLC); endorsed. Recorded in SJL as received 22 July 1787. Enclosure (DLC): Printed circular letter outlining the advantages, as a trading center, of the situation of Nantes which has "a water communication to almost all the trading and manufacturing towns in the kingdom," and offering his services to American merchants desiring to carry on trade with France.

For the LIST OF THE DIFFERENT AMERICAN VESSELS, see Carnes to TJ, 23 Aug. 1787.

From Guillaume Delahaye

Paris ce 20 Juillet 1787

Memoire de
Carte de la Virginie Maryland et Pensylvanie, Corrigée par Guillaume Delahaye, Graveur du Roi, en fevrier et mars de la presente année, pour Son Exelence Monseigneur de Jeifferson, Ministre des Etats Unies d'Amerique

Frais

Voiture pour aller chercher la planche, le dessein et l'epreuve de Correction	3.^{tt}
Quatre Epreuves à 9 Sols chacune papier et impression	1.^{tt} 18
Quinze Epreuve desdites corrections à 9S. chacune pour la verification faites à differente fois	6.^{tt} 15
Deux cent cinquante Epreuves de cette carte demandé par Son Excellence sur papier grand aigle à cent vingt livre la rame, les 250. feuille ou demie rame	60.^{tt}
Impression des 250 Epreuves, à 15 le cent,	37.^{tt} 10

Gravure des Corrections

Pour Vingt cinq jours de travail sur cette carte, cent dix livres	110.^{tt}
total	219.^{tt} 3

Recu acompte le 25 mars 1787 du Maitre d'hotel de Son Exellence quatre vingt seize livre lorsqu'il a recu les 250 Epreuves susdites en l'absence de Son Exellence

GUILL: DELAHAYE

J'ay recu de Son Excellence Monseigneur de Jefferson par les

20 JULY 1787

mains de Monsieur Chort la somme de Cent vingt trois Livres pour Solde de compte du present Memoire

Paris ce 29 Juillet 1787.
G: Delahaye

MS (DLC); endorsed.

From Langlade

Monsieur a montpeiller le 20 Juillet 1787.

Votre Excelence me permettra de la Suplier de me donner des renseignemens Sur une personne Qui m'interesse.

Mr. Jeaques tourny, Capitaine de fregate au Service des Etats unis de l'amerique de la province de virginie prez piterbore Essex Conti, voyageoit En France Et En Italie En 1786 Et 1787. Il m'a assuré Etre chargé par la province de virginie de poursuivre un negotiant de livourne qui etoit debiteur de Cette province pour des Expeditions pendant la guerre, il m'a dit Qu'il avoit Informé votre Excelence de Ses Demarches auprez de Ce negotiant, Que meme vous Luy aviez répondu. Il m'a assuré Etre fils Second de Mr. de tourny, Ecuyer Colonel ayant une habitation Considerable En virginie, deux Enfans males Et trois filles, l'ainé Est Etabli, Se nomme le major tourny, luy le Capitaine tourny de taille Cinq pied quatre pouce Et demi ou Environ, un peu Chauve, grand frond, gras, Bland de figure, le menton un peu avancé. Votre Excelence auroit pû Le voir a paris ou il a été Ce mois de Juin.

Je Suplie votre Excelence de vouloir Bien m'ecrire Ce qu'elle Sçait Sur Ce Mr. Jeaques tourny Et de permetre, lorsque vous m'aurez repondû Que J'adresse a votre Excelence un memoire pour avoir de l'amerique de plus grands renseignemens.

Je Suis avec un très profond respect, de votre Excelence, Le tres humble, et tres obeissant Serviteur,

Langlade
pensionaire du roy au Chateau de Biard prez montpeiller

RC (MHi). Recorded in SJL as received, from "Langlae," 26 July 1787.

From André Limozin

Le Havre, 20 July 1787. Acknowledges TJ's letters of 4 and 17 July; submits his account, amounting to 684.ᵗᵗ3s.6d., for which sum he will draw on TJ, payable to his banker, whenever TJ directs. Has made application at the customs house about the package of seeds TJ mentioned; hopes he can soon answer TJ's query about the town called Tessey; will forward the books sent by TJ's bookseller. Asks for information about the prospects of the continuance of peace; a large part of his fortune is at sea and he would arrange to secure it if war seemed imminent.

RC (MHi); 4 p.; addressed and endorsed. Recorded in SJL as received 22 July 1787.

To Stephen Cathalan, Jr.

Sir   Paris July 21. 1787.

I received your favor of May 9. just as I was stepping into the barge on my departure from Cette: which prevented my answering it from that place. On my arrival here, I thought I would avail myself of the opportunity of paying your balance to make a little acquaintance with Sr. John Lambert. One or two unsuccessful attempts to find him at home, with the intermediate procrastinations well known to men of business, prevented my seeing him till yesterday, and has led me on to this moment, thro' a perpetual remorse of conscience for not writing to you, and on the constant belief that it would be tomorrow and tomorrow. At length I have seen him, paid him the 85^{lt}-4-6 which you have been so kind as to advance for me, and am actually at my writing-table returning you thanks for this kindness, and to yourself and the family for the thousand others I received at their hands at Marseilles. My journey, after leaving you, wanted nothing but the company of Madame Cathalan and yourself, to render it perfectly agreeable. I felt the want of it peculiarly on the canal de Languedoc, where, with society, the mode of travelling would have been charming. I was much indebted to M. Minaudier the son, for a good equipment from Agda and unceasing attentions to that place; for which I was indebted to your recommendations as well as to his goodness.

I am honoured with your father's letter of June 30. and as he does not read English, and I cannot write French, I must beg leave to answer him through you. I thank him for his hints on the subject of tobacco. I am now pressing for arrangements as to that article to take place on the expiration of Mr. Morris's contract and the order of Bernis. What form this business will take, or what will be the nature of the arrangements, or whether there will be any, I am as yet unable to say. I will take care to inform you the moment there is a decision.

The public business with which Mr. Barclay has been charged, rendering it necessary for him to repair to Congress, and the interest of his creditors, his family and himself requiring his return to America, he is departed for that place. I knew nothing of Mr. Barclay's affairs in this country. He has good possessions in America, which he assured me were much more than sufficient to satisfy all the demands against him. He went determined to convert these immediately into money, and to collect the debts due to him there, that he might be enabled to pay his debts. My opinion of his integrity is such as to leave no doubt in my mind that he will do every thing in his power to render justice to his creditors, and I know so well his attachment to M. Cathalan as to be satisfied if he makes any difference among his creditors, he will be among the most favored. Mr. Barclay is an honest and honorable man, and is more goaded towards the paiment of his debts by his own feelings than by all the processes of law which could be set on foot against him.

No arrangements having ever been made as yet for cases like that of the Carpenter of the American ship Sally, I am unable to answer on that subject. I am in hopes his money will last till he recovers his senses, or till we can receive instructions what to do in that and similar cases.

M. Cathalan wishes a copy of my Notes on Virginia. If you will be so good as to advise me by what channel they will go safely, I will do myself the honor of sending a copy either of the original or of the translation. With respect to the translation it is so changed, both in form and substance, as to present only what I ought to have written, in the opinion of a better judge, and not what I have written.

Present me affectionately to Mrs. Cathalan, the mother and daughter; tell the latter I feed on the hopes of seeing her one day at Paris. My friendly respects wait also on your father, and on yourself assurances of the esteem and consideration with which I have the honour to be Dear Sir your most obedient & most humble servt., TH: JEFFERSON

PrC (DLC).

To Joseph Fenwick

SIR Paris July 21. 1787.

I am this moment honoured with your letter of the 16th. and

wish it was in my power to give you the information desired [on the] subject of tobacco. The complaint has been universal that the Farmers general have not complied with the order of government. I have therefore desired that they may be called on to report precisely what tobaccos they have purchased on the terms prescribed by the order, that if it shall appear they have not bought the whole quantity, they may be compelled to do it immediately. It is impossible to foresee whether any new regulations will be made to take place on the expiration of the contract of Mr. Morris. I shall certainly press for something to be done by way of antidote to the monopoly under which this article is placed in France. The moment any thing is decided which may be interesting to our commerce, I shall take care to communicate it to them thro' Mr. Bondfeild: tho' I do not expect any thing interesting to take place very soon. I am with much regard Sir Your most obedient humble servt,

TH: JEFFERSON

PrC (DLC).

From R. & A. Garvey

Rouen, 21 July 1787. Have forwarded four cases of wine from Feger Gramont & Cie. of Bordeaux, which cases should be delivered in five days "by Bleig's Cart"; will send a note of the charges when freight has been paid. Woodmason, of London, has sent a bill of lading for a copying press which will be forwarded on arrival.

RC (MHi); 2 p.; endorsed. Recorded in SJL as received 22 July 1787.

From Ferdinand Grand

MONSIEUR Paris le 21 Juillet 1787.

J'ai l'honneur de vous remettre la notte des articles qui ont eu lieu pour le Compte des Etats de virginie depuis le dernier rèlevé dont vous avez pris connoissance; il rèsulte seulement de cette petite notte £11655.2. à porter au debit, et £5300. à porter au crèdit.

Vous m'avez communiqué, Monsieur, que vous dèsiriés quelques Transitions du Compte des Etats Unis à celui de virginie et de celui-ci à l'autre. Je prendrai la liberté de vous observer que si par cet arrangement le Bloc du Compte des Etats de Virginie devenoit plus considèrable cela pourroit augmenter l'objet de la somme de mon avance en general; ce que je voudrois èviter. Je vous demande donc la grace de ne rien changer à ce qui èxiste

[607]

jusqu'à d'autres moments. J'èspère que vous aurés la bonté d'entrer dans mes motifs à cet egard.

J'ai l'honneur d'être avec beaucoup de Considèration Monsieur Vôtre très humble et très obéissant Serviteur, GRAND

RC (DLC); endorsed. Recorded in SJL as received 21 July 1787. Enclosure not found.

To William Macarty

SIR Paris July 21. 1787.

I am favored with your letter of the 8th. instant. I had applied to the Marquis de la Fayette to sollicit the Sauf conduit for you. A desire of avoiding every possible occasion myself of asking what may be refused, or of giving ground to make a reciprocal demand on any occasion, induced me to do this; and the Marquis's zeal in every business respecting us, his weight and his access to every bureau satisfied me it would be in better hands. But tho he has not been finally refused, yet he thinks the prospect not good. He says that the Intendant (I think it was) of the province had opposed your obtaining it. Be assured that nothing shall be wanting on my part as far as I can meddle with propriety.

The plates you mention being dear, and the articles very incompleat, I will wait till there are better assortments to be had, and on better terms. I thank you for your attention to this matter and am with much esteem Sir Your most obedient & most humble servant,

TH: JEFFERSON

PrC (DLC).

To Parent

à Paris ce 21. Juillet 1787.

Les six paniers de vin rouge et blanc sont arrivés Monsieur bien conditionnés. Nous en avons gouté et nous les trouvons bons. C'est probable qu'en automne j'aurai besoin encore de vin blanc de la meme espece, parce que c'est du blanc dont nous faisons notre principale consommation. Je conterai toujours qu'en m'adressant à vous vous pourrez m'en trouver de la meilleure qualité. Ayez la bonté de m'envoyer la memoire pour la derniere, et de tirer sur moi pour le montant, et votre traite sera payée. Je suis, avec bien des remerciements pour vos attentions, et votre exactitude, Monsieur votre tres humble et tres obeissant serviteur, TH: JEFFERSON

PrC (MHi).

To Ferdinand Grand

SIR   Paris July 22. 1787.

I am honoured with your letter of yesterday on the subject of the accounts of the United states and of Virginia. My only object in allotting to each the articles which had been paid for them respectively was to enable you to send to the commissioners of the treasury an exact state of the advances which have been made for them: otherwise those advances will appear less than they really are. Another object was to enable you to state those accounts ultimately right, no body but myself knowing for which of them the expenditures have been. With respect to the balance due to the state of Virginia, I reserve it for Houdon: and there will be no draught on it till he shall be entitled to one, which will not be till his work is further advanced. As to the United states having some time ago desired Mr. Carmichael and Mr. Dumas to cease drawing, I know of no demand which will come on their account except a bill of Mr. Barclay's for 1200 livres, which as I knew to be on public account and for a very necessary purpose, I accepted; and the usual draughts of Mr. Short and myself: should it be inconvenient to you to advance for these, be so good as to write me a line signifying it, and they shall not be pressed.   We propose to ourselves the honor of dining with you to-day, unless the incertain state of the weather should prevent it. I have the honor to be with sentiments of the most perfect esteem, Sir Your most obedient & most humble servant,   TH: JEFFERSON

PrC (DLC).

To the Rhode Island Delegates in Congress

GENTLEMEN   Paris July 22. 1787.

I was honoured, in the month of January last, with a letter from the honorable the delegates of Rhodeisland in Congress, inclosing a letter from the Corporation of Rhodeisland college to his most Christian majesty, and some other papers. I was then in the hurry of preparation for a journey into the South of France, and therefore unable at that moment to make the enquiries which the object of the letter rendered necessary. As soon as I returned, which was in the last month, I turned my attention to that object, which was the establishment of a professorship of the French language in the college, and the obtaining a collection of the best French authors, with the aid of the king. That neither the college nor myself might be compromitted uselessly, I thought it necessary to sound previously those who were able to inform me what would be the success of the application. I was assured, so as to leave no doubt, that it would not be complied with; that there had never been an instance of the king's granting such a demand in a foreign country, and that they would be cautious of setting the precedent, that in this moment too they were embarrassed with the difficult operation of putting down all establishments of their own which could possibly be dispensed with in order to bring their expenditures down to the level of their receipts. Upon such information I was satisfied that it was more prudent not to deliver the letter and spare to both parties the disagreeableness of giving and receiving a denial. The king did give to two colleges in America, copies of the works printing in the public press. But were this to be obtained for the college of Rhode island, it would extend only to a volume or two of Buffon's works still to be printed, Manilius's astronomicon, and one or two other works in the press which are of no consequence. I did not think this an object for the college worth being pressed. I beg the favor of you gentlemen to assure the corporation that no endeavors of mine should have been spared, could they have effected their wish: and that they have been faithfully used in making the preliminary enquiries which were necessary, and which ended in an assurance that nothing could be done. These papers having been transmitted to me thro' your delegation, will I hope be an apology for my availing myself of the same channel for communicating the result.

I have the honour to be with sentiments of the most perfect esteem and respect, Gentlemen, your most obedient & most humble servant,

TH: JEFFERSON

PrC (DLC).

To John Adams

DEAR SIR   Paris July 23. 1787.

Frouillé, the bookseller here who is engaged in having your

book translated and printed, understanding that you were about publishing a sequel to it, has engaged me to be the channel of his prayers to you to favor his operation by transmitting hither the sheets of the sequel as they shall be printed; and he will have them translated by the same hand, which is a good one.

It is necessary for me to explain the passage in Mr. Barclay's letter of July 13th. of which he writes me he had sent you a duplicate, wherein he mentions that I had given him a full dispensation from waiting on you in London. Mr. Barclay was arrested in Bourdeaux for debt and put into prison. The parliament released him after five days on the footing of his being Consul and minister from the U.S. to Marocco. His adversaries applied here to deprive him of his privilege. I spoke on the subject to the minister. He told me that the character of Consul was no protection at all from private arrest, but that he would try to avail him of the other character. I found however that the event might be doubtful, and stated the whole in a letter to Mr. Barclay, observing at the same time that I knew of nothing which rendered it necessary for him to come to *Paris* before his departure for America. He determined therefore to go to America immediately which indeed was his wisest course, as he would have been harrassed immediately by his creditors.—Our funds here have been out some time and Mr. Grand is at the length of his tether in advancing for us. He has refused very small demands for current occasions, and I am not clear he will not refuse my usual one for salary. He has not told me so, but I am a little diffident of it. I shall know in a few days. Whether he does or not, I cannot approve of his protesting small and current calls. Having had nothing to do with any other banker, I cannot say what their practice is: but I suppose it their practice to advance for their customers, when their funds happen to be out, in proportion to the sums which they pass thro' their hands. Mr. Grand is a very sure banker, but a very timid one, and I fear he thinks it possible that he may lose his advances for the United states. Should he reject my draught, would there be any prospect of it's being answered in Holland, merely for my own and Mr. Short's salaries, say 4500 livres a month?—You will have heard that the emperor has put troops into march on account of the disturbances in Brabant. The situation of affairs in Holland you know better than I do. How will they end?—I have the honour to be with sentiments of the most perfect esteem & respect Dear Sir your most obedient & most humble servt., TH: JEFFERSON

RC (MHi: AMT); endorsed in part: "ansd Aug. 25. 1787." PrC (DLC).

To Mary Jefferson Bolling

Dear Sister   Paris July 23. 1787.

I received with great pleasure your letter of May 3. informing me of your health and of that of your family. Be assured that it is and ever has been among the most interesting things to me. Letters of business claiming their rights before those of affection, we often write seldomest to those whom we love most. The distance to which I am removed has given a new value to all I valued before in my own country, and the day of my return to it will be the happiest I expect to see in this life. When it will come is not yet decided as far as depends on myself. My dear Polly is safely arrived here and in good health. She had got so attached to Captn. Ramsay that they were obliged to decoy her from him. She staid three weeks in London with Mrs. Adams, and had got such an attachment to her that she refused to come with the person I sent for her. After some days, she was prevailed on to come. She did not know either her sister or myself, but soon renewed her acquaintance and attachment. She is now in the same convent with her sister, and will come to see me once or twice a week. It is a house of education altogether the best in France, and at which the best masters attend. There are in it as many protestants as Catholics, and not a word is ever spoken to them on the subject of religion. Patsy enjoys good health, and longs much to return to her friends. We shall doubtless find much change when we do get back; many of our older friends withdrawn from the stage, and our younger ones grown out of our knowledge. I suppose you are now fixed for life at Chesnut grove: I take a part of the misfortune to myself, as it will prevent my seeing you as often as would be practicable at Lickinghole. It is still a greater loss to my sister Carr. We must look to Jack for indemnification, as I think it was the plan that he should live at Lickinghole. I suppose he is now become the father of a family, and that we may hail you as grandmother. As we approach that term it becomes less fearful. You mention Mr. Bolling's being unwell, so as not to write to me. He has just been sick enough all his life to prevent his writing to any body. My prayer is therefore only that he may never be worse. Were he to be so, no body would feel it more sensibly than myself, as nobody has a more sincere esteem for him than myself. I find as I grow older, that I love those most whom I loved first. Present me to him in the most friendly terms, to Jack also, and my other nephews and neices of your fire side and be assured of the sincere love with which I am, dear sister, your affectionate brother, TH: JEFFERSON

PrC (MHi). Mrs. Bolling's LETTER OF MAY 3. is recorded in SJL as having been written from Chestnut Grove, Va., and as received 30 June 1787, but it has not been found.

To H. Fizeaux & Cie.

GENTLEMEN Paris July 23. 1787.

The letter which you mention, of January 1, came duly to my hands, and I forwarded it by the first conveiance to the Commissioners of the Treasury of the U.S. at New York. I could do nothing else with it, being a matter entirely out of the functions of my office, and on which I was not authorized to give any answer. It is all I can now do with the letter of the 16th. inst. with which you have been pleased to honor me on the same subject. I will forward it to the Commissioners of the Treasury by the Pacquet boat which sails the 10th. of the next month. I have the honour to be with sentiments of the most perfect consideration and respect Gentlemen Your most obedient & most humble servant,

TH: JEFFERSON

PrC (DLC).
THE LETTER OF THE 16TH INST.: Not found but recorded in SJL as received 22 July; it was enclosed in TJ to the Commissioners of the Treasury, 5 Aug. 1787.

To Ladevese

à Paris ce 23me. Juillet 1787.

Je viens de recevoir, Monsieur, la lettre que vous m'avez fait l'honneur de m'ecrire, et celle pour Monsieur et Mademoiselle Laurens. Je me charge tres volontier de la faire passer en Amerique ou est Monsieur Laurens actuellement, et de vous faire parvenir la reponse s'il me fera l'honneur de me la remettre. J'ai celui de vous assurer des sentiments tres respectueux avec lesquels je suis Monsieur votre tres humble et tres obeissant serviteur,

TH: JEFFERSON

PrC (DLC); at foot of text: "M. Ladevese, pasteur de l'eglise reformée de Vigon en Severe."

To Montmorin

SIR   Paris July 23. 1787

I had the honor a few days ago of putting into the hands of Your Excellency some observations on the other articles of American produce brought into the ports of this country. That of our tobaccoes, from the particular form of their administration here and their importance to the king's revenues, has been placed on a separate line, and considered separately. I will now ask permission to bring that subject under your consideration.

The mutual extension of their commerce was among the fairest advantages to be derived to France and the United States from the independance of the latter. An exportation of eighty millions, chiefly in raw materials, is supposed to constitute the present limits of the commerce of the U.S. with the nations of Europe, limits however which extend as their population increases. To draw the best proportion of this into the ports of France, rather than of any other nation is believed to be the wish and the interest of both. Of these eighty millions, thirty are constituted by the single article of tobacco. Could the whole of this be brought into the ports of France, to satisfy first its own demands, and the residue to be revended to other nations, it would be a powerful link of commercial connexion. But we are far from this. Even her own consumption, supposed nine millions, under the administration of the monopoly to which it is farmed, enters little as an article of exchange into the commerce of the two nations. When this article was first put into farm, perhaps it did not injure the commercial interests of the kingdom; because nothing but British manufactures were then allowed to be given in return for American tobaccoes. The laying the trade open then to all the subjects of France could not have relieved her from a paiment in money. Circumstances are changed, yet the old institution remains. The body to which this monopoly was given was not mercantile. Their object is to simplify as much as possible the administration of their affairs. They sell for cash: they purchase therefore with cash. Their interest, their principles and their practice seem opposed to the general interest of the kingdom, which would require that this capital article should be laid open to a free exchange for the productions of this country. So far does the spirit of simplifying their operations govern this body that relinquishing the advantages to be derived from a competition of sellers, they contracted some time ago with a single person (Mr. Morris) for three years supplies of American tobacco to be paid for in cash. They obliged themselves too, expressly, to employ no other person to purchase in America during that term. In consequence of this, the mercantile houses of France concerned in sending her productions to be exchanged for tobacco, cut off for three years from the hope of selling these tobaccoes in France, were of necessity to abandon that commerce. In consequence of this too a single individual, constituted sole purchaser of so great a proportion of the tobaccoes made, had the price in his own power. A great reduction in it took place; and that not only on the quantity he bought, but on the whole quantity made. The loss to the states producing the article did not go to cheapen it for their friends here. Their price was fixed. What was gained on their consumption was to enrich the person purchasing it; the rest, the monopolists and merchants of other countries. The effect of this operation was vitally felt by every farmer in America concerned in the culture of this plant. At the end of the year he found he had lost a fourth or a third of his revenue; the state, the same proportion of its subjects of exchange with other nations. The manufactures of this country too were either not to go there at all, or to go through the chanel of a new monopoly, which, freed from the controul of competition in prices and qualities, was not likely to extend their consumption. It became necessary to relieve the two countries from the fatal effects of this double monopoly. I had the honor of addressing a letter on the fifteenth day of august one thousand seven hundred and eighty five to his late Excellency the Count de Vergennes upon this subject. The effectual mode of relief was to lay the commerce open. But the King's interest was also to be guarded. A committee was appointed to take this matter into consideration; and the result was an order to the Farmers general that no such contract should be made again. And to furnish such aliment as might keep that branch of commerce alive till the expiration of the present contract they were required to put the merchants in general on a level with Mr. Morris for the quantity of twelve or fifteen thousand hogsheads a year. That this relief too might not be intercepted from the merchants of the two suffering nations by those of a neighbouring one, and that the transportation of so bulky an article might go to aliment their own shipping, no tobaccoes were to be counted of this purchase but those brought in French or American vessels. Of this order, made at Bernis, his Excellency Count de Vergennes was pleased to honor me with a communication, by a letter of the thirtieth of May one thousand seven hundred and eighty six, desiring that I would publish it as well in America as to the American merchants in France. I did so; communicating it to Congress at the same time. This order thus viewed with the transactions which produced it, will be seen to have been necessary: and its punctual and candid execution has been rendered still more so by the speculations of the merchants entered into on the faith of it. Otherwise it would become the instrument of their ruin instead of their relief. A twelvemonth has elapsed some time since: and it is questioned whether the farmers general have purchased, within that time, the quantity prescribed, and on the conditions prescribed. It would be impossible for the merchants to prove the negative: it will be easy for the farmers general to shew the affirmative if it exists. I hope that a branch of commerce of this extent will be thought interesting enough to both nations, to render it the desire of Your Excellency to require, as it makes it my duty to ask, a report of the purchases they have made according to the conditions of Bernis, specifying in that report. 1. The quantities purchased. 2. The prices paid. 3. The dates of the purchase and paiment. 4. The flag of the vessel in which imported. 5. Her name. 6. Her port of delivery; and 7. The name of the seller. The four first articles make part of the conditions required by the order of Bernis; the three last may be necessary for the correction of any errors which should happen to arise in the report.

But the order of Bernis was never considered but as a temporary relief. The radical evil will still remain. There will be but one purchaser in the kingdom, and the hazard of his refusal will damp every mercantile speculation. It is very much to be desired that before the expiration of this order some measure may be devised which may bring this great article into free commerce between the two nations. Had this been practicable at the time it was put into farm, that mode of collecting the revenue would probably have never been adopted; now that it is become practicable it seems reasonable to discontinue this mode, and to substitute some of those practised on other imported articles on which a revenue is levied without absolutely suppressing them in commerce. If the revenue can be secured, the interests of a few individuals will hardly be permitted to weigh against those of as many millions, equally subjects of His Majesty, and against those too of a nation allied to him by all the ties of treaty, of interests, and of affection. The privileges of the most favored nation have been mutually exchanged by treaty. But the productions of other nations, which do not rival those of France, are suffered to be bought and sold freely within the kingdom. By prohibiting all His Majesty's subjects from dealing in tobacco except with a single company, one third of the exports of the United States are rendered uncommerciable here. This production is so peculiarly theirs that its shackles affect no other nation. A relief from these shackles will form a memorable epoch in the commerce of the two nations. It will establish at once a great basis of exchange, serving like a point of union to draw to it other members of our commerce. Nature too has conveniently assorted our wants and our superfluities to each other. Each nation has exactly to spare the articles which the other wants. We have a surplus of rice, tobacco, furs, peltry, potash, lamp oils, timber, which France wants; she has a surplus of wines, brandies, esculent oils, fruits and manufactures of all kinds, which we want. The governments have nothing to do but *not to hinder* their merchants from making the exchange. The difference of language, laws and customs will be some obstacle for a time; but the interest of the merchants will surmount them. A more serious obstacle is our debt to Great Britain. Yet since the treaty between this country and that, I should not despair of seeing that debt paid in part with the productions of France, if our produce can obtain here a free course of exchange for them. The distant prospect is still more promising. A century's experience has shewn that we double our numbers every twenty or twenty-five years. No circumstance can be foreseen at this moment which will lessen our rate of multiplication for centuries to come. For every article of the productions or manufactures of this country then, which can be introduced into habit there, the demand will double every twenty or twenty-five years. And to introduce the habit we have only to let the merchants alone. Whether we may descend by a single step from the present state to that of perfect freedom of commerce in this article, whether any, and what, intermediate operation may be necessary to prepare the way to this, what cautions must be observed for the security of His Majesty's revenue, which we do not wish to impair, will rest with the wisdom of his Ministers, whose knowledge of the subject will enable them to devise the best plans, while their patriotism and justice will dispose to the pursuit of them. To the friendly dispositions of Your Excellency, of which we had such early and multiplied proofs, I take the liberty of committing this subject particularly, trusting that some method may be devised of reconciling the collection of His Majesty's revenues with the interests of the two nations: and have the honour of assuring you of those sincere sentiments of esteem and respect with which I am Your Excellency's Most obedient & most humble servant,

TH: JEFFERSON

Papers inclosed.
1. Letter of M. le comte de Vergennes of May 30. 1786.
2. The order of Berni.
3. The contract with Mr. Morris referred to in the order of Berni.

RC (Arch. Aff. Etr., Corr. Pol., E.-U., xxxii; Tr in DLC); in the hand of William Short, with complimentary close, signature, and list of enclosures in TJ's hand; accompanied by a translation into French, also in Short's hand, unsigned, without the list of enclosures, and having at head of text: "Traduction de la lettre precedente. Envoyé copie à M. de Villedeuil le 28 Aout 1787." PrC of the letter, having top of first page clipped and salutation and date substituted in TJ's hand, and of the translation; Tr of the letter only, attested by Short and in his hand (DLC). Enclosures, as listed at end of letter, are to be found above in Vol. 9: 586-8, 597-8.

TJ's OBSERVATIONS ON THE OTHER ARTICLES OF AMERICAN PRODUCE are printed above under 3 July 1787.

To Abigail Adams Smith

MADAM
Paris July 23. 1787.

I am honored with your letter of the 11th. inst. covering a draught from General Sullivan, and a letter from him. I will take care to remit a bill for paiment before it becomes due, which I observe will be on the 10th. of the next month. I should be very happy to find occasion of forwarding this by Colo. Smith in person, because that circumstance would relieve the disagreeableness of this new scene of business in which you have been involved: and your letter supposes the possibility of his return. I am afraid however you must expect him still longer, and that you will have the trouble of finishing the business you have so kindly undertaken. I beg your pardon for having been the cause of your being involved in it, and with my thanks for the trouble you have already taken, have the honour of assuring you of those sentiments of sincere esteem and respect with which I am Madam Your most obedient & most humble servt.,
TH: JEFFERSON

PrC (MHi).

From John Jay

DR SIR
Office for foreign Affairs 24th. July 1787

Since my Letter to you of 24th. April I have been honored with yours of 14th. and 23d. of February last, and with two from Mr.

[618]

Short, to whom I had the Pleasure of writing on the 5th. Instant.

I have now the Honor of transmitting to you here enclosed the following Papers.

Letter for the Emperor of Morocco with a Ratification of the Treaty enclosed, and Copies of both for your Information.

This Letter you will be so good as to forward by the first eligible Opportunity, to Don Francisco Chiappe the american Agent at Morocco, to be by him presented to the Emperor.

A Letter for Mr. Fennish to be forwarded in like Manner.[1]

A Copy of an Act of Congress of the 18th. July Instant, authorizing you to redeem our unfortunate fellow Citizens at Algiers in the Manner which you suggested.

An Ordinance for the Government of the western Country passed the 13th. Instant.

The printed Journals of Congress from 6th. November to 10th. May last.

The late Newspapers.

The other Matters on which you have long had Reason to expect Instructions, are yet under Consideration.

Chevr. Jones cannot have his Affairs arranged in Season for him to go in this Packet. He will probably sail in the next, and I flatter myself with the Pleasure of being enabled by that Time, if not sooner, to write you fully and satisfactorily. Nine States for a long Time past have been but seldom represented in Congress, and hence Delays much to be regretted have taken place.

The Convention is sitting, but their Proceedings are secret. Our Indian Affairs in the West still give us Uneasiness, and so I fear they will continue to do for Reasons which you will not be at a Loss to conjecture. Our Affairs in general will admit of much Melioration, and they will afford the Convention ample Field for the Display of their Patriotism and Talents.[2]

I have the Honor to be &c, JOHN JAY

P.S. Congress Yesterday passed a Resolution approving Mr. Barclay's Conduct in the Negociation with Morocco. They have likewise confirmed his Appointment of Don Francisco Chiappe to be their Agent at Morocco, Don Joseph Chiappe to be their Agent at Mogador and Don Girelamo Chiappe to be their Agent at Tangier, with which Agents it is their Desire that their Ministers at Versailles and London should regularly correspond. Want of Time prevents my having and sending you certified Copies of these

24 JULY 1787

Acts by this Opportunity. My next shall contain what may be necessary to say further on these Subjects.

FC (DNA: PCC, No. 121). Dft (NK-Iselin). Recorded in SJL as received 1 Sep. 1787. Enclosures: (1) Letter from Congress to the Emperor of Morocco, 23 July 1787, transmitting ratification by Congress of the treaty with Morocco. (2) Copy of the ratification (both printed in JCC, XXXII, 355-64; XXXIII, 393-4; the copies of these two documents "for your Information" were not sent until 24 Oct. 1787; see Jay's first letter of that date to TJ). (3) Jay to Taher Fennish, 24 July 1787, transmitting the thanks of Congress for his "friendly attentions to their Envoy in the Course of the negociation"; expressing their pleasure "with the Probity Candor and Liberality which distinguished" his Conduct on that occasion; and requesting him to inform "his Majesty's chaplain or Preacher" that Barclay's letters had made honorable mention of him and had thereby impressed Congress (Dft, NK-Iselin); in Dft Jay added this paragraph: "I flatter myself Sir that the Peace so happily concluded between our two Countries will gradually produce advantages to both, especially when our commerce to the Mediterranean shall cease to be interrupted by the African states who now so molest it"; he then deleted the final clause beginning with the word "especially" and substituted for it these words: "and you may rest assured that your name and Character will allways be remembered and respected in these States"; he then deleted the whole. (4) Resolution of Congress of 18 July 1787 on Jay's report respecting "a Petition from Hannah Stephens praying that her Husband be redeemed from Captivity at Algiers, and also a Letter from the Honorable T. Jefferson, proposing that a certain Order of Priests be employed for such Purposes"; authorizing TJ to "take such Measures as he may deem most adviseable for redeeming the American Captives at Algiers, and at any Expence not exceeding that which European Nations usually pay in like Cases"; and directing the "Board of Treasury . . . to provide Ways and Means for enabling Mr. Jefferson to defray the said Expences, either by remitting Money from hence or by a Credit in Europe" (Tr in Clerk's hand, signed by Charles Thomson, in DLC: TJ Papers, 31: 5292; TJ wrote in margin opposite the reference to his letter: "Feb. 1.1787"; see JCC, XXXII, 364-5). (5) *An Ordinance for the Government of the Territory of the United States, North-West of the River Ohio*; the copy enclosed was evidently one of the edition of 100 copies printed by John Dunlap on 13 July 1787 (same, XXXIII, 757; Evans, No. 20779).

¹ Dft has the following deleted at this point: "A Letter to Mr. Carmichael covering a Letter for the king of Spain, of which a Copy is also sent for your Information."

² Dft has the following deleted at this point: "I hope the Changes at Versailles will not produce a less friendly system of Policy with Respect to us. ⟨The appointment of Count Demontmorin will . . . the late minister . . . and I shall be deceived and disappointed if this country should⟩ I have no Reason to apprehend that either France or America will have Reason to regret the appointment of Count Demontmorin especially while his official conduct shall be permitted to correspond with his private Judgment and opinions."

From Robert Montgomery

Alicante, 24 July 1787. Thanks TJ for his letter of 6 July; hopes that under the protection of TJ and John Jay the consulate of Alicante will not slip from him to another; has spent eleven years in "Close application to know the Language and Laws of this Country, the Commerce it is Capable of and disposition of the People"; asks TJ to write to Congress on his behalf; seeks no emolument at present. He happened to be in Madrid when the last letters arrived from Algiers or he would have immediately contradicted the former report of the death of the Dey of Algiers, "which arose from an Indisposition from which he has since recoverd; he is very old and a Change there can be of no disadvantage to our Political Intrests"; knows people of high rank there who will be useful when circumstances permit. "The Plague continues to Rage and has Already Spread so far Westward as Mascara."

RC (DLC); 4 p.; endorsed. Recorded in SJL as received 8 Aug. 1787.

To Moustier

SIR   Paris July 24. 1787.

I must beg your pardon for having forgotten one of the two articles I was to write to London for for you. One I know was the American Atlas; but what was the other?

The bearer brings you a bottle of the Frontignan wine of which I spoke to you. It has the etiquette of Monsieur Lambert the person who makes it, with whom I made acquaintance and passed some hours in his house. He is a good and sensible physician, depending more on the productions of his vineyard than of his profession. There are made at Frontignan 600 peices of this wine, of which 260. are bought by two particular merchants so that there remain 240 peices only for market. Yet they export from Cette (about half a league from Frontignan) 30,000 peices of wine under that name. The only persons who raise the genuine Frontignan of the first quality, are Madame de Soubeinan 200. peices. M. Reboulle 90., M. Lambert medecin, 60., M. Thomas 50., M. Argilliers 50., M. Audibert 45. and some other small proprietors. If any of these persons are among your acquaintance you may be sure of genuine wine from them; if they are not, I will ensure it from Lambert, of whose I send you a specimen. I bought it in his house. He delivers it bottled at 24s. the bottle included, on the spot. With transportation and duties on the road it costs me here 40s. but he will send it for you to Bourdeaux.

Mr. Payne (author of Common sense) is here and desires to be presented to you. What day and hour could you permit me to bring him? I am engaged out on Thursday for the whole day. I have the honor to be with sentiments of the most perfect

PrC (DLC); lacks end of complimentary close and signature (see Vol. 9: 217, note 1).

From Moustier

à Paris le 24. Juillet 1787

Je suis bien reconnoissant, Monsieur, de votre attention pour moi et des marques que vous voulez bien m'en donner. Lorsque j'ai eû l'honneur de vous voir chez vous, je vous ai temoigné le desir d'avoir une collection des ouvrages qui peuvent etendre mes connoissances sur un pays que j'ai depuis bien longtems le desir de connoître par moi-même. Vous ne m'avez parlé que de l'ouvrage de Mr. Ramsay et de celui de Mr. Adams, comme méritant quelque estime, j'ai souhaité les joindre à l'Atlas. L'auteur m'a promis les observations sur la Virginie. Je me nourrirai tant que je pourrai de bonnes lectures avant d'asseoir mon jugement que je desire de fixer bientot sur les lieux. J'attends à chaque instant une decision finale à cet egard.

Je ne connois personne des proprietaires du vin de Frontignan; ainsi je m'en remets entierement à vous, Monsieur, pour en obtenir. Je supose qu'il ne s'alterera pas en passant la mer et qu'il suportera le climat de l'Amerique. Il faudroit je pense en faire un essai par 60. bouteilles; s'il reussit tant pour le transport que pour l'accueil qu'on lui fera j'en prendrai ensuite autant que je pourrai m'en procurer.

Je serai très flatté et très empressé de faire connoissance avec Mr. Payne. Je ne sortirai pas de chez moi demain ni vendredi dans la matinée, mais pour avoir l'honneur de vous posseder l'un et l'autre plus longtems, j'hazarde de vous proposer un mauvais diner sans façon pour Samedi où nous serons seuls. Je vous prie de vouloir bien me marquer si cet arrangement vous convient. Je prends la liberté de vous donner la peine de venir chez moi avec Mr. Payne, parcequ'il y a quelqu'un dans ma maison qui a toujours grand plaisir à vous voir et qui sera bien aise de faire connoissance avec un Americain du merite de Mr. Payne.

Agreez les assurances du très sincere et parfait attachement avec lequel j'ai l'honneur d'etre, Monsieur, Votre très humble et très obeissant Serviteur,   Le Cte. de Moustier

RC (DLC); endorsed. Recorded in SJL as received 24 July 1787.

From the Abbé de Reymond de St. Maurice

Paris, 24 July 1787. Asks for "un instant d'audience" at a day or hour convenient to TJ, to discuss a matter concerning a friend and in which TJ can be of much help.

RC (MHi); 2 p.; in French; endorsed. Addressed as from "Rüe de Bourbon f:B.St.G. près Les Théatins." Not recorded in SJL.

To Martha Jefferson Carr

DEAR SISTER Paris July 25. 1787.

Your letter of May 5. 1786. came to my hands January 24. 1787. My memory tells me that I have answered the article in it relative to Mr. Bernard Moore's purchase of books of Mr. Carr's estate; yet as I find neither a copy nor note of my letter to you on that occasion, I will repeat what I therein assured you, that I am almost perfectly certain that Mr. Moore never accounted to me for the amount. Supposing the possibility of my memory's deceiving me in this instance (which however I do not suspect) it would be found in my memorandum book of the date of the transaction which book is in the hands of Mr. Lewis. If Mr. Moore can point out the date, Mr. Lewis could soon examine it. But I am morally certain, that on recollection and examination he will be satisfied no settlement of this matter ever took place between him and me. His honour and justice will in that case set the matter to rights. Your favors of May 22. 1786. and Jan. 2. and Feb. 26. 1787. came to hand the first of them May 3. 1787, and the two last the 30th. of last month. You will not wonder therefore at the delay of my acknoleging the receipt of them. I am happy to hear the favorable accounts given of Sam Carr, which I think very possibly true, as I always believed the difficulty with him was not a want of capacity, but of attention; and that if any circumstance should ever arise to recall his attention to useful objects he would do well. Mr. Wythe gives me good accounts of Peter, and Mr. Madison transmits me similar ones of Dabney from the college [. . . .][1] from time to time to the convent to habituate her to it. She is now there, contented, and in great favor. She had a fine passage, without a storm. Patsy enjoys good health, as I do also myself, except as to the accident of a dislocated wrist which happened to me ten months ago. It was badly set, and therefore neither it's motion nor strength will ever be recovered in any great degree.— I recollect another circumstance which will inform you whether Mr. Moore settled with me. I gave you an account of every thing subsisting between Mr. Carr's estate and myself, taken from my books with great care. If I have given no credit in that for Mr. Moore's debt, be assured it was never accounted for to me. This

25 JULY 1787

you can know by looking into the account in your hands. Remember me affectionately to Nancy, Lucy and Polly and be assured yourself of the sincere esteem with which I am Dear Sister your affectionate brother, TH: JEFFERSON

P.S. I thank you for the small news. Be so good as to continue this kind of correspondence, as it is most welcome to me.

PrC (Mrs. John C. White, Charlottesville, Va., 1946); probably lacks at least one page.

Mrs. Carr's letters of 5 and 22 May 1786, 2 Jan. and 26 Feb. 1787 have not been found, but are recorded in SJL as received on the dates mentioned by TJ.

[1] Two words illegible at foot of text of first page, which may be "at Williamsburgh"; it also appears from the text that follows (beginning at the top of a succeeding page) that at least one page of PrC is lacking. For the substance if not the exact words of at least that part of the missing matter that pertains to Mary Jefferson, see TJ to Elizabeth Wayles Eppes, 28 July 1787.

From Mantel Duchoqueltz

MONSIEUR à Newyork le 25 Juillet 1787.

J'ai l'honneur d'envoyer à votre Excellence un Connoissement contenant les objets qui sont chargés à Bord du Paquebot du Roi No. 7. Capitaine Lefournier, pour lesquels objets J'ai déboursé 23.^{lt} 12s. 6. Je Suplie Votre Excellence de vouloir bien donner des ordres lorsqu'on retirera les dits objets de payer cette avance à la direction du Havre.

Je suis avec respect Monsieur Votre très humble et très obeissant Serviteur,

MANTEL DUCHOQUELTZ
chargé de l'agence des paquebots.

RC (ViWC); endorsed. Recorded in SJL as received 1 Sep. 1787. Enclosure not found.

To John Stockdale

SIR Paris July 25. 1787.

Not hearing any thing yet of the books which should have come from Lackington's and from yourself I suspect they may be lying in the warehouse of the Diligence in London, perhaps forgotten, and will beg the favor of you therefore to send there for enquiry.

Send me if you please a copy of the American Atlas, latest edition and one of Mr. Adams's books on the American constitutions. Note the prices in the books, as they are not for myself. I am Sir Your very humble servant, TH: JEFFERSON

PrC (DLC).

To Nathaniel Barrett

Dear Sir   Paris July 26. 1787.

The bearer Monsr. Chantrot brings your watch. I had bespoke it expressly at the price and of the quality of mine: that is to say as good as it could be made and at 576. livres. He has however so far misunderstood this as to make it cost 620 livres which is two Louis more than had been agreed on. He sais that it has been occasioned by making the gold case thicker. I have told him that I did not think you bound to take it at a higher price than mine, but that perhaps as there was so much more gold in the case, you might consent to do it. I am with much respect Dear Sir your most obedt. humble servt.,   Th: Jefferson

PrC (MHi).

From John Sandford Dart

[*Charleston, 26 July 1787.* Recorded in SJL as received 13 Oct. 1787. This may have been a notification by Dart that he, as clerk of the South Carolina assembly, would forward to TJ through Jay the session laws of the state as issued; see Izard to TJ, 10 Nov. 1787. Not found.]

From Thomas Barclay

Dear Sir   L'Orient 27th. July 1787

We have had a continued set of hard blowing Westerly Winds for three Weeks, but the weather is now moderate and promises a change favorable to my Embarkation.

The only excuse for the trouble I have given you lately, is the situation I have been in, and to increase it I must now mention the Error committed by me in the Sketches of the little Accounts which I sent you.

The expence of the China at Rouen I estimated at 25 Livres. You will find by the inclosed account of Messrs. Garveys that the amount on three Boxes for you and one for Doctor Franklin was £89.12.6; therefore your proportion will be Livres 67.4. I find also that I paid for 2 Anchors of Brandy which I sent to you from hence 209 Livres and which I Suppose is charged to you with the China, and paid for by you in the Money you gave Mrs. Barclay on that account.

[625]

27 JULY 1787

In my account which I sent you with the State of Virginia I omitted the following Articles.

3 Muskets which I order'd to be made at Liege, as a sample for the State of the work, and value of it at that place cost there	66.
Carriage to Paris	21.4
Ditto from Paris to L'Orient	[21.4][1]

I hope and beleive there is nothing farther to add on these Subjects. I must renew my request that you will send me some Letters to your friends in America, and if you will put them under cover to Mr. Jay at New York, or to Mr. Loreilhe of this place they will be taken proper care of, this will be more necessary as Messrs. French have written Circular Letters to their Correspondents in America Exculpating themselves, and loading me with the blackest Calumnies. I do not by any means intend to involve you in my affair with them, but I want you to give your testimoney of my Public conduct, so far as it has come under your notice, with freedom, and to recommend that I may have as speedy a settlement made of my accounts as will be consistant with the more important business of Congress.

Our last Letters from America are of the 14th. June. The Convention had met at Philadelphia in May and had chosen General Washington President. He together with Mr. Edmond Randolp, Mr. Maddison, Mr. John Blair, Mr. George Mason, Mr. George White, and Mr. James McClurg composed the Deligation of Virginia. Doctor Franklin, Mr. Morris, Mr. Governr. Morris, Mr. Fitzsimmonds, Mr. Wilson (the Lawyer) Mr. Clymer and General Mifflin that of Pensylvania, and Major Jackson was chosen Secretary. Rhode Island was not represented, nor had all the Members from the other States appeared. I think the Day appointed for the first meeting was the fourteenth, and that the General arrived in Town the Thirteenth. The friends to their country look up to this Convention with anxiety, and with respect to the Delegation from Pensylvania I think it coud hardly be mended.

I have received Letters from Mogadore of the 15th. and 16th. of May. The Ratification of the Treaty by the Ministers was got to hand, but Mr. Fennish to whom it was inclosed had sailed for Constantinople on the Business of the Emperor. The Papers lye in the Hands of Mr. Joseph Chiappi at Mogadore, who desires my Instructions for their Disposition. They will be to forward them to the Emperor (who is just returned from Taffilet) by the hands of his Brother Francis at Morocco. The Swedish Ambassador was arrived at that City, and a new Consul General from England was waiting at Mogadore for permission to proceed to court with the Peace offerings, which will probably accommodate the late misunderstandings.

I had the pleasure of receiving your Letter address'd to me at Bordeaux. What I have written to you from hence, with my last from Bordeaux, will fully reply to your obliging favor.

It is my intention when I arrive at Philadelphia to call together five or six Men of known honor, and to submit to them my transactions at Bordeaux, in hopes thereby of cleansing myself from the vile Slanders attempted to be fixed upon me, by the House of French. A sense of justice due to these Gentlemen, among other considerations, prevented me from leaving Bordeaux, untill every attempt of accommodation, which I cou'd make, were rejected in the most insolent manner, and the most gross and vulgar verbal replies made to my Letters, notwithstanding which I declare if there was now the least chance of their listening to reason, I wou'd without hesitation return to Bordeaux, but there is none, and these People will never forgive me, because they have put me in Prison.

I applied at the Post Office at Bordeaux for your Letters Postrestant, but cou'd find none. Mr. Delap, who is a well informed Man on the Subject was making out a state of the Trade of that place, with the prices current and has my directions to put it under cover to Mr. Loreilhe here, who will send you a copy of it.

I forgot to inform Mr. Short that the exportation of Asses from Bayonne are permitted though not from Spain.

My best wishes wait upon him. I am always Dear Sir Your most obt. and very humble Sert., THOS BARCLAY

RC (Vi); in a clerk's hand, signed by Barclay. Recorded in SJL as received 31 July 1787. The enclosed statement of R. & A. Garvey has not been found.
¹ Blank in MS; see Barclay to TJ, 8 July 1787, wherein TJ refers to "filling up the blank" with the amount given in brackets (supplied).

From John Jay, with Enclosure

SIR　　　　　　　Office for foreign Affairs 27th. July 1787

Congress being desirous that the Commerce between the United States and France may be promoted by every reciprocal Regulation conducive to that End, wish that no Time may be lost in ascertaining the Privileges, Powers and Duties of their respective Consuls, Vice Consuls and commercial Agents and Commissaries.

27 JULY 1787

They regret the Circumstance which calls you to the South of France, but are perfectly satisfied that you should make that or any other Journey which your Health may require. It is their Wish and Instruction that on your Return to the Court, your Attention may be immediately directed to the abovementioned Subject. Considering that Conventions of this Nature, however apparently useful in Theory, may from some Defects or unforeseen Circumstances be attended with Inconveniences in Practice, they think it best that they should be probationary, at least in the first Instance, and therefore that the Term to be assigned for the Duration of the one in Question should not exceed twelve Years. They also think it adviseable, in Order to obviate any Difficulties that might arise from your not having been more formally authorized to compleat this Business, to give you an express and special Commission for the Purpose, which I have now the Honor to enclose.

I have the Honor to be &ca: JOHN JAY

ENCLOSURE

We the United States of America in Congress assembled at the City of New York To our well beloved Thomas Jefferson Esquire our Minister Plenipotentiary at the Court of his Most Christian Majesty, &c. &c. send Greeting:

Being desirous to promote and facilitate the Commerce between our States and the Dominions of his said Majesty, and for that Purpose to conclude with him a Convention for regulating the Powers, Privileges, and Duties of our respective Consuls, Vice-Consuls, Agents, and Commissaries; and, having full Confidence in your Abilities and Integrity, We do by these Presents authorize and empower you the said Thomas Jefferson, in our Name and Behalf, to treat with any Person having equal Powers from his Most Christian Majesty, of and concerning such a Convention, and the same in our Name and Behalf to conclude, sign, and seal: And We do promise to ratify and confirm whatever Convention shall in Virtue of this Commission be by you so concluded, provided the Duration of the same be limited to any Term, not exceeding twelve years.

Witness our Seal and the Signature of his Excellency Arthur St. Clair, our President, this Twenty seventh Day of July in the Year of our Lord one thousand seven hundred and eighty seven, and of our Independence, the Twelfth.

AR. ST. CLAIR
JOHN JAY

CHAS. THOMSON Secy.

FC (DNA: PCC, No. 121). Recorded in SJL as received 19 Dec. 1787. Enclosure, signed by St. Clair, Jay, and Thomson, with seal of the United States attached, is in MHi.

Jefferson's letter of 9 Jan. 1787, requesting new powers and authority to reopen the negotiations concerning a consular convention without reference to the previous authorization or the draft that had been developed under it or the differences between the two that Jay had noted, was referred back to Jay by Congress on 20 Apr. He reported on 10 May that in his "opinion the Court of France regard the Consular convention in its present form as an interesting object and that no Article or provision in it will escape their recollection. He nevertheless thinks that the policy of yielding to such circumstances as cannot without risque and hazard be neglected or controuled will induce them at least to consent to the proposed Article for limiting the duration of the Convention. And as he perceives no inconvenience likely to result from giving Mr. Jefferson a commission authorising him in general terms to negotiate and conclude a Convention . . . for ascertaining the authority and powers of french and American Consuls, he thinks it will be adviseable to send him such a Commission, that he may thereby have an opportunity of endeavouring to realize the advantages he expects from it and which under a new administration (perhaps not well advised of what has passed) may be attainable" (JCC, XXXIII, 423-7; Jay's report included the text of the commission and that of the present and following letter to TJ, all of which Congress approved).

From John Jay

SIR   Office of foreign Affairs 27th. July 1787

You will herewith receive another Letter from me of this Date together with the Commission mentioned in it; both of them are in Pursuance of the Ideas suggested in your Letter of the 9th. January last. If the whole Subject should be reconsidered, and a new Convention formed, it is the Pleasure of Congress that the Duties, Powers and Privileges of Consuls, Vice Consuls, Agents and Commissaries be accurately delineated, and that they be as much circumscribed and limited as the proper Objects of their Appointment will admit, and the Court of France will consent to. How far it may be in your Power to obtain a Convention perfectly unexceptionable, must depend on several Circumstances not yet decided. Congress confide fully in your Talents and Discretion, and they will ratify any Convention that is not liable to more Objections than the one already in part concluded, provided that an Article limiting its Duration to a Term not exceeding twelve Years be inserted.

I have the Honor to be &c: JOHN JAY

FC (DNA: PCC, No. 121). Recorded in SJL as received 19 Dec. 1787.

From André Limozin

Le Havre, 27 July 1787. Encloses bill of lading for the three boxes of books shipped to James Madison on the brig *Mary*, John Howland, master. Invoice for disbursements for these boxes, amounting to 55.ᵗᵗ9s. 6d., annexed.

RC (MHi); 2 p.; addressed and endorsed. Recorded in SJL as received 29 July

27 JULY 1787

1787. The enclosed bill of lading has not been found. The annexed statement of account has the following in TJ's hand at foot of page:

"charge J. Madison 1/2   27-14-9
  Dr. Franklin & Hopk. 1/4   13-17-4   6-18-8
  Wm. Hay & Monroe 1/4   13-17-4"

From James Monroe

DEAR SIR   Fredricksburg. July 27. 1787.

I can scarcely venture on an apology for my silence for sometime past but hope notwithstanding to be forgiven. Since I left N. Yk. I have been employ'd in the discharge of duties entirely new to me, oftentimes embarrassing and of course highly interesting, but which have sought the accomplishment of only a few objects. In Octr. last I was admitted to the bar of the courts of appeal and chancery and the April following of the general court. In the course of the winter I mov'd my family to this town, in which I have taken my residence with a view to my profession. These pursuits tho' confin'd have not been attended with the less difficulty. A considerable part of my property has consisted in debts, and to command it or any part of it, hath been no easy matter. Indeed in this respect I have fail'd almost altogether. Several considerations have induc'd me to prefer this place for the present, the principal of which is the command of an house and other accomodations (the property of Mr. Jones) upon my own terms. My standing at the bar hath been so short that I cannot judge of it in that respect, tho' am inclin'd to believe it, not an ineligible position for one of that profession. But I consider my residence here as temporary, merely to serve the purpose of the time, and as looking forward to an establishment somewhere on this side the mountains, and as convenient as possible to Monticello. Mr. Jones is in ill health and begins to be satisfied his existence depends in a great degree upon a similar position. I have earnestly advis'd him to move up and at least make the experiment. Mrs. Monroe hath added a daughter to our society who tho' noisy, contributes greatly to its amusement. She is very sensibly impress'd with your kind attention to her, and wishes an opportunity of shewing how highly she respects and esteems you. With the political world I have had little to do since I left Congress. My anxiety however for the general welfare hath not been diminished. *The[1] affairs of the federal government are, I believe, in the utmost confusion; the convention is an expedient* that will produce a decisive effect. *It will either recover us from our present embarrassments or complete our ruin*; for I do suspect that if what they *recommend* should be *rejected* this would be the case. But I trust that the presence of Genl. Washington will have great weight in the body itself, so as to overawe and keep under the demon of party, and that the signature of his name to whatever act shall be the result of their deliberations will secure its passage thro' the union.   The county in which I reside have plac'd me in the Legislature. I have been mortified however to accept this favor from them, at the expence of Mr. *Page*. I supposed it might be serviceable to me in the line of my profession. My services have been abroad, and the establishment others have gain'd at the bar in the mean time requires every effort in my power to repair the disadvantage it hath subjected me to. *The governor*, I have reason to believe *is unfriendly to me* and hath shewn (If I am well inform'd) *a disposition to thwart me*; *Madison*, upon whose friendship I have calculated, whose views I have favored, and with whom I have held the most confidential correspondence since you left the continent, is in strict league *with him* and hath I have reason to believe concurr'd *in arrangements* unfavorable *to me*; a suspicion, supported by some strong circumstances, that this is the case, hath given me great uneasiness. However in this I may be disappointed and I wish it may be so.   I shall I think be strongly impress'd in favor of and inclined to vote for whatever they will recommend. I have heard from *Beckley* tho' not from himself (who accompanied *the Governor* up, in *expectation of being appointed clerk*) they had agreed on[2] *giving the United States a negative upon the laws of the several States*, if it can be done consistently with the constitutions of the several States. Indeed it might be well to revise them all, and incorporate the federal constitution in each. This I should think proper. It will if the body is well organized, be the best way of introducing uniformity in their proceedings that can be devised, *of a negative kind*, or by a power to operate *indirectly*. But a few months will give us the result be it what it may.   You mentioned in your last the injury you had sustained in your wrist. How did it happen? I hope you found your trip to the south of advantage. Your Daughters I hope are well. Nothing be assur'd will give me more pleasure than to hear from you frequently. If I can be of service in your private affairs in any line, or with respect to Peter Carr I beg of you to command me. It will always be convenient for me to attend to any thing of that kind, either in person or by a suitable messenger. I am Dear Sir your affectionate friend & servant,

JAS. MONROE

Where is Short? How is he. Remember me to him.

RC (DLC); partly in code; endorsed. Recorded in SJL as received 13 Dec. 1787.

[1] This and subsequent words in italics are written in code and have been decoded by the Editors, employing Code No. 9.

[2] Monroe, *Writings*, ed. Hamilton, I, 175, prints this as "upon"; Monroe employed the symbol "1779" by mistake, having obviously intended to hit upon "1179" in the next column, the reading for "on."

To John Adams

DEAR SIR   Paris July 28. 1787.

I take the liberty of troubling you with the inclosed bill of exchange for £46-17-10 sterling, rather than engage Mrs. Smith in so disagreeable a business. It will arrive in time I hope to cover the one drawn by General Sullivan on Colo. Smith, who certainly ought not to have been involved in the business.—The parliament are obstinately decided against the stamp tax. Their last remonstrance is said to be a master peice of good sense and firmness. We have it from the Imperial Ambassador that his master has marched 45,000 men against his resisting subjects. I have the honour to be with sincere sentiments of esteem and respect Dear Sir Your most obedient & most humble servt.,   TH: JEFFERSON

RC (MHi: AMT); addressed. PrC (DLC).

To Alexander Donald

DEAR SIR   Paris July 28. 1787.

I received with infinite satisfaction your letter of the 1st. of March. It was the first information I had of your being in America. There is no person whom I shall see again with more cordial joy whenever it shall be my lot to return to my native country; nor any one whose prosperity in the mean time will be more interesting to me. I find as I grow older that I set a higher value on the intimacies of my youth, and am more afflicted by whatever loses one of them to me. Should it be in my power to render any service in your shipment of tobacco to Havre de Grace, I shall do it with great pleasure. The order of Berni has I believe been evaded by the farmers general as much as possible. At this moment I receive information from most of the seaports that they refuse taking any tobacco under pretext that they have purchased their whole quantity. From Havre I have heard nothing, and beleive you will stand a better chance there than any where else. Being one of the ports of manufacture too it is entitled to a higher price. I have now desired that the farmers may make a distinct return of their purchases which are conformable to the order of Berni. If they have really bought their quantity *on those terms*, we must be satisfied: if they have not, I shall propose their being obliged to make it up instantly. There is a considerable accumulation of tobacco in the ports.

Among many good qualities which my countrymen possess, some of a different character unhappily mix themselves. The most remarkable are indolence, extravagance, and infidelity to their engagements. Cure the two first, and the last would disappear, because it is a consequence of them, and not proceeding from a want of morals. I know of no remedy against indolence and extravagance but a free course of justice. Every thing else is merely palliative: but unhappily the evil has gained too generally the mass of the nation to leave the course of justice unobstructed. The maxim of buying nothing without money in our pocket to pay for it, would make of our country one of the happiest upon earth. Experience during the war proved this; as I think every man will remember that under all the privations it obliged him to submit to during that period he slept sounder, and awaked happier than he can do now. Desperate of finding relief from a free course of justice, I look forward to the abolition of all credit as the only other remedy which can take place. I have seen therefore with pleasure the exaggerations of our want of faith with which the London papers teem. It is indeed a strong medecine for sensible minds, but it is a medecine. It will prevent their crediting us abroad, in which case we cannot be credited at home. I have been much concerned at the losses produced by the fire of Richmond. I hope you have escaped them. It will give me much pleasure to hear from you as often as you can spare a moment to write. Be assured that nobody entertains for you sentiments of more perfect and sincere esteem than Dear Sir Your friend & servant, TH: JEFFERSON

RC (NN: Arents Tobacco Collection); addressed: "Alexander Donald esq. Merchant at Richmond Virginia"; endorsed. PrC (DLC).

To Elizabeth Wayles Eppes

DEAR MADAM   Paris July 28. 1787.

Your favors of March 31. and May 7. have been duly received. The last by Polly, whose arrival has given us great joy. Her disposition to attach herself to those who are kind to her had occasioned successive distresses on parting with Capt. Ramsay first, and afterwards with Mrs. Adams. She had a very fine passage, without a storm, and was perfectly taken care of by Capt. Ramsay. He offered to come to Paris with her; but this was unnecessary. I sent a trusty servant to London to attend her here. A parent may be permitted to speak of his own child when it involves an act of justice to another. The attentions which your goodness has induced you to pay her, prove themselves by the fruits of them. Her reading, her writing, her manners in general shew what everlasting obligations we are all under to you. As far as her affections can be a requital, she renders you the debt, for it is impossible for a child to prove a more sincere affection to an absent person than she does to you. She will surely not be the least happy among us when the day shall come in which we may be all reunited. She is now established in the convent, perfectly happy. Her sister came and staid a week with her, leading her from time to time to the convent, till she became familiarized to it. This soon took place as she became a universal favorite with the young ladies and the mistresses. She writes you a long letter, giving an account of her voiage and journey here. She neither knew us, nor should we have known her had we met with her unexpectedly. Patsy enjoys good health, and will write to you. She has grown much the last year or two, and will be very tall. She retains all her anxiety to get back to her country and her friends, particularly yourself. Her dispositions give me perfect satisfaction: and her progress as well. She will need however your finishing to render her useful in her own country. Of domestic oeconomy she can learn nothing here; yet she must learn it somewhere, as being of more solid value than every thing else. I answer Jack's letter by this occasion. I wish he would give me often occasion to do it. Tho' at this distance I can be of no use to him, yet I am willing to shew my dispositions to be useful to him, as I shall be for ever bound to be to every one connected with yourself and Mr. Eppes, had no other connection rendered the obligation dear to my heart. I shall present my affections to Mr. and Mrs. Skipwith in a letter to the former. Kiss the children for me, and be assured of the unchangeable esteem and respect of, Dear Madam, your affectionate friend & servant,

TH: JEFFERSON

PrC (CSmH). Unfortunately, Polly's LONG LETTER giving an account of her voyage has not been found; it was probably enclosed with the present one to her aunt.

To John Wayles Eppes

DEAR JACK   Paris July 28. 1787.

The letter which you were so kind as to write to me the 22d. of May 1786. was not delivered to me till the 3d. of May 1787. when it found me in the neighborhood of Marseilles. Before that time you must have taken your degree as mentioned in your letter. Those public testimonies which are earned by merit and not by sollicitation may always be accepted without the imputation of vanity. Of this nature is the degree which your masters proposed to confer on you. I congratulate you sincerely on it. It will be a pleasing event to yourself; it will be the same to your parents and friends, and to none more than to myself. Go on deserving applause, and you will be sure to meet with it: and the way to deserve it is, to be good, and to be industrious. I am sure you will be good, and hope you will be industrious. As to your future plan, I am too distant from you, to advise you on sure grounds. In general I am of opinion that till the age of about sixteen we are best employed on languages. Latin, Greek, French and Spanish, or such of them as we can. After this I think the college of William and Mary the best place, to go there thro' courses of Mathematics, Natural philosophy in it's different branches, and Law. Of the languages I have mentioned I think Greek the least useful. Write me word from time to time how you go on. I shall always be glad to assist you with any books you may have occasion for, and you may count with certainty on every service I can ever render you, as well as on the sincere esteem of Dear Jack your's affectionately,

TH: JEFFERSON

PrC (DLC).

To Henry Skipwith

DEAR SIR   Paris July 28. 1787.

A long journey has prevented me from writing to any of my

[635]

friends for some time past. This was undertaken with a view to benefit a dislocated and ill-set wrist by the mineral waters of Aix in Provence. Finding this hope vain, I was led from other views to cross the Alps as far as Turin, Milan, Genoa, to follow the Mediterranean as far as Cette, the canal of Languedoc, the Garonne &c. to Paris. A most pleasing journey it proved, Arts and Agriculture offering something new at every step, and often things worth our imitation. But the accounts from our country give me to believe we are not in a condition to hope for the imitation of any thing good. All letters are filled with details of our extravagance. From these accounts I look back to the time of the war as a time of happiness and enjoiment, when amidst the privation of many things not essential to happiness, we could not run in debt because no body would trust us; when we practised of necessity the maxim of buying nothing but what we had money in our pockets to pay for; a maxim which of all others lays the broadest foundation for happiness. I see no remedy to our evils but an open course of law. Harsh as it may seem, it would relieve the very patients who dread it, by stopping the course of their extravagance before it renders their affairs entirely desperate. The eternal and bitter strictures of our conduct which teem in every London paper, and are copied from them into others, fill me with anxiety on this subject.—The state of things in Europe is rather threatening at the moment. The innovations of the Emperor in his dominions have excited a spirit of resistance. His subjects in Brabant and Flanders are arming, and he has put 45,000 troops in motion towards that country. I believe they will come to blows. The parties in Holland have already spilt too much blood to be easily stopped. If left to themselves I apprehend the Stadhoulderians will be too strong; and if foreign powers interfere, the weight is still on their side. England and Prussia will be too much for France. As it is certain that neither of these powers wish for war, that England and France are particularly averse to it, perhaps the matter may end in an armed mediation. If the mediators should not agree, they will draw their negociations into length and trust to the chapter of accidents for their final solution.   With respect to our country, it stands well with the present ministry here. The nonpaiment of our debt is against us. We are occupied in procuring favorable terms of reception for our produce. I beg leave to recall myself most affectionately to the remembrance of Mrs. Skipwith whose friendship will ever be a precious possession to me, and furnishes me pleasing recollections. Name me also to your little family, who have all, probably, forgotten me. Patsy and Polly are well and both write to Mrs. Skipwith. Polly's arrival has been matter of much happiness to us. Adieu, my dear Sir, and be assured of the sentiments of sincere esteem of Your affectionate friend & servant, TH: JEFFERSON

PrC (DLC). The letters from PATSY AND POLLY . . . TO MRS. SKIPWITH were probably enclosed, but have not been found.

To La Boullaye

SIR   Paris July 29. 1787.

In the observations which I submitted to the consideration of his Excellency the Count de Montmorin some time ago, a copy of which I had the honor of transmitting to Monsieur le Comtroleur general, nothing was said on the subject of tobacco, that article being placed on a very different footing from all others. I have since brought this subject also under the view of his majesty's ministers in a letter written the 23d. instant to Monsieur le Comte de Montmorin, a translation of which I have now the honor to inclose to you and to submit to your consideration. If it would not be trespassing too much on your time and goodness I would take the liberty of asking a moment's conference with you on these subjects, at such time as shall be most convenient to you. The sooner after Tuesday next the more agreeable it would be to me. Monsr. le Marquis de la fayette will be so good as to come with me, my imperfect knowlege of the language, as well as his information as to what relates to the two countries, rendering his aid very desireable. I have the honour to be with sentiments of the most perfect esteem and respect Sir Your most obedient & most humble servant, TH: JEFFERSON

PrC (DLC). Enclosure: Translation of TJ to Montmorin, 23 July 1787.

From John Ledyard

SIR   Town of Barnowl in Siberia July 29th. 1787

You will find this town by the Russian charts situated in about the Latitude 52°: and Longitude 100. It is near the town of Kolyvan and in the province of Kolyvan: the residence of the Governor of the province. It is near the silver mines and has a foundery in it which produces anualy 650 poods of silver bullion

29 JULY 1787

besides some gold. A pood is 36 pounds english. It is also situated near the salt lakes which produces more to the revenue than the mines. I am 4539 versts from petersburg and have 4950 versts to go before I arive at Okotsk, and if I go to Peter and Paul in Kamchatka I have 1065 versts more to go before I see that ocean which I hope will bear me on its boosom to the coast of America. How I have come thus far and how I am still to go farther is an enigma that I must disclose to you on some happier occasion. I shall never be able without seeing you in person and perhaps not even then to inform you how universaly and circumstantialy the Tartars resemble the aborigines of America. They are the same people—the most antient, and most numerous of any other, and had not a small sea divided them, they would all have still been known by the *same name*. The cloak of civilization sits as ill upon them as our American tartars. They have been a long time Tartars and it will be a long time before they are any other kind of people. I shall send this Letter to Petersburg to the care of Doctor Pallas, Professor, of the royal Academy president, and historyographer to the Admiralty. I hope he will transmit it to you together with one to the Marquis in the mail of the count de Segur. I hope you and your friends and mine enjoy as much good health as I do which is of the purest kind. But notwithstanding all the vigour of my body, my mind keeps the start of me and anticipates my future fate with the most sublimated ardour. Pity it is that in such a career one should be subjected like a horse to the beggarly impediments of sleep and hunger.[1]

The Banks of the large Rivers in this country every where abound with something curious in the fossil world. I have found the leg-bone of a very large animal on the banks of the Oby and have sent it to Dr. Pallas and told him to render me an Account of it hereafter. It is either the Elephant or Rinoceros bone, for the latter Animal has also been in this country. There is a compleat head of one in a high state of preservation at Petersburg. I am a curiosity myself in this country. Those who have heard of America flock round me to see me. Unfortunately the marks on my hands procures me and my Countrymen the appelation of wild-men. Among the better sort we are somewhat more known. The Governor and his family get a peep at the history of our existance thro the medium of a Septennial pamphlet of some kind. We have however two Stars that shine even in the Galaxy of Barnowl, and the healths of Dr. Franklin and of Genl. Washington have been drank in compliment to me at the Governors table. I am treated with great hospitality here. Hitherto I have fared comfortably when I could make a port any where. But when totaly in the Country I have been a little incommoded. Hospitality however I have found as universal as the face of man.

When you read this, perhaps 2 months before you do If I do well I shall be at Okotsk where I will do myself the honour to trouble you again and if possible will write more at large.

If Mr. Barclay should be with you I pray you present me to him. My compliments wait on all my Parisian friends. Remember that I am and always shall be with the highest esteem & gratitude Sir. yr. much obliged most obt. hbl servt., LEDYARD

RC (NHi); endorsed. Tr (Mrs. Jane Ledyard Remington, Cazenovia, N.Y.); with slight variations in spelling and phrasing.

[1] Ledyard first wrote: "It is certainly a pity that in such a career I should be. . . ." Following this sentence he began another: "I feel the indignity," then deleted it.

To Nicholas Lewis

DEAR SIR Paris July 29. 1787.

In my letter of Dec. 19. 1786. I informed you that, as you had supposed in your's of March 14. that the balance of bonds and profits of the estate to that time would pay all the debts then known to you except my sister Nancy's, I was desirous of laying our shoulder seriously to the paiment of Farrell & Jones's, and McCaul's debts; that I should make propositions to them on that subject. I did so. These propositions were 1. To pay to Jones 400£ sterl. a year and to McCaul 200£ sterl., or to the former if he preferred it two thirds of the profits of my estate and to the latter one third. 2. That the crop of 1787. should commence these paiments. 3. That no interest should be allowed on their debts from Apr. 19. 1775 to Apr. 19. 1783 (being 8. years). 4. That their accounts should remain perfectly open to settlement and rectification, notwithstanding the paiments which should be made. McCaul has acceded very contentedly to these proposals. I added some other conditions to Jones, not worth mentioning as he does not accede as yet. I think however he will accede. I consider myself as so much bound in honor to the sacred execution of this agreement that what the profits fall short of enabling us to pay at any time I would chuse to have made up by a sale of something or another. I mentioned to you in my letter also that I could always get 36/ Virginia money for my tobacco delivered at Havre and proposed your having

29 JULY 1787

it sent there. Further reflection and information of the Virginia prices convince me it would be best to send them either to Havre or to Bordeaux, at either of which places I could have them attended to. I find that my old friend A. Donald is settled at Richmond, is concerned in the tobacco trade, and particularly sends to Havre. I am confident he would take on himself the having my tobaccoes shipped to me. The earlier they would come in the season, the better alwais. So far I had settled in my own mind the plan for extinguishing as fast as we could these two great debts, when I received from Mr. Eppes a letter of May 2. 1787. wherein he tells me he had been with you in Sep. 1786. that you had computed together all the former debts (except my sister Nancy's) due from the estate, and all due to it; and that there was still a balance of 1200£ against it, to pay which there would be nothing but the crop of 1786. two thirds of which would be consumed by negroes clothing and taxes. This account threatens a total derangement of my plan for payment of my great debts. I had observed that by a statement in your letter of March 14. of the probable proceeds of the crop of 1785 (about 50 hogsheads of tobacco) that the profits of the few house servants and tradesmen hired out were as much as those of the whole estate, and therefore suggested to you the hiring out the whole estate. The torment of mind I endure till the moment shall arrive when I shall not owe a shilling on earth is such really as to render life of little value. I cannot decide to sell my lands. I have sold too much of them already, and they are the only sure provision for my children. Nor would I willingly sell the slaves as long as there remains any prospect of paying my debts with their labour. In this I am governed solely by views to their happiness which will render it worth their while to use extraordinary cautions for some time to enable me to put them ultimately on an easier footing, which I will do the moment they have paid the debts due from the estate, two thirds of which have been contracted by purchasing them. I am therefore strengthened in the idea of renting out my whole estate; not to any one person, but in different parts to different persons, as experience proves that it is only small concerns that are gainful, and it would be my interest that the tenants should make a reasonable gain. The lease I made to Garth and Moseley would be a good model. I do not recollect whether in that there was reserved a right of distraining on the lands for the whole rent. If not, such a clause would be essential, especially in the present relaxed state of the laws. I know there was in that no provision against paper money. This is still more essential. The

[640]

29 JULY 1787

best way of stating the rent would be in ounces of silver. The rent in that lease, tho expressed in current money, was meant to be 11.£ sterling a titheable. When we consider the rise in the price of tobacco, it should balance any difference for the worse which may have taken place in the lands in Albemarle, so as to entitle us there to equal terms. In Cumberland, Goochland, Bedford, where the lands are better, perhaps better terms might be expected. Calculating this on the number of working slaves, it holds up to us a clear revenue capable of working off the debts in a reasonable time. Think of it, my dear Sir, and if you do not find it disadvantageous be so good as to try to execute it, by leases of 3, 4, or 5 years: not more, because no dependance can be reposed in our laws continuing the same for any length of time. Indeed 3. years might be the most eligible term. The mill should be separated from the lease, finished, and rented by itself. All the lands reserved to my own use in Garth and Mousley's lease should still be reserved, and the privileges of that lease in general. House negroes still to be hired separately. The old and infirm, who could not be hired, or whom it would be a pity to hire, could perhaps be employed in raising cotton, or some other easy culture on lands to be reserved; George still to be reserved to take care of my orchards, grasses &c. The lands in Albemarle should be relieved by drawing off a good number of the labourers to Bedford, where a better hire might be expected and more lands be opened there. I feel all the weight of the objection that we cannot guard the negroes perfectly against ill usage. But in a question between hiring and selling them (one of which is necessary) the hiring will be temporary only, and will end in their happiness; whereas if we sell them, they will be subject to equal ill usage, without a prospect of change. It is for their good therefore ultimately, and it appears to promise a relief to me within such a term as I would be willing to wait for. I do not mention the rate of hire with a view to tie you up to that, but merely to shew that hiring presents a hopeful prospect. I should rely entirely on your judgment for that, for the choice of kind and hopeful tenants, and for every other circumstance. The bacon hams you were so kind as to send to Mr. Buchanan for me, I never heard of. The difficulty of getting them here renders it not worth attempting again. I will put into this letter some more seeds of the Spanish Sainfoin lest those formerly sent should have miscarried. The present situation of Europe threatens a war, which if it breaks out will probably be a very general one. France and England are so little in a condition for war that we may still expect they will do much to avoid it. Should it take place, I fear the scale against this country would be too heavy.

I must pray of you to make all the arrangements possible for enabling me to comply with the first years paiment of my debts, that is to say the paiment for this present year, which is to be made in the city of London the next spring. Apologies for all the trouble I give you would only shew you how sensible I am of your goodness. I have proposed the extraordinary trouble of the leases with less reluctance, because it will be taken once for all, and will be a relief in the end. Be so good as to assure Mrs. Lewis of my attachment and my wishes for her health and happiness as well as that of your whole family. I am with sentiments of the most sincere esteem and respect Dear Sir Your friend & servant,

TH: JEFFERSON

P.S. My daughters are in good health, and join me in affectionate wishes for your family.

PrC (DLC).
The OTHER CONDITIONS . . . NOT WORTH MENTIONING are explained in TJ to Eppes, 30 July 1787. Francis Eppes' LETTER OF MAY 2. was received on 30 June 1787; it has not been found.

To André Limozin

SIR Paris July 29. 1787.

I am favored with your letter of the 20th. inst. and will pay your draught for the sum due you at sight. I wish the three boxes of books may have arrived so as that the expences of them may be added to your bill, that I may be enabled to put them into the accounts I shall send by the packet which sails next. The vessel in which my seeds should have come, belonged to Shore, McConnico & Ritson, merchants of Petersburg in Virginia, and was to sail last March from Virginia for Havre de Grace. I think it probable that the Emperor and his subjects of the Austrian Netherlands may be engaged in a contest of arms. It is possible also that the affairs of Holland may in the end involve France, England, and Prussia in a war. But France and England are so little in a condition for war that they will avoid it if possible: at any event they will by negotiation draw the discussions into length, and if they cannot prevent a war they will retard the moment of commencing it. I do not apprehend that any thing now at sea will be in danger before it gets into port. If this subject continues interesting to you,

I shall chearfully communicate to you from time to time any change of appearances which may occur.—I would wish always to send my American dispatches without their passing thro' the post office, where they are opened. They should go by a courier from hence. But would the officers of the Packet (when there is no passenger) be at liberty to receive and carry my letters? I should think myself safe in their hands. I have the honor to be with sentiments of[1]

P.S. In the moment of sealing my letter, I receive your favor of the 27th. inclosing the bill of lading for the three boxes of books, and the account for the expences. Be so good therefore as to add this to the former sum in your draught.

PrC (DLC); lacks end of complimentary close and signature.

[1] PrC ends at bottom of the page at this point; the postscript is written in PrC on the left-hand margin.

From St. Victour

[*Paris, 29 July 1787.* Recorded in SJL as received 30 July 1787. Not found.]

From Thomas Barclay

SIR   L'Orient 30th. July 1787

I do myself the honor to inclose to your Excellency a letter from Mr. Andrew Huntington of Norwich in Connecticut, covering a Memorial to the Marechal De Castries relative to a demand which he makes for supplies furnish'd some French Prisoners in America by order of Mr. Holker, and which Letter and Memorial I did not receive untill this day though it is dated in May 1786. I do not think that Mr. Huntington has taken the proper steps for the recovery of this demand, but that he ought to have laid the State of the matter before the french Consul in Connecticut, and interested him in the affair, however as it is out of my power to be useful to Mr. Huntington though I have all the disposition in the world you will judge what will be right, and proper to do on this occasion, and therefore I take the liberty of submitting intirely to your Excellency and have the honor to be with the greatest respect Sir Your Excellency's most obt. Servant,   THOS. BARCLAY

30 JULY 1787

RC (DLC); in a clerk's hand, signed by Barclay. Recorded in SJL as received 17 Aug. 1787. The enclosed letter and papers were returned in TJ to Barclay, 17 Sep. 1787.

To William Drayton

Sir   Paris July 30. 1787.

Having observed that the consumption of rice in this country, and particularly in this Capital was very great, I thought it my duty to inform myself from what markets they draw their supplies, in what proportion from ours, and whether it might not be practicable to increase that proportion. This city being little concerned in foreign commerce, it is difficult to obtain information on particular branches of it in the detail. I addressed myself to the retailers of rice, and from them received a mixture of truth and error, which I was unable to sift apart in the first moment. Continuing however my enquiries, they produced at length this result; that the dealers here were in the habit of selling two qualities of rice, that of Carolina, with which they were supplied chiefly from England, and that of Piedmont; that the Carolina rice was long, slender, white and transparent, answers well when prepared with milk, sugar &c. but not so well when prepared au gras; that that of Piedmont was shorter, thicker, and less white, but that it preserved it's form better when dressed au gras, was better tasted, and therefore preferred by good judges for those purposes; that the consumption of rice in this form was much the most considerable, but that the superior beauty of the Carolina rice, seducing the eye of those purchasers who are attached to appearances, the demand for it was upon the whole as great as for that of Piedmont. They supposed this difference of quality to proceed from a difference of management; that the Carolina rice was husked with an instrument which broke it more, and that less pains were taken to separate the broken from the unbroken grains, imagining that it was the broken grains which dissolved in oily preparations; that the Carolina rice costs them somewhat less than that of Piedmont; but that being obliged to sort the whole grains from the broken, in order to satisfy the taste of their customers, they ask and receive as much for the first quality of Carolina, when sorted, as for the rice of Piedmont; but the 2d. and 3d. qualities obtained by sorting are sold much cheaper.   The objection to the Carolina rice then being that it crumbles, in certain forms of preparation, and this supposed to be the effect of a less perfect machine for husking, I flattered myself I should be able to learn what might be the machine of Piedmont when I should arrive at Marseilles, to which place I was to go in the course of a tour through the seaport towns of this country. At Marseilles however they differed as much in the account of the machine, as at Paris they had differed about other circumstances. Some said it was husked between millstones, others between rubbers of wood in the form of millstones, others of cork. They concurred in one fact however, that the machine might be seen immediately on crossing the Alps. This would be an affair of three weeks. I crossed them, and went thro the rice country from Vercelli to Pavia, about 60 miles. I found the machine to be absolutely the same with that used in Carolina, as well as I could recollect a description which Mr. E. Rutledge had given me of it. It is on the plan of a powder mill. In some of them indeed they arm each pestle with an iron tooth, consisting of 9. spikes hooped together, which I do not remember in the description of Mr. Rutlege. I therefore had a tooth made which I have the honor of forwarding you with this letter; observing at the same time that as many of their machines are without teeth as with them, and of course that the advantage is not very palpable. It seems to follow then that the rice of Lombardy (for tho' called Piedmont rice, it does not grow in that country, but in Lombardy) is of a different species from that of Carolina, different in form, in colour, and in quality. We know that in Asia they have several distinct species of this grain. Monsr. Poivre, a farmer general of the Isle of France, in travelling through several countries of Asia, observed with particular attention the objects of their agriculture, and he tells us that in Cochinchina they cultivate 6. several kinds of rice, which he describes, three of them requiring water, and three growing on highlands. The rice of Carolina is said to have come from Madagascar, and DePoivre tells us it is the white rice which is cultivated there. This favors the probability of it's being of a different species originally from that of Piedmont, and time, culture and climate may have made it still more different. Under this idea I thought it would be well to furnish you with some of the Piedmont rice unhusked, but was told it was contrary to the laws to export it in that form. I took such measures as I could however to have a quantity brought out, and lest these should fail I brought myself a few pounds. A part of this I have addressed to you by the way of London; a part comes with this letter; and I shall send another parcel by some other conveyance to prevent the danger of miscarriage. Any one of them arriving safe may serve to put in seed, should the society think it an object. This seed too, coming from Vercelli, where the best rice is supposed to grow, is more to be depended on than what may be sent me hereafter. There is a rice from the Levant which is considered as of a quality still different, and some think it superior to that of Piedmont. The troubles which have existed in that country for several years back have intercepted it from the European market, so that it is become almost unknown. I procured a bag of it however at Marseilles, and another of the best rice of Lombardy, which are on their way to this place, and when arrived, I will forward you a quantity of each, sufficient to enable you to judge of their qualities when prepared for the table. I have also taken measures to have a quantity of it brought from the Levant, unhusked. If I succeed, it shall be forwarded in like manner. I should think it certainly advantageous to cultivate in Carolina and Georgia the two qualities demanded at market; because the progress of culture with us may soon get beyond the demand for the white rice; and because too there is often a brisk demand for the one quality, when the market is glutted with the other. I should hope there would be no danger of losing the species of white rice by a confusion with the other. This would be a real misfortune, as I should not hesitate to pronounce the white, upon the whole, the most precious of the two for us.

The dry rice of Cochinchina has the reputation of being whitest to the eye, best flavored to the taste, and most productive. It seems then to unite the good qualities of both the others known to us. Could it supplant them, it would be a great happiness, as it would enable us to get rid of those ponds of stagnant water so fatal to human health and life. But such is the force of habit, and caprice of taste, that we could not be sure beforehand it would produce this effect. The experiment however is worth trying, should it only end in producing a third quality, and increasing the demand. I will endeavor to procure some to be brought from Cochinchina. The event however will be incertain and distant.

I was induced, in the course of my journey thro' the South of France, to pay very particular attention to the objects of their culture, because the resemblance of their climate to that of the Southern parts of the United states, authorizes us to presume we may adopt any of their articles of culture which we would wish for. We should not wish for their wines, tho they are good and abundant. The culture of the vine is not desireable in lands capable of producing any thing else. It is a species of gambling, and of desperate gambling too, wherein, whether you make much or nothing, you are equally ruined. The middling crop alone is the saving point, and that the seasons seldom hit. Accordingly we see much wretchedness amidst this class of cultivators. Wine too is so cheap in these countries that a labourer with us, employed in the culture of any other article, may exchange it for wine, more and better than he could raise himself. It is a resource for a country, the whole of whose good soil is otherwise employed, and which still has some barren spots and a surplus of population to employ on them. There the vine is good, because it is something in the place of nothing. It may become a resource to us at a still earlier period: when the increase of population shall increase our productions beyond the demand for them both at home and abroad. Instead of going on to make a useless surplus of them, we may employ our supernumerary hands on the vine. But that period is not yet arrived.

The Almond tree is also so precarious that none can depend for subsistence on it's produce, but persons of capital.

The Caper, tho a more tender plant, is more certain in it's produce, because a mound of earth, of the size of a cucumber hill, thrown over the plant in the fall, protects it effectually against the cold of the winter. When the danger of frost is over in the spring, they uncover it and begin it's culture. There is a great deal of this in the neighborhood of Toulon. The plants are set about 8. feet apart, and yeild one year with another about 2 ℔. of capers each, worth on the spot 6d. sterl. the pound. They require little culture, and this may be performed either with the plough or hoe. The principal work is the gathering of the fruit, as it forms. Every plant must be picked every other day from the last of June till the middle of October. But this is the work of women and children. The plant does well in any kind of soil, which is dry or even in walls where there is no soil, and they last the life of a man. Toulon would be the proper port to apply for them. I must observe that the preceding details cannot be relied on with the fullest certainty, because in the canton where this plant is cultivated the inhabitants speak no written language, but a medley which I could understand but very imperfectly.

The fig and the mulberry are so well known in America, that nothing need be said of them. Their culture too is by women and children, and therefore earnestly to be desired in countries where there are slaves. In these, the women and children are often employed in labours disproportioned to their sex and age. By presenting to the master objects of culture, easier and equally beneficial, all temptation to misemploy them would be removed, and the lot of this tender part of our species be much softened. By varying too the articles of culture, we multiply the chances for making something, and disarm the seasons in a proportionable degree of their calamitous effects.

The Olive is a tree the least known in America, and yet the most worthy of being known. Of all the gifts of heaven to man, it is next to the most precious, if it be not the most precious. Perhaps it may claim a preference even to bread; because there is such an infinitude of vegetables which it renders a proper and comfortable nourishment. In passing the Alps at the Col de Tende, where they are mere masses of rock, wherever there happens to be a little soil, there are a number of olive trees, and a village supported by them. Take away these trees, and the same ground in corn would not support a single family. A pound of oil which can be bought for 3d. or 4d. sterling is equivalent to many pounds of flesh by the quantity of vegetables it will prepare and render fit and comfortable food. Without this tree the county of Provence and territory of Genoa would not support one half, perhaps not one third, their present inhabitants. The nature of the soil is of little consequence, if it be dry. The trees are planted from 15. to 20. f. apart, and, when tolerably good, will yeild 15. or 20. ℔. of oil yearly, one with another. There are trees which yeild much more. They begin to render good crops at 20. years old, and last till killed by cold, which happens at some time or other even in their best positions in France. But they put out again from their roots. In Italy I am told they have trees 200 years old. They afford an easy but constant employment thro' the year, and require so little nourishment that, if the soil be fit for any other production, it may be cultivated among the olive trees, without injuring them. The Northern limits of this tree are the mountains of the Cevennes from about the meridian of Carcassonne to the Rhone, and from thence the Alps and Appennines as far as Genoa, I know, and how much farther I am not informed. The shelter of these mountains may be considered as equivalent to a degree and a half of latitude at least; because Westward of the commencement of the Cevennes there are no olive trees in 43½° or even 43.° of latitude; whereas we find them *now* on the Rhone at Pierrelatte in 44½° and *formerly* they were at Tains, above the mouth of the Isere in 45.° sheltered by the near approach of the Cevennes and Alps, which only leave there a passage for the Rhone. Whether such a shelter exists, or not, in the states of South Carolina and Georgia, I know not. But this we may say, either that it exists, or that it is not necessary there: because we know that they produce the orange in open air; and wherever the Orange will stand at all, experience shews that the Olive will stand well; being a hardier tree. Notwithstanding the great quantities of oil made in France, they have not enough for their own consumption, and therefore import from other countries. This is an article, the consumption of which will always keep pace with it's production. Raise it; and it begets it's own demand. Little is carried to America because Europe has it not to spare. We therefore have not learnt the use of it. But cover the Southern states with it, and every man will become a consumer of oil, within whose reach it can be brought in point of price. If the memory of those persons is held in great respect in South Carolina who introduced there the culture of rice, a plant which sows life and death with almost equal hand, what obligations would be due to him who should introduce the Olive tree, and set the example of it's culture! Were the owner of slaves to view it only as the means of bettering their condition, how much would he better that by planting one of those trees for every slave he possessed! Having been myself an eyewitness to the blessings which this tree sheds on the poor, I never had my wishes so kindled for the introduction of any article of new culture into our own country. South Carolina and Georgia appear to me to be the states wherein it's success, in favorable positions at least, could not be doubted, and I flattered myself it would come within the views of the society for agriculture to begin the experiments which are to prove it's practicability. Carcassonne is the place from which the plants may be most certainly and cheaply obtained. They can be sent from thence by water to Bordeaux, where they may be embarked on vessels bound for Charleston. There is too little intercourse between Charleston and Marseilles to propose this as the port of exportation. I offer my service to the society for the obtaining and forwarding any number of plants which may be desired.

Before I quit the subject of climates, and the plants adapted to them, I will add as a matter of curiosity, and of some utility too, that my journey thro' the Southern parts of France and the territory of Genoa, but still more the crossing of the Alps, enabled me to form a scale of the tenderer plants, and to arrange them according to their different powers of resisting cold. In passing the Alps at the Col de Tende, we cross three very high mountains successively. In ascending, we lose these plants one after another as we rise and find them again in the contrary order, as we descend on the other side, and this is repeated three times. Their order, proceeding from the tenderest to the hardiest, is as follows: Caper, Orange, Palm, Aloe, Olive, Pomegranate, Walnut, Fig, Almond. But this must be understood of the plant only: for as to the fruit, the order is somewhat different. The Caper, for example, is the tenderest plant, yet, being so easily protected, it is among the most certain in it's fruit. The Almond, the hardiest plant, loses it's fruit the oftenest, on account of it's forwardness. The Palm, hardier than the Caper and Orange, never produces perfect fruit here.

I had the honour of sending you the last year some seeds of the Sulla of Malta, or Spanish St. foin. Lest that should have miscarried, I now pack with the rice a cannister of the same kind of seed raised by myself. By Colo. Franks, in the month of Feb. last I sent a parcel of acorns of the Cork oak, which I desired him to ask the favor of the Delegates of South Carolina in Congress to forward to you.

I have the honour to be with sentiments of the most perfect esteem and respect Sir Your most obedt. & most humble servt.,

TH: JEFFERSON

PrC (DLC). In DLC: TJ Papers, 36: 6231 there is a PrC of the following undated note in TJ's hand that evidently accompanied the present letter and was addressed to James Madison: "Th: J knowing that Mr. Madison sometimes turns his attention to matters of agriculture, leaves the enclosed letter open for his perusal. He will be so good as to give it into the hands of the delegates of South Carolina."

To Francis Eppes

DEAR SIR　　　　　　　　　　　　　　Paris July 30. 1787.

Your favor of May 23. 1786. was not received till May 3. 1787. Those of 1786. Oct. 23, 1787. Mar. 30. Apr. 14. and May 2. have duly come to hand. I wrote you on the 14th. of Dec. 1786. and again the 26. of May 1787. The latter was merely to announce a batch of wine sent you by Capt. Gregory from Bordeaux while I was there. It is now so long since I have had occasion to think on subjects of law that I am not able, with any degree of confidence, to answer your questions on the execution against Mr. Cary's estate. I suppose that the execution directed to the Coroner bound the whole property of Mr. Cary from the moment of it's date. If the slaves taken under the erroneous execution were afterwards sold under the good one, the proceeds of that sale will be secure to us, and any question about the property of the slaves, under pretence they were passed away by the deed of trust, will be a question between the purchaser and trustees and will not affect us. If the good execution could not be satisfied from those particular slaves, yet it could lay hold of all his other slaves and personal property. But were we reduced to seek our remedy against those identical slaves only which were taken under the erroneous execution, I think that they would be subject to the good execution: because the deeds of trust were palpably made to defraud us of a just debt, and are therefore made void by the statute 13. of Elizabeth except against bona fide purchasers for valuable consideration, and having no notice of the fraudulent object of the deed. Even a deed of trust, if not within this description, is not saved out of the condemnation of the statute. With respect to Colo. T. M. Randolph's securityship for this debt, I suppose it to be a very certain fact, tho' I cannot charge myself with the recollection of having seen the bill endorsed by him. 1. I was charged by Mr. Wayles with the having the bill of exchange executed for him at Varina by Mr. Cary, and to be endorsed by Colo. TMR. They did not come to Varina as expected and therefore it was not done then. 2. I am almost certain, I think quite certain, Mr. Wayles told me afterwards he had got the bill so drawn and endorsed. 3. I am also certain that this endorsement has been frequently the subject of conversation between Colo. TMR and myself, that he always spoke of himself as security and often wished we would press for the money. Colo. TMR is too honest a man to question this fact, and would not put you to the trouble of a Bill of Discovery. 4. How it happens that two copies of the bill are without endorsement is unaccountable to me, nor do I know any thing of the third. I delivered every paper of that kind to Frank Harris. Should it be necessary to have recourse against the security, should he declare himself not bound, it may be proper to try whether a copy of the bill and protest cannot be obtained from the notary's office in England. Mr. Wayles's letters about that date should be examined. Doubtless there is one to whatever friend he inclosed the bill in order to obtain the protest. Probably the answer of his friend re-inclosing the bill and protest will explain it. I should wish that this money, when recovered, should be applied in the first place to pay the debt due to Cary of London because we have always assured him it should be so, and should it not, he will justly accuse us of a gross violation of faith. From the conversation I had with him in London he knows that we will not pay interest from Apr. 19. 1775. to April. 19. 1783. I paid him that interest on a small debt of mine, but took care to explain to him explicitly, that it was on

30 JULY 1787

account of the peculiar confidence he had reposed in me, having sent me the articles after the commencement of our national quarrel.

Jones has never sent me a copy of his account current. All I know of it is from memory. I think the balance on the account rendered us after Mr. Wayles's debt was about 9000£ sterling. I think after the date of that account there were in his hands about 300 hhds. of tobacco made the year preceding Mr. Wayles's death and the year of his death, that is 1772 and 1773, or perhaps 1773 and 1774. and moreover 120 hhds. or thereabouts shipped by us separately the first year after the division. Stating this tobacco only at the ordinary price and deducting it from the 9000£, and stopping the interest at Apr. 19. 1775. and not recommencing it till Apr. 19. 1783. the debt should not be so very formidable. On the information I received from Mr. Lewis in his letter of Mar. 14. 1786. that the bonds due and the crops to the end of 1785. would pay all my debts except that to my sister Nancy, and those to Jones and McCaul, I made propositions to them for commencing the paiment of their debts. The conditions were 1. To pay to Jones two thirds of the profits of my estate and to McCaul one third annually; or if they should prefer it, 400£ sterl. to the former and 200£ sterl. to the latter annually. [2.] To pay no interest between Apr. 19. 1775. and Apr. 19. 1783. 3. That the crop of 1787. should begin the paiment. 4. That their accounts, notwithstanding these paiments, should be open to settlement and rectification. McCaul has acceded, and the matter is so far settled with him. To Jones I added two other articles, viz. that the paiment I made into the treasury should not affect him at all, and that in proportion as I should proceed paying my third of the just balance, I should be discharged from the remaining two thirds. This last article I thought we should all wish to make with him, that, the estate being now divided the debt should also be divided and our families be left clear of all responsibility but for themselves. Jones answered that he could not decide till he should hear from his agent in Virginia. He neither approved nor disapproved the conditions, except that of the release as to the two thirds, saying he apprehended if he released any part of the estate it would release the whole; but he said he would answer me finally when he should hear from his agent. I rather believe he will accept my conditions. But I am quite thrown off the hinges by your information that notwithstanding the state of things from Mr. Lewis in March 1786. that all would be paid, you had found on an estimate in Sep. 1786. there would yet be a balance of 1200£ to pay. When I consider the quantity of tobacco to be counted on, the charges to come out of that, it appears evident that the debts can not be paid in this way. I am decided against selling my lands. They are the only sure provision for my children, and I have sold too much of them already. I am also unwilling to sell negroes, if the debts can be paid without. This unwillingness is for their sake, not my own; because my debts once cleared off, I shall try some plan of making their situation happier, determined to content myself with a small portion of their labour.[1] I think it better for them therefore to be submitted to harder conditions for a while in order that they may afterwards be put into a better situation. I hired my estate in Albemarle once for 11.£ sterl. for every titheable hand. Tobacco is since risen, and the lands of Goochland, Cumberland, and Bedford are more profitable. I may hope therefore a good rent may be obtained for the whole estate, letting it out in small parcels to different tenants known to be kind and careful in their natures. I propose my former lease to Garth and Mousley as the model, reserving all the advantages and privileges reserved in that, as also the lands reserved in that to my own use; inserting a clause for distraining on the lands for the whole hire, which I believe was not in that, and which, so far as concerned the hire of the slaves, would not result from the general provisions of the law, unless expressly provided for; guarding also against paper money by stating the rent in ounces of silver, restraining the leases to three years, or at any rate not more than five; retaining rigorously the clauses which had for their object the good treatment of my slaves, particularly that which denied a diminution of rent on the death of a slave; otherwise it would be their interest to kill all the old and infirm by hard usage. Supposing there are about 90 titheable slaves, a reasonable rent on them, my lands and stocks, the tenants paying every tax and charge of every kind, will make a nett annual sum which may clear off the debts within such a term of years as I should be willing to wait for. It will substitute certain calculation for incertainty, and relieve my friends from the perplexity of my affairs added to their own. The only objection is the difficulty of guarding my negroes against ill usage. I put it in all it's force, and I shall go through the operation, as a man does that of being cut for the stone, with a view to relief. I have therefore written to Mr. Lewis to pray him to put my affairs on this footing immediately, in which I know your goodness will aid him. It is taking one great trouble in the lump, to be relieved from it in the detail. It may be lessened too by each undertaking the part to which he is convenient. When this

30 JULY 1787

arrangement shall be taken, I shall feel like a person on shore, escaped from shipwreck. But this cannot be in time for the first year's paiment to McCaul, in which I would on no account fail. I hope resources may be found to effect that. I am to thank you for the Magnolia seeds which came by the way of London. I have heard nothing yet of the Cedar berries which should have come to Havre in a ship of Ross McConnico & Ritson. There are some seeds arrived for me at Bordeaux but I have no information what they are, nor from whence. Perhaps they are the cedar berries. Thanks for all the trouble you have taken and take for me are next to nothing. A sensibility of it is deeply engraven in my heart. I write to Mrs. Eppes, to Jack, and to Mr. Skipwith, making them the channel of my good wishes to the families. I have only to add therefore assurances to yourself of the sincere esteem with which I am Dear Sir your affectionate friend & servant,

Th: Jefferson

PrC (CSmH).

Eppes' letter of 14 Apr. 1787 (missing) is recorded in SJL as received 26 June; that of 2 May 1787 (also missing) is recorded as received 30 June 1787, but for a reference to its contents, see TJ to Lewis, 29 July 1787.

[1] This word interlined in substitution for "liberty," deleted.

From Parent

Beaune, *30 July 1787.* Sends statement of account for two quarter-casks of red and white wine sent to TJ; has drawn on him for the total, 258.^{lt} to the order of D'Aulne; hopes TJ will order from him again when he needs wine from this area; will do his best to give satisfactory service.

RC (MHi); 2 p.; in French; endorsed. Recorded in SJL as received 2 Aug. 1787. At the head of the letter TJ made the following recapitulation of the charges stated in Parent's letter:

"126. bottles   rouge   84.   blanc 124. bottles   78^{lt}
       bouteilles   27. 10   27. 10
       paniers   6.   6.
       emballage   8.   8.
       collé, tiré &c.   4.   4.
       paille &c.   2. 10   2. 10
                              ─────   ─────
                               132   126.

By the bottle
Vollenaye   Meursault
en futaille   13s.4d   en futaille   12s.7d
bottles &c.   7 .8   bottles &c.   7 .8
              ──────   ──────
                21   19 .15"

At the foot of the letter TJ made his calculations for determining the costs per bottle.

[654]

From Mainville

[*Orléans, ca. July 1787*]. Cabarrus, Peyrinnaut & Cie., merchants of Edenton, N.C., issued two notes in favor of Jacques de Mainville, Jr., of Orléans, totalling 12,741ᵗᵗ and payable in two and three years respectively; both were dated 24 Feb. 1785 and both were payable at Orléans. The first, maturing last Feb., was protested for non-payment. To avoid similar difficulty when next falls due, he begs TJ to indicate to Cabarrus, Peyrinnaut & Cie. that it will be to their advantage to settle the account and avoid legal proceedings. Payment may be made by a consignment of merchandise or commercial produce.

RC (MHi); 2 p.; in French. Not recorded in SJL. See Abbé de Reymond de St. Maurice to TJ, 26 Aug. 1787.

From Madame Oster

[*Paris, July 1787*], "tuesday afternoon." Received that morning the packet TJ forwarded and his letter; thanks him for his offer and will remember the kindness even though there is little occasion to make use of it. She had decided to ask a living in proportion to her husband's allowance but has accepted 1,500ᵗᵗ a year; is going to Nancy to be with her mother and relatives; has been under the very expensive care of a physician. Learned from a letter from Mrs. Banister that "Miss Jefferson" had sailed and supposes she is now with TJ; as soon as she is "able to walk out" will go to see her; had hoped that she could have her as a travelling companion. "You inform me Sir of your coming See me. I am sory indeed of trouble in rain." She lost much by not seeing TJ but had asked Mr. Short to wait until she went to the "Abbaye St. Antoine, rue Et faubourg St. Antoine."

RC (MHi); endorsed; undated and not recorded in SJL, but written after 30 June 1787, when TJ received John Banister's letter of 6 May 1787, and before 6 Aug. 1787 when he wrote to Mrs. Banister. Presumably, therefore, the letter was written early in July.

TJ's letter to Mrs. Oster to which she refers has not been found and is not recorded in SJL, but it was evidently the one forwarding Mrs. Banister's letter that had been enclosed in Banister to TJ, 6 May 1787.

To Francis Hopkinson, with Enclosure

DEAR SIR Paris Aug. 1. 1787.

A journey into the Southern parts of France and Northern of Italy must apologize to you for the length of time elapsed since my last, and for the delay of acknowleging the receipt of your favors of Nov. 8. and Dec. 9. 1786. and Apr. 14. 1787. Your two phials of essence de Lorient arrived during that interval and got separated from the letters which accompanied them, so that I could not be

1 AUGUST 1787

sure which was your first preparation and which the second. But I suppose from some circumstances that the small phial was the first, and the larger one the second. This was entirely spoiled so that nothing was distinguishable from it. The matter in the small phial was also too much spoiled for use, but the pearl merchant, from whom I get my details, said he could judge from what remained that it had been very good, that you had a very considerable knowlege in the manner of preparing, but that there was still one thing wanting which made the secret of the art. That this is not only a secret of the art, but of every individual workman who will not communicate to his fellows, beleiving his own method the best; that of ten different workmen all will practice different operations, and only one of the ten be the right one; that this secret consists only in preparing the fish, all the other parts of the process in the pearl manufactory being known. That experience has proved it to be absolutely impossible for the matter to cross the sea without being spoiled; but that if you will send some in the best state you can, he will make pearls of it and send to you that you may judge of them yourself. He says the only possible method of making any thing of it would be for a workman to go over. He would not engage in this, nor would he buy, because he says it is their custom to have contracts for 9. years supply from the fishermen, and that his contract furnishes him with as much as he can sell in the present declining state of the pearl trade: that they have been long getting out of fashion, polite people not wearing them at all, and the poor not able to give a price, that their calling is in fact annihilating, that when he renews his contract he shall be obliged to reduce the price he pays 25. pr. cent, that the matter sells from 5. to 8. livres the French pound, but most generally at 6. livres. He shewed me a necklace of 12. strands which used to sell at 10. livres, and now sells for two and a half. He observed that the length of time the matter will keep depends on the strength of the spirit of wine. The result is then that you must send me a sample of your very best, and write me what you would propose after weighing these circumstances. The leg and feathers of the bird are also arrived; but the comb which you mention as annexed to the foot has totally disappeared. I suppose this is the effect of it's drying. I have not yet had an opportunity of giving it to Monsieur de Buffon, but expect to do it soon. I thank you for the trouble you have taken with Madame Champnes's letters, and must give you another, that of enquiring for James Lillie belonging to the privateer General Mercer of Philadelphia, the property of Irvin, Carson & Semple. Richard

1 AUGUST 1787

Graham & Co. merchants of Philadelphia seem to have been also interested, and Isaac Robinson, Graham's son in law, to have commanded her. For the details I refer you to the inclosed paper I received from a Madme. Ferrier brother[1] to James Lillie, from which you will perceive he has not been heard of since 1779. I receive many of these applications, which humanity cannot refuse, and I have no means of complying with them but by troubling gentlemen on the spot. This I hope will be my apology.   I am obliged to you for subscribing for the Columbian magazine for me. I find it a good thing; and am sure it will be better from the time you have undertaken it. I wish you had commenced before the month of December; for then the abominable forgery inserted in my name in the last page would never have appeared. This I suppose the compilers took from English papers,[2] those infamous fountains of falshood. Is it not surprising that our news writers continue to copy from those papers tho' every one, who knows any thing of them, knows they are written by persons who never go out of their garret, nor read a paper? The real letter alluded to was never meant to have been publick, and therefore was hastily and carelessly dictated while I was obliged to use the pen of another. It became public however. I send you a genuine copy to justify myself in your eyes against the absurd thing they have fathered upon me in the magazine.—Mr. Payne is here with his bridge which is well thought of. The Academy, to whom it is submitted, have not yet made their report. —I have shipped on board the Mary, Capt. Howland, bound from Havre to New York, a box containing the subsequent livraisons of the Encyclopedie for yourself and Doctr. Franklin from those formerly sent you to the 22d. inclusive. I think there are also in it some new volumes of the Bibliotheque physico-oeconomique for you. I had received duplicates of some books (in sheets) for the colleges of Philadelphia and Williamsburgh. Whether I packed one copy in your box and one in Madison's, or both in his, I do not remember. You will see and be so good as to deliver the one to the college of Philadelphia if in your box. The box is directed to Doctor Franklin, and will be delivered to Mr. Madison at New York. I will send you either by this occasion or the next, the cost, expences &c. Present me in the most respectful and friendly terms to Doctr. Franklin, and his grandson, to Mr. Rittenhouse and family, Mrs. Hopkinson the elder and younger. My daughter (my elder one I mean, for both are here now) presents her respects also to your mother. I am with sentiments of sincere affection, dear Sir your friend & servant,   TH: JEFFERSON

1 AUGUST 1787

ENCLOSURE

Francis Hopkinson to Th: J. Dr.

		livres	sous
1786. Jan. 25.	To paid for Crayons	41	16
26.	2. volumes of Bibliotheque Physico-oeconomique	5	4
Feb. 3.	14th. 15th. & 16th. livraisons of Encyclopedie	71	10
Mar. 1.	17th. do. 36^{tt}-10.—May 8. 18th. do. 24^{tt}	60	10
May 8.	for pencils	12	12
Sep. 1.	for 19th. livraison of Encyclopedie	24	
Oct. 20.	for 20th. do.	24	
1787. Jan. 2.	for 21st. do.	36	10
	for 2. vols. Bibliotheque physico-oeconomique	5	4
June 29.	for 22d. livraison of Encyclopedie	24	
		305	6
July.	half the expence of carriage of books to Havre (paid by me to Limozin)	6	18 8
		312	4 8

His Excellency Dr. Franklin to Th: J. Dr.

1786. Feb. 3.	To 14. 15. 16. livraisons of Encyclopedie	71	10
Mar. 1.	17th. do. 36^{tt}-10—May 8. 18th. do. 24.^{tt}		
Sep. 1.	19th. do. 24.^{tt}	84	10
Oct. 20.	20th. do.	24	
1787. Jan. 2.	21st. do. 36^{tt}-10—June 29. 22d. do. 24.^{tt}	60	10
		240	10
July	To half the carriage of a box of books to Havre (pd. by me to Limozin	6	18 8
		247	8 8

Mr. Hopkinson is able to state against this what he has advanced for me, and will be so good as to keep the balance in his hands.

PrC (DLC). Enclosures: (1) Statements of accounts with Hopkinson and Franklin, printed above. (2) Tr of TJ to the Prévôt des Marchands et Echevins de Paris, 27 Sep. 1786, q.v. for a note on the extract that TJ regarded here as an "abominable forgery." (3) The "inclosed paper" concerning James Lillie has not been found.

[1] Thus in MS; TJ must have intended to write "sister."

[2] TJ first wrote: "some English papers, and I know no"; he then revised the sentence to read as printed above.

[658]

To Ralph Izard

DEAR SIR Paris Aug. 1. 1787.

I am to thank you for the laws and newspapers sent me by M. de Chateaufort. Your favor of April 4. has also been duly received. I am happy to find that the idea of diverting the rice trade from England to France is thought to be not impracticable. A journey which I made from Marseilles lately into Lombardy in order to acquire information relative to their rice has corrected some misinformation which the retailers of rice in this capital had given me. I am satisfied that the rice of Lombardy is of a different species from yours. The exportation of it, in the husk being prohibited, I could not bring with me but as much as my pockets would hold, which I have sent to your society of agriculture. It may serve to raise seed from. I have taken measures for a couple of sacks; but I do not make sure of them, nor rely so much on their quality as on that of the parcel I brought myself. I have written so fully on this subject to Mr. Drayton that, without repeating it here I will take the liberty of referring you to that letter. I have endeavored to prevail on the merchants of this country to engage in the rice trade. I inclose you the proposals of Messrs. Berard & Co. for that effect. They are a very solid house. One of them resides here. Their principal establishment is at Lorient, where they would prefer receiving consignments of rice: but they will receive them any where else, and I should suppose Honfleur the best port, and next to that Bourdeaux. You observe they will answer bills to the amount of 12. or 15. livres the French quintal, if accompanied with the bill of lading, and will pay the surplus of the proceeds as soon as received. If they sell at Havre or Rouen, they may receive ready money and of course pay the balance soon: if they sell at Paris it must be on a year's credit (because this will be to the retailers) the money will therefore be received later but it will be at least 6. livres the quintal more; a difference well worth waiting for. I know of no mercantile house in France of surer bottom.

Affairs in Europe seem to threaten war. Yet I think all may be settled without it. The Emperor disapproved of the concessions made to the Netherlanders by their governors, but called for deputies to consult on the matter. They have sent deputies without power to yeild a jot, and go on arming. From the character of their sovereign it is probable he will avail himself of this deputation to concede their demands. The affairs of Holland are so thoroughly embroiled that they would certainly produce a war if France and

England were in a condition for it. But they are not, and they will therefore probably find out some arrangement either perpetual or temporary to stop the progress of the civil war begun in that country. A spirit of distrust in the government here and of confidence in their own force and rights is pervading all ranks. It will be well if it awaits the good which will be worked by the provincial asemblies, and will content itself with that. The parliament demand an assembly of the states: they are supported by the sentiments of the nation, and the object of asking that assembly is to fix a constitution, and to limit expences. They refuse to register any edict for a new tax. This has so far lessened the credit of government that the purse of the money lender is shut. They speak here as freely as Junius wrote. Yet it is possible that in the event of war the spirit of the nation would rise to support a cause which is approved, I mean that of Holland.

I have had the Messrs. Le Coulteux sounded on the subject of lending money. I had before tried the same thing with others. But nothing is to be obtained for persons on our side the water. They have no confidence in our laws. Besides, all the money men are playing deeply in the stocks of this country. The spirit of agiotage (as they call it) was never so high in any country before. It will probably produce as total a depravation of morals as the system of Law did. All the money of France almost is now employed in this, none being free even for the purposes of commerce, which suffers immensely from this cause.

Before I conclude I must add on the subject of rice that what cannot arrive here a month before the Careme, would miss it's sale and must therefore go to another market. The merchant however to whom it is consigned will be competent to this measure whenever he finds it a necessary one. I beg leave to be presented very respectfully to Mrs. Izard and your family and to assure you of the sincere sentiments of esteem and attachment with which I am dear Sir your friend & servant, TH: JEFFERSON

RC (Lloyd W. Smith, Madison, N.J., 1946); endorsed. PrC (DLC). Enclosure: Bérard's notes on the rice trade, 15 July 1787, q.v.

For a note on the house of MESSRS. BERARD & CO. see Simon Bérard to TJ, 6 May 1786.

From André Limozin

Le Havre, 1 Aug. 1787. In accordance with TJ's instructions of 29 July, has drawn sight draft on him for 739^{tt} 13s.; will make inquiries about the box which TJ mentioned; thanks him for the information on current affairs; hopes "Peace could continue untill April next" for he has "Ventures at Sea the value of which exceed 25000£ Sterling," the returns of which cannot be had until "March or April next"; hopes he can be informed of any new developments. Is certain "no officers of the Packet" would take TJ's dispatches for America because they are forbidden to do this; is willing to put these dispatches into the post office under his own cover "two hours before the Box for the Letters is seal'd." Has an American ship which will sail for Philadelphia the 20th of the month; TJ may rely on her master who seems a very good man.

RC (MHi); 4 p.; addressed; endorsed. Recorded in SJL as received 3 Aug. 1787. The sight draft on TJ, dated 1 Aug. 1787, for the amount stated, payable to Sartorius & Cie., is in MHi.

From Abbé Morellet

MONSIEUR mercredy soir. 1er aoust. [1787]

Je vous remercie bien de m'avoir communiqué l'*inquiry in to the principles of a commercial system*. Je vous avoue que je n'en goute pas la doctrine sur beaucoup de points, ni son projet d'etablir des droits sur les vaisseaux etrangers pour reserver aux americains la navigation de port à port et même la navigation aux autres pays de l'europe ni son grand desir de favoriser et de regler déjà l'etablissement de manufactures dans un pays qui a beaucoup mieux à faire; ni ses calculs des avantages des manufacturiers d'amerique sur ceux d'europe &c. Tout cela dis je me paroit pour contraire aux veritables maximes de l'administration. Je suis plus content de ce qu'il dit de la guerre et il me semble qu'il peint avec verité la situation de votre amérique à cet egard. Il parle encore fort bien du credit public et de la necessité de prendre des mesures pour le payement de votre dette nationale. Ainsi ce petit ouvrage est comme tous les ouvrages melé de bon et de mauvais. Je vous le renvoye en vous priant de m'en procurer un exemplaire si vous aves quelque moyen sous la main pour cela.

Je profite en même tems de la permission que vous m'avez donnée de vous addresser mes lettres pour notre respectable ami Mr. Franklin. Je vous envoye donc une lettre et un petit paquet à part que je desire lui etre envoyé avec quelque autre chose qui ne soit pas lettre afin que cela ne soit pas taxé aux prix exorbitans de la poste. Je vous prie aussi si vous aves quelque occasion d'envoyer même la lettre par quelque autre voie que la poste mais après tout si vous n'en aves pas faites la je vous prie partir par la voye ordinaire. Mr. Grant a beaucoup de choses à envoyer à Madame

Beache et à Mr. Franklin. Il m'a dit ce me semble qu'il se concerteroit avec vous. Mille pardons Monsieur de la liberté que je prens mais vous me l'aves accordée. Agrées l'hommage du respectueux devouement avec lequel j'ai l'honneur d'etre Monsieur Vôtre très humble et très obeissant Serviteur,

L'ABBÉ MORELLET

RC (DLC); endorsed; the year has been supplied in the date from internal evidence and an entry in SJL for the receipt of a letter from Morellet of 1 Aug. on 2 Aug. 1787. Enclosure (PPAP): Abbé Morellet to Benjamin Franklin, 31 July 1787 (translation printed in *The Works of Benjamin Franklin*, ed.

Sparks, x, 313-19).

The INQUIRY IN TO THE PRINCIPLES OF A COMMERCIAL SYSTEM was Tench Coxe's *An Enquiry into the Principles on which a Commercial System for the United States of America should be founded*, Philadelphia, Robert Aitken, 1787; see Sowerby No. 3623.

From Thomas Barclay

[*L'Orient*, 2 Aug. 1787. Recorded in SJL as received 7 Aug. 1787, together with a letter of Zachariah Loreilhe [ca. 3] Aug., q.v., in which Barclay's letter was probably enclosed. Not found.]

To James Madison, with Enclosure

DEAR SIR   Paris Aug. 2. 1787.

My last was of June 20. Your's received since that date are May 15. and June 6. In mine I acknoleged the receipt of the Paccan nuts which came sealed up. I have reason to believe those in the box are arrived at Lorient. By the Mary Capt. Howland lately sailed from Havre to N. York I shipped three boxes of books one marked I.M. for yourself, one marked B.F. for Doctr. Franklin, and one marked W.H. for William Hay in Richmond. I have taken the liberty of addressing them all to you as you will see by the inclosed bill of lading, in hopes you would be so good as to forward the other two. You will have opportunities of calling on the gentlemen for the freight &c. In yours you will find the books noted in the account inclosed herewith. You have now Mably's works complete except that on Poland, which I have never been able to get, but shall not cease to search for. Some other volumes[1] to compleat your collection of Chronologies. The 4th. vol. of D'Albon was lost by the bookbinder, and I have not yet been able to get one to replace it. I shall continue to try. The Memoires sur les droits et impositions en Europe (cited by Smith) was a scarce and excessively dear book. They are now reprinting it.

[662]

I think it will be in three or four quartos of from 9. to 12 a volume. When it is finished I shall take a copy for you. Amelot's travels into China I can learn nothing of. I put among the books sent you, two somewhat voluminous, and the object of which will need explanation; these are the Tableau de Paris and L'espion Anglois. The former is truly a picture of private manners in Paris, but presented on the dark side and a little darkened moreover. But there is so much truth in it's ground work that it will be well worth your reading. You will then know Paris (and probably the other large cities of Europe) as well as if you had been here years. L'Espion Anglois is no Caricature. It will give you a just idea of the wheels by which the machine of government is worked here. There are in it also many interesting details of the last war, which in general may be relied on. It may be considered as the small history of great events. I am in hopes when you shall have read them you will not think I have mis-spent your money for them. My method for making out this assortment was to revise the list of my own purchases since the invoice of 1785. and to select such as I had found worth your having. Besides this I have casually met with and purchased some few curious and cheap things. I have made out the Dr. side of the account, taking for my ground work yours of March 18. 1786. correcting two errors of computation in that which were to your prejudice. The account of the Mr. Fitzhughs stood thus. 1785. Sep. 1. cash 600.₶ Nov. 10. paid their bill of exchange in favor of Limozin 480.₶ making 1080.₶ The money they paid you was worth 1050.₶ according to our mode of settling at 18.₶ for 20/ Virginia money. The difference of 30.₶ will never be worth notice unless you were to meet with them by chance, and hardly then. I must trouble you on behalf of a Mr. Thos. Burke at Loughburke near Loughrea in Ireland, whose brother James Burke is supposed to have died in 1785. on his passage from Jamaica, or St. Eustatius to New York. His property on board the vessel is understood to have come to the hands of Alderman Groom at New York. The inclosed copy of a letter to him will more fully explain it. A particular friend of mine here applies to me for information, which I must ask the favor of you to procure and forward to me.

Writing news to others, much pressed in time, and making this letter one of private business, I did not intend to have said any thing to you on political subjects. But I must press one subject. Mr. Adams informs me he has borrowed money in Holland, which if confirmed by Congress will enable them to pay not only the interest due here to the foreign officers but the principal. Let me beseech you to reflect on the expediency of transferring this debt to Holland. All our other debts in Europe do not injure our reputation so much as this. These gentlemen have connections both in and out of office, and these again their connections, so that our default on this article is further known, more blamed, and excites worse dispositions against us than you can conceive. If you think as I do, pray try to procure an order for paying off their capital. Mr. Adams adds that if any certain tax is provided for the paiment of interest, Congress may borrow enough in Holland to pay off their whole debts in France both public and private, to the crown, to the farmers and to Beaumarchais. Surely it will be better to transfer these debts to Holland. So critical is the state of that country that I imagine the monied men of it would be glad to place their money in foreign countries, and that Mr. Adams could borrow there for us without a certain tax for the interest, and saving our faith too by previous explanations on that subject. This country is really supposed on the eve of a *bankruptcy*.[2] Such a spirit has risen within a few weeks as could not have been believed. They see the great deficit in their revenues, and the hopes of oeconomy lessen daily. The parliament refuse to register any act for a new tax, and require an assembly of the states. The object of this assembly is evidently to give law to the king, to fix a constitution, to limit expences. These views are said to gain upon the nation. The *king's passion* for *drink* is *divesting him* of all *respect*. The *queen* is *detested* and an *explosion* of some sort is not impossible. The *ministry* is alarmed, and the surest reliance at this moment for the *public peace* is on their *two hundred thousand men*. I cannot write these things in a public dispatch because they would *get* into a *newspaper* and *come back here*. A final decision of some sort should be made in Beaumarchais' affairs. I am with sentiments of the most perfect esteem Dear Sir Your friend & servt,

Th: Jefferson

P.S. The watch and pedometer not done. In the box of books are some for the colleges of Philadelphia and Williamsburg and two vols. of the Encyclopedie for Congress, presented by the author of that part.

2 AUGUST 1787

ENCLOSURE[3]

James Madison esq. to Th: Jefferson Dr.

	To 58£-6s-8 Virga. currency received from the Fitzhughs	1050₶ 0 0	
1785. Nov. 4.	To repaid Mr. Short for a Spy-glass bought in England	50	
Nov. 21.	To Limozin at Havre transportation of 2. trunks of books Sep. 1785.	34 8 9	
1786. Aug. 2.	To paid for an Umbrella cane	30	
	a copying press & apparatus, paper & ink	144	
Oct. 13.	a chemical box	69	
1787. July 4.	To paid Cabaret for binding books[4]	46 14	
	To paid for books, to wit.		

	₶	s	d
Guerre de 1775 83. 4to.[5]	10	0	0
Voyage en Suisse par Mayer. 2. v. 8vo.	7	4	
Ordonnance de marine 8vo.	4	4	
Voiage aux Alpes par Saussure. 4. v. 8vo.	18		
Experiences d'Ingenhousz. 8vo.	4	10	
Chymie de Fourcroy. 4. v. 8vo.	24	0	
Peines infamantes par La Cretelle. 8vo.	3	12	
Savary sur l'Egypte 3. v. 8vo.	15	0	
Voiages de Volney. 2. v. 8vo.	10	4	
la France et les etats Unis par Warville. 8vo.	4	10	
Loix criminelles par Warville 2. v. 8vo.	7	4	
Vie de Turgot par Condorcet. 8vo.	4	10	
L'Espion Anglois. 10. v. 12mo.	25	0	
Annales Romaines par Macquer 12mo.	5		

142–18   1424 2 9

2 AUGUST 1787

	₶ s	₶ s d
Brought forward	142–18	1424 2 9
Troubles de l'Amerique par Soulés. 4. v. 8vo.	16 0	
Bibliotheque physico-oeconomique (1786) 2. v. 12mo.	5 4	
Mably. Principes de legislation. 12mo.	3	
de la Grece. 12mo.	2	
De Juvigny sur la decadence des lettres. 8vo.	6	
Abregé chronologique d'Angleterre de Salmon. 2. v. 8vo.	12	
Abregé chronol. de l'histoire ecclesiastique	18	
Abregé chronol. de l'Allemagne par Pfeffel. 2. v. 12mo.	12	
Histoire ancienne de Milot. 4. v. 12mo.	12	
Moderne 5. v. 12mo.	15	
de France 3. v. 12mo.	7–10	
De Thou. 11. v. 4to.	55	
Bibliotheque Physico-oeconomique. (1787.) 2. v. 12mo.	5 4	
Pieces interessantes. 4. v. 12mo.	12	
Tableau de Paris 4. v. 12mo.	13	
Demarcation entre l'Espagne et le Portugal en Amerique.⁶		
Histoire de Kentuckey. 8vo.	4 5	
Smith's history of New York. 8vo.	6	
Voiages de Chastellux. 2. v. 8vo.	11	
Memoires de Brandenburgh. 8vo.	6	
Examen de Chastellux par Warville. 8vo.	2 8	
Hennepin. 12mo.	2	
Vie de Voltaire par l'Abbé Duvernet. 8vo.	7 5	
	375–14	1424 2 9

2 AUGUST 1787

	₶ s	₶ s d
Brought forward	375–14	1424 2 9
Histoire de la Nouvelle France par Lescarbot 8vo.	2 10	
Gibson's Saxon chronicle. 4to. 6/ sterl.	7 4	
Avantages et desavantages de la decouverte de l'Amerique	1 4	
Encyclopedie. 16th. 18th. 19th. 20th. 22d. livraisons @ 24.₶ each. 120 15th. 23₶ 10 17th. & 21st. 36₶ 10 each 96–10	216 10	
*5th. Oiseaux to 1. part 2.	7 0	610 2
1787. Aug. 4. To paid Limozin carriage of books to Havre (exclus. of Dr. F's & Hay's)		27 14 9
		2061 19 6
Graecorum respublicae Ubbonis Emmii (qu. if sent?) 9₶ *when your duplicate vol. shall be returned they will give you credit for it.		
Cr.		
By error in computing the value of 10 Guineas in former account (20s: 18₶:: 28s: 25₶—4s)		18₶
By do. 25£ = 441₶–8 remitted to Mrs. Carr (25£ = 450₶)		8–12

N.B. Having been very desirous of collecting the original Spanish writers on American history, I commissioned Mr. Carmichael to purchase some for me. They came very dear, and moreover he was obliged to take duplicates in two instances. I have packed one copy of these in Mr. Madison's box, and will beg the favor of him to sell them for me if he can. I state below the exact prices they cost me in Spain, adding nothing for transportation to France, which was high.

2 AUGUST 1787

La Florida de Garcilasso de la Vega. fol.
Historia General de la Florida por De Cadenasz Caro. fol. } 200. reals = 10. Dollars

Herrera Historia General 4. v. fol. 500. reals = 25. Dollars

TH: JEFFERSON
Aug. 3. 1787.[7]

1784.	Cr.	livres	sous	den.
By balance brought forward 77⅔ Doll. @ 5ᵗ—5		407	15	0
By[8] advance to le Maire 10 Guineas		234		
By do. for 6 Revisals at 2½ drs		81		
		722	15	
By £25 Va. Currency remitted to Mrs. Carr for use of Peter & Dabney equal to the	Balance	441	8	
		1164	3	

RC (DLC: Madison Papers); partly in code; endorsed. PrC (DLC: TJ Papers). Enclosures: (1) Bill of lading for three boxes of books (missing), enclosed in Limozin to TJ, 27 July 1787 (see postscript to TJ to Limozin, 29 July 1787). (2) TJ's account with Madison (RC in DLC: Madison Papers; PrC in DLC: TJ Papers). (3) Copy of a letter from Thomas Burke to John Broom, 30 Sep. 1786 (DLC: Madison Papers); at foot of text in the same hand as this copy: "This letter was sent to Alderman Groom at New York, the 30th. September 1786—to which Mr. Burke got no answer"; and endorsed in another hand: "Alderman Broome Hanover Square." A copy of a later letter from Burke to his wife (DLC: Madison Papers), transmitting a copy of a letter from John Broom to Thomas Burke, 16 May 1787, corrects the name from "Groom" to "Broom" (see TJ to Madison, 17 Sep. 1787).

The PARTICULAR FRIEND that TJ had in mind was the Abbess of the Abbey of Pentemont, Marie-Catherine Béthisy de Mézières (see TJ to Madison, 20 Dec. 1787).

[1] Thus in MS, though TJ evidently intended to write some such phrase as "are wanting," which is the unexplained reading in Ford, IV, 420.

[2] This and subsequent words in italics are written in code and have been decoded by the editors, employing Code No. 9.

[3] The enclosed account begins with a separate page, not printed here, which has at its head: "State of account between James Madison esq. & Th: Jefferson copied from J.M.'s letter of Mar. 18. 1786," followed by the account as printed in Madison's letter of that date.

[4] In DLC: Madison Papers there is a bill, dated 4 July 1787, from Cabaret for bookbinding, which may also have been enclosed in the present letter.

[5] In margin of RC, opposite this entry, Madison wrote: "From hence to the end, the books are to pay duty. The preceding articles were received in Virga."

[6] TJ wrote in the margin, opposite this entry: "(given)."

[7] PrC ends at this point.

[8] From this point on the statement of account is in Madison's hand.

To Thomas Barclay, with Enclosure

Dear Sir Paris Aug. 3. 1787.

I am now to acknolege the receipt of your several favors of June 29. and July 6. on French's affair, July 8. on the accounts of Virginia, July 12. with Ast's bill, July 13. your account in the Marocco business, July 16. on La Vayse and Puchelberg's affair and Geraud and Roland's, July 27. and another without date on my private account. That of July 27. contained also an article of 3. muskets from Liege to be added to your account against the state of Virginia. Supposing you are now departed for America, I send this thither by Doctr. Gibbons.

I am of opinion that the affair of Geraud and Roland in Holland had better be committed to Mr. Dumas in Holland, as law suits must always be attended to by some person on the spot. For the same reason I think that of La Vayse and Puchelberg should be managed by the agent at Lorient, and Gruel's by the agent at Nantes. I shall always be ready to assist the agents of Lorient and Nantes in any way in my power, but were the details to be left to me, they would languish necessarily on account of my distance from the place, and perhaps suffer too for want of verbal consultations with the lawyers entrusted with them. You are now with Congress and can take their orders on the subject. I shall therefore do nothing in these matters in reliance that you will put them into such channel as they direct, furnishing the necessary documents and explanations.

Your bill on me for 1200 livres on account of the U.S. I have accepted and shall pay, myself, the moment it is presented, Mr. Grand chusing not to add to his advances for the United states. The bill for 1800 livres in favor of Ast shall be paid the moment any remittances arrive. Of this I will give him notice. Your draught for 500. livres on the fund of Virginia, refused at first by Mr. Grand, was afterwards paid by him. That in my favor for 2370 livres on Mr. Grand as banker for the state of Virginia I accept as paiment of that sum, and credit it in your private account with me, as also the sum of 108^{tt}-8 for the three muskets from Liege, omitted in the account you had sent me. For these sums amounting to 2478^{tt}-8 be so good as to credit the state of Virginia. You will perceive that they are credited to you in the inclosed account, which I have made out from your several letters and my own memorandums. The balance is in your favor 724^{tt}-7-6 which sum I will pay immediately into the hands of Mrs. Barclay.

3 AUGUST 1787

With respect to French's affair, being perfectly satisfied myself, I have not ceased nor shall cease endeavoring to satisfy others that your conduct has been that of an honest and honourable debtor, and theirs the counterpart of Shylock in the play. I inclose you a letter containing my testimony on your general conduct, which I have written to relieve a debt of justice pressing on my mind, well knowing at the same time you will not need it in America. Your conduct is too well known to Congress, your character to all the world, to need any testimonials.

The moment I close my dispatches for the packet, which will be the 7th. instant I shall with great pleasure go to pay my respects to Mrs. Barclay at St. Germains, to satisfy her on the subject of your transactions, and to assure her that my resources shall be hers, as long as I have any.—A multitude of letters to write prevent my entering into the feild of public news, further than to observe that it is extremely doubtful whether the a[ffairs] of Holland will or will not produce a war between France on one side and England and Prussia on the other.

I beg you to accept assurances of the sincere esteem & respect with which I have the honor to be Dear Sir your friend & servant,

TH: JEFFERSON

ENCLOSURE

Thomas Barclay esq. in account with Thos. Jefferson. Dr.

				₶		
1785. Oct. 31.	To	paid for discharge of black servant from prison		24	0	0
Nov. 24.	To	paid Mrs. Barclay (bill for china, tea, & brandy)		1054	0	0
1786. Aug. 2.	To	paid your bill in favor of Richard		750	0	0
1787. Feb. 8.	To	paid Mrs. Barclay by order on Mr. Grand		1000	0	0
May. 27.	To	cash at Bordeaux		1002	0	0
		Balance to be paid to Mrs. Barclay		724	7	6
				4554	7	6

Cr.

1784. Nov. 19.	By	China, tea & brandy bought for me	1053	1	6
1785. Aug. 20.	By	2. doz. bottles Madeira @ 30₶	60		
		1½ doz. do. Frontignan @ 24₶	36		
		1½ doz. do. Muscat @ 18.₶	27		
	By	2. ℔ tea	16		
1786.	By	books from Spain. 127.9 Dollars	671	10	
		Dalrymple's travels	12		
		Sims' rates of merchandize	7	4	
	By	30. ℔ of coffee from Lorient	90	0	

[670]

By freight of china from Lorient to Rouen	67	4
By cash to Williamos	36	
By your draught on the state of Virginia in my favor	2370	
By 3. muskets from Liege & transportation, for state of Virginia	108	8
	4554	7 6

PrC (DLC). Enclosures: (1) TJ's account with Barclay, (PrC in DLC), printed above. (2) TJ to Barclay, same date, following.

Barclay's letter of JULY 12. WITH AST'S BILL, recorded in SJL as received 20 July, has not been found. ANOTHER WITHOUT DATE ON MY PRIVATE ACCOUNT: Barclay to TJ, printed above under 14 July 1787.

To Thomas Barclay

DEAR SIR   Paris Aug. 3. 1787.

As you have acted, since my arrival in France, in the characters of Consul general for that country, and minister to the court of Marocco, and also as agent in some particular transactions for the state of Virginia, I think it a duty to yourself, to truth, and to justice, on your departure for America, to declare that in all these characters, as far as has come within my notice, you have acted with judgment, with attention, with integrity and honour. I beg you to accept this feeble tribute to truth, and assurances of sincere attachment and friendship from Dear Sir Your most obedient & most humble servant,

TH: JEFFERSON

RC (Charles Caldwell Marks, Birmingham, Ala., 1945). PrC (DLC). Tr (PHi); together with Tr of similar testimonials to Barclay from John Jay, 5 Oct. 1787, and Benjamin Franklin, 10 Nov. 1787. Another Tr (MHi: Knox Papers) of the same letters and in the same hand.

This letter was enclosed in TJ's other letter to Barclay of this date, above. Barclay was not a MINISTER, but an agent deputed by the American Commissioners; see note to TJ to Jay, 21 June 1787.

From Zachariah Loreilhe

L'Orient, [3] *Aug.* 1787. Has sent Grandhome, an officer in the Royal Marine, two packets left by Mr. Barclay to be forwarded to TJ by a safe opportunity; asks TJ to acknowledge their receipt. "Mr. Barclay Sailed yesterday, with a fair wind, for Tercera and Boston."

RC (MHi); 2 p.; endorsed by TJ: "L'Oreilhe." Recorded in SJL as received 7 Aug. 1787, together with a letter from Thomas Barclay, 2 Aug., and from William F. Ast, 3 Aug. (both missing), which were probably the "two Packets" enclosed.

[671]

To Edmund Randolph

DEAR SIR   Paris Aug. 3. 1787.

A journey into the Southern parts of France and Northern of Italy has prevented my sooner acknoleging the receipt of your private favors of July 12. 1786. and Jan. 28. and May 3. 1787.— I am anxious to hear what you have done in your federal convention. I am in hopes at least you will persuade the states to commit their commercial arrangements to Congress, and to enable them to pay their debts, interest and capital. The coercive powers supposed to be wanting in the federal head, I am of opinion they possess by the law of nature, which authorizes one party to an agreement to compel the other to performance. A delinquent state makes itself a party against the rest of the confederacy.—We have at present two fires kindled in Europe. 1. In Brabant. The emperor in the moment of his return to Vienna disavowed the concessions which had been made by his Governors to quiet the Brabantines. They prepared therefore for regular resistance. But as the emperor had at the same time called for deputies to be sent to Vienna to consult on their affairs, they have sent them, but without powers to conclude any thing, and in the mean time they go on arming. The enterprizing, unperservering, capricious, Thrasonic character of their sovereign renders it probable he will avail himself of this little condescendence in the Brabantines to recede from all his innovations.—2. The Dutch are every now and then cutting one anothers throats. The party of the Stadholder is strongest within the confederacy, and is gaining ground. He has a majority in the States general and a strong party in the States of Holland. His want of money is supplied by his cousin George. England and Prussia abet his usurpations, and France the Patriotic party. Were England and France in a condition to go to war, there is no question but they would have been at it before now. But their insuperable poverty renders it probable they will compel a suspension of hostilities, and either arrange and force a settlement on the Dutch, or if they cannot agree themselves on this, they will try to protract things by negociation.—Can I be useful to you here in anything? In the purchase of books, of wines, of fruits, of modes for Mrs. Randolph, or any thing else? As to books, they are cheaper here than in England, excepting those in Latin, Greek, or English. As to wines I know the best Vignerons of Bordeaux, Burgundy and Frontignan. Genuine wines can never be had but of the Vigneron. The best of Bourdeaux cost three livres the bottle, but good may be

bought for two. Command me freely, assured that I shall serve you chearfully and that I am with respects to Mrs. Randolph & attachment to yourself Dr. Sir your most obedient & most humble servt.,
TH. JEFFERSON

PrC (DLC).

To the Governor of Virginia

SIR   Paris Aug. 3. 1787.

I am to acknolege the receipt of your Excellency's letters of Jan. 28. and May 4. which have come to hand since the date of mine of Feb. 7. Immediately on the receipt of the former I caused enquiry to be made relative to the bayonets, and found that they had certainly been packed with the muskets. Your Excellency's favor of May 4. renders unnecessary the sending the proofs. There have been shipped in the whole from Bordeaux 3400 stand of arms, and from Havre 3406 cartouch boxes which I hope have come safely to hand. Besides these there has been a shipment from Bordeaux of powder &c. made by Mr. Barclay. This was but the half of what was intended, and of what Mr. Barclay had contracted for. But his bill on Mr. Grand was protested on a misconception of Mr. Grand's who by a mixture of your account with that of the U.S. had supposed he had but about 12,000 livres of your money in his hands. I was absent on a journey, and happened in the course of that to meet with Mr. Barclay at Bourdeaux, and we concluded to send you half the quantity. Since my return I have not been able to have your account exactly settled so as to render it now; but am able to say in general and with certainty, that every thing sent you has been paid, and that after paying Houdon 3000ᵗᵗ for the second bust of the Marquis de la Fayette now nearly ready to be sent off for you, and 10,000ᵗᵗ the second paiment due towards Genl. Washington's statue, there will remain enough in Mr. Grand's hands to pay for a quantity of powder, &c. equal to that sent you by Mr. Barclay from Bordeaux, which shall accordingly be done. This balance on hand includes 5300. livres paid by Mr. Littlepage, which, tho' he had sent us a bill for, six or eight months ago, we had refused to receive till the arrival of your Excellency's letter informing me it had not been paid in America. It was therefore applied for and received by Mr. Grand a few days ago. Mr. Barclay drew on me for the balance of his account with the state of Virginia 2370 livres which I paid; besides this he afterwards

[673]

discovered an omission of 108ᵗᵗ-8s in his account, which I pay also, so as to leave your account with him balanced. There is however the article of expences for young Mercier, which he has neither entered in your account, nor charged to me in my private account. It remains yet due to him therefore, and I shall pay it to him if he applies to me. I should have called for it, but that he was gone to America before I discovered the omission. Should the state have further occasion for arms, your Excellency will be able to judge, combining quality and price, whether those of Liege or of France are to be preferred. I shall with chearfulness obey your future orders on this or any other account, and have the honor to be with sentiments of the most perfect esteem & respect your Excellency's most obedient & most humble servant, TH: JEFFERSON

P.S. The original of the report on the inauguration of the bust of the M. de la Fayette accompanies this.

P.S. Aug. 4. Mr. Grand's clerk has called on me this morning and shewed me a rough, tho' probable state of his account, by which he convinces me I had mistaken the balance, which probably will be only between six and seven thousand livres. I doubt whether it will be worth while to invest this in military stores, whether it may not be as well to let it remain for the balance of the statue? But I shall follow the orders of your Excellency if you will be so good as to give them. TH: JEFFERSON

RC (Vi); docketed: "Letter from Mr. Jefferson—on subject of Arms &c. No. 11." PrC (DLC). Enclosure: Minutes of the ceremony for the presentation of the bust of Lafayette (see Le Pelletier to TJ, 1 Feb. 1787).

From William Stephens Smith

DR. SIR   Lisbon August 3d. 1787.

I propose embarking in the Packet for Falmouth the day after to-morrow. It is probable I shall be in London in about 18 or 20 day's. My last Letters from Mrs. Smith inform me that she had received a Letter from General Sullivan addressed to me as follows: Dr. Sir I take the Liberty of enclosing a draught in your own favor upon Govr. Jefferson for 46£. 17. 10s. stgr. payable at 10 day's sight, and have drawn upon you for the like sum payable at 30 day's sight, the reason of my doing this is because Bills upon France will not sell here at this time without great loss, and having advanced Cash for Govr. Jefferson to amount of the Contents, and

3 AUGUST 1787

forwarded the articles by Capt. Pierce, I have taken the Liberty to trouble you to negotiate this matter. Yours &c. John Sullivan.

Your advice on this subject will be agreable. I shall do my self the honor of informing your Excellency after my arrival in London, particularly of my visit to this court and what has passed between me and the Prime Minister on our affairs &c. I am with great regard Your Excly. obedt. & hm   W. S. SMITH

RC (MHi); endorsed. Recorded in SJL as received 26 Aug. 1787.

See John Sullivan to TJ, 27 Apr. 1787. The phrasing of John Adams' acceptance of Sullivan's draft; Mrs. Abigail Adams Smith's letter to TJ of 11 July 1787 with its enclosures; her taking the trouble to send a copy of Sullivan's letter to Smith in Lisbon; and, especially, Smith's extraordinary and repeated use of the phrase YOUR EXCELLENCY—all betray a strong resentment at the liberty Sullivan had taken and, equally, reveal the assumption that Sullivan had adopted this course with TJ's approval. On his side, though TJ acknowledged Mrs. Smith's letter, he sent the compensating bill of exchange directly to Adams; there is no evidence that he ever corresponded with Mrs. Smith again, though he repeatedly expressed friendly feelings for her. In his acknowledgment of the present letter, TJ discoursed on other matters, casually asked for an adjustment that would make possible "a final state of my account" with Smith, and, after stating the facts about Sullivan which showed that TJ himself had been far more imposed upon than anyone else and with no more explanation, casually concluded: "However I have no doubt he will explain the matter to me" (TJ to Smith, 31 Aug. 1787). The incident was passed over without exacerbated feelings principally because TJ remained unruffled, as he characteristically did in such situations. The exorbitant and extraordinary price that Sullivan exacted for the decayed skin and bones of a moose might have included in addition the marring of a friendship because of the method he chose of obtaining payment. But TJ was genuinely fond of Colonel Smith and his wife; he knew well that Smith possessed a rather volatile temper; and his own habit was to suffer imposition rather than permit small incidents to interfere with friendships: even in war and politics he believed that different views should not be permitted to intrude upon social intercourse, and while this was a rule of conduct sometimes violated, his failures to observe it—as in differences with Alexander Hamilton and John Marshall—arose almost entirely out of his concern for the public interest, almost never out of concern for his own. In Congress TJ had once drafted a severe reprimand for Sullivan which the latter must have known about even though it was never delivered; yet neither of the men, so far as can be discerned from the record, allowed this to interfere with their relationship; on the contrary, there is much to show that they held each other in esteem (see Vol. 1: 477-8; Vol. 6: 447-55). TJ's letter to Sullivan when he finally learned the facts about the cost of the moose and related items is a remarkable example of his refusal to permit annoying circumstances to interfere with cordial relationships (see TJ to Sullivan, 5 Oct. 1787). The trait that he displayed on such occasions was one that Smith himself had admired in TJ.

From Stael de Holstein

MONSIEUR   Paris le 3. Août 1787.

Permettez que j'aye l'honneur de réclamer vos bons offices auprès des Etats unis dans une circonstance où la sureté du commerce est essentielement compromise.

3 AUGUST 1787

Le Sr. Adolphe fréderic Dahlberg, Capitaine de la Galeasse Suédoise la *Marie-Elisabeth*, appartenante au Baron de Roxendorff, s'est mis en Mer pour une expédition au compte du propriétaire de ce bâtiment. Il s'est écoulé, Monsieur, un temps considérable sans qu'on ait eu la moindre nouvelle de ce Capitaine, qui paroit avoir formé le complôt de s'emparer du navire et de sa cargaison en se réfugiant dans des mers éloignées, suivant ce qui résulte des renseignements qu'on a pu se procurer, et des déclarations fournies aux Amirautés.

Le College de Commerce de Stockholm, ayant de fortes raisons de présumer que le Capitaine Dahlberg se sera retiré dans un des Ports des Etats unis, s'est adressé à moi, Monsieur, pour aviser aux moyens de s'assurer de sa personne.

J'ai l'honneur de joindre ici son signalement et la description de la Galeasse, tels qu'ils m'ont été envoyés. J'espère, Monsieur, que vous trouverez dans la sûreté du commerce et de la navigation des motifs assez puissants pour envoyer ces pieces aux Etats unis, et pour appuyer auprès du gouvernement la réclamation du College de Commerce, qui demande que des ordres soient donnés pour que le Capitaine Dahlberg et ses complices soyent arrêtés dans quelque port de l'Amérique qu'ils puissent se trouver, et quelque soit l'époque de la découverte qui en sera faite, pour delà être envoyès prisonniers sur ledit bâtiment au gouverneur de l'Isle St. Barthelemy appartenante à S.M. le Roi de Suede.

J'attendrai votre Réponse, Monsieur, pour en faire part au College de Commerce de Stockholm.

Je saisis cette occasion pour vous offrir l'assurance de la parfaite considération avec laquelle j'ai l'honneur d'être Monsieur Votre très humble et très obeissant serviteur,

Le Bon. Stael de Holstein

RC (DLC); in a clerk's hand, signed by Stael de Holstein; endorsed by TJ: "Sweden Ambassador of." PrC of Tr (DLC); in William Short's hand. Tr (MHi). Tr (DNA: PCC, No. 107, II). Recorded in SJL as received 3 Aug. 1787. Enclosures (RC and PrC of Tr in Short's hand in DLC; Tr in DNA: PCC, No. 107, II): Description of Capt. Dahlberg and description of the ship, *Marie-Elisabeth*. This letter and its enclosures were enclosed in TJ to John Jay, 6 Aug. 1787. See *Dipl. Corr., 1783-89*, II, 72-4; also Dumas to TJ, 7 June 1787, note.

From John Stockdale

Sir   Piccadilly London 3rd. Augt. 1787.

I duly received your's of the 17th. and 25th. Ultimo and should have sent the Articles off sooner had it not been for the difficulty

[676]

3 AUGUST 1787

I had to meet with Gordon's Tacitus, it being entirely out of Print; it is bound, but I hope it will answer your purpose, the Price is £1. 4.

Just as I was going to ship 400. of your Work, for Richmond and Philidelphia, I had the disagreable intelligence to learn that your Book was already printed in Philidelphia, and a skeliton of a Map added to it, which tho' not equal to mine, I am inform'd, as it comes much cheaper, it will answer their Purpose.

Aitken of Philidelphia is unfortunately fail'd. I sent off in a box by the Dilligence Yesterday the following Books, American Atlas £2. 12. 6. Adams on the Constitutions 5/ 10, Notes on Virginia for yourself (not charged) and *34. at 5/4*[1] each for the Books[eller] you was so good as to recommend. They sell in London Retail at 7/. in boards. When they are sold he will be so good as to pay the Money into your hands. I hope he will soon want more, it is well spoke of in London. But they much lament that you have not gone more at large into the work and brought it lower down.

I have order'd two Copies to be deliver'd in your Name to Mr. Thos. Mann Randolph (Gratis).

I return you my sincere thanks for the Book you sent me. There are many Pleasing and entertaining stories for Children which will be of use for my intended Publication.

I am with great Respect Sir Your much obliged & very humble Servt.,
JOHN STOCKDALE

RC (MHi); endorsed. Recorded in SJL as received 8 Aug. 1787.

[1] TJ wrote the following in the margin:
"5/4=6^{lt}—8s
Postage 16
Commn."

From Wilt, Delmestre & Cie.

MONSIEUR   L'Orient le 3. Aoust 1787.

L'interêt que nous prenons au maintien des faveurs qu'a obtenu en France le Commerce des Etats unis, nous impose le devoir de vous instruire, Monsieur, que le Directeur des fermes en cette ville travaille assiduement à un Tableau, tant des importations que des exportations qu'on[t] fait les Americains depuis l'etablissement de la franchise en ce Port.

Comme nous connoissons par experience tout l'attachement de cet Agent de la ferme generale aux principes peu favorables de

[677]

ses superieurs, nous ne doutons point un instant que par un état erroné, ou peutêtre volontairement infidele, il ne cherche, de concours avec eux, a nous faire priver de nos priviléges sous le pretexte que le Commerce que les Américains font en ce Port n'offre pas une Ballance avantageuse a la Nation françoise, il est de l'interêt du Gouvernement d'abolir une franchise nuisible au Commerce des regnicoles.

Nous ne nous dissimulons pas, Monsieur, Que si les fermiers generaux parviennent a se faire écouter, il n'en resulte la suppression de la franchise, ou aumoins des restrictions tendantes a la rendre purement illusoire, mais d'un autre côté nous nous rassurons en reflechissant que vous etes a portee par votre place et vos Talents de deffendre les Droits qu'on nous a accordé.

Nous sommes avec respect Monsieur Vos très humbles et très Obeissants serviteurs, WILT DELMESTRE & Co

RC (DLC); endorsed. Recorded in SJL as received 7 Aug. 1787.

To Edward Carrington

DEAR SIR   Paris Aug. 4. 1787.

Since mine of the 16th. January I have been honoured by your favors of Apr. 24. and June 9. I am happy to find that the states have come so generally into the scheme of the Federal Convention, from which I am sure we shall see wise propositions. I confess I do not go as far in the reforms thought necessary as some of my correspondents in America; but if the Convention should adopt such propositions I shall suppose them necessary. My general plan would be to make the states one as to every thing connected with foreign nations, and several as to every thing purely domestic. But with all the imperfections of our present government, it is without comparison the best existing or that ever did exist. It's greatest defect is the imperfect manner in which matters of commerce have been provided for. It has been so often said, as to be generally believed, that Congress have no power by the confederation to enforce any thing, e.g. contributions of money. It was not necessary to give them that power expressly; they have it by the law of nature. When two nations make a compact, there results to each a power of compelling the other to execute it. Compulsion was never so easy as in our case, where a single frigate would soon levy on the commerce of any state the deficiency of it's contributions; nor more safe than in the hands of Congress which has always shewn that it would wait, as it ought to do, to the last extremities before it would execute any of it's powers which are disagreeable.—I think it very material to separate in the hands of Congress the Executive and Legislative powers, as the Judiciary already are in some degree. This I hope will be done. The want of it has been the source of more evil than we have ever experienced from any other cause. Nothing is so embarrassing nor so mischievous in a great assembly as the details of execution. The smallest trifle of that kind occupies as long as the most important act of legislation, and takes place of every thing else. Let any man recollect, or look over the files of Congress, he will observe the most important propositions hanging over from week to week and month to month, till the occasions have past them, and the thing never done. I have ever viewed the executive details as the greatest cause of evil to us, because they in fact place us as if we had no federal head, by diverting the attention of that head from great to small objects; and should this division of power not be recommended by the Convention, it is my opinion Congress should make it itself by establishing an Executive committee.—The affairs of Europe are in a critical state. The Emperor, on his return from[1] Vienna, disavowed what his governors had conceded to the people of Brabant. They therefore organized and armed themselves. They determined on regular resistance. This was the more easy, as the innovations proposed had placed all the nobles and priests in the opposition and they easily drew in the body of the nation. But the Emperor had at the same time held out an olive branch by inviting them to send deputies to Vienna to consult on the affairs in dispute. They sent deputies, without powers to concede any thing, and go on at this moment, arming and training. The unsteady, Thrasonic character of the emperor authorizes the conjecture that he will avail himself of this appearance of condescension in the Brabantines to undo all he has done. The affairs of Holland are in a state from which nobody can see the issue. If France and England were in a condition to go to war, they would do it. But neither are. England might perhaps raise supplies: but I doubt if France could. Her assembly des Notables probed and exposed their wounds. The nation were flattered with the hope that being known they could be cured. That hope has lessened, and to the popularity of government which was mounted high at the close of the assembly des notables, has succeeded in the course of a few weeks a spirit of discontent such as the oldest man never saw under their worst administrations. The parliament refuses obstinately to register any law for a tax. We expect hourly to hear of a determination to force them by holding a bed of justice. This will fill up the measure of discontent. Under this situation we may pronounce it impossible for France to undertake a war against England and Prussia, a war by sea and by land, and that the law of self-preservation must oblige her to abandon the Dutch or to patch up by negociation the best terms she can for them. Yet she goes on arming at sea: but as she negotiates at the same time, it is very possible the affair may be drawn out to great length, especially if they can effect a suspension of hostilities in the United Netherlands.—I wish it were possible for us, in this state of fiscal distress of our allies, wherein even a bankruptcy is not impossible, to borrow in Holland wherewithal to pay our whole debt. It would have a capital effect in our favor, and increase the dispositions to favor our commerce and to help us again whenever we shall be in distress. I think Mr. Adams could effect this. I have the honour to be with sincere esteem & respect Dear Sir your most obedt. humble servt., TH: JEFFERSON

PrC (DLC).

[1] An error for "to."

From Madame de Corny

a down place le 4 aoust 1787

En arrivant ici, monsieur, jay vüe avec grand regret que ma lettre avoit ete oubliee, je lay retrouvee a la même place et je me desolle davoir a vos yeux un si grand tort. Je vous prie de rendre justice a mes sentiments et de croire que je ne puis être coupable envers vous dune telle impolitesse. Quoique ma premiere lettre nait aucune valeur je vous lenvoye pour ma justification. Jay fait un voyage tres agreable de 3 semaines pendant lesquels jay parcouru le plus beau pays du monde en glostershire. Le paysage ma plus frapé que dans aucun paiy. Jaurois voulu a toute place y fixer mon sejour et y avoir une chaumiere. Jay suivi a pied tout le nouveau canal jusquau lieu ou lon va percer un souterrain dans la montagne. Jetois ravie de me promener au bord de leau et de chaque cote la colline la mieux meublée de bois et de paturage. Je vous rendrai compte de tout ce que jay parcouru. Mon entousiasme etoit tel que javois lair extravagante. Jay perdu mon rhume, mieux que cela encor, jay repris des forces et jay soutenüe a merveille la fatigue qui doit resulter dun voyage ou lon est toujours en mouvement. Je ne scais encor ce que je vais devenir jattend une lettre pour fixer irrevocablement mon depart. Je vais me hater de parcourir les environs de londre, tels que richemont, Kew, Hampton Court, claremont et pareil. Mais il faut convenir que toutes ces paiys ne peuvent etre imites en france, il faut des pays entiers, 3 ou 4 collines, 5 ou 6 troupeaux de moutons, des espaces immenses, une riviere et ce que je prise beaucoup c'est le bon effet des grands arbres forestiers dont nous avons grand soin de nous defaire. Lorsque nous voulons composer un jardin a langloise tout y est neuf, et ici on a le bon esprit de saider de ce qui est ancien pour faire valoir les nouvelles plantations. Je vois aussi qu'on est moins effraye de tomber dans les lignes droites et nous pour les evitter nous contournons trop chaque allée.

Vous ne me ditte rien de votre poignet, je suis faché contre vous de cette indifference sur une chose qui a vraiment excitte mon interet.

Je regrette bien de n'avoir vüe Mde. Cosewaië que deux instan[ts], et aussi de nêtre pas a paris dans le moment ou elle doit y aller.

Jaccepte tout vos rendez vous au bois de bologne, jespere que la pluië na pas derangé vos promenades, elle a bien contrarier mon voyage. Depuis 2 jours le soleil a reparu mais il ne poura jamais reparer le tort quil ma fait.

Adieu, monsieur, jouissez du plaisir davoir vos deux filles, il est peut [être] fort bien que je naye pas ete chargee de la d[euxieme]. Qui scait sil ne vous eut pas ete bien diff[icile] de la ravoir.

RC (DLC); unsigned; addressed to TJ, "en Son hotel près la grille de chaillot"; endorsed: "de Corny Madame"; postmarked: "Au 15 87." Enclosure: Mme. de Corny to TJ, 9 July, which is recorded in SJL as received with this letter on 21 Aug. 1787.

To James Currie

Dear Sir Paris Aug. 4. 1787.

I am favored with your letter of May 2. and most cordially sympathize in your late immense losses. It is a situation in which a man needs the aid of all his wisdom and philosophy. But as it is better to turn from the contemplation of our misfortunes to the resources we possess for extricating ourselves, you will of course have found solace in your vigour of mind, health of body, talents, habits of business, time yet to retrieve every thing, and a knowledge that the very activity necessary for this is a state of

4 AUGUST 1787

greater happiness than the unoccupied one to which you had thought of retiring. I wish the bulk of my extravagant countrymen had as good prospects and resources as you. But with many of them a feebleness of mind makes them afraid to probe the true state of their affairs and procrastinate the reformation which alone can save something to those who are yet saveable. How happy a people were we during the War from the single circumstance that we could not run in debt. This counteracted all the inconveniences we felt, as the present facility of ruining ourselves overweighs all the blessings of peace. I know no condition happier than that of a Virginia farmer might be, conducting himself as he did during the war. His estate supplies a good table, clothes itself and his family with their ordinary apparel, furnishes a small surplus to buy salt, sugar, coffee, and a little finery for his wife and daughter, enables him to receive and to visit his friends, and furnishes him pleasing and healthy occupation. To secure all this he needs but one act of self denial, to put off buying anything till he has money to pay for it. Mr. Ammonet did not come. He wrote to me however and I am making enquiry for the town and family he indicated. As yet neither can be heard of, and were they to be found, the length of time would probably bar all claims against them. I have seen no object present so many desperate faces. However if enquiry can lighten our way that shall not be wanting, and I will write him as soon as we discover anything or despair of discovering. Littlepage has succeeded well in Poland. He has some office, it is said, worth 500 guineas a year. The box of seeds you were so kind as to forward me came safe to hand. The arrival of my daughter in good health has been a source of immense comfort to me. The injury of which you had heard was a dislocated wrist, and tho it happened eleven months ago, was a simple dislocation, and immediately aided by the best surgeon in Paris, it is neither well, nor ever will be so as to render me much service. The fingers remain swelled and crooked, the hand withered, and the joint having a very confined motion. You ask me when I shall return? My commission expires next spring, and if not renewed, I shall return then. If renewed, I shall stay somewhat longer: how much, will not depend on me altogether. So far as it does, I cannot fix the epoch of my return, tho I always flatter myself it is not very distant. My habits are formed to those of my own country. I am past the time of changing them and am therefore less happy anywhere else than there.—I have sent to the care of Mr Madison at New York a box containing subsequent livraisons of the Encyclopedie for Mr.

4 AUGUST 1787

Hay and Colo. Monroe, to the 22d. inclusive. I will state on the next page their cost and expences hitherto, in order to enable yourself and Mr. Hay to settle the transfer between you. I shall continue to send them as they come out to Mr. Hay. You tell me your knolege of the French has declined, and we have no new publications here but French. This cuts off from me that resource for gratifying you.

It is very incertain yet whether we shall have war. I think the Emperor will arrange his differences with his Brabantine subjects. The internal commotions of Holland are more difficult. Yet the inability of both England and France to go to war renders it still presumeable they will prevent it. I shall always be happy to hear from you being with very sincere esteem Dear Sir your friend & servt., TH: JEFFERSON

1786. Mar. 1.	paid the first 17 livraisons of the Encyclopedie		439^{tt}-10
May 8.	18th. 23^{tt}-May 9. one half of postage to Havre 20^{tt}-2		43^{tt}- 2
Sep. 1.	19th. livraisons 23^{tt}—Oct. 20. 20th. do. 23.^{tt}		46
1787. Jan. 2	21st. livraison 35^{tt}-10.—June 29. 22d. do. 23^{tt}		58 -10
July	half the charges of transportation to Havre (I charge other half to Monroe)		6 -18-8
			594 - 0-8

PrC (DLC). TJ enclosed a similar statement of charges, in the same amounts and on the same dates, in his to Monroe, 5 Aug. 1787.

To Benjamin Hawkins

DEAR SIR Paris Aug. 4. 1787.

I have to acknowlege the receipt of your favors of Mar. 8. and June 9. and to give you many thanks for the trouble you have taken with the Dionaea muscipula. I have not yet heard any thing of them, which makes me fear they have perished by the way. I beleive the most effectual means of conveying them hither will be by the seed. I must add my thanks too for the vocabularies. This is an object I mean to pursue, as I am persuaded that the only method of investigating the filiation of the Indian nations is by that of their languages.

4 AUGUST 1787

I look up with you to the Federal convention for an amendment of our federal affairs. Yet I do not view them in so disadvantageous a light at present as some do. And above all things I am astonished at some people's considering a kingly government as a refuge. Advise such to read the fable of the frogs who sollicited Jupiter for a king. If that does not put them to rights, send them to Europe to see something of the trappings of monarchy, and I will undertake that every man shall go back thoroughly cured. If all the evils which can arise among us from the republican form of our government from this day to the day of judgment could be put into a scale against what this country suffers from it's monarchical form in a week, or England in a month, the latter would preponderate. Consider the contents of the red book in England, or the Almanac royale of France, and say what a people gain by monarchy. No race of kings has ever presented above one man of common sense in twenty generations. The best they can do is to leave things to their ministers, and what are their ministers but a Committee, badly chosen? If the king ever meddles it is to do harm.—It is still undecided whether we shall have war or not. If war, I fear it will not be a succesful one for our friends. England and Prussia, such a war by sea, and such a one by land, are too much for this country at this time. Add to this that the condition of her finances threatens bankruptcy, and that the hope of mending them lessens daily. Good will result from other late operations of the government, but as to money matters they have lost more confidence than they have gained. Were it possible for us to borrow money in Holland to pay them the principal of our debt at this time, it would be felt by them with gratitude as if we had given them so much. I think it probable they would do something clever for us in our commerce; and would be very sure to help us again whenever our affairs would require it. Mr. Adams thinks the money could be borrowed in Holland if there was a tax laid to pay the interest. But I think it possible that the present storm in Holland may make the monied men wish to transfer their money any where else. I wish Mr. Adams put on this business before he leaves Europe. Adieu, my dear Sir, & be assured of the esteem of your friend & servt.,

TH: JEFFERSON

PrC (DLC).

To William Hay

SIR Paris Aug. 4. 1787.

I am now to acknowledge the receipt of your two favors of Apr. 26. and May 3. I have forwarded, by a vessel lately sailed from Havre to New York, a box marked WH. containing the livraisons of the Encyclopedie subsequent to those Dr. Currie has delivered you, to the 22d. inclusive. They are sent to the care of Mr. Madison at Congress who will forward the box to you. There is in it also the same livraisons for Colo. Monroe. I will continue to forward them once or twice a year as they come out. I have stated in a letter to Doctor Currie the cost and expences of the first 22 livraisons to enable yourself and him to settle. The future shall be charged either to you or him as your agreement shall be. It is really a most valuable work, and almost supplies the place of a library.— I receive from too many quarters the account of the distresses of my countrymen, to doubt their truth. Distresses brought on themselves by a feebleness of mind which calculates very illy it's own happiness. It is a miserable arithmetic which makes any single privation whatever so painful as a total privation of every thing, which necessarily must follow the living so far beyond our income. What is to extricate us I know not, whether Law, or Loss of credit. If the sources of the former are corrupted so as to prevent justice, the latter must supply it's place, leave us possessed of our infamous gains, but prevent all future ones of the same character. Europe is in a moment of crisis. The innovations made by their sovereign in the Austrian Netherlands have produced in the people a determination to resist. The Emperor, by disavowing the concessions, made by his governors to quiet the people, seemed to take up the gauntlet which they had thrown. Yet is it rather probable he will recede, and all be hushed up there. The Dutch parties are in a course of hostilities which it will be difficult to suspend; a war would have been begun before this between this country on one side and England and Prussia on the other, had the parties been in a condition for war. Perhaps England might raise supplies, but it would be on a certainty of being crushed under them. This country would find greater difficulty. There is however a difference in her favor which might place her on a level with England; that is, that it would be a popular war here and an unpopular one in England. Probably the weakness of the two countries will induce them to join in compelling a suspension of hostilities, and to make an arrangement for them, or if they cannot agree in that they will spin the matter into length by negociation. In fact, tho both parties are arming, I do not expect any speedy commencement of hostilities.—I am with very great respect & esteem Sir your most obedient & most humble servt., TH: JEFFERSON

PrC (DLC).

To David Ramsay

DEAR SIR   Paris Aug. 4. 1787.

I have to acknolege the receipt of your favors of Nov. 8. and Apr. 7. and the pleasure to inform you that the translation of your book sells well, and is universally approved. Froullé will send you some copies of it, by the first opportunity. I am happy to hear you are occupied on the general history. It is a subject worthy your pen. I observe Stockdale in London has printed your work and advertized it for sale. Since I wrote to you on the subject of rice, I have had an opportunity of examining the rice feilds of Lombardy, and having committed my observations to writing in a letter to Mr. Drayton as President of the Agricultural society I will take the liberty of referring you to that letter, in which probably there is little new to your Countrymen, tho all was new to me. However if there be a little new and useful, it will be my reward. I have been pressing on the merchants here the expediency of enticing the rice trade to Bordeaux and Honfleur. At length I have received the inclosed propositions. They are from a very solid house. I wish they may produce the effect desired. I have inclosed a copy to Mr. Izard but forgot to mention to him on the subject of white plains and hoes (particularly named in his letter to me) that this house will begin by furnishing them from England, which they think they can do as cheap as you can receive them directly from England. The allowance made to wholesale purchasers will countervail the double voiage. They hope that after a while they can have them imitated here. Will you be so good as to mention this to Mr. Izard? I fear that my zeal will make me expose myself to ridicule in this business, for I am no merchant, and still less knowing in the culture of rice. But this risk becomes a duty by the bare possibility of doing good.—You mention in your letter your instalment law as needing apology. I have never heard the paiment by instalments complained of in Europe. On the contrary, in the conferences Mr. Adams and myself had with merchants in London, they admitted the necessity of them. It is only necessary that the terms be faithfully observed and the paiments be in real money. I am sensible that there are defects in our federal government: yet they are so much lighter than those of monarchies that I view them with much indulgence. I rely too on the good sense of the people for remedy, whereas the evils of monarchical government are beyond remedy. If any of our countrymen wish for a king, give them Aesop's fable of the frogs who asked a king; if this does not cure them, send them to Europe: they will go back good republicans. Whether we shall have war or not is still doubtful. I conclude we shall not, from the inability of both France and England to undertake a war. But our friend George is rather remarkeable for doing exactly what he ought not to do. He may therefore force on a war in favor of his cousin of Holland. I am with very great esteem Dear Sir your most obedt. humble servt.,   TH: JEFFERSON

PrC (DLC). Enclosure: Bérard's proposals concerning the rice trade; see under 15 July 1787.

To James Monroe

DEAR SIR   Paris Aug. 5. 1787.

A journey of between three and four months into the Southern parts of France and Northern of Italy has prevented my writing to you. In the mean time you have changed your ground, engaged in different occupations, so that I know not whether the news of this side the water will even amuse you. However it is all I have for you. The storm which seemed to be raised suddenly in Brabant will probably blow over. The Emperor on his return to Vienna pretended to revoke all the concessions which had been made by his governors general to his Brabantine subjects: but he at the same time called for deputies from among them to consult with. He will use their agency to draw himself out of the scrape, and all there I think will be quieted. Hostilities go on occasionally in Holland. France espouses the cause of the Patriots as you know, and England and Prussia that of the Stadholder. France and England are both unwilling to bring on a war, but a hasty move of the king of Prussia will perplex them. He has thought the stopping his sister sufficient cause for sacrificing a hundred or two thousand of his subjects, and as many Hollanders and French. He has therefore ordered 20,000 men to march without consulting England, or even his own ministers. He may thus drag England into a war, and of course this country against their will. But it is certain they will do every thing they can to prevent it, and that in this at least they agree. Tho' such a war might be gainful to us, yet it is much to be deprecated by us at this time. In all probability France would be unequal to such a war by sea and by land, and it is not our interest, or even safe for us that she should be weakened.— The great improvements in their constitution, effected by the Assembleé des Notables, you are apprized of. That of partitioning the country into a number of subordinate governments under the administration of provincial assemblies chosen by the people, is a capital one. But to the delirium of joy which these improvements gave the nation, a strange reverse of temper has suddenly succeded. The deficiencies of their revenue were exposed, and they were frightful. Yet there was an appearance of intention to oeconomize and reduce the expences of government. But expences are still very inconsiderately incurred, and all reformation in that point despaired of. The public credit is affected; and such a spirit of discontent arisen as has never been seen. The parliament refused to register the edict for a stamp tax, or any other tax, and call for the States general, who alone, they say can impose a new tax. They speak with a boldness unexampled. The king has called them to Versailles tomorrow where he will hold a lit de justice and compel them to register the tax. How the chapter will finish, we must wait to see.—By a vessel lately sailed from Havre to New York I have sent you some more livraisons of the Encyclopedie, down to the 22d. inclusive. They were in a box with Dr. Currie's and addressed to Mr. Madison who will forward them to Richmond. I have heard you are in the assembly. I will beg the favor of you therefore to give me at the close of the session a history of the most remarkeable acts passed, the parties and views of the house, &c. This with the small news of my country, crops and prices, furnish you abundant matter to treat me, while I have nothing to give you in return but the history of the follies of nations in their dotage. Present me in respectful & friendly terms to Mrs. Monroe, and be assured of the sincere sentiments of esteem & attachment with which I am dear Sir your friend & servt.,

Th: Jefferson

PrC (DLC). TJ enclosed in this letter a statement of account containing identical charges, under the same dates and for similar items, with those in the account sent to Currie, 4 Aug. 1787, q.v. (MHi).

To the Commissioners of the Treasury

GENTLEMEN   Paris Aug. 5. 1787.

In my last of June 17. 1787. I had the honor of communicating to you the information I had received from Mr. Grand that your funds here were out, and he considerably in advance. I took occasion to mention to him the paragraph in your letter of Feb. 17.[1] wherein you were so kind as to say your attention should be immediately turned to the making a remittance. However I understood soon after that he had protested a draught of Mr. Carmichael's, as also a smaller one of 500. livres. He called upon me and explaining to me the extent of his advances, observed that he should not be willing to add to them, except so far as should be necessary for the private expences of myself and my secretary, which he wished to be reduced as much below the ordinary allowance as we could, until remittances should be received. He will send you by this packet a state of his accounts by which he informs me that your account is in arrear about 32,000ᵗᵗ advanced by him and about 15,000.ᵗᵗ from a fund of the state of Virginia placed here for the purchase of arms, making Genl. Washington's statue &c. In examining his accounts, I found by the one he had sent you formerly that you were debited two articles of 10,000.ᵗᵗ and 2724ᵗᵗ-6-6 which belonged to the account of the state of Virginia. This I must explain to you. That state had directed me to have the statue of Genl. Washington made, and given me assurance, such as I could rely on, that I should receive funds immediately. Dr. Franklin was setting out to America, and Houdon the statuary expressed a willingness to go with him. But it was necessary to advance him a sum of money for that purpose. Rather than lose the opportunity I ventured to borrow from the fund of the U.S. those two sums for the state of Virginia which I knew would be immediately replaced. The funds of the state arrived (being near 200,000ᵗᵗ) and enabled me not only to replace those sums immediately, but to furnish much larger supplies to the wants of the U.S. when their funds failed, insomuch that the state of Virginia is now in advance here for the U.S. about 15,000.ᵗᵗ as beforementioned. As yet it has not suffered by any of these advances, but having no money here left but this balance, I shall be censurable by that state if it be not replaced in time to answer the demands on them, which will now be made within a few weeks. Mr. Grand has, by my direction, credited you in the account he now sends for the two sums of 10,000.ᵗᵗ and

2724ᵗᵗ-6-6 improperly charged in your former account. He has also debited you in his account for the whole sums paid for the United states, as well those paid by Virginia, as by himself. The purpose of this was to keep the accounts unmixed, tho in fact the funds have been applied occasionally in aid of each other.

I had proposed to Mr. Barclay the settlement of my account before his departure for Marocco, but we concluded it would be better to do it on his return, as that would enable me to bring it down to a later day. It was not then expected he would have been so long detained by that business. Unfortunately for me, when at Lorient, on his return to Paris, he found it more adviseable to proceed directly to America; so that I have lost this opportunity of having my account settled. I shall either do it with him on his return, if he returns soon, or with such other person here as you shall point out, or I will transmit it, with copies of my vouchers, to be settled by you, or do whatever else with it you shall please to direct. The articles which, from their minuteness, have not admitted the taking vouchers, I shall be ready to prove by my own oath. In this account I have presumed to charge the U.S. with an Outfit. The necessity of this, in the case of a minister, resident, and of course obliged to establish a house, is obvious on reflection. There cannot be a surer proof of it's necessity than the experience and consent of all nations, as I believe there is no instance of any nation sending a minister to reside any where without an outfit. A year's salary is the least I have been able to hear of, and I should be able to shew that the articles of clothes, carriage and horses, and houshold furniture, in a very plain stile have cost me more than that. When I send you my account, either settled here, or to be settled there, I shall take the liberty of referring this article to the consideration of Congress. It's reasonableness has appeared to me so palpable, that I have presumed it would appear so to Congress, and have therefore kept up the expences of my house at the current rate of 9000. dollars a year, established by Congress, without replacing my outfit by reductions from that. If my expectations should be thought unreasonable, I shall submit, and shall immediately reduce my establishment, with such rigour, as to make up this article in the shortest time possible.—I inclose you a letter from Fiseaux & co. on the subject of their loan. I wish the loan lately obtained by Mr. Adams may enable you to get rid of the debt to the Foreign officers, principal and interest. Indeed if Mr. Adams could be charged with the transfer of our whole debts from this country to Holland, it would be a most salutary operation. The confusions

6 AUGUST 1787

of that country might perhaps facilitate that measure at present, tho' no regular tax could be obtained in the moment for paiment of the interest. I have the honour to be with sentiments of the most perfect esteem & respect, Gentlemen Your most obedient & most humble servant, TH: JEFFERSON

PrC (DLC). Enclosure (missing): Fizeaux & Co. to TJ, 16 July 1787.

¹ An error for 16 Feb.

To Anne Blair Banister

DEAR MADAM   Paris Aug. 6. 1787.

I was honoured with your commands on the subject of Madame Oster. Immediately on her arrival I waited on her with a tender of my services. She told me she had so far arranged her matters as no longer to fear any injustice; that she meant to go and settle among her friends. I begged if any occasion of being useful to her should arise, that she would command me, that your recommendations were a sufficient title. Since I am not likely to have this opportunity of shewing my devotion to you, do all your desires center in your friends? Is there nothing you wish for yourself? The modes of Paris, it's manufactures, it's good things, do they furnish you no temptation to employ me? I hope Mr. J. Bannister has read in my mind all it's wishes to be retained in your memory, and been a faithful interpreter to you of all it's affection, an affection not weakened by—how many years absence is it? My daugher joins me in respect and esteem for you. She will one day have the honor of presenting it in person. Lay up for her a store of new friendship, and preserve all the old stock for him who has the honour to be with all the good faith of old times, my dear Madam, Your affectionate friend & humble servt,   TH: JEFFERSON

PrC (DLC).

To John Banister, Sr.

DEAR SIR   Paris Aug. 6. 1787.

On the receipt of your favor of May 6. I communicated to M. de Vernon so much of it as concerned him. I now inclose you his answer, and will pray you to do the best you can for him. I hope your son has found the air of his native country agrees with him.

[691]

I am sure you will have found him to have laid in a store of observation and wisdom in his journey.—War or peace is the question here. Peace I believe. Yet a hasty order from the king of Prussia to march 20,000 men to revenge what he calls an insult to his sister embarrasses England and France, both of which are desirous to avoid war, yet both determined to meet it, and in opposition to each other, if the Dutch difficulties cannot be arranged. This is the sum of the news of this country, and as my courier parts at daybreak and I am to be up all night writing letters, you will pardon me I know for concluding here, with what I wish I could express to you in person, all my wishes for your happiness, and the sentiments of sincere esteem with which I am dear Sir Your friend & servt,   TH: JEFFERSON

PrC (DLC). Enclosure not found.

To St. John de Crèvecoeur

DEAR SIR   Paris Aug. 6. 1787.

I was not a little disappointed to find on my return that you had gone punctually in the packet as you had proposed. Great is the change in the dispositions of this country in the short time since you left it. A continuation of inconsiderate expence seems to have raised the nation to the highest pitch of discontent. The parliament refused to register the new taxes. After much and warm altercation a lit de justice has been held this day at Versailles; it was opened by the reading a severe remonstrance from the parliament, to which the king made a hard reply, and finished by ordering the stamp tax, and impot territorial to be registered.—Your nation is advancing to a change of constitution. The young desire it, the middle aged are not averse, the old alone are opposed to it. They will die; the provincial assemblies will chalk out the plan, and the nation ripening fast, will execute it.—All your friends are in the country, so I can give you no news of them: but no news are always good news. The Dutchess Danville is with some of her friends: the Duke and Dutchess de la Rochefoucault gone to the waters, the Countess d'Houdetot with Madme. de la Briche. Your sons are well and go on well: and we are laboring here to improve on M. de Calonne's letter on our commerce. Adieu my dear Sir & be assured of the sentiments of sincere esteem with which I am your friend & servt,   TH: JEFFERSON

RC (Louis Saint-John de Crèvecoeur, Montesquiou-sur-Losse, France, 1947). PrC (DLC).

To Benjamin Franklin

Dear Sir   Paris Aug. 6. 1787.

This will be handed you by Doctor Gibbons a young gentleman, who after studying physic and taking his degrees at Edinburgh has passed some time here. He has desired the honor of being known to you, and I find a pleasure in being the instrument of making him so. It is a tax to which your celebrity submits you. Every man of the present age will wish to have the honor of having known, and been known to you. You will find Doctor Gibbons to possess learning, genius and merit. As such I ask leave to present him to you, and of assuring you at the same time of the sentiments of profound respect & esteem, with which I have the honor to be your Excellency's most obedient & most humble servant,

Th: Jefferson

RC (MH). PrC (DLC). John Hannum GIBBONS was graduated M.D. at Edinburgh in 1786 and gave private lectures on medicine in Philadelphia until his death there on 5 Oct. 1795 (communication of Whitfield J. Bell, Jr. to the Editors, 21 July 1955).

To John Hannum Gibbons

Aug. 6. 1787.

Mr. Jefferson's compliments to Doctr. Gibbons and sends him another packet, with a renewal of his wishes for his happiness and success.

PrC (DLC); not recorded in SJL. TJ had sent one packet of letters for America with his to Limozin, 6 Aug. 1787, and the present letter covered ANOTHER PACKET.

To John Jay

Sir   Paris Aug. 6. 1787.

The last letter I had the honour of addressing you was dated June 21. I have now that of inclosing you a letter from the Swedish Ambassador praying that enquiry may be made for a vessel of his nation pyratically carried off, and measures taken relative to the vessel, cargo and crew.   Also a letter from William Russell and others citizens of America, concerned in trade to the Island of Guadeloupe, addressed to the Marechal de Castries, and complaining of the shutting to them the port of Point a Pitre, and receiving them only at Basse-terre. This was inclosed to me by the

[693]

subscribers to be delivered to the Marechal de Castries. But the present is not the moment to move in that business: and moreover I suppose that wherever parties are within the reach of Congress, they should apply to them, and my instructions come through that channel. Matters arising within the kingdom of France, to which my commission is limited, and not admitting time to take the orders of Congress, I suppose I may move in originally. I also inclose you the copy of a letter from Mr. Barclay, closing his proceedings in our affairs with Marocco. Before this reaches you, he will have had the honour of presenting himself to you in person. After his departure, the parliament of Bourdeaux decided that he was liable to arrest. This was done on a letter from the Minister informing them that Mr. Barclay was invested with no character which privileged him from arrest. His constant character of Consul was no protection, and they did not explain whether his character to Marocco was not originally diplomatic, or was expired. Mr. Barclay's proceedings under this commission being now closed, it would be incumbent on me to declare, with respect to them, as well as his Consular transactions, my opinion of the judgment, zeal and disinterestedness with which he has conducted himself, were it not that Congress has been so possessed of those transactions from time to time as to judge for themselves.—I cannot but be uneasy, lest my delay of entering on the subject of the Consular convention may be disapproved. My hope was, and is, that more practicable terms might be obtained: in this hope, I do nothing till further orders, observing by an extract from the Journals you were pleased to send me, that Congress have referred the matter to your consideration, and conscious that we are not suffering in the mean time, as we have not a single Consul in France, since the departure of Mr. Barclay.—I mentioned to you, in my last, the revival of the hopes of the Chevalr. de la Luzerne. I thought it my duty to remind the Count de Montmorin, the other day, of the long absence of their minister from Congress. He told me the Chevalier de la Luzerne would not be sent back, but that we might rely that in the month of October a person would be sent, with whom we should be content. He did not name the person, tho' there is no doubt that it is the Count de Moustier. It is an appointment which, according to the opinion I have formed of him, bids as fair to give content as any one which could be made.

I also mentioned in my last letter, that I had proposed the reducing the substance of M. de Calonne's letter into the form of an

Arret, with some alterations, which on consultation with the merchants at the different ports I visited, I had found to be necessary. I received soon after a letter from the Comptroller general informing me that the letter of Monsr. de Calonnes was in a course of execution. Of this I inclose you a copy. I was in that moment inclosing to him my general observations on that letter, a copy of which are also inclosed. In these I stated all the alterations I wished to have made. It became expedient soon after to bring on the article of tobacco, first to know whether the farmers had executed the order of Berny, and also to prepare some arrangements to succeed the expiration of this order. So that I am now pursuing the whole subject of our commerce. 1. To have necessary amendments made in M. de Calonne's letter. 2. To put it into a more stable form. 3. To have full execution of the order of Berny. 4. To provide arrangements for the article of tobacco after that order shall be expired. By the copy of my letter on the two last points you will perceive that I again press the abolition of the farm of this article. The conferences on that subject give no hope of affecting that. Some poor palliative is probably all we shall obtain. The Marquis de la Fayette goes hand in hand with me in all these transactions, and is an invaluable auxiliary to me. I hope it will not be imputed either to partiality or affectation, my naming this gentleman so often in my despatches. Were I not to do it, it would be a suppression of truth, and a taking to myself the whole merit where he has the greatest share.

The Emperor on his return to Vienna, disavowed the concessions of his governors-general to his subjects of Brabant. He at the same time proposed their sending deputies to him to consult on their affairs. They refused in the first moment; but afterwards nominated deputies; without giving them any power however to concede any thing. In the mean time they are arming and training themselves. Probably the Emperor will avail himself of the aid of these deputies to tread back his steps. He will be the more prompt to do this that he may be in readiness to act freely, if he finds occasion, in the new scenes preparing in Holland. What these will be cannot be foreseen. You well know that the original party-divisions of that country were into Stadhoulderians, Aristocrats, and Democrats. There was a subdivision of the Aristocrats, into Violent and Moderate, which was important. The Violent Aristocrats would have wished to preserve all the powers of government in the hands of the Regents, and that these should remain self-

6 AUGUST 1787

elective but chusing to receive a modification of these powers from the Stadhoulder rather than from the people, they threw themselves into his scale. The Moderate Aristocrats would have consented to a temperate mixture of Democracy, and particularly that the Regents should be elected by the people. They were the declared enemies of the Stadhoulder, and acted in concert with the Democrats, forming with them what were called the Patriots. It is the opinion of dispassionate people on the spot, that their views might have been effected. But the Democratic party aimed at more. They talked of establishing Tribunes of the people, of annual accounts, of depriving the magistrates at the will of the people &c., of enforcing all this with the arms in the hands of the corps francs, and in some places, as at Heusden, Sprang, &c. began the execution of these projects. The Moderate Aristocrats found it difficult to strain their principles to this pitch. A schism took place between them and the Democrats, and the former have for some time been dropping off from the latter into the scale of the Stadhoulder. This is the fatal coalition which governs without obstacle in Zeeland, Friesland and Guelderland, which constitutes the states of Utrecht at[1] Amersfort, and, with their aid, the plurality in the States general. The States of Holland, Groningen and Overyssel vote as yet in the opposition. But the coalition gains ground in the States of Holland, and has been prevalent in the council of Amsterdam. If it's progress be not stopped by a little moderation in the Democrats, it will turn the scale decidedly in favor of the Stadhoulder, in the event of their being left to themselves, without foreign interference. If foreign powers interfere, their prospect does not brighten. I see no sure friends to the Patriots but France, while Prussia and England are their assured enemies. Nor is it probable that characters so greedy, so enterprising, as the Emperor and Empress, will be idle during such a struggle. Their views have long shewn which side they would take. That France has engaged to interfere and to support the patriots is beyond doubt. This engagement was entered into during the life of the late king of Prussia, whose eye was principally directed on the Emperor, and whose dispositions towards the Prince of Orange would have permitted him to be clipped a little close. But the present king comes in with warmer dispositions towards the Princess his sister. He has shewn decidedly that he will support her even to the destruction of the balance of Europe, and the disturbance of it's peace. The king of England has equally decided to support that house at the risk of plunging his nation into another war. He supplies the Prince with money [at] this moment. A particular remittance of 120,000 guineas is known of. But his ministry is divided. Pitt is against the king's opinion; the D. of Richmond and the rest of the ministers for it. Or at least such is the belief here. Mr. Adams will have informed you more certainly. This division in the English ministry, with the ill condition of their finances for war, produce a disposition even in the king to try first every pacific measure: and that country and this were labouring jointly to stop the course of hostilities in Holland, to endeavor to effect an accomodation, and were scarcely executing at all the armaments ordered in their ports: when all of a sudden, an inflammatory letter written by the Princess of Orange to the K. of Prussia induces him, without consulting England, without consulting even his own council, to issue orders by himself to his Generals to march 20,000 men to revenge the insult supposed to be offered to his sister. With a pride and egotism planted in the heart of every king, he considers her being stopped in the road as a sufficient cause to sacrifice a hundred or two thousand of his own subjects and as many of his enemies, and to spread fire, sword and desolation over the half of Europe. This hasty measure has embarrassed England, undesirous of war if it can be avoided, yet unwilling to separate from the power who is to render it's success probable. Still you may be assured that that court is going on in concurrence with this to prevent the extremities if possible, always understood that if the war cannot be prevented, they will enter into it as parties, and in opposition to one another. This event is in my opinion to be deprecated by the friends of France. She never was equal to such a war by land, and such a one by sea; and less so now than in any moment of the present reign. You remember that the nation was in a delirium of joy on the convocation of the Notables, and on the various reformations agreed on between them and the government. The picture of the distress of their finances was indeed frightful, but the intentions to reduce them to order seemed serious. The constitutional reformations have gone on well, but those of expences make little progress. Some of the most obviously useless have indeed been lopped off, but the remainder [is a] heavy mass difficult to be reduced. Despair has seized every mind, and they have past from an extreme of joy to one of discontent. The parliament therefore oppose the registering any new tax, and insist on an assembly of the States-general. The object

6 AUGUST 1787

of this is to limit expences, and dictate a constitution. The edict for the stamp tax has been the subject of reiterated orders and refusals to register. At length the king has summoned the Parliament to Versailles to hold a bed of justice, in which he will order them in person to register the edict. At the moment of my writing they are gone to Versailles for this purpose. There will yet remain to them to protest against the register as forced, and to issue orders against it's execution on pain of death. But as the king would have no peaceable mode of opposition left, it remains to be seen whether they will push the matter to this extremity. It is evident I think that the spirit of this country is advancing towards a revolution in their constitution. There are not wanting persons at the helm, friends to the progress of this spirit. The provincial assemblies will be the most probable instrument of effecting it.—Since writing thus far I have received an intimation that it will be agreeable not to press our commercial regulations at this moment, the ministry being too much occupied with the difficulties surrounding them to spare a moment on any subject which will admit of delay. Our business must therefore be suspended for a while. To press it out of season would be to defeat it.—[It would be felt as a vital benefit here could we relieve their finances by paying what we owe. Congress will judge by Mr. Adams's letters how far the transferring all our debts in this country to Holland is practicable. On the replenishing their treasury with our principal and interest, I should not be afraid to ask concessions in favor of our West India trade. It would produce a great change of opinion as to us and our affairs. In the Assembly des Notables, hard things were said of us. They were induced however, in committing us to writing, to smother their ideas a little. In their votes now gone to be printed, our debt is described in these words. 'L'article 21. de la recette, formé des interets des creances de sa Majesté sur les Etats Unis de l'Amerique ne peut etre tiré, quant au present que pour Memoire: ces creances, quoiqu' elles paraissent avoir les suretés les plus solides, peuvent neanmoins etre d'un recouvrement long, soit en capitaux, soit peutetre meme en interets, et ne doivent pas par consequence entrer dans le calcul des revenus courants annuellement assurés. Cet article est de 1,600,000.'[4] Above all things it is desireable to hush the foreign officers by paiment. Their wants, the nature of their services, their access to high characters, and connections with them bespeak the reasons for this. I hear also that Mr. Beaumarchais means to make himself heard, if a Memorial which he

6 AUGUST 1787

sends by an Agent in the present packet is not attended to as he thinks it ought to be. He called on me with it, and desired me to recommend his case to a decision, and to note in my dispatch that it was the first time he had spoken to me on the subject. This is true, it being the first time I ever saw him; but my recommendations would be as displaced as unnecessary. I assured him Congress would do in that business what justice should require and their means enable them to.]²—The information sent me by Mr. Montgomery from Alicant, of the death of the Dey of Algiers, was not true. I had expressed my doubt of it in my last, when I communicated it. I send herewith the newspapers to this date, and a remonstrance of the parliament, to shew you in what language the king can be addressed at this day. I have received no journals of Congress since the beginning of Novemb. last and will thank you for them if printed. I have the honor to be with sentiments of the most perfect esteem & respect, Sir Your most obedient & most humble servt.,

TH: JEFFERSON

P.S. Aug. 7. The parliament were received yesterday very harshly by [the King.] He obliged them to register the two edicts for the Impot terri[torial, and the] Stamp tax. When speaking in my letter of the reiterated orders and refusals to register which passed between the king and parliament I omitted to insert the king's answer to a deputation of parliament which attended him at Versailles. It may serve to shew the spirit which exists between them. It was in these words, and these only. 'Je vous ferai savoir mes intentions. Allez-vous-en. Qu'on ferme la porte.'

PrC (DLC). Tr (DLC). Tr (DNA: PCC, No. 107, II). Tr of Extract (DNA: PCC, No. 138, I). Enclosures: (1) Stael de Holstein to TJ, 3 Aug. 1787. (2) Petition of American traders in Guadeloupe to Castries, 3 May 1787. (3) Barclay to American Commissioners, 13 July 1787. (4) Villedeuil to TJ, 2 July 1787. (5) TJ's Observations on Calonne's Letter (see under 3 July 1787). (6) Dumas' "last dispatches" were those transmitted with his letters to TJ of 30 June and 12 July, qq.v.

The REMONSTRANCE OF THE PARLIAMENT which TJ sent with the newspapers was *Remontrances du Parlement de Paris; arrêtées le 24 Juillet 1787* (Sowerby No. 2486); the full text of the remonstrance was printed in *Gazette de Leide*, No. LXIII, 7 Aug., and No. LXIV, 10 Aug. 1787.—On 2 Oct. 1787, the extract of TJ's letter respecting the foreign debt was "Referred (as far as it relates to the money due to the foreign Officers) to the board of treasury to report." The Commissioners (Samuel Osgood and Walter Livingston) reported on 8 Aug. 1788 "That the critical situation in which the provision for the payment of the Dutch Interest has been for some time placed, has hitherto prevented the Board from recommending any appropriation of the Funds in Europe for any other object; but as information has lately been received that the Loans now open in Holland, will furnish timely and sufficient Funds for the above object,—The Board are of opinion, that no time should be lost in making Provision for the Payment of the Arrears of Interest due to Foreign Officers, agreeably to the Recommendation of the Minister of the United States at the Court of France."

The Commissioners accordingly proposed, and on 20 Aug. 1788 Congress adopted, a resolution that "so much of the Loans in Holland as shall be necessary to discharge the Interest due on Certificates issued to Foreign Officers to the 31st December 1788 be specially appropriated for that purpose, under the Direction of the Minister of the United States at the Court of France" (report, signed by Osgood and Livingston, and endorsed by Charles Thomson, in DNA: PCC, No. 138, I, 631-8).

[1] Thus in MS; "and" intended.
[2] Extract in DNA: PCC consists of that part of text in brackets (supplied).

To André Limozin

SIR   Paris Aug. 6. 1787.

Your bill in favor of Sartorius was presented to me and paid to-day. There is no change since my last which occasions a fear of sudden hostilities. You may be assured that the courts of London and Versailles are sincerely striving to prevent a war. The king of Prussia has made a late move which wore a threatening aspect; but it is hoped these two powers will be able to recall him to his pacific dispositions. I send one of my servants with my packet of letters which I have taken the liberty to put under cover to you. They are all under address to Doctor Gibbons, an American, who promised me he would call on you for them. Should he fail, I will pray you to put them by a faithful messenger into his hands. Should any accident prevent his arrival at Havre in time, be so obliging as to break open his cover, and to put them under one of your own to any person you please at New York (perhaps best to Mr. Jay) and commit them to the post office. I have the honor to be with much esteem & respect Sir Your most obedient humble servant,   TH: JEFFERSON

PrC (DLC). See TJ to Gibbons, this date.

To John Rutledge

DEAR SIR   Paris Aug. 6. 1787.

I am honored with your letter by your son, and shall be happy to render him every assistance in my power of whatever nature. The objects of his stay in this country and of his visit to London are perfectly well judged, so of that to Amsterdam. Perhaps it is questionable whether the time you propose he should spend at some of the German courts might not be better employed at Madrid at Lisbon and in Italy. At the former there could be no object for him but politics, the system of which there is intricate and can never be connected with us: nor will our commercial connections be considerable. With Madrid and Lisbon our connections both political and commercial are great and will be increasing daily. Italy is a feild where the inhabitants of the Southern states may see much to copy in agriculture, and a country with which we shall carry on considerable trade. Pardon my submitting these thoughts to you. We shall pursue your own plan unless you notify a change in it.

The present question in Europe is War or not war? I think there will be none between the Emperor and his Brabantine subjects. But as to Holland it is more doubtful, for we do not as yet consider as a war the little partisan affairs which are taking place every day. France and England, conscious that their exhausted means would poorly feed a war, have been strenuously exerting themselves to procure an accomodation. But the king of Prussia, in a moment of passion, has taken a measure which may defeat their wishes. On receiving from the Princess of Orange a letter informing him of her having been stopped on the road, without consulting the court of London, without saying a word to his own ministers, he issued orders himself to his generals to march 20,000 men to be at her orders. England unwilling to bring on a war, may yet fear to separate from him who is to be her main ally. Still she is endeavoring in concurrence with this court to stop the effects of this hasty movement, and to bring about a suspension of hostilities and settlement of differences, always meaning, if they fail in this, to take the feild in opposition to one another. Blessed effect of kingly government, where a pretended insult to the sister of a king is to produce the wanton sacrifice of a hundred or two thousand of the people who have entrusted themselves to his government, and as many of his enemies! And we think our's a bad government. The only condition on earth to be compared with ours, in my opinion, is that of the Indians, where they have still less law than we. The European, are governments of kites over pidgeons. The best schools for republicanism are London, Versailles, Madrid, Vienna, Berlin &c. Adieu, my dear Sir, & be assured of the sincere esteem of Your most obedient humble servt,

TH: JEFFERSON

PrC (DLC).

Preliminary indexes will be issued periodically for groups of volumes. An index covering Vols. 1-6 has been published. A comprehensive index of persons, places, subjects, etc., arranged in a single consolidated sequence, will be issued at the conclusion of the series.

THE PAPERS OF THOMAS JEFFERSON is composed in Monticello, a type specially designed by the Mergenthaler Linotype Company for this series. Monticello is based on a type design originally developed by Binny & Ronaldson, the first successful typefounding company in America. It is considered historically appropriate here because it was used extensively in American printing during the last thirty years of Jefferson's life, 1796 to 1826; and because Jefferson himself expressed cordial approval of Binny & Ronaldson types.

✧

Composed and printed by Princeton University Press. Illustrations are reproduced in collotype by Meriden Gravure Company, Meriden, Connecticut. Paper for the series is made by W. C. Hamilton & Sons, at Miquon, Pennsylvania; cloth for the series is made by Holliston Mills, Inc., Norwood, Massachusetts. Bound by the J. C. Valentine Company, New York.

DESIGNED BY P. J. CONKWRIGHT

R0164166101 sscca   S
                     973
                     .46
                     J45
Jefferson, Thomas
The papers of Thomas
        Jefferson. Julian P. B
    VOL. 11

R0164166101 sscca   S
                     973
                     .46
                     J45
Houston Public Library
Social Sci